# NATURAL AND MORAL HISTORY

## OF THE INDIES

CHRONICLES OF THE NEW
WORLD ORDER

# NATURAL AND MORAL
# HISTORY
# OF THE INDIES

JOSÉ DE ACOSTA    *Edited by Jane E. Mangan,*

*with an Introduction and Commentary by Walter D. Mignolo.*

*Translated by Frances M. López-Morillas*

DUKE UNIVERSITY PRESS    *Durham and London*    2002

©2002 Duke University Press
All rights reserved
Printed in the United States of America
on acid-free paper ∞
Designed by Mary Mendell
Typeset in Galliard by
Keystone Typesetting, Inc.
Library of Congress Cataloging-in-Publication Data
appear on the last printed page of this book.

# CONTENTS

BOOK V

BOOK VII

# INTRODUCTION TO JOSÉ DE ACOSTA'S

## *HISTORIA NATURAL Y MORAL*
## *DE LAS INDIAS*

### Walter D. Mignolo

THE *HISTORIA NATURAL Y MORAL DE LAS INDIAS* was published in 1590, almost a century after an Italian navigator from Genoa at the service of the Crown of Castile, Christopher Columbus, landed on one of the many Caribbean islands. If we take this date and look at the situation toward the end of the sixteenth and the beginning of the seventeenth centuries (approximately between 1570 and 1610), we can conclude that Acosta's book was published toward the end of an imperial cycle of which Christianity (the Roman Catholic Church), Spain, and Portugal were the driving forces. Thus, missionary orders (Franciscan, Dominican, and Jesuit, mainly) had an enormous importance in the colonization of the "New World." (The "new" world was, of course, only new for those who did not know about it, not for those who were its inhabitants!)

José de Acosta was a Jesuit. The Jesuit order was created by Ignatius of Loyola in 1534 and was approved by the Catholic Church in 1540. Coincidentally, 1540 was the same year in which Acosta was born.[1] The foundation of the order took place during the tumultuous years of the Reformation and Counter-Reformation. Thus, the *Natural and Moral History of the Indies* falls in the middle of a significant number of historical transformations. It responds not only to the "news" from the New World but to the tensions and conflicts in one part of the "Old World" (Christian Europe, the other two parts being Asia and Africa). Acosta's book was also written at the intersection of the Renaissance revival of the Greco-Latin tradition and the emergence of something unexpected within that tradition: a heretofore unknown but impressive mass of land and an intriguing variety of people. Of course, for the people inhabiting Anahuac (the domain of the Mayas and Aztecs in Mesoamerica) and Tawantinsuyu (the domain of the Incas in the Andes), as well as for the variety of indigenous communities all along the continent, the Greco-Latin tradition was irrelevant. They did not share the same principles of knowledge as Acosta. The greatness of Acosta's book lies in its conceptualization of the "Indies" within a larger philosophical picture. Its feebleness lies in its assumption that Amerindian knowledge did not count in the same way that the Greco-Latin tradition did.

Acosta left Spain for Peru in 1571 and arrived in 1572 (five Jesuits were sent to Peru in 1568, preceding Acosta). Coincidentally, 1572 is the year in which the Jesuit order in the New World was institutionalized formally. Franciscans and Dominicans had been active before the arrival of the Jesuits. The conquest of Mexico-Tenochtitlan by Hernán Cortés in 1519 had much earlier opened the doors for the arrival of mendicant orders. In the Yucatan Peninsula the mendicant orders established themselves after 1530 and in Peru after 1532, the date associated with Francisco Pizarro's conquest of Tawantinsuyu, the territory of the Inca Empire. The Jesuits were in general more open to learning from the cultures they sought to convert than the Dominicans and Franciscans were, and eventually they experienced a significant transformation between the sixteenth and the eighteenth centuries. In fact, the order was expelled in 1767 when the Crown of Castile came to believe that the Jesuits in the New World, who were no longer Spaniards but Creoles (i.e., born in the New World from Spanish descent), were no longer supporting the interests of Spain.

Not a minor factor of these sixteenth-century historical transformations was the approach to the concept of knowledge and understanding that Acosta addressed, head on, in his initial chapters. His concept of the moral and natural aspects of history represented the intersection of philosophy and theology: philosophy because understanding nature, for Acosta, was not just a question of describing minerals, plants, and animals but of understanding the order of the universe and the chain of being, of which the human being was the point of arrival of God's creation; and theology because understanding nature was a way of knowing and revering God, its creator. The relevance of his book can be measured by its immediate translation from Spanish into Italian, French, English, Dutch, and Latin — that is to say, into the languages of what we know today as modern and imperial Europe. Although the Jesuit order was also active in India and China toward the end of the sixteenth century, there was no interest in translating Acosta into Chinese or Hindi. Why? It was neglected because at that point in history the western Christendom that would become Europe was marginal in relation to the center of trade and of ancient civilizations like China and India. The reasons why Christians/Europeans and merchants were interested in reaching China and India, and not the other way around, was because Christians/Europeans did not have much to offer the Chinese and Indian people. Today the European and North American audience is not very interested in minor languages and marginal cultures. The situation was similar, but reversed, in the sixteenth century. The printed book in Europe at the time of Acosta was only some 120 years old and at the time was as crucial for the dissemination of information as the Internet is today. Furthermore, and parallel to the Internet, there was a selection and a relation of power being maintained among those who were in a position to receive and retrieve information.

Before going further let's pause and ponder why Acosta referred in the title of his book to "las Indias" and not to America or to the New World. We know that one of the reasons why America or the New World was first named Indias (or, more exactly, Indias Occidentales) was because Christopher Columbus believed he had arrived at the Asian "India." However, the Spanish Crown long after this misperception had been corrected used the name Indias Occidentales in all its legal documents. The need to specify Occidentales was due to the fact that the Spanish colonial possessions were not limited to America or the New World but extended to the Moluccas and Philippines in Asia, which indeed was part of the Old World. If we keep in mind that for the Incas and the Aztecs the territory they inhabited and governed was conceptualized as Tawantinsuyu and Anahuac, respectively, we can better understand not only in what sense Indias Occidentales was superimposed on indigenous conceptions but what the consequences were. The erasure of the indigenous conceptualization of space extended, on the one hand, the European concept of the globe. On the other, this erasure imposed the idea that the truth of the matter was indeed whatever European cartographers and politicians decided as they mapped and named the ancient lands of Tawantinsuyu and Anahuac. Acosta was not exempt from these assumptions.

As a Renaissance scholar, Acosta was trained in Greek philosophy, Latin rhetoric, and Christian theology. And, like many other great intellectuals of the time, for instance, the Dominican Fray Bartolomé de Las Casas or the Franciscan Fray Bernardino de Sahagún, he was at the intersection of classical scholarship and new discoveries. Acosta's book should be read, therefore, as one of the many efforts, but certainly also one of the most brilliant, to make sense of the novelty of lands, people, religious practices, and methods of social organization that had been unknown to the Greek philosophers, Latin rhetoricians, and Christian theologians. In the Indies, Acosta took advantage of conversations with people in Tawantinsuyu (today Peru, Bolivia, and Ecuador, mainly) and Anahuac (today Mexico, Guatemala, and Nicaragua, mainly). He spent a year in the Caribbean islands before going to the center of Tawantinsuyu (Cuzco, today in Peru), and in Peru he visited the main urban centers of Cuzco, Arequipa, La Paz, Charcas, Potosí, and Chuquisaca.

Acosta also benefited from the previous experience of two scholars of similar stature, Juan de Tovar in Mexico and Juan Polo de Ondegardo in Peru. Indeed, Acosta's chapter on the people of the valley of Mexico is based on the so called "Tovar Manuscript," which either Tovar sent to Acosta or Acosta obtained directly from Tovar when he went to Mexico. That Acosta had the "Tovar Manuscript" is without a doubt. How he obtained it is not clear, but in the last analysis it is not extremely important. There was enough circulation of information between the Spanish colonies in the Indies to assume that one way or another this important manuscript (which has been edited several times since the nineteenth century) was in his hands.

Soldiers, explorers, and missionaries produced an impressive amount of writing, codifying the information they learned about the people, places, plants, animals, atmospheric conditions, and "elements" (as Acosta puts it, meaning air, water, earth, and fire) of the New World. The enormous impact this writing produced in the European mind (mainly men's minds and mainly Spanish and Portuguese) is not easy to imagine five centuries later. Of course, the issue is not whether Europeans (Spanish and Portuguese) were the "first" to arrive in what is today the Americas and what back then, for the Spaniards, was the New World, Indias Occidentales, or las Indias, as Acosta has it. European intellectuals (or men of letters) put themselves in a situation in which an expected existing entity (e.g., the Indies), had to be imagined and constructed otherwise (e.g., as Indias Occidentales — the Spanish possessions in America — and Indias Orientales — the Spanish possessions in East Asia). The fact that Spaniards and Portuguese found people already "there" is a clear indication that these Europeans were not the first to arrive. What should be understood is why the Spaniards thought, as Francisco de Gómara (a Dominican friar) put it in 1555, that the discovery of the Indias Occidentales was the most extraordinary event since the creation of the world. Thus, although Europeans historically were not the first to "discover" the Indias Occidentales or the Americas, it has become "as if" this were the case. And that case at the end of the sixteenth century was the assumption under which Acosta was working and under which he wrote *Historia natural y moral de las Indias*.

It is important to recognize, however, that Acosta's goal was not to write a "history" of the Indies but to convert the Indians to Christianity. He did not write the *Historia* guided by the sole desire to understand what until then was beyond the limited knowledge of Renaissance men. As a matter of fact, in Acosta's mind the *Historia natural and moral de las Indias* was conceived as an introduction to (in his own words) a more important manuscript he had written before, perhaps toward the mid-1570s. That manuscript, published with the title *De procuranda Indorum salute,* was a treatise on what at the time was considered a form of liberation theology. Writing the history, which indeed is mainly a description of nature and mores, was for him a preliminary step toward the conversion of the Indians to Christianity. The project of "liberating" (with reference to the theology of salvation) the Indians from the devil was simultaneously an ethical project destined to achieve the "spiritual conquest" of the Indias Occidentales.[2] To understand why this was the case, it should be kept in mind that Acosta was working within the conflicting ideologies of the Church and the Crown. From the perspective of the Church, the "discovery" of America was understood as part of a divine and global design for the conversion of the heathen to Christianity. From the perspective of the Crown, America was part of southern Europe's commercial hegemony. The Crown of Portugal was far ahead in the oceanic commercial navigation of the emerging southern powers. Genoa, Florence, and Venice were indeed strong city-states, in the fifteenth century, but none had the geographical location of Portugal in relation to the Atlantic nor Portugal's history at the margin of the Mediterranean powers. By the second half of the fifteenth century, the kingdom of Portugal had navigated the Atlantic to the south of Africa and crossed the Indian Ocean toward India and Ceylon. At that time, the kingdom of Castile (later Spain) was still an incipient project propelled by the strong desire to Christianize the world.

Prologues or introductions to reprinted and translated texts are expected to be basic guides for the reader not familiar with the text. In the particular case of Acosta's *Historia* this task has already been accomplished, in a stellar way,

by Mexican historian and philosopher Edmundo O'Gorman in his prologue
to the Mexican edition of 1940. The prologue, eighty pages long, is a detailed
exercise in textual interpretation. Unusual at the time — though being unusual was one of O'Gorman's trademarks — he blatantly stated a position that
has a family resemblance to British New Criticism. However, O'Gorman was
defending a position contrary to one of its main principles, the "intentional
fallacy." While the intentional fallacy discredited textual interpretation based
on the intention of the author as a romantic legacy in literary criticism,
O'Gorman was addressing the field of historiography. Historians were chas-
tised in the following paragraph.

> In general one could say that the kind of texts known as historical
> sources have received serious and critical attention on the part of the
> historians but an attention that I consider insufficient. Historians tend
> to accept that historical sources are, so to speak, gold mines from which
> to extract data. The least one could say today about this position is that it
> is absolutely inefficient. It is impossible to ignore, at this time and age,
> that a text, or a source, is the response of a will, which, in its turn,
> is supported by an indefinite series of presuppositions. ([1940] 1972,
> 166–67)

Putting his money where his mouth was, O'Gorman devoted about sixty
pages of his lengthy and useful introduction to tracing the meaning of *natural* and *moral* from antiquity to Acosta. He sees in the two components of the
title the basic structure of the narrative itself as well as a correspondence
between the structure and the dominant mental frame at the end of the
sixteenth century. Later O'Gorman's historiographical principles would receive the name, in France, of *histoires des mentalitées.* Allow me to repeat with
some variations, for those who are not interested in going back to O'Gorman's prologue, the summary he offered of Acosta's book.

In book I, Acosta deals with issues related to cosmology and geography,
geography and history, and what today we would understand as anthropological matters. Regarding the first set of issues (cosmology and geography),
the shape and size of the earth were not clear at the time, as it was also
uncertain whether the antipodes (i.e., the opposite ends of the earth from the
point of view of the European observer) were inhabited.

The second aspect developed in Acosta's book I, the geohistorical aspect, was devoted to elucidating the "existence" of a continent that had been unknown until then to most of Mediterranean Europe. There are reasons to believe, however, that other Europeans had reached what is today known as America before Columbus. And surely the fact that the continent was inhabited from north to south is more than proof that it had been "discovered" centuries before!! The question, then, is not *who* was the first but *why* and *by whom* Columbus's "discovery" of America *was constructed as the first.* It was taken for granted that the inhabitants of the Americas, the Amerindians, would have been there from eternity, from the very creation of the world. The presupposition, in other words, was that during the creation of the world people were placed in specific territories and stayed in those places until southern Europeans and Christians "discovered" both the continent and the people who came with it. This is not the approach Acosta took on this issue, but it is certainly a crucial issue he addressed and one of the main concerns for sixteenth-century Europeans in the Iberian Peninsula as well as in the south of Europe and the Ottoman Empire.[3]

The third theme of book I was prompted by questions about the origins of the inhabitants of the New World. Acosta surmised that the people of the Indies had moved from Asia through the Bering Strait, a hypothesis that at the time was quite advanced. However, the *idea* that Columbus had discovered the Indies was such a *reality* that Acosta did not consider the people who arrived from Asia to have discovered it. That is why the question is not so much who was the first but who had the opportunity, the desire, and the power to construct himself as the first.

Book II is devoted to a crucial issue of the time: whether the equator ("the burning zone") was inhabited. It was also uncertain whether the tropical zone between the Atlantic and the Pacific was habitable because of the extreme heat. This was the wisdom, transmitted by those who inhabited the northwest end of the Mediterranean, that Acosta refuted, although he did not question Aristotle's authority, based on his experience in Greece, about areas of the planet he did not know. Acosta only questions the veracity of Aristotle's statement, not the foundation of his epistemic principles. Books I and II were originally written in Latin, and their function was to provide a context for the project of converting the Amerindians to Christianity that, as I have said, he had developed in *De procuranda Indorum salute,* published around 1585. It was a treatise on religious conversion. These two chapters, entitled "Natura Novi Orbis," were the introduction to *De procuranda,* as Acosta himself explains in the prologue of his *Historia.* Both chapters played the role of wild cards by serving as the prologue of both a treatise on religious conversion and an *historia.*[4] This fact reveals the complexity of a project that involved epistemology and religion. Both chapters bear witness to Acosta's awareness of the enormous epistemic transformations that were changing the *known* (i.e., the available knowledge on the planet and the universe) and opening up to the *unknown.* Grasping that epistemic transformation was essential to the project of conversion to Christianity. And that is precisely the place and the role that Acosta's book occupied in both the history of the Spanish conquest and the history of Western epistemology.

Book III is entirely devoted to the "natural" configuration of the Indies. It is a treatise on climatology and discusses the novelty of the atmosphere in the Indies, the winds, the waters (oceans, lakes, rivers, ponds, etc.), the properties of the land, and volcanic heat. The apparent random order of the description is indeed only apparent since Acosta follows a well-established cognitive pattern going back to Greek natural philosophy and the four basic elements in the creation of the universe: air, water, earth, and fire. The four basic elements that explain the creation of the universe are complemented, in book IV, by the Christian trilogy of the chain of being. The natural order of things, inscribed in God's creation of the universe, was an ascending order that moved from the inanimate (rocks, minerals) to plants to animals.

Following a symmetrical pattern common to the Renaissance organization and presentation of knowledge, Acosta devotes the next two books (V and VI) to "man" (or human beings), conceived, according to the chain of being's model, to occupy a niche above animals (see my commentary at the end of this volume). "Rational animals" was the expression employed at the time to distinguish human beings from the rest of the animal kingdom. Briefly stated, these two books deal with the "moral" aspect of the *Historia.* Book V is entirely devoted to "religion" and book VI to a variety of topics (education, the writing system, chronology, politics, the economy) that today one would be inclined to summarize under the name "culture." However, in European Renaissance terminology what I call here religion and culture were both subsumed under the moral dimension and differentiated from the natural.

Up to this point Acosta's *Historia* follows a symmetric pattern. The first two books are devoted to the place of the Indies in the configuration of the earth. The next two books are devoted to minerals, plants, and animals, and the following two are devoted to human beings. Thus far, Acosta's *Historia* has been about the present rather than the past. Book VII breaks the symmetry in two ways. First, it introduces an uneven number of chapters, and second it introduces the past. Acosta, like many other missionaries, soldiers, and men of letters, did not belong to the society of which the history was to be written. On the one hand, "history" was not yet a discipline authorizing, from a local perspective, the writing of the history of the world (as in Hegel's lessons in the philosophy of history, published in 1822). On the other hand, Amerindian conceptualizations and uses of the past did not correspond to European history.

Last but not least, the *Historia natural y moral de las Indias* was read within the confines of Spanish history and its Roman and Greek antecedents. It was, in other words, read within the confines of the colonial histories framed from the perspective of the national ideology that came after the colonial period. It was translated into several European languages, as mentioned earlier, during the Spanish colonial period (the sixteenth to eighteenth centuries), but it was not interpreted or studied during that period. The book became an object of study when the era of imperial Spain was replaced with the period of nation building. In Latin America the colonial period ended with the independence of several Spanish American countries. It is time to understand Acosta's work in the larger frame of imperial conflicts, of the process that we call globalization. Acosta's book was published about twenty years before the publication of Francis Bacon's *The Proficiency and Advancement of Learning Divine and Human,* which announced a change of paradigm and imperial power. Although Latin was common to Acosta and Bacon, the former belonged to the Latin cultures of the south (people who spoke Spanish, Italian, and Portuguese) while Bacon belonged to the Anglo cultures of the north (people who spoke Anglo-Saxon and Germanic languages). The Reformation and the Counter-Reformation helped widen the divide between north and south, between Protestant and Catholic, and between a new approach to science and knowledge in the north and the humanistic culture of the south. To understand Acosta's book at this intersection it is necessary to keep in mind a change that is noticeable in the principles upon which knowledge was being produced as well as a change that took place in the reasoning that justified the production and transformation of knowledge itself. First of all there was a change of languages. Acosta was writing in Latin and Spanish, Bacon in Latin and English. At that point the difference may not have been as clearly visible as it became two hundred years later when England was displacing Spain in world hegemony. Second, Acosta found himself in a very epistemologically multicultural scenario. He situated himself within the Greco-Roman-Christian tradition, although he was aware that Judaism and Islam were strong and competing alternatives. Furthermore, he faced the novelty of having to think about nature and people who had been, until then, outside the frame of knowledge he was embracing. Bacon, instead, found himself in a much less diversified scenario, as the reformation of the Church in the second half of the sixteenth century had already established a frontier between Catholic and Protestant Christians. Protestants in the north had been much less exposed to the variegated multiculturalism of the Mediterranean than Catholics in the south. And, third, with the increasing national ideology elaborated around the idea of nation-states, in the eighteenth century history also became entrenched in national languages. Consequently, when one goes to the library and reads about Acosta and Bacon one never finds that the work of one illuminates the work of the other. Acosta remains within the Spanish memory of the "discovery." Bacon is part of the foundation of "modernity," and he is either read in the context of British history or in the context of European philosophy, which means English, French, and German but certainly not Spanish, Italian, or Portuguese. My invitation to the reader in this introduction, and in the commentary at the end of this book, is to move away from national ideologies in understanding the past and to look at the constitution and transformation of the modern/colonial world and globalization from 1500 to the present. If we do not intend to read Acosta in this new context, why would we be interested in reprinting his classical book, *Historia natural y moral de las Indias*?

Acosta, as well as many others, found himself not only confronting unknown people but confronting an unknown past. Toward the end of the sixteenth century a significant number of narratives existed about the memories of Europe as well as narratives accounting for other civilizations such as those of China, India, or Islam. Amerindians' past was ignored. Furthermore, the conception Acosta had of history was linked to alphabetic writing (see book VI). Since history presupposed, for Acosta and other men of letters, alphabetic literacy and Amerindians were not alphabetically literate, they were considered to be people without history. Acosta was one of those who appointed themselves to write the history Amerindians did not have.

The reader of Acosta's fascinating *Historia* should keep in mind what is constantly absent and silenced in the narrative, that is, Amerindians' descriptions and conceptualizations of everything Acosta writes about without acknowledging Amerindians' knowledge of them. I have devoted some pages of the commentary to elaborating this point. While it is necessary to update the reading of the classical texts of the "discovery and conquest," the time has arrived to read them bearing in mind what has been omitted as well as what has been recorded. The issue is not trivial. The silencing by Acosta (as by many others) did not mean absence or replacement. At the beginning of the twentieth century the "silence" and the "absences" (i.e., the unknown) have come back in various and unexpected forms. Amerindians' social movements are fighting not only for their rights to land but for their epistemic rights. Ecological movements are articulating a discourse that approximates epistemic and ethical principles that were common ground before modernity and progress considered them diabolic, folkloric, or obsolete. Gaia science, curiously enough, could have been developed by Amerindian intellectuals if they had had the opportunity to expand their knowledge instead of being suppressed and negated.

Acosta's classical *Historia* should be read not only for what he says but, and perhaps mainly, for what he hides, certainly unintentionally, at the limits of his Christian beliefs.

## Notes

1   For the life of Acosta and his role and contributions in and to the Jesuit order, see Burgaleta 1999.

2   On *De procuranda Indorum salute,* see Pereña 1984.

3   See, for instance, Kafadar 1995 and Brotton 1998.

4   For the conception of history in the sixteenth century, see O'Gorman's introduction to Acosta's book ([1940] 1972) and Mignolo's essays on the letters, chronicles, and histories of the discovery and conquest (1981; 1982).

## Bibliography

Brotton, Jerry. 1998. "Disorienting the East: The Geography of the Ottoman Empire." In *Trading Territories: Mapping the Early Modern World,* 87–118. Ithaca: Cornell University Press.

Burgaleta, Claudio M. 1999. *José de Acosta, S.J. (1540–1600): His Life and Thought*. Chicago: Loyola University Press.

Kafadar, Cemal. 1995. *Between Two Worlds: The Construction of the Ottoman State*. Berkeley: University of California Press.

Mignolo, Walter D. 1981. "El metatexto historiográfico y la historiografía Indiana." *Modern Languages Notes* 96 (1981): 358–402.

———. 1982. "Cartas, crónicas, y relaciones del descubrimiento y de la conquista." In *Historia de la Literatura Hispanoamericana*. Vol. 1: *Epoca colonial*. Coordinated by Luis Iñigo Madrigal, 57–116. Madrid: Cátedra.

O'Gorman, Edmundo [1940] 1992. "La 'Historia natural y moral de las Indias' del P. Joseph de Acosta." In *Cuatro Historiadores de Indias*, 165–236. Mexico City: Secretaría de Educación Pública, 1972.

Pereña, Luciano. 1984. "Proyecto de Sociedad Colonial: Pacificación y colonización." In José de Acosta, *De procuranda Indorum salute: Pacificación y colonización*, 1–48. Madrid: Centro Superior de Investigaciones Científicas y Técnicas.

# NATURAL AND MORAL HISTORY
## OF THE INDIES

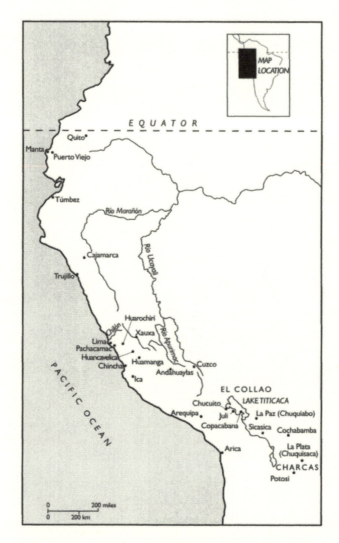

Regional map of the Andes with major preconquest and colonial locations. Adapted from Sabine MacCormack, *Religion in the Andes: Vision and Imagination in Early Colonial Peru* (Princeton University Press, 1991), p. xvi.

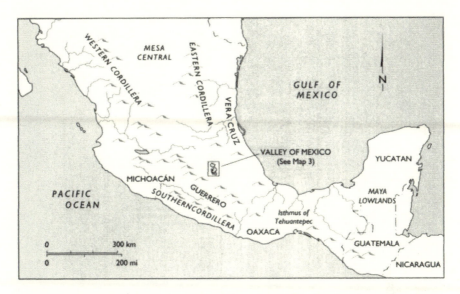

Regional map of Mesoamerica. Adapted from Inga Clendinnen, *Aztecs: An Inter-pretation* (Cambridge University Press [1991] 1993), p. xiv.

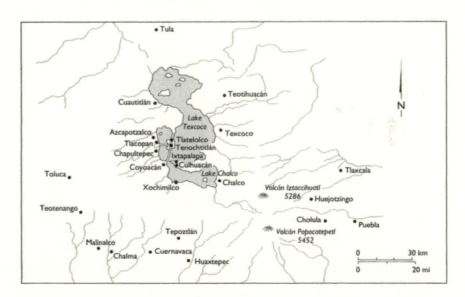

Map of the Valley of Mexico with preconquest locations. Adapted from Inga Clendinnen, *Aztecs: An Interpretation* (Cambridge University Press [1991] 1993), p. xv.

# PRINTING PERMISSION GRANTED BY KING PHILIP II

BECAUSE WE WERE INFORMED that you, José de Acosta of the Society of Jesus, had written a book in the Spanish language entitled *Natural and Moral History of the Indies,* into which you had put much labor and care, and you requested and implored Us, we grant you permission to allow it to be printed in these Our realms under ecclesiastical privilege for ten years or for as long as We please or Our pleasure extends.[1] The book having been seen by the members of Our council, and since by its order investigations of the present volume were made according to the terms of the pragmatic recently issued by Us, it was agreed that We should issue this Our license in this matter, and I gave My agreement. Hence, We give you license and permission for the period of ten years, counting from the day of the issuance of the permission, to print and sell in Our realms the aforesaid book of which mention is made above, from the original, which was examined in Our

1. Acosta was a member of the Society of Jesus, commonly known in English as the Jesuits, an order founded by the Spaniard Ignatius Loyola in 1534. King Philip II (1527–98) was hesitant to allow the Jesuits to travel to the New World because he feared conflict with the Dominican, Franciscan, and Augustinian orders, which were already well established in Mexico and Peru. Moreover, the Spanish Crown was wary of potential confrontations over jurisdiction with Rome, the home of the Jesuits' centralized power structure. Despite these concerns, King Philip granted his approval, and the first five Jesuits went to the New World in 1568 as missionaries in Peru. In 1571, at the age of thirty-one, Acosta followed these pioneers. The Jesuits are best known for their establishment of schools in colonial cities and their missionary work with indigenous peoples in the *reducciones* of Paraguay. The ouster of the Jesuit order in 1759 from Brazilian territories and 1767 from the Spanish colonies was grounded in long-standing political conflicts with the Crown and was ushered in by policy changes of the Bourbon monarchy. On the Jesuits, see the various works of Nicholas Cushner, including *Lords of the Land: Sugar, Wine, and Jesuit Estates of Coastal Peru* (Albany: State University of New York Press, 1980); Herman W. Konrad, *A Jesuit Hacienda in Colonial Mexico: Santa Lucia, 1576–1767* (Stanford: Stanford University Press, 1980); and Magnus Morner, ed., *The Expulsion of the Jesuits from Latin America* (New York: Knopf, 1965).

council, with each page certified, and signed at the end of the book by Christóbal de León, Our personal scribe, of those who reside in Our council; and that, before it is sold, you bring it before them together with the original that you presented to them previously, so that it can be seen if the printed book is in agreement with the original, or bring public proof that a corrector appointed by Us saw and corrected the printed version by the aforesaid original version. And the errors pointed out by him for each book so printed shall also be printed and the price set for each volume that you have and will carry away. And We order that during the aforesaid period of time no one may print it without your permission and that anyone who prints or sells it incurs the penalty of losing all and any type of molds and machinery that he possesses as well as the books that he shall have sold in these realms and will in addition incur a fine of fifty thousand *maravedises* in each case that occurs. Of this fine one-third shall be for Our chamber, another one-third for the person who discovers the fault, and the remaining one-third for the judge who issues the sentence. And we order those of Our council, the president and members of Our courts of justice, mayors, officers of Our household and court, and chancelleries, and all the governors, assistants, major and minor officers, and other judges and justices in any of Our cities, towns, and villages of Our realms and possessions, present ones as well as those to come, to keep and fulfill this Our license and favor that We do for you, and let no one transgress it or allow it to be transgressed in any way whatsoever, on pain of being deprived of Our favor and a fine of ten thousand *maravedises* for Our chamber. Issued in San Lorenzo on the twenty-fourth day of the month of May in the year one thousand five hundred and eighty and nine.

I THE KING
By order of the King Our Lord
Juan Vázquez

# PRINTING PERMISSION GRANTED
# BY GONZALO DÁVILA, SOCIETY OF JESUS

I, GONZALO DÁVILA, PROVINCIAL OF the Society of Jesus in the Province of Toledo, by special instruction that I have received for the purpose from Father Claudio Aquaviva, our director general, give permission to print the book of the *Natural and Moral History of the Indies,* which Father José de Acosta, a religious of that society, has written; and it has been examined and approved by learned and grave persons of our society. In testimony of which, I gave this permission signed with my name and sealed with the seal of my office. In Alcalá, eleventh of April of 1589.

Gonzalo Dávila
Provincial

# CONTENT APPROVAL GRANTED
## BY FRAY LUIS DE LEÓN

I HAVE SEEN THIS *Natural and Moral History of the Indies* written by Father José de Acosta of the Society of Jesus, and it is Catholic in matters pertaining to the doctrine of the Faith, and as for the rest worthy of the great learning and prudence of the author and worthy of causing all who read it to praise God, who is so wonderful in all his works. Given in San Phelipe de Madrid, on May fourth, 1589.

Fray Luis de León[1]

1. In the sixteenth century, the Inquisition regularly submitted texts to a university committee for review. Acosta's work fell under the review of Fray Luis de León (1528–91), an Augustinian friar best known for his *siglo de oro* poetry and his exposition on marriage, *La perfecta casada*. Even though he had never been to the Americas, León read and approved Acosta's chronicle of New World history in his capacity as a chaired professor of sacred scripture at the University of Salamanca. A history of the New World, be it an account of Spanish actions or a philosophical treatment of the origins of native peoples, carried weighty political consequences. Acosta wrote during an era of hypersensitivity to the study of indigenous history because in 1577 King Philip II had ordered the censorship of all publications on native customs and rituals. See Fray Diego Durán, *The History of the Indies of New Spain,* translated and edited by Doris Heyden (Norman: University of Oklahoma Press, 1994), xxxii, citing Georges Baudot, *Utopia e historia en México: Los primeros cronistas de la civilización mexicana (1520–1569)* (Madrid: Espasa-Calpe, 1983), 471–500.

# DEDICATION TO THE INFANTA
## DOÑA ISABEL CLARA EUGENIA
## DE AUSTRIA

*To Her Most Serene Highness*
*the Infanta Doña Isabel Clara Eugenia de Austria*
*My lady:*

The Majesty of the King our lord having given me permission to offer to Your Highness this little work entitled *Natural and Moral History of the Indies,* I should not like to have any lack of consideration attributed to me in wishing you to occupy your time, which Your Highness in so saintly a manner spends on matters of importance, by directing it to subjects that because they have to do with philosophy are somewhat obscure and that seem not to be suitable owing to the fact that they deal with heathen peoples.[1] But because knowledge and speculation concerning the works of Nature, especially if they are remarkable and rare, cause natural pleasure and delight in persons of exquisite perception, and because news of strange customs and events also pleases by way of its novelty, I believe that my book can serve Your Highness as honorable and useful entertainment. It also offers an opportunity to observe the works that the Most High has performed in the fabric of this world, especially in those parts that we call the Indies. Because these are new lands they are worthy of consideration, and because they belong to new vassals whom Almighty God has given to the Crown of Spain I believe that they are

1. The recipient of Acosta's dedication, the infanta Doña Isabel Clara Eugenia de Austria (1566–1633), was the elder daughter of King Philip II, born to his third wife, Isabel de Valois. She was twenty-four years old when Acosta made the dedication in the *Historia natural y moral de las Indias.* As a young girl, in the wake of the death of the queen (Philip's fourth wife, Anna of Austria, who died in 1580), she had become her father's closest confidante. Acosta anticipated that the infanta would read his work and recommend it to her father. Her energies, however, focused largely on Spain's European possessions and she served as queen of the Netherlands from 1598 to 1621.

not completely alien and removed from your consideration. It is my desire that Your Highness may pass a few hours of time in reading it, which is the reason it is written in the vulgar tongue, although, if I am not mistaken, it is not for common intellects. And it may even be that in this as in other things, if my little book pleases Your Highness and you show your pleasure in it, perhaps the King our lord also may deign to spend some time on the account and consideration of things and people so intimately connected with his royal Crown. To His Majesty I dedicated another book on the preaching of the Gospel in the Indies, which I composed in Latin.[2] And my desire is that all I have written may serve to make known which of his treasures God Our Lord divided and deposited in those realms; may the peoples there be all the more aided and favored by the people of Spain, to whose charge divine and lofty Providence has entrusted them. I entreat Your Highness that, if in some places this little book does not seem pleasant to read, you will not fail to read the other parts, for it may be that some of them will please you. And if this proves to be the case they cannot help but be of great use, for this favor of yours will work to the good of lands and people who are so much in need of it. May God Our Lord keep and prosper Your Highness for many years, as your servants daily and affectionately beseech His Divine Majesty.

Amen. In Seville, March first, in the year of 1590.

José de Acosta

2. Acosta refers here to his 1588 text. See his *De procuranda Indorum salute,* edited by L. Pereña (Madrid: Consejo Superior de Investigaciones Científicos, 1984).

## PAPER TAX ORDERED
## BY CHRISTÓBAL DE LEÓN

I CHRISTÓBAL DE LEÓN, PRIVY SCRIBE of the King Our Lord of those who reside in his Council, attest that, having been viewed by the lords of the Council, a book entitled *Natural and Moral History of the Indies,* which Father José de Acosta of the Society of Jesus has had printed with its permission, each sheet of the aforesaid book printed on paper be taxed at the rate of three *maravedises* and ordered that before it is sold the testimony of this tax be printed on the first page of each book. And so that this may be official, by order of the aforesaid lords of the Council and at the request of Father Diego de Lugo, procurator general of the aforesaid Society of Jesus, I do now so attest. Done in the city of Madrid on the thirtieth day of April in the year one thousand five hundred and ninety.

Christóbal de León

# PROLOGUE TO THE READER

MANY AUTHORS HAVE WRITTEN sundry books and reports in which they disclose the new and strange things that have been discovered in the New World and the West Indies and the deeds and adventures of the Spaniards who conquered and settled those lands. But hitherto I have seen no author who deals with the causes and reasons for those new things and natural wonders, nor has any made a discourse and investigation of these matters; nor have I encountered any book whose matter consists of the deeds and history of those same ancient Indians and natural inhabitants of the New World.[1] Indeed, both of these things are of no small difficulty. The first, because it deals with natural phenomena that fall outside the philosophy

1. A summary of Acosta's precursors in New World literature provides a mark by which to measure his particular contribution among the "sundry books and reports." By the publication date of Acosta's *Historia natural y moral de las Indias,* numerous scholars had taken pen to paper in a quest to define some aspect of the New World experience for a European audience. The first writings came from early explorations in the Caribbean, namely, the letters and journals of Christopher Columbus; the first study of the native peoples by Fray Ramón Pané, *An Account of the Antiquities of the Indians;* and Fray Bartolomé de Las Casas's famous polemic *The Destruction of the Indies.* Then came the heroic tales of conquest on the mainlands of Mexico and Peru from the perspective of conquerors like Hernán Cortés and foot soldiers like Bernal Díaz del Castillo and Francisco Jérez. By the mid–sixteenth century, when abuse and disease threatened the native population, a group of missionaries in New Spain created a corpus of ethnographic and linguistic studies that preserved histories of native Mexican culture. The most famous of these early Indies ethnohistorians is the Franciscan friar Bernardino de Sahagún, who, along with native elites, compiled an encyclopedic study of Aztec culture entitled *The General History of the Things of New Spain,* also known as *The Florentine Codex.* In Peru during the same period some of the most detailed reports of native history and customs, including Pedro Sarmiento de Gamboa's *Historia Indica* and Juan de Betanzos's *Narrative of the Incas,* were written at the behest of the Crown.

Scholars who have examined indigenous influence on the production of history in this era include, for the Andes, Sabine MacCormack, *Religion in the Andes: Vision and Imagination in Early Colonial Peru* (Princeton: Princeton University Press, 1991); and Frank Salomon, "Chronicles of the Impossible: Notes on Three Peruvian Indigenous Historians," in *From Oral to Written Expression: Native Andean Chronicles of the Early Colonial Period,* edited by Rolena Adorno (Syracuse: Maxwell School of Citizenship and Public Affairs,

formerly received and argued, such as the fact that the region called the Torrid Zone is very humid, and in places very temperate, and that it rains there when the sun is closest, and other similar things. And those who have written of the West Indies have not claimed this much philosophy, nor have most of them even made mention of such things. The second, because it deals with the deeds and history of the Indians themselves, and required many and very intimate dealings with the Indians, which was not the case of most of those who have written of the Indies, either because they did not know their language or because they did not bother to learn about their ancient history; hence, they were satisfied to recount a few superficial things. Because I wanted to have more specialized knowledge of the Indians' affairs, I resorted to experienced men who were very knowledgeable in these matters, and from their conversation and abundant written works I was able to extract material that I judged sufficient to write of the customs and deeds of those people and of the natural phenomena of those lands and their characteristics, with the experience of many years and my diligence in inquiring and discussing and conferring with learned and expert persons.[2] I also felt that I was offered some information that could be used and taken advantage of by intellects superior to mine, either to search for the truth or to pass over, if what they found in these pages was to their liking. Thus, although the New World is

---

1982), 9–40. For Mexico, see Enrique Florescano, *Memory, Myth, and Time in Mexico: From the Aztecs to Independence* (Austin: University of Texas Press, [1992] 1994); and Serge Gruzinski, *The Conquest of Mexico: The Incorporation of Indian Society into the Western World, 16th–18th Centuries,* translated by Eileen Corrigan (Oxford: Blackwell, [1988] 1993).

Acosta accurately assessed his precursors in the field when he concluded that his work was distinct. He had earned his authorial voice on the basis of his ten-year stay in the Indies. Yet he knew that despite his travels and observations he had spent relatively little time working directly with the native population in comparison with scholars like Sahagún. And no evidence suggests that he had other than a cursory knowledge of native languages. Acosta's valuable contribution stemmed from his ability to incorporate both central and peripheral regions of Mexico and Peru, and even China and Japan, into his realm of observation. To this expansive view of the New World, he added "cause and reason." New World realities often contradicted Old World philosophy or proved difficult to reconcile with Catholic religious doctrine. The immense popularity of Acosta's systematic cataloging of New World plants, animals, minerals, and native customs speaks to the potential of the New World experience to influence the late-sixteenth-century European intellectual climate and hasten the dawn of scientific reasoning.

2. In this passage Acosta reveals his method and sources for writing the *Historia natural y moral* and provides his definition of what it meant to write history in 1590. On the issues of genre in the Renaissance, see Walter D. Mignolo, "Cartas, crónicas, y relaciones de descubrimiento y de la Conquista," in Luis Iñigo Madrigal, *Historia de la literatura hispanoamerica, Epoca Colonial,* vol. 1 (Madrid: Catedra, 1982), 57–116; and "El metatexto historiográfico y la historiografía Indians," *Modern Language Notes* 96 (1981): 358–402. See also his

not new but old, for much has been said and written about it, I believe that this history may be considered new in some ways because it is both history and in part philosophy and because it deals not only with the works of nature but with problems of free will, which are the deeds and customs of men. That is why I gave it the name *Natural and Moral History of the Indies,* including the

---

"On the Colonization of Amerindian Languages and Memories: Renaissance Theories of Writing and the Discontinuity of the Classical Tradition," *Comparative Studies in Society and History* 34, no. 2 (1993): 301–330.

To compensate for his lack of expertise on the native population, Acosta relied on informants, only some of whom he acknowledged directly in the text. Two of the "learned and expert persons" who most influenced Acosta's history of the Indies were Juan de Tovar and Juan Polo de Ondegardo. Although these men were not cited in the notes of the original 1590 version, as were the ancient philosophers and passages from Scripture, they were acknowledged in the body of the work. Acosta met the Peruvian expert Juan Polo de Ondegardo during his travels around Peru in the late 1570s and early 1580s. After arriving in Peru in 1545, Polo's early activities included helping Gasca to sort out the civil war and serving as governor and captain general of Charcas, where he visited the region to try and squelch rebellion. The Viceroy Marqués de Cañete appointed him the *corregidor* of Cuzco from 1558 to 1561, during which time he supervised expeditions to locate and destroy temples of the dead Inca kings, ostensibly looking for treasure as well. This was one of the most formative experiences for his work on Inca religious and state practices. When Viceroy Toledo visited Peru, Polo was placed in charge of the *visita* of the entire viceroyalty. Toledo, and other Spanish administrators, sought opinions from Polo about governing the native population because he had earned a reputation as an expert through his numerous writings, including *Instrucción contra las ceremonias y ritos que usan los indios conforme al tiempo de su infidelidad: Informaciones acerca de la religión y gobierno de los Incas,* edited by Horacio H. Urteaga (Lima: Imprenta Sanmarti y Ca., 1916); and *Relación del linaje de los Incas y como extendieren ellos sus conquistas* [ca. 1560–72], published in English as *Narratives of the Rites and Laws of the Incas,* translated and edited by Clements R. Markham (London: Hakluyt Society, 1873). Acosta would have been familiar with Polo's work because his tract on idolatry was included in the Third Council of Lima. Acosta's proximity to Toledo would have allowed him access to other reports prepared for the viceroy, notably Pedro Sarmiento de Gamboa's *Historia Indica.*

Acosta made the acquaintance of fellow Jesuit Juan de Tovar during his stay in Mexico where the two exchanged information, including the well-known "Tovar Manuscript," Acosta's main source on ancient Mexican history (ms. no. 1586 in the John Carter Brown Library, Brown University). The manuscript was published for the first time in 1860 under the title *Historia de los yndios mexicanos,* after its discovery in 1856 by José Fernando Ramírez. Hence it was known as the *Codex Ramírez.* For contemporary editions of the manuscript, see George Kubler and Charles Gibson, *The Tovar Calendar: An Illustrated Mexican Manuscript, ca. 1585,* vol. 2 (New Haven: Connecticut Academy of Arts and Sciences, 1951), as well as *Relación del origen de los indios que habitan esta Nueva España según sus historias* (Mexico City: Editorial Porrúa, 1975).

Tovar read and used the work of his relative the Dominican Fray Diego Durán. Thus, many of Acosta's Mexican revelations come, albeit indirectly, from Durán's work. Acosta likely met him as well, since Durán returned to Mexico City from rural assignments in 1585 and remained there until his death in 1588. Durán, a native of Seville, grew up in Texcoco, Mexico, and spoke fluent Nahuatl, the language of the Aztec civilization and the Mexica people. His writings on the religion, calendar, and history of the native peoples of New Spain are exemplary for their ethnographic detail. Given his proximity to native informants who lived in the preconquest era and his facility with the language, he was able to provide information not available to other

two things in this aim. In the first two books I deal with everything concerning the heavens and climate and living conditions of that hemisphere; initially I wrote these books in Latin and now have translated them, using more license as a writer than the accuracy of a translator, to better adjust my writing to those for whom books are written in the vulgar tongue. In the two subsequent books I deal with whatever is remarkable about the elements and natural mixtures, such as metals, plants, and animals, that are found in the Indies. The remaining books describe what I have been able to discover and what seems worthy of telling about men and their deeds (I mean the Indians themselves and their rites and customs, government and wars, and great events).[3] The history itself will explain how the ancient sayings and doings of the Indians have come to be known, since they had no writing like us, for it is

---

authors. His work has been published in translation as *The History of the Indies of New Spain,* translated and edited by Doris Heyden (Norman: University of Oklahoma Press, 1994).

In addition to the texts produced by Durán and Tovar with the help of native historians, the Amerindian Martín de la Cruz authored an equally critical text on native civilization, healing techniques specifically, now known as the *Codice Badiano.* Although it was written in 1552, it is unlikely that Acosta was familiar with it. For further analysis of the significance of this text, see Walter Mignolo's "Commentary" in this volume.

Although many of Acosta's descriptions of natural history come from what he saw with his own eyes, he surely benefited from the studies of natural history produced by Dr. Francisco Hernández. In response to the great variety of new natural species found in Mexico, King Philip II appointed Dr. Hernández to travel around New Spain studying its plants, animals, and minerals. His field research in New Spain from 1570 to 1577 resulted in the *Rerum medicarum Novae Hispaniae thesaurus.* When he died in 1587, most of his work was unpublished, although copies of it were located in both Mexico and Spain, where Acosta could have consulted them. Hernández's natural history, *De historia plantarum plantae Novae Hispaniae,* was finally printed in 1651, and has now been published in Spanish as *Historia de las plantas de Nueva España,* 3 vols. (Mexico City: Imprenta Universitaria, 1942–46). Although he was sent to the New World solely to explore flora and fauna, Hernández was fascinated by native culture and composed *Antigüedades de la Nueva España,* translated and edited by Don Joaquín García Pimentel (Mexico City: Editorial Pedro Robredo, 1946). It is likely that Acosta consulted the work by Hernández, and, indeed, its existence suggests that Acosta, who is credited with creating a model for the natural history of the New World, had a model himself.

Acosta's use of published and unpublished manuscript sources was always tempered by his own observations and his determination to add reason to descriptions of the New World. In the case of Peru, his lengthy stay provided more eyewitness fodder for his history than did his short visit to Mexico. In addition to incorporating his own experience into the text, Acosta's structure was unique. He aimed to present an encyclopedic, albeit abbreviated, history of the New World. It was the breadth of his observations, in contrast to the depth of Durán or Sahagún, that propelled Acosta's imagination of the Indies to a comparative scope and pushed him to devise his structure of comparative ethnology of native peoples in the Americas, arguably the most novel contribution of the work.

3. Acosta consistently uses the term *Indian,* a word Spanish colonizers introduced in the late fifteenth and early sixteenth centuries to identify the peoples they encountered in the New World. The notes and commen-

no small part of their abilities to have been able to preserve records of ancient times even though they did not use or possess letters of any kind. The aim of this work is that, by disclosing the natural works that the infinitely wise Author of all Nature has performed, praise and glory may be given to Almighty God, who is marvelous in all places. And that, by having knowledge of the customs and other matters pertaining to the Indians, they may be helped to continue and remain in the grace of the high calling of the Holy Gospel, to which he who enlightens from the lofty peaks of his eternity deigned to bring these blind people in these latter days. In addition to this, each reader can also achieve some useful knowledge, for no matter how unimportant the subject a wise man can learn wisdom for himself, and even from the lowest and smallest creatures very lofty thoughts, and very useful philosophy, may be extracted. I need only remind the reader that the first two books of this history or discourse were written while I was in Peru and the other five later in Europe, obedience to my Order having caused my return here.[4] And so some of the books speak of things in the Indies as things present and the others as of things absent. So that this difference in style will not offend, I felt that I should remind the reader here of the reason for it.

---

tary of this edition of Acosta's work use the word *Indian* when citing Acosta. Otherwise, *indigenous* is used to refer to any originary community; *Amerindian* to refer to the general native population of the Americas; and specific terms, like *Mexica* or *Pueblo,* to refer to individual peoples.

4. Acosta's itinerary, dictated by his order and Rome, led him to many of the places he would discuss in his *Historia*. He sailed to the New World from Spain in 1571, arriving in Lima in 1572. Although the main indigenous mission of the Jesuits during this early period was at Juli, on the western side of Lake Titicaca, Acosta spent the next fourteen years in Lima or journeying among the major cities of Cuzco, Arequipa, La Paz, Chuquisaca, Pilcomayo, and Potosí. After assisting in an Inquisition trial that sentenced two fellow Jesuits to death, Acosta requested a transfer to Spain. In 1586, he traveled to New Spain, landing in Huatulco, on the southern Pacific coast of Mexico, and then taking up residence in Mexico City for almost one year. In May of 1587, Acosta returned to Spain. He lived and worked in Spain and Rome until his death in 1600. On his biography, see Francisco Mateos, "Introducción," in *Obras del Padre José de Acosta*, Biblioteca de Autores Españoles, vol. 73 (Madrid: Ediciones Atlas, 1954), vii–xlix.

# BOOK I

### CHAPTER I \* OF THE OPINION HELD BY SOME AUTHORS THAT THE HEAVENS DID NOT EXTEND TO THE NEW WORLD

The ancients were so far from thinking that this New World was peopled that many of them refused to believe that there was any land in these regions; and, what is more surprising, there were even some who also denied that these heavens that we behold exist here.[1] For, although it is true that most of the philosophers, and the best of them, believed that heaven was all round, as in fact it is, and that hence it surrounded the earth everywhere and enclosed it within itself, despite all this some of them — and no small number, or those of least authority among the holy doctors — had a different opinion, imagining the fabric of this world like that of a house in which the roof that covers it encircles only the upper part and does not surround it everywhere. They offered as justification for this that otherwise the earth would be hanging in

---

1. Throughout the *Historia,* Acosta excuses the "doctors of the Church" when his New World experiences disprove their beliefs. He does not forgive scholars like Aristotle and Plato, whom he terms the "wise men and vain philosophers." The ancient scholars are representative of Acosta's intellectual formation in Old World philosophy. Acosta would have been influenced by the work of the sixteenth-century Spanish philosopher Francisco Suárez, who exemplified the Aristotelian roots of knowledge popular in the wake of the Council of Trent and the Counter-Reformation. This school of thought came under attack by the early seventeenth century in the writings of Francis Bacon. In the late sixteenth century, Acosta strove to reason and explain the quandaries faced by Europeans with the "discovery" of the New World, and, although the Bible served as the foundation of his theoretical path, he negotiated a trajectory between the texts of the ancients and his personal experiences in the Indies. Anthony Grafton charts this process whereby New World philosophers like Acosta chipped away at the block of paradigmatic ancient texts in the sixteenth and seventeenth centuries in *New Worlds, Ancient Texts: The Power of Tradition and the Shock of Discovery* (Cambridge: Belknap Press of Harvard University Press, 1992).

the midst of the air, which seems a thing devoid of all reason, and also that in every building we see that the foundations are in one place and the roof opposite them; and thus logically in this great edifice of the world, all the heavens must be in one place above and all the earth in a different place below. The glorious Chrysostom, as one who occupied himself more with sacred letters than the human sciences, shows himself to be of this opinion, for in his commentaries on the Epistle to the Hebrews he derides those who affirm that the heavens are round everywhere.[2] He believes that Holy Writ means to indicate something different when it calls the heavens a tabernacle and a tent or awning placed there by God.[3] And the saint goes even further, saying that it is not the heavens that move and progress but the sun and moon and stars that move in the heavens, just as birds move through the air and do not, as the philosophers believe, rotate with the heavens themselves like spokes in a wheel.[4] Theodoret, a weighty author, agrees with this opinion of Chrysostom's, as does Theophilactus in almost every case.[5] And more than all of these Lactantius Firmianus, believing as they do, constantly jeers and mocks at the opinion of the Peripatetics and academicians, who assign a round shape to the heavens and place the earth in the middle of the universe, for it seems laughable to him that the earth can hang in the air as described by them.[6] Hence, his opinion agrees more with that of Epicurus, who said that there is nothing beyond the earth but infinite chaos and abyss. And what Saint Jerome says seems to incline to this opinion, for when writing on the Epistle to the Ephesians he says, "The natural philosopher considers the

2. Saint John Chrysostom, *Homilies on the Letter to the Hebrews,* 14 and 27. Hereinafter, notes from the original annotations of Acosta's work, as printed in the 1962 Edmundo O'Gorman edition of *Historia natural y moral de las Indias* on which this translation is based, will be followed by the notation O'G. The distinction between "sacred letters" and "human sciences" had, at the end of the sixteenth century, a long history that could be traced back to the fourteenth century and the *studia humanitatis,* or *humaniora,* which indicates an intellectual attitude similar to philosophy. Grammar and rhetoric are the central disciplines of the human sciences, or *studia humanitatis,* and language is considered by the humanists as the basic principle of wisdom and instrument of knowledge. See Luis Gil Fernández, *Panorama social del humanismo español (1500–1800)* (Madrid: Alhambra, 1981); Gabriel González, *Dialéctica escolástica y lógica humanista de la edad media al renacimiento* (Salamanca: Ediciones Universidad de Salamanca, 1987); and H. I. Marrou, *A History of Education in Antiquity* translated by George Lamb (New York: Sheed and Ward, 1956).

3. Saint Paul, Letter to the Hebrews, 8, 2 (O'G).

4. Saint John Chrysostom, *Homilies on Genesis,* 6 and 13; *Homilies to the People of Antioch,* 12 (O'G).

5. Theodoretus and Theophilactus, *Commentary on the Letter to the Hebrews,* 8 (O'G).

6. Lactantius Firmianus, *Divinarum Institutionum,* book 3, chapter 24 (O'G).

heights of heaven, and, on the other hand, in the deepest part of the earth and its abysses he finds an immense void."[7] It is said of Procopius (though I have not seen it) that he states in connection with the Book of Genesis that Aristotle's opinion on the shape and circular movement of the heavens is contrary and repugnant to Holy Writ.[8] But we need not be astonished that the aforesaid authors believe and say things like these, for it is well known that they did not pay great heed to the sciences and demonstrations of philosophy, being engaged in more important studies. What seems more remarkable is the fact that Saint Augustine, who was so superior in all the natural sciences and knew so much about astronomy and physics, was yet always doubtful and unable to decide whether or not the heavens surround the earth on every side. "What matters it to me," he says, is "whether we believe that the heavens are like a ball and surround the earth on all sides, with the earth in the middle of the universe like the needle of a balance, or whether we say that it is not so, but rather that the heavens cover the earth only in part, like a large plate hanging above it."[9] In the same place where he says this he gives us to understand (and even states clearly) that there can be no proof, only conjectures to affirm that the heavens are round in shape. And there and elsewhere he considers that the circular motion of the heavens is a doubtful thing.[10] No one should be offended, or think less of the doctors of the Church, if on some point of philosophy and the natural sciences they hold opinions different from what is chiefly received and approved by sound philosophy; for their whole study was to know and serve and preach the Creator, and this they performed excellently. And because they were wholly employed in this, which is the important thing, it is of small concern that they were not always wholly correct in the study and knowledge of creaturely things. Certainly the wise men of our day, and vain philosophers, are more to be blamed, for, although they know and grasp the nature and order of these creatures and the course and movement of the heavens, these unfortunates have not come to know the Creator and Maker of all this. And while all of them were occupied in these excellent deeds and writings they did not rise with their thought to discover their sovereign Author, as divine wisdom

7. Saint Jerome, *Three Books on the Letter to the Ephesians,* book 2, chapter 4 (O'G).

8. Sixtus of Siena, *Biblioteca sancta ex praecipuis catholicae auctoribus collecta,* book 5, note 3 (O'G).

9. Saint Augustine, *De Genesi ad litteram imperfectus liber,* book 2, chapter 9 (O'G).

10. Saint Augustine, *Enarrationes in Psalmos,* 135 (O'G).

teaches;[11] or, even when they acknowledged the Creator and Lord of all, they did not serve and glorify him as they should have done, being vain in their thoughts, for which the Apostle justly blames and accuses them.[12]

## CHAPTER 2 * HOW THE HEAVENS ARE ROUND EVERYWHERE AND ROTATE AROUND THEMSELVES

But to come to our purpose: there is no doubt that what Aristotle and the other Peripatetics believed, along with the Stoics,[1] as to the whole heaven being round in shape and moving circularly in its course, is so patently true that we who live in Peru see it with our own eyes, and it is made even more manifest by experience than it could be through any philosophical argument or demonstration. For in order to know that the heavens are round everywhere, and that they girdle and encircle the earth on every side, and to have no doubt of it, we need only observe from this hemisphere that part and region of the heavens that turns around the earth and that the ancients never saw.[2] We need only to have seen and noted the two poles on which the heavens turn as upon their axes: I mean the Arctic and northern pole that is

11. Book of Wisdom, 13, 1 (O'G).

12. Saint Paul to the Romans, 1, 21 (O'G).

1. Plutarch, *De Placitis Philosophorum,* book 2, chapter 2 (O'G).

2. Acosta believed, along with Aristotle and the Bible, that the earth is located at the center of the universe. While this view, based on the Ptolemaic system of astronomy, was widely held, it had been challenged by the work of Nicolaus Copernicus, who published *De revolutionibus orbium caelestium* in 1543. Copernicus's theory that the earth revolved around the sun on a yearly basis was significant because it placed the sun at the center of the universe and recognized that the earth was not singular but existed along with many celestial bodies. See Nicolaus Copernicus, *On the Revolutions,* translated by Edward Rosen, edited Jerzy Dobrzycki (Baltimore: Johns Hopkins University Press, 1978). For further analysis of the ideas of Copernicus during Acosta's lifetime, see Mignolo's "Commentary" in this volume.

In addition to ignoring Copernicus, Acosta omits references to alternative cosmologies, either Native American or African. Thus, he concluded that "we need only observe from this hemisphere" to prove inherited Western knowledge. At the same time he ignored the fact that the Incas, the Maya, and the Mexica (to name just the communities with sophisticated *calendaris* calculus) had themselves created knowledge through observations from this hemisphere. For a wide spectrum of Mesoamerican ancient and current cosmological knowledge, see the useful reader compiled by Johanna Broda, Stanislaw Iwaniszeski, and Lucrecia Maupome, *Arqueoastronomía y etnoastronomía en Mesoamérica* (Mexico City: Universidad Nacional Autónoma de México, 1991). For the Andes, see Gary Urton, *At the Cross-Road of the Earth and the Sky: An Andean Cosmology* (Austin: University of Texas Press, 1981).

seen by those in Europe and this other Antarctic and southern pole (whose existence Augustine doubts).[3] Once the equator has been passed we exchange the south for the north here in Peru. Last, suffice it to say that I myself have sailed more than sixty degrees from north to south, forty on one side of the equator and twenty-three on the other, leaving aside for the moment the testimony of others who have sailed much farther and reached almost sixty degrees south. Who can claim that the ship Victoria, surely worthy of eternal memory, did not win victory and triumph over the roundness of the world, and still more over that illusory void and infinite chaos that the ancient philosophers placed under the earth, since she circumnavigated the globe and encompassed the great ocean's immensity? Who could not accept that by this deed she demonstrated that all the vastness of the earth, no matter how great it is represented to be, is subject to a man and under his feet, since he has succeeded in measuring it? Thus, there is no doubt that the heavens are of a round and perfect shape and that they and the earth, clasping the water, make a perfect globe or ball formed by the two elements, and that it has its boundaries and limits, its roundness and its vastness, which can be sufficiently proved and demonstrated by means of philosophy and astronomy, not to mention those subtle arguments, commonly heard, that the most perfect body (like the heavens) must have the most perfect shape, which is undoubtedly round, that circular motion cannot be equal and firm if it has a corner anywhere or if it bends, as it would have to do if the sun and moon and stars do not rotate around the earth. But leaving this aside, as I say, it seems to me that in this case the moon alone suffices to serve as a faithful witness in the heavens, for it darkens and suffers an eclipse only when the circumference of the earth comes between it and the sun, thus preventing passage of the sun's rays.[4] This would certainly not be true if the earth were not in the middle of the universe, surrounded on all sides by the celestial orbs (though some have questioned whether the moon's light is received from that of the sun). But this is to doubt excessively, for it is impossible to find any other rational cause for eclipses and the quarters and fullness of the moon except transmission of the sun's light. Also, if we think about it, we will see that night is nothing but the darkness caused by the earth's shadow because

3. Saint Augustine, *De Genesi ad litteram imperfectus liber,* book 2, chapter 10 (O'G).

4. Saint Augustine, *Letter 109 to Januarius,* chapter 4 (O'G).

the sun has passed to the other side. But if the sun does not pass to the other side of the earth except by turning at the moment of its setting, making an angle and bending, which would have to be conceded by the person who says that the heavens are not round but cover the face of the earth like a plate, it therefore clearly follows that there could not be the differences that we observe between day and night, which in some regions of the world are long and short at different times and in others are always equal. What the holy doctor Augustine writes[5] in the books of his *Genesi ad litteram* is that all the oppositions and conversions, and elevations and descents, and whatever other aspects and dispositions of the planets and stars, can be reconciled if we understand that they move while the heavens themselves are still and motionless. This is very easy for me to understand and should be easy for anyone who allows himself to give his imagination free rein. For if we assume that each star and planet is a body in itself, and that an angel moves it as an angel carried Habakkuk to Babylon,[6] who can be so blind as not to see that all the differences that appear in the aspects of the planets and stars may come from the diversity of motion given them by He who moves them by his will? Therefore, sound reason cannot admit that the space and region where it is supposed that the stars move, or fly, ceases to be elemental and corruptible, because it divides and withdraws when the stars pass, for certainly they do not pass through a vacuum; and, if the region in which the stars and planets move is corruptible, then they also must surely be so by their nature and consequently must change and alter and at last come to an end. For naturally what is contained is not more durable than the container. Therefore, to say that those celestial bodies are corruptible neither agrees with what Scripture tells us in the psalm, that God established them forever, nor is consistent with the order and preservation of this universe.[7] Moreover, to confirm this truth that the heavens themselves are what move, and that the stars rotate in them, I say that we can prove it with our own eyes, for we manifestly see that not only do the stars move but so do parts and entire regions of the heavens; I refer not only to the shining and resplendent parts, such as the so-called Milky Way, which in common parlance we call the Way of Santiago, but say it even more insistently about other dark and black parts that are in the

5. Saint Augustine, *De Genesi ad litteram imperfectus liber,* book 2, chapter 10 (O'G).
6. Daniel, 14, 35 (O'G).
7. Psalms, 148, 6 (O'G).

heavens. For really we see in the heavens some areas like spots that are very noticeable, that I never remember having seen in the sky when I was in Europe, yet here in this hemisphere I have seen them very clearly. These spots are like the eclipsed part of the moon in color and form and resemble it in their blackness and gloom. They are very close to the stars themselves and are always of the same appearance and size, as we have observed and seen very clearly. Someone may perchance think them a new thing and will ask from where such spots in the heavens may come. Indeed, for now I can only speculate that, according to what the philosophers say, parts of the heavens, like the galaxy or Milky Way, are denser and more opaque, and hence receive more light, and that on the other hand there are other, very diaphanous or transparent parts with low density and, because they receive less light, seem to be blacker parts. Whether or not this is the cause (and I cannot affirm a certain cause), at least the fact that those spots do exist in the sky, and that they move in unison at the same rate as the stars, is an absolutely certain phenomenon and has been observed many times. It may be inferred from everything we have said that there is no doubt that the heavens enclose all parts of the earth within themselves, always moving around it, and there will be no need to question this again.

CHAPTER 3 * HOW HOLY WRIT GIVES US TO
UNDERSTAND THAT THE EARTH IS IN THE
MIDST OF THE UNIVERSE

And, although Procopius of Gaza and others of his opinion believe that it is contrary to Holy Writ to place the earth in the middle of the universe and make all the heavens round, in truth this doctrine is not only not false, but agrees very well with what sacred letters teach us. For, apart from the fact that Scripture itself often uses the expression "the roundness (or fullness) of the earth" and in another place tells us that everything corporeal is surrounded by the heavens and as it were included in its roundness,[1] at least the verses in Ecclesiastes cannot be considered as anything but very clear, where he says, "The sun riseth, and goeth down, and returneth to his place: and there rising again, maketh his round by the south, and turneth again to the north: the

1. Esther, 13, 2, and 4; Book of Wisdom, 1, 2, 7, 11, 18; Psalms, 9, 17, 23, 39, 97; Job, 37; Ecclesiastes, 1, 5 and 6 (O'G).

spirit goeth forward, surveying all places round about, and returneth to his circuits."[2] The paraphrase and exegesis of Gregory the Neocaesarian, or Gregorius Nazianzenus, says of this point: "The sun, having run through the whole earth, returns to his same term and place." This, which Solomon says and Gregory repeats, could not be true if some part of the earth were not surrounded by the heavens. And Saint Jerome understands it thus, writing in these words on the Epistle to the Ephesians: "Common opinion affirms, agreeing with Ecclesiastes, that the heavens are round and move circularly like a ball. And it is perfectly clear that no round shape has width or length, or height or depth, because it is everywhere like and equal, etc."[3] Therefore, according to Saint Jerome, what most authorities think about the heavens is that they are round, and this is not only not contrary to Scripture but very much in agreement with it, for Saint Basil and Saint Ambrose, who usually follows the former in his books entitled *Hexameron,* although they appear to be a trifle doubtful on this point, eventually incline to concede the earth's roundness.[4] The truth is that Saint Ambrose is not in agreement about the fifth essence that Aristotle attributes to the heavens.[5] As for the place of the earth and its unshakable nature, it is truly a wonderful thing to see how elegantly and gracefully Holy Writ speaks, to cause us great admiration and no less pleasure in the Creator's ineffable power and wisdom. For there is a place in Scripture where God tells us that it was he who established the pillars that bear up the earth,[6] giving us to understand, as Saint Ambrose clearly declares, that the immense weight of the whole earth is sustained by the hands of the Divine Power;[7] for this is what Scripture calls the pillars of heaven and earth.[8] Surely these pillars are not those of Atlas, which the poets feigned, but others worthy of God's eternal Word, which by its power upholds heaven and earth.[9] But elsewhere that same Divine Scripture,[10] to show us that the earth is joined to and in large part encompassed by the

---

2. Ecclesiastes, 1, 5 and 6 (O'G).

3. Saint Jerome, *Three Books on the Letter to the Ephesians,* chapter 3 (O'G).

4. Saint Basil, *Homily on Hexameron,* 1 (O'G).

5. Saint Ambrose, *Hexameron,* book 1, chapter 6 (O'G).

6. Psalms, 74, 4 (O'G).

7. Saint Ambrose, *Hexameron,* book 1, chapter 6 (O'G).

8. Job, 9, 6 and 26, 11 (O'G).

9. Saint Paul, Letter to the Hebrews, 1, 3 (O'G).

10. Psalms, 135, 6, 23, 2 (O'G).

element of water, says elegantly that God founded the earth upon the seas and in another place that he established the earth above the waters. And, although Saint Augustine does not wish to have this passage interpreted as an article of faith,[11] that earth and sea form a globe in the midst of the universe, and hence tries to give another explanation of the words of the Psalm, their plain meaning is doubtless what I have stated and that is to give us to understand that we need imagine no other foundations or supports of the earth but water, which, because it is so ductile and changeable, is caused by the wisdom of the Supreme Maker to uphold and enclose this immense machine of the earth. And we say that the earth is established and held above the waters and above the sea, although it is true that the earth is rather more under the water than above it; for in our imagination and thoughts what is on the other side of the earth where we dwell seems to us to be under the earth, and thus we imagine that the sea and the waters that bind the earth on the other side are below and the earth above them. But the truth is that what is actually below is always that which is more nearly in the middle of the universe. But Scripture speaks according to our way of imagining and speaking. Someone will ask, since the earth is above the waters according to Scripture, upon what are the waters and what support do they have? And if earth and sea make a round ball where can this terrible machine be supported? Holy Writ answers this question in another place, causing even greater admiration for the Creator's power.[12] It says, "He stretcheth out the north over the empty space and hangeth the earth upon nothing." It is certainly marvelously expressed, for it really seems that the mass of earth and sea is hung over nothing when it is imagined as being in the midst of the air, and so indeed it is. This marvel, so much admired by men, is emphasized even more by God in speaking to Job: "Who hath laid the measures thereof, if thou knowest? Or who hath stretched the line upon it? Upon what are its bases grounded?"[13] Finally, so that we may fully understand the plan of this wonderful edifice that is the world, the prophet David, a great extoller and singer of the works of God, says this in a psalm that he composed for the purpose: "Who hast founded the earth upon its own bases: it shall not be moved forever and ever."[14] This

11. Saint Augustine, *Enarrationes in Psalmos*, 135 (O'G).

12. Job, 26, 7 (O'G).

13. Job 38, 4, 5 and 6 (O'G).

14. Psalms 103, 5 (O'G).

means that the reason why the earth, being set in the middle of the air, does not fall or falter is because it has sure foundations for its natural stability given it by the infinitely wise Creator so that it is sustained by itself without the need for other supports or buttresses. Therefore, human imagination is deceived if it seeks other foundations for the earth and commits the error of measuring divine works by human standards. Thus, there is nothing to fear, no matter how much it appears that this great machine is hanging in the air or that it may fall or be shaken, for it will not be shaken, as the Psalm says, forever and ever.[15] So David was right when, after having contemplated and sung of the wonderful works of God, he added: "The Lord shall rejoice in his works," and then, "Oh Lord, how great are thy works! Thy thoughts are exceeding deep." Certainly, if I am to give my opinion on this point, I will say that on the occasions when I have passed through those great gulfs of the Ocean Sea and traveled through regions of strange lands and have looked upon and considered the greatness and strangeness of these works of God I could not help feeling great pleasure in the contemplation of the Maker's sovereign wisdom and greatness, which shines through all his works, so much so that in comparison with them all the kings' palaces and all human works seem insignificant and vile. Oh, how often that passage from the psalms came from my thoughts into my mouth: "For thou hast given me, O Lord, a delight in thy doings: and in the works of thy hands I shall rejoice."[16] Indeed, the works of divine art have an indescribable grace and freshness that are as it were hidden and secret, and although they are regarded once and again and many times again they always cause new pleasure. Unlike human works, which even though they are built with great skill after one has grown accustomed to seeing them they appear worthless and almost arouse distaste, be they pleasant gardens, elegant palaces and churches, splendidly constructed fortresses, paintings or sculptures, or gems of exquisite skill and workmanship, although these possess all possible beauty, it is a proved and certain thing that after they are looked at two or three times it is hard to keep one's eye on them, for soon they turn away to look at other things, as if sated by the sight of them. But if one contemplates the sea, or turns one's eyes to a high crag that emerges from it strangely, or the fields when they are clothed

---

15. Psalms, 103, 31 (O'G).
16. Psalms, 91, 5 (O'G).

in their natural verdure and flowers, or the torrent of a river that flows furiously and ceaselessly strikes against the rocks and seems to roar in combat: in a word, any works of nature whatsoever, no matter how many times viewed, always cause new delight and never tire the eyes, for there seems no doubt that they are like an abundant and magnificent feast offered by Divine Wisdom, which quietly and untiringly soothes and delights our contemplation.

CHAPTER 4 * IN WHICH A RESPONSE IS GIVEN
TO WHAT IS ALLEGED IN SCRIPTURE AGAINST
THE HEAVENS BEING ROUND

But, to return to the shape of the heavens, I do not know from what scriptural authorities the conclusion has been drawn that they are not round and their movement circular.[1] For when Saint Paul calls the heavens a tabernacle or tent pitched by God and not by man I fail to see that it fits the case,[2] for, although they tell us that it is a tabernacle pitched by God, this does not mean that we must understand that, like an awning, it covers only a part of the earth and that it stays there unmoving, as some have apparently tried to believe. The Apostle was referring to the appearance of the old tabernacle of the law, and for this reason he said that the tabernacle of the new law of grace is heaven, into which the high priest Jesus Christ entered once and for all by his blood. And from there he infers that the new one is equally greater than the old tabernacle since God, the author of the new one, is greater than the maker of the old tabernacle, who was a man, although it is true that the old tabernacle was made by God's wisdom, which he taught to his master craftsman Bezaleel.[3] Nor is there any need to search in similarities or parables or allegories, to make them agree in every respect, as the blessed Chrysostom so wisely tells us in another context.[4] The other authority cited by Saint Au-

1. Acosta's overwhelming concern with sacred knowledge being challenged is paradoxical if we think of what such insistence is hiding: the superb and sophisticated cosmological knowledge of the *amautas* and *tlamatinimes* (men of wisdom) of pre-Hispanic Peru and Mexico, which is denied in the anti-idolatry missionary practices of Acosta and many of his colleagues. On the *amautas*, see Tom Zuidema, *Inca Civilization in Cuzco* (Austin: University of Texas Press, 1986); and on the *tlamatinimes* see Miguel León-Portilla, *La Filosofía Nahuatl* (Mexico City: Universidad Nacional Autónoma de México, 1956).

2. Saint Paul, *Letter to the Hebrews*, 8, 2 and 5 (O'G).

3. Exodus, 36, 1 (O'G).

4. Saint John Chrysostom, *Homily on Saint Matthew*, chapter 20 (O'G).

gustine, which is alleged by some to prove that the heavens are not round, says "Who stretchest out the heaven like a hide," from which it is inferred that the heavens are not round, but flat above.[5] This same holy doctor replies easily and correctly that in these words of the Psalm it is not the shape of the heavens that is to be understood but rather the ease with which God created so large a heaven, for it was no more difficult for God to provide so immense a cover for the heavens than it would be for us to spread a folded hide.[6] Or perhaps his intent was to make us understand God's great majesty, for whom the heavens, beautiful and great as they are, serve him just as in the countryside we are served by an awning or tent made of hides. This a poet splendidly declared, saying, "The tent of the bright heavens." And there is also what Isaiah says, that "Heaven is my throne, and the earth my footstool."[7] If we shared the error of the anthropomorphites, who assigned corporeal members to God in accordance with his divinity, we might succeed in declaring how it was possible for the earth to be God's footstool, being in the middle of the universe. If God fills the whole world, why would he have to have feet in one place or another and many heads all around, which is an absurd and ridiculous notion. We require only to know, therefore, that in Holy Writ we need not follow the letter that killeth but the spirit that quickeneth, as Saint Paul says.[8]

## CHAPTER 5 * OF THE SHAPE AND APPEARANCE OF THE HEAVENS IN THE NEW WORLD

Many folk in Europe ask what the appearance and aspect of the heavens on the southern side of the equator can be, since they cannot read anything reliable in the ancients, although they prove reliably that there is a heaven in this part of the world; but they could not discover what shape and size it had,

5. Psalms, 103, 2 (O'G).

6. Saint Augustine, *De Genesi ad litteram imperfectus liber,* book 2, chapter 9 (O'G).

7. Isaiah, 66, 1 (O'G).

8. Saint Paul, 2 Corinthians, 3, 6. Acosta's conclusion in chapter IV, from Saint Paul, that "we need not follow the letter that killeth but the spirit that quickeneth" justifies his metaphorical use of the scripture on the shape of the heavens and prepares readers for his reasoning throughout the *Historia*. In Acosta's quest for the "causes and reasons" of New World discoveries, he must often make leaps of reason that are similar to those required to move from a literal to a metaphorical reading of the Bible. The biggest of these logistical leaps is perhaps in answer to one of the most vexing questions for Acosta, the repopulation of the Indies from Noah's Ark following the Flood, discussed in book I, chapters 16, 18, 19, and 20.

although it is true that they make frequent mention of a large and beautiful star that we see here, which they call Canopus.[1] Those who sail to these parts nowadays are wont to write splendid things about this heaven, namely, that it is very brilliant and has many and very large stars. Indeed, remote things are often described with exaggeration, but I think the contrary, and consider it obvious that there are more stars on the northern side and that they are greater. Nor do I see any stars here that are brighter than the Little Bear and the Great Bear. It is indeed true that the Southern Cross we have here is beautiful and admirable to see. We call "the Cross" four bright stars that form the shape of a cross, all very similar and in proportion. The ignorant believe that this cross is the southern pole, for they see the sailors take their altitude from it, as is done in the Northern Hemisphere, but they are mistaken.[2] And the reason the sailors do this is that on this side of the equator there is no fixed star that indicates the pole in the way that the North Star does, and so they take the altitude by the star at the bottom of the Cross, which star is some thirty degrees distant from the true and fixed pole, just as the North Star is distant three and a half; and thus it is more difficult to take the altitude because the aforementioned star at the bottom of the Cross must be directly overhead, which it is only at one time of the night and at different times of the year is overhead at different hours; and during a large part of the year it does not achieve elevation at any hour of the night, which makes it difficult to take the altitude. And so the most skillful pilots do not rely on the Southern Cross but take the sun's height with the astrolabe and find in it at what latitude they are. The Portuguese are best at this, as people who have the most experience in navigation of all the nations in the world.[3] In this region of the south there

1. Pliny, *Natural History,* 6, 22 (O'G).

2. Acosta refers to the practice in which sailors used the astrolabe, a device made of a disk with a bar running through its center, to calculate latitude by measuring the distance between the horizon and the sun or stars. The astronomer Hipparchus is credited with inventing the astrolabe circa 140 B.C.

3. During the time of Prince Henry the Navigator in the fifteenth century, Portugal initiated remarkable advances in maritime technology and mapmaking. The Portuguese Crown desired a route to Asia to participate in trade and to crusade against Muslims. Prince Henry, whose court at Sagres was renowned as a center of maritime expertise, oversaw the initial Portuguese expeditions to the west coast of Africa, which voyaged as far as Sierra Leone and settled the Azores in 1434. Portuguese explorers marked another major accomplishment when they unseated the reigning geographer, Ptolemy, from his throne with the discovery of a route around Africa to the Indian Ocean in 1490. On the history of maritime exploration in the fifteenth century, see Boies Penrose, *Travel and Discovery in the Renaissance, 1420–1620* (Cambridge: Harvard University Press, 1952).

are other stars that in some sense correspond with those of the north. The so-called Milky Way extends very far into it and shines brightly on this side of the equator, and those remarkable black splotches that we mentioned before can be seen in it. Other writers will give other details, or will describe them with more care; let this small amount of information that we have given suffice for the moment.

### CHAPTER 6 * HOW THE WORLD HAS BOTH LAND AND SEA IN THE DIRECTION OF BOTH POLES

We have accomplished no little, for we have established that here in the Southern Hemisphere we have heavens and that they overspread us just as those of Europe and Asia and Africa do. And we take advantage of this circumstance at times when some, or many, of those here sigh for Spain and can speak only of their own land and are surprised at us and even angry, for they feel that we are forgetful and pay little heed to our common fatherland; to them we answer that this is the reason why the desire to return to Spain does not bother us, because we find that heaven is as close to us in Peru as in Spain, for, as Saint Jerome says so well when writing to Paulinus, the gate of heaven is as close to Brittany as to Jerusalem. But since we have now established that the heavens completely surround the earth we must understand that it does not follow from this that there is land in all parts of the world. Since it is a fact that the two elements of earth and water compose a round globe or ball, as most of the ancients, and the best of them, believed (according to what Plutarch tells us),[1] and this can be proved with very accurate demonstrations, it might be thought that the sea occupies the whole region extending to the Antarctic or South Pole, in such a way as to leave no space at all for land on that side, as Saint Augustine learnedly argues in opposition to those who place the antipodes there.[2] They do not realize (he says), that even though it be believed or proved that the world has a round shape like a ball, it does not necessarily follow that in that other part of the world the land is uncovered and has no water. Saint Augustine is no doubt correct in this, but neither does the opposite follow, nor is it proved that there is no land at the Antarctic pole, and eyewitness experience has demonstrated that land does indeed exist

1. Plutarch, *De Placitis Philosophorum*, book 3, chapters 9, 10, and 11 (O'G).
2. Saint Augustine, *De Civitate Dei*, book 16, chapter 9 (O'G).

there. For, even though the greater part of the world around the aforesaid Antarctic pole is occupied by the sea, not all of it is, for there is land, so that in every part of the world land and water embrace, as it were, with each entering the other, which truly gives us reason to marvel and glorify the Supreme Creator's art. We know from Holy Writ that at the beginning of the world the waters were gathered together into one place and that thereupon the dry land appeared.[3] And the same holy writings tell us that these gatherings of waters were called seas and, as there were many of them, there are of necessity many seas. And there is this diversity of seas not only in the Mediterranean, with one being called the Euxinian, another the Caspian, another the Erythraean or Red Sea, another the Persian, another that of Italy, and many more, but also the great ocean itself, which in Divine Writ is often called the abyss, though in truth it is one ocean but in many variations and manners. For example, with respect to Peru and all America it is the one called the Northern Sea, and the other is the Southern Sea. And in the East Indies one is the Indian Ocean and the other the China Sea. I have observed, during my own travels by sea as well as what I have learned from the accounts of others, that the sea is never separated from the land for more than a thousand leagues and never surpasses that measure no matter how extensive the ocean. I do not mean that the Ocean Sea cannot be navigated for more than a thousand leagues; that would be a foolish statement because we know that the ships of Portugal sail for four thousand leagues and more, and it is possible to sail completely around the world, as we have seen in our own time, and of this there can be no doubt. But what I say and affirm is that, in the parts of the world that have already been discovered, no land is more distant in a straight line from the nearest continent or nearby islands than a thousand leagues at most, and so there is never a sea distance greater than that between land and land, measuring from the place where one land is closest to the next; for, from the end of Europe and Africa, and of their coasts, the Canary Islands and the Azores, along with those of Cape Verde and other neighboring islands, are never farther from a continent than three or four hundred leagues at most. From the aforesaid islands, sailing in the direction of the West Indies, there are scarcely nine hundred leagues before reaching the islands called Dominica and the Virgins and La Beata and the others. And these run

3. Genesis, I, 9 and 10 (O'G).

in a series to the Windward Islands, which are Cuba and Hispaniola and Puerto Rico.[4] From these islands to the continent there are scarcely two or three hundred leagues and in places much less. Then the continent runs for an infinitely long distance, from Florida to the land of the Patagones; and on the other side of the Southern Sea, from the Strait of Magellan to Cape Mendocino, there is a very long but not very broad land, the widest part of which is here in Peru, which is some thousand leagues distant from Brazil. In this same Southern Sea, although an approach from the west has not been found, the islands called the Solomons were discovered not many years ago.[5] There are many of these, and very large, and they are some eight hundred leagues distant from Peru. And because it has been observed, and is a fact, that wherever there are many large islands there will be a continent not far away, many persons, and I among them, believe that near those same Solomon Islands there is a large continent that corresponds to our America on the west and that continent may possibly extend as far to the south as does the Strait of Magellan. New Guinea is believed to be a continent, and some learned men place it very near the Solomon Islands. Thus, it is most reasonable to believe that a good part of the world still remains to be discovered, for already our people sail this Southern Sea to China and the Philippines, and in traveling from here to there they do not report the voyage to be longer than that from Spain to these Indies. But where one Ocean Sea continues and connects with the other — I mean the Southern Sea with that of the north — in the direction of the Antarctic pole we well know that it is through the famous Strait of Magellan, which lies at fifty-one degrees of latitude. If these two seas also continue and flow on the other side of the world, at the Arctic pole, it would be a wonderful thing, which many have sought, but as far as I know no one has discovered it, only by conjecture. Some have put forward, by I know not what signs, that there is another strait to the north similar to that of Magellan. For our purposes, we need only know for certain that there is land here in the south and that it is a land as large as all of Europe and Asia and even Africa, and that in the world's two poles there are lands and seas

4. Dominica, a southeastern Caribbean island that Columbus crossed on his second voyage, retains its colonial name. Hispaniola, named as such on Columbus's first voyage, is the modern island of Haiti and the Dominican Republic.

5. Álvaro Mendaña, the nephew of the governor of Peru, Lope García de Castro, discovered the Solomon Islands in 1567.

embracing each other.[6] Since the ancients lacked experience of this, they could express doubt and issue contradictory statements.

### CHAPTER 7 * WHICH REFUTES THE OPINION OF LACTANTIUS, WHO SAID THAT THERE WERE NO ANTIPODES

But now that we know that there is land near the southern or Antarctic pole it remains to be seen whether there are men living in it, which was a hotly discussed question in past times. Lactantius Firmianus,[1] and Saint Augustine,[2] mock those who say that there are antipodes, meaning men who have their feet opposite to ours. But, although these two authors agree in considering them a joke, they take very different directions in the reasons and motives for their opinions, just as they were very different in their intelligence. Lactantius agrees with the common opinion, considering it laughable to say that the heavens are around us everywhere, with the earth in the middle surrounded by the heavens like a ball, and so he writes in these terms: "What sort of idea is it that some say there are antipodes, whose footprints are contrary to ours? Can anyone be so foolish as to believe that there are men whose footprints are above them and their heads down? And that things that here are in their proper places can be hanging upside down there? And that trees and grain grow downward there? And that rain and snow and sleet fall upward upon the earth?" And, after some other remarks, Lactantius adds these: "Imagining a round heaven was the reason why men invented antipodes hanging in the air, and so I have no more to say of those philosophers

6. The discovery of new territory threatened the central location of Europe in both epistemological tradition and physical representation (maps). Acosta's outline of the continent from Florida south to the tip of Argentina and north to California affirmed the contemporary European perspective of the world map. His ideas likely came from *Theatrum orbis terrarum* by Abraham Ortelius, the most popular world image of the era, and the *Descripción y demarcación de las Indias Occidentales* (1574), compiled by Juan López de Velasco, the official cosmographer of the Council of the Indies. A master map of the Spanish colonies, updated continuously over the course of the sixteenth century, was guarded at the House of Trade in Seville. On the reaction of Europeans to alternative traditions of mapmaking in the Indies and the relationship of mapmaking to the creation of meaning in the colonial empire, see Walter D. Mignolo, "The Movable Center: Geographical Discourses and Territoriality during the Expansion of the Spanish Empire," in *Coded Encounters: Writing, Gender, and Ethnicity in Colonial Latin America*, edited by Francisco Cevallos-Candau, Jeffrey A. Cole, Nina M. Scott, and Nicomedes Suárez-Araúz (Amherst: University of Massachusetts Press, 1994), 15–45.
1. Lactantius Firmianus, *Divinarum Institutionum*, book 7, chapter 23 (O'G).
2. Saint Augustine, *De Civitate Dei*, book 16, chapter 9 (O'G).

than that, having erred once, they persist in their foolishness, each defending the others." So far, the words of Lactantius. But, no matter what he says,
we who live nowadays in the part of the world that is the opposite of Asia and
is its antipode, as the cosmographers tell us, know that we do not walk
hanging upside down, nor do we go about with our heads down and our feet
in the air.[3]

It is surely a marvelous thing to consider that on the one hand it is not
possible for human understanding to perceive and achieve the truth without
making use of imagination, and on the other hand neither is it possible to
avoid error if we follow only our imaginations. We cannot understand that
the heavens are round, as they are, and the earth in the midst of them, except
by imagining it. But if reason does not correct and reform this same imagination, but instead lets understanding be carried away by it, we must necessarily
be mistaken and commit error. Hence, experience teaches us that there is a
certain divine light in our souls by which we see and judge the very inner
images and shapes that are offered us so that we may understand, and by that
same inner light we approve or disapprove what they tell us. Therefore, we
can easily see that the rational soul is superior to all corporeal nature and how
the eternal strength and vigor of truth rules over the highest place in man.
And we plainly see how this shows and declares that this pure light partakes
of that highest and primary light, and if someone does not know this, or
doubts it, we can correctly say that he does not know, or doubts, whether he
is a man. So, if we ask our imagination its opinion of the roundness of the
heavens, surely it will tell us nothing other than what it told Lactantius, that
is, that if the heavens are round the sun and stars would have to fall when they
set and rise when they move toward the meridian, that the earth is hanging in
the air, that the men who live on the other side must walk with their feet in
the air and their heads down, that the rain there does not fall from above but

3. When Acosta and other scholars used their New World observations to disprove the antipodes theory, they
happily pronounced the inhabitants of the Indies right-side up, in a physical sense, and mocked the notion of
humans walking around in inverted positions. This European-centered discussion of things right-side up and
upside down provoked irony for indigenous peoples. The Andean chronicler Don Felipe Guaman Poma de
Ayala employed the baroque literary theme of a world upside down to describe native Andean social structure
in the aftermath of conquest. Discovery may have righted the antipodes, but from a native perspective it
upended Andean life. For an analysis of the world-upside-down theme in Guaman Poma, see Rolena
Adorno, *Guaman Poma: Writing and Resistance in Colonial Peru* (Austin: University of Texas Press, 1986),
esp. 106.

rather rises from below, and other absurdities that provoke us to laughter even when they are spoken. But if we apply the force of reason it will pay no heed to all these idle pictures and will not listen to imagination any more than to a crazy old crone; and, with its integrity and gravity, reason will answer that it is a great error to build a whole world in our imagination just as we would build a house, in which the earth is below its foundations and the sky above its roof. And it will also say that, just as in animals the head is the loftiest and most important part of the animal, all animals do not have a head of the same kind, for some have it placed above, as men do, others on a level with the body, like cattle and sheep, and others in the middle like the octopus and spider. In the same manner the heavens are above no matter where they may be, and equally the earth is below no matter where it may be. For our imagination is tied to time and space, and does not perceive time and space universally but only in part. Hence, when the imagination rises to consider things that exceed and surpass the time and space that we know, it soon falls and cannot be sustained for a moment unless reason upholds and lifts it. Thus, we see that when our imagination deals with the creation of the world it has to seek a time before the world was created and it must also fix a place for the making of the world and cannot see that the world could be made in any other way, although it is true that reason clearly shows us that neither could there be a time before there was movement, whose measurement is time, nor could there be any place before there was a universe, which includes every place. Hence, that excellent philosopher Aristotle clearly and briefly refutes the argument that is made against the location of the earth, taken from our manner of imagining it, by saying with complete accuracy that in the universe the same place is in the middle and below and the more a thing is in the middle the lower it is;[4] when Lactantius Firmianus mentions this, he does not reject it with reasoning but merely says that he cannot stop to refute it owing to his haste in going on to other things.

## CHAPTER 8 * OF SAINT AUGUSTINE'S MOTIVES
### IN DENYING THE ANTIPODES

Very different was the reasoning that inspired Saint Augustine, who was so highly intelligent, to deny the antipodes, for the reasoning that we men-

4. Aristotle, *On the heavens*, book 1, chapter 3 (O'G).

tioned above, that men of the antipodes would move about upside down, is refuted by that same holy doctor in his book of *Preachings*. The ancients, he says, state that everywhere the earth is below and the sky above, according to which the antipodes, who are said to walk in a contrary manner to ourselves, also have the sky over their heads.[1] Since Saint Augustine realizes that this is in accordance with sound philosophy, why would so learned a person come to the opposite conclusion? Surely his motive was taken from the innermost parts of sacred theology, through which Holy Writ teaches us that all mankind descends from the first man, who was Adam. Therefore, to say that men were able to pass over to the New World by crossing that infinite expanse of the Ocean Sea seemed an incredible thing and completely nonsensical. And, indeed, if palpable events and the experience of what we have seen in our own time had not opened our eyes, this reasoning would have been considered irrefutable to the present day. And now that we know that the reasoning I speak of is neither conclusive nor true, yet we will be at some pains to give an answer: I mean to declare how and by what means the lineage of men could arrive here and how and whence they came to people these Indies. And because later on I shall have to deal with this very particularly, for the moment we must hear what the holy doctor Saint Augustine says about this matter in the books of *The City of God,* as he does in these words: "As for the fabled antipodes, that is, men who live on the other side of the earth where the sun comes up at the same time that it sets for us, men who plant their footsteps opposite to ours, there is no rational ground for such a belief, for those who hold it true do not affirm it by experience, but solely through a discourse of philosophy that they perform, and so they conclude that since the earth is in the midst of the heavens, surrounded everywhere and equally by them, then there must be a lower place the farther into the middle of the world one goes." And then he adds, "Divine Writ cannot possibly deceive; its truth about what has happened is wholly proved when we see how accurately the things that the Bible prophesies have come to pass; and it is ridiculous to believe that men could have reached that other New World from these parts of the world and could have crossed the immensity of the Ocean Sea. For in no other way could there be men in those parts, since it is true that all men descend from that first man."[2] According to this passage, Saint Augustine's

---

1. Saint Augustine, *Liber Categoriarum,* chapter 10 (O'G).
2. Saint Augustine, *De Civitate Dei,* book 16, chapter 9 (O'G).

whole difficulty was simply the incomparable size of the Ocean Sea, and Saint Gregory Nazianzus was of the same opinion, stating as something beyond doubt that it is impossible to sail upon the sea once the Strait of Gibraltar is passed. In one of his epistles he writes as follows, "I am much in agreement with what Pindar says, that after Cádiz the sea is unnavigable by men."[3] And the same author, in the funeral oration he made for Saint Basil, says that to no one was it granted to pass the Strait of Gibraltar by sailing on the sea. And, although it is true that this was taken as a sort of adage by the poet Pindar, who says that it is forbidden to wise men as well as fools to know what lies beyond Gibraltar, the very origin of this proverbial saying clearly shows how stubbornly the ancients held to that opinion, and it is the same in the books of poets and historians and ancient cosmographers, who place the end and boundaries of the earth in Cádiz, the city in our Spain. It is there that they place the Pillars of Hercules; it is there that the ends of the Roman Empire are bounded; it is there that they represent the end of the world.[4] And not only profane letters but even sacred letters also speak in these terms when put into our language, where they say[5] that the decree of Caesar Augustus was published that the whole world should be enrolled, and of Alexander the Great, who extended his empire to the ends of the earth;[6] and elsewhere they say that the Gospel has grown and borne fruit in the whole world, for by its way of speaking Scripture calls "the whole world" the greater part of the world that had been discovered and known up to that time.[7] The ancients did not believe that the other sea of the East Indies, or this one of the West Indies, could be navigated, and on this point they were generally agreed; hence Pliny writes, as something obvious and true, "The seas that cut off the land split the habitable earth in half, for they cannot be crossed from here, nor from there to here."[8] Tullius, Macrobius, and Pomponius Mela believed the same, and, finally, it was the common belief of all the ancient writers.

---

3. Saint Gregory Nazianzus, *Letter to Postumianus*, 17 (O'G).

4. The Pillars of Hercules is a reference to Gibraltar and Mount Hacho, the rocky formations on either side of the Strait of Gibraltar that separate the Mediterranean Sea from the Atlantic Ocean. According to legend, Hercules pushed the rocks apart to open a passageway for water from the Atlantic and so created the Mediterranean. The pillars defined the real limits of maritime exploration for ancient sailors and represented the metaphorical limits of the known world to the ancient philosophers.

5. Saint Luke, 2, 1 (O'G).

6. 1 Machabees, 1, 3 (O'G).

7. Saint Paul, *Letter to the Colossians*, 1, 6 (O'G).

8. Pliny, *Natural History*, 2, 67 (O'G).

## CHAPTER 9 * OF ARISTOTLE'S OPINION OF THE NEW WORLD AND WHAT IT WAS THAT CAUSED HIM TO DENY IT

In addition to the reasons I have mentioned there was another that moved the ancients to believe that it was impossible for men to pass from there to this New World; and they said that in addition to the immensity of the Ocean the heat of the region that they call torrid, or burnt, was so extreme that it would not allow men — no matter how daring — to cross it either by land or sea, from one pole to the other. For even those philosophers who affirmed that the world was round, as indeed it is, and that there was habitable land near the two poles, denied in spite of this that human beings could live in the middle region that includes the two tropics, which is the greatest of the five zones or regions into which the cosmographers and astronomers divided the world. The reason they gave as to why this Torrid Zone was uninhabitable was the burning heat of the sun, which is always so close overhead and scorches that whole region and hence causes it to lack water and vegetation. Aristotle was of this opinion, and, though a great philosopher, he was mistaken in this; to understand it we must state in what ways he was correct in his discourse and in what ways he erred. When the philosopher is discussing the south wind, whether we should believe that its origin is in the south or no, he writes in these words: "Reason teaches us that the latitude and breadth of the habitable world has its limits; yet all this habitable world cannot continue uninterrupted because the middle is intemperate. For it is certain that in its longitude, which is from east to west, there is no excess of cold or heat, but it does have this excess in its latitude, which is from the pole to the equatorial line, and thus the whole world could be continuous throughout its longitude were it not interrupted in some parts by the vastness of the sea, which cuts them off."[1]

Up to this point we could not ask more of Aristotle, and he is perfectly correct in saying that the earth's longitude, which runs from east to west, is more akin and better adapted to human life and habitation than is its latitude, which runs from north to south. And this is true not only for the reason that Aristotle cites, that the heavens have the same temperature from east to west, for they are always equally distant from the cold of the north and

---

1. Aristotle, *Meteorologica*, book 2, chapter 2 (O'G).

the heat of the south, but also for another reason; for when one travels in longitude there are always successive days and nights, but this cannot be when traveling in latitude, for inevitably the traveler would reach that polar region where for part of the year there is a continuous night that lasts for six months, which is a very great obstacle to human life. Later the philosopher rebukes the geographers who described the earth during his time and says, "What I have said can easily be observed in travels by land and navigations on the sea, because there is a great difference between their longitude and latitude, for the space that exists from East India to the Pillars of Hercules" (which is Gibraltar) "exceeds, in a proportion of five to three, the space that exists between Ethiopia and Lake Maeotis and the farthest limits of the Scythians; and this is proved by the accounts of journeys and navigations, as far as experience has been able to achieve until now; and we have knowledge of the breadth of the habitable torrid zone as far as the parts of it that are uninhabited."

Aristotle must be pardoned for this, for in his time only the first part of Ethiopia, which is known as the exterior part, had been discovered; it is near Arabia and Africa. The other, interior Ethiopia was not known in his time, nor had he any knowledge of that immense territory located where the lands of Prester John now are, and still less had they knowledge of the rest of the land that is below the equator and continues until it passes the tropic of Capricorn and ends in the Cape of Good Hope, so well known and famous thanks to the Portuguese navigations.[2] From that cape, if the land is mea-

---

2. The kingdom of Prester John was both an actual and a mythical place at distinct times in history. In Acosta's time, the name Prester John was applied to the region of Africa situated on the Red Sea coast near the Indian Ocean. For centuries, however, a myth circulated in Europe about the existence of a Christian nation led by a Christian ruler, Prester John, somewhere in Asia, near Persia and Abyssinia. The legend is said to have originated during the time of the Crusades, from the eleventh to the thirteenth centuries, based more on the hope for allies in the fight against non-Christians than on any evidence of such a kingdom. After the mid–fourteenth century, the location of the myth switched from Asia to Ethiopia. As the forerunner in early maritime exploration, Portugal hoped to establish contact with the supposed Prester John after it established a route from the Atlantic to the Indian Ocean. The name, Prester John, was then applied to the area on the Indian Ocean and adjacent interior after its discovery by the Portuguese Antonio Fernandes.

The reference to Prester John illustrates the significance of myth in the creation of history. The myth was attractive to the European Christians who created and recorded it because of its suggestion that Christian allies could be found even in heathen lands. Such myths also operated to ease concerns over initiating trade and commerce. The historical trajectory whereby a mythical place became an actual place offers insight into the many myths of Acosta's generation that drove exploration, like El Dorado, or the creation of theories about the New World, like Atlantis.

sured until Scythia and Tartary are passed, there is no doubt that this latitude and space are greater than the longitude and space that exist from Gibraltar to the West Indies. It goes without saying that the ancients were unaware of the sources of the Nile and the innermost parts of Ethiopia, and that is why Lucan rebuked Julius Caesar because he wanted to investigate the source of the Nile and says in one line, "What is the matter with you, oh Roman, to want to know the source of the Nile?"[3] And the same poet, speaking to the Nile itself, says, "Your source is so hidden that the world does not know all that you are." But, as Holy Scripture tells, we can well believe that that land is habitable, for if it were otherwise the prophet Zephaniah, speaking of those peoples' aptness for the Gospel: "From beyond the rivers of Ethiopia shall my suppliants, the children of my dispersed people" (for so he calls the apostles) "bring me an offering."[4] But, as has been said, it is only right to pardon the philosopher, for he believed the historians and cosmographers of his time. Let us now look at the following quotation: "One part of the world," he says, "which is the septentrional region in the north, once the temperate zone is passed, is uninhabitable owing to the excessive cold; the other part, which lies to the south, is also uninhabitable below the Tropics by reason of excessive heat. But the parts of the world that exist after India is passed on the one side, and the Pillars of Hercules on the other, are certainly not joined together, for the great Ocean Sea prevents them." In this last quotation he speaks much truth, but then he adds, "As for the other part of the world, there must be a region of the same proportion with its Antarctic pole as this habitable part of ours has with its own, which is the North Pole." There is no doubt that the other world must correspond to this one here in all other things, and especially in the source and order of the winds, and after some arguments that are not germane to our purpose Aristotle ends by saying, "We must necessarily conclude that the south wind is the one that blows from the region that burns with heat and that region, because it is so close to the sun, lacks water and vegetation." This is the opinion of Aristotle, and truly human conjecture could scarcely achieve more. From this I often conclude, when considering the matter from a Christian viewpoint, how weak and inadequate is the philosophy of the wise men of our world in divine

3. Lucan, *Pharsalia (Civil War)*, book 10, 269–334 (O'G).
4. Zephaniah 3, 10 (O'G).

matters, for even in human affairs, where they think they know so much, they are sometimes mistaken.

Aristotle believes and states that the land that lies at this South Pole is habitable throughout its very great longitude, which is from east to west, and that according to its latitude, which is from the South Pole to the equator, it is very short. This is so contrary to the truth that almost all the habitable land that exists on this side of the Antarctic pole is according to latitude—I mean from the pole to the equator. And, as for longitude, which is from east to west, it is so small that latitude exceeds and surpasses longitude in this new hemisphere by a proportion of ten to three and even more. As for the other statement, when he says that the middle region, which they call the Torrid Zone, is completely uninhabitable owing to excessive heat and proximity to the sun, and for this cause lacks water and vegetation, all of this is the reverse. For the greater part of the New World—and it is very well supplied with men and animals—lies between the two tropics in that selfsame Torrid Zone, and it is the region most abundant in vegetation and waters in the entire world, and for the most part is a very temperate region, from which it can be seen that even in these natural phenomena God rendered foolish the wisdom of this world. In conclusion, the Torrid Zone is habitable and very abundantly inhabited, even though the ancients said that this was impossible. But as for the other zone or region, which lies to the south between the Torrid and polar zones, even though by its position it is well adapted to human life there are few who live in it, for we scarcely know of any land except the realm of Chile and a small portion near the Cape of Good Hope. The rest is occupied by the Ocean Sea. Although there are many who believe, and I must confess that I am inclined to agree, that there is a great deal more land that has not been discovered, and that this land must be a continent opposite Chile and extending southward, below the circle or Tropic of Capricorn; and if there is such a land it is doubtless of an excellent kind because it is in the middle of the two extremes and corresponds to the best parts of Europe.[5] With regard to this, Aristotle's conjecture was a very shrewd one, but, with reference to what has already been discovered, there is very little land in that location, while in the Torrid Zone there is a great deal of land and it is well populated.

5. Acosta suspects a land mass opposite Chile dominated by fertile lands. Traveling due west from Chile, one would reach Australia, which had not yet been discovered in Acosta's time, but his logic produced a tenable supposition.

## CHAPTER 10 * HOW PLINY AND MOST OF THE
## ANCIENTS BELIEVED THE SAME AS ARISTOTLE

Pliny followed to the letter the opinion of Aristotle, for he says,[1] "The climate of the middle region of the world, where the sun always shines, is burned as if by nearby fire, and is all scorched and smoking. Next to this middle region are two others, one on each side, which are temperate because they lie between the burning heat and the cruel cold of the other two extremes. But these two temperate zones cannot communicate between themselves owing to the heavens' excessive heat." This was also the opinion of the other ancients and was splendidly celebrated by the poet in his verses.[2]

Five zones surround all the sky,
and one reflects the sun's
perpetual splendor and perpetual heat.

And the same poet, in another strophe:[3]

He heard it, if such there be
where the broadest region lies
that the sun melts, amid the other four.

And another poet expresses the same thought even more clearly.[4]

On earth the regions are equal
to those of heaven, and of these five,
the central zone may not be dwelt in
by reason of fierce heat.

This common opinion of the ancients was founded on a reasoning that they considered certain and indisputable. They observed that the closer a region was to the south the hotter it was; and this is true to the point that even in an Italian province Apulia is hotter than Tuscany for this reason. And in Spain by the same token Andalusia is hotter than Biscay; and this is true to such a degree that, although the difference is of eight degrees or less, one has the reputation for being very hot and the other very cold. From this the ancients logically inferred that a region that lay so far to the south that it had

1. Pliny, *Natural History*, 2, 68 (O'G).
2. Virgil, *Georgics*, I, 232–33 (O'G).
3. Virgil, *Aeneid*, VII, 225–27 (O'G).
4. Ovid, *Metamorphosis*, I: "The creation of the world" (O'G).

the sun directly overhead would necessarily have to experience perpetual and excessive heat. In addition to this they also observed that all the differences in the year represented by spring, summer, autumn, and winter proceed from the nearness or distance of the sun. And, noticing that even though they were far distant from the Tropics, where the sun reaches in summer, even so they felt terrible heat in summer as the sun came nearer. They therefore calculated that if the sun were so close to them that it was directly over their heads, and this for the entire year, the heat would be so unbearable that man would undoubtedly burn and be consumed by such an excess of heat. This was the reasoning that convinced the ancients and made them believe that the middle region (which is why they called it the Torrid Zone) was uninhabitable. And, indeed, if eyewitness experience had not disclosed the truth to us, even today we would say that it was a conclusive and mathematical kind of reasoning, for we see how feeble is our ability to grasp even these natural occurrences. But now we can say that it was the good fortune of our time to achieve two great marvels, namely, to sail the Ocean Sea with great ease and to see that men enjoy a beautiful climate in the Torrid Zone, things of which the ancients were never able to persuade themselves. In our next book, with the help of God, we will deal at length with the second of these two marvels, the inhabitants and characteristics of the Torrid Zone. Hence, in this book it would be well to describe the other marvel, that of navigating the ocean, for it is very important to us for the purposes of this book. But before arriving at that point I had better speak of what the ancients believed about these new peoples whom we call Indians.

## CHAPTER II * HOW SOME MENTION OF THIS NEW WORLD IS FOUND IN THE ANCIENTS

To sum up what has been said, it is clear that the ancients either believed that there were no men beyond the Tropic of Cancer, as Saint Augustine and Lactantius thought, or that if there were men at least they did not live in the region between the Tropics, as Aristotle and Pliny and before them the philosopher Parmenides affirm.[1] I have offered sufficient proof that both of these assumptions were untrue. Yet many persons ask out of curiosity whether, in ancient times, there was any knowledge of this truth, which is so apparent to us nowadays. For surely it seems a very strange thing, since this

1. Plutarch, *De Placitis Philosophorum*, book 3, chapter 11 (O'G).

New World is of the great size that we see with our own eyes, that in the course of so many centuries it did not become known to the ancients. There are some, however, perhaps trying to tarnish the good fortune of our time and dim the glory of our nation, who try to demonstrate that this New World was known by the ancients, and indeed it cannot be denied that there are some traces of this. Saint Jerome, writing on the Epistle to the Ephesians, says, "We may rightly ask what the Apostle meant by those words 'you walked for a season according to the course of this world,' whether perchance he would have us understand that there is another world that does not belong to this one, but to other worlds, of which Clement writes in his Epistle: 'The Ocean and the worlds that are beyond the Ocean.'"[2] This is from Saint Jerome. Certainly I do not know which epistle of Clement's it is that Saint Jerome cites, but I have no doubt that Saint Clement wrote it, since Saint Jerome says so. And clearly Saint Clement refers to the fact that there is another world, and even worlds, on the other side of the Ocean Sea, as is in fact the truth, for there is a very great distance from one New World to the other: I mean from this Peru and the West Indies to the East Indies and China. Pliny, too, always so eager to inquire about strange things, tells in his *Natural History*[3] that Hanno, a captain of the Carthaginians, sailed from Gibraltar along the African coast as far as the end of Arabia and that he left a written account of his navigation. From this, if what Pliny says is true, it clearly follows that this Hanno sailed all the distance that the Portuguese sail today, crossing the equator twice, which is an astonishing feat. And according to what Pliny[4] takes from Cornelius Nepos, a weighty author, another man named Eudoxus made the same voyage, though in the opposite direction, for as this Eudoxus was fleeing from the king of Latyros he came out of the Red Sea into the Ocean Sea and turning reached the Strait of Gibraltar, which the aforesaid Cornelius Nepos states happened in his time. Reliable writers also say that a Carthaginian ship, being carried into the Ocean Sea by a powerful wind, came to a land that had never been known before, and that when they returned to Carthage they were very eager to discover and settle that land, and that the Senate by a firm decree refused to permit such a voyage, fearing that the people would spurn their own country out of greed

2. Saint Jerome, *Three Books on the Letter to the Ephesians,* chapter 2 (O'G).
3. Pliny, *Natural History,* 2, 69 (O'G).
4. Ibid., 2, 67 (O'G).

for new lands. From all this it may safely be assumed that there was some knowledge of the New World among the ancients, although there is almost nothing in the ancient authors' works that has particular reference to this America of ours and the West Indies as a whole. But as for the East Indies, both those on the other side and those on this side, which in those days were the more remote because the journey was made from the opposite direction, I repeat that there is mention, and mention neither short nor doubtful. For who cannot easily find references to Malacca, which they called the Golden Chersonese, and Cape Comorin, which they called Promontorium Cori, and the large and famous island of Sumatra, so well known under its ancient name of Taprobana? What shall we say of the two Ethiopias? What of the Bracmanes? What of the great land of the Chinese? Who can doubt that these things are often discussed in the books of the ancients? But, as for the West Indies, we do not find in Pliny that men sailed beyond the Canary Islands, which he calls the Fortunate Isles and says that the largest of them was named Canaria for the large number of *canes,* or dogs, found there.[5] Beyond the Canaries there is hardly a trace in the ancients of voyages such as those made today over the gulf that is rightly called the Great Gulf.

Yet many believe that Seneca the Tragedian prophesied the existence of these West Indies, based on what we read in his *Tragedy of Medea,* in anapestic verse, which in translation reads as follows.[6]

After many long years will come
a new and happy time,
when our broad Ocean
will surpass its limits.

A large land will be espied,
another New World seen,
when we sail the great deep
that now is closed to us.

Thule, so famed
as the last place on earth
by this voyage will be found
to be a near neighbor.

5. Ibid., 6, 32 (O'G).
6. Seneca, *Medea,* 375–79 (O'G).

This is what Seneca writes in his verses, and we cannot deny that things have turned out exactly as he says, for the long years to which he refers, if reckoned from his time, are about one thousand and four hundred and if reckoned from the time of Medea more than two thousand. With our own eyes we have seen the prophecy fulfilled, that the broad ocean has opened the way that it had kept closed, that a great land, larger than Europe and Asia, has been discovered, and that this New World is inhabited; and of this there is no doubt. What we may reasonably doubt is whether Seneca really divined this or whether his poetry expressed it by chance. If I were to offer my opinion, I believe that he divined it with the kind of divination practiced by wise and perceptive men.[7] He saw that as early as his time new navigations and sea journeys were being attempted; as a philosopher he was well aware that there was another land of the same sort opposite Europe, which they called Antichthon, or Antiworld. Using this as a basis, he could well believe that men's daring and skill would eventually allow them to succeed in crossing the Ocean Sea and after crossing it discover new lands and another world, especially in view of the fact that in Seneca's day the account of those shipwrecks that Pliny told of, in which the great Ocean Sea was crossed, were well known. And that this has been the reason for Seneca's prophecy seems to be indicated in some verses that precede those quoted above, where, having praised the ancients' peaceful and untroubled life, he says:

But now is another time;
and the sea, willingly or no
must yield before the bold man
and he will easily cross it.

And later he says as follows:

All ships now dare
the broad and stormy sea;
all journeys now are short
for the questing sailor.

7. Acosta's assertion that Lucius Annaeus Seneca (ca. 55 B.C. to 39 A.D.) was able to imagine the existence of the New World adds strength to the basis for Acosta's imagination of regions yet to be discovered, the location of which he posits with some accuracy for the land bridge across the Bering Strait and the continent of Australia.

No land is left to know,
no realm left to be won;
who seeks for his defense
must find new walls.

All is in confusion,
nothing is left in place,
the world is open and free;
no corner is left closed.

The thirsty Indian drinks
from the icy river Araxis,
the Persian bathes in Elbe
and Rhine, colder than snow.

Man's extreme daring leads Seneca to conjecture what he then predicts will eventually come to pass, saying, "After long years will come," and so on, as I have said.

CHAPTER 12 ∗ WHAT PLATO BELIEVED
CONCERNING THESE WEST INDIES

But if there was someone who wrote of these West Indies in more detail it appears that this glory is owed to Plato, who in his *Timaeus* wrote as follows: "At that time it was not possible to sail upon that gulf" (and he is speaking of the Atlantic Ocean, which is the one outside the Strait of Gibraltar), "for the passage was blocked at the Pillars of Hercules, as you are accustomed to call it" (this is the Strait of Gibraltar itself) "and the island that at the time lay near that strait was so large that it was greater than all of Africa and Asia together. From this island there was a passage to other islands for those who traveled to them, and from those other islands men sailed to all of the continent that was opposite them, surrounded by the true sea." Critias speaks these words in Plato; and those who are convinced that this account by Plato is history, and true history stated in this form, say that the large island called Atlantis, which was larger than Africa and Asia together, then occupied the greater part of the Ocean Sea known as the Atlantic, upon which Spaniards now sail; and that the other islands that were supposed to be near this large

one are those called the Windward Islands in our day, namely, Cuba, Hispaniola, San Juan de Puerto Rico, Jamaica, and others in that area.[1] And they
say that the continent mentioned is the one that today is called Tierra Firme,
the country of Peru, and America. They say that the true sea that is reputed to
be near that land is the Southern Sea and that this is why it is called a true sea,
because in comparison with its vastness those Mediterranean seas, and even
the Atlantic Ocean itself, are laughable in size. These authors interpret Plato
with real skill and conviction, though with what degree of truth and accuracy
I will discuss elsewhere.

### CHAPTER 13 * HOW SOME HAVE BELIEVED THAT IN HOLY SCRIPTURE OPHIR IS THIS PERU OF OURS

There are also some who believe that there is mention of these West Indies in
Holy Writ, taking the Ophir so highly praised by the scriptures as this land of
Peru. Robert Stephano, or rather Francisco Batablo, a man learned in the
Hebrew tongue according to our preceptor, who had been a pupil of his, said
in his commentaries on the ninth chapter of the third Book of Kings that the
island of Hispaniola that Christopher Columbus discovered was Ophir, from
which Solomon brought 420 or 450 talents of very fine gold.[1] For such is the
gold of Cibao that our countrymen bring from Hispaniola. And there are
learned writers who state that Ophir must be this Peru of ours, deducing one
name from the other and believing that at the time the book of Paralipomenon was written it was called Peru, as it is today.[2] They base this on the fact
that Scripture tells us how fine gold and very precious stones were brought
from Ophir, and very precious wood, all of which abound in Peru according

1. Greek legend told that the island of Atlantis, located west of the Strait of Gibraltar, was home to an
advanced civilization that tried to conquer the peoples of the Mediterranean. The Athenians halted their
advance, and soon after an earthquake sent Atlantis to its resting place under the Atlantic Ocean. Since Plato
incorporated the legend into his dialogues, *Timaeus* and *Critias,* it was well known by Acosta's contemporaries, some of whom imagined the Indies to be this sunken continent. Acosta sought a more scientific
explanation for its history and the origins of its peoples and animals.

1. 3 Kings, 9, 28; 2 Paralipomenon, 8, 18 (O'G). Francisco Batablo, also known as Francisco Vatable or
Francisco Watebled, compiled an edition of the Bible published in 1545 by Roberto Estienne, *Biblia sacra cum
duplici translatione et scholis Francisci Vatabli.*

2. Benito Arias Montano (O'G).

to these writers.[3] But in my opinion Peru is far from being the Ophir that Scripture praises,[4] for, although it has an abundance of gold, there is not so much as to surpass in this respect the reputation for riches possessed by the East Indies in ancient times. Those precious stones, and that wood so excellent that its like had never been seen in Jerusalem, I have never seen here, although there are fine emeralds and some trees with hard and aromatic wood. But I find nothing worthy of the praises written in the scriptures. Nor do I think it accurate to believe that Solomon should have sent his fleets to this farthest land, leaving behind the riches of the East Indies. And if he had come so many times it seems reasonable to suppose that we would have found more traces of the fact. But the etymology of the word *Ophir,* and its reduction to the equivalent of *Peru,* I find unconvincing, for the fact is that the name Peru is not so very old, nor is it applied generally to all of this land. In the discoveries of the New World it has been a very common custom to name places and seaports according to circumstances upon arrival, and I believe that this is what happened with this realm of Peru. The belief here is that at the beginning of the discovery by the Spaniards a river, called Piru by the natives, gave rise to the name Peru for the whole land, and it argues in favor of this that the Indians, natives of Peru, neither use nor know this name for their country.[5] A similar case seems to be that of stating that Sefer, in Scripture, is the Andes, which are some very high mountain ranges in Peru. Nor is it sufficient that there is some affinity or resemblance between the words, for in that case we could also say that Yucatán is Yectan, who is named

3. 2 Paralipomenon, 9, 10; 3 Kings, 10, 11 (O'G).

4. 2 Paralipomenon, 8, 18; 3 Kings, 22, 49; 3 Kings, 9, 28 (O'G).

5. Acosta's reasoning in this chapter is intriguing. The reference to eyewitness status, continual throughout the *Historia,* points to the growth of experiential logic in the multitude of new experiences. In this instance, Acosta uses his eyewitness experience to discount similarities between the biblical descriptions of Ophir and Peru. He never saw, he informs the reader, beautiful wood, precious jewels, and gold in abundant quantities that would rival those supposed to be found in Ophir. To further disprove those who would call Peru Ophir, Acosta acknowledges a native linguistic tradition whereby the name Peru is not used throughout the whole of the land and its colonial usage originated from the river where the first Spanish explorers landed. Fabled kingdoms, based either on biblical or philosophical writings, carried enormous weight for European intellectuals who tried to rationalize the discoveries of the New World. Acosta's rejection of these traditions, here with regard to Ophir and in other sections of the book with regard to Atlantis or the Amerindian peoples being a lost tribe of Israel, represented a significant departure from the accepted wisdom of his education in Spain. It was not enough of a leap, as it turned out, to place him among the modern historians of his age. See Mignolo's "commentary" in this volume.

in Scripture; nor ought it to be believed that the names of Titus and Paul, which the Incas of this Peru used, came from the Romans or Christians, for it is a very weak argument to apply to such great matters.

What some authors write, that Tarshish and Ophir were not reached on the same voyage or were located in the same province, is clearly contrary to the intent of Scripture, because chapter 22 of the fourth Book of Kings agrees with chapter 20 of the second book of the Paralipomenon. For when it says in the Books of Kings that Jehosaphat built a fleet in Asiongaber to go to Ophir for gold this same event is described in the Paralipomenon as a fleet built to go to Tarshish. Hence, it can clearly be inferred that Scripture considered Tarshish and Ophir to be the same place. According to this, someone is sure to ask me in what region or province must Ophir have been, where Solomon's fleet went with the sailors of Hiram the king of Tyre and Sidon to bring gold, and where the fleet of King Jehosaphat also tried to go and was shipwrecked in Asiongaber, as Scripture tells us?[6] On this matter I am more inclined to agree with Josephus in his books on antiquities, where he says that it is a province of the East Indies founded by Ophir, the son of Yectan, who is mentioned in Genesis, and that this province was abundant in very fine gold.[7] This is why the gold of Ophir, or Ophaz, was so highly praised, and according to some the word *obrizo,* which we use to designate fine gold, is connected with Ophir, for, since Saint Jerome tells us that there were seven grades of gold, the gold of Ophir was considered the most pure, just as here we rate most highly the gold of Valdivia or Carabaya. The chief reason why I believe that Ophir was in the East Indies and not in these western ones is that Solomon's fleet could not have come here without crossing all of the East Indies, all of China, and another infinitely broad sea; it is not likely that it would cross the whole world to come and look for gold here, especially in view of the fact that this land was such that there could have been no knowledge of it by land. And we will show later that the ancients did not attain the skill in navigation that we practice today, without which they could not have taken such a risk. Finally, in matters such as these, for which there are no certain proofs but only idle conjectures, we are not obliged to believe more than what each of us considers likely.

6. 3 Kings, 9, 26 and 27; 3 Kings, 22, 49 (O'G).
7. Genesis, 10, 29 (O'G).

## CHAPTER 14 ∗ WHAT TARSHISH AND OPHIR
### MEAN IN SCRIPTURE

And if conjectures and guesses are worth anything, mine are that in Holy Writ the words *Ophir* and *Tarshish* often do not mean any particular place but that they are of general meaning to the Hebrews, just as in our vulgar tongue the word *Indies* is general, for to name the Indies in our usage and language simply means lands that are very far away and very rich and very different from our own. And so we Spaniards indifferently call Peru and Mexico the Indies and China and Malacca and Brazil, and when letters come from any part of these lands we say that they are letters from the Indies, although those lands and realms are at immense distances from each other and entirely different. Yet we cannot deny that the name Indies was taken from the East Indies and this because among the ancients India was famed for being a very remote land. Hence came the circumstance that when this other remote land was discovered it was also called India, because it was so far away and thought of as the end of the world.[1] Likewise, it seems to me that in Holy Writ Tarshish seldom means a particular place or area but some extremely remote regions that were considered to be very strange and rich. For what Josephus and other writers mean, that Tarshish and Tarsus are the same in Scripture, is in my opinion rightly refuted by Saint Jerome, not only because the two words are written with different letters, one having a letter *h* and the other not, but also because a great many things that are written of Tarshish cannot be reconciled with Tarsus, a city in Cilicia.[2] It is indeed true that in some part of Scripture it is indicated that Tarshish is in Cilicia, for the following is said of Holofernes in the Book of Judith:[3] "And when he had passed through the borders of the Assyrians, he reached the great mountains of Ange" [perhaps Mount Taurus],[4] "which are on the left of Cilicia. And he went up to all their castles, and took all the strong places. And he took by assault the renowned city of Melithi, and pillaged all the children of Tharsis

1. Such was the conviction in Spain that Columbus had located the Indies in 1492 that no one postulated that the Indies were in fact an entirely different continent from Asia until Amerigo Vespucci in 1500. Juan de la Cosa, a navigator for Columbus, drew one of the earliest extant world maps that pictured the postdiscovery view of the world with a distinct image of the Americas.

2. Saint Jerome, *Letter to Marcela* (o'G).

3. Judith, 2, 12, 13, and 14 (o'G).

4. Pliny, *Natural History,* 5, 27 (o'G).

[Tarshish] and the children of Ismahel, who were over against the face of the desert, and on the south of the land of Cellon. And passed over the Euphrates, etc." But, as I have said, what is written about Tarshish rarely agrees with the city of Tarsus. Theodoret and others,[5] following the interpretation of the Septuagint, sometimes place Tarshish in Africa and say that it is the same city as the ancient Carthage,[6] now the kingdom of Tunis. And they say that Jonah was on his way there when Scripture tells that he wished to flee from the Lord to Tarshish. Others say that Tarshish is a certain region of India, as Saint Jerome appears to believe.[7]

For the moment I will not contradict these opinions but repeat that it does not always mean a particular region or part of the world. The Wise Men who came to adore Christ certainly were from the East, and we also learn from Scripture that they were from Sheba and Epha and Midian, and learned men believe that they were from Ethiopia and Arabia and Persia.[8] And of these the Psalm and the Church sing: "The kings of Tarshish shall bring gifts." We may therefore concede with Saint Jerome that *Tarshish* is a word with many meanings in Scripture and that sometimes it stands for the stone called chrysolite or hyacinth, sometimes a certain region in India, and at other times the sea, which has a hyacinth color when the sun shines on it. But that same holy doctor rightly denies that Tarshish was a region of India whence Jonah was fleeing. It was impossible to sail to India by departing from Joppa, for Joppa, which today is called Jaffa, is not a port on the Red Sea, which connects with the Indian Ocean, but on the Mediterranean, which has no outlet to that Indian Ocean. From this it can plainly be deduced that the voyage made by Solomon's fleet from Asiongaber,[9] where King Jehosaphat's ships were wrecked, went by the Red Sea to Ophir and Tarshish, both of which are expressly stated in Scripture.[10] It was very different from the voyage Jonah wanted to make to Tarshish, for Asiongaber is the port of a city of Idumea, which is situated on the strait where the Red Sea joins the great ocean. From that Ophir and that Tarshish (whatever else they sent), they brought to

5. Theodoretus, *Commentary on Jonah,* 1 (o'g).

6. Benito Arias Montona (o'g).

7. Saint Jerome, *Letter to Marcela* (o'g).

8. Psalms, 44, 13; Isaiah, 60, 6 (o'g).

9. 3 Kings, 22, 49 (o'g).

10. 2 Paralipomenon, 9, 10, and 21; 3 Kings, 10, 11 and 22 (o'g).

Solomon gold and silver, and ivory, and apes, and peacocks, in a very rich voyage lasting three years. All of this no doubt came from the East Indies, which abound in every one of these things, as Pliny demonstrates at length and as our times sufficiently prove. Ivory could not be brought from this Peru of ours, for there is no memory of elephants here; gold and silver, and very amusing monkeys, could well have been brought. But all in all my belief is that in Scripture what is usually meant by Tarshish is either the great sea or extremely remote and very strange regions. And so I believe that the prophecies dealing with Tarshish, since the spirit of prophecy includes all things, can often be true of things in the New World.

### CHAPTER 15 * OF THE PROPHECY OF ABDIAS, WHICH SOME SAY CONCERNED THESE INDIES

There are some who say and affirm that a long time ago it was prophesied in Holy Writ that this New World would be converted to Christ, and by people of Spain.[1] And in support of this they quote the ending of the prophecy of Abdias, which reads as follows: "And the transmigration of this host of the children of Israel shall possess all the places of the Chanaanites even unto Sarepta" (which is France) "and the transmigration of Jerusalem, that is, in Bosphorus, shall possess the cities of the south. And saviours shall come up into Mount Zion to judge the mount of Esau: and the kingdom shall be for the Lord."[2] This is set down literally from our Vulgate. The authors I have mentioned interpret the Hebrew as follows: "And the transmigration of the army of the children of Israel, Canaanites unto Sarfat" (which is France) "and the transmigration of Jerusalem which is in Sefarad" (which is Spain) "will inherit the cities of the south, and those who seek salvation will ascend the Mount of Zion to judge the mount of Esau, and the kingdom shall be the Lord's." Since the word *Sepharad,* which Saint Jerome interprets as the Bosphorus or Strait and the Septuagint interprets as Euphrata, means Spain, some do not claim testimony from the ancients or any other convincing justification except that they believe it. Others cite the Chaldean paraphrase, which states it, and the ancient rabbis, who interpreted it thus. As for Sarfat, which

1. Guido Boderiano, *Letter to Philip, Catholic King,* in volume 5, *Holy Bible,* Juan de Zumárraga, *Hispanica historia* (O'G).

2. Fr. Luis de León, *In Abdiam Prophetam (In Epistolam ad Galatas, etc.)* Salamanca, 1589 (O'G).

our Vulgate and the Septuagint call Sarepta, they understand it to be France. And leaving this dispute aside, for it involves skill in languages, why do we have to understand that by the cities of the south, or the Negev (as the Septuagint has it), is meant the peoples of the New World? Moreover, what need is there to interpret "the transmigration of Jerusalem into Sepharad" to mean the Spanish people unless we take *Jerusalem* spiritually and understand it to mean the Church? So "the Holy Spirit through the transmigration of Jerusalem that is in Sepharad" means the sons of the Holy Church who dwell in the ends of the earth or in the seaports; for this is what the word *Sepharad* means in Syriac, and this agrees well with our Spain, which according to the ancients is the last place on earth and is almost entirely surrounded by the sea. It would be possible to understand by "the cities of the south" these Indies, for most of this New World is toward the south and a large part of it faces the South Pole. As for what follows, "And saviours shall come up into Mount Zion to judge the mount of Esau," it would not be difficult to interpret this as meaning that those who attempt to undo the errors and profane acts of the Gentiles accept the doctrine and strength of the Holy Church, for that is what "judging the mount of Esau" means. From this it follows that the kingdom will not be for Spaniards or Europeans but for Christ Our Lord. Whoever wishes to declare the prophecy of Abdias in this form should not be blamed, for it is certain that the Holy Spirit knew all of these secrets far in advance, and it seems a very reasonable supposition that there would be some mention in Holy Writ of a matter as great as the discovery and conversion to the Faith of Christ of the New World. Isaiah says, "Woe to the land, the winged cymbal, which is beyond the rivers of Ethiopia!"[3] Many learned authors, to whom I defer, understand that whole chapter to be about the Indies. The prophet himself says elsewhere that those who escape Israel will go far off to Tarshish and faraway isles and that they will convert to the Lord many and varied peoples, among whom he names the people of Greece and Italy and Africa and many other nations; and no doubt this could well be applied to the conversion of the Indies.[4] For what the Savior so strongly impressed upon us, that the Gospel will be preached to the whole world and then shall the consummation come, surely states that as long as the world

3. Isaiah, 18, 1 (o'g).
4. Isaiah, 66, 19 (o'g).

lasts there will be people in it who have not received news of Christ.[5] Therefore, we must conclude that much was unknown to the ancients and that
today a good part of the world is still to be discovered.

### CHAPTER 16 * HOW THE FIRST MEN COULD
### HAVE COME TO THE INDIES AND HOW THEY DID
### NOT SAIL PURPOSELY TO THESE PARTS

Now it is time to respond to those who say that there are no antipodes and
that this region where we live is uninhabitable. Saint Augustine was so terrified by the immensity of the ocean that he could not believe that the human
race could cross to the New World. And because on the one hand we know
for certain that there have been men in these parts for many centuries, and on
the other we cannot deny what Holy Writ clearly teaches, that all men were
preceded by a first man,[1] we will undoubtedly be forced to admit that men
crossed to these parts from Europe or Asia or Africa; but how and by what
route they came we must still ask and seek to know. Certainly we are not to
think that there was a second Noah's Ark in which men were brought to the
Indies, nor much less that some angel brought the first inhabitants of this
world holding them by the hair, as did an angel with the prophet Habakkuk.[2]
For it is not a question of what God could do but of what conforms to reason
and the order and style of human affairs. And so two things must truly be
considered marvelous and in conformity with the secrets of God: first, that
the human race could have crossed such a great immensity of land and sea;
and, second, that since there are innumerable peoples here they could have
been hidden from us for so many centuries. For I ask myself with what
motive, with what means, with what strength, could the men of the Indies
have crossed such an immense sea? Who could have been the inventor and
inspirer of so strange a crossing? Truly I have debated this point with myself
and others many times and have never found an answer that satisfies me.
However, I will state what I believe, and since there is no testimony for me to
follow I shall have to proceed by the thread of reason, though it be very thin,
until it disappears from before my eyes. It is certain that the first Indians came

5. Saint Matthew, 24, 14 (O'G).
1. Acts, 17, 26 (O'G).
2. Daniel, 14, 35 (O'G).

to the land of Peru in one of three ways. They came either by land or by sea and if by sea either accidentally or by their own will. I say accidentally, perhaps cast up here by some great tempest, as happens in contrary and stormy times; I say by their own will, that they might have tried to sail and find new lands. Apart from these three, no other possible way occurs to me if we are to speak of the course of human affairs and not set ourselves to imagining poetic and fabulous tales or unless someone takes the notion to seek another eagle like that of Ganymede, or some winged horse like Perseus's, to carry the Indians through the air. Or perhaps they would enjoy using fishes or mermaids or the fish called Nicolaos to transport them by sea? Leaving aside these jests, let us examine each of the three ways that we have noted; perhaps this investigation will be useful and agreeable.

First, I think that we can save time by saying that the ancient settlers in these Indies may have come and discovered and populated them in the same way that we come to them now, with pilots guiding themselves by taking readings of latitude and by knowledge of the heavens and with the skill to handle the sails according to the prevailing weather. Why not? Is it only in our age, perchance, and only our men, who have achieved this secret of sailing on the ocean? We see that even in our time the ocean is sailed upon to discover new lands, as only a few years ago Álvaro Mendaña and his companions sailed from the port of Lima toward the west searching for the land that corresponds to Peru in the east; and at the end of three months they found the islands they named the Solomons, which are many and large. And it is very likely that they lie near New Guinea, or at least have a continent very close to them. And today we see that by order of the king and his council a new journey to those islands is being considered. And since things like this happen why may we not say that the ancients, in trying to discover the land opposite theirs, which should have been there according to sound philosophy, the land they call Antiworld, were moved by this desire to make the voyage and not to stop until they found the land that they were seeking? Certainly there is nothing repugnant in the thought that what happens today could have happened in ancient times, especially since Holy Writ tells us that Solomon received from the people of Tyre and Sidon master mariners and pilots who were very skilled at sea and that with them he made that three-year voyage.[3] Why would Scripture stress the skill of the sailors and their knowl-

---

3. 2 Paralipomenon, 9, 10 and 21; 3 Kings, 10, 11 and 22 (O'G).

edge, and report such a long voyage of three years, if it were not to give the impression that the great ocean was sailed upon by Solomon's fleet? No few persons believe this to be true, and even believe that Saint Augustine was wrong in being frightened and cowed by the immensity of the great Ocean, for he might well have conjectured that the aforesaid voyage of Solomon was not so difficult to accomplish. But to tell the truth I am of a very different opinion and cannot persuade myself that the first Indians came to the New World in a planned voyage deliberately undertaken. Nor will I concede that the ancients attained the degree of skill in navigation with which men cross the Ocean Sea nowadays, from whatever point on one side to whatever point on the other that they wish, which they do with incredible speed and accuracy; for I find no traces in all of antiquity of anything as important and celebrated as this would have been.

I find no mention made of the use of the lodestone and compass among the ancients, nor do I believe that they were aware of them; and without knowledge of the compass, it is obvious that there is no possibility of crossing the ocean. Those who know something of the sea will easily understand what I am saying. For it is as hard to imagine that the sailor, in the middle of the sea, knows how to point his prow in the desired direction if he has no compass as it is to imagine that a blind man could point with his finger at what is closer and what farther away on a distant hill. It is astonishing that something with such excellent qualities as the lodestone should have been unknown to the ancients for so long and to have been discovered by modern men. That it was unknown to the ancients is clearly seen in Pliny, who, although he was a conscientious historian of natural things, when he tells wonders about the lodestone never says a word about the functions and uses that it has, the most remarkable of which is that any iron that it touches turns toward the north.[4] Nor did Aristotle speak of it, or Theophrastus, or Dioscorides, or Lucretius, or any historian or natural philosopher that I have read, although they do discuss the lodestone.[5] Nor does Saint Augustine mention it, although on the other hand he praises at length the wonderful qualities of the lodestone in the books of *The City of God*.[6] And it is true that, no matter how many wonders the ancients recount about this stone, none of

4. Pliny, *Natural History*, 36, 16; 34, 14; 37, 4 (o'g).

5. Dioscorides Pedanius, *Da Materia Medica*, book 5, chapter 105; Lucretius, *De Rerum Natura*, book VI, 906–1089 (o'g).

6. Saint Augustine, *De Civitate Dei*, book 21, chapter 4 (o'g).

them have much to say about this strange quality of always turning toward the north, which is a great miracle of nature. There is another argument as well, and it is that because Pliny describes the first inventors of the art of navigation, and refers to their other instruments and gear, he speaks not a word about the compass or the lodestone; he merely says that the art of noting the stars during navigation came from the Phoenicians.[7] There is no doubt that everything the ancients knew about the art of navigation consisted of observing the stars and noting the beaches and capes and differences in the land. If they found themselves so far out at sea that they lost sight of land on every side, they did not know how to point their prow by any other guides than the stars and sun and moon. When these were lacking, as happens in cloudy weather, they were guided by the quality of the wind and guesses about the distance they had sailed. Finally, they were guided only by their judgment, just as in these Indies also the Indians make long sea journeys guided only by their skill and instinct. Further evidence of this is what Pliny says about the inhabitants of Taprobana, which is now called Sumatra, concerning the art and skill with which they sail, writing as follows: "The inhabitants of Taprobana cannot see the north, and in navigating they compensate for this lack by carrying with them certain birds, which they loose at frequent intervals; and since birds by natural instinct fly toward land, the sailors turn their prows to follow them."[8] Who can doubt that if these people had had knowledge of the compass they would not have taken birds as guides when seeking land? In conclusion, it suffices to make us understand that the ancients did not discover this secret of the lodestone when we see that there is no word in Latin or Greek or Hebrew for such a remarkable object as the compass. If they had known it, such an important thing would inevitably have had a name in these languages. This explains why pilots nowadays, to announce the course to the helmsman, sit on the highest part of the stern the better to watch the needle from there; and in ancient times they sat in the prow to observe the differences in land and sea and gave orders about the course from that position, as pilots also often do in our day when entering or leaving ports. That is why the Greeks called their pilots *proritas,* because they remained in the prow.

7. Pliny, *Natural History,* 7, 56 (O'G).
8. Ibid., 6, 22 (O'G).

## CHAPTER 17 * OF THE PROPERTIES AND REMARKABLE VIRTUE OF THE LODESTONE IN NAVIGATION AND HOW THE ANCIENTS DID NOT KNOW OF IT

From what I have said it can be understood that safe and short navigation to the Indies is owed to the lodestone, for today we see many men who have sailed from Lisbon to Goa, from Seville to Mexico and Panama, and on that other Southern Sea as far as China and the Strait of Magellan; and they do this with as much ease as the farmer goes from his village to the town. We have seen men who have made fifteen and even eighteen voyages to the Indies; we have heard of others who have made more than twenty back and forth, crossing that Ocean Sea, in which there is certainly no trace of those who have gone before, nor are any travelers found of whom to ask the way. For as the sage says, "And as a ship that passeth through the waves: whereof when it is gone by, the trace cannot be found, nor the path of its keel in the waters."[1] But by the power of the lodestone a clear path is opened through the whole great ocean, because the Most High Creator has given it such virtue that as soon as iron touches it it moves and faces toward the north, nor does this quality fail anywhere in the world. Others may dispute and inquire as to the cause of this marvel, and may talk as much as they like about some sort of sympathy, but I receive more pleasure, when contemplating these great things, in praising the power and providence of the Supreme Maker and exulting in contemplation of his marvelous works. Here, surely, it is appropriate to say to God, along with Solomon: "But thy providence, O Father, governeth it: for thou hast made a way even in the sea, and a most sure path among the waves. Shewing that thou art able to save out of all things, yea, though a man went to sea without art. But that the works of thy wisdom might not be idle: therefore men also trust their lives even to a little wood, and passing over the sea by ship are saved."[2] Also what the psalmist says is very appropriate here: "They that go down to the sea in ships, doing business in the great waters: these have seen the works of the Lord, and his wonders in the deep."[3] Surely it is not the least of God's wonders that the

1. Book of Wisdom, 5, 10 (O'G).
2. Book of Wisdom, 14, 3, 4, and 5 (O'G).
3. Psalms, 106, 23 and 24 (O'G).

power of such a little stone has command over the sea and makes the immense abyss obey it and follow its orders. Because this happens every day and is such an easy thing, men do not marvel at it or even remember to think of it, and because it is so simple thoughtless men scorn it. But those who consider it properly are impelled by reason to bless the wisdom of God and to give him thanks for so great a benefit and gift. Since Heaven decreed that the nations of the Indies be discovered after lying hidden for so long, and that this route had to be made familiar so that many souls would come to know Jesus Christ and attain his eternal salvation, Heaven also provided a sure guide for those who follow this path, which was the guide of the compass and the virtue of the lodestone. We do not know with certainty how long ago this navigational device was discovered and used. It seems obvious to me that it cannot be a very ancient thing, for in addition to the arguments noted in the previous chapter I have not read any mention of the lodestone in the ancients when they speak of sun clocks, although it is true that in the portable sun clocks that we use the commonest instrument is the needle touched by the lodestone.[4] Eminent authors write in the history of the East Indies that the first to discover its use at sea was Vasco da Gama,[5] who met certain Arab sailors in the vicinity of Mozambique who used the compass and with it sailed upon those seas.[6] But they do not say from whom they had learned of this device. Rather, some of these authors state what I believe, that the ancients did not know this secret.

But I will speak of another marvel even greater than the compass, which might be thought incredible if it had not been seen and manifested so frequently by plain experience. Iron touched and rubbed with the part of the

4. *De Italiae Illust. Reg.*; Pliny, *Natural History*, 2, 72 and 76; 7, 60 (o'g).

5. Jerónimo Osorio, *De rebus gestis Emmanuelis*, 1 (o'g).

6. The Portuguese navigator Vasco da Gama (1469–1524) was the first European to reach India by sailing an ocean route from the Atlantic. He arrived in India in 1498 by sailing from Lisbon to the Canaries, south along the western coast of Africa, and around Cape Verde and the Cape of Good Hope. On his return to Portugal in 1499, he begged off a return trip to India, sending in his stead Pedro Álbares Cabral, who ran into foul weather and first sighted the coast of Brazil. Da Gama did return twice more to India, serving once as admiral of the seas of Arabia, Persia, and India, and then, shortly before his death, as viceroy. Portugal's belief that its navigators would find the Atlantic route to India prompted their demands for the division of New World territory between their realm and Spain in the 1494 Treaty of Tordesillas. For biography and background on Portuguese exploration, see K. G. Jayne, *Vasco da Gama and His Successors, 1460–1580* (London: Methuen, 1910); and Sanjay Subrahmanyan, *The Career and Legend of Vasco da Gama* (New York: Cambridge University Press, 1997).

lodestone that is toward the south assumes the quality of pointing in the opposite direction, which is the north, always and everywhere; but it does not point directly at it in every place. There are certain places and climes where it points directly to the north and fixes upon it; outside of these it leans a little toward east or west and the more so as it moves farther from that clime. This is what sailors call northeasting and northwesting. If northeasting it inclines toward the east; if northwesting, it inclines toward the west. This declination or leaning of the needle is very important to know, for, although it is small, navigation will be in error if it is not taken into account and the ship will go where it was not intended to go. A very skilled pilot, a Portuguese, told me that there were four points on the whole globe where the compass needle was perfectly aligned to the north, and he told me their names, which I do not remember well. One of them is near the island of Cuervo in the Terceiras or Azores Islands, which is something very well known. Going from there to a higher latitude it northwests, that is to say, inclines to the west. On the other hand, passing to a lower latitude in the direction of the equator it northeasts, that is, inclines toward the east. How much and to what point masters in this art can tell. For my part I would gladly ask university graduates, who presume to know so much, what this can be, and would have them tell me the cause of this effect: why a bit of iron, after being rubbed on a lodestone, acquires the virtue of always pointing north, and this with such skill that it knows the different climes and places in the world where it will be fixed and where it must lean to one side or the other, for there is no philosopher or cosmographer who knows it so well. And if we cannot find the reason for these things, which we see daily and would no doubt be hard for us to accept if we did not see them so palpably, who can doubt the folly and madness of wanting to make ourselves judges and trying to subject divine and sovereign matters to our puny reason? It is better, as Gregory the Theologian says, for reason to be subject to faith, for she cannot understand even in her own house. But enough of this digression. Let us return to our subject, concluding that the use of the compass was not achieved by the ancients, from which we may infer that it was impossible to make the journey from the other world to this one by way of the ocean, even with the aim and determination to cross it.

### CHAPTER 18 * WHICH ANSWERS THOSE WHO BELIEVE THAT IN ANCIENT TIMES THE OCEAN WAS CROSSED AS IN OUR DAY

What is alleged in opposition to the foregoing, that Solomon's fleet sailed for three years, is insufficient proof; for Holy Writ does not state that three years were spent on that voyage but rather that the voyage was made once every three years. And even if we grant that the voyage took three years it is quite possible, and more in agreement with reason, that in sailing to the East Indies the fleet may have stopped in some of the many ports and regions that it sighted and reached, just as the whole Southern Sea is sailed upon almost from Chile to New Spain; and this method of sailing, although it is safer because land is always in sight, requires a very long time because of the roundabout way that must be taken along the coasts and much delay in many ports. I certainly have found no proof in the ancients that they penetrated very far into the Ocean Sea, nor do I believe that they navigated any differently than the navigations in the Mediterranean Sea today. Hence learned men tend to believe that they did not sail without using oars, always sailing coastwise. And it appears that Divine Writ testifies to this in telling of the famous voyage of the prophet Jonah,[1] where it says that the sailors rowed toward land because of the storm.

### CHAPTER 19 * HOW IT MAY BE BELIEVED THAT THE FIRST INHABITANTS OF THE INDIES CAME THERE BROUGHT BY STORMS AND AGAINST THEIR WILL

Having demonstrated that there is no reason to believe that the first dwellers in the Indies came to them by purposeful navigation, it then follows that if they came by sea it must have been by chance and as a result of storms, which is not impossible to believe notwithstanding the immensity of the Ocean Sea. For this is how the discovery happened in our own time, when that sailor (whose name we still do not know, to the end that no other author but God can have so great a matter attributed to him), having sighted the New World as a result of a terrible and unseasonable storm, repaid Christopher Co-

---

1. Jonah, 1, 13.

lumbus's generous offer of lodging by imparting that great news.[1] Thus it could have been that in ancient times folk from Europe or Africa were carried by the force of the wind and cast upon unknown shores on the other side of the Ocean Sea. Who is not aware that many, or even most, of the regions that have been discovered in the New World were found in this way, owing their discovery to the violence of storms rather than the skill of those who discovered them? And let it not be thought that such voyages have been made only in our own time, by the large size of our ships and the skill of our men, for anyone who reads what Pliny recounts as happening to many of the ancients will easily be disabused of the idea. He writes as follows: "When Gaius Caesar, son of Augustus, was commanding on the Arabian Sea, they say that the remains of Spanish ships that had been shipwrecked were seen and recognized." And later he says, "Nepos tells of the northern voyage in which Quintus Metellus Celere, coconsul of Gaius Afranius (when the aforesaid Metellus was proconsul in Gaul) was brought some Indians, presented to him by the king of Suevia; these Indians, sailing from India for trading purposes, were cast ashore in Germany by the force of tempests."[2] Surely, if Pliny is telling the truth, the Portuguese sail no farther today than the men did who experienced those two shipwrecks, some from Spain to the Red Sea and the others from the East Indies to Germany. In another book the same author writes that a servant of Annius Plocanius, who had leased customs rights to the Red Sea, was sailing around Arabia when furious north winds assailed him, and in fifteen days he passed Carmania and reached Hippuros, a port on the island of Taprobana, which is called Sumatra today.[3] They also tell of a Carthaginian ship that was driven by the wind from the Mauretanian Sea to within sight of the New World.

It is no new thing for those who have some experience of the sea that strong and very persistent storms often blow, without letting up in their fury for a moment. It happened to me when I went to the Indies that we reached the

1. According to Edmundo O'Gorman, the first published source of the myth of the unknown sailor is Oviedo and the information was repeated soon after by Las Casas. The story suggests that Columbus went to discover unknown lands, not to reach Asia, based on the suggestion of an unnamed sailor who had seen an undiscovered coast while on a stormy trip. Most scholars accept that Columbus intended to discover a route to Asia and that the myth was an attempt to discredit his initial intentions during postvoyage political struggles. See Edmundo O'Gorman, *The Invention of America* (Bloomington: Indiana University Press, 1961), 11–12.
2. Pliny, *Natural History,* 2, 69 (O'G).
3. Pliny, Ibid., 6, 22 (O'G).

first land populated by Spaniards fifteen days after leaving the Canaries, and undoubtedly the journey would have been shorter if we had set our sails to take more advantage of the gale that was blowing.[4] Hence it seems to me a very likely thing that men have been carried away by winds and reached the Indies against their will. In Peru there are many reports of giants who came to these parts, whose enormously large bones are found today near Manta and Puerto Viejo; and those men must have been proportionately three times larger than the Indians of today.[5] They say that those giants came by sea, that they made war on the inhabitants of the land, and that they built splendid buildings; and to this day they show us a well built with very valuable stones. They also say that those men, who committed abominable sins, especially the sin against nature, were burned and consumed in fire that came from Heaven. The Indians of Yca and Arica also tell that in ancient times they used to sail to some very faraway islands in the west and that they sailed on inflated seal hides.[6] So there is no lack of indications that the Southern Sea had been sailed upon before the Spaniards came. Thus it is possible to believe that the New World began to be peopled with men cast there by contrary weather and the power of northern gales, as was also discovered in our time. It is very much worth considering that things of great importance in nature have mostly been found by chance and without intention, not by human skill and diligence. Most of the medicinal herbs and most stones, plants, metals, pearls, gold, the lodestone, amber, diamonds, and other such things, as well as their properties and benefits, have come to be known through chance events and not by means of the art and ingenuity of man; by this we see that the praise and glory of such marvels is owed to the Creator's providence, and not to the talents of men. For, whatever seems to us to happen by chance, that very thing has been ordained by God after much reflection.

4. The Canary Islands served as a stopping point for Spanish voyages to and from the New World where ships made necessary repairs and restocked supplies.

5. While oversized skeletal remains seemed to corroborate native myths about giant ancestors, they were in fact the bones of prehistoric mammals. The port city Manta, and its inland counterpart, Puerto Viejo, were located on the coast of Ecuador some one hundred miles north of Guayaquil.

6. In regions that lacked lumber or *totora* reeds, people turned to sealskins to construct *balsas,* or small boats, which held one man and were used for traveling ten to twenty miles out to sea. Yca, or Ica, is located in modern Peru, some 170 miles southeast of Lima on the Pacific coast. The peoples of the Ica region are known for a tradition of pottery production that dates back to 2500 B.C. The region was ruled by the Inca Empire and used as a center of agricultural and seafood production. Arica, a port city in modern Chile, is situated south of Ica. In colonial times, Arica served as a crucial destination for silver-laden llama trains traveling from mines at Potosí and Oruro en route to Spain.

## CHAPTER 20 * HOW IT IS MORE REASONABLE TO BELIEVE THAT THE FIRST DWELLERS IN THE INDIES CAME BY LAND

I will conclude by saying that the early peoples very probably came to the Indies by means of shipwreck and tempest on the sea; but a difficulty arises here that is very hard for me to understand. Although we admit that men may have come by sea to these very remote lands, and that from these men the nations that we see have multiplied, I do not know how they could contrive to ship and carry the beasts and reptiles that the New World breeds, which are many and large, across the sea to the Indies. The reason why we are forced to admit that the men of the Indies traveled there from Europe or Asia is so as not to contradict Holy Writ, which clearly teaches that all men descend from Adam; and thus we cannot assign any other origin to the men of the Indies, for the same Divine Writ also tells us that all the beasts and animals on earth perished except those that were preserved in Noah's Ark for the continuation of their kind.[1] Thus also we must reduce the propagation of all those animals to those that emerged from the Ark, where it came to rest on the mountains of Ararat; so, just as for men, we must seek a way for the beasts to have come from the Old World to the New. Saint Augustine deals with this question of how wolves and tigers and other beasts of no use to man can be found on some islands;[2] as for elephants, horses, oxen, dogs, and other animals that men use, there is no difficulty in thinking that they were brought by sea in ships by means of men's ingenuity, like those that we see today brought from the Orient to Europe, and from Europe to Peru, in such long voyages. But there is a question as to animals that are not at all useful and indeed very dangerous, like wolves, and how they reached the islands if it is true, as it manifestly is, that the Flood covered the whole earth.

In discussing this, the above-mentioned saint and very learned man tries to free himself from these perplexities by saying that such beasts swam to the islands, were carried there because of man's desire to hunt, or appeared because it was God's will to have them produced from the land, just as in the first creation, when God said, "Let the earth bring forth the living creature in its kind, cattle and creeping things, and beasts of the earth, according to their

1. Genesis, 7, 21, 22, and 23 (O'G).
2. Saint Augustine, *De Civitate Dei*, book 16, chapter 7 (O'G).

kinds."[3] But it is true that the matter becomes even more complicated when we try to apply this solution to our purpose. For, beginning with the last item, it conforms to neither the laws of nature nor the order of government established by God that perfect animals such as lions, tigers, and wolves should be brought forth from the earth without procreation. This is the way frogs and mice and wasps and other imperfect creatures are engendered. But why does Scripture say so often that "Of all clean beasts take seven and seven, the male and the female: that seed may be saved upon the face of the whole earth" if the world was destined to have such animals after the Flood by some new mode of producing them without the joining of male and female?[4] And still another question remains, for if such animals were brought forth according to this opinion all the lands and islands would not have them, for then it would not be the natural order of breeding but only the Creator's bounty. I do not find it incredible that some animals may have been brought to provide hunting (which was another possible answer), for we often see that princes and great lords have lions, bears, and other wild beasts in their cages simply for their own prestige, especially when they have been brought from distant lands. But to believe this of wolves and foxes and other such vile and worthless animals, which have no usefulness and only serve to make inroads on the flocks, and to say that they were brought over the sea for hunting, is something that makes no sense. Who can convince himself that, with such a very long voyage, there could have been men who took the trouble to carry foxes to Peru, and especially those animals called *añas,* which is the dirtiest and most stinking species of animal I ever saw?[5] Who can argue that tigers and lions were brought? It was enough and more than enough that men escaped with their lives on such a long voyage, subjected to storms, as we have said, without trying to carry foxes and wolves and feed them while at sea. Really, it is laughable even to imagine it. So if these animals came by sea the only other possibility is that they swam. That this is possible and practicable, with regard to some islands that are not very far from each other or from the mainland, cannot be denied, for we see from experience that in some desperate need these creatures can swim for whole days and nights and at last make their escape by swimming. But this occurs only with short distances, for our ocean would make a mockery of such swimmers, since even birds that fly

3. Genesis, 1, 24 (O'G).
4. Genesis, 7, 2 and 3 (O'G).
5. *Añas* are Andean animals similar to European foxes.

great distances have not the wings to cross so great an abyss. Indeed, there are birds that fly more than a hundred leagues, as we have seen many times while sailing; but it is impossible, or at least very difficult, to cross the whole Ocean Sea by flying. Since all that I have said is true, how will we find the way in which wild beasts and birds crossed to the Indies? How could they have gone from one world to the other?

The argument that I have pursued leads me to a great conjecture, that the new world that we call the Indies is not completely divided and separated from the other world. And, to state my opinion, I came to the conclusion some time ago that one part of the earth and the other must join and continue, or at least that they come very close. To the present day at least, there is no certainty that things are otherwise, for toward the Arctic or North Pole the whole longitude of the earth has not been discovered and there are many who affirm that above Florida the land runs very far in a northerly direction, which they say reaches the Scythian or German Sea. Others add that a ship has sailed there and state that the sailors had seen the coast of Newfoundland running almost to the ends of Europe. Above Cape Mendocino in the Southern Sea no one knows how far the land extends, but everyone says that it is an immense distance. Returning to the other pole, the South Pole, no man knows how far the land extends on the other side of the Strait of Magellan. Men on a ship belonging to the bishop of Plasencia, which sailed through the strait, said that it had been constantly in sight of land, and Hernando Lamero, a pilot who was obliged by a storm to pass two or three degrees above the strait, told the same story. Therefore there is no reason or experience to contradict my conjecture or opinion that the whole earth must join and connect somewhere or at least that the parts are very close. If this is true, as indeed it appears to me to be, there is an easy answer for the difficult problem that we propounded, how the first dwellers in the Indies crossed over to them, for then we would have to say that they crossed not by sailing on the sea but by walking on land.[6] And they followed this way quite unthinkingly, changing places and lands little by little, with some of them settling in the lands already discovered and others seeking new ones, so that in

6. Acosta's systematic reasoning led him to postulate a theory on the existence of a land link between the continents at the North Pole. His idea was proven centuries later, when in 1728 the Bering Strait was discovered by the Danish navigator Vitus Bering. Contemporary research has shown that a land bridge, called Beringia, was exposed during the Ice Age due to falling water levels and that people used the bridge to travel from Asia to the Americas.

the course of time they arrived and swelled the lands of the Indies with many nations and peoples and languages.

## CHAPTER 21 * HOW WILD BEASTS AND DOMESTIC ANIMALS CROSSED TO THE LANDS OF THE INDIES

The opinions already expressed are of great help to those who examine with curiosity the Indians' way of living, for wherever there is an island very distant from the mainland and also from other islands, such as Bermuda, we find that it is uninhabited. The reason is that the ancients sailed only to nearby coasts and almost always within sight of land. Add to this the fact that in no land of the Indies have large ships been found, such as are required to cross great gulfs. What we do find are rafts or pirogues or canoes, all of them smaller than a shallop. The Indians used only these boats, with which they could not put out to sea without manifest and certain danger of perishing. Even if they had had ships large enough to sail the open ocean they knew nothing of the compass or astrolabe or quadrant.[1] Were they to travel for eighteen days without sight of land they would inevitably be lost, having no knowledge of where they were. I have seen islands heavily populated with Indians whose navigations are very frequent, but they were of the sort that, as I say, Indians could make in pirogues or canoes and without a compass. When the Indians who lived in Túmbez first saw our Spaniards, who had sailed to Peru, and saw how great were the spread sails and the large vessels also, they were astonished; and as they could never have imagined that they were ships, because they had never before seen any of that shape and size, it is

---

1. Acosta's assertion that indigenous peoples had no boats larger than shallops (a small rowboat or sailboat used exclusively in shallow waters) is incorrect. While the majority of native peoples used small boats for fishing close to sea or canoes for river travel, larger ships were used for trade along the Pacific coast of Peru. Sarmiento suggests that one of the Inca rulers, Topa Inca, used seagoing balsa rafts that held some fifty men and cargo to explore the Pacific. Sarmiento, *Historia indica,* chapter 46. Reports of the first Spanish contact with the seafaring Inca rafts came in 1526 from Bartolomé Ruíz, Francisco Pizarro's pilot. See John Hemming, *The Conquest of the Incas* (New York: Harcourt Brace Jovanovich, 1970), 25. Controversial twentieth-century experiments, most notably the Kon-tiki expedition headed by Thor Heyerdahl, have suggested that small indigenous boats could be sailed successfully across the ocean even without the technological assistance of quadrants and astrolabes.

said that they believed they must be rocks and crags in the sea.[2] And when they saw that the ships moved and did not sink they were beside themselves with fear for a long while, until, looking more closely, they saw bearded men walking in them, whom they thought must be gods or people come down from Heaven. From which it is easy to see how far the Indians were from using large ships or even having heard of them.

There is something else that tends to support very strongly what I have said, and this is that those useless beasts (of which we said it was unbelievable that men could have brought them to the Indies in ships) are found on the mainland and not on islands as far away from the mainland as four days' sailing. I have taken great pains to verify this, thinking that it was a very important factor in convincing me of the opinion I had, that the lands of the Indies and Europe and Asia and Africa have a connection among themselves, or at least come very close together at some point. There are many wild beasts in America and Peru, such as lions, although they are not as large and savage nor have they the same reddish color as the famous lions of Africa; there are many tigers, and very fierce ones, although they are commonly more so to Indians than Spaniards. There are bears, but not so many; there are wild boars and innumerable foxes. Yet, of all these kinds of animals, were we to search for them on the island of Cuba or in Hispaniola or Jamaica, or in Margarita or Dominica, we would not find any. Add to this that those islands, although they are large and fertile, did not have any other useful animals until the Spaniards brought them; and now they have herds of horses, oxen and cattle, and dogs, and pigs, and so abundantly that the cattle do not have known owners because they have multiplied so much and belong to the first person who hamstrings them in the hills or the countryside. The dwellers in those islands do this in order to use their skins for the traffic in hides, leaving the flesh behind uneaten. Dogs have multiplied so excessively that they hunt in packs and have become so savage that they do as much harm to the herds as wolves, which is a serious problem on those islands.

Not only do they lack wild beasts, but for the most part they lack poultry

2. Túmbez is the site on the modern Ecuadorian coast where Francisco Pizarro and Diego de Almagro landed in 1526 in their second attempt to reach Peru. It is likely that the Spanish named the site after the Tumbez people who lived in this coastal region south of the Gulf of Guayaquil. The Tumbez were conquered early by the Inca and related welcome tales of Inca "civilization" and wealth to the Spanish explorers who arrived on their shores.

and birds. There are many parrots, which can fly far and travel in bands; they also have other birds, but not many, as I have said. I cannot remember having seen or heard of partridges there, as in Peru, and of course they do not have the animals that in Peru are called guanacos and vicuñas, extremely agile animals resembling mountain goats, in whose stomachs we find the stones called bezoars, which are much prized by some and are occasionally larger than hens' eggs by half again the size.[3] Nor do they have another kind of livestock, which we call "Indies sheep," which in addition to supplying the wool and meat that the Indians use for clothing and food also serve as pack animals and beasts of burden to carry loads; they can carry half as much as a mule and cost their owners little, for they need no shoes or packsaddles, nor any kind of harness, nor barley to eat. Nature gave them all this as a free gift, wishing to favor the poor Indian people. The continent of the Indies abounds in all of these kinds of animals as well as others, which will be mentioned in their proper place; the islands, except those where Spaniards have disembarked, have none. It is true that on some islands a brother of our society saw tigers, as he told us, in the course of a long peregrination and a very dangerous shipwreck. But when he was asked how far from the mainland those islands lay, he said that they were a matter of six or eight leagues at most, and there is no doubt that tigers could swim that distance. From these and similar indications we may draw the conclusion that the Indians came to settle that land by a land route rather than by sea, or if they did sail the journey was not very long or difficult, for indeed one hemisphere must connect with the other, or at least they must be very close to each other somewhere.

3. Guanacos and vicuñas along with llamas and alpacas make up the four species of camelids native to the central and southern Andean highlands. Llamas and alpacas were domesticated by the Inca and other native peoples for their wool, hides, and meat and for use as pack animals and in ritual sacrifice. During the colonial period, they were crucial to Spaniards as pack animals and a source of wool. Wild guanacos were hunted for meat, and Andean peoples rounded up the wild vicuñas once a year to shear their wool, the softest of all Andean "sheep." The bezoar stones found inside the Andean camelids were mineral deposits located in the digestive organs of certain animals. In Acosta's time, the stones were coveted for their supposed curative and magical powers.

## CHAPTER 22 * HOW THE RACE OF INDIANS
## DID NOT COME BY WAY OF ATLANTIS,
## AS SOME BELIEVE

There are some,[1] following the opinion of Plato mentioned above, who say that these people went from Europe or Africa to that famous and much celebrated island of Atlantis and that from there they crossed to other and still other islands until they reached the mainland of the Indies. For Plato's Critias mentions all this in the *Timaeus*. If the island of Atlantis was as large as all of Asia and Africa together, or even larger, as Plato believes, then it would have had to occupy all of the Atlantic Ocean and reach almost as far as the islands of the New World. And Plato says further that a terrible flood destroyed this Atlantis of his and left that sea impossible to sail owing to the many shallows, with rocks and reefs and quantities of mud, and that it was like this in his time. But later, with the passage of time, the ruins of the sunken island settled and it was possible to sail there. Some very intelligent men speak of this and discuss it very seriously, but these are such absurd things, if one thinks about them a little, that they seem more like fables or stories by Ovid than history or philosophy worthy of the name. Most of the interpreters and explicators of Plato say that everything Critias recounts is true history, about the strange origin of the island of Atlantis and its greatness and prosperity, the wars waged between the people of Europe and those of Atlantis, and all the rest. They are led to take it as true history by the words of Critias that Plato writes, when he says in his *Timaeus* that he wishes to discuss strange but entirely true things. Other followers of Plato, believing that the whole story has more fiction than history in it, say that all of it must be taken as allegory and that it was the divine philosopher's intention that it be so understood. Among these are Proclus and Porphyrius and even Origen. These writers are so convinced by Plato that they treat his writings as if they were the books of Moses or Esdras, and where Plato's words do not conform to truth they insist that it all has to be understood in a mystical and allegorical sense and can be nothing else.

To tell the truth, I have no such reverence for Plato no matter how divine they may call him, nor do I find it very difficult to believe that he may have related that whole story of the island of Atlantis as true history; and perhaps

1. Plato, Dialogues, *Critias* and *Timaeus* (O'G).

even so it is merely a fine tale, especially because he says that he learned that story from the elder Critias, who sang the song of Atlantis among many other songs and ballads when Plato was a boy. However that may be, whether Plato wrote it as history or allegory, what I find obvious is that everything he says about that island, beginning with the dialogue of *Timaeus* and continuing in the dialogue of *Critias,* cannot be told as truth except to children and old women. Who would not think it a fable that Neptune fell in love with Cleito, had five sets of male twins by her at one birth, and made three concentric circles by sea and two by land around a hill, so identical that they seemed to have been turned on a lathe? What shall we say of that temple a thousand paces long and five hundred broad, whose outer walls were covered with silver and the upper parts with gold, where the ceiling inside was made of ivory worked and intertwined with gold and silver and brass? And last there is the finishing touch in the *Timaeus:* "In a single day and night came a great flood, and the earth swallowed up all our soldiers, and the island of Atlantis sank into the sea in like manner and disappeared." The island certainly did a fine job of disappearing so quickly, for, since it was bigger and Asia and Africa together and made by magic arts, it was fitting that it disappeared in the same way. And it is all very well to say that the ruins and indications of that great island can be seen underneath the sea, when those who might see it are sailors who cannot sail there. Then he adds pleasantly, "Even today that is the reason why the sea is impassable and impenetrable, because the masses of mud that the island gradually built up after it sank form an impediment." I would gladly ask what sea could be great enough to swallow such a vast extent of land, which was larger than Asia and Africa together and stretched as far as the Indies, and to swallow it so completely that not a trace has remained? For it is common knowledge that in that sea where they say the island used to be sailors find no bottom today, no matter how many fathoms they let down the lead. But it is beside the point to try to argue about things that were either told as a pastime or, taking into account the seriousness of Plato, told merely to illustrate, as an example, the prosperity of a city and how it fell. The argument they make to prove that there really was an island of Atlantis, that today that sea is called the Atlantic Ocean, is of little importance, for we know that on the edge of Mauretania is a mountain called Atlas, from which Pliny[2] believes the name Atlantic was

---

2. Pliny, *Natural History,* 6, 5 and 6, 31 (O'G).

given to the ocean. Even without this, Pliny also reports that opposite that hill is an island called Atlantida, which he says is very small and wretched.

### CHAPTER 23 * HOW THE OPINION OF MANY, WHO BELIEVE THAT THE INDIANS COME FROM THE RACE OF THE JEWS, IS FALSE

Given that it is very unlikely that the Indians crossed to the New World from the island of Atlantis, others believe that it must have been in the way described by the writer of Esdras, in the fourth book, where he says:

> And because you saw that he also brought together another peaceful multitude, know that these are the ten tribes that were carried into captivity at the time of King Hosea, who took captive Salmanasar, king of the Assyrians, and he crossed them over to the other side of the river, and they were taken to another land. They were agreed and determined to leave the multitude of the heathen and go to another, more remote region where mankind had never dwelt, to keep their law there, which they had not kept in their own land. And so they entered through some narrow gates of the river Euphrates, for the Most High did marvels for them then and held back the currents of the river until they crossed. For the road through that region was very long, requiring a year and a half; and that region is called Arsareth. There they dwelt until the latter day, and now when they begin to come the Most High will again hold back the currents of the river so that they can pass; and that is why that multitude is clothed with peace.[1]

Some try to make this text by Esdras fit the Indians, saying that they were carried by God to a place where humankind had never lived, that the land where they dwell is so remote that the journey to it lasts a year and a half, and that these people are naturally peaceful. Ignorant folk commonly believe that the Indians proceed from the race of Jews because they are cowardly and weak and much given to ceremony, and cunning, and lying.[2] In addition to

1. 4 Esdras, 13 (O'G).

2. The historian of ancient Mexico, Diego Durán, was one of those who believed that the indigenous peoples of the Indies were related to the Jewish people. Durán wrote that "we can almost positively affirm that they are Jews and Hebrews, and I would not commit a great error if I were to state this as fact, considering their way of life, their ceremonies, their rites and superstitions, their omens and hypocrisies, so akin to and

this they say that their dress appears to be the same as that of the Jews, for they use a tunic or shirt with a cloak wrapped around it and go barefoot or wear shoes that are simply soles tied on the foot, which they call *ojotas*. And they say that this was once the costume of the Jews, shown in their histories as well as in old paintings that represent them dressed in this clothing, and that these two garments, which only the Indians wear, are the same that Samson wagered, which the Scripture[3] calls *tunicam et syndonem,* shirts and coats, and that they are the same that the Indians call shirt and cloak.

But all these are very idle conjectures and have much more evidence against them than for them. We know that the Hebrews used writing, but among the Indians there is no trace of this. The others were very fond of money; these pay it no heed. The Jews, if they were seen not to be circumcised, were not considered to be Jews. The Indians do not circumcise at all, and have never practiced this ceremony, as many in Ethiopia and the Orient have. Moreover, how can it be, when the Jews have been so assiduous in preserving their language and ancient traditions, to the point that in every part of the world where they live today they differ from the rest, that in the Indies alone they have forgotten their ancestry, their law, their ceremonies, their Messiah, and finally all their Jewishness? As to what is said about the Indians being fearful, superstitious, cunning, and liars: as for the first, it is not general among all of them; there are nations among these savages who are very far removed from all that, for tribes of Indians exist who are extremely fierce and fearless, and some are very stupid and blunt of intellect. The heathen have always been given to ceremonies and superstitions. As for the fashion of their clothing, it is the simplest and most natural in the world, with almost no artifice; and this fashion of clothing was common in ancient times not only among the Hebrews but among many other nations. Therefore the history of Esdras (if we are to take notice of apocryphal writings) contradicts rather than assists their intent, for in that book it is written that the ten tribes fled from the multitude of the heathen in order to keep their ceremonies and law. But the Indians are

---

characteristic of those of the Jews." See Durán, *The History of the Indies of New Spain,* 3. While Acosta provided methodical proofs to discount the possible link between Amerindians and Jews suggested by Durán and others, his impassioned dismissal of the idea suggests that he was eager to dismiss the implicit taint of Judaism on Indian souls. It was in the interest of missionaries to show that they were ministering to a pure population, with no prior knowledge, or rejection, of Christianity.

3. Judges, 14, 12 and 13.

given over to all the idolatries in the world; and, as for the entrances of the River Euphrates, those who believe this must consider well how they could reach to the New World and how the Indians could return from there, as it says in the aforesaid book. And I do not know how these people can be called peaceful, since the truth is that they have been perpetually at war among themselves. In conclusion, I do not see how the apocryphal Euphrates of Esdras could have provided a better opportunity for men to cross to the New World than Plato's enchanted and fabled Atlantis.

## CHAPTER 24 * WHY THERE IS NO SURE WAY TO ESTABLISH THE INDIANS' ORIGIN

But it is easier to refute what is false about the Indians' origin than to discover the truth, for among them there are neither writings nor any certain memories of their first founders. On the other hand, there is no trace of the New World in the books of those peoples who did use writing, for many of the ancients believed that there were neither men nor land nor even sky in these parts; and therefore anyone who promises to tell the truth about the Indians' first origin, and the first men to dwell in the Indies, must inevitably be taken for a rash and very reckless man. But along general lines, and by making plausible conjectures, we can extract from all of the arguments above that the race of men arrived by crossing gradually until they reached the New World, that the continuity or nearness of lands helped in this, that there were occasional voyages, and that this was the method of arrival, not in a fleet built for the purpose. Nor was there any great shipwreck, although there could have been some element of this also. For, since these regions are very extensive and there are innumerable tribes in them, we may well believe that some came to settle in them by one method and some by another. But, finally, I come to the conclusion that the chief and truest reason why the Indies were settled is that the lands of the Indies are connected to other lands in the world or at least lie very close to them. And I believe that the New World and the West Indies have not been inhabited by men for very many thousands of years, that the first men who entered them were savage hunters rather than civilized folk, and that they came to the New World because they had strayed from their land or because they felt cramped and in need of seeking new lands; and when they found it, they began to settle it little by little, with no more laws than a bit of natural instinct (and even that somewhat clouded) and at most a few customs left over from their original country. Even though they came from civilized and well-governed countries, it is not difficult to believe that they forgot everything in the course of a long time and little use; for it is well known that even in Spain and Italy groups of men are sometimes found who, except for their shape and faces, have no other resemblance to men; and so in this way there came to be an infinite amount of savagery in the New World.

## CHAPTER 25 * WHAT THE INDIANS ARE WONT TO SAY ABOUT THEIR ORIGIN

It is not very important to know what the Indians themselves are wont to tell of their beginnings and origin, for what they relate resembles dreams rather than history.[1] Commonly there is a great deal of information among them, and much talk, about the Flood; but it is not easy to discover whether the flood that they tell of is the Universal Flood recounted in Divine Scripture or some other flood or inundation confined to the regions where they dwell. But the fact that in these lands, experts say, there are clear signs of some great inundation in the past inclines me to agree with those who feel that the traces and signs of a flood that do exist are not those of Noah's Flood but of some other particular flood such as that described by Plato, or Deucalion's, of which the poets sing. However that may be, the Indians say that at the time of their flood all men were drowned, and they tell that a certain Viracocha came out of the great lake Titicaca and that he settled in Tiahuanaco, where even today ruins and fragments of ancient and very strange buildings can be seen; and from there they came to Cuzco, and thus the human race was

1. Acosta's treatment of native peoples as unreliable informants who tell dreams not histories represents a European bias rather than a historian's careful treatment of sources. Two points are in order here. First, Acosta's use of the word *dreams* to describe native histories was freighted with significance. As a participant in the Third Council of Lima, he was one of the religious elites who composed orders that indigenous people stop "keeping dreams." Priests condemned Andean practices of dream interpretation as idolatrous. See Bruce Mannheim, "A Semiotic of Andean Dreams," in *Dreaming: Anthropological and Psychological Interpretations,* edited by Barbara Tedlock (New York: Cambridge University Press, 1988), 137. Second, Acosta's mistrust of native histories is in contrast to the work of Fray Bernardino Sahagún, who collaborated with native Mexica and relied almost exclusively on their information. For an insightful collection of essays analyzing the method and meaning in images and text of the corpus of Sahagún's work, see J. Jorge Klor de Alva, H. B. Nicholson, and Eloise Quiñones Keber, *The Work of Bernardino de Sahagún, Pioneer Ethnographer of Sixteenth-Century Aztec Mexico* (Albany: Institute for Mesoamerican Studies, State University of New York, 1988).

multiplied anew.[2] In that same lake they show a little island where they claim the sun hid and was preserved, and hence in ancient times they made many sacrifices there, not only of sheep but also of men.[3] Others tell that six or some such number of men emerged through a window in a certain cave and that these began the propagation of men, and they call it Pacari Tambo for this reason. And thus they believe that the Tambos are the oldest race of men. They say that Manco Capac, whom they recognize as the founder and head of the Incas, came from there, and that from him came two families or lineages, one the Hanan Cuzco and the other the Urincuzco. They tell that the Inca kings, when they went to war and conquered different provinces, gave as justification for the war that all the people owed them recognition because the world had been renewed from their lineage and country and hence the true religion and cult of heaven had been revealed to them. But of what use is it to add more, since all of it is full of lies and goes against reason? What learned men affirm and write is that the entire memory and tradition of these Indians is about four hundred years and everything previous to that is pure confusion and shadows, with no possibility of discovering anything certain. And this is not to be wondered at, as they lack books and writing, in place of which their special method of calculation, the *quipu,* is far from sufficient to cover four hundred years.[4] When I made efforts to learn of them from what lands and people they had come to the place where they live, I found that, so far from being able to do so, they were instead certain that they had been created from their very beginnings in this New World where they dwell. We opened their eyes with our faith, which teaches us that all men come from one man.[5] There are clear indications that for a long time these men had no

2. Tiahuanaco, or Tiwanaku, was a stratified society that dominated the Lake Titicaca region in the highlands of colonial Peru beginning in 100 A.D., long before Inca rule. After 375 A.D., Tiahuanaco culture spread throughout the Andes until its decline around 1200. Viracocha was the main deity of the Inca empire, whose capital city, Cuzco, was founded by Manco Capac. Ceremonial and religious structures made of massive and expertly carved stone dominated the city center. Four roads leading from the town designated the four corners of Tawantinsuyu, the Inca Empire. For a colonial era source on the founding of Cuzco, see Bernabé Cobo, *History of the Inca Empire,* edited by Roland Hamilton (Austin: University of Texas Press, 1979), esp. 108–12.

3. When Acosta writes of sheep, he actually refers to llamas, the sheep of the Andes.

4. Acosta analyzes the *quipu,* a memory device made of colored string and knots, and other forms of native writing in book VI. On the possible calculations from the *quipu,* see Marcia Ascher and Robert Ascher, *Code of the Quipu: A Study in Media, Mathematics, and Culture* (Ann Arbor: University of Michigan Press, 1981).

5. Acts, 17, 26 (O'G).

kings or any form of government but lived in free groups like the Indians of Florida nowadays and the Chiriguanas and Brazilians and many other tribes, who do not have regular kings but in accordance with the occasions that arise in war or peace choose their chiefs as they like. But in time some men who in strength and skill were superior to the others began to lord it over the rest and command, as Nimrod did in ancient times;[6] and, increasing little by little, they eventually founded the kingdoms of Peru and Mexico, which our Spaniards found. Although they were barbarians, these had a very great advantage over the other Indians. Thus the reasoning I have outlined persuades us that the Indian race has risen and multiplied, for the most part, from savage and fugitive men.

And let this suffice as to the origin of these people, leaving the rest for the time when we deal more extensively with their histories.

6. Genesis, 10, 8 (O'G).

# BOOK II

### CHAPTER 1 * WHICH WILL DEAL WITH THE NATURE OF THE EQUINOCTIAL LINE, OR EQUATOR

Since the larger portion of the New World that has been discovered, under the middle region of the heavens, is the part called the Torrid Zone by the ancients and held by them to be uninhabitable, it is necessary to understand the nature and condition of this region in order to comprehend some things about the Indies. It does not seem to me that those men were wrong who affirmed that knowledge of the Indies depended principally on knowledge of the equator, for almost all the difference between one sphere and the other proceeds from its properties. And it is notable that all the space existing between the two tropics must be reduced and examined by its own rules, by the line in its middle, which is the equinoctial line, so called because when the sun moves along it days and nights are equal all over the world and also because those who live under it enjoy equal length of nights and days throughout the year. On this equinoctial line we find so many and such remarkable properties that there is every reason for men's imaginations to be stirred and stimulated to inquire about their causes, guiding ourselves not so much by the doctrine of the ancient philosophers as by true reason and a degree of experience.

### CHAPTER 2 * WHAT CAUSED THE ANCIENTS TO HAVE NO DOUBT THAT THE TORRID ZONE WAS UNINHABITABLE

Now, to take the matter from its beginnings, no one can deny what we see very clearly, namely, that when the sun draws near it warms and when it withdraws it cools. Witnesses to this are the days and nights; witnesses, too, are winter and summer, whose variation and cold and heat are caused by whether the sun moves closer or farther away. The second and no less certain point is that the more closely the sun approaches and pierces most directly with its rays, the more the earth is scorched. This is clearly seen in the heat of midday and the ardor of summer. Hence it is (to all appearances) correctly assumed and inferred that the colder a land is the more distant it is from the sun's movement. Thus we observe that the lands closest to the septentrional and north are colder lands and on the other hand those closest to the Zodiac, where the sun is, are hotter. By this rule Ethiopia is hotter than Africa and Barbary and these are hotter than Andalusia, and Andalusia is hotter than Castile and Aragon, and these are hotter than Biscay and France.[1] And the more northerly they are the less warm are these and other provinces; consequently, those that come closest to the sun and are more directly pierced by its rays surpass the others in receiving more of the sun's heat. Some authors add another reason, and this is the movement of the heavens, which within the Tropics is very swift and near the poles extremely slow. From this they conclude that the region around the Zodiac has three reasons for being scorched by heat: one is the nearness of the sun, another that its rays pierce more directly, and the third that the region participates in the more rapid movement of the heavens. As for heat and cold, what I have written is that upon which sense and reason appear to agree. As for the other two qualities, which are wetness and dryness, what shall we say of them? Undoubtedly the same, since dryness is apparently caused by the sun's approach and wetness by its withdrawal, for, since night is cooler than day, it is also more humid, and day, because it is warmer, is also drier. Winter, when the sun is farther away, is colder and rainier, and summer, when the sun is nearer, is hotter and drier. For fire, just as it cooks and burns, also sucks up moisture and dries. So, if we consider what has been written on the subject, Aristotle and the other philosophers attributed to the middle region, which they called Torrid, an excess of both heat and dryness, and hence they said that that it was remark-

---

1. Acosta turns from his focus on cosmology in book I to an environmental comparison in book II. Here he categorizes countries according to climate (Ethiopia is hotter than Africa and so on), and later in book II he develops links between climate, civilization, and race. His early theorizing about climate and race informs the categories by which he classifies indigenous peoples. It also reveals the tension present throughout the *Historia* between satisfaction with the potential for the New World to be an earthly paradise and frustration that the continent does not exhibit what he perceives as a high civilization.

ably scorched and dry and in consequence utterly lacking in water and vegetation; since this was so, naturally it had to be very uncomfortable and unfit for human habitation.

### CHAPTER 3 * HOW THE TORRID ZONE IS VERY WET, AND HOW IN THIS THE ANCIENTS WERE MUCH MISTAKEN

Although it seems that everything so far said and suggested is true and certain and clear, yet everything that has been inferred from it is false; for the middle region, the one called Torrid, is in very fact inhabited by men, and we Spaniards have inhabited it for a very long time, and living in it is very comfortable and moderate.[1] Since this is true, and we well know that falsehoods cannot spring from truths if the conclusion is false (which it is), we must retrace our steps and carefully examine the beginnings, where there may have been error and misunderstanding. First we will write the truth as actual experience has revealed it to us, and then we will try (although it is a very arduous task) to offer reasons for it according to sound philosophy. The last point proposed above was that dryness is greater when the sun is closest to the earth. This appears to be a plain and certain truth, yet it is not true but false, for rains and downpours in the Torrid Zone are never greater than when the sun is very close overhead. Certainly it is a remarkable thing, and much worthy of notice, that in the Torrid Zone the calmest and least rainy part of the year is that in which the sun is farthest away; and, conversely, no part of the year is more full of rain and clouds and snow (in the places where these last are wont to fall) than the part where the sun is closest. Those who have not been in the New World may think this unbelievable, and even those who have been there, if they have not stopped to think about it, may also find it new to them. But both will easily be rebutted when they observe the clear proof of what I have said.

In this land of Peru, which faces toward the South or Antarctic Pole, the sun is farthest away when it is nearest in Europe, namely, in May, June, July,

1. Acosta proclaims the Torrid Zone an inhabitable region based on the ability of Spaniards to live there comfortably. Moreover, his claim that Spaniards had inhabited any region of the New World for "a very long time," when at most continuous settlement had existed for one hundred years, discounts the centuries of experience by native peoples. Preconquest history, then, does not constitute valid evidence for disproving the theories of the "ancients." For Acosta, the beginnings of orderly observation of natural history are connected to the onset of the Spanish experience in the Indies.

and August, when it is very near the tropic of Cancer. In these months I have mentioned that there is great calm in Peru. There is no rain, and no snow falls; all the rivers carry little water, and some dry up altogether. But later, as the year progresses and the sun approaches the circle of Capricorn, the water, rain, and snow begin and strong currents in the rivers, that is, from October to December. And when the sun, returning from Capricorn, beats down on the heads of those in Peru, then comes the fury of downpours and heavy rains and many snowfalls and fierce floods in the rivers, which is the time when the greatest heat of the year occurs, that is, from January to the middle of March. This happens every year in this province of Peru, and no one can gainsay it. In the regions that face the Arctic Pole, exactly the opposite occurs after the equinox has passed and for the same reason. Whether we take Panama, and all of that coast, or New Spain or the Windward Islands — Cuba, Hispaniola, Jamaica, and San Juan de Puerto Rico — we will invariably find that from the beginning of November to April these places enjoy a calm and clear sky; and the cause is that the sun, crossing the equator toward the tropic of Capricorn, then moves farther away from those regions than in any other part of the year. On the other hand, in those same lands severe storms and copious rains occur when the sun turns toward them and moves closer to them, which is from June to September, for it beats down on them more closely and directly during those months. The same phenomenon has been observed in the East Indies, and to judge from the accounts given in letters from there it appears to be the case. Hence it is the general rule (although in some places, owing to special causes, there may be exceptions) that in the middle region or Torrid Zone, which is the same thing, there is calm weather and it is drier when the sun draws away; when it approaches more closely, the weather is rainy and there is more humidity. And, according to whether the sun is far away or near, it is then that the earth has more or less abundance of water.

CHAPTER 4 * HOW OUTSIDE THE TROPICS
THERE IS MORE RAIN WHEN THE SUN DRAWS
FARTHER AWAY, WHICH IS THE REVERSE OF
THE TORRID ZONE

Outside the Tropics quite the opposite happens, for rain and cold come together, as do heat and drought; this is very well known all over Europe and in all of the Old World. Everywhere in the New World the same thing happens, of which the realm of Chile is the best example, for, because it lies outside the circle of Capricorn and has the same latitude as Spain, it is subject to the same laws of winter and summer except that winter occurs there when it is summer in Spain, and vice versa, for it faces toward the opposite pole. Thus, in that province the rains come in great abundance along with the cold, at the time when the sun draws farthest away from the region, which is from the beginning of April to the end of September. Heat and drought return when the sun again draws near, in fact, exactly the same as in Europe. This is the reason why that country, in products of the earth as well as in the spirits of men, is closer to conditions in Europe than any other in these Indies.[1] It is said that the same thing, and for the same reason, happens in that large area that stretches like a point from the interior of Ethiopia to the Cape of Good Hope. And they say that this is the reason why the floods of the Nile, about which the ancients so often disputed, occur during the summer season. For in April, when the sun has passed the sign of Aries, that region begins to have winter rains, for it is winter there; and these waters, which come in part from snow and in part from rain, gradually swell those large lakes from which the Nile proceeds according to true and accurate geography. And so they go on broadening the river's currents little by little, and after traveling for a long distance over a period of time they come and flood Egypt during the summer season, which seems a thing against nature but, in fact, conforms with it; for at the same time that it is summer in Egypt, which is in the tropic of Cancer, it is full winter in the sources and lakes of the Nile, which is in the other tropic, that of Capricorn. In America there is another inundation very similar to that of the Nile, and it is in the river called Paraguay or Río de la Plata; each year, gathering an immense amount of water, which comes from the moun-

---

1. Acosta's regional preference for the province of Chile surfaces at various points in the *Historia*. Even in 1590, when he published the book, Chile was considered to be on the periphery of the Spanish colonies, and it suffered considerably from active resistance to colonization by the native Araucanians in particular. Why would Acosta become an advocate for the region? His suggestion that Chile was the best place to replicate Spanish civilization in the Americas, because of natural and moral similarities to Spain, reveals an underlying assumption that climate affects civilization. Acosta believed that the best approximation to Europe in the New World would come in a region of comparable climate. Interestingly, Acosta himself never visited the still largely unconquered region; secondary sources and his own geographical comparisons formed the basis for his Chilean predilection. Perhaps his imaginings of Chile were possible because he never experienced it, never trekked through its unfamiliar territory, and never witnessed the culture of its native peoples.

tains of Peru, it rushes out of its course so impetuously, and so overcomes all that land, that the people who live there must spend those months in boats or canoes, abandoning their dwellings on land.

### CHAPTER 5 * HOW IN THE TROPICS THE RAINS COME IN SUMMER, OR TIME OF HEAT, AND THE CALCULATION OF WINTER AND SUMMER

To sum up: in the two temperate zones or regions, summer goes hand in hand with heat and drought and winter with cold and wetness. But within the Torrid Zone those qualities do not go hand in hand, for rains follow heat, and cold (I call "cold" the lack of excessive heat) is followed by calm weather. Hence it follows that, although in Europe winter means cold and rain and summer means heat and fair weather, our Spaniards in Peru and New Spain, observing that these two qualities do not match or go together as they do in Spain, call winter the time of heavy rains and summer the time of light rains or none. But plainly they are wrong in doing so, for by this rule they say that summer lasts in the mountains of Peru from April to September because the waters cease at that time, and from September to April they say that it is winter because the waters return; thus they affirm that in the mountains of Peru it is summer at the same time as in Spain, and winter, too, neither more nor less. And when the sun is directly over their heads they believe that it is the depth of winter, for the rains are greater; but this is laughable and only an illiterate person would say it.[1] For, just as the day differs from the night by the presence and absence of the sun in our hemisphere, according to the movement of the First Movable, and this is the definition of day and night, exactly thus does summer differ from winter, by the sun's nearness or withdrawal, according to the movement of the sun itself, and that is its cause. Hence, in reality it is summer when the sun is at its nearest and winter when it is at its farthest remove. Heat and cold and mild temperatures necessarily follow the

1. The majority of Spaniards arriving to the Indies, presumably the illiterates referred to by Acosta, did not register a change of seasons when they crossed the ocean but merely applied the European calculations of winter and summer to their new home. The sixteenth-century description of the mining town of Potosí by the Spaniard Luis Capoche proves that this confusion was not limited to illiterates. Historian Peter Bakewell's keen analysis of the text reveals that Capoche described winter rains pounding down on the town when in fact rains come to Potosí during the summer months. See his *Miners of the Red Mountain: Indian Labor in Potosí, 1545–1650* (Albuquerque: University of New Mexico Press, 1984), 6.

approach or withdrawal of the sun; but whether it rains or not, whether the weather is wet or dry, does not necessarily follow. And thus it may be deduced, contrary to what many believe, that in Peru winter is calm and without rain and summer is rainy and not the reverse, as the common belief has it, that winter is hot and summer cold. Those who draw a distinction between the mountains and the plains in Peru commit the same error. They say that when it is summer in the mountains it is winter on the plains, that is, April, May, June, July, and August; for then the mountains enjoy calm weather and the sun shines without thunderstorms and at the same time there is fog on the plains, which they call *garúa,* a sort of mist or very gentle humidity that covers the sun. But, as has been said, summer and winter are determined by the approach or withdrawal of the sun; and, since everywhere in Peru, both in the mountains and on the plains, the sun approaches and withdraws at the same time, there is no reason to say that when it is summer in one part of the land it is winter in the other, though there is no use arguing about the words employed. Let them call it whatever they like and say that when there is no rain it is summer, even though the weather is warmer; that matters little. What does matter is to know the truth, which is obvious, that the waters do not always withdraw when the sun approaches more closely; rather, in the Torrid Zone the opposite is customary.

### CHAPTER 6 * HOW THE TORRID ZONE HAS A GREAT ABUNDANCE OF WATER AND VEGETATION, THOUGH ARISTOTLE DENIES IT

Following what has been said, it is easy to understand that the Torrid Zone has water and is not dry; this is true to the point that in the abundance and duration of waters it is superior to the other regions of the world, except in some places where there are sandy wastes or deserts and barren lands, as also happens in other parts of the world. As for rainfall, we have already demonstrated that it has a large supply of rain, snow, and frost, which especially abound in the province of Peru. Nothing has been said up to now of groundwaters, such as rivers, fountains, brooks, wells, pools, and lakes, but, as the waters below usually correspond to those above, it can easily be understood that these exist also. In fact there is such an abundance of natural waters that nowhere in the world are there more rivers, or larger ones, or more swamps and lakes. Owing to this superabundance of water the greater part of America is almost uninhabitable, for with the storms of summer the rivers overflow their beds very violently and sweep everything away and the sediment from swamps and narrows prevents the water from passing through it in a great number of places. Therefore, when those who dwell near the Paraguay River, which we mentioned above, realize that the river is rising, they take to their canoes before it floods, placing their homes and possessions in them, and for a period of almost three months preserve their persons and goods by floating on the water. When the river returns to its bed they also return to their dwellings, which are not yet entirely dry. The size of this river is so great that if the Nile, Ganges, and Euphrates were joined into one they would not be nearly so large. And what shall we say of the vast Magdalena River, which enters the sea between Santa Marta and Cartagena and is rightly called the Great River? When I sailed upon it I was amazed to see that its currents could be observed clearly as far as ten miles out to sea, and even the waves and immensity of the ocean could not obliterate them. But, speaking of rivers, that great river that some call the river of the Amazons, others the Marañón, others the River of Orellana, which our Spanish compatriots first discovered and navigated, silences them all; indeed, I do not know whether to call it a river or a sea. This river flows out of the mountains of Peru, from which it gathers immense amounts of water from rainfall and streams, collecting them into itself and traversing the fields and plains of Paitití and El Dorado; from the region of the Amazons it flows at last into the ocean and enters it almost opposite the islands of Margarita and Trinidad. Its banks are so far apart, especially in the last third of its course, that there are many large islands in it; and, something that seems incredible, when navigating this river those who look upon it can see only sky and river. They say that even very high hills near its banks cannot be seen owing to the great size of the river. We learned about the amazing breadth and grandness of this river, which may justly be called the Emperor of Rivers, from a very reliable source: this was a brother of our society who as a youth traveled through and sailed upon the whole length of it. He was present at all the events of that strange expedition made by Pedro de Orsúa and witnessed the seditious and dangerous deeds of the wicked Diego de Aguirre.[1] And God Our Lord delivered him from all those labors

1. In the tradition of myths like that of Prester John, Spaniards circulated stories about El Dorado, which spread throughout the Indies animated by Spanish imagination and signs or references within native culture.

and perils to make him a member of our society. These, then, are the rivers of the so-called Torrid Zone, that dry and charred region that Aristotle and all the ancients held to be poor and lacking in water and vegetation.

And because I have made mention of the Marañón River in order to show the abundance of waters that exist in the Torrid Zone, I believe that I must also mention the lake that they call Titicaca, which is in the middle of the province of Collao. More than ten rivers of considerable volume enter this lake, but it has only one outlet, and that not a very large one, though from what they say it is very deep. It is not possible to make a proper bridge over it owing to the depth and breadth of the water. Nor can it be crossed in boats because of the powerful current, according to what people say. It is crossed on a bridge very cleverly constructed in a style peculiar to the Indians, made of straw and at water level; because this is such a light material it does not sink and forms a safe and easy crossing. This lake's circumference is almost eighty leagues; the lake itself must measure almost thirty-five and about fifteen at its broadest part. It has islands, which in ancient times were inhabited and cultivated but are now deserted. It grows a large quantity of a kind of reed that the Indians call *totora,* which they use for any number of things, for it is fodder for pigs and horses and even food for men, and they make houses from it and use it for fuel and boats and whatever they need. All these uses do the Uros find for their *totora.* These Uros are so brutish that they do not even think of themselves as men. It is told of them that when asked what sort of people they were, they replied that they were not men but Uros, as if this were another species of animal.[2] Whole communities of Uros were found

---

El Dorado was a mythical kingdom that included, among other riches, a river whose sands were made up of precious stones that covered stores of gold in its depths. Tales that El Dorado sat within reach, in the interior of Peru, led Viceroy Don Andrés Hurtado de Mendoza to commission Pedro de Orsúa to head a 1559 expedition to find and conquer the province, Omagua, home of the mythical golden kingdom. The group headed into the upper Amazon basin by way of Peru, and, disillusioned by the mirage of the promised land, they emerged again at the mouth of the Orinoco. Orsúa did not make it very far on the journey. Hardships and infighting led to a rebellion led by Lope de Aguirre, mistakenly referred to by Acosta as Diego de Aguirre. Aguirre's behavior, namely, killing expedition members, abandoning native assistants, and ultimately declaring rebellion against Spain, earned him what is perhaps the worst reputation among sixteenth-century explorers. For an account of the journey, see *Relación de todo lo que sucedió en la jornada de Omagua y Dorado hecha por el gobernador Pedro de Orsúa* (Madrid: La Sociedad de Bibliófilos Españoles, 1881).

2. The Uros, or Urus, made their home in the *totora* swamps of Lake Titicaca and in other wetland areas on the surrounding Andean Plateau. They spoke Uru, a language distinct from Quechua and Aymara. Both their name, meaning "dirty," "ragged," or "rustic" in seventeenth-century usage, and their "brutish" reputation likely originated from other indigenous groups, who acted as Spanish informants. Acosta's characterization

living on the lake on their rafts made of *totora,* which were fastened together and tied to a rock; it sometimes happened that a whole settlement would leave there and go to another place, and thus if they were sought one day in the place where they had been yesterday no trace of them could be found. After Titicaca's outlet river runs for another fifty leagues it forms a smaller lake; this is called Paria. It also has islands and is not known to have an outlet. Many believe that it runs underground and flows into the Southern Sea, and offer as proof of this the tributary of a river that is seen to enter the sea very near there and whose source is unknown. But I incline to believe that the waters of this lake evaporate by themselves due to the sun's heat. Let this digression serve to prove how unjustly the ancients condemned the middle region as lacking in water, when the truth is that it has very abundant water from both heaven and earth.

## CHAPTER 7 * WHICH DEALS WITH THE REASON WHY THE SUN, OUTSIDE THE TROPICS, CAUSES RAIN WHEN IT IS MOST DISTANT, AND IN THE TROPICS THE REVERSE, WHEN IT IS NEAREST

Thinking carefully many times about the reasons why the equatorial zone is as wet as I have said, proving the ancients to be mistaken, no other cause has occurred to me except that the sun's great strength there attracts and raises very large amounts of vapor from the whole ocean, which is so extensive in those parts, and that, together with raising large quantities of vapor, the sun quickly disperses them and they fall in the form of rain. That rains and downpours are the result of very fierce heat has been proved by many and manifest experiences. The first proof is that which I have already stated, that rains come there when the sun's rays fall most directly and therefore most strongly, and that when the sun withdraws and the heat lessens neither rains nor downpours occur. It may easily be inferred from this that the sun's very great strength is what causes the rains there. The same has been observed to be the case in Peru and New Spain and throughout the Torrid Zone, that downpours and rains are apt to come after noon, when the sun's rays have

---

of the Urus may have been reflected in the writings of Garcilaso de la Vega, who calls them "rude and wild." See El Inca Garcilaso de la Vega, *Royal Commentaries of the Incas and General History of Peru,* translated by Harold V. Livermore (Austin: University of Texas Press, 1966), 410.

acquired all their strength. It is very rare for rain to fall in the morning, and therefore travelers are advised to set forth early and try to complete their day's journey by noon, for that is the time when they can be sure of a wetting; those who have traveled in these lands know this well. Some observers also say that the greatest rainfall occurs when the moon is fullest; the truth is that I cannot form an adequate judgment of this, although I have experienced it several times. Thus the year, the month, and the day all prove the truth I have expressed, that excess of heat in the Torrid Zone causes the rains. Indeed, experience demonstrates this in artificial things, such as the retorts and alembics that extract liquids from herbs or flowers, for the force of the enclosed flame draws up abundant vapors and then, by compressing them, turns them to water and liquor because they find no outlet. The same phenomenon occurs in gold and silver that is extracted by means of quicksilver, for if the fire is small and feeble almost nothing is extracted from the quicksilver, but if the fire is strong the quicksilver evaporates a great deal, and when it encounters what is called the "top" it turns to liquid and drips down. Thus the great strength of heat, when it finds material prepared for it, performs two effects: one is to draw the vapors up, and the other is to dissolve them and turn them into liquid when an obstacle is placed to their being consumed and exhausted.

Although it seems contradictory to say that the sun itself causes rains in the Torrid Zone because it is near and the same sun causes them elsewhere because it is far away, and although the two seem impossible to reconcile, if we look at the matter carefully this is not really so. Very many natural phenomena come from contrary causes, by opposite ways. We set wet clothing to dry by the fire, which dries, and also in the open air, which cools; adobe bricks are dried and hardened both by the sun and by cold weather; sleep is induced by moderate exercise, but if exercise is excessive or if there is little or none, sleep is prevented; fire goes out if more wood is not placed upon it, but if too much wood is piled on it goes out, too. If the amount of wood is in proportion, the fire is fed and grows stronger. To see a thing it must not be very close to the eyes or very far away; one sees it at a moderate distance. If it is too far off it is lost to sight, and if too near it cannot be seen either. If the sun's rays are very weak they do not cause mists to rise from rivers; if they are very strong, as soon as they raise vapor they dissolve it, and hence moderate heat both raises the mist and preserves it. This is the reason why mists seldom rise at night or midday but in the morning, when the sun's rays are becoming stronger. There are a great number of examples of natural things of this sort, which as we see often proceed from opposite causes; hence we need not be astonished that when the sun is close it causes rain, and also causes it when it is far away, and that it does not permit rain if its presence is moderate, that is, neither near nor far away.

But we must still ask why, within the Torrid Zone, the nearness of the sun causes rain and while outside the Torrid Zone it causes rain when it is very far away. As I understand it, the reason is that outside the Tropics the sun's heat does not have sufficient strength in winter to consume the vapors rising from land and sea. Thus these vapors join together very abundantly in the cold regions of the air and the cold itself squeezes and thickens them; with this, being squeezed or compressed, they turn to water. For in that winter period the sun is far distant and the days are short and the nights long, all of which makes for feeble warmth; but as the sun arrives little by little in countries outside the Tropics, that is to say, in summer, its strength is great enough to raise vapors, and consume and dissipate them, and thus causes the very vapors that it raises to disappear. The greater nearness of the sun and the longer days help to increase heat, but within the Tropics, in the Torrid Zone, the sun's withdrawal is equal to the greater presence of those other regions outside the Tropics, and so it does not rain in the Torrid Zone when the sun is farthest away, for the same reason that it does not rain when the sun is nearer in regions outside the tropics. Thus, for the same reason it does not rain when the sun is farthest away in the Torrid Zone, as it does not rain when the sun is nearest in regions outside the Tropics, for it is at an equal distance and thus causes the same phenomenon of calm weather. But when in the Torrid Zone the sun attains its maximum strength and falls directly on people's heads there is no calm weather or drought as it seems there ought to be but instead great and sudden rains. For, with the excessive strength of the sun's heat, it attracts and quickly raises a great abundance of vapors from the earth and the Ocean Sea. And, because the quantity of vapors is so large, and because the wind does not dissipate or destroy them, they readily dissolve and cause unseasonable rains, for the excessive vehemence of heat can quickly raise so many vapors that it cannot consume and disperse them rapidly; thus, rising and piling up in such abundance, they dissolve and become water, all of which can be understood very easily by means of a familiar example.

When we begin to roast a piece of pork or mutton or veal, if the fire is hot and very close, we see that the fat melts and runs down and drops to the ground; the cause is that the great heat of the fire attracts and raises that juice and vapor from the meat, and because there is a great abundance of it the fire cannot deal with it and thus it is distilled and falls more freely. When the fire is moderate and what is being roasted is at a proper distance, we see that the meat roasts and the fat does not run or become distilled, for the heat gradually draws out the liquid and it is consumed and resolved by that same moderation. Therefore, those who are experienced in the art of cookery demand that the fire be moderate, and that what is being roasted be not too near or too far away, so that it will not melt. Another example is that of wax or tallow candles. If the wick is large it melts the tallow or wax, for it cannot use up the humors that are produced. But if the flame is in proportion it does not melt, nor does the wax fall, because the flame continues to consume what it produces. This, then (I believe), is the reason why in the equatorial and Torrid zones the great force of heat causes the rain that in other regions is caused by weaker heat.[1]

### CHAPTER 8 * HOW WHAT IS SAID OF THE TORRID ZONE MUST BE UNDERSTOOD

Since it is true that we must not seek an infallible and mathematical rule for natural and physical causes, but rather that a rule is established by ordinary and common experience, it must be understood that what we are saying has to be accepted in the same spirit, namely, that in the Torrid Zone there is more humidity than in those other regions and that it rains there when the sun is closest; but this is true in the most ordinary and common sense and is not a reason for us to deny the exceptions that Nature has made to the rule I have mentioned, making some parts of the Torrid Zone extremely dry, as is told of Ethiopia and as we have seen in a large part of Peru, where the whole coast and what they call the plains have little rain and even very little groundwater, except for a few valleys that can exploit the waters of rivers flowing

1. Acosta's use of systematic logic is on display in this chapter. Here he eschews biblical exegesis and instead offers multiple examples of practical experiments, like drying wet clothing and cooking meat, through which he attempts to prove to his European audience the effects of the sun in the Torrid Zone. Incidentally, Acosta's idea that excessive heat was due to the distance of the sun from the earth, not the angle of the sun's rays, implies an underestimation of the size of the sun and the universe, as well as the distance from the sun to the earth, all views consistent with his geocentric conception of the universe.

down from the mountains. All the rest is sandy waste and barren ground, where there are almost no springs and the wells, where they exist, are extremely deep. Why it never rains on these plains (something that many persons ask) will be dealt with in its proper place, God willing; here I am only trying to demonstrate that there are many exceptions to natural rules. And thus it may happen that in some part of the Torrid Zone it does not rain when the sun is near but when it is more distant, although I have not seen or heard of it; if there is such a place it would have to be attributed to some special quality of the land there if it were a permanent condition. But if it is sometimes so and sometimes not, then we must conclude that a number of impediments occur in natural matters, which can obstruct each other. Let us offer this example: it might be that the sun causes the rains and the wind hinders them or makes them fall more copiously than usual. The winds have their properties and different elements, with which they cause different effects, and often those effects are contrary to what reason and the season of the year require. And, since great variations occur every year because of various aspects of the planets and differences in their positions, it is not strange that something of the kind happens in the Torrid Zone and makes things different from what we have described. Indeed, our conclusion, which represents certain truth and is born from experience, is that in the middle region that we call Torrid the drought that the ancients believed in does not exist. Rather, great humidity and rain occur in that zone when the sun is closest.

CHAPTER 9 * HOW THE TORRID ZONE IS NOT
EXCESSIVELY HOT BUT ONLY MODERATELY SO

So far we have spoken of the Torrid Zone's humidity; now it behooves us to speak of its other two qualities, which are heat and cold. At the beginning of this treatise we spoke of how the ancients believed the Torrid Zone to be dry and hot, and both qualities in great excess; but the truth is that it is not, but is rather humid and hot, and for the most part its heat is not excessive but temperate, something that would be considered unbelievable had we not amply experienced it ourselves. I shall tell what happened to me when I went to the Indies. As I had read the exaggerations of the philosophers and poets, I was convinced that when I reached the equator I would not be able to bear the dreadful heat; but the reality was so different that at the very time I was crossing it I felt such cold that at times I went out into the sun to keep warm, and it was the time of year when the sun is directly overhead, which is in the sign of Aries, in March. I will confess here that I laughed and jeered at Aristotle's meteorological theories and his philosophy, seeing that in the very place where, according to his rules, everything must be burning and on fire, I and all my companions were cold.[1] For the truth is that no place in the world is there a calmer and more moderate region than that under the equator. But there is great diversity in it, and it is not the same in all places. Parts of the Torrid Zone are very temperate, as in Quito and on the plains of Peru; parts are very cold, as in Potosí; and parts are very hot, as in Ethiopia, Brazil, and the Moluccas.[2] And because this diversity is real and well known we must seek another cause of heat and cold in addition to the sun's rays, for it can happen that at the same season of the year places with the same latitude and at an equal distance from the poles and the equator can feel such variety that some are burned with heat, others are almost paralyzed with cold, and others find temperate climates with moderate heat. Plato placed his celebrated island of Atlantis in the Torrid Zone, for he says that at a certain time of the year the sun was directly overhead; yet he says that it was temperate, fertile, and rich.[3] Pliny places Taprobana, or Sumatra, as it is now called, under the equator, as indeed it is, and says of it that it is not only rich and prosperous but heavily populated with men and beasts.[4] From this we may understand that, although the ancients considered the heat of the Torrid Zone to be intolerable, they did realize that it was not as uninhabitable as they represented it. The excellent astronomer and cosmographer Ptolemy and the famous philosopher and physician Avicenna came much closer to the truth, for both believed that there were very moderate dwelling places under the equator.

### CHAPTER 10 * HOW THE TORRID ZONE'S HEAT IS TEMPERED BY THE ABUNDANCE OF RAIN AND THE BREVITY OF THE DAYS

Although what these writers said was true, it was proved beyond doubt after the New World was discovered. But it is very natural, after experience has

1. The undoing of Acosta's conviction that he would burn up when his ship entered the Torrid Zone is a quintessential example of the European challenge to comprehend the physical experience of the New World within the context of Old World intellectual training.

2. The Moluccas, also known as the Spice Islands, are part of modern Indonesia.

3. Plato, Dialogues, *Timaeus* and *Critias* (O'G).

4. Pliny, *Natural History,* 6, 22 (O'G).

proved something, for us to then try to discover the cause of such a secret. Thus we wish to understand why the region where the sun is closest and more directly overhead is not only temperate but in many places cold. Looking at the region as a whole, there are two general reasons why it is temperate. One is the reason stated above, that it is a more humid region and subject to rains, and there is no doubt that rain cools, for the element of water is by nature cold, and, although water can be heated by the agency of fire, yet it tempers the ardor caused by the sun's direct rays. This is thoroughly proved by what we are told of the interior of Arabia, which is terribly burned by the sun because it has no rains to temper the sun's fury. Clouds prevent the rays of the sun from penetrating so strongly, and the rains that come from them also cool both air and earth and moisten the earth no matter how warm the rain that falls seems to be; indeed, drinking rainwater assuages both thirst and heat, as our countrymen have discovered when they had little water to drink. Hence reason as well as experience demonstrate that rain in itself tempers heat, and since we have established that the Torrid Zone is very rainy this proves that there is cause within it to temper its heat. To this I will add another cause that is important to remember, not only for the present question but for many others. And, to express it in as few words as possible, although the equatorial region has greater heat, it does not last as long because the length of the day's heat is shorter and less; hence the sun does not heat or scorch as much. Masters of the sphere teach us, and very truly, that the more oblique and slanted is the rising of the Zodiac in our hemisphere the more unequal are the days and nights; contrariwise, in places where the sphere is straight and the signs mount straight up, the days and nights are equal to one another. It is also an incontrovertible fact that all the regions lying between the two tropics have less inequality of days and nights than those outside them and that this inequality lessens the closer the approach to the equator. In these parts we have proved this by eyewitness testimony. The inhabitants of Quito, which lies under the equator, have no day or night longer than another throughout the year; all are equal. But those of Lima, who are some twelve degrees below it, can see some difference between days and nights, but not much, for in December and January the day will lengthen by a little less than an hour. Those of Potosí have much more difference between winter and summer, for it lies almost below the tropic. Those who live completely outside the Tropics note shorter days in winter and longer ones in summer and all the more so the farther they are from the equator and nearer the pole; and so Germany and England have longer days in summer than Italy and Spain. Since this is true, as the sphere shows and plain experience demonstrates, we will have to add another equally true proposition, that in all natural phenomena it is very important to persevere until we discover their efficient cause.

This established, if I am asked why the equatorial region does not have as extreme heat in summer as other regions, for example, Andalusia in July and August, I will respond that the reason is that summer days are longer in Andalusia and the nights shorter; and because the day is hot, heat is extreme, and the night is damp and chilly, and cooling takes place. And that is why they do not feel so much heat in Peru, for the summer days are not so long or the nights so short, and the day's heat is much tempered by the cool of the night. It is only reasonable that a place where the days are fifteen or sixteen hours long will be hotter than a place where they are twelve or thirteen, and an equal number of night hours remain for a cooling effect. And thus, although the Torrid Zone is closer to the sun, those other regions have a greater length of exposure to it. And reason demonstrates that a fire heats more, even if it is somewhat smaller, than a larger fire that lasts less time, especially when it is interspersed with cold. So, if we place these two properties of the Torrid Zone in a balance, that it is rainier at the time of most heat and the days are shorter, it will seem that the two opposites are reconciled, which are that the sun is closer and its rays fall more directly. At least there will not be much difference between them.

CHAPTER 11 * HOW IN ADDITION TO THE
CAUSES MENTIONED THERE ARE OTHER
REASONS WHY THE TORRID ZONE IS
TEMPERATE, ESPECIALLY THE PROXIMITY
OF THE OCEAN SEA

But because the two properties that I have stated are universal and common to all the Torrid Zone, and despite the fact that it has very warm parts and also others that are very cold, and, finally, because the temperature of the Torrid and equinoctial zones is not the same everywhere, but instead one climate is hot, another cold, and still another temperate, we must necessarily seek other causes for this great diversity that is found in the Torrid Zone. Thinking carefully about this, therefore, I find three clear and obvious causes and a fourth cause that is more obscure. The clear and obvious causes, I say, are first the ocean, second the position and location of the land, and third the properties and nature of the different winds. In addition to these three, which I consider obvious, there is a fourth cause, which is obscure, a characteristic of the inhabited land itself and the particular efficacy and influence of its heavens. The general causes to which I alluded above are insufficient, as will be very clear to anyone who thinks about what happens along different points of the equator. Manomotapa and a large part of Prester John's realm are located on the equator or very close to it, and terrible heat reigns and all the people born there are black; not only there, which is a continent lacking a sea, but the same thing happens in islands surrounded by the sea. The island of Santo Tomé lies on the equator; the Cape Verde Islands are nearby and have fierce heat, and all the people there are black, too. Parts of Peru and the new kingdom of Granada are under the equator, and they are very temperate lands and tend rather toward cold than heat, and the people of those lands are white.[1] The land of Brazil is at the same distance from the equator as Peru, yet Brazil and that whole coast are extremely hot lands, even though they lie on the Northern Sea. This other coast of Peru, which looks on the Southern Sea, is very temperate. Therefore I say that whoever examines these differences and attempts to find a reason for them cannot content himself with the general rules that I have specified in order to prove that the Torrid Zone is temperate. Among special causes I have placed the sea first because there is no doubt that its proximity helps to temper and cool the heat; for, although its water is salty, it is water after all and water is by nature cold, of that there is no doubt. Add to this the fact that the Ocean Sea's immense depth does not allow the water to be warmed by the sun's heat in the way that river waters are warmed. Finally, just as saltpeter serves to cool water because it partakes of the nature of salt, we also see by experience that seawater cools, and so in some ports like Callao we have seen them cool water or wine to drink in flasks or vessels placed in the sea. From all of this it may be inferred that the ocean undoubtedly has the property of tempering and cooling excessive heat; this is

1. The reference to Manomotapa, or Monomotopa, signifies the actual East African empire believed to be the mythical land of Prester John, a region well known in Acosta's time due to the Portuguese, who were the first Europeans to explore, and subsequently trade ivory, silver, and gold, in East Africa.

why we feel the heat more on land than at sea, other things being equal. And usually lands that enjoy proximity to the sea are cooler than those that lie far away from it, other things being equal, as I have said. Thus, because the greater part of the New World is very close to the Ocean Sea even though it lies in the Torrid Zone, we can correctly state that it receives great benefit from the sea in tempering the sun's heat.

### CHAPTER 12 ∗ HOW THE HIGHER LANDS ARE COLDER AND THE REASON FOR THIS

But to pursue our argument further, we will find that on land, though at an equal distance from the sea and in the same degree of latitude, there is nonetheless not the same degree of heat; rather, it will be very hot in one place and much less so in another. As to the cause of this, there can be no doubt that the circumstance of a place being lower or higher makes one hot and the other cold. It is obvious that mountain peaks are colder than the depths of valleys, and this is so not only because there is a greater repercussion of the sun's rays on low and concave places, although it is a considerable cause. There is another cause also, and this is that the region of the air most distant from the earth, and highest, is certainly colder. There is sufficient proof of this in the high plains of Collao in Peru, and those of Popayán and those of New Spain, for clearly all of them are high ground and hence cold, though surrounded by hills and much exposed to the sun's rays. But, if we now ask why the plains of the Peruvian coast and New Spain are hot lands and the high plains of the mountain ranges of Peru and New Spain cold lands, I can see no other reason than that some of those plains are low lying and the others are high. Experience persuades us that the middle region of the air is colder than its lower region, for the closer the mountains are to it the more they are subject to snow and ice and perpetual cold.

Reason also persuades us of it, for if a sphere of fire exists, as Aristotle and the other philosophers suggest, then by antiparistasis the middle region of the air must be colder because the cold is attracted to it, as we see in deep wells in summer. Hence the philosophers say that the two extreme regions of the air, the highest and the lowest, are hotter and the middle region colder. And if this is true, as experience indeed demonstrates, we have another very powerful reason why the Torrid Zone is temperate, which is that most of the land in the Indies is high and full of many mountain peaks that cool the districts near them by their proximity. Perpetual snow and frost can be seen on the peaks to which I refer, and the waters that come from them are icy and sometimes completely frozen; the cold there is so intense that it withers the grass. And when men and beasts travel in those parts they are numbed from the cold. This, as I have said, occurs in the middle of the Torrid Zone and is more likely to occur when the sun is in its zenith. The fact that the peaks are colder than the valleys and plains is common knowledge. And the cause of it is also common knowledge, that mountains and high places partake more of the middle region of the air, which is extremely cold; and the reason why the middle region of the air is colder has also been stated, which is that the region of the air closest to the fiery exhalation that Aristotle tells us is above the sphere of the air thrusts out and expels all the cold. And thus all the cold is gathered together in the middle region of the air by the force of what the philosophers call antiparistasis. After this, if someone should ask me if the air is hot and humid, as Aristotle believes and is commonly stated, whence comes that cold that gathers in the middle region of the air?[1] For it cannot proceed from the sphere of fire, and if it proceeds from water and earth, as reason seems to indicate, the lowest region would have to be colder than the middle region. Actually, if I must answer I will confess that I have so much difficulty with this objection and argument that I am almost ready to follow the opinion of those who criticize the similar and dissimilar qualities that Aristotle assigns to the elements and say that they are but imagination. And so they affirm that the air is cold by nature, and certainly they bring many and great proofs to bear. Leaving the others aside, one of these proofs is very well known, that in the hottest weather we can fan ourselves with a fan and find that it cools us. So these authors state that heat is not a property of any element except that of fire, which is scattered and encountered in everything, according to what Dionysius the Great tells us.[2] But whether it be so or not (for I cannot bring myself to contradict Aristotle unless on some very obvious matter), everyone agrees in the end that the middle region of the air is much colder than the lower region nearest to earth, as experience also demonstrates, for it is where snows are made and sleet and frost and other signs of

1. Aristotle, *Meteorologica,* chapter 4 (O'G).

2. Dionysius the Great, *Of heavenly Hierarchy,* chapter 15 (O'G).

extreme cold; and because the sea is on one side and very high mountains on the other there is considerable reason to believe that these suffice to refresh and temper the heat of the middle region known as the Torrid Zone.

### CHAPTER 13 * HOW COOL WINDS ARE THE CHIEF REASON WHY THE TORRID ZONE IS TEMPERATE

But the temperate climate of this region is chiefly and above all other factors owed to the properties of the wind that blows there, which is very cool and pleasant. The providence of the great God, Creator of all, has ordained that in the region where the sun always shines, and with its fire would seem to ravage everything, the most reliable and frequent winds are wonderfully cool and their coolness serves to temper the sun's ardor. It appears that those who said that the Earthly Paradise lay below the equator were not so far out of the way, had they not been deceived into believing that the only reason why that region was very temperate was that the days and nights were of equal length; others contradicted this opinion, the famous Poet among them,[1] when he said,

> and that region
> is ever scorched by a fierce sun
> and fire never leaves that place.

The cool of the night is not sufficient in itself to moderate and correct such strong rays from the sun. And so, because of the cool and calm wind, the Torrid Zone receives such mild weather that, although for the ancients it was a fiery furnace, for those who live there now it is a delightful spring. That the quality of the wind is chiefly responsible for this is proved by obvious signs and reasons. Within the same climate we see some lands and cities that are warmer than others simply because they receive fewer of the cooling winds. And there are other lands where no wind blows or they are far inland and stifling in temperature and are so wilted by heat that to be in them is like being in a lighted oven. There are no few of such cities and lands in Brazil, Ethiopia, and Paraguay, as everyone knows; and, what is even more remarkable, these differences are seen very clearly not only on land but on the seas

1. Virgil, *Georgicas*, I, 232–33 (o'g).

themselves. There are seas that experience terrible heat, as is reported of the seas of Mozambique and Hormuz, far off in the East, and in the West the sea of Panama, which is the reason why it engenders alligators, and the sea of Brazil. Even at the same degree of latitude there are other very cool seas, like that of Peru, where, as I have mentioned, we were very cold the first time we sailed on it. This was in March, when the sun is directly overhead.

Here, certainly, where the heavens and the water are of the same kind, one can find no explanation for so great a difference except for the property of the wind, which either cools or burns. And, if we think carefully about this property of the wind that I have mentioned, we can satisfy some of the reasonable doubts that many persons have raised about seemingly strange and wonderful things. For example: why, when the sun beats down so strongly in the Torrid Zone and especially in Peru, more strongly indeed than during the dog days in Spain, do people despite this defend themselves against it with much less difficulty, so much so that with the covering of a reed mat or a straw roof they are more protected from the heat than in Spain under a wooden roof and even a vault of stone? For example: why are the summer nights in Peru not hot and uncomfortable, as they are in Spain? For example: why, on the highest peaks of the mountains, even among piles of snow, can there often be intolerable heat? Why is it that everywhere in the province of Collao one is always cold in the shade, no matter how meager it may be, and then when one comes out into the sun one feels excessive heat? For example: why, when the entire coast of Peru is full of barren sandy wastes, is it so temperate? For example: why, when Potosí is only eighteen leagues away from Ciudad de La Plata and has the same degree of latitude, is there such a notable difference, for Potosí is terribly cold, sterile, and dry? Why is La Plata, on the other hand, temperate, with a tendency to warmth, and very even in temperature and very fertile? Indeed, the wind is the chief cause of all these differences and peculiarities; for when the benefit of the cool wind stops the sun's heat burns even in the midst of snow. When coolness returns to the air, all heat lessens, no matter how great it has been. And where this cool wind is usual and persistent it does not allow the thick and earthy exhalations of the earth to join and cause heat and discomfort. In Europe it is the opposite, for owing to these exhalations of the earth, which is burned by the sun all day, the nights are hot and irksome and uncomfortable, and so it often seems that the air comes, as it were, from the mouth of an oven. In

Peru, for the same reason, the freshness of the breeze makes any shade seem cool because there are no rays from the sun; but in Europe the calmest and coolest time in summer is the early morning, for the afternoon is hotter and more annoying. But in Peru and all the equatorial lands it is the opposite, for, since the sea breeze ceases to blow in the morning and rises again when the sun begins to be troublesome, greater heat is felt in the mornings until the so-called *virazón*, or soft or sea wind — it is all one — comes and begins to bring a cool sensation. We had long experience of this during the time we were in the islands that they call the Windwards, where we sweated freely in the mornings and at midday felt pleasantly cool, for then the sea breeze, which is a fresh and pleasant wind, generally began to blow.

## CHAPTER 14 * HOW LIFE IN THE EQUATORIAL REGION IS VERY AGREEABLE

If those who maintain that the Earthly Paradise lies below the equator were guided by what I have written,[1] they would seem to be partially right, not because I believe that the Paradise of Delights described in Scripture is there, for it would be rash to affirm this as true. But I say it because, if we can speak of any paradise on earth, it would be a place where gentle and moderate weather can be enjoyed; for, just as in human life there is nothing so burdensome and painful as a contrary, irksome, and unhealthy sky and wind, so nothing is pleasanter and sweeter than to enjoy a soft, healthy, and exhilarating sky and air. It is clear that of all the elements there is none that we experience more often, or more intimately in our bodies, than air. It surrounds our bodies; it enters our very entrails and visits our hearts at every moment and thus imprints its properties there. If air is foul it quickly kills; if it is healthful it restores our strength. Finally, of air alone can we say that it is the whole life of men. Thus, although we may possess many riches and belongings, if the sky is stormy and unwholesome we must necessarily live an irksome and unhappy life. But if air and sky are healthful and joyful and temperate, even in the absence of other riches, they yield contentment and pleasure. When I consider the very temperate and pleasant climate of many lands in the Indies, where winter when it presses with its cold or summer that makes us suffer from heat are equally unknown, where a reed mat protects

1. Juan Luis Vives, *Commentary on the City of God by Saint Augustine,* book 13, chapter 21 (O'G).

from all assaults of the weather, and where it is hardly necessary to change one's type of clothing in a whole year, I can truly say that in consideration of this I have thought many times and still think today that if men could escape from the bonds placed on them by greed, and if they would abandon useless and irksome pretensions, they could undoubtedly live a very carefree and pleasant life in the Indies.[2] For men would surely find in these lands what other poets sing of the Elysian Fields and famed Tempe as well as what Plato tells, or invents, of his island of Atlantis if with generous hearts they preferred to be masters rather than slaves of their money and greed. As for the qualities of the equatorial zone and its heat and cold, drought and rains, and the causes of its moderate climate, what has been presented here must suffice. A more detailed treatment of the diversity of winds, waters, and lands, as well as the metals, plants, and animals that proceed from them, of which there are great and marvelous examples in the Indies, will have to be left to other books. This book, though short, may perhaps appear tedious owing to the difficulty of the matters dealt with herein.

*Note to the Reader:* The reader should take note that the two preceding books were written in Latin while I was in Peru, and thus speak of things of the Indies as things present. Later, having returned to Spain, I decided to translate them into the vernacular and did not wish to change their mode of expression. But in the five subsequent books, because I wrote them in Europe, I had to change the mode of expression, and so in those books I deal with things of the Indies as with lands and things that are absent. Because this change of style may quite properly displease the reader, I thought I had better remind him of it here.

2. Acosta's natural history in books III and IV often focuses on negative aspects of the New World, like altitude sickness brought on by thin air. In the conclusion to book II—recall that this was written while Acosta still lived in Peru—he strikes a positive tone on the air and, by extension, the New World environment. His description of the Indies as a place that could foster a "carefree and pleasant" life if only men could escape greed recalls earlier sixteenth-century missionary portrayals of the New World as an earthly utopia free from the ills of European civilization. The regular orders, like the Jesuits, commonly entered into heated debate with Spanish colonials over the abuse of native peoples in the pursuit of profit and the negative role models they provided for neophyte Christians. Interestingly, Acosta never restated the idea of the Indies as an earthly paradise in the remaining books, which were all written after his return to Europe.

# BOOK III

## CHAPTER I * HOW THE NATURAL HISTORY OF THE INDIES IS PLEASANT AND ENJOYABLE

All natural history is in itself agreeable, and for anyone who thinks about it in a somewhat loftier sense it is also useful for praising the Author of all nature, as we see that wise and saintly men have done, especially David in different psalms, where he lauds the excellence of these works of God.[1] And this is true of Job, too, when he spoke of the secrets of the Maker, and the Lord himself answered Job at length.[2] Persons who enjoy discovering the true features of this Nature, which is so varied and abundant, will receive the pleasure that history gives and history that is all the greater insofar as the events in it are made not by men but by the Creator. Anyone who goes further, and comes to understand the natural causes of effects, will be exercising good philosophy. We may say of anyone whose thought rises higher and contemplates the Highest and Supreme Artificer of all these marvels, that he will rejoice in God's wisdom and greatness and will be studying excellent theology. Thus the description of natural things can serve many good ends, although the low quality of many tastes usually stops with the least useful of these, which is a desire to know new things, a trait that we properly call curiosity. Apart from this common desire, the description of natural things in the Indies responds to another desire because these are very remote things and among the ancients even the most learned masters of this subject did not discover many or even most of them. If it were possible to write fully about natural things in

1. Psalms, 103, 135, 91, 32, 18, 8 (O'G).
2. Job, 28, 38, 39, 40, 41 (O'G).

the Indies, and with the consideration required by such notable things, I do not doubt that a work could be written equal to those of Pliny, Theophrastus, and Aristotle. But I do not find that vein in myself, nor would it agree with my aim even if I did, for I intend only to take note of some natural things that I saw and contemplated while in the Indies, or that I heard from very reliable persons and which I believe are not commonly known in Europe. And so I will pass over many of them briefly, either because they have been written by others or because they require more consideration than I have been able to give them.[3]

## CHAPTER 2 * OF WINDS AND THEIR DIFFERENCES AND PROPERTIES AND CAUSES IN GENERAL

Since in the previous books I have dealt with matters pertaining to the heavens and climate of the Indies in general, I will go on to speak of the three elements — air, water, and earth — and their compounds, which are metals, plants, and animals. For I see no special qualities of fire in the Indies that differ from those of other places, unless some few readers might be interested in the method of making fire that some Indians use, by rubbing one stick against another, or of cooking in gourds by tossing red-hot stones into them;

3. Most historians and chroniclers of the Indies devoted several chapters to the environment to provide a context for their audience, but few provided, as Acosta does, a methodical treatment of climate and geography (book III) and plants, animals, and minerals (book IV) for both Mexico and Peru. The work of Gonzálo Fernández de Oviedo may have provided an early example for Acosta. His publication *Natural and General History of the Indies* (1535) dealt with both the flora and fauna of the Caribbean islands and to a lesser extent Mexico. In contrast to the historian Acosta, he is best known as a chronicler of the New World because of his attention to the timeline of developments in Spain's discovery of the Americas. Acosta also would have been familiar with some of the best-known naturalists of New Spain, like Francisco Hernández and Nicolás Monardes, who focused their work on cataloging plant life and ascertaining its medicinal value. Another scholar of the New World, Fray Bernardino de Sahagún, offered the closest approximation to Acosta's encyclopedic treatment of plants and animals in book 11, "Of Earthly Things" of his *Florentine Codex* (1579).

The most significant model for Acosta, and other sixteenth-century natural historians, was the comprehensive *Natural History* of Pliny. Acosta never intended to replicate the scope of Pliny's work for the Indies. He did, however, follow a general outline of Pliny, whose work deals with cosmology first; treats earth, water, and air subsequently; and finally discusses animal and plant life.

Acosta's decision to scale back his treatment of New World natural history, however sensible in 1590, meant that he would discuss only certain plant and animal examples, like the mysterious manatee. Over time, this had the effect of presenting an encyclopedia of the exotic to a largely European audience.

what needs to be said about these has already been written. However, I will write at length of the fires that exist in volcanoes in the Indies, which are indeed worthy of consideration, when I deal with the different lands where these fires and volcanoes are found.

And so, beginning with the winds, the first thing to say is that Solomon, among the other traits of great wisdom given him by God, rightly believes it necessary to know about the force of winds and their properties, which are indeed marvelous.[1] For some are rain bearing, others dry, some unwholesome and others wholesome, some hot and others cold, calm, and stormy, sterile and fertile, with innumerable other differences. In certain regions there are winds that blow and are, as it were, lords of the land, with no competition from contrary winds. In other places they blow at intervals, and at times they prevail and at other times their opposites. Sometimes different and even contrary winds blow at the same time and divide their course between them, so that at times one blows at a higher level and the other at a lower. Sometimes they are violently opposed to each other, which is a great danger for those who travel on the sea. There are winds that serve to engender animals, and others that destroy them. When a certain wind blows on a particular coast it rains fleas, and I do not exaggerate, for indeed they fill the air and pile up on the beaches; in other places it rains frogs. These and other well-attested differences are commonly attributed to the places through which these winds pass, for it is said that they take from them their qualities of being dry or cold, moist or hot, wholesome or unwholesome, and so on. This is partly true and cannot be denied, for within the space of a few leagues notable differences can be observed in a single wind. In Spain, for example, the Solano, or east wind, is usually hot and causes distress; however, in Murcia it is the healthiest and coolest wind there is, for it blows across garden plots and the large cool plain that tempers it. A few leagues away, in Cartagena, that same wind is oppressive and unwholesome. The Abrego, which men who sail on the Ocean Sea call the southwest wind and those of the Mediterranean the Mezzogiorno, is usually rain bearing and irksome, but in the city referred to above it is healthful and gentle. Pliny says that in Africa the north wind brings rain and the south wind is gentle.[2] And from what I

---

1. Book of Wisdom, 7, 20 (O'G).
2. Pliny, *Natural History*, 2, 47 (O'G).

have said of these winds as an example, within such small distances, it is
obvious to anyone who looks at the matter with some attention that very
often the same wind has very different properties, and sometimes even quite
contrary ones, over a short distance either on land or sea. From this it can
well be argued that the place over which it passes gives the wind its quality
and properties. But this is true only to the extent that it is impossible to call
this the whole cause, or even the chief one, of the differences and properties
of the winds. For within a single region, let us say fifty leagues in circumference, it can clearly be seen that in one place the wind is hot and moist and
in another cold and dry, even though there is not so much difference in the
places it passes over; rather, those qualities must be brought by the winds
themselves. And so general names are given to each, to wit: Septentrion or
Cierzo or north wind (which are all one) as cold and dry and blowing away
clouds; its contrary wind is called Abrego or Leveche or south wind, which
unlike the other is moist and hot and creates clouds.

Therefore, since this is general and widespread, another, more universal
cause must be sought to explain these effects, and it does not suffice to say
that the place over which these winds pass gives them their properties, for in
passing over those places they in fact cause very well known contrary effects.
Hence we will have to admit that the region of the heavens from which they
blow is what gives them these attributes and qualities. And so the wind that
blows from the north, which is the region farthest from the sun, is by its
nature cold. The wind that blows from the south is by its nature hot, and
because heat attracts vapors it is both moist and rain laden, while the north
wind is the opposite, dry and keen because it does not allow vapors to form.
The other winds can be described in the same way, attributing their properties to the regions of the air from which they blow. But if we examine it a little
more closely this reasoning does not satisfy us fully, for I would ask: what
role has the region of the air from which the wind blows if its particular
quality is not found there? I mean that in Germany the south wind is moist
and rainy and in Africa the north wind is cold and dry; obviously, whatever
region of Germany in which the south wind arises must be colder than any
region of Africa where the north wind arises. Then why does the north wind
have to be colder in Africa than the south wind in Germany, since it comes
from a hotter region? You will say that it blows from the north, which is cold.
This is neither a sufficient nor a true explanation, for according to it when the

north wind blows in Africa it would have to blow in the entire region all the way to the north, which is not so, for at the same time north winds blow in lands with fewer degrees of latitude, while strong southwest winds blow in places with more degrees of latitude and are hot. This is true and evident and a matter of daily experience. From this, I believe, we may clearly infer that it does not suffice to say that the winds acquire their qualities by means of the places they pass through. Nor is it satisfactory to say that the winds have these differences because they blow from different regions of the air, although, as I have said, both are true; we need to go further. Whatever may be the true and original cause of these strange differences in the winds, I can think of no other than that the efficient cause, and the one that produces the wind, confers its first and most original property upon it, for the material of which winds are made, which according to both Aristotle and reason are exhalations of the inferior elements, although their differences of being heavier or lighter, or drier or moister, can cause and indeed do cause a large part of this diversity. But neither is this sufficient, for the same reason that I have mentioned: that contrary winds arise in a single region and where the vapors and exhalations are of the same kind.

And so it seems that the question has to be reduced to the higher and celestial efficient cause, which must be the sun, and the movement and influence of the heavens, which move and influence the winds from different directions. And because these principles of movements and influences are so hidden from men, and are so powerful and effective in themselves, as the holy prophet David said with great wisdom,[3] among other signs of the Lord's greatness, the prophet Jeremiah[4] answered the same: "Qui profert ventos de thesauris suis," He bringeth forth the wind out of his treasures. Certainly these are rich and hidden treasures that the Author of all things has in his power, so that when he wishes he can easily bring them forth either for men's chastisement or enjoyment and can send the wind that he wishes. This wind not like that Aeolus, who, as the poets foolishly imagined, had the winds shut in his cave like wild beasts in a cage. We cannot see the onset and origin of these winds, nor do we know how long they will last nor whence they come nor where they will go. But we do see and know for certain what their

3. Psalms, 134, 7 (O'G).
4. Jeremiah, 10, 13 (O'G).

different effects are, as the Supreme Truth and Author of all creation told us:[5] "Spiritus ubi vult spirat: et vocem eius audis: et nescis unde venit, aut quo vadit," the spirit (or wind) breatheth where he will and thou hearest his voice: but thou knowest not whence he cometh and whither he goeth. This is to make us realize that, understanding not a jot of a thing that is so commonplace and close to our experience, we must not presume to comprehend something as lofty and arcane as the causes and motives of the Holy Spirit. We need only know its operations and effects, which are sufficiently revealed to us in their greatness and perfection; and it will also suffice to have philosophized a little about winds in general and the causes of their differences and their properties and operations, which we have reduced to a total of three, namely, the places through which they pass, the regions from which they blow, and celestial virtue, the mover and causer of winds.

### CHAPTER 3 * OF SOME PROPERTIES OF THE WINDS THAT BLOW IN THE NEW WORLD

It is a question much disputed by Aristotle whether the south wind, which we call Abrego or Leveche (for the moment they are all one), blows from the Antarctic Pole or only from the equator and the south.[1] This amounts to asking whether that warm and rainy quality that it possesses stays with it once it has crossed the equator. And certainly there is room for doubt, for even though it crosses the equator it does not cease to be an austral or south wind; it comes from the same side of the world, like the north wind, which blows from the opposite direction and does not cease to be a north wind even though it crosses the Torrid Zone and the equator. And so it appears that both winds must preserve their primary properties, the one of being hot and moist and the other cold and dry, the south wind causing fogs and rain, and the boreal or north wind dispersing them and clearing the sky. But Aristotle leans toward the opposite opinion, holding that it is the reason why the north wind is cold in Europe, since it comes from the pole, which is an extremely chilly region, and that the south wind, on the other hand, is hot because it comes from the south, which is the region most heated by the sun. This reasoning would oblige us to believe that for those on the other side of

5. Saint John, 3, 8 (O'G).
1. Aristotle, *Meteorologica*, chapter 5 (O'G).

the equator the south wind is cold and the north wind hot, for there the south wind comes from the pole and the north wind from the equator. And, although it seems that the south wind must be colder there than the north wind here, for the region of the South Pole is colder than that of the North Pole because the sun inclines more toward the tropic of Cancer than the tropic of Capricorn for an additional seven days a year, as is clearly shown in the equinoxes and solstices that it causes in both regions, it appears that Nature wished to declare the advantage and nobility enjoyed by this half of the world, which is the north, over the other half, which is the south. If this is true, it seems a conclusive reason to believe that these qualities of the winds change after the equator is crossed.

But in fact this is not the case insofar as I have been able to understand by means of the experience of several years of living in that part of the world below the equator. It is indeed true that the north wind is not usually as cold and calm there as here. In some parts of Peru the inhabitants find the north wind unhealthy and irksome, as in Lima and on the plains; and throughout that coast, which is more than five hundred leagues long, the south wind is held to be wholesome and cool and especially very gentle. It never brings rain, completely contrary to what happens in Europe and on this side of the equator; but what I have said about the coast of Peru is the exception that proves the rule and a wonder of Nature, for it never rains on that coast and the same wind always blows there, yet the opposite never happens, as I will describe in its proper place. For the moment let us establish that on the other side of the equator the north wind does not have the same properties that the south wind has with us, although both blow from the equator to opposite regions, for it is not usually the case there that the north wind is warm and moist, as the south wind is here. Rather, it also rains there with a south wind, as can be seen in the whole mountain chain of Peru and in Chile, and in the Congo, which is on the other side of the equator and located very far from the sea. And in Potosí the wind that they call Tomahavi, which if I remember correctly corresponds to our north wind, is extremely dry and cold and very disagreeable, just as it is here. The truth is that the north wind there is not so likely to disperse the clouds as it is here; rather, if I am not mistaken, it often brings rain. There is no doubt that, from the places through which they pass and the nearby regions from whence they originate, the winds acquire such great differences and contrary effects as are felt daily in a great many places.

But speaking in general of the quality of the winds we must pay more attention to the parts of the world they come from than to their coming from one side or the other of the equator, as (I believe) the Philosopher correctly held. These important winds, which are the west and east winds, do not have as obvious and universal qualities, either here or there, as the other two I have named. But here in Europe the Solano, or east wind, is usually disagreeable and unwholesome, and the west wind, or Zephyr, is milder and healthier. In the Indies and everywhere in the Torrid Zone the east wind, which they call the trade wind, is unlike the east wind here and is very healthful and mild. I am unable to say anything very accurate or general about the west wind, chiefly because that wind blows only very rarely in the Torrid Zone. For all the voyages made in the Tropics, the ordinary and regular wind there is the one called the trade wind, and because it is one of the most wonderful works of Nature we would do well to thoroughly understand how it arises.

## CHAPTER 4 * HOW EASTERLY WINDS ALWAYS BLOW IN THE TORRID ZONE AND OUTSIDE IT BOTH WESTERLIES AND EASTERLIES

Traveling on the sea is not like traveling on land, where the traveler returns by the same road he took. The journey is, as the Philosopher said, from Athens to Thebes and from Thebes to Athens. On the sea this is not so; we go by one route and return by another. The first discoverers of the West Indies and even the East Indies had to expend great effort and undergo difficulties to find a reliable route there, and no less for returning,[1] until experience — which is the teacher of these secrets — showed them that navigating the Ocean was not the same as sailing on the Mediterranean to Italy, where both outward bound and on the return voyage they recognize the same ports and headlands and need only await the wind, which changes with the weather. Even when the wind fails they can use oars, and so ships ply to and fro by hugging the coast. In some places on the Ocean Sea there is no use waiting for a different wind, for it is known already that the wind that blows is going to continue to do so to a greater or lesser degree. In a word, what is good for the outward journey is not good for the return, for beyond the Tropics and in the Torrid Zone the winds that come from the direction where the sun rises are always masters of

1. Juan de Barros, *Decades of Asia,* I, book 4, chapter 6 (O'G).

the sea and blow perpetually and never allow contrary winds to prevail there or even to be felt. There are two wonderful elements in this: one, that in the region that is the greatest of the five into which the world is divided, easterly winds called the trades prevail and the westerly and southerly winds cannot blow at any time of the year. The other wonderful thing is that easterly winds never fail there and blow most reliably in places nearest the equator, where it would seem that calms would be more likely, since it is the part of the world most subject to the sun's heat. And yet this is not so, for calms are extremely rare and the easterlies are much cooler and more reliable. This has proved to be the case in all navigations to the Indies. Hence this is the reason why the journey from Spain to the West Indies is much shorter and easier, and even safer, than the return journey from them to Spain.[2]

The fleets sail out of Seville and find the greatest difficulty until they reach the Canaries because that gulf called Yeguas is changeable and plagued by several contrary winds. After the Canaries are left behind the ships sail southward until they enter the Torrid Zone and then pick up the trades and sail before the wind and hardly need to touch the sails throughout the voyage. That is why that whole great gulf is called Damas, or Ladies' Gulf, for its calm and tranquillity. And so they reach the islands of Dominica, Guadalupe, Deseada, Marigalante, and the others in those regions, which are, as it were, the suburbs of the Indies. There the fleets separate, and those that go to New Spain bear right toward Hispaniola, and after sighting Cape San Antón arrive in San Juan de Ulúa, constantly making use of the trade winds. Those going to the southern continent bear to the left and sail until they sight the high mountain range of Tairona and put in at Cartagena and go on to Nombre de Dios, whence the journey to Panama is by land and from there by the Southern Sea to Peru. When the fleets return to Spain they make the voyage in the following manner: the fleet from Peru sights Cape San Antón and when it reaches the island of Cuba puts in at Havana, which is a very

2. The routes that Acosta describes here became standard following a period of trial and error in the early years of discovery. The trip from Seville to Nombre de Dios, the port at Panama, lasted approximately 75 days, while the return voyage to Spain took as long as 130 days. Despite advances in technology and the publication of navigational guides like Pedro de Medina's *Arte de Navegar,* historian Murdo MacLeod suggests that most European sea pilots relied on dead reckoning to plot their courses and that maritime wisdom grew out of informal communication from port to port. See MacLeod's thorough treatment of trade routes and navigation in "Spain and America: The Atlantic Trade, 1492–1720," in *Cambridge History of Latin America,* vol. 1 (New York: Cambridge University Press, 1984).

beautiful harbor on that island. The fleet from New Spain also comes from Veracruz or the island of San Juan de Ulúa to Havana, though with difficulty, for easterlies commonly blow there and are contrary winds. Once the fleets are joined in Havana the return to Spain is made by seeking a latitude outside the tropics where strong southwest winds are found, and by using them they sight the Azores, or Terceira Islands, and from there sail to Seville. So the outward voyage is accomplished at a low latitude, always less than twenty degrees, which is within the Tropics; and the return voyage is outside the Tropics, at least at twenty-eight or thirty degrees of latitude. The reason for this is, as has been said, that within the Tropics trade winds always prevail and are favorable for sailing from Spain to the West Indies because this involves traveling from east to west. Outside the Tropics, at twenty-three degrees of latitude, strong southwest winds blow and are all the more reliable the more degrees of latitude are reached; and these are good for returning from the Indies because they are southerly and westerly winds and serve for returning east and north.

The same thing happens in navigations on the Southern Sea, sailing from New Spain or Peru to the Philippines or China and returning from the Philippines or China to New Spain. Outward bound the voyage is easy, from east to west, and near the equator the ships always find that they can sail before the wind, which is easterly. In 1584 a ship set out from Callao to the Philippines and sailed for 2,700 leagues without seeing land; the first land it sighted was the island of Luzón, which was its destination, and there it dropped anchor after having made its crossing in two months, the wind never failing or a storm occurring. And it made the whole voyage almost below the equator, for from Lima, which is 12 degrees below it, they arrived in Manila, which is almost the same number of degrees to the north of it. Álvaro de Mendaña had almost the same good fortune on his journey to discover the Solomon Islands, for when he discovered them they constantly sailed before the wind until they sighted those islands, which must be a thousand leagues from Peru, from which they sailed, and are in the same degree of latitude to the south of the equator. The return is made like that from the Indies to Spain, for to find southwest winds those who return from the Philippines or China to Mexico sail far to the north, until they reach the latitude of the Japanese islands, and then they sight the Californias and on the coast of New Spain turn south to the port of Acapulco, from which they had departed.

So in this kind of navigation it has been established that from east to west a ship sails successfully within the Tropics because easterly winds prevail there, and when they return from west to east they must seek southwesterly or westerly winds outside the Tropics, at twenty-seven degrees of latitude above the equator. The Portuguese do the same in their navigations to India, though in the opposite direction, for the journey from Portugal to India is difficult and the return journey easier because they are sailing from west to east when outward bound; so they try to reach a higher latitude to catch the prevailing winds, which they also say are found at twenty-seven degrees or more. On the return they sight the Terceiras, but it is easier for them because they come from the east and can make use of the easterlies or northeasterlies. Finally, it is the rule and correct observation of sailors that within the Tropics easterly winds prevail and so it is easy to sail in a westerly direction. Outside the Tropics there are at times easterly winds; at other times (and this is more likely) there are strong southwesterly winds, and that is why a ship that sails from west to east tries to leave the Torrid Zone and reach a latitude of twenty-seven degrees. By following this rule men have dared to make strange navigations to very remote places never seen before.

CHAPTER 5 * OF THE DIFFERENCES BETWEEN
EASTERLIES AND SOUTHWESTERLIES AND
OTHER KINDS OF WINDS

Although what I have said is well proven and universal, we are still led to ask the cause of this secret: why is it so easy to sail from east to west in the Torrid Zone and not from west to east? This is the same as asking why easterly winds prevail there and not southwesterlies, for according to sound philosophy all that is perpetual and universal *de per se* (as the philosophers express it) must also have a proper cause *de per se*. Before taking up this question, an important one in our opinion, it will be necessary to state what we understand by easterly and southwesterly winds, which will serve both for this purpose and for many other matters concerning winds and navigation. Those who practice that art number 32 differences in winds, for in order to reach the desired port they must make a very careful calculation, with as many gradations and fine distinctions as they can manage. No matter how little they deviate to one side or another, it makes a great difference at the end of the voyage, and they do not count more than 32 because these divisions are sufficient and they could not keep track of more than these. But actually, just as they use 32, they could use 64 or 128 or 256 and finally could go on multiplying these divisions infinitely, because, considering the place where the ship is located as the center and the whole hemisphere as its circumference, who can deny that innumerable lines can go from this center to the circumference?

And so any number of divisions can be counted and an equal number of winds, for the wind comes from all parts of the hemisphere. As for making them into this or that number of divisions, it is my opinion that men can divide them into as many parts as they wish. But men's good sense (and Divine Scripture is in agreement with this) designates four winds that are the chief of them all and form as it were the four corners of the world, which can be visualized by making a cross with two lines, one going from pole to pole and the other from one equinox to the other. These are the north wind, or Aquilon, and its opposite the Austral, or what we commonly call the south wind. On the other side there is the east wind, where the sun rises, and the west, where it sets. However, Holy Writ points out other kinds of winds in some places,[1] like the Euroaquilo, which those of the Ocean Sea call northeast and those of the Mediterranean Gregal, which is mentioned in the voyages of Saint Paul. But the four great differences that everyone knows are celebrated in Divine Writ, and they are, as has been said, north, south, east, and west. But, because there are three differences in the rising of the sun, from whence the Orient receives its name, namely, the two major declinations that the sun makes and the mean between them, according to which it rises in different places in winter and summer and the mean between these seasons, two other winds are properly counted, which are the summer east wind and the winter east wind. Consequently there are two other west winds opposite to these, summer and winter. Hence there are eight winds in eight notable points of the heavens, which are the two poles and the two equinoxes and the two solstices, along with their opposites in the same circle. Therefore eight important divisions of winds exist, which have different names in different parts of the sea and land. Men who sail the Atlantic usually name them as follows: the wind that comes from our pole they call north, like the pole itself; the following one, which comes from the summer east direction,

1. Acts, 27, 14 (O'G).

northeast; the one that comes from the direct and equinoctial east they call east; from the winter east, southeast; from the south or Antarctic pole, south; from the winter west, southwest; from the direct and equinoctial west, west; and from the summer west, northwest. The other winds are measured between these and share the names of those I have mentioned, such as north-northwest, north-northeast, east-northeast, east-southeast, south-southwest, west-southwest, and west-northwest, which by the very way they are named indicate the places from whence they proceed.

In the Mediterranean Sea, although the same method of counting them is followed, there are different names for these winds. They call the north wind Tramontana, and its opposite, the south wind, is called Mezzogiorno. The east wind is called Levante and the west wind Poniente. As for those that come between these winds, the southeast wind is called Jiroque or Jaloque and its opposite, which is northwest, Maestral; northeast is called Greco or Gregal, and its opposite, the southwest, is called Leveche (which in Latin means Libyan or African). In Latin the four winds are Septentrio, Auster, Subsolanus, and Favonius, and the four in between are Aquilo, Vulturnus, Africus, and Corus. According to Pliny, Vulturnus and Eurus are the same wind, which is southeast or Jaloque; Favonius is the same as the west wind or Poniente; Aquilo and Boreas are the same as the northeast or Gregal or Tramontana; Africus and Libs are the same as southwest or Leveche; Auster and Notus are the same as the south wind or Mezzogiorno; and Corus and Zephyrus are the same as northwest or Maestral. To the remaining wind, which is northeast or Gregal, he gives no other name than Fenicias.[2] Others give different names, and it is not our intention at present to establish the Latin and Greek names of the winds.

Now we will state which of these winds are called easterlies and which southwesterlies by our sailors of the Ocean Sea of the Indies. The fact is that for a long time I was confused by these names, observing that the sailors used these words very differently, until I realized that they are general terms rather than specific names of winds or their divisions. Those that serve for the voyage to the Indies and blow almost astern are called easterlies or trades, which in fact include all the east winds and their neighboring and quarterly winds. Those that serve the return from the Indies are called westerlies,

2. Pliny, *Natural History,* 2, 47; *Gell,* book 2, chapter 22 (O'G).

which are the winds ranging from the south to the summer west wind. So the winds form, as it were, two groups, each from one direction, whose chief winds come from the northeast, or Gregal, and the others from the southwest or Leveche. But we must realize that of the eight winds and the subdivisions that we count five are useful for navigation and three are not. I mean that when a ship is sailing on the sea it can sail and accomplish the voyage it intends from any one of five directions from which the wind blows, although they will not be equally favorable; but if one of the other three blows the ship cannot sail where it wishes. If, for example, it is going south it can sail with a north and northeast wind, with a northwest and also an east and a west wind, for the side winds serve equally to go and to return. But if a south wind is blowing, which is directly contrary, the ship cannot sail in a southerly direction, nor can it do so with the two lateral winds, which are southwest and southeast. This is a very familiar situation for those who sail on the sea, and there is no need to write of it here except to state that the lateral winds or the real and true east wind usually blow in the Torrid Zone and are called trade winds. The winds from south to west, which allow one to sail from west to east, are not usually found in the Torrid Zone. Hence ships must seek them outside the Tropics, and sailors commonly call them westerlies.

## CHAPTER 6 * WHY THERE IS ALWAYS AN EAST WIND FOR SAILING IN THE TORRID ZONE

Now let us say something about the question I have propounded, namely, how is it possible to sail successfully from east to west in the Torrid Zone and not contrariwise? For this we must presuppose two certain causes. One is that the movement of the First Movable, which is called diurnal, not only draws after it and moves the celestial spheres that are inferior to it, as we see daily in the sun, moon, and stars, but the elements also participate in that movement as long as they are not hindered. The earth does not move in this way owing to its great weight, which renders it incapable of moving circularly and also because it is very far from the First Movable. Nor does the element of water have this diurnal movement, for it is clasped to the earth and forms a single sphere and the earth does not allow it to move circularly. The other two elements, fire and air, are more subtle and nearer to the celestial spheres and thus participate in their movement, being borne along circularly like the celestial bodies themselves. As to fire, there is no doubt that it has a sphere of its own, as Aristotle and the other philosophers state. The air is what we are talking about, and that it moves with the diurnal movement from east to west is proved by the movement of comets, which can clearly be seen to move from east to west, appearing and rising, reaching their zenith and descending, and finally crossing our hemisphere in the same way as the stars that we see in the firmament. And, because the comets are in the region and sphere of the air where they are born and appear and disappear, it would be impossible for them to move circularly, as they do, if the element of air did not move with the same movement as the First Movable. Because comets, as we know, are made of a flaming substance, they would remain motionless and would not move circularly if the sphere in which they are located remained motionless unless we imagine that some angel or intelligence travels with the comet and draws it across the heavens. In the year of fifteen hundred and seventy-seven that wonderful comet, with a form like a plume, could be seen from the horizon almost to the middle of the heavens, and it lasted from the first of November until the eighth of December. I say from the first of November because, although it was noted and seen on the ninth of November in Spain, as histories of that time tell, I remember well that in Peru, where I was at the time, all of us saw and observed it eight days earlier. Others may explain the cause of this difference; what I say now is that during the forty days that it lasted we all saw, those who were in Europe as well as those of us who were in the Indies, that it moved each day with the universal movement from east to west, like the moon and the other stars, which proves that since its region was the sphere of air the element itself moved in that direction. We also noticed that apart from that universal movement it had another movement of its own, moving with the planets from west to east, because every night it was more easterly, as the sun and moon and the star of Venus are. We also observed that it had a third and very special movement in the Zodiac toward the north, for after several nights it was closer to the northern signs. Perhaps this is the reason why this great comet was first seen by those who were farther south, as people in Peru are, and, since with the third movement that I mentioned it moved farther north, people in Europe began to see it later. But all of us could observe the differences in movement that I have mentioned, so it could easily be seen that the impression of different celestial bodies reached the sphere of the air. Hence there is no doubt that the air moves with the circular movement of the heavens, from east to west, which is the first proposition that I mentioned.

The second is no less certain and obvious, namely, that this movement of air through the parts that are below the equator and near it is very rapid, all the more so the closer it comes to the equator, and consequently this movement is slower and tardier as it draws away from the equator and comes closer to the poles. The reason for this is perfectly clear, for, since the efficient cause of this movement is the movement of the celestial body, it must necessarily be more rapid where the celestial body moves more swiftly. To try to demonstrate that the Torrid Zone has a swifter movement in the heavens, and on the equator more than in any other part of the heavens, would be to assume that men are blind, for on a wheel it is evident that the greater circumference moves more rapidly than the lesser, finishing its larger revolution in the same space of time as the lesser finishes its own. From these two propositions comes the reason why those who sail from east to west on large bodies of water always encounter a following wind when they travel at a few degrees of latitude; the closer they are to the equator the more reliable and persistent is the wind. And, on the contrary, when sailing from west to east they always find that they are sailing into the wind and it is contrary, for the very rapid movement of the equator draws the element of air after it, as it does the other higher spheres. Thus the air always follows the diurnal movement, blowing from east to west and never changing, and the rapid and effective movement of the air also draws after it the vapors and exhalations that rise from the sea. This causes the easterly wind to be constant in those parts and that region, blowing from the east. Father Alonso Sánchez, a religious of our society who has traveled in both the East and West Indies and is a very experienced and intelligent man, said that he thought the reason why it was possible to sail with such constant and persistent good weather below the equator, or near it, was that the very air moved by the heavens was what moved the ships, and that that wind was not properly speaking an exhalation but the element of air itself, moved by the diurnal course of the heavens. He added as confirmation of this that in the gulf of Las Damas and those other great gulfs that are sailed upon in the Torrid Zone, the weather is unchanging and the sails stay strangely the same without having to be touched, and hardly need to be changed in almost the whole course of the voyage. And if the air were not moved by the heavens it would sometimes fail, and sometimes would turn into a contrary wind, and sometimes be stormy. Though this is learnedly expressed, we cannot deny that it is a wind, for there are vapors and exhalations from the sea; and we clearly see that the same easterly wind is at times stronger and at times weaker, so much so that sometimes the ships cannot carry all their sails. So it must be understood, and it is the truth, that the air when moved draws after it the vapors that it encounters, for its strength is great and it finds no resistance; and that is why the wind from east to west is continuous and almost uniform near the equator and in almost all the Torrid Zone, which is the course followed by the sun between the two circles of Cancer and Capricorn.

CHAPTER 7 * WHY WESTERLY WINDS ARE MORE
USUALLY FOUND WHEN LEAVING THE TORRID
ZONE, AT HIGHER LATITUDES

Anyone who thinks about what I have said can also understand that when sailing from west to east at a latitude higher than that of the tropics, westerly winds may reasonably be expected; for since the rapid movement of the equator is the reason why underneath it the air moves by following its move-ment, which is from east to west, and that it commonly draws after it the vapors that arise from the sea, just so, contrariwise, the vapors and exhala-tions that arise from the two sides of the equator or Torrid Zone, with the repercussion they cause when they encounter the current of the Zone, turn almost around and cause the westerly or southwesterly winds that are so often experienced in those parts. Just as we see that currents of water, if they are struck and shaken by others that are stronger, turn almost completely around, the same thing seems to happen with the vapors and exhalations where the winds arise in some places and in others. These westerlies are more likely to prevail at middling latitudes of twenty-seven to thirty-seven degrees, though they are not as reliable and regular as the easterlies at lesser latitudes, and the reason is clear: westerlies are not caused by the characteristic and uniform movement of the heavens, as are the easterlies near the equator, although they are, as I have said, more common and often very furious and stormy. Nor, when a ship reaches a higher latitude such as forty degrees, is there any more certainty of winds on the sea than on land. Sometimes the easterlies or north winds blow, while at other times they are westerly or southwesterly, and thus those navigations are more uncertain and perilous.

CHAPTER 8 * OF EXCEPTIONS TO BE FOUND IN
THE RULE JUST EXPRESSED AND THE WINDS
AND CALMS THAT EXIST ON SEA AND LAND

What I have said of the winds that commonly blow inside and outside the Torrid Zone must be understood to apply to the open sea and the great gulfs; the case is different on land, where all sorts of winds are found owing to its great irregularities in the form of mountains and valleys and a multitude of rivers and lakes and other features of the land, from which arise thick and varied vapors. These are moved to one place or another according to different principles and hence cause different winds, and the movement of the air caused by the heavens is not always sufficient to draw them after itself. These differences are found not only on land but along the seacoasts in the Torrid Zone, and with the same cause, because there are land winds that blow from the land and sea winds that blow from the sea. Usually the sea winds are gentle and wholesome and those of the land oppressive and unhealthy, although this depends upon the difference in coasts (such is the variation that exists in this respect). The land winds commonly blow from after midnight until sunrise; the sea winds blow from the time the sun begins to warm until after it has set. Perhaps the cause is that the land, as it is made of heavier matter, steams more after the sun's heat is gone, like ill-dried wood that smokes most after the flame is extinguished. The sea, as it consists of lighter parts, does not raise vapors except when it is being heated, just as straw or hay, if in small quantities and not well dried, raises smoke when it is burned, and when the flame ceases the smoke stops, too. Whatever may be the cause of this, it is certain that the land wind prevails more at night and on the other hand the sea wind is more likely to prevail in the daytime.

Just as on the coasts there are contrary winds, and violent and very stormy ones at times, there can also be very great calms. Men of much experience who have sailed below the equator say that they cannot remember having seen calms but that the ship always moved forward, whether little or much, thanks to the breeze raised by celestial motion, which suffices to cause the ship to sail before the wind, as is in fact the case. I have already mentioned that in a voyage of 2,700 leagues, always sailing either below or no more than ten or twelve degrees from the equator, a ship traveled from Lima to Manila in February and March, which is the time of year when the sun is most directly overhead, and in that whole space of time they encountered no calms, only a fresh gale, and so made that long voyage in two months. But in the vicinity of land, on coasts or in places where the vapors from islands or a continent can reach, there are often many and very cruel calms both inside and outside the Torrid Zone. Likewise, hurricanes and sudden downpours, and cyclones and other stormy disturbances in the air, are more likely and common along the coasts, and in places where land vapors can reach, than on the high seas. By this, I mean within the Torrid Zone, for outside it calms as well as hurricanes are also found on the open sea. This does not mean that there are no downpours or sudden rainstorms at times between the Tropics and the equator, even far out at sea; the exhalations and vapors of the sea suffice for this, since they often move rapidly through the air and cause thunderstorms and hurricanes. But this is much more common near land and on the land itself.

When I sailed from Peru to New Spain I noticed that all the time we were sailing along the coast of Peru the voyage was, as it always is, calm and easy owing to the south wind that prevails there, and with that wind the return trip from Spain and New Spain is made before the wind. When we crossed the open sea, as we were far from land and almost below the equator, the weather was very calm and cool and we had a following wind. When we reached the vicinity of Nicaragua, and all along that coast, we had contrary weather and many clouds and heavy rains, and wind that sometimes roared terribly. This whole voyage took place within the Torrid Zone, for we sailed from Lima, at twelve degrees south, to seventeen degrees north, the location of Huatulco, a seaport of New Spain. And I believe that those who have carefully observed the voyages they have made within the Torrid Zone will find that their experience agrees more or less with what I have said. Let this suffice for a general explanation of the sea winds that prevail in the Torrid Zone.

CHAPTER 9 * OF SOME WONDERFUL EFFECTS
OF WINDS IN PARTS OF THE INDIES

I would need great knowledge to explain in detail the remarkable effects caused by different winds in different places and to give the reason for them. There are winds that by their nature disturb the water of the sea and turn it greenish-black; others make it as clear as a mirror. Some have the faculty of causing pleasure and delight; others cause sadness and oppression. The breeders of silkworms are very careful to close their windows when the southwest winds are blowing and open them when the contrary winds blow, and they know from experience that with some winds the creatures die or deteriorate while with other winds they improve and fatten. Anyone who takes notice of it can prove for himself that the different kinds of winds make noticeable impressions and changes in the body's feelings, especially in those parts that are ill or indisposed, and all the more when they are in a delicate condition. Scripture describes one sort of wind as a burning wind and another as a gentle dew.[1] And it is no wonder that such noticeable effects of the wind are felt in plants and animals and men, for they can be observed visibly even in iron itself, which is the hardest of metals. In different parts of the Indies I have seen iron gratings so rusted and ruined that if the iron was squeezed between the fingers it crumbled like hay or dry straw, and all this was caused solely by wind, which consumed and corroded it beyond repair. But, leaving aside other great and remarkable effects, I wish to recount only two: one that, although it causes anguish worse than the pains of death, does not threaten life; and another that cuts life short although it is not felt.[2]

It is a very frequent thing for men to become seasick at the beginning of a voyage, and if we did not know how common it is, and the little harm it does, men would think it the pangs of death because of the way it confounds and distresses and afflicts us during the time it lasts, with severe nausea and headache and any number of other troublesome symptoms. This well-known and frequent effect is caused in men by their first experience of the sea breeze, although the movement of the ship and its rolling motion greatly influence the degree of seasickness, as do infections and the bad odor of things on

1. Exodus 10, 13 and 14, 21; Job 27, 21; Jonah 4, 8; Hosea 13, 15; Daniel, 3, 50 (O'G).

2. In this chapter Acosta describes seasickness, which he holds to be a universal affliction, and altitude sickness and frostbite, which he finds particular to Peru. His analysis of altitude sickness, known in the Andes as *soroche*, is one of the first attempts at a causal explanation of the ailment. The sum of these "remarkable" effects of the winds, in particular the *soroche* attack that Acosta describes in vivid detail, offered to a suggestible European mind the notion that the very environment of the Americas was antagonistic to civilization. The negative implications of the inferior Andes air is in contrast to the pleasant air of the Torrid Zone, which Acosta had described earlier. This tension in his own work between favorable and unfavorable climatic elements in the New World exemplifies numerous sixteenth-century debates on the Americas as a land of earthly paradise or savage barbarity.

board. But the actual and fundamental causes are the wind and sea vapors, which the body — and especially the stomach that is unused to them — finds so strange that it becomes upset and suffers terribly. For air, after all, is the element in which we live and breathe, and we draw it into our very entrails and bathe them in it. Thus there is nothing that so quickly or powerfully affects us than a change in the air we breathe, as can be seen in those who die of plague. The fact that sea air is the chief cause of that strange indisposition and nausea is proved by much experience. One proof is that when a certain wind blows strongly from the sea men on land sometimes suffer nausea, as has often happened to me. Another is that the more one penetrates into the sea and leaves the land behind the more one is seasick. Another is that when sailing in the lee of an island, when one begins to breathe air from the open sea one feels much more likely to succumb. It cannot be denied that movement and the rolling of the ship also cause seasickness, for we see that there are persons who become ill when crossing a river by boat and others who have the same symptoms when riding in carts or carriages, according to the different complexion of their stomachs, just as, on the other hand, there are some who never know what it is to be seasick no matter how heavy the seas. In a word, it is a plain and proven fact that sea air commonly causes this effect in those who first breathe it.

I have said all this in order to speak of a strange effect caused by the air or wind that prevails in certain lands in the Indies, which is that men become ill from it, not less but much more than at sea. Some think it a legend and others call it an exaggeration, but I will tell what happened to me. In Peru there is a very lofty mountain range that is called Pariacaca; I had heard of this alteration that it causes and went prepared as best I could according to the advice given me by those called *vaquianos* there, or experts; yet after all my preparation, when I climbed the Staircases, as they are called, the highest part of that range, almost in an instant I felt such mortal anguish that I thought I would have to throw myself off my mount onto the ground. Although many of us were making the journey, each one was hurrying and not waiting for the others in order to get out of that bad situation. I was left with only one Indian, whom I begged to help hold me on my mount. This was soon followed by convulsive retching and vomiting that made me think I would give up the ghost, for after vomiting up my food and a watery residue there came bile and more bile, some yellow and some green, and I even vomited blood from the violence felt by my stomach. Finally, I will say that if it had continued I would have been certain of dying, but it lasted only a matter of three or four hours until we had gone a good way down the mountain and reached a more tolerable altitude, where I found all my companions, of whom there were some fourteen or fifteen, completely exhausted. Some had asked for Confession along the way, thinking that they were dying; others had dismounted and were in a wretched condition with vomiting and flux. Some told me that they were sure their end was at hand from that illness. I saw another who threw himself to the ground and screamed from the terrible pain that the transit of Pariacaca had cost him. But commonly it does not result in any great harm, apart from the feelings of nausea and extreme discomfort that it causes while it lasts. It is not only the crossing of the Pariacaca range that has this effect but that of the whole mountain range that extends for more than five hundred leagues, and wherever one crosses it one feels this strange sensation of discomfort, though in some places more than in others and much more in those who climb from the seacoast up to the mountains than in those who go down from the mountains to the plain. In addition to Pariacaca, I also suffered from it in the Lucanas and Soras, and elsewhere in the Collaguas ranges, and yet again in the Cauanas, and indeed in four different places in different comings and goings. And at that height I always felt the disturbance and nausea I have described, though never as acutely as that first time in Pariacaca. Others who have endured it have had the same experience.

There is no doubt that the cause of this strange discomfort and disturbance is the wind or air that prevails there, for the only remedy (and it is very helpful) is to cover ears and nose and mouth as much as possible, and to cover oneself well with clothing, especially the stomach. For the air is so keen and penetrating that it goes straight to the entrails, and not only do men feel that affliction but also their mounts, which sometimes stop short, and no spur suffices to move them. I believe that that place is one of the highest in the world, for the distance that one climbs is immense, and it is my opinion that in comparison the snow-covered mountain passes in Spain and the Pyrenees and the Alps in Italy are like ordinary houses compared to lofty towers. Thus I am convinced that the element of air is so thin and delicate there that it does not lend itself to human respiration, which needs heavier and warmer air. This, I believe, is the reason why the stomach becomes so upset and the person's whole body is indisposed. The snowy passes or mountain ranges that I have seen in Europe certainly have cold air, which causes discomfort and makes it necessary to dress very warmly; however, that cold does not take away the appetite but increases it, nor does it cause vomiting or retching in the stomach, only pain in feet and hands; finally, its operation is external. But the illness of the Indies of which I speak, without causing pain in feet or hands or any external part, stirs up the inner organs, and, what is even more remarkable, it happens even when there is pleasant sunshine and warmth in the same spot. Hence I am persuaded that the harm is due to the quality of air that a person breathes, because it is very keen and sharp, and its cold is not so much perceptible by the senses as it is penetrating.

That mountain chain is largely uninhabited, with no towns or human dwellings, and even for those who pass through it there are almost no inns or huts in which to take shelter at night. Nor are animals, either good or bad, found there, except for vicuñas, whose properties are very strange, as will be told in its proper place. Often the grass is withered and very dark owing to the air of which I speak. This uninhabited area is twenty to thirty leagues across, and its length, as I have said, is more than five hundred leagues. There are other uninhabited regions, deserts, or high plains, which in Peru they call *punas* (to speak of the second point I promised), where the properties of the air cut off bodies and human lives without being felt.

In former times the Spaniards of Peru went to the realm of Chile over the mountains; now people usually go by sea and sometimes by the coast, which, although it is a difficult and very troublesome way, does not spell danger as the road over the mountain does, in which there are high plains where many men have perished and others have escaped by great good fortune, although some of them lost a limb or were lamed. A little wind blows there that is not at all strong, which penetrates in such a way that men fall dead almost without realizing it or fingers and toes fall off their hands and feet, which is something that seems like fiction but is not; rather, it is true history. I met and had a good deal to do with Gen. Gerónimo Costilla, one of the earliest settlers in Cuzco, who was missing three or four toes from his feet; they fell off when he was passing through that uninhabited region on the way to Chile because they had been penetrated by that little wind.[3] When it occurred to him to look at them they were dead and fell off as a withered apple falls from

3. General Gerónimo Costilla arrived to Peru in 1535, where he was appointed to the expedition to Chile led by Diego de Almagro. On his return, Costilla fought in the battle for Cuzco. Costilla may have been an important source about Chile for Acosta, who never visited the region, but, as noted above, did not hesitate to comment on both its natural history and its people and even praised its similarities to Spain.

the tree, giving neither pain nor discomfort. This officer used to say that a large part of an army that had crossed some years before, after that realm had been discovered by Almagro, had died there and that he had seen the bodies lying there, with no bad odor or decay. And he even added another strange thing: that they found a boy alive and asked him how he had survived. He said that he had hidden in some hut or other, from which he emerged only to cut some flesh from a dead horse with a knife, and that he had fed himself like this for a long time. Any number of his companions had survived in that way, but all had eventually perished, with one dying on one day and another on another. He wished for nothing but to die there like the others, for he did not feel able to go anywhere or enjoy anything. I heard the same tale from others, among them one who was a member of our society who had passed through there when he was still a layman. That cold wind's capacity to kill and at the same time to preserve dead bodies without decay is remarkable. I was told the same thing by a worthy religious, a Dominican and a prelate in his order, who had seen it while passing through those uninhabited regions; and he even told me that, in the necessity of spending the night there and of protecting himself from the wind, which as I have said blows in that fatal place, and finding nothing else at hand, he gathered a number of the dead bodies that were lying about and made a sort of wall of them, like the head of a bed, and slept in that way with the dead giving him life. No doubt it is a kind of cold so penetrating that it smothers vital heat and cuts off its influence; and because it is exceedingly dry it does not corrupt or rot dead bodies, for corruption arises from heat and moistness.

As for another kind of wind, which can be heard under the ground and causes tremors and earthquakes more often in the Indies than elsewhere, I shall speak of it when dealing with the properties of the earth in the Indies. For the moment we will content ourselves with what I have said of the winds and air and will go on to what needs to be said about water.

## CHAPTER 10 * OF THE OCEAN THAT SURROUNDS THE INDIES AND OF THE NORTHERN AND SOUTHERN SEAS

Among waters, primacy is held by the great Ocean Sea, by means of which the Indies were discovered; and all its lands are surrounded by it, for they are either islands in the Ocean Sea or a mainland, which also, no matter where it comes to an end, is bounded by this same ocean. Until now there has been no discovery in the New World of a Mediterranean sea such as Europe, Asia, and Africa possess, where arms of that great ocean enter and form different seas, taking the names of the provinces and lands that its waters bathe; and almost all these Mediterranean seas are contiguous among themselves and to the ocean itself at the Strait of Gibraltar, which the ancients called the Pillars of Hercules. However, the Red Sea, which is separated from those other Mediterranean seas, enters the Indian Ocean, and the Caspian Sea is connected with no other. But in the Indies, as I say, there is no other sea but the ocean, and this is divided into two, one that they call the Northern Sea, the other the Southern Sea; for the land of the West Indies, which was first discovered through the ocean that touches Spain, lies all to the north, and it was from that land that a sea was discovered on the other side of it. They called this one the Southern Sea because they sailed down it until they reached the equator, and having lost the North Star, or Arctic Pole, they discovered the Antarctic Pole, which is called the South Pole; and hence all of that ocean on the other side of the West Indies is called southern, even though a very large part of it lies to the north, such as the entire coast of New Spain and Nicaragua and Guatemala and Panama. They say that the first discoverer of this Southern Sea was a certain Vasco Núñez de Balboa; it was discovered through the part that we now call Tierra Firme, where the land is so narrow, and the two oceans so close to each other, that they are no more than 7 leagues apart. For, although the journey from Nombre de Dios to Panama is 18 leagues, it is made so by going roundabout and trying to find the most comfortable path; but in a straight line the distance from one sea to another is no more than I have said.

Some have discussed breaking through this distance of 7 leagues and joining one sea with the other to make the passage to Peru easier, because the 18 leagues of land that lie between Nombre de Dios and Panama give rise to more expense and difficulty than the 2,300 leagues of ocean.[1] Someone is sure to reply to this argument that it would mean flooding the land, for they say

---

1. Vasco Núñez de Balboa crossed the Isthmus of Panama from the Atlantic to the Pacific in 1513, thus becoming the first of the Spanish explorers to see the Pacific. In subsequent years, Nombre de Dios became the main port town on the isthmus, the narrowest portion of what Acosta termed Tierra Firme, or Central America. Despite the short distance, the terrain was inhospitable to Spanish settlement and travel. The Spanish maintained an unremarkable presence on both the northern and southern coasts of the isthmus. Nombre de Dios was abandoned in 1598 for the town of Portobelo, which offered a better harbor to protect the inhabitants. The singular role of these port cities was to host the annual trade fairs, which acted as the main point of commerce between Peru, Mexico, and Spain in the sixteenth century.

that one sea is lower than the other, as we find in the histories that in ancient times the project of joining the Red Sea to the Nile was abandoned for the same reason at the time of King Seostris and later during the Ottoman Empire.[2] But I think that such a plan is useless, even though the obstacles they describe did not exist, which I do not know for certain; I believe that no human power is capable of tearing down the strong and impenetrable mountain that God placed between the two seas, with hills and rocky crags able to withstand the fury of the seas on either side. And even if it were possible for men to do it I believe it would be very reasonable to expect punishment from Heaven for wishing to improve the works that the Maker, with sublime prudence and forethought, ordered in the fabric of this world.

This plan of opening the earth and joining the seas having been abandoned, there was another project less rash but equally difficult and dangerous: to explore whether these two great gulfs were joined in some part of the world; and this was the undertaking of Ferdinand Magellan, a Portuguese gentleman whose courage and persistence in searching for this secret, and his no less happy feat in uncovering it, gave his name in eternal memory to the strait that is called, and rightly for its discoverer, the Strait of Magellan.[3] As it is one of the great wonders of the world, we will describe it briefly. Some believed that the strait that Magellan found in the Southern Sea either did not exist or had already been closed, as Don Alonso de Ercilla says in his *Araucana*.[4] Even today there are some who say that there is no such strait but merely islands in the sea, for the continent ends there and the rest is all islands, and at the end of them one ocean joins with the other very fully; or, to express it better, all become a single sea. But it is certainly true that there is a strait, and a great deal of land on both sides, although we do not know how

2. Herodotus, *History of the Persian War,* II, 158; Paolo Jovio, *Historia* (o'g).

3. The navigator Ferdinand Magellan, angry with rulers in his native Portugal, approached King Philip II with a plan to prove that the Moluccas (Spice Islands) lay within Spain's portion of the New World, as outlined in the 1494 Treaty of Tordesillas. In 1520, Magellan sailed from the Madeiras to Brazil, and then south, where he explored the Río de la Plata region. Not finding a passageway there, he continued south and entered the strait between the mainland of South America and Tierra del Fuego. The expedition successfully navigated the tricky passage and emerged in the Pacific. After reaching Guam, the group went to the Philippines, where Magellan died in a local territorial struggle in 1521.

4. Don Alonso de Ercilla (1533–94) wrote his famous epic poem *Araucana,* which portrays the battles between the Spaniards and the native Araucanians, while he was a soldier in Pedro de Valdivia's campaign in Chile from 1557 to 1558. The poem heroicizes the valiant stance of the Araucanians toward continual Spanish incursions and became a nation-building literary text for Chile in the nineteenth and twentieth centuries.

far the land extends on the southern part of the strait. After Magellan, a ship of the bishop of Plasencia, Don Gutierre Carbajal, passed through the strait; they say its mast is in Lima, at the entrance of the palace. An expedition was sent to discover the southern side under orders from Don García de Mendoza, who at the time was governor of Chile, and so it was found and traversed by Captain Ladrillero, whose account I have read, although he says that he did not dare to emerge from the strait; having recognized the Northern Sea, he turned back owing to the inclement weather, for winter was well under way and, as he says, furious waves were coming from the north and the sea was all foamy from the heavy swells.[5] In our day Francis Drake, the English pirate, has traversed the strait. After that it was crossed by Captain Sarmiento on its southern side, and finally, during this past year of fifteen hundred and eighty-seven it has been crossed by other English pirates, instructed by Drake, who at present are sailing off the coast of Peru. Because I feel that the account I heard from the chief pilot is worth the telling, I will include it here.

### CHAPTER II * OF THE STRAIT OF MAGELLAN AND HOW IT WAS CROSSED ON ITS SOUTHERN SIDE

In the year fifteen hundred and seventy-nine, after Francis Drake had crossed the Strait of Magellan, sailed along the coast of Chile and all of Peru, and captured the ship San Juan de Antona, which carried a large number of silver bars, the viceroy Don Francisco de Toledo armed and dispatched two good vessels to explore the strait; Pedro Sarmiento, a man well versed in astronomy, went as captain.[1] They left Callao, the port of Lima, early in October,

5. Although Juan Ladrillero did not pass through the strait from the Pacific to the Atlantic in 1557, his expedition did record the first Spanish sighting of the island of Chiloe and the Chonos Archipelago.

1. The infamous pirate of the seas, Sir Francis Drake, vocally opposed Catholicism and the Spanish Crown and actively attacked Spanish territory along the many coastlines of the Americas. Drake's initial threats against Spain in the Americas occurred at the Isthmus of Panama, where he tried to capture the weak port settlement at Nombre de Dios. In 1577, Drake was chosen by England to lead an expedition around South America through the Strait of Magellan. His personal goal was to make treaties with people living south of the Spanish territory outlined in the Treaty of Tordesillas. After the expedition passed through the strait in 1579, Drake turned his expedition north and looted his way up the Chilean coast. Drake's attacks on the Spanish colonies, in conjunction with competition from other European powers, paralleled the paradigm

and because that coast has an unfavorable wind constantly blowing from the south they put out to sea for a long distance and after a very successful voyage reached the vicinity of the strait in little more than a month. But because it is difficult to recognize, in order to do so they approached land and found a very large bay where there is an archipelago of islands. Sarmiento insisted that the strait was there and spent more than a month looking for it in different coves and bays and climbing high hills on land. In view of the fact that they did not find it, he put to sea again at the request of others in the fleet and sailed along the coast. That same day a very great storm came up; they ran before it and in the early evening spied the lantern of the flagship, which then disappeared, and the other ship never saw it again. Next day, with the wind (which was a side wind) continuing, they saw a cove formed by the land, and thought it advisable to enter it and take shelter until the storm was over. It happened that once they had discovered the cove they observed that it extended farther and farther into the land; suspecting that it was the strait they were seeking, they took the sun and found that they were at fifty-one degrees and a half, which is the very latitude of the strait. To assure themselves further they launched the brigantine, and after it had sailed up that arm of the sea for many leagues without finding an end to it, they at last became convinced that the strait was there. Because they had orders to cross it, they set up a tall cross with a message at its foot, so that if the other ship reached there it would have news of their ship and follow it. They then traversed the strait in good weather and without difficulty and after they had come out into

---

shift from the period of conquest to the period of colonization. Spanish concerns about military defense switched from defending themselves from the inside against unknown native enemies to protecting their possessions from outside European threats.

Following Drake's attack on Chile, Viceroy Toledo was determined to halt Drake and chose Pedro Sarmiento de Gamboa (1530–1608) to captain the expedition. Toledo trusted Sarmiento, who had served the viceroy in his tour of Peru and authored the famous *Historia Indica* (1572) at his behest. Toledo hoped that Sarmiento would traverse the strait from the Pacific to the Atlantic and determine a suitable location for a settlement. The Spanish determined that a strong fort in the Patagonia region would be vital for Chile's growth as a colony. Sarmiento accomplished the first of the objectives, which he described in his *Derrotero al Estrecho de Magallanes* (1580). The attempt to establish a colony failed, and Spain chose the more hospitable island of Chiloe farther north as a site for settlement. Acosta would have known Sarmiento from his participation in the Toledan *visita*. Indeed, in chapter 13 of this book Acosta acknowledges that Sarmiento's account of the voyage, the first detailed description of the Strait of Magellan, was one of his sources. It is available in English as *Narratives of the Voyages of Pedro de Gamboa to the Straits of Magellan*, translated with notes and introduction by Clements R. Markham (London: Hakluyt Society, 1895).

the Northern Sea reached a certain island, where they took on water and repaired the ship. From there they set a course to the Cape Verde Islands, whence the chief pilot returned to Peru by way of Cartagena and Panama. He brought the viceroy an account of the strait and everything that had happened and was well rewarded for the good service he had rendered. But Capt. Pedro Sarmiento sailed from Cape Verde to Seville in the same ship that had traversed the strait and went to the court, where His Majesty granted him many boons and at his suggestion had a large fleet prepared, which he sent with Diego Flores de Valdés to settle and fortify the strait, although for a number of reasons the fleet cost a great deal of money and accomplished little.

Now, to return to the vice admiral's ship, which was sailing with the flagship: having become separated from the other in that storm I mentioned, she tried to put out to sea as far as possible, but as the wind was broadside to her and very strong she was certain to perish, and everyone confessed and prepared to die. The storm continued without ceasing for three days, during which they thought they would run aground at any moment; but the opposite happened, for they found that they were driven ever farther from land until at the end of the third day, when the storm had abated, they took the sun and found themselves at fifty-six degrees. And, seeing that they had not been cast on the shore but indeed were farther from land than ever, they were astonished. Hence they came to the conclusion (as Fernando Lamero, pilot of that vessel, told me) that the land on the other side of the strait, as one entered it from the Southern Sea, did not go on in the same direction as it did before reaching the strait but turned back toward the east, for otherwise it was impossible not to have been stranded on it owing to the crosswind that had lasted so long. They went no further, nor did they discover whether the land ended there (for some insist that after the strait is passed there is an island, and that the two oceans, North and South, meet there) or whether it turned toward the east until it joined the land of Vista, as it is called, which corresponds to the Cape of Good Hope, as others believe. Even today the truth of this has not been established, nor has anyone been found who has sailed around that land. The viceroy, Don Martín Enríquez, told me of his belief that the rumor that the strait formed an island, and that the two oceans joined there, was an invention of the English pirate. For when he was viceroy of New Spain he had carefully interrogated the Portuguese pilot whom

Francis Drake left there and never understood anything of the sort from him, rather that it was a real strait with a continent on either side. And so the vice admiral's ship I mentioned turned around and explored the strait, as the aforesaid Fernando Lamero told me, but through another mouth or entrance higher up, because of a certain large island that is at the mouth of the strait, which they call La Campana, the Bell, because of its shape. According to him he wanted to go beyond it, but the vice admiral and the soldiers would not let him, for they thought that they had spent a great deal of time on this already and were in great danger, and so they returned to Chile and Peru without having passed through the strait.

### CHAPTER 12 * OF THE STRAIT THAT SOME SAY EXISTS IN FLORIDA

Just as Magellan found the strait that is in the south, so others have tried to discover another strait that they say exists in the north, which they fancy to be in the land of Florida, which extends so far that its end is unknown. The *adelantado* Pedro Meléndez, a very experienced man and a fine seaman, stated that there was certainly a strait there, and that the king had sent him to discover it, a task for which he showed great enthusiasm. He had arguments to prove his opinion, because he said that pieces of the kind of ships used by the Chinese had been seen in the Northern Sea, which would not be possible if there were no passage from one sea to the other. He also said that in a certain large bay in Florida, which penetrates three hundred leagues into the land, whales were seen at certain times and that these came from the other sea.[1] He also described other indications, at last concluding that it was within the wisdom of the Maker and the good order of Nature that, since there was communication and a passage between the two seas at the Antarctic Pole, these should also exist at the Arctic Pole, which is the more important one. Some say that the great pirate Drake had some indication of it and that he indicated this when he passed the coast of New Spain on the Southern Sea. It is even believed that the English pirates, who during this last year of fifteen hundred and eighty-seven robbed a ship coming from the Philippines with a large quantity of gold and other treasures, came by way of it. They made this

---

1. The whales Meléndez claimed to have seen in Florida were probably the manatees, or sea cows, that live in the intercoastal waterways of the Florida peninsula.

capture near the Californias, where the ships returning to New Spain from the Philippines and China always make landfall. Men's daring and their desire to find new ways of making themselves famous is so great that I am sure this secret will also become known before many years have passed. Surely it is an astonishing thing how men, like ants, never cease to follow the trail and rumor of new things, until they attain the sweet rewards of greed and human glory. And the Creator's lofty and eternal wisdom employs this natural curiosity of man to communicate the light of his Holy Gospel to folk who still live in the dark shadows of their errors.[2] However, so far the strait of the Arctic Pole, if it exists, has not been discovered, and thus it would be well to state the properties and reports of the Antarctic, which has been discovered and known, as told to us by the same men who saw them with their own eyes.

### CHAPTER 13 * OF THE PROPERTIES OF THE STRAIT OF MAGELLAN

The strait, as I have said, is located at barely fifty-two degrees south; its length from one sea to the other is ninety or a hundred leagues; at its narrowest point it is about a league wide, perhaps less, and here it was hoped that the king would place a fort to defend the passage. It is so deep in places that it cannot be sounded; in other places the bottom is found, in some it is no more than eighteen fathoms, and in still others no more than fifteen. Of the hundred leagues of its length from sea to sea, it is clear that the Southern Sea enters for thirty of them and indicates this by its waves; the Northern Sea with its waves indicates the other seventy leagues. Yet there is this difference, that the thirty leagues of the Southern Sea run between very high cliffs whose summits are perpetually covered with snow and are so tall that they appear to join together; this is why it is so difficult to recognize the entrance to the strait from the Southern Sea. These same thirty leagues are of immense depth, and ships cannot drop anchor there, but they can be beached in places where the shoreline can be sounded. Bottom can be found in the other seventy leagues, which lead to the Northern Sea, and on both sides are large fields and savannas, as they are called there. Many and large rivers with very

2. Although Acosta finds the ultimate motivation and enlightenment for discovery in God, it is clear that the striving to locate a geographical parallel to the Strait of Magellan was, by 1590, driven by the desire of Spain to best European rivals in the contest of exploration.

fine water enter the strait. There are wonderful stands of trees and some trees with excellent and sweet-smelling wood, unknown in Europe, samples of which have been brought by those coming from Peru. Inland there are great prairies and a number of islands in the middle of the strait. The Indians who live on the southern side are few in number, small of stature, and very wretched; those on the northern side are tall and valiant, and some have been captured and brought to Spain.[1] Pieces of blue cloth and other reliable signs that people from Europe have passed through there have been found. The Indians greeted our people with the name of Jesus. They use bows and arrows and dress in the skins of deer, which are abundant there. The waters of the strait rise and fall with the tides, and it is possible to see the tides come in from the Northern and Southern Seas; and in the place where they meet, which as I have said is thirty leagues from the Southern Sea and seventy from the Northern, it seems that there would be more danger than in all the rest of the strait. But when Sarmiento's flagship passed, as I have said, they did not encounter a great storm, but indeed found much less difficulty than they had anticipated because, in addition to the fact that the weather was favorable at the time, the waves of the Northern Sea were very broken when they reached them because of the long space of seventy leagues from whence they came, nor did the waves of the Southern Sea show great fury owing to its great depth, for they were swallowed up in it. It is indeed true that in winter the strait cannot be navigated owing to the force of the winds and the swelling of the sea that exists there, and that is why some vessels that have tried to cross the strait have been lost. Only one has crossed from the Southern Sea, which is the flagship that I mentioned, from whose chief pilot, named Fernando Alonso, I had a very long account of everything that I have written. And I have seen the true description of the coast of the strait, which they made as they were sailing through it, a copy of which they took to the king in Spain and to his viceroy in Peru.

1. The native peoples on the north side, or mainland, of the strait were the Tehuelche. Those on the south side, or on the island of Tierra del Fuego, were the Ona. Although both groups of people were hunters, gatherers, and fishers, the Tehuelche adopted the horse from the Spanish and adapted their hunting style to the use of horses and lances. The Ona continued to focus on small game and fish for their subsistence. Further descriptions of the Tehuelche and Ona, along with other groups in the southern peninsula, can be found in Jorge Hidalgo, "The Indians of Southern South America in the Middle of the Sixteenth Century," in *Cambridge History of Latin America*, vol. 1 (New York: Cambridge University Press, 1984).

## CHAPTER 14 * OF THE EBB AND FLOW OF THE
## OCEAN SEA IN THE INDIES

One of Nature's remarkable secrets is the ebb and flow of the sea, not only because of its strange property of rising and falling but still more because of the variety that is found in this respect in different seas and even on different coasts of the same sea. There are seas that do not have a daily ebb and flow, like the lower Mediterranean, which is the Tyrrhenian; but the upper Mediterranean, which is the sea of Venice, does have a daily ebb and flow. This is a matter that rightly causes astonishment, for, although both are Mediterranean and the sea of Venice is no larger, it ebbs and flows like the ocean yet this Italian sea does not. But some Mediterranean seas manifestly have a rise and fall each month; others do so neither daily nor monthly. Other seas, like the ocean that surrounds Spain, have a daily ebb and flow and in addition to this have two monthly ones, namely, at the new and the full moon, which are called spring tides. I do not know of any sea that rises and falls daily and not monthly. In the Indies the variation in this regard is amazing: there are places where the sea rises and falls two leagues every day and even more during the spring tides, as can be seen in Panama. There are other places where the amount of rise and fall is so small that the difference can scarcely be noticed. The most usual thing is that the Ocean Sea rises and falls daily and monthly; the daily tide occurs twice in the natural day and always three-quarters of an hour less from one day to another, according to the movement of the moon. And so the tide on one day is never at the same time as on another.

Some believe that this ebb and flow is the local movement of the sea's water, so that the water that rises in one place falls at another and thus is ebbing on the opposite side of the sea when it is rising here, just as we know that water makes waves in a cauldron, for when one side of it rises the other falls; others say that the sea rises everywhere at the same time and also ebbs everywhere at the same time, so that it is like the boiling of a pot, in which all its contents rise at the same time and when it cools they also subside everywhere. This second idea is the true one, and in my opinion can be held to be certain and proven, not so much for the reasons given by the philosophers, who base their opinion on their studies of the subject, as by reliable experience that has been achieved on the matter. For, to satisfy myself on this point and question, I asked the above-mentioned pilot with special curiosity what the tides that they found in the strait were like and if by any chance the tides of the Southern Sea ebbed and fell at the same time that those of the Northern Sea rose and swelled and vice versa. For, if this were true, it would be obvious that the sea rising on one side meant that it fell on the other, which is what the first opinion states. He replied that it was not like that; rather, the tides of the Southern and Northern Seas very clearly rose at the same time until the waves of one met those of the other, that each ebbed again into its sea, and that this swelling and rising, and then ebbing and falling, was something they observed every day. The point of contact and meeting of the rising tide from both seas was (as I have said) seventy leagues from the Northern Sea and thirty from the Southern, from which it is perfectly obvious that the ebb and flow of the ocean is not a purely local movement but an alteration and agitation by means of which all its waters rise and swell at the same time, and at other times fall and ebb, as the comparison of the boiling kettle has shown. It would not be possible to understand this matter through experience except in the strait, where all the waters of the Ocean Sea come together, because to be on opposite shores in order to find out whether the tide rises on one as it falls on the other would only be possible to the angels. Men do not have eyes to see so far, nor feet to carry our eyes in the short time that a tide allows, which is only six hours.

CHAPTER 15 * OF THE DIFFERENT FISH AND
METHODS OF FISHING OF THE INDIANS

There is such an innumerable multitude of fish in the ocean that only the Maker can declare their species and properties. Many of them are of the same kind as those found in European seas, such as skate, shad that swim up the rivers from the sea, giltheads, sardines, and numerous others.[1] There are other fish about which I am uncertain as to whether they exist here, such as those called *cabrillas,* which somewhat resemble trout, and those that in New Spain are called *bobos,* which swim up rivers from the sea. I have seen neither bream nor trout; it is said that they exist in the land of Chile. There are some

1. Acosta acknowledges that many of the fish in the Indies are also found in Europe. But, in keeping with his agenda of describing the natural things "not commonly known," he details strange animals, notably the manatee. This strategy magnifies the exotic image of the Americas for the imagination of a European audience.

tunas off the coast of Peru, although they are rare, and it is believed that at times they go up the Strait of Magellan to spawn, as they do in Spain in the Strait of Gibraltar. That is why they are found more often on the coast of Chile, although the tuna that I have seen brought from there do not resemble the tuna of Spain. In the islands known as the Windwards, which are Cuba, Hispaniola, Puerto Rico, and Jamaica, the creatures called manatees are found. This is a strange kind of fish, if we can call a fish an animal that gives birth to its young alive, has teats and milk to feed them, and grazes on grass on land but in fact lives most of the time in the water, and therefore they eat it as fish, although when I was in Santo Domingo I ate some on a Friday and almost felt scruples, not so much because of the description I have given but because the chops taken from the shoulder portion of this animal were very like slices of veal in color and taste.[2] The manatee is the size of a cow.

I had good reason to marvel at sharks and their incredible voracity when I saw one that had been captured in the port I mentioned; they took out of its maw a large butcher's knife, a big iron hook, and a large portion of a cow's head with one horn intact — and I am not sure that there were not two horns. I once saw, as a pastime, a quarter of a horse hung high over a deep inlet formed by the sea and how a group of sharks were immediately attracted by the smell; to make the entertainment merrier, the horsemeat did not touch the water but hung a good many handbreadths above it. All around were these creatures I am describing, which leaped into the air and in one leap cut through flesh and bone with extraordinary speed. They lopped off the horse's leg as if it had been a stalk of lettuce, so sharp are the knives that they carry in their teeth. Little fish called *romeros,* pilgrims, or pilot fish, swim clinging to these savage sharks, and no matter how hard the sharks try they cannot dislodge them; these fish feed on what escapes from the sides of the sharks' mouths. Other fish found in tropical seas are the flying fish, and I do not know whether they exist elsewhere. Giltheads pursue these fish, and to escape them they leap out of the sea and fly through the air for a good distance;

---

2. Acosta confesses to his readers that eating the veal-like manatee on a day when meat was prohibited to Catholics made him feel guilty. Although Acosta does not share the zeal of missionary authors who obsess over excesses of pleasure in New World cultures, his example of the manatee suggests an implicit view of the New World as filled with outlandish beings (animal or human) that can entice even a priest to sin. What is even more telling is that Acosta need not confess, despite the sensation that he has indulged in meat on a Friday, because his actions are sanctioned by local custom.

that is why they are called flying fish, for they have fins made of something resembling cloth or parchment that sustain them in the air for a time. One of them flew or leaped into the ship in which I was sailing, and I saw the form of its fins as I have described them.

As for lizards, or alligators as they are called, much has been written about them in histories of the Indies; really, they are the animals that Pliny and the ancients called crocodiles. They are found on warm water beaches and rivers; they are not found on beaches and rivers with cold water. That is why there are none of them on the coast of Peru as far north as Paita, and from there on they occur very frequently in rivers. It is a very ferocious animal, though extremely slow; it seizes its prey outside the water and drowns its catch alive, although it only swallows its prey outside the water because its throat is such that the creature could easily drown if water came into it. A fight between an alligator and a tiger—and there are many fierce animals of this kind in the Indies—is astonishing to see. A member of our society told me that he had seen these beasts fight very savagely on the seashore. The alligator delivered heavy blows to the tiger with its tail and tried with all its great strength to draw it into the water; the tiger seized the alligator firmly in its claws and dragged it to land. At last the tiger won and tore open the lizard's body, I suppose by the belly, which is soft, for the rest of the creature's body is impenetrable by a lance or even a harquebus. More astonishing was the victory that an Indian had over an alligator, for it snatched a child from him and carried it underwater, whereupon the Indian, grieving and furious, jumped in after it with a knife and, as Indians are excellent divers and the alligator captures only outside the water, he succeeded in wounding it underneath the belly so that it crawled out on the bank, wounded, and loosed the child, although he had drowned and was dead.

Still more remarkable is the battle that the Indians have with whales, which is certainly a wonderful thing on the part of the Maker of all, to give people as weak as the Indians the skill and daring to attack the fiercest and most monstrous beast in the whole world and not only to battle him but to conquer and triumph so gallantly. On seeing this, I have often thought of what the Psalm says of the whale: "Draco iste, quem formaste ad illudendum eum," this sea dragon, which thou hast formed to play therein.[3] What better jest

3. Psalms, 103, 26 (O'G). It is notable that Acosta chose to include, among his classification of natural things, several examples of Amerindians battling animals. His tales of "weak Indians" successfully conquering the

than for an Indian, with only a rope, to bring in a whale as large as a hill, conquered and tied? The way the Indians of Florida, where there are many whales, do this (as persons expert in the matter told me) is to board a dugout canoe or small boat and paddle out to reach the side of the whale and then to leap lightly and climb on the back of its neck; mounted there, awaiting the proper moment, the Indian introduces a sharp, strong stick that he has brought with him into the opening of the whale's nostril. (I call nostril the hole through which whales breathe.) Then he strikes it hard with another stick and drives it in very deeply. The whale roars and slaps the sea and raises tremendous waves and furiously submerges and leaps out again, not knowing what to do in his rage. The Indian stays quiet and continues to ride the whale and improves upon the harm he has already done by introducing another stick into the other nostril and hammering it in until the whale cannot get its breath. With this he returns to his canoe, which he has tied to the whale's side with a rope, but first he leaves his rope well fastened to the whale. Standing to one side in his canoe he plays the whale with his rope, which while it is in deep water thrashes from one side to the other as if mad with fury and at last begins to approach land, where it soon becomes beached because of the enormous size of its body and cannot move either forward or backward. Now a great crowd of Indians rushes to the trapped animal to gather its spoils. Indeed, they finish it off and divide it into pieces. By drying and grinding its less than desirable flesh they make certain powders that they use in their food, and it lasts them a long time. Here, too, is the proof of what another Psalm says of the whale: "Dedisti eum escam populis Aethiopum," thou hast given him to be meat for the people of the Ethiopians.[4] The *adelantado* Pedro Meléndez often described this kind of fishing, which Monardes also mentions in his book.[5]

Although it is on a smaller scale, another method of fishing that the Indians often use in the sea is worthy of mention. They carefully tie together bundles of reeds or dry grasses, which are called *balsas* there, and carry them on their

---

powerful alligators and whales serve to highlight the exotic nature of the practices and strengths of native peoples. Note also his reference in this chapter to the Chiriguana who "seemed more like fish than like men."

4. Psalms, 73, 14 (O'G).

5. Doctor Nicolás Monardes (1493–1588) wrote his most widely read book, *Medicinal History of the Indies*, in 1565, prior to Francisco Hernández's Crown-sponsored fieldwork in New Spain. As its title suggests, it focuses on the medicinal use of New World plants, with additional information on the curative properties of iron, bezoar stones, and snow.

backs to the sea, where they quickly throw them in, climb onto them, and perched on them go out to sea. Paddling with small oars on either side, they go one or two leagues out to sea in order to fish. On these bundles they carry their nets and ropes, and riding on their rafts cast their nets and spend a large part of the night or day fishing until they are loaded to capacity, after which they return very happy. Certainly I very much enjoyed watching the Indians go out to fish in Callao, near Lima, for there were many of them there, each perched on his raft or sitting confidently breasting the waves of the sea, which is very rough in the place where they fish. They resembled Tritons or Neptunes, who are represented upon the water. When they reach land they load their boat on their shoulders and then pull it apart and spread out the reeds on the beach to be wiped off and dried. Other Indians, in the valleys of Ica, used to go out fishing on inflated hides or sealskins and from time to time would blow them up like balls to keep them from sinking. In the valley of Cañete, which formerly was called El Guarco, there were a very large number of Indian fishermen, and because they resisted the Inca he pretended to make peace with them when he was in process of conquering that land. To pay him honor they organized a solemn fishing expedition of many thousands of Indians, who entered the sea on their rafts. On their return the Inca had soldiers waiting in ambush and perpetrated a cruel massacre of them, as a result of which the country, which had been very prosperous, was left almost uninhabited.

I saw another kind of fishing, which the viceroy Don Francisco de Toledo took me to see, although in truth it was not in the sea but on a river that they call Río Grande in the province of Los Charcas. There some Chiriguana Indians dived under the water and, swimming with remarkable speed, followed the fish with hooks or harpoons that they held in their right hands, swimming only with their left. They speared the fish and brought them to the surface pierced through; they surely seemed more like fish than land-dwelling men. Now that we have emerged from the sea, let us proceed to other kinds of waters, which are yet to be described.

### CHAPTER 16 ∗ OF THE POOLS AND LAKES THAT ARE FOUND IN THE INDIES

In place of the Mediterranean Sea, which the regions of the Old World enjoy, the Creator has provided many lakes in the New, some of them so large that they can properly be called seas, for Scripture gives this name to the lake of Palestine, and it is no larger than some of these, or even as large. The principal lake is that of Titicaca in Peru, in the province of Collao, which was described in the preceding book as having a circumference of almost eighty leagues, and eight or ten important rivers empty into it. At one time the Indians began to sail on it in boats or ships and did so with such lack of skill that the first ship that entered it split open in a storm that occurred on the lake. The water is not entirely bitter and salty, like that of the sea, but it is so coarse that it is not fit to drink. Two kinds of fish breed there in abundance; one is called the *suche*, which is large and has a good taste but is ropy and unwholesome; the other is called the *boga*, which is more wholesome but small and very bony. There are innumerable kinds of ducks everywhere in the lake. When the Indians wish to do honor to some important person who passes through Chucuito or Omasuyo, which are the two sides of the lake, they assemble a large number of rafts and pursue and enclose the ducks by circling around them until they can catch by hand as many as they like; they call this kind of hunting *chaco*. The best Indian towns in Peru are on opposite shores of this lake.[1] From its outlet is formed another smaller lake called Paria, though still quite a large one, where there is also a great deal of livestock, chiefly swine, which flourish greatly there because of the reeds that grow in the lake, on which these animals fatten. There are many other lakes in the high places of the mountains, from which flow rivers or streams that later become very important rivers. On the way from Arequipa to Collao there are two high and beautiful lakes, one on each side of the road. From one of them flows a stream that later becomes a river and empties into the Southern Sea, and they say that the famous River Apurímac starts from the other; it is believed that it flows into that great joining of rivers that have their origin in these mountains, the Amazon River, also called the Marañón.

I have wondered many times why there were so many lakes high in those mountains and ranges into which no rivers empty; abundant streams flow from them and yet these lakes scarcely lose water at any time of year. It is not entirely satisfactory to assume that these lakes are formed from melted snow or rain, for many of them do not receive sufficiently large amounts of snow or

---

1. Acosta indulged in self-promotion with his judgment on the "best Indian towns" in Peru. He refers to his own order's settlement at Juli in the royal province of Chucuito on the shores of Lake Titicaca.

rain, yet their level does not diminish; everything points to the fact that it must be spring water that Nature provides there, although it is easy to believe that the springs are aided by snow and rain at some times of the year. These lakes are so common in the highest peaks of the mountains that there is scarcely an important river that does not have its source in one of them. The water of these lakes is clean and clear; they do not provide much fish, and those that are found in them are small ones, owing to the constant cold temperature. However, to mention another marvel, some of these lakes are found to be extremely hot. At the end of the valley of Tarapaya, near Potosí, there is a lake so round that it seems to have been drawn with calipers, and, although the earth where it emerges is very cold, the water is extremely hot. People swim in it near the edge, for if they penetrate farther into the lake they cannot bear the heat. In the middle of this lake is a whirlpool and a bubbling area more than twenty feet long and broad, and this is the true source of the lake, which despite the large size of its source never increases. It would appear that the water evaporates there or has some hidden outlets. But its level is not seen to decrease, which is another marvel, even though a large stream of water was taken out of it to grind ore in certain mills and judging from the amount of water that is taken from it reason dictates that it would have to decrease.[2]

Leaving Peru, and going on to New Spain, the lakes found there are no less remarkable, especially that most famous lake of Mexico, in which there are two different kinds of water: one is brackish and resembles seawater, the other clear and fresh, caused by the rivers that enter the lake. In the midst of the lake there is a rock of very pleasing shape, with baths in which the hot water rises from the lake; these are said to be very good for the health. There are fields built in the middle of the lake whose foundations are the water itself, and after furrows have been made in them they are filled with all kinds of seeds and grasses and any number of flowers, a sight that has to be seen to be believed.[3] The City of Mexico was founded upon this lake, although the

2. The Spanish diverted water from Tarapaya to run numerous silver refineries in the nearby silver capital of Potosí. Despite the extensive use of the water source for the mining industry, the hot springs that Acosta observed at Tarapaya exist to this day.

3. The "fields" that Acosta describes are *chinampas*, sections of earth extended into the lakes and wetlands through a structure of logs and marsh plants to take advantage of irrigation throughout the year. The population of the Valley of Mexico utilized the lake and surrounding wetlands to their maximum benefit. The

Spaniards have gradually filled in all of the city and have left only a few large canals and some smaller ones, which enter and surround it; with these canals they find it very easy to bring in necessary supplies of firewood, grass, stone, timber, agricultural products, and all the rest. Cortés built brigantines at the time he conquered Mexico; later it appeared that it was safer not to use them, and so only canoes are used, of which there are a very large number. The lake has a great deal of fish and game, although I did not see fish of value there; however, they say that the harvest of fish is worth more than three hundred thousand ducats. There are other lakes not far from there from which a good deal of fish is brought to the city. The province of Michoacán is so named because the word means "land abounding in fish"; there are large and beautiful lakes that have a great deal of fish, and that part of the country is healthful and cool. There are many other lakes, and it is not possible to mention all of them or even know the details of them. I will draw attention only to what was noted in the preceding book, that there is a greater abundance of lakes below the Torrid Zone than in any other part of the world. With what I have already said, and a little more about rivers and fountains, I will have finished all I can say on this subject.

### CHAPTER 17 * OF VARIOUS FOUNTAINS AND SPRINGS

As in other parts of the world, there is a great variety of springs and fountains and rivers in the Indies, and some of them have strange properties. In Huancavelica in Peru, where the quicksilver mines are, there is a fountain that spews hot water, and as the water flows it gradually turns to stone. Almost all the houses in that town are built of this stone. It is soft and easy to cut; they cut and shape it with iron tools as easily as if it were wood, and it is light and durable. If men or animals drink of this water they will die, for it congeals in their bellies and turns to stone, and several horses have been killed in this way. As the water gradually turns to stone, the water that flows out blocks the passage of the water behind it, and so it changes course and flows through several different places as the stone accumulates. On the point or cape of Santa Elena there is a spring or fountain of a kind of pitch that in Peru is

---

Spanish, however, were intent on draining the lake and forced the native population to labor on drainage projects throughout the colonial period.

called *copey.* It must be like what Scripture tells us of that valley where there were pits of slime.[1] Sailors take advantage of that fountain or pit of pitch to tar rigging and tackle because it serves them in the same manner as does the resin or tar of Spain. As we sailed to New Spain along the coast of Peru, the pilot showed me the island that they call Lobos, or Isle of Lions, where there is another fountain or pit of that *copey,* or pitch, that I have mentioned, which they use to tar the rigging of ships. And there is another fountain or spring of tar, of which this pilot, a man very skilled in his calling, told me that several times it had happened, while he was sailing in these waters and so far at sea that he could not see land, he had realized where he was by the smell of *copey* as certainly as if he had sighted it, so strong is the odor emitted by that tar pit. In some springs, which they call "baths of the Inca," there is a stream of water that emerges boiling hot and near it another that is cold as snow. The Inca used to temper the one with the other at will, and it is remarkable that there are springs of such different properties so close to one another. There are innumerable others, especially in the province of Los Charcas, in whose water a person cannot endure to hold his hand for the space of an Ave Maria, as I saw demonstrated for a wager. There is a farm in Cuzco where a fountain of salty water springs from the earth, which as it emerges turns to salt, and it is wonderfully white and good. If it were in any other place it would represent no little riches, but this is not the case in Peru owing to the abundance of salt. The waters that flow in Guayaquil, which is in Peru almost under the equator, are considered useful in treating the French disease and other similar ailments, and so folk go there from very distant places to recover their health; they say the reason is that in this region a vast quantity of the root called sarsaparilla grows, whose properties and effect are well known, and the water partakes of that quality of healing. Vilcañota is a peak that, according to general opinion, is in the highest part of Peru. Its summit is covered with snow, and in places it is as black as coal. Two springs emerge on opposite sides of it, which in a short time form large streams and not long afterward rushing rivers; one goes to Collao, to the great lake of Titicaca, and the other to the Andes. It is the river that they call Yucay, which joins with others and emerges in the Northern Sea with an exceedingly swift current. When this spring comes out of the aforesaid Vilcañota it is exactly like lye, of an ashy

1. Genesis, 14, 10 (O'G).

color, and the whole stream smokes and gives off a smell as of something burnt; it runs like this for a long time until the many waters that flow into it put out the flame and smoke that it had in the beginning. In New Spain I saw a spring the color of ink, almost blue, and the source of a river in Peru that was red as blood, which is why it is called the Río Bermejo, Scarlet River.

## CHAPTER 18 * OF RIVERS

Among all rivers, not only in the Indies but in the whole world, pride of place is held by the Marañón or Amazon River, which was dealt with in the previous book. Spaniards have navigated this river a number of times in an attempt to discover lands that according to rumor possess great riches, especially those called El Dorado and Paitití. The *adelantado* Juan de Salinas made a famous exploration of it, though with little result. It has a narrows called El Pongo, which must be one of the most dangerous in the world, for it is squeezed between two extremely high and steep crags and then falls to a terrible depth, where the water makes such whirlpools on impact that it seems impossible not to be sunk and drowned there. Despite all that, daring men attempted the passage of that narrows out of greed for the famed El Dorado. They slid down from the heights and were swept along by the river's fury, and clinging fiercely to the canoes or boats in which they were traveling, although they were overturned in the fall and they and their canoes sank, they came to the surface and at last emerged by means of skill and strength. Indeed, the whole army escaped except for some few who drowned, and the most remarkable thing is that they managed so well that their weapons and the powder they carried with them were not lost. On the way back (for after tremendous efforts and dangers they had to return by the same route) they climbed one of those enormously high crags, pulling themselves up by their daggers, which they drove into the rock. Captain Pedro de Orsúa made another voyage down the same river, and after he had died and his people had mutinied other captains continued along the branch of the river that reaches the Northern Sea. A religious of our society who made that whole journey when he was a layman told us that the tides come up the river almost a hundred leagues and when it eventually mingles with the sea, which is almost below or very near the equator, its mouth is seventy leagues wide, an incredible feature and one that exceeds the width of the Mediterranean Sea, although the descriptions of others assign it only twenty-five or thirty leagues at its mouth. After this river, second place in the world is held by the Río de la Plata, also called the Paraguay, which flows from the mountains of Peru and enters the sea at a latitude of thirty-five degrees south. It rises as they say the Nile does, but incomparably more, and leaves the fields into which it over-flows underwater for three months; then it returns to its bed, and large ships can ascend it for many leagues.

There are other rivers that, though not as large, equal and even surpass the largest rivers of Europe, such as the Magdalena near Santa Marta, the Río Grande and Alvarado in New Spain, and innumerable others. In the south-ern continent, in the mountains of Peru, the rivers are not usually as large, for their course is short and they do not accumulate as much water, but they are swift because they descend from the mountains and have sudden freshets and hence are dangerous and have been the cause of many deaths. In the hot season they rise and cause flooding. I crossed twenty-seven rivers along the coast, and none was fordable.

The Indians use any number of devices to cross rivers. In some places there is a heavy rope stretched from bank to bank and on it a basket or pannier; the person who wants to cross gets into it and is pulled across from the other side, and so he crosses over in his basket. In other places an Indian rides, as if on horseback, on a straw raft and takes behind him the person who is going to cross; he crosses by paddling with a little oar. In other places they have a big net filled with gourds on which they place the persons or clothing that is to cross, and the Indians, tied to it by ropes, swim and pull the gourd raft as horses pull a coach or carriage, and others swim behind pushing it to help it on its way. When they have crossed they pick up their gourd raft and swim back again; they do this on the Santa River in Peru. We crossed the Alvarado, in New Spain, on a plank that the Indians take on their shoulders, and when they are out of their depth they swim. These and a thousand other ways they have of crossing rivers are rather frightening to see, for they seem such slender and fragile methods, but in fact they are very safe. They use no bridges except those made of reeds and straw. Occasionally there are stone bridges over rivers, thanks to the diligence of some government officials, but many fewer than there ought to be in a land where so many men drown for lack of them and which yields so much wealth that superb constructions can be built not only in Spain but in other lands. From the rivers that flow out of the mountains the Indians make many large ditches in the valleys and plains to irrigate the land, which they build with so much order, and so well, that there are no better ones even in Murcia or Milan; this is the greater part, or the sum, of the wealth that exists in the plains of Peru, as also in many other parts of the Indies.

## CHAPTER 19 * OF THE GENERAL NATURE OF THE EARTH IN THE INDIES

The nature of the earth in the Indies (for this is the last of the three elements that we proposed to deal with in this book) can easily be understood from what I have said in the previous book about the Torrid Zone, for the greater part of the Indies lies beneath it; but, for a fuller understanding, I have observed three different kinds of land in the course of my travels in those regions: one is low and the other very high, and one is between those two extremes. The lowlands are on the seacoast and are found everywhere in the Indies, and ordinarily this kind of land is very humid and hot, and so it is the least healthful and least populated at the present time; however, formerly it had large populations of Indians, as is made clear in the histories of New Spain and Peru. Since that region was native to those who were born and raised in it, they survived in it very well. They made their livings by fishing in the sea and from the fields that they made by drawing water from the rivers by means of canals, with which they compensated for the meager rainfall that is the rule on the coast, where in some places it never rains at all. This low-lying land contains large uninhabitable areas, either cruel deserts and hills composed entirely of sand or marshes; for as water flows from the heights it often finds no outlet and spreads and forms swamps and permanently sub-merged lands. Indeed, the greater part of the whole seacoast is like this in the Indies, especially in the region of the Southern Sea.

In our time the population of these coasts or plains is so much diminished and impaired that twenty-nine out of thirty of its inhabitants have disap-peared; and many believe that the remaining Indians will disappear before long.[1] People attribute this to various causes, some to the fact that the Indians have been overworked, others to the changes of food and drink that they adopted after becoming accustomed to Spanish habits, and others to the

---

1. The two main causes of the decline in native population — disease and migration — do not come to mind for Acosta. In general the sixteenth-century debate about depopulation focused on Spanish abuses (the Lascasian theory) or "excessive vices" on the part of the native population, the theory espoused by Acosta.

excessive vice that they display in drink and other abuses. As for me, I believe that this latter disorder is the chief cause of their reduced numbers, but I will not discuss the point just now.

In these low-lying lands to which I refer, which are generally unhealthy and unfit for human habitation, there are exceptions in some places that are moderate in climate and fertile, such as the greater part of the Peruvian plains, where there are cool and fertile valleys. The population of the coast sustains most of the sea trade with Spain, on which the whole status of the Indies depends. There are some fairly large cities on the coast, such as Lima and Trujillo in Peru, Panama and Cartagena on the mainland, Santo Domingo and Puerto Rico and Havana in the islands, and many smaller cities such as Veracruz in New Spain and Yca and Arica and others in Peru. Generally the seaports have some population, though not much.

At the other extreme the second kind of land is very high and in consequence cold and dry, as mountainous regions generally are. This land is neither fertile nor mild, but it is healthful and so it is thickly inhabited. It has ample pasturage and in consequence much livestock, which forms a large part of human sustenance. By trading and trafficking in this commodity the inhabitants compensate for the lack of agricultural land. What causes these lands to be populated, and some of them heavily, is the mining wealth that is found in them, for everything is subordinate to gold and silver. In these lands, thanks to the mines, there are several very large cities inhabited by Spaniards and Indians, such as Potosí and Huancavelica in Peru and Zacatecas in New Spain. There is a large Indian population in all the mountain regions; they maintain their numbers today, and some even say that the Indians are increasing, except that work in the mines kills many of them, and some common diseases (such as the fever called *cocoliste* in New Spain) have caused many deaths; but in fact it does not seem that their numbers are decreasing. This high, cold, and dry region possesses the two advantages that I have mentioned, pasturage and mines, which fully compensate for two others that the flatlands along the coast have, which are the benefit conferred by coastal trade and the fertility of the vines, which are found only in these warmer regions.

Between these two extremes lie the lands at the middle level, which, though in varying degrees, suffer neither from the heat of the coast nor the extreme temperatures of the exclusively mountainous regions. On this kind of land agriculture is very successful, yielding crops of wheat, barley, and maize, which, although they grow well at the lower levels, do not flourish at very high altitudes. They also have an abundance of pasturage and livestock and are rich in fruits and trees and vegetables as well. It is the best place to live for health and comfort, and hence the most thickly populated places in the Indies are of this kind. I have considered this with some attention in the different journeys and excursions I have made and have found it very true that the most heavily populated and best parts of the Indies are of this sort. In New Spain, for example (which is undoubtedly the best country under the sun), no matter where one enters it one soon begins to climb and climb from the coast, and even though one descends again after reaching the highest point it is not much and the land is still a great deal higher than the coast.[2] The whole vicinity of Mexico City, including the part that faces the volcano, is like this, and it is the best land in the Indies. It is the same in Peru, in Arequipa, Huamanga, and Cuzco, although some of these places are a little higher and others a little lower; but it is all high country after all, and from it one can descend to deep valleys and climb to lofty mountains, and they tell me the same of Quito and Santa Fe and the best parts of the new kingdom of Granada. Finally, I consider it great wisdom on the part of the Creator to provide that most of this land of the Indies is high, making it moderate in climate, for were it low it would be extremely hot below the Torrid Zone, especially if distant from the sea. Also, almost all the regions I have seen in the Indies have high mountains on one side or the other and sometimes on every side. So true is this that I often remarked while I was there that I would like to be in a place where the horizon was closed by the juncture of sky and earth, as one can see in any number of landscapes in Spain; I never remember having seen such a sight in the Indies, either in the islands or on the continent, although I traveled the length of the land for more than seven hundred leagues. But, as I say, the closeness of hills and mountains is very useful in moderating the sun's heat in that region; and so the most thickly populated

2. Acosta showers high praise on Mexico, calling it "the best country under the sun," because it is neither too high, which would cause *soroche,* nor too low, which could lead to tropical disease. Many of Acosta's complaints of the Peruvian climate stem from his lengthy tours of the region. One wonders, had Acosta traveled equally throughout Mexico, if he would have offered the same opinion. It should also be noted that Acosta's reflections on Peru were framed within the rather unpleasant context of his departure. He requested to be transferred home to Spain after playing a role in an Inquisition trial that condemned fellow Jesuits.

parts of the Indies are as I have described them, and in general all of it is a land with a great deal of vegetation and pasturage and trees, contrary to what Aristotle and the ancients believed. So when men travel from Europe to the Indies they marvel to see such a green and pleasant land, and so cool, although this rule has some exceptions, the chief one being the land of Peru, which is unusual among all the others, and of which we will now speak.

## CHAPTER 20 * OF THE PROPERTIES OF THE LAND OF PERU

By Peru we do not mean that whole part of the world called America, for that would include Brazil and the kingdom of Chile and New Granada; yet none of those are Peru but only the part that is located on the southern side and begins at the kingdom of Quito, which is below the equator, and extends as far as the kingdom of Chile, which is outside the Tropics. It is about six hundred leagues long, and its width extends only to the Andes, which in most places is about fifty leagues, although in some places, as at Chachapoyas, its breadth is greater. This piece of the world called Peru is most worthy of study because it has very strange properties and is almost the exception to the general rule among the lands of the Indies. First, its entire coast has only one wind, not the one that usually blows below the Torrid Zone but rather its opposite, namely, the south and southwest wind. Second, although this wind is by its nature the stormiest and most irksome and unwholesome of them all, it is wonderfully gentle, health giving, and pleasant there, so much so that it is responsible for the habitation of that coast, for without the wind it would be uninhabitable by reason of heat and discomfort. Third, along that whole coast it never rains or thunders, nor is there sleet or snow, which is a remarkable thing. Fourth, at a very short distance from the coast it snows and storms terribly. Fifth, two mountain ranges run alongside each other and at the same distance from the pole, yet in one there are many trees and it rains most of the year and it is very hot. The other, on the contrary, is barren and very cold and the year is divided between winter and summer into a rainy season and a calm season. So that all this may be better visualized, we must realize that Peru is divided into three long and narrow zones, which are the plains, the sierras, and the Andes; the plains are on the seacoast; the sierras are all inclines, with some valleys; and the Andes are extremely high peaks. The plains are about ten leagues wide, less in some places and more in others; the sierra must be about twenty leagues wide and the Andes another twenty, in some places more and in others less. Their length runs from north to south, their width from east to west.

It is a wonderful thing, therefore, that in a distance as short as fifty leagues, equally distant from the equator and the pole, there can be such great diversity that it rains almost constantly in one place and almost never in another and in one place it rains at one season and never at another. On the coast and the plains it never rains, although now and then a very fine mist falls that they call *garúa* and in Castile is called *mollina,* and this occasionally forms into droplets of water that fall; in fact there are no roofs nor rain to make them necessary. Roofs are a straw mat with a bit of earth on top, and that is sufficient. In the Andes it rains almost all the year, although one season is calmer than the other. In the sierra, which falls between these extremes, it rains at the same seasons as in Spain, namely, from September to April. The other season is fine, which is the time when the sun is farthest away, and the opposite occurs when it is nearest, a point fully discussed in the preceding book.

The names Andes and sierras are given to two ranges of high mountains that run in sight of each other and almost parallel for more than a thousand leagues. In the sierra are bred nearly innumerable flocks of vicuñas, which are animals resembling the agile mountain goat. The animals called guanacos and *pacos,* which serve both as sheep and pack animals in that land, will be described in the appropriate place. In the Andes there are many and very amusing monkeys and a vast number of parrots. Here also is found the herb or tree called coca, so highly valued by the Indians and very lucrative as a trading product. The part known as the sierra, in places where it opens out and forms valleys, such as the valleys of Jauja, Andahuaylas, and Yucay, is the best place to live in Peru. Maize, wheat, and fruit are raised in these valleys, more in some and less in others. Beyond the city of Cuzco (which was formerly the court of the lords of those realms) the two mountain ranges I have mentioned draw farther apart, leaving between them a broad level area or plain that is called the province of Collao. On these plains are a large number of rivers, the great lake of Titicaca, and vast extensions of land and abundant pastures, for, although it is flat country it has the altitude and cold climate characteristic of the sierra. It does not have trees or wood, but the inhabitants compensate for the lack of bread with some roots that they plant, called *papas,* potatoes, which grow underground; these are the Indians' food, and by drying and curing them they make something that they call *chuño,* which is the bread and chief food of that region. There are also some other roots and herbs that they eat. It is a healthful region, the most heavily populated in the Indies, and the richest for the abundance of livestock that is successfully raised there, European animals like sheep, cows, and goats as well as the native animals that they call guanacos and *pacos;* there is good hunting of partridges. Behind the province of Collao comes that of Los Charcas, where there are warm valleys and great fertility of the soil and rugged mountains with a great wealth of mines; larger or richer mines do not exist, nor have ever existed, in any other part of the world.

## CHAPTER 21 * OF THE REASONS GIVEN AS TO WHY IT DOES NOT RAIN ON THE PLAINS

Because it is such an extraordinary thing that a land can exist where it never rains or storms, men naturally desire to know the cause of that strange circumstance. The explanation given by some who have considered it carefully is that heavy vapors, sufficient to create rain, do not arise on that coast for lack of substance; instead the vapors are very thin, sufficient to cause fog and a very fine mist, just as in Europe we see vapors rise on many mornings that do not bring rain but only mist. This comes from the fact that their substance is not thick enough to become rain. And the fact that this condition is constant on the coast of Peru, just as it is occasionally in Europe, is the reason, they say, why that whole region is so very dry and incapable of producing heavy vapors. Its aridity can easily be observed from the immense stretches of sand it contains and the fact that springs and wells cannot be found except at very great depths, fifteen fathoms and more; and even those must be near rivers, where wells are found formed by seepage from them. However, experience has shown that when the river is deflected from its bed and made to run in another channel the wells dry up until the river is returned to its usual bed. They offer this as the material reason why it does not rain. As for the efficient cause, they offer another no less worthy of consideration, that the very high altitude of the sierra that runs all along the coast shelters those plains in such a way that they do not allow a wind to blow from the land side, for it is not high enough to cross those lofty peaks. Hence the only wind comes from the sea, which, as it has no contrary wind does not sufficiently squeeze and compress the vapors that arise and make them produce rain. The result is that the sheltering action of the sierra prevents the vapors from condensing and converts them all into scattered mists.

Some experiences coincide with this explanation, such as the rain that sometimes falls on some of the slightly less sheltered hills along the coast like those of Arica and Arequipa. One example is the fact that it has rained during some years when northeast or north winds have blown through all the area that they could reach, as happened in the year fifteen hundred and seventy-eight on the plains of Trujillo, where it rained copiously, something that had not been seen for centuries. Another example is that on the coast itself it rains in places that the north or northeast winds generally reach, such as Guaya-quil, and where the land rises steeply and the shelter of the sierra is deflected, as happens north of Arica. Some explain it in this way, although anyone is entitled to do so as best he can. But this much is true, that on coming down from the sierra to the plains one often sees two kinds of sky, one very clear and calm in the upper reaches of the air, the other murky and resembling a dark veil spread below, which covers the entire coast. But even though it does not rain that mist is wonderfully useful in making the earth produce grass and turn the fields green. For, even though they have as much river water as they wish, taken from the irrigation canals, I do not know what quality rainwater possesses, for if the *garúa* fails the fields fail too; and the most remarkable thing is that dry, sterile expanses of sand, when the *garúa* or mist arrives, become covered with grass and flowers, which is an exquisite thing to see and very useful for the pasturing of livestock, which gorge themselves on that grass, as can be seen in the sierra called Arena, near Ciudad de los Reyes.

CHAPTER 22 * OF THE PROPERTIES OF NEW
SPAIN AND THE ISLANDS AND THE
OTHER LANDS

New Spain is superior in pasturage and thus breeds large numbers of horses, cattle, sheep, and other animals. It is also very abundant in fruit and no less so in fields of every sort of grain; indeed, it is the best-endowed and supplied land in the Indies. However, in one thing Peru has a great advantage, and that is in wine, for there is much good wine in Peru and cultivation of grapes increases daily in the very warm valleys where there are canals for irrigation. In New Spain, although grapes do grow there, they do not ripen at the time of year required to make wine; the reason is that it rains there in July and August, which is the time when the grapes ripen, and so they do not mature sufficiently.[1] And if anyone should persevere in trying to make wine, it would be like the wines of the Genoa region and Lombardy, which are very thin and so rough in taste that they seem not to have been made from grapes.

The islands called the Windwards, which are Hispaniola, Cuba, Puerto Rico, and others in that region, have a great deal of vegetation and pasturage and a great abundance of the larger livestock. There are vast numbers of cattle and pigs that have gone wild. The wealth of these islands consists of sugar mills and hides; they have a great deal of *cassia fistula* and ginger, and when you see the amount of these brought by a fleet it does not seem possible that all of Europe could use so much. The islands also produce wood of excellent quality and appearance such as ebony and other woods for construction or cabinet work. There is a great deal of the wood called *lignum sanctum,* which serves to cure swollen glands. All of these islands, as well as the innumerable ones in their vicinity, have a cool and beautiful appearance because they are covered with vegetation all year long and full of trees. They have no knowledge of autumn and winter, owing to the constant humidity along with the heat of the Torrid Zone. Although their territory is large, the population of these islands is scanty because they tend to produce large and impenetrable *arcabucos* (which is what they call thick woods there) and in the level regions there are many marshes and swamps. Another important reason for their underpopulation is the fact that few of the native Indians have survived, owing to the thoughtlessness and indiscipline of the early conquistadors and colonists.[2] They chiefly use blacks for labor, but these are costly and are not of

1. Acosta may not have been aware of another crucial distinction between the production of wine in New Spain and Peru, namely, that the Crown initially prohibited vineyards (and olive groves) in New Spain and the Caribbean islands to ensure a New World market for its wine. The long trip to South America meant that wine exports arrived less frequently and costlier to Peru, however, so the Crown relaxed its prohibitions on vineyards.

2. The Arawaks (also referred to as the Tainos) and the Caribs were the two main indigenous peoples on the islands at the time of Spanish arrival. The history of their fate after the conquest was well publicized by the Spanish *encomendero* turned Dominican friar Bartolomé de Las Casas. His account of native life on the islands, *The Devastation of the Indies,* detailed the abuse of the indigenous population at the hands of profit-

much use for cultivating the land. These islands do not produce bread or wine, for the excessive fertility and luxuriance of the earth does not permit seed to grow to maturity; rather, it all goes to grass and is very uneven. Nor are there olive trees, or at least the trees do not produce fruit; they have many leaves and grow greenly but do not bear. The bread they use is cassava, of which we will speak in the appropriate place. The rivers of these islands contain gold, which some collect, but they do not produce much, for lack of the means to refine it. I spent less than a year in these islands, and the accounts I have received of the mainland of the Indies, such as Florida, Nicaragua, Guatemala, and other regions where I have not been, are almost the same as I have described. I do not write of more particular aspects of nature in those places because I do not have full information about them.

In all the West Indies the land that most resembles Spain and other European regions is the realm of Chile, which is unlike the other lands because it lies outside the Torrid Zone and the tropic of Capricorn. It is a naturally cool and fertile land and grows all the kinds of fruit that we have in Spain. It produces bread and wine in abundance and abounds in pasturage and live-stock; its climate is wholesome and moderate, neither hot nor cold. It has well-defined summer and winter seasons and a great deal of very fine gold. Despite all this it is poor and underpopulated, owing to the constant warfare carried on by the Araucanians and their allies, for they are belligerent Indians and jealous of their freedom.

CHAPTER 23 * OF UNDISCOVERED REGIONS
AND THE DIFFERENCE OF A WHOLE DAY
BETWEEN EAST AND WEST

There are many conjectures that large and prosperous regions exist in the temperate zone of the Antarctic Pole, but none have been discovered to this day, nor is any other land known in that region except for Chile and some

driven Spaniards. Las Casas forced debate on these issues in the Council of the Indies, including a famous debate with Juan Ginés de Sepúlveda, a Spanish humanist who founded his defense of Spain's activities in the Indies on the Aristotelian doctrine of just war.

Experts on colonial demographics generally agree that disease from Europe engendered the single most devastating attack on the native population. A good overview of population studies for the Indies is Linda A. Newson, "Indian Population Patterns in Colonial Spanish America," *Latin American Research Review* 20, no. 3 (1995): 41–74.

small part of the land that extends from Ethiopia to the Cape of Good Hope, as was stated in the first book. Neither do we know if there is inhabited land in the other two regions of the poles, nor whether it can be reached from the Antarctic or southern side of the land that begins after the Strait of Magellan has been crossed, for the highest number of degrees attained so far is fifty-six, as has been said. Nor do we know how far the land that runs northward from Cape Mendocino and the Californias extends toward the Arctic or North Pole, nor the end and boundaries of Florida, nor how far it extends to the west. Only a short time ago a large area called New Mexico was discovered, where it is said that there are many people and that they speak the Mexican tongue. The Philippines and neighboring islands, according to well-informed persons who have reported on them, extend for more than nine hundred leagues; but to deal with China and Cochinchina and Siam and the other provinces belonging to the East Indies would be a never-ending subject and is no part of my intention, which is only to describe the West Indies. As for the American continent itself, whose boundaries have been established on all sides, the greater part of it, which is the portion lying between Peru and Brazil, is still unknown. And there are divergent opinions by some who say that it is all flooded land, full of lakes and swamps, and others who insist that there are great and flourishing realms there and situate Paitití and El Dorado and Los Césares in that region and say that it contains wonderful things. I heard a member of our society, a person worthy of belief, say that he had seen great cities and roads as broad and well traveled as those between Salamanca and Valladolid; and this was at the time when the entrance or discovery of the great Amazon or Marañón River was made by Pedro de Orsúa and later by others who followed him. Believing that the El Dorado they sought lay before them, they did not try to settle there and then lost out on El Dorado (which they never found) as well as that great province that they left behind. Indeed, the inhabited region of America is almost unknown even today, except for its edges, which are Peru and Brazil, and the places where the continent narrows, which are Río de la Plata and then Tucumán, leading to Chile and Los Charcas. Quite recently, by means of letters from our members who are in Santacruz de la Sierra, we have new reports that large provinces and great numbers of inhabitants are being discovered in the area between Peru and Brazil. Time will disclose this, for since it is the task of zeal and courage to cover the entire world we may well believe that just as part has been discovered up to now the rest will be discovered, too, so that the Holy Gospel may be declared throughout the whole world. For the two Crowns of Castile and Portugal have already met from both east and west, making a perfect circle of the world by joining their discoveries together; certainly it is an important achievement that some have reached China and Japan by the eastern route and others by the western route to the Philippines, which are neighboring and almost contiguous with China. For from the isle of Luzón, which is the chief island of the Philippines, where the city of Manila is located, to Macao, which is the island of Canton, only eighty or a hundred leagues of sea intervene.

And it is a remarkable thing that, despite the little distance between them, there is a whole day's difference in their reckoning, so that it is Sunday in Macao at the same time that it is Saturday in Manila and the same for the other days; the people of Macao and China are always one day ahead and those of the Philippines a day behind. It so happened that Fr. Alonso Sánchez (who was mentioned above) was traveling from the Philippines; he arrived in Macao on the second of May according to his computation, and, wishing to pray to Saint Athanasius, he found that the festivity of the Finding of the Cross was being celebrated, for there they reckoned it to be the third of May. The same thing happened to him on another occasion when he journeyed there. Some have marveled at this difference and believed that there must be an error on one side or the other; this is not so but is a true and carefully observed calculation. For, according to the different routes that both groups have taken, it is inevitable that when they meet there is a day of difference. The reason for this is that those who sail from west to east are gradually gaining a day because the sun continues to rise sooner; for those who sail from east to west it is the opposite because they gradually lose time or fall behind, for each day the sun rises later, and the farther they proceed in an easterly or westerly direction the earlier or later is the day. In Peru, which is to the west of Spain, there is a delay of more than six hours, so that when it is midday in Spain the sun is just coming up in Peru and when the sun comes up here it is midnight there. I have established palpable proof of this by computing the eclipses of the sun and moon. Now, the Portuguese have performed their navigations from west to east and the Spaniards from east to west; when they have come together (as in the Philippines and Macao) one side has gained twelve hours and the other has lost an equal number; thus, at the same place and time they find a difference of twenty-four hours, which constitutes a whole day. And so one group must necessarily be at the third of May while the others reckon it as the second. And one group fasts on Holy Saturday and the other eats meat on Easter Sunday. And if we were to imagine that they continued their voyage, circumnavigating the globe again and making their calculation, when they came together again they would have two days' difference in their reckoning; because, as I have said, those who sail toward the sunrise reckon the day earlier each time, and contrariwise those who sail westward reckon it later because the sun continues to come up later. Finally, the difference in the meridians causes the different calculation of days, and because those who sail either to east or west gradually change the meridian without being aware of it, and yet continue to make the same calculation as when they set out, they must necessarily have incurred an error of an entire day by the time they have completely circumnavigated the globe.

## CHAPTER 24 * OF VOLCANOES OR VENTS OF FIRE

Although volcanoes are found in other places, such as Mounts Etna and Vesuvius, which nowadays is called Mount Soma, they are extraordinarily frequent in the Indies. Usually volcanoes are very high mountains, higher than the peaks of the other mountains. They have a level space at their summit and in the middle of it a pit or large vent descending into the depths, a frightening thing to see. Smoke issues from these vents and sometimes fire. There are some that emit very little smoke and have no more than the form of a volcano, like the one in Arequipa, which is immensely tall and almost all composed of sand. Two days are required to climb it, but no noticeable signs of fire have been found, only traces of sacrifices that the Indians made there while they were still heathens, and occasionally a little smoke comes from it.[1] The volcano of Mexico, which is near Puebla de los Angeles, is also remarkably high, rising from an area of thirty leagues all around. A great cloud of smoke emerges from it, not constantly but at intervals and almost daily, and

1. A recent discovery of Andean sacrifices to these volcanoes occurred on the mountain of Ampato in Peru in 1995. Archaeologists came upon the mummified body of a young woman whose icy tomb had been exposed due to recent climatic changes. Further excavations revealed two more sacrificial victims on the same mountain, and numerous ritual goods, such as pottery, textiles, and even coca leaves, accompanied the bodies.

rises straight up like an arrow; then little by little it forms a very large shape resembling a plume of feathers until it disappears completely and turns into a sort of dark cloud. Most often this smoke appears in the morning after daybreak and at night when the sun sets, although I have also seen it at other times of day. A great deal of ash is emitted along with the smoke; so far flame has not been seen to emerge, but there is fear that it will escape and scorch the soil, for the best land in that kingdom is found around the volcano. It is firmly believed that there is a certain connection between this volcano and the nearby mountains of Tlaxcala, for this would explain why so many thunderings and lightnings and even thunderbolts are often experienced in them. Spaniards have climbed this volcano and entered it and have extracted sulphur from it to make gunpowder. Cortés tells of the efforts he made to discover what was in it.[2] The volcanoes of Guatemala are more famous, both for their large size — those who sail on the Southern Sea can see them a long way off — and for the fury of the fire that they emit. On December twenty-third in the year fifteen hundred and eighty-six, almost all the city of Guatemala tumbled down as the result of an earthquake and several persons died. For six months the volcano had not ceased either by day or by night to eject from its summit, like a vomit, a river of fire. The material of which it was composed rolled down the slopes of the volcano and became ash and burnt stone. It taxes the human imagination to understand how the volcano could have ejected from its center all the material that it threw out during those months. This volcano did not ordinarily emit anything but smoke, and not always even that, and occasionally produced some flickers of flame. During the time I spent in Mexico I received an account of this in a letter from a secretary of the law courts in Guatemala, a trustworthy person, and even then the fire that I mentioned had not ceased to flow from the volcano. Years ago in Quito, when I was in Ciudad de los Reyes, the nearby volcano cast up so much ash that it rained ashes for many leagues around and completely blotted out the sun, and the ash fell so thickly in Quito that it was impossible to walk in the streets. Other volcanoes have been seen that do not emit flames or smoke or ash, but fire is constantly burning deep within them. It was this kind of volcano about which, in our day, a greedy priest became convinced

2. In his second letter to King Charles V, Cortés wrote of his attempts to "discover the secret of the smoke." See Hernán Cortés, *Letters from Mexico,* translated and edited by Anthony Pagden, introduced by J. H. Elliott (New Haven: Yale University Press, 1986), 77.

that the burning material had to be gold, concluding that anything that burned for so many years without being consumed could be no other substance or metal. In this belief he had certain kettles and chains made, and some sort of instrument to gather and remove the gold from that pit. But the fire outwitted him, for no sooner had the iron chain and kettle reached it than they melted and fell apart as if made of straw. Yet he persisted, I was told, and was planning other methods of removing the gold that he imagined was there.

## CHAPTER 25 * WHY THE FIRE AND SMOKE OF THESE VOLCANOES PERSISTS FOR SO LONG

There is no need to mention other volcanoes, for what happens in them can be understood from those I have described; but the reason why the fire and smoke of these volcanoes persists is worth discussing because it seems a prodigious thing, and one that exceeds the course of nature, that they bring up from their interiors the amount of material that they vomit forth. Where does that material come from or who provides it? How is it made? Some are of the opinion that volcanoes constantly consume the internal matter of which they are made and thus believe that they will naturally come to an end when they have exhausted the fuel (so to speak) that they possess. As a consequence of this opinion they point today to some mountains from which burnt stone is extracted, light in weight but very strong, and excellent for building purposes, such as that which is brought to a few workshops in Mexico. And indeed what they say seems to be true, that those mountains had natural fire for a while, the material they consumed had run out, and so those burnt stones were left. I do not quarrel with this insofar as I think that there was fire there and that those mountains had been volcanoes at one time. But it is very hard for me to believe that the same thing happens in all volcanoes in view of the fact that the material they eject is almost infinite in quantity and could not all fit into the bowels of the mountain at one time. And in addition to this there are volcanoes that stay the same for hundreds and even thousands of years and unvaryingly throw off smoke and fire and ash. Pliny, the writer of natural history (as his nephew, the other Pliny, records), because he wondered about this secret and wanted to see how it came about, came too close to the fire of one such volcano and died, and that was the end of his search.

Looking at the matter from a greater distance, I will state my opinion, which is that, just as on this earth there are places that have the property of being able to attract cloudy matter to themselves and change it into water, and these are sources that flow constantly and never cease running because they attract moisture to themselves, so there are also places that have the property of attracting hot, dry emissions and converting them into flame and smoke, and by the violence of these they also throw off heavy matter that resolves itself into ash or pumice stone or something similar. And the fact that they sometimes but not always emit smoke, and sometimes flame, though not always, is sufficient proof of this. For this is proportionate to what they have been able to attract and digest; and just as fountains flow freely in winter and less freely in summer, and some even dry up completely, according to their condition and degree of activity and the raw material at hand, so volcanoes spew out more or less fire at different times. Some say that it is fire from hell and comes from there as a warning, to make us consider what the other life may be like; but if hell is, as the theologians say, in the center of the earth and the globe has a diameter of more than two thousand leagues, it cannot very well be argued that that fire comes from the center. This is all the more true because the fire of Hell, according to the teachings of Saint Basil and other saints, is very different from the fire that we see, for it has no light and burns incomparably more fiercely than our fire.[1] And so I conclude that what I have offered as an explanation is more reasonable.

CHAPTER 26 * OF EARTHQUAKES

Some have thought that earthquakes, which are very frequent there, may arise from these volcanoes in the Indies. But since they also occur in places where there are no volcanoes nearby this cannot be the entire cause. It is indeed true that earthquakes and volcanoes have a certain resemblance to each other, for the hot blasts that originate in the deep hollows of the earth seem to be the chief element in the volcanoes' fire, which causes other, heavier material to catch fire and produces those smokes and flames that emerge from them; and those same blasts, unable to find an easy outlet underground,

1. Saint Basil, *On Psalm 28; Homilies on Hexameron* (O'G).

shake the earth violently as they emerge, causing the horrible noise that is heard under the ground and the movement of the earth itself, stirred by the fiery blast. Just as does gunpowder, when flame touches it, break rocks and walls in the mines, or a chestnut placed in the fire leaps and breaks and crackles when the air inside its shell feels the force of the fire. Usually these tremors or earthquakes occur in coastal areas, where there is water nearby. We see in both Europe and the Indies that towns far from the sea and other waters have this problem less often and those that are seaports, or have beaches or coastlines, suffer this calamity more frequently. In Peru it has been a remarkable thing, and worthy of notice, that from Chile to Quito, a distance of more than 500 leagues, earthquakes have occurred in a series (I mean the large and famous ones, for there have been many lesser tremors). There was a very terrible one on the coast of Chile, I do not recall in what year, which brought down whole mountains and shut off the course of rivers with its debris and made lakes of them and destroyed towns and killed a large number of people. And it caused the sea to inundate the land for several leagues, leaving ships stranded and very far from their anchorages, and other similar and very terrifying things. And, if I remember correctly, they said that the movement of that earthquake had run along the coast for 300 leagues. The earthquake that laid waste most of the city of Arequipa occurred a few years ago, in fifteen hundred and eighty-two. Later, in fifteen hundred and eighty-six, on the ninth day of July, there was the earthquake of Ciudad de los Reyes, which according to the viceroy's report had run in length 170 leagues along the coast and in breadth 50 leagues into the sierra. By the great mercy of the Lord, in this earthquake the people were alerted by a loud noise, which they heard a short time before the tremor, and since in those parts they are forewarned by experience they quickly saved themselves by going out to the streets or squares or fields, in a word, out of doors. And so, although it devastated that city and demolished or badly damaged the principal buildings, they say that among its inhabitants only some fourteen to twenty persons died. Also at that time the sea made the same movement as in Chile, which was shortly after the earth tremor was over; it rushed furiously away from the beaches and then swept inland for almost 2 leagues, for it rose more than 14 fathoms and covered that whole coastal region with the beams and lumber that were floating in the water there, as I said. Later, the following year in fact, there was another, similar earthquake in the kingdom and city of Quito, for it seems that these severe tremors have occurred in a series all along that coast. And indeed it is subject to such disasters, for, although on the plains of Peru they do not suffer the persecution of the heavens in the form of thunder and lightning, yet they are not without fear from the earth, and so they all have agents of Divine Justice constantly before their eyes to make them fear God. For, as Scripture says, "Fecit haec, ut timeatur," those things that God made so that he may be feared.[1]

Returning to my subject, I say that coastal lands are more subject to these tremors, and in my opinion the cause is that the water closes and obstructs the earth's apertures and holes where the hot blasts that are engendered have to be exhaled and dispersed; also, humidity condenses the earth's surface and causes those hot vapors that eventually escape in fiery form to be enclosed and concentrated within the earth. Some have observed that these tremors are more apt to occur when a rainy period ensues after very dry years, and experience proves, they say, that for the same reason fewer earthquakes occur in places where there are many wells. As for the City of Mexico, it is believed that the cause of some tremors that it experiences, although they are not very large, is the lake on which it stands. Although it is also true that cities and lands a long way inland, and far from the sea, often suffer great damage from earthquakes, such as the city of Chachapoyas in the Indies and Ferrara in Italy, since the latter is near a river and not far from the Adriatic Sea, it seems that in the present case it must be counted among maritime cities. In Chuquiavo, which is also called La Paz, a city in Peru, a strange thing happened in this regard in fifteen hundred and eighty-one, and this was that a very large portion of a high precipice suddenly fell near a town called Angoango, where there were idolatrous Indians dedicated to witchcraft. It covered a large part of this town and killed a large number of those Indians; another thing, almost impossible to believe (although reliable persons attest to it) is that the earth that fell slid for a league and a half without stopping, like water or melted wax, and covered a lake, and that a vast quantity of earth was spread over the whole distance.[2]

---

1. Ecclesiastes, 3, 14 (O'G).

2. The village of Angoango, or Ancu-Ancu, was the capital of the province of Omasuyos, located on the eastern side of Lake Titicaca, toward the city of Chuquiavo (La Paz). In contrast to his usual quest for causality, Acosta offers no explanation for the mudslide in Angoango. Instead, he substitutes a logical scientific explanation with the suggestion of malevolence. To a European audience primed in the battle between good and evil, the idolatrous residents of Angoango themselves appear to be the heavy weight that made the precipice collapse.

## CHAPTER 27 * HOW EARTH AND SEA CLASP
### ONE ANOTHER

I shall close my discussion of this element, earth, by linking it to the one previously dealt with, water, for their order and interaction are remarkable. These two elements have the globe divided between them and clasp one another in any number of ways. In some places the water attacks the land furiously, like an enemy; in others it girdles the land gently. There are places where the sea enters very far into the land, as if to visit it; there are others where the earth repays the sea by thrusting sharp points into its innermost parts. In some places one of these elements ends and the other begins very gradually, each yielding to the other. In places each element has immense depth where they join, for there are islands in both the southern and the northern ocean where ships can sail very close to the land and, although they sound to a depth of seventy or eighty fathoms, they find no bottom. This proves that they are like shafts or points of land that rise from the deep, something that is very wonderful. An expert pilot told me that the islands called Lobos are of this kind and that there is another at the beginning of the coast of New Spain, called Cocos. And there is even a place in the middle of the vast ocean, with no land visible for many leagues around, where two lofty towers or peaks of living rock can be seen; they emerge from the middle of the sea, and there is no land and no bottom near them. We cannot grasp the shape of the entire land of the Indies because we do not know its boundaries, nor have they been discovered to the present day, but in broad terms we can say that it is shaped like a heart and lungs. The widest part of this heart shape extends from Brazil to Peru, and its tip is the Strait of Magellan; the upper part, where it comes to an end, is the part called Tierra Firme, and from there it gradually widens again until it reaches the large land mass of Florida and the lands to the north of it, which are imperfectly known. Other details of these lands of the Indies can be learned from reports made by Spaniards about their experiences and discoveries, among them the pilgrimage, which I recorded, of a brother of our society. It is certainly a strange one and can offer a great deal of information. With this, for the present I have said everything necessary to give some idea of things in the Indies with regard to the common elements of which all the regions of the world are composed.

# BOOK IV

### CHAPTER I * OF THE THREE KINDS OF MIXTURES THAT WILL BE DEALT WITH IN THIS HISTORY

Having dealt in the preceding book with matters concerning the elements and single entities in the Indies, in this book we shall deal with compounds and mixtures, insofar as they seem to conform to our aims. And, although there are many other kinds, we will reduce this subject to three, namely, metals, plants, and animals. Metals are like plants hidden in the bowels of the earth and have some resemblance to plants in the manner in which they are produced because the places from which their roots arise, and their trunk as it were, can be perceived; these are the large and small veins that are very well interlaced and organized among themselves. And in a way it seems that minerals grow in the same manner as plants, not because they have real vegetable and inner life, for this is true only of real plants, but because they are produced in the bowels of the earth in such a way, by the virtue and efficacy of the sun and the other planets, that over a long period of time they gradually grow and almost, one might say, propagate. And, just as metals resemble the earth's hidden plants, we may also say that plants are like animals that remain in one place, whose life is ruled by the nourishment nature supplies them at their birth. But animals are greater than plants, for because they have a more perfect nature they also need more perfect nourishment; and Nature gave them movement to seek it and senses to find and recognize it. Hence, harsh and barren land serves as substance and nourishment for metals, and fertile and more amenable land is substance and nourishment for plants. Plants themselves are the food of animals, and both plants and animals are food for men, with the lower order of nature always serving the higher and the less perfect subordinated to the more perfect. This makes us understand how far are gold and silver, which greedy men in their covetousness hold so dear, from being a worthy object for man, for they are many degrees lower than man, and man is subject and subordinate only to the Creator and universal Maker of all things as his proper end and repose, and all other things are worthy only insofar as they guide him and help him to attain this goal. The man who contemplates created things from this viewpoint, and ponders them, can gain advantage from knowledge and consideration of them, using them to know and glorify the Author of them all. The man who goes no further than to understand their properties and uses, or who is merely curious as to knowledge of them or covetous in acquiring them, will find that in the end these creatures will be as the sage has said: "to the feet of the unwise and foolish they are a snare and a net into which they fall and are entangled."[1] Therefore, with the aim and intention I have expressed, to the end that the Creator may be glorified in his creatures, I mean to write something in this book of the many things worthy of mention in the Indies concerning the metals and plants and animals peculiar to those parts. And because to deal with them accurately would be a very large task, and one that requires greater knowledge than my own and more time than I have at my disposal, I will say that I intend to deal briefly with some things about these three groups that I have proposed and that I know from experience or by true accounts given me, leaving longer exposition of these matters to others more curious and diligent than myself.

### CHAPTER 2 * OF THE ABUNDANCE OF METALS THAT EXIST IN THE INDIES

The wisdom of God created metals for medicine and for defense and for adornment and as instruments of men's activities. We could easily give examples of all four of these uses, but the chief object of metals is the last of them; for human life requires not mere survival, like the life of beasts, but must also be lived according to the capacity and reason bestowed on it by the Creator. And thus, just as man's intelligence extends to different arts and faculties, the Author of all things also provided it with materials of different kinds for man's investigation and for security and ornament and a great number of ac-

---

1. Book of Wisdom, 14, 11 (O'G).

tivities. Such is the diversity of metals that the Creator enclosed in the storage places and hollows of the earth that all of them are useful for human life. Man uses some to cure illnesses, others to provide him with weapons and a defense against his enemies, others for the adornment and decoration of men's bodies and homes, and others for vessels and tools and various instruments invented by human ingenuity. But above all these uses, which are simple and natural, communication among men resulted in the use of money, which (as the philosopher said) is the measure of all things;[1] and, although by its nature it is but one thing, actually it is all things, for money represents food and clothing and shelter, mounts to ride on, and everything of which men have need. And so all things obey money, as the sage said.[2] For this invention, that of making one thing serve for all things, men — guided by natural instinct — chose the most durable and negotiable thing of all, which is metal. And among the metals they decided that those whose nature was most durable and incorruptible, namely, silver and gold, must have primacy in this invention of money. These metals were held in esteem not only among the Hebrews and Assyrians and Greeks and Romans, and other nations in Europe and Asia, but also among the most remote and barbarous nations in the world, such as the Indians, those of both the East and West Indies, where gold and silver were greatly prized and esteemed and were used in temples and palaces and as adornment for kings and nobles. However, some savages have been found who had no knowledge of silver or gold, as is reported of the inhabitants of Florida, who would take the sacks or bags containing money and leave the money itself abandoned on the beach as something useless. And Pliny tells of the Babitacos, who loathed gold and hence buried it where no one could make use of it.[3] But there have been very few of these Floridians and Babitacos, and few exist today, and on the other hand there are many Indians who value and seek and keep gold and silver and have no need to learn of it from those who come from Europe. But the truth is that their greed for it was not as immoderate as ours, nor did they idolize gold and silver as much (even though they were idolaters) as some bad Christians, who have committed so many excesses for the sake of gold and silver.[4]

1. Aristotle, *Nichomachean Ethics*, 5, 5 (O'G).
2. Ecclesiastes, 10, 19 (O'G).
3. Pliny, *Natural History*, 6, 27 (O'G).
4. The most famous commentary in colonial literature on Spanish greed is Guaman Poma's depiction of an

But it is a circumstance worthy of much consideration that the wisdom of our Eternal Lord has enriched the most remote parts of the world, inhabited by the most uncivilized people, and has placed there the greatest number of mines that ever existed, in order to invite men to seek out and possess those lands and coincidentally to communicate their religion and the worship of the true God to men who do not know it. Thus the prophecy of Isaiah has been fulfilled that the Church shall pass on to the right hand and to the left,[5] which is, as Saint Augustine declares, the way the Gospel must be propagated, not only by those who preach it sincerely and with charity but also by those who proclaim it through temporal and human aims and means.[6] Hence we see that the lands in the Indies that are richest in mines and wealth have been those most advanced in the Christian religion in our time; and thus the Lord takes advantage of our desires to serve his sovereign ends. In this regard a wise man once said that what a man does to marry off an ugly daughter is give her a large dowry; this is what God has done with that rugged land, endowing it with great wealth in mines so that whoever wished could find it by this means. Hence there is great abundance of mines in the Indies, mines of every metal: copper, iron, lead, tin, quicksilver, silver, and gold. And among all parts of the Indies the realms of Peru are those that most abound in metals, especially silver and gold and quicksilver, and this is true to such an extent that new mines are discovered every day. And, to judge from the characteristics of the land, there is no doubt that incomparably more mines exist still to be discovered than those already discovered, and it even appears that the whole land there is sown, as it were, with these metals, more than in any other land known at present in the world or in any written about in the past.

---

Andean giving a Spaniard gold to eat, so voracious was the Spanish appetite for precious minerals. See Felipe Guaman Poma de Ayala, *El Primer Nueva Corónica y Buen Gobierno,* edited by John V. Murra and Rolena Adorno (Mexico City: Siglo Veintiuno, 1980), 2:343. Pre-Hispanic societies honored gods and rulers with gold and silver, but they did not use the metals for money and relied instead on barter or used other valuable items, like cacao beans and coca leaves, as currency. On preconquest notions of property and trade, see Pedro Carrasco, *Economía política e ideología en el México prehispánico* (Mexico City: Editorial Nueva Imagen, 1978); Hassig, *Trade, Tribute, and Transportation,* esp. chap. 4; John Murra, *The Economic Organization of the Inca State* (Greenwich, CT, 1955); and María Rostworowski de Diez Canseco, "Mercaderes del Valle de Chincha en la época prehispánica," *Revista Española de Antropología Americana* 5 (1970): 135–78.

5. Isaiah, 54, 3 (O'G).

6. Saint Augustine, *De Concordia Evangelistarum,* book 1, chapter 31 (O'G).

## CHAPTER 3 * OF THE KIND OF LAND WHERE
## METALS ARE FOUND, AND HOW IN THE INDIES
## ALL THE METALS ARE NOT WORKED, AND
## HOW THE INDIANS USED METALS

The reason why there is so much mineral wealth in the Indies (especially in the West Indies of Peru), is, as I have said, the will of the Creator, who distributed his gifts as he pleased. But if we base ourselves on reason and philosophy we will find that what Philo, a wise man, wrote is very true: he says that gold and silver and other metals naturally occur in the most sterile and infertile lands.[1] Thus we see that temperate lands fertile in plants and fruits rarely or never possess mines, for Nature contents herself with giving them the power to produce the commodities most necessary for the organization and life of animals and men.[2] On the other hand, silver and quicksilver mines and gold-bearing sands, and all the wealth that has come to Spain, are found in very harsh, dry, and barren lands, among high mountains, on wild peaks, with very unfavorable weather. Since the discovery of the West Indies, that wealth has been taken from similar hard and difficult and bleak and sterile places, but the love of money renders them soft and abundant and well populated. And, although there are in the Indies, as I have said, lodes and mines of every metal, only silver and gold mines are worked and those of quicksilver, too, because it is needed for extracting silver and gold. Iron is brought from Spain and China. The Indians formerly worked copper, for their tools and weapons were commonly made not of iron but of that metal. Since the Spaniards have held the Indies, copper mines have been little sought or worked, though many exist, for they seek the richer metals and spend their time and labor upon them; as for other metals, they make use of what comes from Spain or what is left as a result of refining silver and gold.

It has not been found that the Indians used gold or silver or any other metal for money, nor to establish the price of things; they used it for adornment, as has been said. And so they had a vast quantity, and innumerable vessels, of gold and silver in their temples and palaces and tombs. For trading and buying they did not have money but instead bartered some things for

1. Philo of Alexandria, *De genesi mundi,* book 5 (O'G).
2. Eusebius of Caesarea, *De evangelica praeparatione,* book 8, chapter 5 (O'G).

others, as Homer tells of the ancients and as Pliny relates.[3] In place of money there were a few things of more esteem that had an established value, and this custom persists among the Indians to this day; for example, in the provinces of Mexico they use cocoa (which is a sort of berry) instead of money and barter with it for what they want. In Peru the same purpose is served by coca, which is a leaf much valued by the Indians. In Paraguay they use iron dies as money, and in Santa Cruz de la Sierra they use woven cotton. Finally, the Indians' method of trading, their buying and selling, was to barter and exchange some things for other things; because their markets were very large and found everywhere, they did not need money or third parties, for all were very clever at knowing how much of something was reasonable to give for a certain amount of something else. After the Spaniards came the Indians also used silver and gold to buy things; at first there was no coinage, but the price was set in silver by weight, as is related of the ancient Romans.[4] Later, for more convenience, money was minted in Mexico and Peru, but to this day no money made of copper or any other metal is used in the West Indies, only silver and gold. Owing to the wealth and richness of that land, the use of the alloyed coin known as *vellón* has not been permitted, nor have other types of alloys that are used in Italy and other parts of Europe. Although it is true that in some islands in the Indies, such as Santo Domingo and Puerto Rico, they use copper money, the coins have value only in those islands, for there is little silver there and, although much gold exists, there is no one to refine it. But, because the wealth of the Indies and the work of the mines consists of gold, silver, and quicksilver, I will say something about these three metals, leaving the others aside for the present.

### CHAPTER 4 * OF THE GOLD THAT IS PRODUCED IN THE INDIES

Gold was always held to be the chief among all metals, and rightly so, because it is the most durable and incorruptible; for fire, which consumes or diminishes the other metals, improves and perfects it, and gold that has passed through great heat maintains its color and is exceedingly pure. This is properly speaking (as Pliny says) called fine gold or tried gold, of which such

3. Pliny, *Natural History,* 33, 3 (O'G).
4. Ibid., 33, 4 (O'G).

frequent mention is made in Scripture.[1] And usage, which wears away all the others (as Pliny himself says) detracts nothing from gold, nor corrodes it nor wears it out; and because its essence is so solid it can be folded and beaten thin to an astonishing degree.

Gold beaters and drawers of gold wire are well acquainted with the strength of gold, which lends itself to being drawn so thin and so often folded without ever breaking, which, along with its other excellent properties, gives men who are spiritually inclined the opportunity to understand why charity is compared to gold in Holy Writ.[2] As for the rest, there is almost no need to recount the excellent properties that cause it to be esteemed and sought after, for its greatest excellence among men is that of being recognized as the world's supreme power and greatness.

To come to our subject, there is great abundance of this metal in the Indies, and it is known from reliable histories that the Incas of Peru were not content to have large and small vessels made of gold, and pitchers and goblets, and cups and flasks, and jugs and even large jars, but they also had chairs and litters made of solid gold and placed solid gold statues in their temples. There was also a great deal of gold in Mexico, though not so much, and when the first conquistadors went to these two realms the riches that they found were immense and those that the Indians hid or buried were incomparably greater. Using silver to shoe horses because there was no iron, paying three hundred gold escudos for a jug or pitcher of wine, and other such tales of excess seem exaggerated in the telling, but things more extravagant than these actually happened.

In those parts gold is obtained in three ways, at least I have seen it done in these three ways, for gold can be found in nuggets, in the form of dust, and in rock. They call nuggets the pieces of gold that are found in this form and are unmixed with any other metal, which do not need to be smelted or treated by fire. In Spanish they are called *pepitas,* seeds, because ordinarily they are small pieces the size of melon or squash seeds; this is what Job calls *glebae illius aurum,*[3] clods of gold, although they can be much larger, and I have seen them, and some have even weighed many pounds. This is the great thing

1. Ibid., 33, 3 (O'G).

2. Apocalypse, 3, 18; Apocalypse, 21, 18; Song of Solomon, 3, 10; Psalms, 67, 14; Lamentations, 4, 1; 3 Kings, 6, 20, 21, 22 (O'G).

3. Job, 28, 6 (O'G).

about this metal when it occurs alone, as Pliny says, that it is found in a finished and perfect state, which does not happen with the other metals, for they always contain dross and need fire to purify them.[4] I have also seen silver in a natural state that resembles hoarfrost, and there also exist in the Indies what are called "silver potatoes," for sometimes fine silver is found in pieces the size of truffles; this is rare in silver, but in gold it is a very common thing. However, the quantity of gold found in nuggets is small compared to its other forms. Gold in rocks consists of a vein that arises in the rock or rock formation itself, and I have seen quite large rocks from the mines of Zaruma, in the Salinas district, that are shot through with gold and others that are half gold and half rock. This sort of gold is found in deep holes and in mines that have veins of gold like veins of silver, which are very difficult to work. The method of extracting gold from rocks that the kings of Egypt employed in ancient times is described by Agatharchides in the fifth book of his *History of the Erythraean Sea,* or Red Sea, as Phocion relates in his *Library,* and it is astonishing how similar his description is to the process now used in extracting these metals, gold and silver.

The greater part of the gold collected in the Indies is gold dust, which is found in rivers or places through which a great deal of water has passed. The rivers of the Indies are very rich in this metal, just as the ancients praised the River Tagus in Spain and the Pactolus in Asia and the Ganges in the East Indies. And what we call gold dust they called *ramenta auri,* morsels of gold. And at that time also, the greater part of the gold was taken from these morsels or gold dust that was found in rivers. In our day, in the Windward Islands and Hispaniola and Cuba and Puerto Rico, there has always been, and still is, an abundance of gold in the rivers, but, owing to the disappearance of the natives and the difficulty of extracting it, not much gold comes to Spain from those islands. There is much gold in the kingdom of Chile and in those of Quito and New Granada.[5] The best known is the gold

---

4. Pliny, *Natural History,* 33, 4 (O'G).

5. Dreams of gold prompted Spanish exploration, but in reality the profits from gold never neared the silver wealth Spain took from the New World. Gold exports from the Caribbean islands to Spain reached their peak in the first half of the sixteenth century. Despite Acosta's assertion that depopulation halted gold mining in the Caribbean (an idea likely founded on Las Casas's writings), the decline in gold profits occurred because most of the mineral resources on the islands had been depleted. The abundant gold deposits in Brazilian territory were not discovered until the 1690s.

of Carabaya in Peru and that of Valdivia in Chile, for there it occurs in the purest form, twenty-three and a half carats, and sometimes even more. The gold of Veragua is also famous for its purity.

A great deal of gold is brought from the Philippines and China to Mexico, but it is usually of low quality and few carats. Gold is found mixed with other metals or with silver or copper. Pliny says that no gold exists without some silver, but the gold that has a mixture of silver is usually lower in carats than that mixed with copper.[6] He says that if it contains one-fifth part of silver it is properly speaking called electrum and has the property of shining in firelight much more than pure silver or pure gold.[7] Gold associated with copper is usually of higher quality. Gold dust is extracted in troughs by washing it copiously with water until the sand or mud falls from the troughs or pans; the gold settles below because it is heavier. It can also be extracted with mercury. Gold is also purified with nitric acid because the alum of which it is made has the property of drawing out the gold from the rest. After it has been purified or smelted, ingots or bars are made of it to take it to Spain, for gold dust cannot be removed from the Indies because it cannot be divided into fifths and stamped or weighed until it has been smelted. According to the above-mentioned historian, Spain used to abound above all other regions in the world with these metals, gold and silver, especially in Galicia and Lusitania, and in particular Asturias, from whence it is related that twenty thousand pounds of gold were brought annually to Rome and there was no such abundance of gold in any other place.[8] This seems to be attested to by the Book of Machabees, where it says that one of the greatest glories of the Romans was that they possessed the metals of silver and gold, which were in Spain.[9] Today this great treasure comes to Spain from the Indies, for Divine Providence has ordained that some realms must serve others and render their wealth and share its use for the good of all men if they use properly the assets they possess.

The amount of gold that is brought from the Indies is difficult to estimate, but we can certainly state that it is much greater than the amount that Pliny says was brought to Rome from Spain every year. In the fleet in which I

6. Pliny, *Natural History,* 33, 4 (O'G).
7. Ibid., 33, 4 (O'G).
8. Ibid. (O'G).
9. 1 Machabees, 8, 3 (O'G).

traveled in the year fifteen hundred and eighty-seven, the share from the continent was twelve boxes of gold, each at least the size of a bushel, and from New Spain 1,156 gold pieces. This amount was only the king's share and did not include the gold that was registered to individuals, nor does it include what was brought to be registered, which is usually a very large amount. And let this suffice concerning the gold of the Indies; we will speak of silver in succeeding chapters.

### CHAPTER 5 * OF THE SILVER OF THE INDIES

In the Book of Job we read the following: "Silver hath beginnings of its veins: and gold hath a place wherein it is melted. Iron is taken out of the earth: and stone melted with heat is turned into copper."[1] Thus admirably, in a few words, does Job declare the properties of these four metals: silver, gold, iron, and copper. Something has been said of the places where gold is formed and engendered, which are either rocks in the depths of mountains and the bosom of the earth, or sand from rivers and places subject to flooding, or very high hills from which the grains of gold are displaced by water, which is the most widespread opinion in the Indies; hence many ignorant folk believe that gold is found in water from the time of the Flood, in places as strange as those where it is now found. We shall now deal with veins or lodes of silver, and the beginnings and roots that Job speaks of, first stating that the reason why silver holds second place among metals is that it is closest to gold in being more durable than any other and less affected by fire, permits of being treated and worked better, and even surpasses gold in shining more and ringing clearer. Also its color more closely resembles that of light and its sound is more delicate and penetrating. There are places where silver is held to be better than gold, but because gold is rarer, and Nature bestows it more sparingly, this is an argument for considering it the most precious metal. There are lands, as is told of China, where gold is found more readily than silver, but the common and ordinary thing is that silver is easier to find and more abundant. The Creator provided such abundance of it in the Indies that everything known from ancient histories, and everything that they say of the silver mines of Spain and other places, is less than what we see in those parts.

Silver mines are commonly found in very rough and arid hills and moun-

1. Job, 28, 1 and 2 (O'G).

tains, although they have also been found on plains or flat places. These are of two kinds: some are known as free deposits, others as fixed veins. The free ones are pieces of metal in places where, after they are collected, no more are found. Fixed veins are those shaped like large tree branches in both depth and length, and where one of these is found there are usually many other veins nearby. The way the Indians refined and extracted the silver was by smelting, which means melting that mass of ore in a fire, a process that leaves the dross on one side and separates the silver from the lead and tin and copper and other mixtures that it has. For this purpose they used to make structures resembling small ovens in places where the wind blew strongly and performed the operation with firewood and charcoal. In Peru these were called *guairas.* Since the Spaniards' arrival (in addition to this kind of smelting, which is also still in use) silver is refined by the use of quicksilver, and even more silver is extracted with it than by the smelting method, for there is a kind of silver ore that is not extracted or removed by smelting but only with quicksilver, and this is usually low-grade ore, of which there exists a much larger amount.[2]

Ore is described as poor when it has little silver in a large quantity of ore and rich when it yields a great deal of silver. And it is a remarkable thing that not only is this difference found, that one kind of silver ore is smelted with fire and another not with fire but with quicksilver, but in the same ores that the fire extracts by smelting there are some that will not melt or become smelted if the fire is fed with artificial air, such as derives from bellows; it must be a natural wind that blows. And then there are ores that are smelted just as well or better with artificial air supplied by a bellows. The ore from the Porco mines is easily smelted and extracted with bellows; that of the mines of Potosí cannot be smelted with bellows, nor can it be extracted except with the air of *guairas,* which are those little ovens built on the sides of hills, exposed to natural wind, with which that ore is extracted. And, although it is hard to

---

2. Acosta offers a slight misrepresentation of silver refining in Potosí in the sixteenth century. The indigenous *guairas* (or *huayras*) were used from 1545 to the early 1570s, well past the Spaniards' arrival. When Spaniards discovered mercury in Huancavelica in 1564, it prompted a changeover from the indigenous method to the European amalgamation method. Whereas thousands of *huayras* dominated the refining industry in the early decades of Potosí mining, sources from late-sixteenth-century Potosí indicate that only hundreds of the clay ovens still kept their fires burning on the hillsides there. On the transition from indigenous to Spanish refining technology, see Bakewell, *Miners of the Red Mountain,* chap. 1.

explain such diversity, it is proved by long experience. Curiosity and greed have prompted the discovery of any number of properties of this metal that men love so much, some of which we will describe hereafter. The chief places in the Indies that supply silver are New Spain and Peru, but the mines of Peru are much richer, and among them the best in the world are the mines of Potosí, with which we will deal at some length, for they are among the most famous and notable things that exist in the West Indies.[3]

## CHAPTER 6 * OF THE MOUNTAIN OF POTOSÍ AND ITS DISCOVERY

The famous mountain of Potosí is located in the province of Los Charcas, in the kingdom of Peru; it is twenty-one and two-thirds degrees distant from the southern or Antarctic Pole, so that it lies within the Tropics near the edge of the Torrid Zone.[1] And yet it is extremely cold, more than Old Castile and more than Flanders, although it ought to be warm or hot considering the distance from the pole at which it lies. What makes it cold is that it is so high and steep and all bathed in very cold and intemperate winds, especially the one they call *tomahaui* there, which is gusty and very cold and prevails in May, June, July, and August. Its surroundings are dry, cold, and very bleak and completely barren, for it neither engenders nor produces fruit or grain or grass and thus is by nature uninhabitable owing to the unfavorable weather and the great barrenness of the earth.

3. The major silver mines in the New World were at Potosí in Peru and Zacatecas and Guanajuato in Mexico. For essays on production and labor in these and smaller mines see the collection edited by Peter Bakewell, *Mines of Silver and Gold in the Americas* (Brookfield, VT: Variorum, 1997). Important monographs on colonial mining include, for Mexico, Peter Bakewell, *Silver Mining and Society in Colonial Mexico: Zacatecas, 1546–1700* (Cambridge: Cambridge University Press, 1971); and David Brading, *Miners and Merchants in Bourbon Mexico, 1763–1810* (New York: Cambridge University Press, 1971). For the Andes, see Enrique Tandeter, *Coercion and Market: Silver Mining in Colonial Potosí, 1692–1826* (Albuquerque: University of New Mexico Press, 1993); and Ann Zulawski, *They Eat From Their Labor: Work and Social Change in Colonial Bolivia* (Pittsburgh: University of Pittsburgh Press, 1995).

1. Acosta was not the first historian of the Indies to discuss Potosí, a city known for its silver wealth throughout the sixteenth-century world, but given his two visits to the city, one in the company of Viceroy Toledo, he contributed a higher degree of familiarity with the town and its mining operations. The most comprehensive *historia* of Potosí, combining elements of history and story, was written in the late colonial period by its native son Bartolomé Arzáns de Orsúa y Vela. Arzáns relied on documents about Potosí's mining industry along with local lore to write the massive, three-volume *Historia de la Villa Imperial de Potosí*, edited by Lewis Hanke and Gunnar Mendoza (Providence: Brown University Press, 1965).

But the power of silver, desire for which draws all other things to itself, has populated that mountain with the largest number of inhabitants in all those realms; and silver has made it so rich in every sort of foodstuff and luxury that nothing can be desired that is not found there in abundance. And, although everything has to be brought in by wagon, its marketplaces are full of fruit, preserves, luxuries, marvelous wines, silks, and adornments, as much as in any other place. The color of this mountain is a sort of dark red; it is very beautiful to look upon, resembling a well-shaped tent in the form of a sugar-loaf. It rises above and dominates all the other mountains in its vicinity. To climb it is difficult even on horseback. It terminates in a round peak, its slopes measure a league in circumference, and from the peak of this mountain to its foot and base there are 1,624 yards of common measure, which, reduced to the measure and reckoning of Spanish leagues, is a quarter of a league. On the lower slope of this mountain is another, smaller one, which rises from it. It formerly had a few mines of scattered ore that was found in little pockets, so to speak, and not in lodes; these were not numerous but were very rich. It is called Guainapotosí, which means "Potosí the Younger." On the slopes of this little mountain begins the town inhabited by Spaniards and Indians attracted by the riches and workings of Potosí. This town has a circumference of two leagues; it contains the largest population, and the most commerce, in all of Peru.

The mines of this mountain were not worked during the time of the Incas, who were lords of Peru before the Spaniards came, although they did work the mines of Porco six leagues away. The reason must have been that they did not know of them, although others tell some sort of tale that they tried to operate those mines and heard certain voices telling them not to touch anything there, that the mountain was reserved for others. Indeed, until twelve years after the Spaniards entered Peru nothing was known of Potosí and its riches.

It was discovered in the following manner: an Indian named Hualpa, of the Chumbibilca tribe near Cuzco, was on the western side of the mountain pursuing some deer, which kept climbing up the mountain; and because it is so steep and was at that time largely covered with a kind of tree that they call *quinua,* and also by many brambles, in order to climb a particularly steep place he caught hold of a branch that was rooted in the lode that acquired the name of La Rica, or Rich Lode. And, because of his experience in the mines of Porco, in the root and the space that it left he recognized the ore as very rich. He found on the ground near the lode some chunks of ore that had fallen away from it and were not easily recognizable because their color had been affected by the sun and water, and he took them to Porco to be tested by fire in an oven. When he saw how extremely rich it was, he worked the lode secretly without telling anyone until an Indian named Huanca, a native of the Jauja Valley, which is within the district of Ciudad de los Reyes, and who was a neighbor in Porco of the Indian Hualpa, a Chumbibilca, saw that he was taking from the smelting that he performed larger ingots than those usually extracted from the ores of that place, and that he was wearing better clothing, for until then he had lived very modestly. Having observed this and seen that the ore his neighbor was working was different from that of Porco, he was led to investigate the secret; and, although the other Indian tried to hide it, he importuned him so earnestly that Hualpa had to take him to the mountain of Potosí thereby ending a month during which time he alone had enjoyed that treasure. There Hualpa told Huanca to take for himself a lode that he had also discovered, which was near the Rich Lode, and this is the one that today is called the lode of Diego Centeno, which was no less rich but harder to mine. And by this agreement they divided between them the richest mountain in the world. It later happened that Huanca had some difficulty in mining his lode, which was very hard, and because Hualpa did not want to give him part of his they fell out with one another; and hence, because of this and other differences of opinion, Huanca, the Indian from Jauja, became angry and informed his master about the matter. He was a Spaniard named Villaroel who resided in Porco. Villaroel, wishing to satisfy himself as to the truth of the matter, went to Potosí, and, finding the wealth that his *yanacona,* or servant, had told him about, had it adjudicated to Huanca, staking a claim along with him in the lode called Centeno.[2] "Staking a claim" means claiming

2. Acosta defines *yanacona* as "servant," collapsing the complex identity of the pre-Hispanic *yanacona* into a one-dimensional Spanish classification. Under Inca rule, *yanaconas* were servants of the Inca king and as such did not retain identity in native kin groups, called *ayllus*. In the wake of Spanish conquest, *yanaconas* sometimes allied themselves with Spanish leaders and worked for them in a variety of capacities. The relationship between the Spaniards and the *yanaconas* operated, in theory, on the basis of loyalty, and to reward their loyalty the *yanaconas* were exempt from tribute payments and enjoyed an elevated social status vis à vis other indigenous servants in the colonial period. It is not clear whether Huanca had official *yanacona* status or if Acosta used the term in a general fashion. Nonetheless, the tale of Huanca's disclosure of the silver secret to his master, Villaroel, rather than to his kin, and Villaroel's subsequent reward to the loyal Huanca, fits within the stereotype of *yanaconas* under Spanish rule.

for oneself the space between the measurements that the law allows to those who find or work a mine. This action, and establishing the claim in a court of law, makes the claimant owner of the mine to work it as his own, paying the royal fifth to the king.

To be brief, the first registration and public knowledge of the mines of Potosí was made in the town of Porco on the twenty-first day of April in the year fifteen hundred and forty-five by these two men, Villaroel the Spaniard and Huanca the Indian. A few days later another lode was discovered, called the Tin Lode, which is very rich, though extremely hard to work, for its ore is as hard as stone. Then, on the thirty-first of August in the same year of fifteen hundred and forty-five, the lode called Mendieta was registered, and these four are the four chief lodes in Potosí. Of the Rich Lode, which was the first to be discovered, they say that the ore stuck out of the ground to the height of a lance, in the form of crags raised like a crest above the surface of the earth, and that it was three hundred feet long and thirteen wide; it is believed that it was left uncovered and bare at the time of the Flood, resisting the surge and force of the water because it was made of hard metal. And the ore was so rich that half of it was silver, and its richness continued to a depth of fifty and sixty *estados* when it ran out.

This is the way in which Potosí was discovered, Divine Providence decreeing, for the good of Spain, that the greatest treasure known to exist in the world was hidden and came to light at the time when the Emperor Charles V, of glorious name, held the reins of empire and the realm of Spain and seigniory of the Indies. Once the discovery of Potosí became known in the kingdom of Peru many Spaniards went there, along with most of the citizens of the city of La Plata, which is eighteen leagues from Potosí, to establish mining claims; a large number of Indians also came from different provinces, especially those who owned smelting ovens in Porco, and in a short time it became the largest town in the realm.

CHAPTER 7 * OF THE WEALTH THAT HAS BEEN
TAKEN, AND IS STILL BEING TAKEN DAILY,
FROM THE MOUNTAIN OF POTOSÍ

I have often asked myself whether, in the histories and accounts of the ancients, there has ever existed such mining wealth as we have seen in Peru in our time. If there were ever rich mines in the world, and famed for their riches, they were those that the Carthaginians and later the Romans had in Spain, which, as I have said, are described as marvels in both sacred and profane writings. The author I have read who most especially mentions these mines is Pliny, who writes as follows in his *Natural History:*

> Silver is found in almost all the provinces, but the finest is in Spain. This metal too is found in barren land, and in crags and mountains, and wherever one vein of silver is found another is bound to be discovered not far away; almost the same thing happens with the other metals, and accounts, it seems, for the word for metals used by the Greeks. It is a remarkable fact that the shafts that began to be worked in Hannibal's time still exist in Spain today, and still retain the names of the men who discovered them, among them a famous one which still bears the name of its discoverer, Baebelo. So much wealth was taken from this mine that it furnished to its owner, Hannibal, three hundred pounds of silver a day, and the mine has been worked up to the present time. The mine has been excavated deep in the mountain for a distance of fifteen hundred paces, and along this whole distance the Gascons pump out the water in the time and to the extent that their candles last, and pump so much water that it makes a river.[1]

All of these are Pliny's words, which I have chosen to reproduce here because they will please those who know something about mines when they see that the ancients had the same experiences as they have today. Especially notable is the richness of that mine of Hannibal's in the Pyrenees, which the Romans took over and continued to work until Pliny's time, a span of three hundred years; its depth was fifteen hundred paces, which is a mile and a half.[2] In the beginning it was so rich that its owner daily received three hundred pounds consisting of twelve ounces each; but, although this was very great wealth, I believe that it does not equal the wealth of our day in Potosí.

For, as appears from the royal books of the House of Trade of that place and is affirmed by old men worthy of belief, at the time when the Licentiate Polo was in charge, which was a good many years after the discovery of the mountain, every Saturday they set aside 150,000 to 200,000 pesos, and the royal fifths were worth 30,000 and 40,000 pesos weekly and half a million

---

1. Pliny, *Natural History,* 33, 6 (O'G).
2. Gilberto Genebrardo, *Chronographiae,* book 4 (O'G).

pesos yearly, more or less.[3] So according to this calculation a matter of 30,000 pesos was extracted daily, and the king's fifth was worth 6,000 pesos a day. One more thing must be stated about the wealth of Potosí, and this is that the calculation I have made is only the silver that was stamped and set aside for the royal fifth. It is very well known in Peru that for a long time the silver called "ordinary" was used, which was not stamped or set aside, and the conclusion of those who know a great deal about the mines is that at that time a very large proportion of the silver that was taken out of Potosí never had the royal fifth set aside. This was the silver that circulated among the Indians and much of the Spaniards' silver, a practice that, as I saw, lasted until my time.[4] Thus we may well believe that a third, if not half, of the wealth of Potosí was not recognized or set aside for the royal fifth.

There is another, even greater factor: Pliny says that the Baebelo Lode was worked to a depth of fifteen hundred paces, and that for all that distance they had to pump out water which is the greatest obstacle to taking silver out of mines. The mines of Potosí, although many of them are deeper than two hundred *estados,* have never reached water, which is the most fortunate fact about that mountain; for the mines of Porco, whose ore is very rich, are no longer being worked and smelted because of the problem of water. Breaking rocks and encountering water are the two most intolerable conditions when seeking ore; even the first of them is trouble enough and to spare.

Finally, today his Catholic Majesty receives, year after year, a million pesos simply from the royal fifths of silver that come from the mountain of Potosí, not counting further wealth from quicksilver and other prerogatives of the Royal Treasury, which constitutes another great treasure. Experts make the calculation and say that everything that has been subjected to the royal fifth in

---

3. The House of Trade, or Casa de Contratación, in Seville was the hub for the New World administration of Spain. The royal fifth, the Crown's profit on all silver and gold mined in the Indies, arrived at the House of Trade, where Crown officials registered the income. Licentiate Juan Polo de Ondegardo oversaw the division of Potosí silver in his capacity as the *corregidor* of Potosí and La Plata in the 1550s. On the royal incomes from Potosí, see volume 1 of John J. TePaske and Herbert S. Klein, *The Royal Treasuries of the Spanish Empire in America,* 4 vols. (Durham: Duke University Press, 1982–90).

4. The trade in "ordinary" silver was widespread among all sectors of the population in Potosí. The practice of *kapcha,* a tradition whereby indigenous mine workers could mine on Sundays for their own benefit, fueled a market of unminted silver that was traded on the streets of Potosí within shouting distance of the royal mint. Historians will never know with certainty how much silver went unrecorded in Spanish account books. On *kapcha,* see the institutional history of the *mita* by Jeffrey A. Cole, *The Potosí Mita, 1573–1700: Compulsory Indian Labor in the Andes* (Stanford: Stanford University Press, 1985), esp. 14.

the customs house of Potosí, even though the books of the first separations are not presented as accurately as they are today, for in the early years the weighing was done with a steelyard, such was the abundance of silver. But, by means of the instructions and calculations made by the viceroy Don Francisco de Toledo in the year fifteen hundred and seventy-four, it was found that up to that year there were 76 million pesos, and, from that year to fifteen hundred and eighty-five inclusive, it appears from the royal registers that 35 million pesos were registered. So, adding what was registered up to the year fifteen hundred and eighty-five, 111 million pesos were assayed, and each peso was worth 13 reales and 1 cuartillo. And this is not counting the silver that remained unregistered, or was registered in other royal customs houses, and not counting what has been spent in ordinary silver and the silver still not registered, which is an incalculable amount. This accounting was sent from Potosí to the viceroy in the year that I mentioned, when I was in Peru, and from that time to this the wealth that has come from Peru in the fleets has been still greater.[5] For in the fleet in which I traveled in fifteen hundred and eighty-seven, 11 million pesos came from Peru and Mexico in the two fleets; almost half was the king's share, and two-thirds of that was from Peru.

I have made this calculation especially so that my readers may understand how great is the power that Divine Majesty has graciously placed in the hands of the kings of Spain, heaping so many crowns and realms upon them that through Heaven's special favor the East and West Indies have been joined, circling the world with their power. We must believe that this has occurred through the special providence of our God, for the good of those people who live so far distant from their head, who is the pope of Rome, vicar of Christ Our Lord, and also for the defense of the Catholic Faith itself and the Roman Church in these parts, where the truth is so much resisted and persecuted by heretics. And, since this is ordained by the Lord on high, who both gives and takes away kingdoms to whomever he wishes and as he wishes, we must humbly petition him to graciously favor the pious zeal of the Catholic king, granting him good fortune and victory over the enemies of his Holy Faith, for it is in this cause that he pours out the treasure of the Indies that God has

5. Acosta lived in Peru during the boom years of Potosí silver production. Encouraged by new technology, access to mercury in Huancavelica, and the *mita* system of forced labor, the production rose from the 1570s through the 1590s. When Potosí's production declined in the seventeenth century, and continued to decline until approximately 1730, Mexico began to register higher silver production than Peru.

given him and requires even more. But let it suffice that I have made use of the riches of Potosí to make this digression, and now let us return to how the mines are worked and how the ores taken from them are refined.

CHAPTER 8 * HOW THE MINES OF
POTOSÍ ARE WORKED

It was well said by Boethius, when he complained of the first inventor of mines,

> Heu primus quis fuit ille
> Auri qui pondera tecti
> Gemmasque latere volentes
> Pretiosa pericula fodit.[1]

He rightly calls them "precious perils," for it is with very great labor and peril that these metals so greatly desired by men are extracted. Pliny says that in Italy there are many metals but that in order to save lives the ancients did not utilize them.[2] They brought ores from Spain and made the Spaniards work the mines as tributaries. Spain now does the same with the Indies, for, although there is surely much mineral wealth left in Spain they do not seek it nor even allow it to be worked, owing to the difficulties they perceive; and they bring great wealth from the Indies, where to seek and extract it costs no little labor and even considerable risk.

As I have said, the mountain of Potosí has four chief lodes, namely, the Rich, Centeno, Tin, and Mendieta. All of these lodes are located on the eastern side of the mountain, as if facing toward the sunrise; none is on the western side. These lodes run from north to south, that is, as from pole to pole. At their widest part they measure six feet, at the narrowest a handbreadth. There are other veins that branch off from these, just as, in trees, small branches commonly grow out of large ones.

Each lode has different mines that form part of it, and these have been taken over and divided among various owners, whose names they usually bear. The largest mine is 80 yards long and cannot be longer by law; the smallest is four yards. Today all of these mines are very deep. There are

---

1. Boethius, *De Consolatione Philosophiae* (O'G).
2. Pliny, *Natural History,* 33, 4 (O'G).

seventy-eight mines in the lode called Rich; in some places they are 180 *estados* deep, and even 200. There are twenty-four mines in the Centeno lode. Some are 60 and even 80 *estados* deep, and other mines and lodes in that mountain are comparable. To compensate for this great depth of the mines, the so-called *socavones,* or galleries, were devised; these are caves that are excavated from below through one side of the mountain, piercing it in order to reach the lodes. For it must be understood that the lodes, although they run from north to south, as I have said, do so by descending from the top to the slopes and base of the mountain, and it is believed by some who have calculated the distance that they are more than 1,200 *estados* long. And by this calculation, although the mines are so deep, they are six times removed from the roots and bottom of the lodes, which they say must be extremely rich, for they are like the trunk and origin of all the lodes. However, up to this time experience has proved the opposite, for the higher the lode the richer it is, and as it descends its ore is poorer.

The galleries were devised to work the mines more cheaply, and with less effort and risk, and the miners enter and leave the mines through them. These are 8 feet wide and more than 6 feet high, with doors to close them off; the ore is taken out through them with great ease, and a fifth of all the ore removed from each gallery is paid to the owner. There are nine of these galleries, and others are being constructed. One gallery, known as El Venino, which has access to the Rich Lode, took twenty-nine years to build, for it was begun in the year fifteen hundred and fifty-six, eleven years after the discovery of those mines, and finished on the eleventh of April, fifteen hundred and eighty-five. This gallery reached the Rich Lode at a distance of 35 *estados* from its mouth to the end, and there is a distance of another 135 *estados* from where it joins the lode to the top of the mine, and the miners had to descend all this distance to work those mines. This gallery measures 250 yards from its mouth to the lode (which is called The Crossing), and twenty-nine years were required, as I have said, to complete the construction.

This shows how much effort men will expend to seek silver in the bowels of the earth. And yet they work there in perpetual darkness, with no idea of when it is day or night; and as these are places never visited by the sun, not only is there perpetual darkness but it is also extremely cold, with a very heavy atmosphere unfit for man's nature; and so it happens that those who enter the mine for the first time feel weak and dizzy, as happened to me, experiencing nausea and cramps in the stomach.

The miners always work by candlelight, dividing their labor in such a way that some work by day and rest at night, and others work at night and rest by day. The ore is usually very hard and is loosened by blows of a mattock, which is like breaking stone. Then they carry the ore on their backs up ladders made of three strands of leather plaited into thick ropes, with sticks placed between one strand and another as steps, so that one man can be descending while another is climbing. These ladders are 60 feet long, and at the end of each is another ladder of the same length, which starts from a ledge or shelf where there are wooden landings resembling scaffolding, for there are many ladders to climb. Each man has a fifty-pound load in a blanket tied over his breast, with the ore it contains at his back; three men make the climb at one time. The first carries a candle tied to his thumb so that they can see, for, as I have said, no daylight comes from above. They climb by catching hold with both hands, and in this way ascend the great distances I have described, often more than 150 *estados,* a horrible thing about which it is frightening even to think.

Such is the power of money, for the sake of which men do and suffer so much.[3] Not without reason does Pliny exclaim, when discussing this, "We penetrate the inner parts of the earth and seek riches even in the place of the damned."[4] And then, in the same book, he writes, "Outdoing the achievement of giants is the work performed by those who extract ores, making holes and galleries deep in the earth, excavating mountains for such great distances by the light of lamps, where night and day are the same and where they do not see daylight for many months, where sometimes the walls of the mine suddenly give way and kill the miners in an instant." And a little later he adds, "They attack the hard rock with machines containing a hundred and fifty pounds of iron; they take the ore out on their backs, working night and day, each passing on his load to the next man in the dark, for only those at the end of the line see the light. With iron wedges and with machines they break the stones and rocks, no matter how strong and hard they may be, for indeed

3. Acosta does not identify the men who "suffer so much" in Potosí. This omission is striking because Acosta traveled to Potosí with Toledo when the viceroy set up the crown's *mita* program, an infamous forced labor draft under which thousands of indigenous men worked in the Potosí mines. Wage laborers worked the silver mines alongside compulsory *mita* laborers, according to Peter Bakewell (*Miners of the Red Mountain*). While Acosta recognized the suffering that went into extracting the silver, he did not acknowledge the injustice of the Spanish colonial apparatus whereby the men rewarded with the silver were not the same men who sweated to unearth it. Instead, Acosta recalls a time in Spain's history when the Spaniards mined for the Romans, and he reasons that, in turn, the native Andeans now mine for the Spaniards in Potosí.
4. Pliny, *Natural History,* preface to book 33 (O'G).

the hunger for money is still stronger and harder."[5] This quotation is from Pliny, who, although he was a historian of olden times speaks like a prophet of today. And Phocion of Agatharchides recounts no less when he tells of the immense labor of those men called Chrysians when they extracted and smelted gold, for always, as this author says, the more effort the acquisition of gold and silver requires the greater the satisfaction once acquired.

### CHAPTER 9 * HOW SILVER ORE IS REFINED

The vein in which the silver is found, as we have said, usually runs between two layers of rock that are called "the box," and one of them is usually as hard as flint, the other soft and easier to break. The ore is between them and is not all alike or of equal value, for within the vein itself there is a very rich kind, which they call *cacilla* or *tacana,* from which a great deal of silver is extracted; there is another, poor kind, from which little can be taken. The richest ore of this lode is the color of amber, and there is another that is blacker; there is another of a reddish color, and still another resembles ashes. Indeed, the ore has many colors, and to the person who does not know what it is all of it looks like the ordinary rocks in the vicinity. But the miners recognize its grade of excellence by marks on it and little veins and certain other signs. All this ore taken out of the mines is carried on the backs of the Peruvian sheep that serve as pack animals and is taken to the mills. The richest ore is refined in those little wind ovens called *guairas;* this is the ore that contains the most lead, and the lead causes it to melt. To make it melt better the Indians throw in what they call *soroche,* which is an ore resembling lead. When subjected to fire the dross falls below, the lead and silver melt, and the silver floats on top of the lead until it is skimmed off; then they refine the silver many more times.

From one hundredweight of ore, 30 or 40 or even 50 pesos' worth of silver can be extracted by smelting. As a sample, they showed me ores that had produced by smelting more than 200 and even 250 pesos per hundredweight, a very rare degree of richness and almost unbelievable if I had not seen the proof of it by fire. A poor grade of ore gives 2 or 3 pesos, or 5 or 6, or not much more, per hundredweight; ordinarily this ore does not contain lead but is dry and thus cannot be smelted by the use of fire. Hence for a long time a very large amount of these poor ores existed in Potosí, which were cast aside and considered to be the dross of the good ores until the method of extract-

5. Ibid., 33, 4 (O'G).

ing silver with quicksilver came into use. This meant that those piles of slag, as they were called, turned out to be immensely rich, for it is the strange and wonderful property of quicksilver to refine the silver and serve for these poor, dry ores; and less quicksilver is expended and consumed in them than with rich ores, for the richer they are the more quicksilver they ordinarily consume.

Today most refining of silver, and nearly all of it in Potosí, is done with quicksilver, as is also true of the mines of Zacatecas and others in New Spain. There used to be more than six thousand *guairas* on the slopes of Potosí and on the peaks and hills; these are the little wind ovens where the ore is smelted. They were placed like illuminations, and it was a pretty sight to see them burning at night and casting their light so far, each of them like a red coal of fire. Now I doubt whether there are more than one or two thousand of them, for as I have said they give little result and smelting by quicksilver is much more profitable. And because the properties of quicksilver are admirable, and the method of refining silver by their use is so interesting, I shall discuss what is useful for my purpose with regard to quicksilver and its mines and action.

## CHAPTER 10 * OF THE WONDERFUL PROPERTIES OF QUICKSILVER

Mercury, whose other name is *argen vivo,* or quicksilver, as it is called in Latin, because it appears to be alive in the way it bubbles and slides quickly from one side to another, has great and wonderful properties among all other metals. The first is that, although it is a metal, it is not hard, nor does it have a shape and hold together like the other metals but is a liquid and runs, unlike silver and gold, which once melted by fire are liquid and run, and does so out of its own nature; even though it is a liquid it is heavier than any other metal, and so the other metals float on the quicksilver and do not sink because they are lighter. I have seen two pounds of iron cast into a barrel of quicksilver and have seen the iron floating on it without sinking, like a stick or cork floating on water. Pliny makes an exception, saying that only gold sinks and does not float on quicksilver; I have not seen this with my own eyes, and perhaps this is because the quicksilver naturally surrounds gold and hides it within itself.[1] This is its most important property, that with remarkable persistence it clings to gold and seeks it out and goes to wherever it senses that gold is. Not only

1. Ibid., 33, 6 (O'G).

this, but it joins with gold and draws it to itself and strips and detaches it from any other metals or bodies with which it is mixed.

Therefore, those who wish to protect themselves from mercury poisoning take gold. The remedy for men who have had quicksilver poured into their ears, in order to murder them secretly, has been to place a little wand of gold in the ear, to which the quicksilver is attracted; then it is taken out, white from the mercury that has stuck to the gold. In Madrid, when I went to see the remarkable works of art that Jacomé de Trezo, a superb Milanese crafts-man, was creating for San Lorenzo el Real, it happened to be a day on which they were gilding some parts of the *reredos* made of bronze, which is done with quicksilver; and, because the vapor of quicksilver is deadly, they told me that the workmen guarded against this poison by swallowing a gold dou-bloon broken into tiny pieces, which after it had passed into the stomach attracted any quicksilver that might have entered their bodies through the ears or eyes or nose or mouth in the form of that deadly vapor; and by this means they protected themselves from the harm done by quicksilver, for all the gold that was in the stomach attracted it, after which it left the body by the natural route. Certainly this is something worthy of astonishment, that after quicksilver has cleaned the gold and purged it of all other metals and mixtures it is also separated from its friend the gold by fire and thus leaves it completely pure.

Pliny says that there was a certain art for separating gold from quicksilver; I do not know whether that art is used nowadays.[2] I believe that the ancients did not discover the process by which silver is refined with the use of quick-silver, which today is its chief use and greatest advantage, for he expressly says that only gold attracts it, and in the passage where he speaks of the method of refining silver he makes mention only of smelting. Thus we may infer that the ancients did not possess this secret. Indeed, although the chief attraction of quicksilver is to gold, when there is no gold it goes to silver and possesses it, though not as quickly as it does gold, and as with gold it cleans the silver and strips it of the earth and copper and lead with which it occurs without the need of fire, which refines metals by smelting them, although fire also has a part in separating and detaching the silver from the quicksilver, as I shall describe later.

2. Ibid. (o'g).

Quicksilver does not have the same effect on metals other than silver and gold; rather, it eats them away and wears them down and makes holes in them, and withdraws and flees from them, which is also a remarkable thing and is the reason why they place it in clay vessels or animal hides, for it soaks into vessels made of copper or iron or any other metal and goes right through them; and it penetrates and corrodes all other materials, which is the reason why Pliny called it the poison of all things and says that it eats away and corrodes everything. Quicksilver is found in the tombs of dead men, and after it has consumed the bodies it emerges unscathed, in its original form. It has also been found in the pith and marrow of men or animals because, after they have received its vapor through their mouths or nostrils, it congeals inside them and penetrates the very bones. This is the reason why any close contact with such a perilous and deadly thing is so dangerous, for another property that it has is to bubble and break into a hundred thousand little globules, and not one of them is lost no matter how small, for in one way or another quicksilver joins into liquid form again. And it is almost incorruptible, and almost nothing can exhaust it, which is why the aforementioned Pliny called it "eternal sweat."

It has another property, which is that, although quicksilver is the metal that draws gold out of copper and other metals, when men want to combine gold with copper or bronze or silver — that is, to gild them — the agent of this combination is quicksilver, for these metals are gilded through its use. Among all the wonders of this strange liquid, for me the one most worthy of consideration is that, although it is the heaviest thing in the world, it instantly turns into the lightest thing in the world, which is vapor, and rises straight up. And then that very vapor, which is a thing so light in weight, immediately becomes as heavy as the liquid mercury into which it turns, for when the vapor of that metal strikes some hard body above it, or reaches a cold atmosphere, it immediately takes shape and again falls in the form of quicksilver; and if the quicksilver is again subjected to fire it turns into vapor, and from the vapor it falls again in the form of liquid quicksilver. Surely the cases in nature of such immediate transmutation of so heavy a thing into one so light, and vice versa, must be very rare. And in all these and other strange properties that this metal possesses, the Author of its nature is justly to be glorified, because all created nature so quickly obeys his hidden laws.

CHAPTER II  *  WHERE QUICKSILVER IS FOUND
AND HOW RICH MINES OF IT WERE
DISCOVERED IN HUANCAVELICA

Quicksilver is found in a kind of stone that also yields cinnabar or vermilion, which the ancients called *minium;* and today this name is used to describe the images that are painted on glass with quicksilver. This *minium,* or vermilion, was held in great esteem by the ancients, for they believed it to be a sacred color, as Pliny relates, and so he says that the Romans used to paint Jupiter's face with it, as well as the bodies of those who received triumphs, and that in Ethiopia the governors painted their own faces as well as those of their idols with it, and that vermilion (which came only from Spain, where there were many quicksilver pits and mines, in existence even today) was so greatly esteemed in Rome that the Romans did not allow that metal to be refined in Spain to prevent any of it from being stolen; but it was sent just as it came from the mine and shipped to Rome, and was refined there.[1] And some ten thousand pounds of it were sent from Spain annually, especially from Andalusia, and the Romans believed this to be very great wealth. I have recounted all this from the above-mentioned author because I believe that those who observe what is happening in Peru today will be pleased to know what happened in ancient times to the most powerful men on earth.

I say this because the Incas, the monarchs of Peru, and the Indians who are natives of the place worked the mercury mines for a long time without knowledge or experience of quicksilver, nor to seek anything but this cinnabar or vermilion, which they call *llimpi.* They prized it greatly for the same reason that Pliny tells us the Romans and Ethiopians did, which was to paint or dye their faces and bodies, and those of their idols, with it; the Indians used it a great deal, especially when they went to war, and today they use it when they hold certain festivals or dances, and they call it "smearing themselves," because they thought that faces painted in this way caused terror, and nowadays they believe that it is very ornamental. Hence, in the hills of Huancavelica in Peru, near the city of Huamanga, they had some strange workings of mines where they extracted this ore, and they are of such a kind that to this day, if men go into the caves or galleries that the Indians made, they become

1. Ibid., 33, 7 (O'G).

lost and cannot find their way out. But they paid no attention to the quick-silver, which is found naturally in that substance or ore of vermilion, nor did they even know that there was such a thing in the world.

And not only Indians but even Spaniards were unaware of those riches for some time, until, during the period when the Licentiate Castro was govern-ing Peru in the years fifteen hundred and sixty-six and fifteen hundred and sixty-seven, the quicksilver mines were discovered in the following manner: some of the red ore that, as I have said, the Indians called *llimpi,* and with which they painted their faces, came into the hands of an intelligent man named Enrique Garcés, a Portuguese by birth; and when he looked at it he realized that it was of the kind called vermilion in Castile. And since he knew that vermilion is extracted from the same ore as quicksilver he guessed that those mines must be quicksilver mines. He went there and made some tests and assays and found that it was true. And after the mines of Palcas were discovered, in the district of Huamanga, many people went to mine the quicksilver in order to take it to Mexico, where silver was refined by the use of quicksilver, and no few of them became rich thereby. And the mining camp called Huancavelica quickly filled with Spaniards and Indians who went there, and still go there today, to work in those quicksilver mines, which are many and prosperous.[2]

Among them the most famous is the one named for Amador de Cabrera, also called the Mine of the Saints, which is a very rugged peak saturated with quicksilver. The mine is so large that it extends eighty yards in length and forty in width; and this whole area is excavated to a depth of seventy *estados,* and more than three hundred men can work in it at the same time owing to its large capacity. This mine was discovered by one of Amador de Cabrera's Indians named Navincopa, from the town of Acoria; Amador de Cabrera registered it in his own name, and the Indian brought suit with the treasury

2. Inca mining occurred at Huancavelica prior to the conquest, but the Inca mined for ore not mercury. The mining town, initially named Villa Rica de Oropesa, was founded in 1571, five years after the Spanish realized that they had located a source of mercury in the Americas. Viceroy Toledo provided *mita* labor for the Huancavelica mines because of the pressing need for mercury to process Potosí silver. Conditions proved to be so deadly in the mercury mines that the Huancavelica *mita* quickly became more infamous than the Potosí *mita.* The classic historical studies of the mercury mines are Arthur P. Whitaker, *The Huancavelica Mercury Mine: a Contribution to the History of the Bourbon Renaissance in the Spanish Empire* (Cambridge: Harvard University Press, 1941); and Guillermo Lohmann Villena, *Las minas de Huancavelica en los siglos XVI y XVII* (Seville: Escuela de Estudios Hispano-Americanos, 1949).

and by judicial decree was given the usufruct of it because he had been the discoverer. Later he sold it for 250,000 ducats, and, believing that he had been cheated in the sale, he again brought suit, for they say that it is worth more than 500,000 ducats, and many even believe that it is worth a million; it is a rare thing for a mine to be so rich.

At the time when Don Francisco de Toledo was viceroy in Peru, a man named Pedro Fernández de Velasco, who had been in Mexico and seen how silver was extracted with quicksilver, offered to refine the silver of Potosí with it; and after the test was made and had given good results, in fifteen hundred and seventy-one, silver began to be refined in Potosí with quicksilver brought from Huancavelica, and this was a complete success for those mines; for with quicksilver they could extract any amount of silver from the ore that had been wasted, which they called slag. For, as has been said, quicksilver extracts all the silver even though it be poor and of low grade, which is something that smelting by fire does not do.

The Catholic monarch draws from the workings of the quicksilver mines, without expense or any risk to himself, nearly four hundred thousand pesos, at a price of fourteen reales or a little less, not counting the subsequent profit from them by the refining done in Potosí, which is another very large sum. Year after year eight thousand hundredweight of quicksilver, and more, are taken from these mines of Huancavelica.

CHAPTER 12 * HOW QUICKSILVER IS
EXTRACTED AND HOW SILVER IS REFINED
WITH ITS USE

Let us now describe how quicksilver is extracted and how silver is refined with its use. The rock or ore where quicksilver is found is ground and placed in closed kettles over a fire, and when the ore is smelted or melted in them the quicksilver is expelled from it by the heat of the fire and emerges as a vapor along with the smoke of that fire. And commonly it rises to the point where it touches some solid body, where it stops and congeals; or if it goes higher without encountering some solid body it rises until it cools and there congeals and falls down again. When the smelting is finished they open the pots and take out the ore, which they try to do after the pots have cooled; for if any smoke or vapor reaches the persons who open the vessels they are poisoned and die or are left in very poor condition or lose their teeth.

And because large amounts of firewood are used in smelting these ores a miner named Rodrigo de Torres discovered a most useful fuel; it was to gather a sort of straw that grows on all those mountains in Peru, which is called *icho* there and resembles esparto grass, and they use it to feed the fires.[1] The capacity of this straw to smelt ore is wonderful to see and resembles what Pliny says about gold, that it is possible to smelt with fire from straw what cannot be smelted with great quantities of firewood.[2] The quicksilver thus obtained is placed in hides, for it keeps successfully in leather, and in this form it is placed in the king's storehouses and taken from there to Arica by sea and thence to Potosí, using droves of the Peruvian sheep as pack animals. From six to seven thousand hundredweight a year are used in refining the ore of Potosí, not counting what is extracted from the lees (the sediment and mud left over from the preliminary washing of ore, which is done in cauldrons). These sediments are burned and refined in kilns to extract the quicksilver that remains in them, and there must be fifty or more of these kilns in the town of Potosí and in Tarapaya.

Men of experience have estimated the quantity of ore that is smelted there to be three hundred thousand hundredweight a year, and more than two thousand hundredweight of quicksilver is extracted from the lees that are smelted. And it must be understood that the quality of these ores is variable, for sometimes a specific ore yields much silver and consumes little quicksilver and other ores give the opposite result, yielding little silver and much quicksilver; another sort will yield a great deal and consume a great deal, and another yield little and consume little. And according to how accurately these ores have been judged a man can earn little or much or can lose money in dealing with ore. Commonly, however, rich ore yields much silver and also consumes much quicksilver and poor ore does the opposite.

The ore is first ground very fine with the pestles of the mills, which strike the ore as with hammers, and after it has been ground fine they sift it through sieves made of wire mesh, making the powder as fine as in an ordinary

1. Given Acosta's tendency to exaggerate European knowledge and resourcefulness at the expense of indigenous tradition, it is worth noting that Rodrigo de Torres did not "discover" that *ichu* could be used as fuel. Andeans had been using it for centuries, along with llama dung, to fuel *huayra* refining.
2. Pliny, *Natural History,* 33, 4 (O'G).

horsehair sieve, and these sieves can sift out thirty hundredweight of ore in the course of a day and a night if they are well constructed and placed. After the powder is sifted it is put into furnaces, where it is treated with brine, adding five hundredweight of salt to each fifty hundredweight of powder; this is done so that the salt will cause the powder to separate from the mud or lees it contains and makes the quicksilver receive the silver more easily. Then they press out the quicksilver that lies on the ore with a coarse cloth, and it emerges in the form of a dew and they continue to stir the ore so that this quicksilver dew will mix with it completely.

Before the invention of furnaces the ore was kneaded with quicksilver many times and oft, in great troughs, and they made round balls like mud balls and left them for several days and kneaded them again and again until they knew that the quicksilver was thoroughly mixed into the silver. This took twenty days or more, and nine days at the very least. Later, because the desire for profit is a spur, it was discovered that fire was useful to shorten the time and caused the quicksilver to incorporate with the silver more quickly; and so they built furnaces with large receptacles in which the ore is placed with salt and quicksilver, and a slow fire is built in certain vaults made for the purpose, so that within the space of five or six days the quicksilver absorbs the silver. When they see that the quicksilver has done its work, which is to absorb all the silver whether it be much or little, leaving none of it behind, but, like water in a sponge, taking the silver into itself and separating it from the dirt and lead and copper that is found with it, they then uncover it and take it out and separate it from the quicksilver, which is done in the following manner: the ore is placed in barrels of water, where it is turned with paddles or waterwheels, turning the ore round and round as if dissolving it or making mustard. The dross or lees emerge in the water that runs away, and the silver and quicksilver, because they are heavier, settle on the bottom of the barrel. The ore that remains resembles sand, and they take it out and wash it again in large troughs or barrels of water, and there the rest of the dross is washed away, leaving the silver and quicksilver behind. However, some silver and quicksilver are always washed away, along with the dross and lees; these are called washings, and they also try to draw them out later and make use of them. When the silver and quicksilver are clean and begin to shine because the dross and earth have been removed, they take all of the ore and turn it out on a cloth, squeezing it very hard; and so all the quicksilver that is not incorporated into the silver runs out, and what is left is a ball of silver and quicksilver, just as the harder parts of almonds are left when they are pressed to make oil; and after the remaining ball is thoroughly pressed only a sixth of it is silver, and the other five-sixths is mercury. So that, if a sixty-pound ball is left, ten pounds of it are silver and fifty are of mercury.

Out of these balls they make pinecone shapes like sugarloaves, hollow inside and usually weighing a hundred pounds; then, to separate the silver from the mercury, they place them in a hot fire and cover them with an earthenware vessel made like the molds used for sugarloaves. These have the form of a hood, and they cover them with coal and light the fires. Then the quicksilver escapes in the form of vapor, and when it touches the clay hood it thickens and distills, like the steam of a covered pot, and all the quicksilver that is distilled is carried through a tube like an alembic and recovered, leaving only the silver, which is the same in form and size but is five parts less in weight. Rather, it is wrinkled and spongy, which is a remarkable thing to see; from two of these cones they make a bar of silver weighing seventy-five or seventy-six marks, and in this form it is taken to be assayed and stamped and the royal fifth deducted.

And the silver refined with quicksilver is so fine that it is never less than 2,380 in purity. And it is so excellent that the silversmiths have to reduce its purity by adding an alloy or mixture, and the same is done in the mints where it is worked and minted. Silver undergoes all these torments and sufferings (so to speak) in order to be pure; if we think about it, it is a shaped mass that is ground and sifted, and kneaded and leavened and cooked, and even in addition to this it is washed over and over and cooked and recooked, passing through mallets and sieves, kneading troughs and furnaces, barrels and pans, wringers and kilns, and finally through water and fire.

I say this because, having seen this process in Potosí, I thought of what Scripture says of just men, "colabit eos, et purgabit quasi argentum," he shall purify them, and refine them as silver.[3] And I thought of what it says elsewhere, "sicut argentum purgatum terrae, purgatum septuplum," as silver purged from the earth, refined seven times.[4] To purify silver, and refine it and cleanse it of the earth and clay where it occurs, they purge and purify it seven

3. Malachi, 3, 3; Ecclesiastes, 2, 8 (O'G).
4. Psalms, 11, 7 (O'G).

times, for indeed it is done seven times; that is, many and many times is silver tormented until it is left pure and fine. So it is with the Word of the Lord, and just so will the souls destined to partake of his divine purity be refined.

### CHAPTER 13 * OF THE MACHINERY FOR GRINDING ORE AND ASSAYING SILVER

To conclude this subject of silver and metals, two things remain to be said: one has to do with the machinery and mills and the other with assaying. I have already stated that the ore is ground to receive the quicksilver. This grinding is done with different types of machines, some that use horses to do the milling and others that are moved by water power, like water mills or flour mills, and there are a great many of both kinds. Because they usually depend on rainwater and there is not enough of it in Potosí except for two or three months of the year, which are December, January, and February, they have made lakes that measure seventeen hundred yards around and three *estados* deep; there are seven of them with their sluices, and when there is need for one of them they raise the sluice gates and a rush of water emerges, and they close them on holy days. When the lakes fill, and there is a year with abundant rain, the milling of the ore lasts for six or seven months, so men yearn for a good year of rain in Potosí because of silver, as in other places for bread.

There are other mills in Tarapaya, which is a valley three or four leagues from Potosí with a river running through it, and other mills in other places. There is this difference, that some mills have six mallets and others twelve and fourteen. The ore is ground in receptacles resembling mortars, where ore is added day and night, and the grindings from them are carried off to be sieved. There are forty-eight water mills on the banks of the stream that runs through Potosí, with eight and ten and twelve mallets; there are four others on the opposite side, which is called Tanacoñuño. In the valley of Tarapaya there are twenty-two mills, all of them water mills, and in addition to these there are thirty mills in Potosí that use horses, and some others outside Potosí, so great has been men's diligence and skill in refining silver, which in the end is assayed and tested by the assayers and experts whom the king has placed there to establish the purity of each piece.

The silver bars are taken to the assayer, who assigns a number to each, for the assay is made with a large number of pieces. He cuts a small amount from each one and weighs it accurately; then he puts it in a crucible, which is a little vessel made of ground and burnt bones. He places these vessels in order in the kiln or oven and subjects them to very great heat. All the metal melts; the part that is lead goes up in smoke, the copper or tin is dissolved, and the refined silver remains, red hot. It is a remarkable thing that when it is refined to this degree, even though it is in liquid form and melted, the silver does not spill out when the crucible or vessel is overturned, but stays inside it, and not a drop falls. The assayer knows when it is refined by its color and other signs; he takes the crucibles out of the furnace and again weighs each piece with great care and observes how much each has lost and how much of its weight is lacking, for the purest silver loses very little and that which is less pure a great deal. And so, judging by how much it has lost, he can see the degree of purity that the silver has, and he makes a note and marks it carefully on each bar.

The scale is so delicate, and the weights or grains so small, that they cannot be handled with the fingers but with pincers, and the weighing is done by candlelight so that no movement of air will cause the scale to move, for the price and value of a whole bar depends on those very small measurements. Indeed, it is a delicate job and requires great skill, which Divine Scripture also mentions in different places to indicate how God tests his chosen and to take note of the differences in the merits and worth of souls;[1] and especially does Jeremiah the prophet give God the title of an assayer,[2] so that he may know and declare the spiritual value of men and their works, which is the proper activity of the spirit of God, who weighs the souls of men.[3] And with this we have said enough on the subject of silver and ores and mines and will go on to the other subjects, those of plants and animals.

### CHAPTER 14 * OF EMERALDS

First it would be well to say something about emeralds, as much because they are prized equally with gold and silver, of which we have spoken, as because according to Pliny they also occur in mines of metals, and so it is not out of

1. Psalms, 65, 10; Proverbs, 17, 3; Proverbs, 27, 21 (O'G).
2. Jeremiah, 6, 27 (O'G).
3. Proverbs, 16, 2 (O'G).

place to deal with them here.[1] In ancient times the emerald was much esteemed, and, as the aforesaid writer says, it occupied third place among gems after the diamond and the pearl. Today neither the emerald nor the pearl is so highly thought of, owing to the abundance of both produced in the Indies; only the diamond has maintained its primacy, which no one can take away from it; after it come fine rubies and other stones that are prized more than emeralds. Men are attracted by singularity, and when they see that something has become common they do not value it. They tell a tale of a Spaniard in Italy who, soon after these gems were found in the Indies, showed an emerald to a lapidary and asked the price of it. The other, seeing that it was of excellent size and quality, told him a hundred *escudos;* the Spaniard showed him another, larger one, and he said three hundred. Delighted with his trade, the Spaniard took the lapidary to his house and showed him a large box full of emeralds; when he saw so many, the Italian said, "Sir, these are worth but one *escudo.* " This is what has happened both in the Indies and Spain, for such an abundance of these gems has been found that their value has declined. Pliny praises them highly and says that there is nothing more agreeable or satisfying to the eye, and he is right; but his opinion is of little importance when there are so many of them.[2] Lollia, a Roman lady of whom it is said that she spent four hundred thousand ducats on a headdress and gown embroidered with pearls and emeralds, could make two such nowadays for less than forty thousand ducats.[3]

Emeralds have been found in various parts of the Indies. The Mexican kings prized them, and some even pierced their nostrils and placed a fine emerald there. They also placed them on the countenances of their idols; but the place where they have been found, and are found today, in the greatest abundance is in the New Kingdom of Granada and also in Peru, near Manta and Puerto Viejo. In those parts there is an inland region known as the emerald region because it is reputed to have so many, although that land has not yet been conquered. Emeralds occur in rocks in the form of crystals, and I have seen them in the rock itself, where they form a sort of vein and apparently congeal there over the course of time and gradually become refined, for I saw some that were half white and half green; others were almost white and others

1. Pliny, *Natural History,* 37, 5 (O'G).
2. Ibid. (O'G).
3. Ibid., 9, 35 (O'G).

already green and perfect. I have seen some the size of a walnut, and larger ones exist as well, but I do not know whether any have been discovered in our time the size of the stone or gem that is in Genoa, which is rightly prized as a gem and not as a relic, for it is not certain that it is a relic, probably not.

But there is no comparison with the emerald of which Theophrastus tells. It was presented to the king of Egypt by the king of Babylon and was four cubits long and three wide. In the temple of Jupiter there was a needle made of four emeralds that was forty cubits long and four cubits wide in some places and in others two; and during his lifetime there was a pillar made of emerald in the temple of Hercules at Tyre. It may have been (as Pliny says) made of a green stone resembling emerald, and this is called "false emerald."[4] Some even say that certain pillars that stand in the cathedral church of Córdoba, from the time when it was a mosque of the Moorish Miramamolín kings who ruled in Córdoba, are made of emerald.

In the fleet in which I came from the Indies in fifteen hundred and eighty-seven, two boxes of emeralds were brought, each weighing at least a hundred pounds, which shows how abundant they are. Divine Scripture praises emeralds as a highly prized jewel, and places them among the precious stones that the High Priest wore on his breast, like those that adorn the walls of the heavenly Jerusalem.[5]

### CHAPTER 15 * OF PEARLS

Now that we are discussing the chief riches that are brought from the Indies we must not forget pearls, which the ancients called margarites, and which were so highly prized in ancient days that they were considered something that only royal personages could own. Today there is such an abundance of them that even black women wear strings of pearls.[1] They grow in oysters or sea shells, amid their flesh, and I have had the experience of eating an oyster

4. Ibid., 37, 5 (O'G).

5. Exodus, 29, 5; Exodus, 39, 10 and 11; Apocalypse, 21, 19 (O'G).

1. The idea that African women could afford to wear pearls sounded like hyperbole to a European audience, so Acosta explained the phenomenon as a matter of supply and demand: since pearls were so abundant in the Indies, even non-Spaniards wore them. Spanish colonials, for whom clothes and jewelry marked social and ethnic identity, objected to African women wearing any valuable clothing or accessories. Seventeenth-century sumptuary laws defined what clothing Africans could and could not wear and aimed to discourage Spanish men from presenting silks and jewels as gifts to African women.

and finding a pearl inside. The shells have the very bright colors of the sky inside them, and in some places they make spoons of these and say that they are made of mother of pearl.

Pearls vary greatly in size, shape, color, and smoothness, and so their price is very different, too. Some are called Avemarias because they resemble small rosary beads, others Paternosters because they are bigger. It is rare to find two that match in size, form, and color. That is why the Romans (as Pliny writes) called them *uniones*.[2] When two are found to be a perfect match their price rises very much, especially for earrings; I have seen some pairs that were valued at thousands of ducats, although they did not approach the value of Cleopatra's two pearls, which according to Pliny were each worth a hundred thousand ducats, with which that mad queen won the bet that she made with Mark Antony that she could consume more than a hundred thousand ducats in the course of a supper; for when the food had been eaten she tossed one of those pearls into strong vinegar, and when it had dissolved she drank it.[3] Of the other it is said that it was split in two and placed in the Pantheon of Rome, in the earrings of the statue of Venus. And they tell of that Claudius, son of the tragic actor Aesopus, who during a banquet gave each of his guests, among the other dishes, a valuable pearl dissolved in vinegar, to render the banquet sumptuous. These were follies of those times, and those of our day are no less, for in the Indies we have seen not only hats and sashes but women's boots and pattens thickly embroidered with pearls.

Pearls are obtained in different parts of the Indies; the place where they most abound is the Southern Sea near Panama, where islands are located that for this reason are called the Pearl Islands. But the best and most abundant are taken in the Northern Sea, near the river that is called the Hacha. There I learned how this crop is harvested, which involves much cost and labor on the part of the poor divers, who go down to depths of seven and nine and even twelve fathoms in search of oysters, which commonly adhere to rocks and crags in the sea. The divers pull them off and load themselves with them and then rise to the surface and toss them into their canoes, where they open them and extract the treasure that they contain. It is very cold there in the sea, and much greater is the effort of having to hold one's breath for a quarter of

2. Pliny, *Natural History*, 9, 35 (O'G).
3. Ibid. (O'G).

an hour at times, or even half an hour, when they are fishing. So that they can hold their breath longer, the poor divers are allowed to eat very little, and that little very dry, and they must be chaste; so greed also has its abstainers and chaste persons, even though it be against their will.

Pearls are worked in various ways, and are bored in order to make strings of them. There is great abundance of them everywhere. In fifteen hundred and eighty-seven I saw an item in a list of products coming from the Indies for the king, 18 marks' worth of pearls and three additional boxes of them, and for the use of individuals 1,264 marks' worth of pearls, not counting seven more bags waiting to be weighed, all of which would formerly have been considered a fabulous treasure.

### CHAPTER 16 * OF BREAD IN THE INDIES, AND MAIZE

In speaking of plants we will first discuss those that are most characteristic of the Indies and then those that are common both to those lands and Europe.[1] And because plants were grown chiefly to sustain man's life, and the chief food that sustains him is bread, we need to show what sort of bread there is in the Indies and what they use in place of bread. The word for bread is also used in their languages; in Peru it is called *tanta,* and in other places it is known by other names. But the quality and substance of the bread that the Indians possessed and used is very different from ours, for it has not been discovered that they had any sort of wheat or barley or millet or any of the other grains used for bread in Europe. Instead of this they used other grains and roots; the chief place among them all is rightly held by maize, which in Castile is called "Indies wheat" and in Italy "Turkish grain."

Just as wheat has been the ordinary grain in the ancient parts of the globe, which are Europe, Asia, and Africa, so in the regions of the New World it has been, and is, maize, which has been found in almost all the realms of the West Indies, in Peru, New Spain, the New Kingdom of Granada, Guatemala, Chile, and everywhere on the continent. I do not know whether in olden

1. Chapters 16 through 26 describe foods and plants native to the Indies. Acosta attempts to be a diplomatic guest at the American banquet, marveling, for example, at the variety of *ají.* In the end, however, he can find no "proper spices." Since most of his European audience came into contact with such foods only through his words, these chapters set up the disposition of his Old World audience toward New World foods.

times they used maize in the Windward Islands, which are Cuba, Hispaniola, Jamaica, and San Juan; today they make more use of yucca and cassava, of which I will speak shortly.

I believe that maize is not inferior to wheat in its strength and power of sustenance, but it is heavier and gives more heat and engenders blood; hence those who first eat it, if they overindulge, often suffer from bloating and the itch.[2] It grows on stalks, each of which bears one or two ears that contain the grains, and although the grains are large there are many of them, for we counted seven hundred grains on some of the ears. It is planted by hand and not scattered freely; it requires a hot and humid land. It grows very abundantly in many parts of the Indies; it is not rare to harvest three hundred bushels from one planting.

There are different kinds of maize just as there are different kinds of wheat: one kind is heavy and nourishing, another small and dry and called *moroche;* maize leaves and its green stalks make excellent fodder for horses and mules and even in dry form serve as straw. The grains themselves are better food for horses and mules than barley, and it is common in those parts to water the animals before they give them corn to eat; for if they drink on top of the corn they will swell up and have cramps, as is also the case with wheat.

The Indians' bread is maize, which they usually eat boiled in the grain and hot, and they call this *mote;* the Chinese and Japanese also eat rice boiled, along with its hot water. Sometimes maize is eaten roasted; there is a round, thick maize like that found in the Lucanas that Spaniards eat roasted as a treat, and it tastes better than roasted chickpeas. A more elaborate way of eating it is to grind the maize and make a dough from the flour and from the flour make little cakes that are placed on the fire and are then set on the table hot and eaten; in some places these are called *arepas.* They also make round buns out of the same dough and by seasoning them in a particular way make them last, and these are eaten as a treat. And, to show that there is no lack of ingenuity in New World cookery, they have also contrived to make a kind of pastry with this dough by mixing the finest of their flour with sugar, and these biscuits are called *melindres.*

Maize serves the Indians not only as bread but also as wine, for they make

---

2. Dietary differences were crucial cultural signifiers in the sixteenth-century world, and Acosta's argument that maize was not inferior to wheat responded to a European assumption that corn was fit for animals but not humans. See John C. Super, *Food, Conquest, and Colonization in Sixteenth-Century Spanish America* (Albuquerque: University of New Mexico Press, 1988), 32–37.

drinks out of it with which they become quite drunk and more rapidly than with wine made of grapes. The maize wine that is called *azua* in Peru, and more commonly in the Indies *chicha*, is made in various ways. The strongest is made like beer, first soaking the grains of corn until they start to sprout and then boiling it in a certain way; it becomes so strong that a few drinks leave a man unable to stand. In Peru they call this drink *sora,* and it is forbidden by law owing to the serious consequences that it entails, for it causes violent drunkenness. But the law is of little use, for the Indians drink it regardless and are capable of dancing and drinking for days and nights together.[3] This method of making a brew with which to get drunk, made of grain that is first soaked and then boiled, is said by Pliny to have been used in ancient times in Spain and France, and in other provinces, too, as beer made of barley grains is used in Flanders today.[4] Another way of making *azua* or *chicha* is to chew the corn and make leaven out of the stuff that is chewed and then boil it, and the Indians even believe that to make good leaven it must be chewed by decrepit old women, which is disgusting even to hear about, and yet they show no repugnance toward drinking that wine. The cleanest and most wholesome way, and the one that does least harm, is to make it from roasted maize; the more scrupulous Indians and some Spaniards use this as medicine, for in fact they find that it is a very healthful drink for the kidneys and urine, and hence such ailments are rarely found among the Indians owing to their habit of drinking *chicha*.

When the maize is tender on the ear and milky, both Indians and Spaniards eat it as a dainty either boiled or roasted, and they also put it in the pot and in stews, and it is a good food. The grains of maize are very rich and serve as lard in place of oil, so that maize is used in the Indies for animals and men, for bread and wine, and for oil. And that is what the viceroy Don Francisco de Toledo used to say, that Peru had two things of substance and wealth, which

---

3. Few Spanish observers refrained from commenting on native patterns of drinking maize beer (*chicha*) in the Andes and cactus wine (pulque) in New Spain or expressing their concern about the extent to which indigenous people indulged in alcoholic beverages. Numerous laws attempted to limit the sale of *chicha* and pulque to the indigenous population. For a study of the regulation of *chicha* sales as well as the social and economic role of the drink in the colonial city of Potosí, see Jane E. Mangan, "Enterprise in the Shadow of Silver: Colonial Andeans and the Culture of Trade in Potosí, 1570–1700," Ph.D. diss., Duke University, 1999. The best historical analysis of the changes from pre-Hispanic ritual use of pulque to everyday colonial consumption is found in William Taylor, *Drinking, Homicide, and Rebellion in Colonial Mexican Villages* (Stanford: Stanford University Press, 1979).

4. Pliny, *Natural History*, 14, 22 (O'G).

were maize and the flocks of that land. And truly he was right, for both of these serve any number of uses. As for how maize came to the Indies, and why this most useful grain is called "Turkish" in Italy, I can ask this question sooner than answer it. For, indeed, among the ancients I find no trace of this sort of grain, although the *milium* that Pliny says had come to Italy from India ten years before he wrote has some resemblance to maize in that he says it is a grain and grows on a stalk, is covered with leaves, has hairlike strands at its tip, and grows very abundantly, all of which does not correspond to millet, which is what is commonly understood by the word he uses.[5] Verily, the Creator scattered his largesse everywhere; to this hemisphere he gave wheat, which is the chief nourishment of man, and to the hemisphere of the Indies he gave maize, which holds second place after wheat for the sustenance of men and animals.

### CHAPTER 17 * OF YUCCA AND CASSAVA, AND POTATOES AND *CHUÑO* AND RICE

In some parts of the Indies they use a kind of bread called cassava, which is made from a certain root called yucca. The yucca root is large and thick. It is cut into small pieces and grated and squeezed in a sort of press, and what is left resembles a thin cake that is very long and broad, almost like a shield. Dried, this is the bread that they eat; it has no taste and is perfectly insipid but is wholesome and nourishing. This is why we used to say, when we were in Hispaniola, that it was an appropriate food for discouraging gluttony because it could be eaten without the slightest concern that desire for it would cause excess. Cassava has to be moistened before it is eaten, for it is harsh and scratchy; it can easily be moistened with water or broth and is good for soup because it soaks up a great deal of liquid, and so they make stews of it. Placed in milk or cane syrup or even wine, it hardly soaks up the liquid or disintegrates as wheat bread does. There is a more refined kind of cassava made of the flower that they call *jaujau,* which is much prized in those parts, but I myself would much prefer a piece of bread no matter how hard or black it was.[1] An astonishing thing is that the juice or water pressed from that root out of which

5. Ibid., 18, 7 (O'G).

1. Acosta attempted to explain the various New World diets to Europeans by classifying all starchy foods (bread, tubers, and rice) as breads. Although these food items shared a common role as dietary staples, they were not equal in Acosta's opinion. Any wheat bread, regardless of its quality or freshness, ranked above cassava.

cassava is made is a deadly poison, which kills if it is drunk, and yet the substance that remains is a wholesome bread, as has been said. There is a kind of yucca known as sweet yucca that does not have this poison in its juice and is eaten as a root, either boiled or roasted, and is a satisfactory food. Cassava will keep for a long time, and so it is taken on voyages in place of sea biscuit.

The places where this food is most commonly used are, as I said, Santo Domingo, Cuba, Puerto Rico, Jamaica, and some other islands in those parts; the reason is that wheat and even maize do not grow well there. When wheat is planted it grows very quickly but so unevenly that it cannot be gathered, for in the same field at the same time some of it will be sprouting, some in full sheaf, and some just beginning. Some plants will be tall and others short; in one place there will be nothing but weeds, in another mere seedlings. And, although farmers have been sent to see whether they can raise wheat there, the quality of the land makes this impossible.

Flour is brought from New Spain or carried from Spain or the Canaries, and it is so damp that the bread has hardly any taste, nor does it give good nourishment. The communion wafers, when we said mass, would bend as if made of wet paper; this is caused by the combination of extreme humidity and heat in that country. Another contrasting extreme in other parts of the Indies means that there is no bread made of wheat or maize, as in the higher parts of the mountains of Peru and the provinces called El Collao, which constitute the greater part of that realm.

There the climate is so cold and dry that it does not lend itself to the cultivation of either wheat or maize, in place of which the Indians use another kind of root, which they call *papas,* or potatoes. These look like lumps of earth with a few leaves on top. The Indians gather these potatoes and let them dry in the sun and then mash them and make what they call *chuño,* which lasts for many days in this form and takes the place of bread; in that kingdom there is a great deal of commerce in *chuño* for the mines of Potosí.[2] Potatoes are also eaten fresh, either boiled or roasted, and they make a certain stew or concoction called *locro* from a milder type of potato that also grows in hot places. In short, these roots are the only bread of that land, and when there is a good year for them the people are happy, for there are many years

2. Potatoes are freeze-dried at night on the high-altitude plains of the Andes to make the popular *chuño.* Acosta does not describe the high-protein grain quinoa, which, when consumed alongside starch-laden potatoes or *chuño,* creates a unique Andean diet that meets nearly all nutritional needs.

when they mildew and freeze in the ground, such is the cold and inclemency of that region.

Maize is brought from the valleys and the seacoast, and the Spaniards bring flour and wheat as a luxury from those and other regions, which, as the mountain climate is dry, can easily be preserved, and good bread is made of it. In other parts of the Indies such as the Philippines they use rice in place of bread, which is excellent in all that land and in China and is very nourishing and makes a good food; they cook it and then serve it hot in porcelain dishes or bowls, in its cooking liquid, and mix it with other food. In many places they also make their wine from the grain of rice, moistening it and then boiling it as beer is made in Flanders or *azua* in Peru.

All over the world, rice is nearly as universal a food as wheat and maize, and perhaps more so, for in addition to China and Japan and the Philippines and a large part of the East Indies it is the commonest cereal in Africa and Ethiopia. Rice requires a great deal of moisture and swampy ground almost saturated with water. In Europe and Peru and Mexico, where there is wheat, rice is eaten in the form of a stew or side dish and not as bread, being cooked in milk or the grease from the pot and in other ways. The finest rice is that which comes from the Philippines and China, as has been said. And in general terms this suffices to recount what is eaten as bread in the Indies.

### CHAPTER 18 * OF DIFFERENT ROOTS THAT GROW IN THE INDIES

Although foodstuffs that grow above ground are more plentiful and abundant here in Spain owing to our great diversity of fruit trees and greenstuffs, I believe there is a greater abundance in the Indies of roots and foods that grow underground, for among those kinds of foods here we have radishes and turnips and carrots and chicory and onions and garlic and some other useful roots, but there so many exist that I cannot count them. Those that occur to me now, in addition to potatoes, which are the chief roots, are *ocas* and *yanaocas* and yams and sweet potatoes and jícama and yucca and *cochuchu* and *cavi* and *totora* and peanuts and a hundred other kinds that I cannot recall.

Some of these, like sweet potatoes, have been brought to Europe and are considered a good thing to eat, just as European roots have been taken to the

Indies, and with this advantage, that European plants grow much better in the Indies than do products of the Indies in Europe. The reason is, I believe, that there are greater differences in temperature there than here, and so in the Indies it is easy to adapt plants to the temperature desired. And there are even some European plants that seem to grow better in the Indies, for onions and garlic and carrots are not as fine in Spain as they are in Peru, and turnips have been grown there in such abundance that they have multiplied enormously in some places, to the point that, as I have been told, on one occasion when they wanted to sow wheat on certain lands they were unable to do so because of the turnips that had multiplied there.

We often saw radishes thicker than a man's arm and very tender and tasty. Of the roots I mentioned many are everyday foodstuffs, such as yams, which are roasted and take the place of fruit or vegetables; there are others that serve as dainties, such as *cochucho,* a little root that is very sweet, which some make into jam as a special treat. Others provide refreshment, like the jícama, which is very cold and moist, and it refreshes and kills thirst in summer during the hot weather; potatoes and *ocas* are better for nourishment and nutrition. Among the European roots, the Indians most prize garlic and consider it a very important thing; and they are not wrong about this, for it protects and warms the stomach, and it is said that they eat it eagerly and almost raw, just as it comes out of the ground.

CHAPTER 19 * OF DIFFERENT KINDS OF
GREENSTUFFS AND VEGETABLES, AND OF
THOSE CALLED CUCUMBERS, AND PINEAPPLES
AND CHILEAN STRAWBERRIES, AND PLUMS

Now that we have begun with small plants, I will deal briefly with greenstuffs and vegetables and what the Romans called *arbusta,* all that does not reach the size of a tree. There are some kinds of these shrubs or green plants in the Indies that have a very good taste; the first Spaniards to arrive gave Spanish names to many of these plants of the Indies, taken from other things that they somewhat resembled, such as pineapples and cucumbers and plums; but in reality these are very different fruits, and are incomparably more unlike them than those that bear these names in Castile.

Pineapples have the same size and external shape as the pinecones of Castile but are wholly different within, for they have no pine nuts or inner divisions and are all flesh once the skin has been removed; it is a fruit of an excellent smell and very pleasant to eat. Its taste is slightly acid, but sweet and juicy; they are eaten by slicing them and soaking them for a time in salted water. Some are of the opinion that they engender bile and say that they are not a healthful food, but I have not observed any bad effects from them. They grow on a single stalk or shoot that emerges from among many leaves, like a lily, and is not much larger, though thicker. The tip of each of these stalks is the fruit of the pineapple; it grows in hot and humid places, and the best ones come from the Windward Islands. They do not grow in Peru; they are brought from the Andes but are neither good nor really mature. The emperor Charles was presented one of these pineapples, which must have required a great deal of effort to bring from the Indies on its plant, for otherwise it could not have come. He praised the smell but declined to discover what it tasted like. In New Spain I have seen an excellent preserve made of these pineapples.

The plant they call *pepino,* or cucumber, is not a tree either but a garden vegetable that takes a year to grow. It was given this name because some or most of these vegetables are of the length and circumference of a cucumber in Spain but are completely different in every other way, for the color is not green but purple or yellow or white, and they are not spiny or rough but very smooth and have a very different and much better taste, for they also have a pleasantly acid flavor that is very tasty when they are fully ripe, though not as sharp as that of the pineapple. They are very juicy, cool, and easy to digest and good for refreshment in hot weather; one pulls off the peel, which is soft, and all the rest is flesh. They grow in temperate climates and require irrigation, and, although because of their shape they are called cucumbers, many of them are completely round and others have a different shape, so that they do not even have the form of cucumbers. I do not recall having seen this plant in New Spain or in the islands but only on the plains of Peru.

The fruit called the Chilean strawberry is also very good to eat, for, although it has a taste somewhat resembling cherries, the plant is entirely different, for it is not a tree but a plant that grows very low and spreads over the ground and produces that small fruit, which in its color and visible seeds somewhat resembles mulberries when they are white and about to be ripe, although it is more tapering in shape and larger than mulberries. They say that in Chile this fruit grows naturally in the fields. Where I have seen it, it is planted in rows and grown like any other garden plant. What they call plums are a true tree fruit and more closely resemble certain kinds of Spanish plums. They are found in various forms: one kind is called the Nicaragua plum, which is red and very small and has scarcely any flesh apart from the skin and pit. But the little flesh they do have is of an exceptionally good taste, and its juice is as good or better than the cherry; they are considered to be very wholesome and hence are given to the sick, especially to tempt the appetite. There are other, large ones, dark in color and with a great deal of flesh, but these are coarse and not very good tasting, for they are like the plums known as *chabacanas*. Each of these has two or three little stones.

To return to greenstuffs and garden plants, although there are many different ones and many others besides those I have mentioned, I have not found that the Indians had separate market gardens of different vegetables but cultivated bits of land for the vegetables they use, such as the kinds they call *frijoles* and *pallares,* which they use in the same ways that chickpeas and beans and lentils are used here; nor have I discovered that these or any other kinds of European vegetables existed here before the coming of the Spaniards, who brought greenstuffs and vegetables from Spain. They grow there exceedingly well, and there are even places where their products exceed the fertility of those here, for example, the melons that grow in the Yca valley in Peru; for they use the root as stock, and it lasts for years, and each stock produces melons, and they prune it like a tree, something that I do not believe is done in any part of Spain. The gourds of the Indies are another monstrosity, in both their size and the luxuriance with which they grow, especially those that are native to the land, which they call *capallos,* whose flesh can be eaten, especially during Lent, either boiled or stewed. There are a thousand differences among these gourds, and some are so extraordinarily large that they leave them to dry and make a sort of basket out of their rind, cut in half and cleaned, into which they put all the preparations for a meal. Of the smaller ones they make vessels for eating and drinking and decorate them attractively for various uses. Having said this much about less important plants, let us go on to the more important ones; but let us first speak of *ají,* which still belongs to this area.

CHAPTER 20 * OF *AJÍ*, OR INDIES PEPPER

In the West Indies no proper spices have been found, such as pepper, cloves, cinnamon, nutmeg, and ginger, although one of our brothers who traveled through many and diverse lands told us that in some desert places on the island of Jamaica he had found some trees that produced peppers but that they are not recognized as such and there is no trade in them. Ginger was brought from India to Hispaniola and has multiplied to the point that they no longer know what to do with so much of it. In the fleet of fifteen hundred and eighty-seven, 22,053 hundredweight of ginger was brought to Seville.

But the native spice that God gave to the West Indies is what in Castile is called "Indies pepper," and the general word for it, taken from the first islands that were conquered, is *ají*. In the language of Cuzco they say *uchu* and in the Mexican language chile. By now this is a well-known thing, and hence not much need be said about it; we need to know only that it was prized by the ancient Indians and carried by them, as important merchandise, to places where it did not grow. It does not grow in cold places such as the mountains of Peru but occurs in warm valleys where there is irrigation. There are peppers of different colors, green and red and yellow; there is a very strong one that they call *caribe,* which stings and bites severely. There is another that is very mild and even a sweet one that can be eaten by mouthfuls. There is a little one that tastes like musk in the mouth and is very good. The parts of the pepper that sting are the veins and seeds; the rest does not bite. It is eaten green and dry, and ground and whole, and in the pot in stews. It is the chief sauce and the only kind of spice used in the Indies; eaten in moderation it aids digestion in the stomach, but if used excessively it has very destructive effects, for it is extremely hot in itself, and smoky and penetrating, and hence much use of it in the young is prejudicial to health, especially to that of the soul, for it heightens sensuality. And it is an amusing fact that, although the heat it possesses in itself is so well known, and when it goes in or out everyone remarks that it burns, yet with all this no few persons insist that it is not hot but cool and very mild. As for me, I will say the same of pepper and have no more experience of the one than the other; thus, it is a joke to say that it is not hot and in the highest degree. Salt is used to temper this pepper, which helps it a great deal, for they are two very opposite things and the one restrains the other; they also use tomatoes, which are cool and wholesome.

These are a kind of round, juicy berry that makes a delicious sauce, and they are good to eat by themselves. This pepper of the Indies is found universally there, in the islands, in New Spain, in Peru, and in every other place that has been discovered, so that, just as maize is the most widespread grain for bread, *aji* is the commonest spice for sauces and stews.

## CHAPTER 21 * OF THE PLANTAIN

Going on to larger plants, the first tree in the Indies of which we must speak is the plantain, or *plantano,* as it is commonly called. At one time I was doubtful as to whether the plane tree that the ancients praised and this tree of the Indies were of the same species, but, having seen what this plant is like and what has been written about the other, there is no doubt that they are very different. The reason why the Spaniards called it plantain (for the natives had no such word) was a certain similarity that they saw, as in other cases such as giving the names of plums and pineapples and almonds and cucumbers to things as different from plants in Castile as these were. Where I think they must have found a resemblance between these plantains of the Indies and the plane trees praised by the ancients is in the size of the leaves, for these are extremely large and cool, and the great size and coolness of their leaves is much praised; it is also a plant that requires a great deal of water and an almost continuous supply of it. This agrees with the saying in the Scripture: "As a plane tree by the water."[1]

But in point of fact one plant has no more to do with the other than an egg with a chestnut, as the saying goes. For, first, the ancient plane tree bore no fruit or at least there is no mention of it; it was chiefly prized for the shade that it cast, to the point that no more sun penetrated a plane tree than a roof. The reason why the plantain of the Indies is appreciated, and much appreciated, is its fruit, which is very good. But, as for making shade, it has none, nor is it possible to be seated under it.

In addition to this the ancient plane tree had such a huge trunk, and such spreading branches, that Pliny tells of a certain Licinius, a Roman captain, who dined very pleasantly in the hollow of a plane tree in the company of eighteen others, and of that emperor Caius Caligula who sat in the upper

1. Ecclesiastes, 24, 19 (O'G).

branches of a plane tree and offered eleven guests a splendid banquet.[2] The plantains of the Indies have neither hollows nor trunks nor branches. Moreover, the ancient plane trees grew in Italy and Spain, although they had come from Greece, and to Greece from Asia; but the plantains of the Indies do not grow in Italy and Spain. I say that they do not grow, although they have been seen here, and I saw one in Seville in the king's garden; but they do not bear fruit and are of no use. Finally, although there is a faint resemblance there are also great differences, for, although the leaves of the plane tree were large, they were not excessively so, since Pliny compares them with grape and fig leaves.[3]

The leaves of the Indies plantain are extraordinarily large, for one of them would cover a man almost from head to foot. Hence there is no reason to doubt that they are different; but, granted that this plantain is different from the ancient plane tree, it deserves no less praise on that account. Rather it merits more, owing to the useful properties that it possesses.

It is a plant whose stock is planted in the earth, and out of it grow a number of shoots, which are separate and have no connection between them. Each shoot grows and makes a tree of its own, becoming thicker and putting forth very smooth and verdant leaves of the size that I have indicated. When this tree has reached a height of ten or twelve feet it puts forth a single bunch of plantains, which sometimes contains very many and other times not so many; three hundred have been counted on some bunches. Each fruit is a handbreadth long more or less and as thick as two or three fingers, although in this there is a great deal of difference between one plant and another. The rind or peel is easily removed, and all the rest is a firm and tender core that is very good to eat, for it is wholesome and nourishing. This fruit tends to be cool rather than warm. The bunches to which I have alluded are usually picked green and stored for protection in large jars until they ripen and mature, especially with the help of a certain herb that is used for this purpose. If they are allowed to ripen on the tree they have a better taste and a very pleasant smell like that of an apple. They are available almost all the year, for the stump of the plantain continues to grow shoots, and when one has finished another begins to give fruit, so that one shoot always follows another and there is fruit all year. The stalk is cut down after it has produced its

2. Pliny, *Natural History,* 12, 1 (O'G).
3. Ibid., 16, 24 (O'G).

bunch, for a shoot bears fruit only once. But the stump, as I have said, remains and sprouts anew until it wears out. It lasts for several years; the plantain requires a great deal of humidity and a very hot climate. Ashes are placed around its base to make it bear better; thick woods are formed of plantain trees, and they are extremely useful, for it is the fruit most used in the Indies and is universal in almost every country, although they say that its origin was in Ethiopia and that it came from there. Indeed, blacks use it a great deal, and in some places it serves as their bread; wine is also made of it.

The plantain is eaten as fruit, simply raw; it can also be roasted and stewed, and they make a number of dishes from it, and even preserves, and it adapts well to all of these methods. There are some small plantains that are softer and more delicate, which in Hispaniola are called Dominicans. Others exist that are thicker and coarser and red in color. They do not grow in Peru; they are brought from the Andes, as to Mexico City from Cuernavaca and other valleys. On the northern part of the continent and on some of the islands there are enormous plantain groves, like thick woods. If the plantain could serve for firewood it would be the most useful plant imaginable; but it does not, for neither its leaves nor its branches can be used as firewood, much less than tree wood, for example, for they are spongy and have no strength. However, the dried leaves could serve Don Alonso de Ercilla (as he says) to write some parts of his *Araucana,* in Chile, and it is not a bad substitute for paper, for the leaf is as broad as a sheet of paper or a little less and is four times as long.

### CHAPTER 22 * OF COCOA AND COCA

Although the plantain is more useful, cocoa is more highly prized in Mexico, and coca in Peru, and both are trees associated with no little superstition.[1] Cocoa is a fruit a little smaller than the almond, and thicker, and when roasted it does not have a bad taste. It is so much prized among the Indians,

1. Acosta's grouping of cocoa and coca in this chapter is an intriguing example of his attempt at comparative classification of the natural world of the Indies. Although the products are distinct in appearance and taste, both the coca leaves and the cocoa beans grow on small trees. Andean and Mexican societies, respectively, dedicated considerable energies to the domesticated production of the two crops. The cultural uses in pre-Hispanic society offer a more compelling comparison. Coca leaves were chewed; cocoa beans were ground into a thick beverage. Yet, despite these distinct modes of consumption, both products played a valuable role in trade as a type of money and a form of tribute; in ritual tradition, as offerings to deities, and in the social hierarchy as products controlled by the native elite.

and even among Spaniards, that it is one of the richest and most frequent objects of trade in New Spain; for because it is a dry fruit it can be kept for a long time without loss and ships loaded with it are brought from the province of Guatemala. And this past year an English pirate burned more than a hundred thousand loads of cacao in the port of Huatulco in New Spain. It is also used as money, for with five cocoa beans one thing can be bought, and with thirty another, and with a hundred another, and without haggling; and it is customary to give cocoa beans to the poor when they ask for alms.

The chief value of this cocoa is a beverage that they make called chocolate, which is prized to the point of folly in that land. It is nauseating to some who are not accustomed to it, for it has froth on top and a sort of lees, which indeed require a good deal of effort to drink. Yet it is the most prized drink and is offered to noblemen as they pass through their lands. Both Indians and Spaniards, and especially Spanish women who have grown accustomed to the land, adore their black chocolate. They say that this chocolate is made in different forms and temperatures: hot and cold and lukewarm. They often put spices in it and much chile; they also make it in the form of a paste, and say that it is good for the chest and stomach and against catarrh. No matter what its uses, those who have not been brought up to it do not much care for it.

The tree on which the fruit grows is of medium size and good proportions and has a beautiful shape. It is so delicate that to keep it from the sun and prevent its being burned, they plant it next to another large tree whose only purpose is to give it shade, and this tree is called "the mother of cocoa." There are commercial plantings of cocoa trees in which they are grown like vines or olive trees in Spain. As far as commerce and volume of trade are concerned, the province that has the most is Guatemala. It does not grow in Peru, but there is coca there, about which there is even greater superstition, and it seems quite incredible. The simple truth is that in Potosí alone there is an annual trade in coca of more than half a million pesos a year, for ninety to ninety-five million baskets of it are sold, and as late as the year fifteen hundred and eighty-three a hundred thousand. In Cuzco a basket of coca is worth from two and a half to three pesos and in Potosí, in cash, four pesos and six tomines and even five minted pesos. And it is the product involved in most trades and exchanges, for it is merchandise that has great circulation. This coca, which is so highly prized, is a small green leaf that grows on little trees about six feet high; it is grown in very hot and humid regions. The trees produce this leaf, which is called *tresmitas* there, every four months. Its cultivation requires much care because it is very delicate and needs even more attention after it is picked. They place it very carefully in long, narrow baskets and load them onto the native sheep, which carry this merchandise in flocks, with a thousand and two thousand and even three thousand baskets. Usually it is brought from the Andes, from valleys where the heat is unbearable, where it rains most of the year, and its cultivation causes the Indians no little labor and even no few lives because they go from the mountains and cold climates to cultivate and pick it and bring it. Hence there were great disputes and opinions among educated and learned men as to whether they should eradicate all the plantings of coca, but in the end they have remained.

The Indians prize it very highly, and in the time of the Inca kings it was unlawful for the common people to use coca without permission from the Inca or his governor. It is used by bringing it to the mouth and chewing and sucking it; it is not swallowed. The Indians say that it gives them strength, and it is a great treat for them. Many grave men think this is a superstition and pure imagination. To tell the truth, I do not think it pure imagination; rather, I believe that it produces strength and spirit in the Indians, for effects can be seen that cannot be attributed to imagination, such as doubling the workload with a handful of coca without ingesting anything else and other similar feats. The sauce they eat it with is a good match for the leaf, for I have tried it and it tastes like leather. The Indians sprinkle it with an ash made of burned, ground bones, or with lime, as others say. They like the taste of it and say that it does them good, willingly spend their money on it, and trade it like money as often as they like. All this would be acceptable were not its cultivation and trade so dangerous and did it not occupy so many people. The Inca lords used coca as a royal prerogative and a luxury, and it was the thing most often offered in their sacrifices by burning it in honor of their idols.

### CHAPTER 23 * OF MAGUEY, TUNAL, AND COCHINEAL AND OF INDIGO AND COTTON

The maguey is a wonderful tree, about which new settlers, or *chapetones* (as they are called in the Indies), write miraculous things, that it gives water and wine, oil and vinegar, honey and syrup, thread and needles, and a hundred other things.[1] It is a tree much esteemed by the Indians in New Spain. They often have one or several of these trees near their dwellings to help them in daily life, and they grow and are cultivated in the fields. They have broad, coarse leaves ending in a strong sharp point, which can be taken and used like a pin, and that is the needle; and a certain kind of fiber or thread is taken from the leaf. The trunk, which is thick, can be cut when it is immature and a large hollow left, whence the sap rises from the root, and it is a liquid that can be drunk like water and is sweet and cool; this same liquid when boiled becomes a sort of wine; if left to turn sour it becomes vinegar, and if reduced by fire it resembles honey. When it is half cooked it can be used as syrup and tastes very good and is wholesome, and I think it is better than the must made of grapes. And so they cook these and other things from that juice or liquor, which is very abundant, for they can take several measures of it daily for a long time. This tree also grows in Peru, but it is not as widely used there as in New Spain. The stalk of this tree is spongy and can be used to keep fire alive, for it holds the fire like the fuse of a harquebus and keeps it for a long time, and I have seen the Indians use it in this way in Peru.

The tunal is another tree famed in New Spain, if a heap of leaves or excrescences piled one on the other can be called a tree. In this regard it has the strangest structure that ever a tree had, for one leaf sprouts, and from that leaf another, and from that another, and so on up to the top, except that as some leaves are growing above or to the sides, the lower leaves grow thicker and almost lose the shape of a leaf, forming a trunk and branches; and all of it is spiny and rough and ugly, which is why in some places they call it a thistle. There are trees of this kind growing wild, and these do not give fruit, or if they do it is very thorny and useless. There are domestic ones, and they produce fruit that is much prized in the Indies, called tunas, or prickly pears, and these are rather larger than plums and just as round. The rind, which is thick, is opened, and inside there is flesh and little seeds like fig seeds, which taste very good and are very sweet, especially the white ones, and have a mild sort of flavor; usually the red ones are not as good.[2]

---

1. The maguey, known in English as the century plant, was indeed a multipurpose wonder plant, as Acosta claims. Families used it to mark the boundaries of their property, its prickly spines for needles, its rough fibers for blankets, and its sweet sap, called *aguamiel,* as a beverage. Mexicans made pulque, an intoxicant that played a central role in ceremonial life, from the *aguamiel*.

2. In addition to eating the fruit of the domesticated tunal, also called the *nopal,* many natives of Mesoamerica cooked and consumed its leaves.

There are other trees of this kind that do not produce fruit yet are much more highly regarded and are cultivated with great care, for, although they do not provide prickly pears, still they produce a crop of cochineal; for some little worms develop on the leaves of this tree when it is carefully cultivated, stuck to the leaf and covered with a sort of thin membrane, which they carefully pick. And this is the famous cochineal of the Indies, with which the best red dye is made; they are allowed to dry and then are taken to Spain in dry form, which is a rich and voluminous trade.[3] Twenty-five pounds of this cochineal, or *grana,* is worth many ducats. In the fleet of the year fifteen hundred and eighty-seven there were 5,677 twenty-five pound measures of cochineal, which amounted to 283,750 pesos, and this amount of wealth in cochineal comes in every year. These tunal trees grow in areas that range from temperate to cold; until now they have not grown in Peru, nor in Spain. I have seen a few plants of this kind but not enough to make them commercially useful.

And, though it is not a tree but a plant, the plant from which indigo is extracted, which is used for dyeing cloth, is also grown in quantity in New Spain and is merchandise associated with cochineal. A matter of 25,273 measures came in the fleet that I mentioned and were worth an equal number of pesos.

Cotton also grows on trees both small and large, which have a kind of pod that opens and produces that thread or fleece, which is spun and woven after it is picked, and clothing is made of it. It is one of the best things in the Indies, for it serves the inhabitants for clothing in place of linen and wool; it grows in hot places, much of it in the valleys and on the coasts of Peru, in New Spain, in the Philippines and China, and much more, as I am given to understand, in the province of Tucumán, in Santacruz de la Sierra, and in Paraguay, and in those places it is the principal crop. Cotton is brought to Spain from the islands of Santo Domingo, and in the year I mentioned sixty-four twenty-five pound measures were brought. In the parts of the Indies where cotton grows, it is the cloth in which both men and women custom-

---

3. Cochineal, the bright red dye made from the crushed insects that crowded the *nopal* cactus, was traded extensively in the pre-Hispanic period, when production took place primarily with wild plants in the regions of Oaxaca and Guatemala. After the conquest, colonists built commercial estates to meet European demand for the dye. On this trade see the work of Jeremy Baskes, *Indians, Merchants, and Markets: A Reinterpretation of the Repartimiento and Spanish-Indian Economic Relations in Colonial Oaxaca* (Palo Alto: Stanford University Press, 2000).

arily dress, and tablecloths are made from it and even canvas and sails for ships. Some of this cloth is heavy and rough textured; other kinds are delicate and thin. It is dyed in various colors, and the same varieties are produced that we see in Europe applied to woolen cloth.

## CHAPTER 24 * OF MAMEYS AND GUAVAS AND ALLIGATOR PEARS

The plants that we described in the previous chapter are the ones most often cultivated in the Indies and those that provide most livelihood. There are many others that are good to eat; among them mameys are much prized, of the size of a large peach and even bigger. They have one or two pits inside, and their flesh is rather hard. Some are sweet and others slightly bitter; the rind is also tough. Preserves are made of their flesh and resemble quince paste; they are good to eat raw and are even better when preserved. They grow in the islands; I have not seen them in Peru. It is a large, well-formed tree with a big canopy.

Other trees that give a poor fruit, full of hard seeds and the size of small apples, are the guavas. In the northern part of the continent and in the islands, both tree and fruit have a bad name; they say it smells like bedbugs, and its flavor is very coarse and its effect unhealthy. In Santo Domingo and in those islands there are mountains thickly sown with guavas, and they say that there was no such tree there when the Spaniards arrived but that it was brought from I do not know where and has multiplied to an infinite degree. For no animal eats the seeds, and when they fall, as the land is damp and hot, they say that the trees have multiplied to their present numbers. In Peru this tree is different, for the fruit is not red but white, it has no bad odor, and its taste is good; and in some kinds of guavas the fruit is as good as the best of its kind in Spain, especially the sort called *matos* and other small white ones. It is a fruit for stomachs that digest well and are healthy, for it is hard to digest and quite cold.

Alligator pears, or avocados, on the other hand, are warm and delicate. The tree is tall and well-formed, with a beautiful canopy, and the fruit is the size of large pears; it has a big pit inside, and the rest is soft flesh. When they are ripe they are like butter, and their taste is delicate and soft. In Peru alligator pears are large and have a hard shell, which can be removed in one piece. In Mexico most of them are small and have a thin rind that can be peeled like an apple; they are considered a wholesome food there and incline toward warmth, as I have said. These — mameys and guavas and alligator pears — are the peaches and apples and pears of the Indies, and, although I would prefer those of Europe, others, either out of habit or choice, would perhaps think the fruit of the Indies preferable. One thing is certain: those who have not seen and tasted these fruits can have little idea of them by reading this, and may even be bored with hearing about them, and I am becoming bored myself.[1] And so I will cut short my discussion by telling of a few other, different fruits, for it is impossible to describe them all.

CHAPTER 25 * OF *CHICOZAPOTE* AND
*ANONAS* AND *CAPOLÍES*

Some lovers of things of the Indies said that there was a fruit that was like quince and another that was like almonds and cream, for the flavor seemed to them worthy of such names. The quince paste or marmalade (if I am not mistaken) was made from what they call *zapotes* or *chicozapotes,* which are very sweet to eat, and the color resembles that of preserved quince. Some Creoles (as the children of Spaniards born in the Indies are called there) said that it was better than all the fruits of Spain. I do not think so: it is said that there is no use arguing over taste, and even if there were, it is not a dispute worth writing about. These *chicozapotes* grow in the hotter parts of New Spain. Those called *zapotes* are not much different, to judge from those I saw in the northern part of the continent; I do not know whether this fruit exists in Peru. There the equivalent of the almond is the *anona* or *guanábana,* which grows in the northern parts of the continent. The *anona,* or *chirimoya,* is the size of a very large pear and somewhat tapering and open; all the flesh inside is soft and tender as butter and sweet and white and of an exquisite taste. It is not almonds and cream, though it is a white food that cannot be praised sufficiently, for it has a delicate and savory taste and some believe that it is the best fruit in the Indies. It has many small black seeds. The best of these fruits

1. When Acosta suggested that readers might be bored with his descriptions of food, he underestimated the power of his words to shape, literally, European tastes — or distastes — for the New World. The fact that Acosta tasted the "peaches and pears" of the Indies and preferred those of Europe implied the innate inferiority of the native fruits of America.

that I have seen were in New Spain, where *capolíes* also grow. These are like cherries and have a pit which is somewhat larger than a cherry's, and their shape and size are like cherries and their flavor good, sweet, and somewhat sharp. I have not seen *capolíes* in any other place.

CHAPTER 26 * OF DIFFERENT KINDS OF FRUIT
TREES, AND OF COCONUTS AND ANDES
ALMONDS, AND CHACHAPOYAS ALMONDS

It is impossible to describe all the fruit and trees of the Indies, for many of them I do not remember and there are many more about which I do not know; and it seems a burdensome thing even to discourse about all the ones I do remember, for there are other, coarser kinds of fruits, such as those called *lucumas,* about which there is a saying that they are wood in disguise. There are also *pacayes,* or *guabas,* and *hobos,* and the kind of nuts called "imprisoned," which many believe to be walnuts of the same type as in Spain; and it is even said that if these were transplanted frequently from one place to another they would eventually give the same walnuts as in Spain, for because they grow wild the nuts are so small that they can scarcely be enjoyed. Indeed, we must consider the providence and riches of the Creator, who distributed such a variety of trees and fruit trees to such varied parts of the world, all for the service of the men who inhabit the earth; and it is a wonderful thing to see so many differences in shape and tastes and properties never before known and heard of in the world before the discovery of the Indies, and of which Pliny and Dioscorides and Theophrastus and other scholars achieved no knowledge despite their diligence and curiosity. In our day there has been no lack of inquiring men who have written treatises on these plants of the Indies and on grasses and roots and their properties and the medicines extracted from them, who may be consulted by anyone who wishes a more complete knowledge of these matters. My aim is only to recount, superficially and briefly, what I have to say about this subject.

Yet I do not think I should pass over coconuts, or Indies palms, because their properties are so remarkable. I say palms, although they are really not date palms, but they are similar to them in being tall and very strong trees and in producing larger branches the higher they grow. These palm or coconut trees produce a fruit that is also called coconut, of which vessels for drinking are customarily made; and they say that some of them have the quality of protecting against poison and against the colic. The center or marrow of these nuts, when it is mature and dry, can be eaten and tastes something like green chestnuts. When the coconut is young and on the tree, its whole interior is milk, and it is drunk as a delicacy and a refreshment in times of heat. I saw these trees in San Juan de Puerto Rico and in other places in the Indies, and I was told a very remarkable thing, that each moon or month this coconut tree puts forth a new cluster of leaves, so that it gives twelve fruits a year, like the tree described in the Apocalypse. And indeed this seemed to be the case, for the clusters were of different ages, some just beginning and others half developed. These coconuts that I speak of are about the size of a small melon; there are others known as *coquillos,* and these are better fruit and are found in Chile. They are a little smaller than walnuts, but rounder.

There is another kind of coconut that does not have this solid marrow but instead has a large number of seeds the size of almonds, which fit inside it like the seeds in a pomegranate. These almonds are three times as large as the almonds of Castile. In taste they resemble them, although the flavor is a little stronger, and they are also juicy and full of oil; they are very good to eat and are used in the absence of almonds to make sweetmeats such as marzipan and other similar things. They are called "Andes almonds" because these coconut trees grow abundantly in the Andes of Peru. And they are so strong that they have to be struck with a very large stone to open them and require a good deal of strength. When they fall from the tree, if they hit someone on the head they can easily crack it open. It seems incredible that, with the size that they are, which is no more than that of other coconuts, for they are not larger than the others, at least not much larger, they can contain such a large number of these almonds.

But in the matter of almonds, and even of any fruit whatever, the almonds of Chachapoya (for I know no other name for them) have no rival. It is the most delicate and delicious fruit, and the most wholesome, of any that I have seen in the Indies. And a learned physician even stated that among all the fruits of the Indies and Spain none could equal the excellence of these almonds. They are smaller than the Andes almonds that I mentioned, and larger, or at least thicker, than those of Castile. They are very tender to eat, have a great deal of juice, and are meaty and soft in texture. They grow on very tall trees with a large canopy, and Nature gave them good protection, as to a thing of great worth. They come in husks with spines that are larger and more numerous than those of chestnuts. When these husks are dry, they can easily be opened and the nut extracted. They say that monkeys, who love to eat this fruit and abound in the Chachapoyas region of Peru (the only place, as far as I know, where these trees exist), to avoid pricking themselves on the spines when taking out the almonds throw them violently from the top of the tree onto the rocks, and when they have broken them in this way they finish opening them and thus eat as many as they wish.

### CHAPTER 27 * OF VARIOUS FLOWERS, AND SOME TREES THAT BEAR ONLY FLOWERS, AND HOW THE INDIANS USE THEM

The Indians love flowers, more in New Spain than in any other part of the world, and so they are accustomed to make nosegays that are called *suchiles* in that land, with so much variety and care and artistry that they leave nothing to be desired. It is customary to honor lords and guests by offering them these *suchiles* or nosegays. And when we traveled in that province we received so many of these that we did not know what to do with them. However, the chief flowers of Castile have been acclimated there for this purpose, for they grow as well there as here, for example, carnations and pinks, and roses and lilies and jasmine, and violets and orange blossom and other kinds of flowers, which grow wonderfully once they have been brought from Spain. In some places rosebushes became so lush that they ceased to produce roses. It once happened that a rosebush was burned, and the shoots it later put forth produced roses in abundance; from this they learned to prune them and curb their growth, and now they give an abundance of roses. But apart from these kinds of flowers that are brought from Spain there are many others whose names I do not know, red and yellow and blue and purple and white, in any number of varieties, which the Indians have a habit of wearing on their heads as adornment, like plumage. It is true that many of these flowers have nothing but their looks, for their smell either is not good or is very heavy. However, there are some that have a very beautiful odor, like those of a tree that some call *floripondio,* which produces no fruit but only flowers. And these are large, larger than lilies, bell-shaped, all white, and inside have stamens like those of the lily, and all year long this tree never stops producing these flowers, whose odor is wonderfully delicate and mild, especially in the cool of the morning. Because it was worthy of being in the royal gardens, the viceroy Don Francisco de Toledo sent a tree to our lord King Philip.

In New Spain the Indians prize very much a flower that they call *yolosuchil*, which means "heart flower," for it is shaped just like one, and even its size is not much smaller than a heart. This kind of flower also grows on another large tree that produces nothing else. It has a strong, and to my mind excessive, smell; others think it very good. It is well known that the flower they call sunflower has the shape of the sun and moves with the sun's movement. There are others called "Indies carnations," which resemble purple and orange velvet; this flower is also well known. These have no odor that can be noted, only their looks. There are other flowers that, along with their appearance, have a taste (although they have no odor), like those that taste of cress, and were they to be eaten without looking at them one would think by their taste that they were nothing else.

The blossom of the *granadilla*, or passion flower, is believed to be a remarkable thing; they say that it has the signs of the Passion, and that the nails and the pillar and the blows can be found in it, and the crown of thorns and the wounds. There is something to be said for this belief, although in order to imagine it one needs a touch of piety to help one see it all; but much is very clearly visible, and its appearance is beautiful in itself, although it has no odor. The fruit it produces is also called *granadilla*, and it can be eaten or drunk, or rather sucked, as a refreshment; it is sweet, and some think it excessively so. The Indians used to carry flowers in their hands during their dances and festivals, and the great lords and kings used them as a sign of greatness.[1] This is why one ordinarily sees pictures of their ancients with flowers in their hands, as in Europe the great ones are depicted with gloves.

And now I have said enough about flowers; sweet basil, though it is not a flower but an herb, is used for the same purposes of recreation and odor and to have it in their gardens and to grow it in pots. It is so common there, and grows so abundantly and needs no care, that it is not thought of as basil at all but merely a weed that grows behind every ditch.

1. The use of flowers in dances and festivals continued well into the colonial period and was likely infused with pre-Hispanic ritual significance. See Inga Clendinnen, "Ways to the Sacred: Reconstructing 'Religion' in Sixteenth Century Mexico," *History and Anthropology* 5 (1990): 105–141, esp. 115, 116.

### CHAPTER 28 * OF BALSAM

The Supreme Maker fashioned plants not only to eat but also for recreation and medicine and for man's activities. We have said enough of those that serve as nourishment, which is their chief use, and also something of those that are recreational; we shall say a little more about those that serve for medicine and activities. And, although everything in plants is medicinal if thoroughly known and well applied, there are some things that appear to have been ordained by their Creator most particularly for medicine and for the health of men, such as the liquors or oils or gums or resins produced by different plants, and it is easy to discover why they are good. Among these plants balsam is rightly praised for its excellent odor and still more for its ability to cure wounds and some other remedies for illnesses that have been found in it. Balsam from the West Indies is not of the same kind as the true balsam that is brought from Alexandria or Cairo and that in ancient times existed in Judea, which was the only place in the world, as Pliny writes, that possessed this great boon until the Vespasian emperors brought it to Rome and Italy.[1] I am bound to say that one kind and the other are not of the same species, for we need only see that the trees from which it flows are very different. The balsam tree of Palestine was small and resembled a vine, as Pliny states as an eyewitness, and today those who have seen it in the East say the same; and in Holy Writ the place where this balsam was produced was called the vineyards of Engaddi, owing to its resemblance to a vine.[2] I have seen the tree from which Indies balsam comes, and it is as large as a pomegranate tree and even taller, and rather resembles one in shape, if I remember rightly, and is not at all like a vine, although Strabo writes that the ancient balsam tree was the size of the pomegranate tree;[3] however, both kinds of balsam are very similar liquids in their properties and operations, such as having a fine smell, in curing wounds, and in color and consistency; and as for what they say about the classical balsam, that it is both white and red, and green and black, Indies balsam has the same characteristics.[4] And just as that balsam was extracted by cutting or slashing the bark and letting the liquid

1. Pliny, *Natural History,* 12, 25 (O'G).
2. Song of Solomon, 1, 13 (O'G).
3. Strabo, *Geography,* lib. 16 (O'G).
4. Pliny, *Natural History,* 12, 25 (O'G).

exude from it, the same is done in the Indies, although the quantity that it exudes is greater. And just as in that balsam there is a pure liquid called apobalsam, which is the very drop that oozes from the tree, and another that is less perfect, for it is the liquid that comes from the branch or bark itself and the leaves that are pressed and boiled, which are called jilobalsam, so also in the balsam of the Indies there is one that is pure, just as it comes from the tree, and another that the Indians get by boiling and pressing the leaves and stems; and they also adulterate it and increase its bulk with other liquids to make it seem like more. Indeed, it is very rightly called balsam, although it is not of that kind, and it is greatly prized and would be still more so did it not have the defect that emeralds and pearls have, namely, that they are very abundant. What is most important is its role in making sacramental chrism, which is so necessary and so much venerated in the Holy Church. The Apostolic See has declared that chrism can be made with this balsam of the Indies and that the sacraments of Confirmation and the other sacraments in which the Church uses it can be performed with it.[5] Balsam is brought to Spain from New Spain and from the province of Guatemala and from Chiapa and other provinces where it is most abundant, although the kind most highly valued is the balsam that comes from the island of Tolú, which is on the continent not far from Cartagena. That balsam is white, and the white is generally considered purer than the red, although Pliny gives first place to red balsam and second to white, third to green, and last place to black.[6] But Strabo appears to value the white balsam most, as our compatriots do.[7] Monardes deals at length with Indies balsam in his first and second parts, especially with that of Cartagena or Tolú, which is the same thing. I have not found that in ancient times the Indians valued balsam highly, or even used it to any important degree, although Monardes says that they cured their wounds with it and that the Spaniards learned of it from them.

5. Acosta calls Indies balsam not a "true" balsam, despite the many similarities between it and its Old World counterpart. The indication that the pope had to offer a declaration before Indies balsam could be used to produce holy chrism reiterates the theme running through book IV, that New World species are inferior or tainted until blessed with European approval.

6. Pliny, *Natural History,* 12, 25 (O'G).

7. Strabo, *Geography,* lib. 16 (O'G).

CHAPTER 29 * OF LIQUIDAMBAR AND OTHER
OILS AND GUMS AND DRUGS THAT ARE
BROUGHT FROM THE INDIES

After balsam, liquidambar is much valued: it is another liquid that is also sweet smelling and medicinal, of thicker consistency in itself, which solidifies and makes a white paste with a pleasant perfume and is applied to wounds and other needs, concerning which I refer my readers to doctors, especially Dr. Monardes, who in the first part of his book wrote about this liquid and many other medicinal liquids that come from the Indies.

Liquidambar also comes from New Spain, and there is no doubt that that province has the advantage in these gums or liquids or sap of trees, and so they have large amounts of different materials for perfumes and medicines, such as *anime,* which occurs in large quantities, and *copal* and *suchicopal,* which is another sort resembling balm or incense, also possessing excellent qualities and a very fine smell for censing.[1] There are also *tacamahaca* and *caraña,* which are very medicinal. The oil called *abeto* also comes from there, and doctors and painters make considerable use of it, the former for poultices and the latter for varnish for their pictures. *Cassia fistula* is also brought for medicinal purposes; it grows abundantly in Hispaniola and is a large tree, and produces those canes, along with their pulp, as its fruit. Forty-eight hundredweight of cassia was brought in the fleet in which I came from Santo Domingo.

Sarsaparilla is no less known for its many uses: fifty hundredweight came in the same ships from the same island. In Peru there is an abundance of very good sarsaparilla in the region of Guayaquil, which is situated below the equator. Many people go there for cures, and it is thought that the herbal waters that they drink themselves bring them health because such waters have passed through these roots, as I mentioned above; add to this the fact that in that climate not much clothing or coverings are needed to make a person sweat.

*Guayacán* wood, also called holy wood or Indies wood, grows in abundance on the same islands, and is as heavy as iron, and quickly sinks in water; the fleet I have mentioned brought 350 hundredweight and could

---

1. Copal played a central role in Mesoamerican spiritual ceremonies; when burned, its smoke was believed to invoke the presence of deities.

have brought 20,000 or even 100,000 if there were a market for so much wood. One hundred and thirty-four hundredweight of Brazil wood, which is bright red in color and so well known and employed in dyes and other uses, came from the same island in the same fleet. There is such an enormous number in the Indies of other aromatic woods and gums and oils and drugs that it is impossible to list them all, nor need I do so for the present purpose. I will only say that during the time of the Inca kings in Cuzco and the monarchs of Mexico there were many famous men who cured with simples and performed excellent cures because they had knowledge of the different virtues and properties of the herbs and roots and woods and plants that grow there, about which the ancients in Europe knew nothing. Any number of these simples are used for purges, such as Michoacán root, pine nuts from Puna, preserves from Guanaco, oil of figs, and a hundred other things, which, if well applied and at the appropriate time, are no less efficacious than the drugs that come from the East, which anyone can appreciate who reads what Monardes has written in the first and second parts of his book; it also deals at length with tobacco, which has been used with remarkable success against poison.

Tobacco is a small tree or plant that is quite common but has rare virtues; there is also one that they call *contrayerba,* and other plants, for the Author of all things distributed his good qualities as he wished and did not allow anything useless to be born into the world; but it is another sovereign gift that the Creator deigns to concede to men that man can know these plants and learn how to use them.

Doctor Francisco Hernández, expressly commissioned by His Majesty, wrote a remarkable book about this subject of plants of the Indies and liquors and other medicinal things. He made paintings from life of the plants of the Indies, of which it is said there are more than twelve hundred, and they say that this work cost more than sixty thousand ducats. A sort of extract of this book was made with rare scientific zeal by Doctor Nardo Antonio, an Italian physician. I recommend these books and works to any of my readers who may wish to know in more detail, and more perfectly, about the plants of the Indies, especially for medicinal purposes.[2]

2. King Philip appointed the Italian physician Dr. Nardo Antonio Recchi, Napolitano de Montecorvo, to edit and publish a version of Dr. Francisco Hernández's natural history of New Spain. Nardo returned to Naples

## CHAPTER 30 * OF THE GREAT FORESTS OF THE INDIES AND OF CEDARS AND CEIBAS AND OTHER LARGE TREES

Since from the beginning of the world the earth brought forth plants and trees by order of the Omnipotent Lord, there is no region that does not produce some fruit, though more in some than in others. And apart from the trees and plants that have been planted and carried from one land to another by men's efforts there are a large number of trees that Nature alone has produced. Of these I believe that there are far more, both in number and variety, in the New World (as we call the Indies) than in the Old World and the European lands, Asia, and Africa. The reason is that, contrary to the opinion of the ancients, the Indies has a warm and humid climate, as was demonstrated in my second book; and hence the land produces in great abundance a huge variety of these wild and natural plants. This is the reason why the greater part of the Indies is uninhabitable and impenetrable, owing to its forests and mountains and heavily wooded hills, which have constantly had to be cleared. To make some roads in the Indies passable, especially in places where they are newly opened, it has been, and still is, necessary to progress by cutting down trees with axes and leveling thickets, which, as members of our society who have experienced it have told us, means progressing no more than a league in six days. And one of our brothers, a man worthy of belief, told us that once he was lost in some mountains without knowing where to go or where he had come from. He found himself among thickets so dense that he had to travel in them for two weeks without ever putting foot to ground. In these thickets, too, in order to see the sun and try to find some direction, because the vast tree cover of that region was so thick, he sometimes had to scramble to the top of very tall trees to find his way out from among them. Whoever reads the account of the time when this man was lost, and the paths that he trod, and the strange things that happened to him (which I, because I thought it ought to be known, jotted down), as well as anyone who has sometimes traveled through the mountains of the Indies,

---

and made an extract of Hernández's books, which were published as *Nova plantarum, animalium et mineralium mexicanorum historia a Francisco Hernández, etc.* A more complete three-volume edition of Hernández's research, *De historia plantarum plantae Novae Hispaniae,* was finally published in 1651.

if only the eighteen leagues that separate Nombre de Dios from Panama, will well understand the immensity of forests in the Indies. Since there is never a cold winter there, and the moisture of sky and earth is so great, naturally the mountain regions produce infinite forests and the flat lands, which they call savannas, infinite grass. So there is never any lack of grazing, and grass, and wood for buildings, and firewood.

It would be impossible to describe the differences and shapes of this abundance of forest trees, for even the names of most of them are unknown. Cedars, so highly praised in ancient times, are very common there both for building and for ships, and there is great diversity among them: some are white and others red and very sweet smelling. They grow in the Andes of Peru and in the mountains of the northern continent and on the islands and in Nicaragua and in large numbers in New Spain. There are bay trees, which are beautiful to see and very tall, infinite numbers of palm trees, and ceibas, of which the Indians make canoes, boats made of a single piece of wood.

Precious woods such as ebony, mahogany, *granadillo,* cedar, and other woods about which I know nothing are brought to Spain from Havana and the island of Cuba, where there are an immense number of these trees. There are also large pines in New Spain, though not as thick as those in Spain; they do not bear pine nuts, only empty cones. The oak that is brought from Guayaquil is a very fine wood, and sweet-smelling when it is worked, and from the same place come very tall canes whose sections make a jug or pitcher for water and also serve for building, and mangrove wood, which makes spars and masts for ships and is considered so strong that it is like iron. The *molle* is a tree with many good qualities; it has little branches of which the Indians make wine. In Mexico they call it the Peru tree because it came from there, but it also grows in New Spain, and better than in Peru. There are any number of other trees, which it would be a useless effort to describe. Some of these are of enormous size; I will mention only one in Tlacochabaya, three leagues from Oaxaca in New Spain. When this tree was measured the center hollow alone measured nine cubits, the outer measurement near the roots sixteen cubits, and higher up twelve. This tree was struck by lightning from top to bottom, and they say that it left the hollow I have described. It is said that before it was struck by lightning it cast shade enough for a thousand men, and so the Indians met there to perform their rites and dances and superstitions; it still has branches and leaves but many fewer than before.

They do not know what kind of tree it was, except that they say it was some sort of cedar.

Anyone who thinks that this is an exaggeration should read what Pliny recounts of the plane tree of Lycia, whose hollow measured eighty-one feet and seemed more like a cave or a house than a hollow tree; and its canopy looked like a whole forest, whose shadow covered the fields.[1] This will suffice to allay the fear and astonishment aroused by the story of a certain weaver who had his house and loom in the hollow of a chestnut tree and of that other chestnut or some other kind of tree where eight men on horseback could enter and wheel around, to emerge from its hollow without the slightest difficulty. The Indians performed many of their idolatrous rites in these trees of strange and unusual shape, as did the ancient pagans also, according to writers of that time.

### CHAPTER 31 * OF THE PLANTS AND FRUIT TREES THAT HAVE BEEN BROUGHT TO THE INDIES FROM SPAIN

Insofar as plants are concerned, the Indies have profited more from them than from any other merchandise, for few of theirs have been brought to Spain and those few did not thrive; those that came from Spain are many, and they do very well in the Indies.[1] I do not know whether we ought to say that the plants were so good that they have given glory to Spain or that the earth there has made them the glory of the Indies. To sum up, almost every good plant produced in Spain also grows there, in many places better than in Spain and in others not as well: wheat, barley, herbs and greenstuffs, and vegetables of all kinds such as lettuce, cabbage, radishes, onions, garlic, parsley, turnips, carrots, eggplant, escarole, chard, spinach, chickpeas, beans, lentils, and in short everything that is raised here in Spain, both for domestic consumption and for commerce; for those who have gone to the Indies have been careful to take all kinds of seeds with them, and the land has favored

1. Pliny, *Natural History*, 12, 1 (O'G).

1. Once again Acosta alludes to the tension between the New World as earthly paradise or land of barbarity. Notice that products of the uncivilized Indies did not thrive in civilized Spain, but Spanish products, stunted in their home soil, flourished in the fertile climate of the New World. For a discussion of trans-Atlantic exchanges of plants, see Alfred W. Crosby, *The Columbian Exchange: Biological and Cultural Consequences of 1492* (Westport, CT: Greenwood, 1972).

them all, though more in some places than in others and in a few places very little.

The trees that have adapted best to the Indies, and bear most abundantly, are oranges and limes and citron and fruit of that kind. In some places there are already whole woods and groves of orange trees, and this seemed so wonderful to me that in one of the islands I asked who had planted so many. They told me that perhaps it had happened when oranges fell from the tree and the fruit rotted, and that the trees had sprouted from seeds, and that the seeds of those trees and others had been carried by the waters to different places and had formed those thick woods. It seemed a reasonable explanation to me. As I said, this fruit is the one that has grown best in the Indies, for no part where I have been lacked oranges; the reason for this is that all the Indies are hot and humid lands, which is what that tree requires. Oranges do not grow in the mountains but are brought from the valleys or the coast. The orange marmalade that they make in the islands is the best I have ever tasted. Peaches have also given good results, as well as their relatives nectarines and apricots, although the latter are more common in New Spain; in Peru, apart from peaches, there is not much fruit, and even less in the islands. Apples and pears grow, but with moderate success; there are very few plums but figs in abundance, especially in Peru. There are quinces everywhere, and in New Spain they were so abundant that we used to choose fifty of them for half a real. And there are a good many pomegranates, too, though all of them are of the sweet variety; the sour ones do not grow well. There are good melons in some places, such as Tierra Firme and some parts of Peru. So far cherries have not been raised successfully in the Indies; I do not think it the fault of the climate, for all sorts of climates exist there, but rather lack of care or ignorance. There are none of the coarser and grosser kinds of fruits such as acorns or chestnuts, which have not been cultivated in the Indies as far as I know. There are almonds but not many. Almonds, walnuts, and filberts are brought from Spain as dainties for the well-to-do. Nor do I know whether there are medlars or wild pears, nor are they important. And let this suffice to show that there is no lack of excellent fruit; now we will say a little more about profitable plants that have been sent from Spain, and then we will end this discussion of plants, which is already overlong.

CHAPTER 32 * OF GRAPES AND VINES AND
OLIVES AND MULBERRIES AND SUGARCANE

By profitable plants I mean those that, in addition to providing food, bring money to their owners. The chief of these is the vine, which gives wine and vinegar and grapes and raisins and verjuice and must; but wine is the most important of these. On the islands and in Tierra Firme neither grapes nor wine are produced; there are vines in New Spain, and they bear grapes, but wine is not made there. The reason must be that the grapes do not fully ripen owing to the rains that come in July and August and prevent them from maturing successfully; they are good only for eating. Wine is brought from Spain or the Canaries, and this is the case in the rest of the Indies except for Peru and Chile, where there are vineyards and very good wine is made. It increases daily both in quantity, because it represents great wealth in that land, and quality, for nowadays there is a better understanding of how to make it. In Peru the vineyards are commonly located in warm valleys where there are irrigation canals, and they are irrigated by hand, for there is no rainwater on the plains and the rains do not come at the right time in the mountains. There are places where the vines are watered neither from above nor below, and they produce in large quantities, such as the valley of Yca; and the same is true in the river basins called Villacuri, where amid dead, sandy soil are some depressions or low-lying lands that are incredibly cool all year long, though it never rains nor is there any irrigation by human hands. The reason is that the soil is spongy and sucks up the water of the rivers that come down from the mountains and soaks those sandy places; or, if it is moisture from the sea (as some believe), it must be understood that the water percolating through the sand is the reason why the soil is neither barren nor useless, as the philosopher says. The vineyards have increased so much that for this reason alone church tithes today are five or six times what they were twenty years ago. The valleys most fertile in vineyards are those of Víctor, near Arequipa; Yca, in the region of Lima; and Caracato, near Chuquiavo. This wine is taken to Potosí and Cuzco and a number of other places, and it yields great profit because, even though it is so abundant, a jug or *arroba* of wine is worth five or six ducats; and if it is Spanish wine (which always comes with the fleets) it sells for ten and twelve ducats. In the kingdom of Chile wine is made just as it is in Spain, for the climate is the same; but if brought to Peru it goes bad.

Grapes can be enjoyed in places where wine cannot, and it is a remarkable thing that in the city of Cuzco there are fresh grapes all year long. The cause of this, they told me, is the valleys of that region, which give crops at different times of the year; and whether it is because they prune the vines at different times or because of the quality of the soil the fact is that all year long different valleys produce fruit. If anyone is astonished by this, he will be still more astonished by what I am about to say and perhaps will not believe it. There are trees in Peru of which one part gives fruit for half the year and the other part the rest of the year. In Mala, thirteen leagues from Ciudad de los Reyes, the half of a fig tree that faces south is green and gives fruit at one point in the year, when it is summer in the mountains, and the other half, which faces toward the plains and the sea, is green and gives fruit at a different time, when it is summer on the plains. Differences in climate, and the wind that comes from one place or another, can have effects as great as these.

Production of wine is not small, but it does not go beyond the province. The silk made in New Spain is exported to other realms such as Peru. This industry did not exist during Indian times; mulberry trees have been brought from Spain, and they grow well, especially in the province of Mixteca, where silkworms are raised and silk thread made and good taffetas woven; so far they do not make damask and satin and velvet. Sugar cultivation is another widespread agricultural activity; not only is sugar used in the Indies but a considerable quantity is also taken to Spain, for sugarcane can be grown in different parts of the Indies. On islands, in Mexico, in Peru, and in other places sugar mills that do a great deal of business have been built. Of the mill in Nazca I was told that it brought in more than thirty thousand pesos every year. That of Chicama, near Trujillo, has also brought a large revenue, and the mills of New Spain are no less profitable, for the amount of sugar that is eaten and used for preserving in the Indies borders on folly. In the fleet in which I came to Spain, 898 boxes and chests of sugar were brought, each of which, if they were the size that I saw loaded in Puerto Rico, must have weighed a couple of hundred pounds. So much has men's appetite for sweet things increased that sugar is the chief agricultural product of those islands. Olives and olive groves have also been established in the Indies, in Mexico and Peru, but up to the present there is no oil mill, nor has one ever been built, for the inhabitants prefer to eat the olives, and they prepare them well. They find that the cost of producing oil is more than it is worth, so all the oil comes from Spain. With this I have finished the subject of plants, and now let us go on to the subject of animals in the Indies.

CHAPTER 33 * OF SHEEP AND CATTLE

I find that there are three kinds of animals in the Indies: some that have been taken there by Spaniards; others that, although they have not been brought from Spain, are of the same species as in Europe, and others that are native to the Indies and are not found in Spain.[1] Among the first group are sheep, cattle, goats, pigs, horses, asses, dogs, cats, and other such animals, for all these kinds are found in the Indies. Sheep have multiplied greatly, and if their wool could be utilized by shipping it to Europe it would be one of the Indies' greatest riches, for sheep have a great abundance of pasturage there and in many places the grass never dries up; the freedom of pastures and grazing lands is so great that there is no individual ownership of them in Peru. Each man grazes his flock where he pleases, and for this reason meat is usually cheap and abundant there, as are other products from sheep such as cheese, milk, and so on. For a time all the wool went to waste, until textile workshops were built to make cloth and blankets, which has been of great help to the poor folk in that land, for Castilian clothing is very expensive. There are various textile workshops in Peru and many more in New Spain, although, either because the wool is coarser or because it is not woven as well, clothing from Spain is much better than that made in the Indies. There used to be men who owned seventy thousand and a hundred thousand head of sheep, and even today there are flocks nearly as large; in Europe this would represent great wealth, and there it is only moderate.

In many parts of the Indies, I believe almost everywhere, sheep cannot be raised successfully because the grass is so tall and the vegetation so rank that only cattle can graze there, and so there are innumerable herds of cattle. And there are two kinds of these, the first being domestic cattle in herds, as in the Charcas district and other provinces of Peru, and as in all of New Spain. The herds are made use of, as in Spain, for meat and butter and calves, the oxen are used for plowing, and so on. There is another kind of cattle that has gone wild, and because of the rough country and great thickets as well as their large numbers these are not branded and have no owners; the first man to hunt

---

1. An innovative historical study considers the ecological transformations caused by the introduction of sheep, and other products, to New Spain and analyzes how they are linked to social changes in the region. See Elinor Melville, *A Plague of Sheep: Environmental Consequences of the Conquest of Mexico* (Cambridge: Cambridge University Press, 1994).

and kill them, like game, becomes their owner. The cattle of Hispaniola and other neighboring islands have multiplied so greatly in this way that thousands of ownerless animals roam the woods and fields. These cattle are used for their hides; both whites and blacks go out in the country and chase the bulls and cows, and the animal that they hamstring, when it falls, belongs to them. They flay it and take the hide home, leaving the meat to go to waste on the spot, for no one uses it or even wants it owing to the glut of cattle. This happens so frequently on that island that I was told infection existed in some places from the quantities of rotting meat. The hides that are imported into Spain represent one of the chief products of the islands and New Spain. In the fleet that came from Santo Domingo in fifteen hundred and eighty-seven, there were 35,444 cattle hides. From New Spain came 64,350, which were valued at 96,532 pesos. When one of these fleets unloads, it is astonishing to see the river in Seville, and the sandy bank where all those hides and all that merchandise are displayed.

Goats are also raised in the Indies, and aside from the usual products, milk and kids, a very important product is tallow, which rich and poor commonly use for illumination because, since it is abundant, it is cheaper than oil, although all the tallow that is used in this way does not come from male animals. Their leather is also worked to make shoes, but I do not think them as good as those of Spain.

There are horses, and they are found in some and indeed almost all parts of the Indies; and some breeds are as good as the best horses in Castile, for racing and show as well as travel and work. The common thing there is to use horses for traveling, although there are mules and many of them, especially in places — like Tierra Firme — where strings of them are used. There are not many donkeys, nor are they much used, and they are employed very little for working. I did see a few camels in Peru, which had been brought from the Canaries and had multiplied there, but not many.

In Hispaniola dogs have multiplied both in number and size to the point that they are the plague of that island, for they eat the cattle and roam the countryside in packs. A bounty is offered to those who kill them, as is done with wolves in Spain. There were no true dogs in the Indies, only an animal similar to a little dog that the Indians called *alco;* and the Indians are so fond of them that they will go hungry in order to feed them, and when they are walking along the roads they will carry them on their backs or in their bosoms. And if they are ill the dog must stay by them, though they use them for nothing, only good friendship and company.

## CHAPTER 34 * OF SOME EUROPEAN ANIMALS THAT THE SPANIARDS FOUND IN THE INDIES AND HOW THEY MIGHT HAVE COME

All of the animals that I have described were certainly brought from Spain, and none was in the Indies at the time of the discovery, less than a hundred years ago; and, besides being a matter that still has living witnesses, the fact that the Indians do not have names for these animals in their own languages is sufficient proof of it. Instead they use the Spanish names, though in corrupt form, because, since they did not know what the thing was, they took its name from Spanish. I have found this a good rule for discovering what things the Indians had before the Spaniards came and those they did not, for they gave their names to the things they already had and with which were familiar; things that they received newly were given new names, which are usually Spanish ones, though pronounced after their fashion, like the words for horse, wine, wheat, and so on. However, animals of the same kind as in Europe were found that had not been brought by the Spaniards.

There are lions, tigers, bears, boars, foxes, and other wild beasts, as we strongly argued in the first book, saying that it was not likely that they went to the Indies by sea, for it is impossible to cross the ocean by swimming and it would have been folly for men to bring them. It therefore follows that they must have come from some place where one hemisphere is near the other and little by little populated that world. For, according to Divine Scripture, all of these animals were saved in Noah's Ark and from there have propagated in the world.[1] The lions that I saw there are not reddish in color, nor do they have those manes with which they are usually pictured; they are dark colored and not as fierce as they have been described. To hunt them the Indians surround them in a maneuver that they call *chaco* and kill them with stones and sticks and other weapons. These lions often climb trees and are killed there with spears or crossbows and even more easily with harquebuses. The tigers are considered to be fiercer and crueler, and their leaps are more dangerous because they leap so treacherously. They are spotted, and look just as

1. Genesis, 6, 19 (O'G).

the historians describe them. I heard it said sometimes that these tigers were accustomed to eating Indians, and that was why they never or almost never attacked Spaniards, and that a group of them would pick out an Indian among Spaniards and make off with him. The bears, which in the language of Cuzco are called *otoroncos,* are of the same kind as here, and eat ants.[2] There is little experience of beekeeping because where honeycombs exist in the Indies they occur in trees or underground, and not in hives as in Castile, and the honeycombs that I saw in the province of Los Charcas, which they call *lechiguanas* there, are dark in color and contain little honey; they are more like sweet straw than honeycombs. They say that the bees are no larger than flies and that they swarm underground; the honey is ill tasting and black. In other places there is better honey and the combs are better formed, such as in the province of Tucumán and in Chile and Cartagena. I have little to relate about wild boars, apart from having heard people say that they have seen them. There are more foxes and animals that kill livestock than herdsmen would wish. Apart from these beasts, which are fierce and harmful, there are also useful ones that were not brought by the Spaniards, such as deer and stags, of which there are a large number in all those regions; but most of them are not the sort to have horns, at least not those I have seen or heard people say they had seen, for all are hornless, like roe deer.

I do not find it difficult to believe that all these animals may have crossed from one hemisphere to the other where they come close together because of their fleetness of foot and the fact that they are naturally wild and game animals. Indeed, this is very probable and almost certain given the fact that they are not found in large islands that are far distant from the mainland, at least as far as I have been able to discover from my own experience and that of others.

CHAPTER 35 * OF BIRDS THAT EXIST IN
EUROPE AND HOW THEY CAME TO THE INDIES

It is less difficult to believe the same of the birds that exist there and are of the same kind as those of Europe, such as partridges and pigeons and doves and many different breeds of falcons, which are much prized and are sent from

2. Otoronco, from the Quechua, signifies the jaguar and not the bear, as Acosta states. See the seventeenth-century dictionary of Diego Goncalez Holguin, *Vocabulario de la lengua general de todo el Perú llamada lengua Qquichua o del Inca,* edited by Raúl Porras Barrenechea (Lima, 1952), 265, 280.

New Spain and Peru to be presented to noblemen in Spain. The same is true
of herons and eagles of different breeds. There is no doubt that these and
other, similar birds could cross, and much more easily than lions and tigers
and deer. Parrots also are capable of very long flights and are found abundantly in the Indies, especially in the Andes of Peru; and flocks of them, like
flocks of doves, fly in the islands of Puerto Rico and Santo Domingo. Finally,
birds with their wings may go where they like, and it would not be very
difficult for many of them to cross the great gulf; for it is certainly true, as
Pliny states, that many cross the sea and go to very remote regions, although
I do not know whether anyone has written that birds fly across so great a gulf
as the ocean of the Indies.[1] But neither do I think it altogether impossible, for
it is the common opinion of sailors that some birds are seen at a distance of
two hundred leagues, and much more, from land. And also, as Aristotle
teaches us,[2] birds easily tolerate staying under water, for their respiration is
not great, as we can see in sea birds who dive and stay underwater for a long
time; and thus we may believe that the birds and fowl that are found in the
islands and on the continent of the Indies could have crossed the sea by
resting on islands and bits of land, which they know by natural instinct, like
some birds of which Pliny speaks.[3] Or perhaps they let themselves fall into
the water when they are tired of flying, and from there, after they have rested
for a while, they resume their flight. And, as for the birds that are found in the
islands where there are no land animals, I have no doubt that they crossed in
one of the two ways I have described.

As for the other birds that are found on the mainland, especially those that
are not great flyers, it is preferable to believe that they came in the same way
as the land animals that are like those of Europe. For there are also very large
birds in the Indies resembling ostriches, which are found in Peru and even
frighten the Peruvian pack animals when they are loaded. But let us leave
these birds, which take care of themselves, and men pay no heed to them
except to use them for hunting.

As for domestic fowl, I have wondered much at the hens, because indeed
they existed before the Spaniards came, and the best proof is that they have
native names; for the hen is called *gualpa,* and the egg *ronto,* and the Indians

1. Pliny, *Natural History,* 10, 23 (O'G).
2. Aristotle, *De partibus animalium,* book 3, chapter 6 (O'G).
3. Pliny, *Natural History,* 10, 25 (O'G).

have the same saying as we do, calling a man a hen to describe him as a coward. And the men who discovered the Solomon Islands say that they saw hens like ours there. It can well be believed that, since the hen is so domestic and useful an animal, men took them with them when they crossed from one place to another, just as today we see the Indians walking along carrying their hen or chick on top of the load on their shoulders, and they often carry them easily in cages made of straw or wood. Finally, in the Indies there are many species of animals and birds resembling those of Europe, which the Spaniards found there, such as the ones I have described and others that I will leave to others to describe.

### CHAPTER 36 * HOW IT CAN BE POSSIBLE THAT THERE ARE ANIMALS IN THE INDIES NOT FOUND IN ANY OTHER PART OF THE WORLD

It is more difficult to establish the beginnings of different animals that are found in the Indies and not in our world here in Europe. For if the Creator produced them there, we need not have recourse to Noah's Ark, nor was it necessary to save all the species of birds and animals at that time if they were going to be created again later; nor does it appear that God would have left the world in a finished and perfect state after the Creation in six days if there were still new species of animals to be formed, chiefly perfect animals and of no less excellence than those already known. But if we say that all these species of animals were preserved in Noah's Ark, it follows that these, like the other animals, went to the Indies from this continent; and also that the animals that are not found in other parts of the world must have done the same. And this being so, I must ask why their species did not remain in Europe. Why are they found only in foreign and strange places? Truly it is a question that has perplexed me for a long time. For example, I say that if those sheep of Peru, and the ones they call *pacos* and guanacos, are not found in any other part of the world, then who took them to Peru or how did they get there, since no trace of them remained in the whole world? And, if they did not come from another region, how were they formed and brought forth there? Did God perchance make a new formation of animals? What I say about these guanacos and *pacos* I can say of a thousand kinds of birds and fowl and forest animals that have never been known before either in name or shape, nor is there any memory of them in the Latins and Greeks, nor in any nations of our world. We must then say that, even though all the animals came out of the Ark, by natural instinct and the providence of Heaven, different kinds went to different regions and in some of those regions were so contented that they did not want to leave them; or that if they did leave they were not preserved, or in the course of time became extinct, as happens with many things. And if we look at the matter carefully it is not only the case of the Indies but the general case of many other regions and provinces of Asia, Europe, and Africa, where we read that in all of them breeds of animals exist that are not found in other regions; and if they are found there it is known that they were brought from other places. Since these animals came out of the Ark, like the elephants, for example, which are found only in the East Indies, we may say the same of these animals in Peru and the rest of the animals in the Indies, which cannot be found in any other part of the world. We must also consider whether these animals differ specifically and essentially from all others or whether their difference is accidental; this could be caused by various accidents, as in the lineage of men some are white and others black, some giants and others dwarfs. Thus, for example, in the monkey family, some have tails and others not, and in the family of sheep some are bare and others have fleece; some are large and strong and long-necked like those of Peru, and others are small and weak and with short necks like those of Castile. But what is most certainly true is that anyone who, by trying to establish only accidental differences, attempts to resolve the propagation of Indies animals and reduce them to those of Europe must take great care because he could be very wrong about the matter. For if we are to judge the species of animals by their characteristics those of the Indies are so diverse that to try to reduce them to species known in Europe would be like calling an egg a chestnut.

## CHAPTER 37 * OF BIRDS NATIVE TO THE INDIES

Whether of different or the same species as in Europe, there are remarkable birds in the Indies. Birds are brought from China that, sad to say, have no feet either large or small, and almost all their bodies are feathers. They never alight on the ground, but hang from branches on little strings that they have, and thus rest; they eat mosquitoes and little flying insects. In Peru there are birds called *tominejos,* or hummingbirds, so very small that I often wondered, when I saw them flying, whether they were bees or butterflies, but they are really birds. On the other hand, those they call condors are immensely large and strong; they not only tear open a sheep and eat it but even a calf. I believe that the birds known as *auras,* and also as turkey buzzards, are some species of crow. They are tremendously swift and no less sharp of sight; they are excellent for cleaning cities and streets, for they leave no dead thing untouched. They spend the night in trees or among rocks; in the morning they come to the cities and spy from the tops of the tallest buildings to locate their prey. The chicks of these birds are whitish in color, as is said of crows, and change their feathers to black. Macaws are birds larger than parrots and somewhat resemble them; they are prized for their feathers of many colors, which are very handsome. In New Spain there are a large number of birds with excellent plumage, finer than any to be found in Europe, as can be seen from the feather pictures that come from there. These are rightly prized and cause amazement that such delicate work can be done with birds' feathers. They are so smooth that they seem to be painted in colors, and better than what the brush and dyes can do. They have such a beautiful sheen, and are so pretty and lifelike, that when they are looked at slightly sideways they delight the eye wonderfully.

Some Indians, good artists, copy perfectly with feathers what they have seen drawn and do it as well as any painters in Europe. His tutor gave the prince of Spain, Don Felipe, three little feather pictures like those one might use between the pages of a book of hours, and His Highness showed them to his father the king, Don Felipe our lord, and as he looked at them His Majesty said that he had never seen anything more exquisite in such small objects. There is another, larger picture that shows Saint Francis gladly receiving sainthood from Pope Sixtus V, and when the king was told that the Indians had made it he tried to test it by brushing his fingers lightly over the picture to see if it was indeed made of feathers; he thought it marvelous that it was so well done that the eyes could not tell whether they were natural colors of feathers or artificial colors painted with a brush. The sheen made by green and a sort of yellowish-orange, and other lovely colors, is extraordinarily beautiful; and if the picture is looked at in a different light the colors seem dead, which is a notable change. The best feather pictures are made in the province of Michoacán, in the town of Pátzcuaro.[1] The method is to take the feathers with small pincers, pulling them out of the dead birds themselves and sticking them together very quickly and skillfully with a very fine glue that they have. They take these tiny, delicate feathers from those little birds that in Peru are called hummingbirds, or from other, similar birds that have perfect colors in their plumage.

Besides pictures, the Indians made many other beautiful things out of feathers, especially for the adornment of their kings and nobles and their temples and idols. For there are other, large birds and fowl that have excellent and very fine feathers, of which they made elaborate plumes and crests, especially when they went to war; and they combined these works of rich plumage with gold and silver, and they were objects of great price. Today there are the same birds and fowl, but they are not used with as much artistry and complexity as before.

In contrast to these beautiful birds with such rich plumage, there are others in the Indies that are entirely different, for in addition to being ugly in themselves they are good for nothing except to void excrement; yet, even so, they may be no less useful. I have thought about this and been astonished by the providence of the Creator, who has decreed in so many ways that the other creatures must serve man. On some islands or rocky islets near the coast of Peru, entirely white hills can be seen; anyone who saw them would think they were covered with snow, or that the earth was white, and they are piles of dung from seabirds that go there to discharge it. And there is so much of it that the piles are yards high, or the height of a lance, which seems hard to believe. Boats go to these islands simply to load that dung, for the islands have no other product either large or small; and it is so effective and easy to use that when the earth is manured with it both grain and fruit are very much improved. This dung is called guano, from which was taken the name of the valley called Lunaguana in the valleys of Peru, where that dung is used, and it is the most fertile valley in the country. The quinces and pomegranates and other fruits are much larger and better, and they say that the reason for it is that the water with which these trees are irrigated passes through dung-laden earth and produces that beautiful fruit. So not only the flesh of birds

1. The Purepeche, or Tarascan peoples, of Michoácan produced feather paintings from their colonial artisan communities, which were founded with the assistance of Bishop Vasco de Quiroga.

to eat, and their songs to delight us, and their feathers for adornment and decoration, but their very excrement also serves to improve the earth; and all this is decreed by the Supreme Maker for the service of men, so that man may remember to be grateful and faithful to Him, who does good to man in every way.

## CHAPTER 38 * OF GAME ANIMALS

Apart from the kinds of game animals that are common to both the Indies and Europe, others are found there, and I do not think that there are any of them here unless they have been brought from those parts. They call *saynos,* or peccaries, animals resembling little pigs, which possess the strange feature of having their umbilicus on their backs. These roam the countryside in herds; they are savage and have no fear, but instead attack, and have tusks as sharp as knives with which they administer very serious wounds and slashings if those who hunt them are not extremely careful. Those who wish to hunt them in safety climb trees, and the peccaries or pigs of the herd come and bite the tree when they cannot bite the man; and then from above, with a short spear, the hunters wound and kill as many as they like. They are very good to eat, but that round place where the umbilicus is located on their back must be cut out very quickly, for otherwise the meat will spoil in a day. There is another species of animal, similar to a suckling pig, that they call *guadatinajas.* I doubt that there were pigs of the same kind as in Europe before the Spaniards went to the Indies, although in the account of the discovery of the Solomon islands it is said that they found hens and pigs like those of Spain.

What is certain is that this kind of animal has multiplied very much in almost all parts of the Indies. Fresh meat from pigs is eaten in many places, as, for instance, in Cartagena, and is considered to be very wholesome and as good as lamb. In some places pigs have returned to the wild and become savage and are hunted like wild boar, as in Hispaniola and the other islands where these animals have taken to the hills. In some places they are fattened with maize and become excessively fat in order to provide lard, which is used for lack of oil. In some places excellent hams are made of them, as in Toluca in New Spain and Paria in Peru. To return to the animals of Paria, just as the peccaries resemble pigs, although they are smaller, so do the *dantas* or tapirs resemble little cows, although because they lack horns they are more like small mules; the hides of these animals are much prized for jackets and other clothing because they are so strong that they turn aside any blow or gunshot. Just as what defends the tapirs is the strength of their hides, the animals called armadillos are defended by their many hard scales, which they open and shut like armor plate. They are small animals that are found in the woods, and are called armadillos because of their natural defenses, with many scales that open and shut at will like a cuirass. I have eaten them and do not think them good. A much better meat is that of iguanas, although they are hideous to look upon, for they greatly resemble Spanish lizards. These animals are of an ambiguous kind, however, for they swim in water and then come up on land and climb trees on the edges of the water; and as they jump into the water hunters catch them by placing their boats underneath.

Chinchillas are another kind of little animal, the size of squirrels. They have wonderfully soft fur, and their skins are considered a great luxury and healthy to cover the stomach and other parts of the body that require moderate heat; coverlets or blankets are also made from the fur of these chinchillas. They are found in the mountains of Peru, where there is also another very common little animal, the guinea pig, called *cuy* by the Indians, which they consider very good to eat; and in their sacrifices they used to offer these guinea pigs very frequently. They are like small rabbits and have their nests underground, and there are places where the ground is full of holes. Some of them are dark in color, others white, and some particolored. There are other small animals called *vizcachas,* which resemble hares, although they are larger, and these also are hunted and eaten. There is very good hunting of true hares in some places. There are also rabbits in the realm of Quito, but the best ones have come from Spain. Another amusing animal is the sloth, so called because of its excessive slowness of movement; it has three nails on each limb. It moves its limbs rhythmically, with extreme sluggishness. It is rather like a monkey and resembles one in the face. It emits great howls and lives in trees and eats ants.

## CHAPTER 39 * OF *MICOS,* OR THE MONKEYS OF THE INDIES

There are innumerable *micos* in all the mountains of the islands and the continent and the Andes. They are of the family of monkeys but are different in that they have very long tails, and among them there are some species that have bodies three and four times the size of those of ordinary monkeys. Some are black all over, others reddish-brown, and others gray; others are spotted and of several colors. The agility and cleverness of these animals is amazing, for they seem to possess speech and reason; and in the way that they travel through the trees it seems that they almost want to imitate birds. In Capira, when I was crossing the isthmus from Nombre de Dios to Panama, I saw one of these monkeys jump from one tree to another that was on the other side of the river, which astonished me. They seize a branch with their tails and leap wherever they wish; and when the space is very great and they cannot manage it in one jump they employ a clever trick: each grabs the tail of another monkey, and thus they make a chain of many animals. Then, with all of them swinging, the first monkey, helped by the efforts of the others, leaps and reaches his objective and catches hold of the branch, and holds the others up until they arrive, joined together as I have said, one caught by the tail of the other. The pranks, antics, and capers performed by these animals would be a long time in the telling; the skills they can acquire when they are trained seem worthy of human intelligence rather than of brute animals. I saw one in Cartagena, in the governor's house, about whom they told me things that were scarcely credible, such as sending him to the tavern for wine and putting the money in one hand and the jug in the other, and that there was no way he would relinquish the money until they gave him the jug with wine in it. If on the way boys shouted at him or threw stones, he would set the jug aside and take up stones and throw them at the boys until he saw that the coast was clear, and then he would carry his jug again. And, in addition, although he was a very good imbiber (as I saw him drink it, with his master pouring it from above), he would not touch the pitcher unless he was given it or was given permission. They also told me that if he saw women with their faces painted he would go and pluck at their headdresses and pull them about and ill treat them. There may be some exaggeration in this, for I did not see it; but I do believe that there is no animal that understands and adapts to human company as well as this breed of monkeys.

They tell so many things about them that I think it preferable to leave this subject, lest it be thought that I believe tall tales, or cause others to believe them; therefore, I will merely bless the Author of all creatures for having made, simply for men's enjoyment and wholesome entertainment, a kind of animal whose entire purpose is to laugh or make others laugh. Some have written that these animals were brought to Solomon from the West Indies; my opinion is that they came from the East Indies.

CHAPTER 40 * OF THE VICUÑAS AND
*TARUGAS* OF PERU

Among the remarkable things in the Indies of Peru are the vicuñas and native sheep of that land, which are gentle and very useful animals. Vicuñas live in the wild, and the native sheep are domestic livestock. Some have thought that vicuñas are the animals that Aristotle and Pliny and other authors are describing when they write of the animals they call *capreas,* which are wild goats; and doubtless there is some resemblance to goats owing to their agility and the fact that they inhabit mountainous areas.[1] But in fact they are not the same animals, for vicuñas possess no horns and goats do, as Aristotle states. Nor are they the goats of East India, whence comes the bezoar stone, or if they are of that kind they must be a different species, just as in the race of dogs the mastiff is of a different breed from the greyhound. Nor are the Peruvian vicuñas the same animal as the one in New Spain that has the stones called bezoars, for those are a kind of deer or stag. Yet I do not know in what other part of the world this kind of animal exists except in Peru and Chile, which is contiguous with Peru.

Vicuñas are larger than goats and smaller than calves; they have a color not unlike that of a lion, though a little lighter. They have no horns as deer and wild goats have; they graze and live in the highest mountains, in the coldest and most uninhabited places, which in Peru are called *punas.* They are undisturbed by snow and ice and indeed seem to enjoy them. They travel in flocks and run very fast; when they encounter travelers or other animals they run away as if very timid. When they flee, they drive their young before them. It is believed that they do not multiply rapidly, and hence the Inca kings banned the hunting of vicuñas except for festivals and at their orders. Some complain that since the Spaniards came too much license has been given to *chacos,* or vicuña hunts, and that their number has diminished. *Chaco* is the Indians' method of hunting, in which they gather a great many men together — sometimes a thousand, sometimes three thousand and more — and surround a large area, and then start the game by yelling until the animals come together from many places, whereupon the Indians take three hundred

---

1. Aristotle, *De partibus animalium,* book 3, chapter 2; Pliny, *Natural History,* 10, 72 (O'G).

and even four hundred of them, or more or less as they desire, and let the rest go, especially the females, so that they may continue to breed.

They have the habit of shearing these animals, and from their wool make coverlets or blankets that are much prized, for the wool is as soft as silk and very durable, and as the color is natural and not dyed it is permanent. These coverings are cool and very good for hot weather; they are held to be very healthful for inflammations of the kidneys and other organs, tempering the excessive heat. And their wool has the same effect when employed in mattresses, which some use for their health's sake because they have experienced their benefits. They also say that this wool, or blankets made from it, is good for other ailments such as gout; I do not have direct experience of this. The flesh of vicuñas is not good, although the Indians eat it and make *cusharqui*, or dried meat, of it. As for medicine, I can recount what I saw: once while traveling through the mountains of Peru I arrived at a *tambo*, or inn, with such a terrible pain in my eyes that I thought they would start out of my head; this is a common accident when one passes through a great deal of snow and looks at it. While I was lying down, with so much pain that I almost lost my patience, an Indian woman came in and said, "Put this over your eyes, father, and you will be well." It was a bit of vicuña meat, recently killed and running with blood. When I applied that medicine the pain lessened and within a very short time stopped altogether, and I never felt it again.[2] Aside from the communal hunts I have described, to catch these vicuñas individually the Indians throw knotted cords with lead weights on them when they get sufficiently close to the animals, which become entangled in their legs and trap them and hinder them from running; and so they approach the vicuña and capture it. The chief reason why these animals are prized is that bezoar stones are found in them, of which we will speak later.

There is another breed of animal called *taruga*, or Peruvian deer, which is also wild, and these are nimbler than the vicuñas; their bodies are also larger and their color darker; they have soft, drooping ears. These do not travel in herds like the vicuñas, at least I saw them only alone and usually on very high rocky peaks. Bezoar stones are also taken from them and are larger and possess greater efficacy and benefit.

2. This is one of the few examples in the book in which Acosta lends credence to indigenous knowledge, here of medical practices, with his testimony that the remedy of a native Andean woman cured his snow blindness.

CHAPTER 41 * OF ALPACAS AND GUANACOS
AND THE SHEEP OF PERU

There is nothing richer or more profitable in Peru than the livestock of that land, which our people call Indies sheep and the Indians in their language llama; for, all things considered, it is the most useful and the cheapest to maintain of any animal known. The Indians get food and clothing from this livestock, as from sheep in Europe; and it is still more useful in the moving and transport of anything they find necessary, for the llama serves to carry loads to and fro. And on the other hand there is no need to spend money on shoeing them, or for saddles or saddlebags, or for feeding them barley; rather, they serve their masters for nothing, being satisfied with the grass that grows in the countryside. So it is that God provided the Indians with a sheep and beast of burden in the same animal, and because they were poor people he ordained that it should cost them nothing; for there is a great deal of pasturage in the mountains, and as for other costs this type of animal neither requires nor needs them.

These sheep or llamas are of two species: of one kind are the alpacas, or woolly sheep, while others are smooth and have little wool and are better for carrying loads. They are larger than large sheep and smaller than yearling calves; they have a very long neck like a camel, and they need it because they are tall animals and high in the body and require a long neck in order to graze. They are of various colors: some are all white, others all black, others gray, and others of several colors, which they call *moromoro*. For their sacrifices the Indians had very careful specifications, such as the color they had to be for different times of year and different purposes.

The flesh of these animals is good, though tough, and that of their young ones is one of the best and most exquisite things that can be eaten; but the Indians do not use much of this, for the animals' chief product is wool to make clothing and the carrying of loads to and fro. The Indians prepare the wool and make from it the clothing they wear. One kind is coarse and ordinary and is called *hauasca;* another is delicate and fine, and they call it *cumbi*. They make tablecloths and coverlets from this *cumbi,* and coverings and other cloths of exquisite workmanship, which last for a long time and have a sheen almost as if made half of silk; and what is particularly interesting is their method of weaving wool. All the work that they do is woven on both sides, and not a single thread or loose end can be seen in an entire piece of material.

The Inca, king of Peru, had artists expert in preparing this clothing made of *cumbi,* most of whom lived in the district of Capachica, near the great lake of Titicaca. They dye this wool with vegetable dyes of different and very exquisite colors, with which they make different kinds of work. And the Indian men and women who live in the mountains are expert weavers, whether their work is rough and coarse or fine and delicate. They have their looms in their houses and do not need to go and buy, or give to others to make, the clothing that they need for their homes. The Indians make *cusharqui,* or dried meat, of the flesh of these animals, which lasts them a long time and is very highly prized.

Droves of these sheep are commonly loaded into a pack train, and in these trains go three hundred or five hundred or even a thousand animals, which transport wine, coca, maize, *chuño,* quicksilver, and every other sort of merchandise, as well as the best merchandise of all, which is silver; for they carry the bars of silver from Potosí to Arica, which is 70 leagues, and in former times carried them to Arequipa, 150 leagues.[1] And I was often astonished to see that these droves of sheep went loaded with a thousand and two thousand bars of silver and more, which are worth more than three hundred thousand ducats, with no more guard and no more escort than a few Indians, simply to lead the animals and load them, and very occasionally a Spaniard or two, and every night they would sleep in the middle of the countryside with no more precautions than those I have described. And in such a long road, and with so little guard, none of that large quantity of silver was ever missing, so great is the safety with which men travel in Peru. The load carried by one of these sheep is about four to six *arrobas,* and if it is a long trip they travel only 2 or 3 leagues in a day, or 4 at the most. The drovers, as the men who have charge of these pack trains are called, have their preferred stopping places where there is pasturage and water; there they unload and put up their rude tents, and build a fire and cook food, and do not have too bad a time of it, although it is a very slow method of travel. When the journey lasts no more than a day, one of these sheep can easily carry eight *arrobas* and more and will do a day's journey, with its load, of 8 or 10 leagues, as poor soldiers who traveled in Peru used to do.

All of these animals like cold weather, and that is why they breed in the

1. On this complex system of intracolonial provisioning, see Luis Miguel Glave, *Trajinantes: Caminos indígenas en la sociedad colonial siglos XVI/XVII* (Lima: Instituto de Apoyo Agrario, 1989).

mountains and die of heat on the plains. These animals can be all covered with frost and ice and be perfectly happy and healthy. The smooth-skinned sheep have a very amusing gaze, for they will stop on the road and stretch their necks and look very attentively at a person, and can stay in this position for such a long time without moving or any appearance either of fear or satisfaction that their placidity makes one want to laugh, although sometimes they suddenly take fright and run, load and all, to the highest crags. Then occasionally, not being able to reach them and not wishing to lose the silver bars they are carrying, it becomes necessary to shoot and kill them. Alpacas sometimes grow angry and tired of their burden and will lie down with it and resist any attempt to make them get up. When this fit of annoyance is on them they would rather be cut into a thousand pieces than move. From this comes the expression that they have in Peru, saying of someone that he has acted like an alpaca to mean that he has become sulky or stubborn or spiteful, for this is what alpacas do when they are angry. What the Indians do then is to stop and sit down next to the animal, and caress and pet it until it stops being sulky and stands up; and on occasion it can be two or three hours until the fit has passed and it stops being angry. They have an illness resembling mange, which the Indians call *carache,* and of which this kind of livestock often dies. The remedy used by the ancients was to bury alive the animal that had the disease, so that it would not spread to the others, for as a disease it is very contagious. If an Indian owns one or two of these sheep it is no small fortune, for one of them is worth seven or eight assayed pesos and more, according to the season of the year and the place.

CHAPTER 42 * OF BEZOAR STONES

In all the animals that we have described as native to Peru the bezoar stone is found, about which authors of our day have written whole books that may be consulted by anyone who wishes more detailed information. For the present purpose I need only say that this stone called bezoar is found in the stomach and belly of these animals, sometimes one and at other times two and three and four. There is a great deal of difference in their shape and size and color, for some are the size of hazelnuts and even smaller; others are like walnuts, others like pigeons' eggs, a few are as large as hens' eggs, and I have seen some the size of an orange. In shape some are round, some oval, some flat like lentils, and other similar shapes. In color there are black and dark brown ones, and white and dark green, and as if gilded; there is no firm rule as to color or size to judge which is a finer stone. All of them are composed of different layers or strata, one on another.

In the province of Jauja and other provinces of Peru they are found in different animals both wild and domestic, such as guanacos, alpacas and vicuñas, and *tarugas;* others add another kind of animal, which they describe as a wild goat, which the Indians call *cypris.* These other kinds of animals are very well known in Peru and have already been discussed. The guanacos and native sheep and alpacas commonly have the smallest and blackest stones, and they are not so highly prized, nor are they thought to be as useful in medicine. Larger bezoar stones are taken from the vicuñas, and they are dark brown or white or purplish and are held to be the best. The most excellent stones are believed to be those of *tarugas,* and some are very large; their stones are more commonly white and shading toward brown, and their layers or strata are thicker. The bezoar stone is found with equal frequency in both males and females; all the animals that have them are ruminants and usually graze in snow and on the high pastures.

The Indians say that, by tradition and what has been taught them by their elders and ancients, in the province of Jauja and others in Peru there are many poisonous herbs and animals that poison the water and grass that they drink and eat and smell. And among these herbs there is one that is very well known by natural instinct to the vicuña and those other animals that harbor the bezoar stone; they eat this herb, and with it are preserved from the poison of the water and pasturage, and grow the stone in their bellies from this herb, and it is from there that all its virtue against poison comes and these other marvelous operations. This is the opinion and tradition of the Indians, as very experienced persons in the realm of Peru have attested. This agrees very much with reason and what Pliny tells of mountain goats, that they graze on poison and it does not harm them.[1] When the Indians are asked how it is that Castilian sheep, and goats and deer and cattle, grazing as they do in the same upland pastures, lack the bezoar stone, they answer that they do not believe that those animals from Castile eat that herb, and that they have also found the bezoar stone in deer and fallow deer. This appears to agree with what we

1. Pliny, *Natural History,* 10, 72 (O'G).

know, that in New Spain bezoar stones are found in places where there are no vicuñas or alpacas or *tarugas* or guanacos, but only deer, and this aforesaid stone is found in some of them.

The chief effect of the bezoar stone is to protect against poison and the illnesses brought on by poisoning, and, although there are different opinions about the stone and some think it all superstition, others recount miracles of it. Certainly it is very useful if applied at the proper time and in the proper way, like other herbs and natural agents; for there is no medicine so efficacious that it invariably cures. It has performed very well in Spain and Italy for the spotted fever but not so well in Peru. For melancholy and heart disease, and for pestilent fevers and other different ailments, it is used ground to a powder and dissolved in some liquid appropriate to the illness being treated. Some take it in wine, others in vinegar, in orange flower water, with bugloss, with borage, and in other ways recommended by doctors and apothecaries. The bezoar stone itself has no taste at all, as the Arab physician Rashid-el-Din also said of it.[2] Some extremely interesting cures have been witnessed, and there is no doubt that the Author of all things placed great curative virtue in this stone.

The most highly prized bezoar stones are those that come from the East Indies, which are the color of olives; in second place come those of Peru and in third place those of New Spain. Since these stones began to be prized, they say that the Indians have made some that are artificial and adulterated; and many persons, when they see stones like these that are larger than normal, believe that they are false; but this is untrue, for there are large stones that are very fine, and small ones that have an ugly shape. Testing and experience are the best ways to recognize them. One remarkable thing is that these stones sometimes form around very strange objects, such as a bit of iron or a pin or a tiny stick, which is found in the very center of the stone; and this is no reason to argue that it is false, for it can happen that the animal swallows this and then the stone forms around it, growing little by little, one layer over another, and so it increases in size. I saw in Peru two stones that had grown around two pine nuts of Castile, and all of us who saw it were astonished, for in all of Peru we had not seen Castilian pinecones or pine nuts unless they had been brought from Spain, which seems a most extraordinary thing.

2. Rashid-el-Din, or Rashid ad-Din (1247–1318), was a Persian who wrote a general history of Mongolia, presumably including its medical practices. Acosta probably had access to his best-known work, *Jami' al-tavarikh*.

Let this short description suffice for bezoar stones. Other medicinal stones are brought from the Indies, such as those used for pain in the side, or for the blood, or for milk or for childbirth, and those known as cornelians for the heart, which, because they have nothing to do with animals such as those I have been discussing, I need not describe. Let what I have said serve to make us understand how the Universal Lord and Omnipotent Author distributed his gifts and secrets and marvels through the globe that he created, for which he must be adored and glorified forever and ever, amen.

# PROLOGUE TO
## THE SUBSEQUENT BOOKS

NOW THAT I HAVE DEALT WITH things pertaining to the natural history of the Indies, the remaining books will treat its moral history: that is, the customs and deeds of the Indians.[1] For after descriptions of the heavens, and climate and location, and the properties of the New World, and of its elements and mixtures (I mean its metals and plants and animals), of which I have said all that I could in the four preceding books, logic dictates that I go on to deal with the men who inhabit the New World. Therefore, in the books that follow everything that seems worthy of being recounted will be told; and because the aim of this history is not only to inform of what is happening in the Indies, but to dedicate that information to the benefit that knowledge of such things can bring, which is to help these peoples to their salvation and to glorify the Creator and Redeemer who led them out of the profound darkness of their heathen beliefs, and imparted to them the wonderful light of his Gospel, I will therefore first describe in the book that follows things pertaining to their religion, or superstition and rites, and idolatries and sacrifices, and then I will deal with their polity, form of government and laws, and customs and deeds. And because the memory of their beginnings and lineages, and wars and other things worthy of remembrance, has been preserved in the Mexican nation, apart from the ordinary matters dealt with in the sixth book I will make special mention of those things in the seventh book, until I have demonstrated the inclination and forewarnings that these people had of the new kingdom of Christ our God, which was destined to spread to those

1. Throughout books V, VI, and VII, Licentiate Juan Polo de Ondegardo and Fray Diego Durán constitute the main sources of information for Acosta on Peru and Mexico, respectively. Their data, gathered through exhaustive fieldwork with native Mexicans and Andeans, provided Acosta with primary source material from which to offer his philosophical interpretations.

lands and subject them to his will, as it has done in all the rest of the world. Surely it is worthy of great consideration to see how Divine Providence ordained that the light of his word should find a way into the farthest parts of the earth. It is not my intention now to write of what the Spaniards did in those parts, for many books have been written about that, nor what the servants of God have labored and brought forth, because that requires a new and different task. I shall merely content myself with placing this history or account at the doors of the Gospel, for all of it is intended to offer information about things both natural and moral in the Indies, to the end that spiritual and Christian values may be planted and grow, as I have explained at length in the book that I wrote, *De procuranda Indorum salute*.[2] If any reader is astonished by some of the Indians' rites and customs, and scorns them as ignorant and wicked or detests them as inhuman and diabolical, let him look to the Greeks and Romans, who ruled the world, and he will find the same or very similar customs, and sometimes worse ones, as can easily be understood not only from our Christian authors Eusebius of Caesaria, Clement of Alexandria, Theodoret of Cyrene, and others, but also from their own writers such as Pliny, Dionysius of Halicarnassus, and Plutarch. But since the prince of darkness is the teacher of all the heathen, it is no new thing to find cruelty and filth and folly and madness among them, learned from that teaching and that school; although in courage and natural intelligence the heathen of antiquity were much superior to these men of the New World, things deserving of being recorded have also happened to them. But, after all, the most important thing is that, as heathen peoples deprived of supernatural light, they also lacked philosophy and natural doctrine.

2. While in Lima from 1576 to 1577, Acosta reflected on his travels around the viceroyalty of Peru and used these reflections to compose *De procuranda Indorum salute*, an influential treatise that proposed revisions to missionary policy in the face of continued native religious practices in quotidian rituals like childbirth, marriage, burial, and ritual drinking. Sabine MacCormack analyzes the development of Acosta's missionary philosophy from *De procuranda Indorum salute* to the *Natural and Moral History* in "The Mind of the Missionary: José de Acosta on Accommodation and Extirpation, c. 1590" in her *Religion in the Andes*.

# BOOK V

## CHAPTER I * HOW THE DEVIL'S PRIDE AND ENVY HAVE BEEN THE CAUSE OF IDOLATRY

The devil's pride is so great and so obstinate that he always longs and strives to be accepted and honored as God and to steal and appropriate to himself in every way he can what is owed only to the Most High God. He never ceases to do this in the blind nations of the world, those that the light and splendor of the Holy Gospel has not yet illuminated. In the book of Job we read of this prideful tyrant that "he beholdeth every high thing, he is king over all the children of pride."[1] His evil intentions and reckless treachery, with which he tried to make his throne equal to the throne of God, are clearly told us in the Holy Scriptures, saying in Isaiah: "And thou saidst in thy heart: I will ascend into heaven, I will exalt my throne above the stars of God, I will sit in the mountain of the covenant, in the sides of the north. I will ascend above the height of the clouds, I will be like the Most High."[2] And in Ezekiel: "Because thy heart is lifted up and thou hast said: I am God, and I sit in the chair of God in the heart of the sea."[3] Satan still feels this wicked desire to become God even though the just and awful punishment of the Most High deprived him of all his pomp and ostentation, by which he had become so haughty, dealing with him as his impudence and folly deserved, as is told at length in the prophets. Yet he has not desisted one jot from his perverse intent, which he demonstrates in all the ways he can, like a mad dog biting the very sword

1. Job, 41, 25 (O'G).
2. Isaiah, 14, 13 and 14 (O'G).
3. Ezekiel, 28, 2 (O'G).

with which he is wounded.[4] For it is written that the pride of those who hate God persists forever. From this comes the strange and perpetual care that this enemy of God has always exercised to make himself worshiped by men, inventing so many kinds of idolatries with which he held most of the world in subjection for so many ages that God retained scarcely a fragment of his people Israel.[5]

And, employing the same tyranny, after the might of the Gospel defeated and disarmed him, and by the power of the cross entered the chiefest and stoutest strongholds of his realm, he attacked the most remote and savage peoples, attempting to preserve among them the false and lying divinity that the Son of God had wrested from him in his Church, enclosing him like a wild beast in its cage to make him an example and a cause of rejoicing for his servants, as he showed through Job.[6] And so, once idolatry was rooted out of the best and noblest part of the world, the devil retired to the most remote places and reigned in that other part of the world, which, although it is very inferior in nobility, is not so in size and breadth. The reason why the devil has encouraged idolatry so much in all heathen lands, to the point that scarcely any people can be found who are not idolaters, is due to two chief causes. One is that he is infected with his incredible pride, which anyone who wishes to think about it can discern from the fact that he attacked the Son of God and true God himself, so shamelessly bidding him fall down and adore him; and he said this to him even though he did not know for certain that he was God himself, but at least having a very good idea that he was the Son of God.[7] Who is not astonished by this strange assault, this excessive and cruel pride? Is it any wonder that he causes himself to be worshiped by ignorant folk, he who assaulted God himself, trying to make himself God, being such a filthy and abominable creature? The other cause and motive for idolatry is the mortal hatred and enmity that he harbors toward men. For, as the Savior says, "He was a murderer from the beginning, and he stood not in the truth; because truth is not in him."[8] And because he knows that the greatest harm man can do to himself is to worship the creature as God, he never ceases to invent ways of idolatry with which to destroy men and make them God's

---

4. Psalms, 73, 23 (O'G).
5. Saint Matthew, 12, 29 (O'G).
6. Job, 40 (O'G).
7. Saint Matthew, 4, 9 (O'G).
8. Saint John, 8, 44 (O'G).

enemies. And there are two evils that the devil does to idolaters: one is to make them deny God, according to the verse, "He forsook who made him";[9] the other is to make man subject to something lower than himself, for all creatures are inferior to the rational creature, and the devil, although in nature he is superior to man, in estate is much inferior, because man even in this life is capable of divine and eternal life. And so, with idolatry in every place, God is dishonored and man destroyed, and in both cases the proud and envious devil is well content.

## CHAPTER 2 * OF THE KINDS OF IDOLATRIES USED BY THE INDIANS

Idolatry, says the sage, and through him the Holy Spirit,[1] is the cause and beginning and end of all evils, and it is for this reason that the enemy of men has multiplied so many kinds and manners of idolatry that to try to recount them in detail would be a never-ending task. But if we reduce idolatry to headings, there are two kinds of it: one has to do with natural things and the other with things imagined or fabricated by human ingenuity. The first of these is divided into two: whether the thing worshiped is general, such as the sun, moon, fire, earth, and elements, or particular, such as a specific river, fountain, tree, or hill, and when these things are worshiped not for their kind but in particular. It was this kind of idolatry that was used in Peru in great excess and is specifically called *huaca*.[2] The second kind of idolatry, which is owed to human invention or imagination, also has two further differences: one consists in pure human art or invention, such as worshiping idols or a

9. Deuteronomy 32, 15 (O'G).

1. Book of Wisdom, 14, 12 (O'G).

2. Acosta's expansive definition of the *huaca,* or *waq'a* in the Quechua, reflects both the ubiquitous place of *huacas* in the Andean world and the European missionary determination to identify any and all significance in the term. *Huaca* was a general term used to indicate a sacred object, whether it be a person, place, or thing. Serge Gruzinski's analysis of the Nahuatl word *ixiptla* is revealing here. The sacred was enacted in Amerindian civilization in persons, places or objects, but there was a lack of correspondence between the signifier and the signified that displaced the missionaries' logic. The cross was, from the Amerindian perspective, the sacred, and not just a signifier of the absent signified (God) according to Christian logic. See Serge Gruzinski, *Images at War: Mexico from Columbus to Blade Runner (1492–2019),* translated by Heather MacLean (Durham: Duke University Press, 2001), 50–52. The Spanish tried to eradicate all vestiges of Andean native religion, including the *huacas,* and they readily burned ancestor mummies or crushed small stone figures of deities. The multitude of sacred locations, such as hills, caves, or streams, proved to be more elusive targets for destruction. The desire to move people away from these natural *huacas* gave a religious motivation to the Spanish campaigns to remove natives from their ancestral lands to colonial settlements called *reducciones.*

wooden or stone or gold statue like those of Mercury or Pallas, which are nothing and never were anything but a mere painting or statue; the other difference is of that which really was and is something, but not what the idolater who worships it pretends, like the dead or things belonging to them, which men worship out of vanity and a desire to flatter. So, in all, we can count four kinds of idolatry that the heathen use, and it behooves us to say something about all of them.[3]

## CHAPTER 3 * HOW THERE IS SOME KNOWLEDGE OF GOD AMONG THE INDIANS

First, although the gross darkness of unbelief has obscured the minds of those nations, in many ways the light of truth and reason works in them to some small degree; and so most of them acknowledge and confess a supreme Lord and Maker of all, whom the Peruvians called Viracocha, adding a very excellent name such as Pachacamac or Pachayachachic, which means the creator of heaven and earth, and Usapu, which means admirable, and other similar names.[1] They worshiped him, and he was the chief god that they venerated, gazing heavenward. And the same belief exists, after their fashion, in the Mexicans and the Chinese today and in other heathen peoples. This is very similar to what is told in the Book of Acts of the Apostles, when Saint Paul was in Athens and saw an altar with the inscription "Ignoto Deo," to the unknown God, from which the Apostle took the subject of his preaching, telling them, "What therefore you worship without knowing it, that I preach to you."[2] And so, similarly, all those who preach the Gospel to the Indians today have little difficulty in persuading them that there is a supreme God and Lord of all, and that he is the God of the Christians and the true God. Yet

3. When Acosta devised this novel classification of New World idolatries, he labored under the conviction that a better understanding of non-Christian practices would serve to help eradicate them. Sabine MacCormack attributes Acosta's schema of two forms of idolatry, with two subcategories each, to his reading of the Book of Wisdom and his direct experience of idolatry in the Andes, which included reading or hearing reports from secondhand sources while in Peru (*Religion in the Andes*, 264–66).

1. Viracocha is the name the Spanish used to refer to the Andean creator god situated at the top of the Inca cosmological hierarchy. Instead of a single name, the Inca referred to him with a number of titles, including Pachayachachic (Teacher of the World) and Pachacamac (Maker of the Earth). While Viracocha was recognized as a supreme god, native Andeans actively worshiped other deities in keeping with the polytheistic nature of their religion.

2. Acts, 17, 23 (O'G).

it has greatly astonished me that even though they do have the knowledge that I mention, they have no word of their own with which to name God. For, if we try to find in the Indian languages any word corresponding to this one, *God,* as it is *Deus* in Latin and *Theos* in Greek, and *El* in Hebrew and in Arabic *Allah,* it cannot be found in the language of Cuzco, nor in the Mexican tongue. And so those who preach or write for the Indians use our Spanish word *Dios,* adjusting its pronunciation and accent to the properties of the Indian languages, which are very diverse. This shows what a weak and incomplete knowledge they have of God, for they do not even know how to name him except by using our word.[3] But indeed they did have a sort of knowledge, and so they built a very splendid temple for him in Peru, calling it Pachacamac, which was the chief sanctuary of that realm. And as I have said, *Pachacamac* means the same as *Creator,* although they also performed their idolatries in this temple, worshiping the devil and representations of him; and they also made sacrifices and offerings to Viracocha, and that temple held supreme place among the temples that the Inca kings possessed. And the fact that they called the Spaniards *viracochas* arose from this, that they thought they were children of heaven and as it were divine, just as others attributed godhood to Paul and Barnabas, calling one Jupiter and the other Mercury and trying to offer them sacrifices as to gods. And likewise those other barbarians of Melita (which is Malta), observing that the viper did the Apostle no harm, called him a god.[4]

It is therefore a truth that conforms to all sound reason that there must be a sovereign Lord and King of Heaven, which the heathen did not deny for all their idolatry and unbelief, as appears in Plato's philosophy in the *Timaeus,* in Aristotle's *Metaphysics,* and in the *Asclepius* of Trismegistus, as well as in the poetry of Homer and Vergil.[5] So it is that preachers of the Gospel do not have much difficulty in affirming and persuading of the truth of a supreme God, however barbarous and bestial the nations to whom they preach. But it

3. Acosta's observation that native languages had no word for God suggested, implicitly, that they were ineffective for teaching doctrine. Other participants in the sixteenth-century debate on native languages, such as the Dominican Santo Tomás, who authored the first Quechua grammar, *Lexicon o vocabulario de la lengua general del Perú* (1560), argued that the native language was comparable to Spanish or Latin and thus acceptable for teaching Christian doctrine.

4. Acts, 14, 12; Acts, 28, 3 and 6 (O'G).

5. Plato, dialogue *Timaeus;* Aristotle, *Metaphysica,* book 21, final chapter; Hermes Trismegisto, *Asclepio,* book 1, called Pimandro (O'G).

is extremely difficult for them to root out of their minds the idea that there is no other god or deity but only one, and that all other things have no power or being of their own, or operation of their own, than what is given and communicated to them by that supreme and only God and Lord. And it is exceedingly necessary to convince them of this in every way possible, completely rejecting their errors in worshiping more than one God, and even more particularly having as gods and attributing godhood and addressing pleas to other things that are not gods, for they can accomplish no more than what the true God, their Lord and Maker, allows them.

### CHAPTER 4 * OF THE FIRST SORT OF IDOLATRY, THAT OF NATURAL AND UNIVERSAL THINGS

After the Viracocha, or supreme god, the sun was and is the entity that the heathen chiefly venerate and worship, and after the sun those other things prominent in celestial or elemental nature, such as moon, morning star, sea, and earth. After Viracocha and the sun, the Inca lords of Peru placed thunder in the third *huaca,* or temple, and gave it three names: Chuquiilla, Catuilla, and Intiillapa. They imagine that it is a man in the sky with a sling and a club and that he has power over rain and sleet and thunder and everything else pertaining to the region of the air, where clouds are formed. This *huaca* (for that is what they call their temples), was common to all the Indians of Peru, and they offered different sacrifices to this god. And in Cuzco, which was the court and capital, children were also sacrificed to him, just as they were to the sun. They adored these three that I have named, Viracocha, Sun, and Thunder, in a different way from all the other gods, as Polo writes that he has ascertained, placing a gauntlet or glove on their hands when they raised them to worship these gods. They also worshiped Earth, which they called Pachamama, just as the ancients celebrated the goddess Tellus, and the sea, which they called Mamacocha, just as the ancients called it Thetis or Neptune.[1] They also worshiped the rainbow, and it was the arms or insignia of the Inca, with two serpents stretched along its sides. Among the stars that all of them commonly worshiped was the group they called Collca, which we call the

---

1. The earth and ocean deities were both female. Pachamama, the Mother Earth, was worshipped for agricultural fertility, often with offerings of *chicha.* Andeans honored Mamacocha, the Mother Sea, in relation to the Pacific Ocean or highland streams and springs, with offerings of shells.

Pleiades. They attributed different functions to different stars, and worshiped those whose favor they needed, just as the shepherds adored and sacrificed to a star that they called Urcuchillay, which they say is a sheep of many colors that is skilled in the preservation of their flocks and is apparently the one the astronomers call Lyra. And the same Indians adore two other stars near it, which they call Catuchillay and Urcuchillay, which they fancy to be a ewe with a lamb. Others worshiped a star that they call Machacuay, which has charge of serpents and snakes, to prevent their harming them, just as another star called Chuquichinchay, which means tiger, is responsible for tigers, bears, and lions. And generally speaking they believed that for each of the animals and birds on earth there was a similar one in the heavens, responsible for that animal's procreation and increase; and so they assigned meanings to certain stars, like the one they call Chacana, and Topatorca and Mamana, and Mirco and Miquiquiray, and others, to the point that in some sense they approached the tenets of Plato's ideas.

In almost the same way, after the supreme god the Mexicans worshiped the sun, and so they called Hernán Cortés (as he states in a letter to the Emperor Charles V) son of the sun because of the speed and energy with which he encompassed the land. But they offered their greatest worship to the idol called Huitzilopochtli, whom that whole nation called the Almighty and lord of creation; and as such the Mexicans built him the largest and loftiest temple, and the most beautiful and sumptuous building, whose position and massive strength can be guessed from the ruins of it that remain in the center of the City of Mexico.[2] But in this respect the idolatry of the Mexicans was more grievously in error and more pernicious than that of the Incas, as will become clear later; for the greater part of their worship and idolatry was given to idols and not to natural phenomena in themselves, although they attributed these natural effects such as rain and flocks and war and procreation to the idols, just as the Greeks and Romans also set up idols to Phoebus and Mercury and Jupiter and Minerva and Mars, etcetera.

Finally, whoever looks carefully at all this will discover that the devil's

---

2. Huitzilopochtli, translated as Hummingbird of the South, was the main tribal deity of the Mexica, who led them on their journey from Aztlán to Tenochtitlán. Represented by a sacred medicine bundle during the days of the journey, he became the god of the sun after their settlement in Tenochtitlán, where the great *Templo Mayor* was built to honor both him and Tlaloc, the rain god. In addition to his role as god of the sun, Huitzilopochtli was the war god, and warriors captured and sacrificed human victims in his name. His role became increasingly bellicose as the Aztec empire expanded and he demanded more sacrifices accordingly.

method of deceiving the Indians is the same as that with which he deceived the Greeks and Romans and other ancient unbelievers, by making them believe that these noble creations — sun, moon, stars, elements — had power and authority of their own to do good or evil to men. And, although God has created these things for the service of man, man has been so unsuccessful in ruling and governing them that on the one hand he has tried to raise himself to be God and on the other has recognized and subjected himself to creatures lower than he, by worshiping and invoking these works and ceasing to worship and invoke the Creator, as the sage so well expresses it in these words: "But all men are vain, in whom there is not the knowledge of God: and who by these good things that are seen could not understand him that is, neither by attending to the works have acknowledged who was the workman. But have imagined, either the fire, or the wind, or the swift air, or the circle of the stars, or the great water, or the sun and moon, to be the gods that rule the world. With whose beauty, if they, being delighted, took them to be gods: let them know how much the Lord of them is more beautiful than they. For the first author of beauty made all those things. Or if they admired their power and their effects, let them understand by them, that he that made them is mightier than they. For by the greatness of the beauty, and of the creature, the creator of them may be seen, so as to be known thereby."[3] Thus far the words of the Book of Wisdom, from which very wonderful and effective arguments can be taken to convince the idolatrous heathen of their great error, for they would rather serve and revere the creature than the Creator, as the Apostle so rightly argues.[4] But because this does not fall within my present intent, and is sufficiently expressed in the sermons that have been written against the Indians' errors, for the moment it will suffice to say that the Indians worshiped the supreme God in the same way that they worshiped those vain and lying gods.[5] For the way of praying to Viracocha and to the sun, and to the stars

3. Book of Wisdom, 13 (O'G).

4. Saint Paul, Letter to the Romans, 1, 25 (O'G).

5. Acosta refers to sermons authored by the Third Council of Lima, which was held from 1582 to 1583. Acosta acted as a theological adviser to the council and carried out numerous duties during its tenure, such as composing catechisms, confession manuals, and the sermons he mentions here. The council convened precisely during an era when missionaries, confronted with their failure to eradicate idolatry, retreated from the notion of conversion through persuasion and moved in the direction of an increasingly conservative missionary practice. The proceedings were published in R. Vargas Ugarte, ed., *Concilios Limeños (1551–1772)*, 3 vols. (Lima: Rávago e hijos, 1951–54).

and the other *huacas* or idols, was to open their hands and make a certain sound with their lips like someone kissing, and to request what each one wanted, and to offer sacrifice to the god. There was, however, a difference in the words when they spoke to the great Ticciviracocha, to whom they chiefly attributed the power to rule over all things, and to the others as gods or private lords, each one in his house, who were intercessors with the great Ticciviracocha. This way of worshiping by opening the hands and making a kissing gesture is in some sense like the one that the holy Job abominates as proper to idolaters, saying, "If I beheld the sun when it shone, and the moon going in brightness: and my heart in secret hath rejoiced, and I have kissed my hand with my mouth (which is a very great iniquity, and a denial against the most high God)."[6]

CHAPTER 5 * OF THE IDOLATRY PRACTICED BY
THE INDIANS WITH PARTICULAR THINGS

Not content with causing those blind Indians to worship the sun and moon and stars, and earth and sea, and other general features in nature, the devil went further and gave them to them as gods and subjected them to things of no importance, many of which were very vile. No one need be surprised by this blindness in the heathen if he remembers what the Apostle says of the sages and philosophers, that having known God they did not glorify him or give thanks to him as God, but became vain in their thoughts, and their foolish heart was darkened, and they exchanged the glory and godhood of the eternal God for images and figures of things that are perishable and corruptible, such as men and birds and beasts and creeping things.[1] The dog Osiris, whom the Egyptians worshiped, is well known, and the cow Isis, and the sheep Amon; and in Rome the goddess Februa of the fevers, and the Goose of the Tarpeian Rock; and in Athens the wise woman, the crow, and the cock. And the histories of the heathen are full of such vileness and travesties, and men have incurred great ignominy because they would not subject themselves to the law of their true God and Creator, as Saint Athanasius learnedly discusses when he writes against idolaters.

But among the Indians, especially those of Peru, the sinfulness and perdi-

6. Job, 31, 26, 27, and 28 (o'g).
1. Saint Paul, Letter to the Romans, 1, 21, 22 and 23 (o'g).

tion involved in all this was exaggerated to the point of folly; for they worship rivers, fountains, ravines, rocks, large stones, hills, and the mountain peaks that they call *apachitas* and consider them worthy of great devotion. And, last, they worship anything in nature that seems to them notable and different from others, as if recognizing some special deity in it. In Cajamarca de la Nasca they showed me a large hill of sand, which was the particular place of worship, or *huaca*, of the ancients. When I asked what divinity was there, they told me that they worshiped the wonderful circumstance that a very tall hill of sand existed among others that were all rocks. And indeed it was astonishing to think how such a great hill of sand was placed in the middle of massive hills made of stone. In Ciudad de los Reyes we needed a large amount of good firewood to cast a bell, and a large distorted tree was cut, which, owing to its age and size, had for many years been a temple and *huaca* of the Indians. Thus they thought that anything strange among things of its kind was divine, and they did this with pebbles and metals, and even roots and products of the earth, as, for example, among the roots that they call *papas* there are some of strange shape, which they call *llallahuas*, and kiss and worship them. They also worship bears, lions, tigers, and snakes to prevent them from harming them.

And because such absurd things are their gods the objects that they offer them in worship are equally absurd. When they travel they are wont to toss onto the roads or at crossroads, on the hills, and especially on the peaks that they call *apachitas* old shoes and feathers and chewed coca (which is an herb that they make much use of). And when they have nothing else they will toss a stone, and all this is like an offering to allow them to pass and give them strength, and they say that they pay with this, as is reported in the Provincial Council of Peru.[2] And so on the roads there are great piles of the stones that have been offered as well as the other sorts of rubbish that have been mentioned. Such folly is like that employed by the ancients, of whom it is said in the Book of Proverbs, "As he that casteth a stone into the heap of Mercury, so is he that giveth honor to a fool."[3] This means that no more result or useful-

2. *Concilium provinciale Limense celebratum in civitate Regum. Anno MDLXXXIII,* Madrid, 1591, 2, p. 2, chapter 99 (O'G). The reports on native Andean traditions are likely the work of Juan Polo de Ondegardo, which was presented and debated in the Third Council of Lima, as discussed in note 2 of the prologue to book V.

3. Proverbs, 26, 8 (O'G).

ness is obtained from the second than from the first, for the Mercury fashioned of stone does not recognize the offering, nor does the fool appreciate the honor done to him. They make another offering that is no less absurd, which is to pull out their eyelashes or eyebrows and offer them to the sun, or to the hills and *apachitas,* to the winds or other things that they fear. The pitiful condition in which many Indians have lived, and still live today, enables the devil to make them believe, like children, in anything he wishes no matter how absurd it may be, as Saint Chrysostom in a homily makes a similar comparison about the heathen.[4]

But the servants of God who occupy themselves with the Indians' instruction and salvation ought not to scorn these childish practices, for they are sufficient to entrap the Indians into eternal perdition; rather, they must undeceive them, with good and simple arguments, of such great manifestations of ignorance. For indeed it is worth noting how submissive they are to those who bring them to reason. Among corporeal creatures there is nothing more splendid than the sun, which is the entity that all heathen customarily adore. A wise captain, and a good Christian, told me how he had convinced the Indians by a sound argument that the sun was not a god but had only been created by God, and did so as follows: he asked the chief and principal lord to give him a swift Indian to send a letter; he gave him one, and then the captain asked the chief, "Tell me, who is the lord and chief, that Indian who is carrying the letter, or you who have commanded him to take it?" The chief answered, "I, without a doubt, for he does only what I command." "Exactly this," replied the captain, "happens between the sun that we see and the Creator of all. For the sun is only a servant of that infinitely high Lord, who by his commandment moves swiftly and untiringly, carrying light to all peoples. And so you will see how it is unreasonable, and a lie, to give to the sun that honor that is owed to its Creator and the Lord of all." They were all much impressed by the captain's reasoning, and the chief and the Indians who were with him said that it was indeed true and that they had derived much pleasure from understanding it. It is told of one of the Inca kings, a man of very fine intelligence, that when he observed that all his ancestors had worshiped the sun, he said that he did not think that the sun was God, nor could it be. For God is a great lord and does all that he does with great

4. Saint John Chrysostom, *Homily on the first letter to the Corinthians,* 4 (O'G).

tranquillity and authority, and the sun never stopped moving; and that it did not seem to him that anything so restless could be a god. It was well said. And, if their misapprehensions and blindness are presented to the Indians with gentle reasoning that can be grasped easily, they will soon be convinced and will recognize the truth.

## CHAPTER 6 * OF ANOTHER KIND OF IDOLATRY WITH THE DEAD

Another kind of idolatry, very different from those I have described, is the kind that the heathen have employed with the dead whom they loved and respected. And, although it appears that the sage gives us to understand that this was the beginning of idolatry, saying,

> For the beginning of fornication is the devising of idols: and the invention of them is the corruption of life. For neither were they from the beginning, neither shall they be forever. For by the vanity of men they came into the world: and therefore they shall be found to come shortly to an end. For a father, being afflicted with bitter grief, made to himself the image of his son who was quickly taken away: and him who then had died as a man, he began now to worship as a god, and appointed him rites and sacrifices, among his servants. Then in process of time, wicked custom prevailing, this error was kept as a law, and statues were worshiped by the commandments of tyrants. And those whom men could not honor in presence, because they dwelt far off, they brought their resemblance from afar, and made an express image of the king whom they had a mind to honor: that by this their diligence they might honor as present him that was absent. And to the worshiping of these, the singular diligence also of the artificer helped to set forward the ignorant. For he, being willing to please him that employed him, labored with all his art to make the resemblance in the best manner. And the multitude of men, carried away by the beauty of the work, took him now for a god that a little before was but honored as a man. And this was the occasion of deceiving human life: for men serving either their affection, or their kings, gave the incommunicable name to stones and wood.[1]

1. Book of Wisdom, 14, 12 (O'G).

All this is from the Book of Wisdom, which is worthy of notice; and anyone who is curious about searching out antiquities will find that the origin of idolatry was precisely these images and statues of the dead. I am speaking of the idolatry that involves worshiping idols and images because it is not certain that the other kind of idolatry, that of adoring creatures like the sun and the host of heaven, mentioned by the prophets,[2] came after, although there is no doubt that making statues and idols in honor of the sun and moon and earth did so.

To return to our Indians, they reached the pinnacle of their idolatries by the same process that is described in Scripture. First, they tried to preserve the bodies of their kings and great lords, and they were kept whole, without smelling or corrupting, for more than two hundred years. This was the way the Inca kings of Cuzco were kept, each in his chapel and temple. The viceroy, Marqués de Cañete, in order to extirpate idolatry, had three or four of them removed and brought to Ciudad de los Reyes, and it caused great astonishment to see human bodies so many years old with such a beautiful appearance and completely whole.[3] Each of these Inca kings left all his treasures and assets and revenues to support his temple, where his body was placed along with those of many of his ministers and all his family dedicated to his cult. No subsequent king usurped the treasures and precious vessels of his predecessor but instead gathered new treasures for himself and his palace. They were not content with this idolatrous worship of dead bodies but also made statues of them; and each king during his lifetime had a stone idol or statue of himself made, which was called *guaoiqui,* meaning "brother," for both in life and death the same veneration had to be paid to that statue as to the Inca himself. These statues were taken to war and carried in procession to

2. Jeremiah, 19, 5; Zephaniah, 1, 5 (O'G).

3. The preservation of deceased rulers and relations through mummification constituted an important part of Inca religious practice. The cult of the dead was worshipped, in part, through the practice of satisfying the earthly needs of the mummified bodies, called *mallquis.* To the surprise of the Spanish, the supply of food and comforts to these mummies continued on a perpetual basis. The Spanish newcomers identified these *mallquis* as powerful components of Inca rule and determined to locate and destroy them, since the worship represented a religious and political threat. MacCormack classifies the cult as the "pivot of Andean idolatry" (*Religion in the Andes,* 268). The largest "find" of mummified leaders was made in Cuzco under Polo de Ondegardo by order of the viceroy Marqués de Cañete. The looted mummies were brought to the capital of the viceroyalty, the Ciudad de los Reyes, or Lima, for display as symbols of the rise of Spanish power and the demise of Inca idolatry.

pray for rain and good growing seasons, and different feasts and sacrifices were made to them. There were a great many of these idols in Cuzco and its district, but it is believed that the superstitious practice of worshiping these stones has entirely or almost entirely ceased since they were discovered by the efforts of Licentiate Polo, and the first of them was that of Inca Roca, chief of the tribe of Hanan Cuzco. Other tribes likewise have great respect for the bodies of their ancestors, together with their statues, which they worship and venerate.

### CHAPTER 7 * OF THE SUPERSTITIONS THAT WERE EMPLOYED WITH THE DEAD

Among the Indians of Peru there was a widespread belief that their souls lived on after this life, and that the good received glory and the bad punishment, and so there is little difficulty in persuading them of these articles of faith. But they did not grasp the idea that bodies would arise along with souls, and so they expended a great deal of effort, as has been said, in preserving bodies and honoring them after death. To this end their descendants clothed them and made sacrifices; the Inca kings especially, in their burials, had to be accompanied by a large number of servants and women for their service in the other life. And so on the day they died their favorite women and servants and officials were killed so that they might go to serve them in the other life. On the death of Huayna Capac, the father of Atahualpa, during whose reign the Spaniards came into Peru, more than a thousand persons of all ages and conditions were put to death for his service and company in the other life. They were killed after much singing and excessive drinking and considered themselves fortunate; many things were sacrificed to the dead, especially children, and with their blood they drew a line from ear to ear on the dead man's face. This same superstition and inhumane practice, of killing men and women for the company and service of the dead in the other life, has been used and is still used by other barbarian nations. And according to Polo it has been almost universal in the Indies, and the Venerable Bede even says that the Angles, before they were converted to the Gospel, had the same custom of killing people to accompany and serve the dead. The story is told of a Portuguese who, when he was a captive among savages, received an arrow wound from which he lost an eye. When they wanted to sacrifice him to accompany a dead chief, he replied that those who dwelt in the other life would have a poor opinion of the dead man if his people gave him a one-eyed man for a companion and that it was better to give him one with two eyes; and as this reasoning seemed good to the savages they let him go.

Apart from this superstition of sacrificing men to the dead, which is done only with very important chiefs, there is another that is much more common and widespread all over the Indies, that of placing food and drink for the dead on their tombs and in their caves and believing that they feed themselves with it, which according to Saint Augustine was also an error of the ancients.[1] And even today many heathen Indians secretly disinter their dead from churches and cemeteries and bury them on hills or in ravines, or in their own houses, in order to give them food and drink.[2] They also used to put silver in their mouths, in their hands, and in their bosoms, and dress them in new and usable clothing, folded under the shroud. They believe that the souls of their dead wander about and feel cold and thirst and hunger and travail, and that is why they celebrate their anniversaries by bringing them food and drink and clothing. For this reason the prelates in their synods rightly insist upon the priests making the Indians understand that the offerings placed on tombs in the church are food and drink not for souls but for the poor, or ministers of the Church, and that it is God alone who nourishes souls in the other life, for they do not eat or drink any corporeal thing. And it is very important for them to learn this thoroughly, so as not to change holy usage into heathen superstition, as many of them do.

CHAPTER 8 ∗ OF THE FUNERAL RITES THAT THE
MEXICANS AND OTHER NATIONS USED

Having recounted what many of the nations of Peru did with their dead, in this respect I must now make special mention of the Mexicans, whose funeral

1. Saint Augustine, *Epistolae,* 64 (O'G).

2. While the practice of worshiping mummified Inca rulers waned with the Spanish conquest, local cults of the dead endured. In one Jesuit priest's seventeenth-century anti-idolatry manual, he identified *mallquis* as an important target for novice missionaries. See Pablo José de Arriaga, *The Extirpation of Idolatry,* translated and edited by L. Clark Keating (Lexington: University of Kentucky Press, 1968). For an analysis of the cult of the dead as an example of resistance to Spanish rule, see Frank Salomon, "Ancestor Cults and Resistance to the State in Arequipa, ca. 1748–1754," in *Resistance, Rebellion, and Consciousness in the Andean Peasant World,* edited by Steve J. Stern (Madison: University of Wisconsin, 1987), 148–165.

rites were extremely solemn and full of absurdities. It was the office of the priests and other religious in Mexico (who had very strange customs, as will be described later) to bury the dead and perform their obsequies. And the places where they buried them were in fields and in the courtyards of their own houses. Others were carried to the places of sacrifice in the hills, and others were burned and their ashes buried in the temples; and all of them were buried with all the clothing and jewels and precious stones they possessed. And when bodies were burned they put the ashes into jars and placed in the jars their jewels and gems and ornaments, no matter how rich. They chanted the funeral offices like responses and lifted the bodies of the dead many times, performing elaborate ceremonies. They ate and drank during these funerals, and if the dead were persons of quality clothing was given to all those who had come to the burial. When someone died they laid him in a room until all his friends and acquaintances arrived from all around, and these brought the dead man gifts and greeted him as though he were alive; and if he was a king or the lord of some town they offered slaves to be killed so as to serve him in the other world. They also killed his priest or chaplain, for all the nobles had a priest to perform ceremonies within the house, and they killed him so that he could minister to the dead man. They killed the chamberlain, the butler, the dwarfs and hunchbacks (for they made great use of such persons), and those among his brothers who had served him most, for it was a mark of greatness among the nobles to be served by their brothers and the others I have mentioned. Last, they killed everyone in his household so that they could go and establish one in the other world. And, lest they suffer poverty there, they buried great wealth in gold, silver, precious stones, richly embroidered curtains, gold bracelets, and other rich pieces; and if the dead man was burned they did the same with all the people and ornaments that were given to him for the other world. They took all those ashes and buried them with great solemnity; the ceremonies lasted for ten days, during which plaintive and mournful chants were sung.

The priests dispatched the dead with different ceremonies, as they themselves had requested, and these were so numerous that they can hardly be counted. Captains and nobles had their insignias and trophies placed upon them, according to their exploits and the valor they had demonstrated in war and governance, for they had their special devices and weapons for this purpose. All of these objects and tokens were carried before the corpse to the place where it was to be buried or burned, accompanied by a procession in which the priests and temple dignitaries walked with different tokens, some swinging censers and others singing, and still others playing on woeful flutes and drums, which greatly increased the weeping of vassals and relatives. The priest who was conducting the office was arrayed in the insignias of the idol whom the dead man had represented, for all the nobles represented idols and enjoyed their reputations, which caused them to be greatly esteemed and honored. These insignias that I mention were usually carried by members of the orders of chivalry; and, if the body was to be burned, after they had taken it to the place where the ashes were to be produced, they surrounded it and everything pertaining to it with candlewood, as I have said, and set fire to it, constantly feeding the flame with resinous woods until all had been reduced to ashes. Then a priest came out dressed in the accoutrements of the devil, with mouths painted on all the joints and many eyes made of mirrors. He carried a large stick with which he stirred all those ashes very vigorously and boldly, presenting such a savage spectacle that it struck horror into all present. And sometimes this same priest wore other different costumes, according to the dead man's rank. This digression concerning the dead and mortuary rites has been made in connection with idolatry of the dead; now we must return to our chief aim and finish this subject.

### CHAPTER 9 * OF THE FOURTH AND LAST KIND OF IDOLATRY THAT THE INDIANS, ESPECIALLY THE MEXICANS, USED WITH IMAGES AND STATUES

Although there is great offense to God in the kinds of idolatry I have described, in which mere creatures were worshiped, the Holy Spirit condemns and abominates much more another kind of idolater, those who worship only figures and images made by the hands of men, although they are mere stones or sticks or metal and have only the shape bestowed on them by the artist who made them. The sage speaks of these as follows: "But unhappy are they, and their hope is among the dead, who have called gods the works of the hands of men, gold and silver, the inventions of art, and the resemblance of beasts, or an unprofitable stone the work of an ancient hand."[1] And he continues to

1. Book of Wisdom, 13, 10 (O'G).

speak, divinely inspired, against this deceit and folly of the heathen, as the prophet Isaiah and the prophet Jeremiah and the prophet Baruch and holy King David also argue fully and elegantly.[2] And it behooves the minister of Christ who reproves the errors of idolatry to have these places in Scripture well marked and digested, and the arguments that the Holy Spirit so graciously mentions can all be reduced to a short sentence spoken by the prophet Hosea: "A workman made it, and it is no god: for the calf of Samaria shall be turned to spiders' webs."[3] To return to our subject, great zeal was shown in the Indies to make idols and paintings of different forms and materials, and these were worshiped as gods. In Peru they were called *huacas,* and ordinarily these were ugly and deformed in appearance; at least all the ones I have seen were so. I believe there is no doubt that the devil, in whose veneration they were made, liked to be worshiped in ill-featured figures. And, indeed, the devil spoke and answered in many of these *huacas* or idols, and his priests and ministers flocked to those oracles of the Father of Lies, and his counsels and warnings and prophecies were of the same nature as himself.

The place where this kind of idolatry flourished more than anywhere else in the world was in the provinces of New Spain, in Mexico and Texcoco and Tlaxcala and Cholula and neighboring parts of that realm.[4] And to tell of the

2. Isaiah, 44, 9; Jeremiah, 10, 15; Baruch, 6, 3 and 5; Psalms, 113, 4–7 (O'G).

3. Hosea 8, 6 (O'G).

4. Acosta's grouping of these four cities prompts an explanation of their distinct identities in pre-Hispanic Mexico. Texcoco, located on the eastern side of Lake Texcoco, was the second largest town in the Valley of Mexico. Allied with the Mexica of Tenochtitlán, it shared in the leadership of the Aztec Empire. The sixteenth-century elite mestizo chronicler Fernando de Alva Ixtlilxochitl, a native of Texcoco, praised the cultural supremacy of the town in the Valley of Mexico. His writings were published in *Obras históricas,* edited by Edmundo O'Gorman, 2 vols. (Mexico City: Universidad Nacional Autónoma de México, 1985).

The city-states of Tlaxcala and Cholula, located in the mountainous highlands west of Tenochtitlan and Lake Texcoco, were independent of Aztec rule, although they conducted trade and ritual warfare with the people of the capital city. The scholarly study of Texcoco in the pre-Hispanic period is Jerome A. Offner, *Law and Politics in Aztec Texcoco* (New York: Cambridge University Press, 1983). The best-known sixteenth-century source on Tlaxcala is Diego Muñoz Camargo, *Suma y epíloga de toda la descripción de Tlaxcala,* edited by Andrea Martínez Barcas and Carlos Sempat Assadourian (Tlalpan: Centro de Investigaciones y Estudios Superiores en Antropología Social, 1994). In 1519, Tlaxcala saw an alliance with the Spanish as a way to end years of ongoing battle with the Mexica. In the aftermath of conquest the Tlaxcallans lobbied for, and received, special treatment based on their loyalty to the Spanish. The Cholulans also welcomed the Spanish into their town and impressed them with their temple to Quetzalcoatl. The main plaza soon became the site of a gruesome massacre of the Cholulans by the Spaniards, who purportedly attacked after hearing rumors of an ambush.

superstitions that they had there is a monstrous thing, but it would be useful to recount some of them.[5] The chief idol of the Mexicans, as stated above, was Huitzilopochtli; this was a wooden statue carved into the likeness of a man, seated on a blue bench set upon a litter, from each of whose four corners emerged a beam ending in a serpent's head; the bench symbolized that he was sitting in heaven. The idol itself had its forehead painted all blue, and above the nose a blue fillet that stretched from ear to ear. On its head was rich plumage in the shape of a bird's beak, tipped with highly polished gold. In its left hand it held a round white shield with five tufts of white feathers placed in the form of a cross, and on top a gold pennon, and from the shield's handholds issued four arrows, which were said by the Mexicans to have been sent them from heaven to do the deeds that will be described in their proper place. In its right hand the idol held a staff carved in the shape of a serpent, all curved and painted blue. According to the Mexicans, all these ornaments and others, which were many, had their special meanings. The name Huitzilopochtli means "left claw of shining feathers." Later I will describe the splendid temple and the sacrifices and feasts and ceremonies of this great idol, for they are very remarkable. At present I will merely say that this idol, richly dressed and adorned, was set upon a very high altar in a little room amply hung with draperies and jewels and feathers and gold ornaments, with many shields made of feathers, all as beautifully and carefully arranged as possible, and with a curtain always placed before it to show greater veneration. Adjacent to the apartment of this idol was a less richly ornamented chamber where there was another idol called Tlaloc.[6] These two idols were always together, for they were considered to be companions and to have equal power.

There was another very important idol in Mexico, which was the god of penitence and jubilees and forgiveness of sins. This idol was called Tezcatlipoca and was made of a very shiny stone as black as jet and splendidly arrayed

5. A systematic early-seventeenth-century compilation of such practices in the adjacent region of Mexico and southern points like Cuernavaca and Taxco is Hernando Ruíz de Alarcón, *Treatise on the Heathen Superstitions and Customs That Today Live among the Indians Native to This New Spain,* translated and edited by J. Richard Andrews and Ross Hassig (Norman: University of Oklahoma Press, 1984).

6. Tlaloc, meaning "he who lies on earth," was the ancient Mesoamerican rain god linked to agricultural fertility. He shared the great temple in Tenochtitlán, the site of yearly sacrifices to him to ensure the success of the agricultural harvests, with Huitzilopochtli. Tlaloc preferred young victims, and the child sacrifices were chosen, unlike the vast majority of sacrificial victims, from within the population of Tenochtitlán.

after their fashion.⁷ It had gold and silver earrings, and in its lower lip a little crystal tube a handbreadth long with a feather stuck through it that was sometimes green and sometimes blue and seemed to be of emerald or turquoise. Its tress of hair was bound with a ribbon of polished gold, ending in a golden ear with symbols painted on it representing smoke, which signified the pleas that the idol heard from the afflicted and sinners when they applied to it for help. Between this ear and the other were a large number of plumes; around its neck hung a gold ornament so large that it covered the whole breast. There were gold bracelets on both arms and a rich green stone in the navel; in its left hand was a fly whisk of beautiful green, blue, and yellow feathers, emerging from a plaque of gleaming, highly polished gold, so brilliant that it resembled a mirror. This signified that the god saw in that mirror everything that was happening in the world. This mirror or gold plaque was called Itlacheaya, which means "his looking glass." In its right hand were four arrows, signifying the chastisement that he meted out to evildoers for their sins. Hence this was the idol they most feared, lest he discover their wrongdoings; pardon for sins was issued during his festivities, which took place every four years, as will be described later. They held this god, Tezcatlipoca, to be the god of droughts and famines and barrenness and pestilence. And so they represented him in another way, seated with much pomp upon a bench and wrapped in a crimson mantle embroidered with skulls and dead men's bones. In his left hand was a shield with five tufts of cotton and in his right a throwing spear with which he seemed to be threatening, his arm stretched out as if about to throw. Four arrows stuck out of the shield. The idol's face was angry, its body all daubed with black, its head full of quail feathers. The superstitions they entertained concerning this idol were very great, owing to their acute fear of it.

In Cholula, which is near Mexico and was a separate country, they worshiped a famous idol who was the god of merchandise, for they were great merchants and even today are very fond of business dealings; they called it Quetzalcoatl.⁸ This idol stood in a large courtyard in a very lofty temple. All

---

7. Tezcatlipoca, meaning "smoking mirror," was a very powerful Aztec deity who observed people's actions through his mirror. He often played the role of a trickster in Aztec myth and as such had a reputation for causing disorder in daily life.
8. Quetzalcoatl, whose name means "plumed serpent," was an ancient Mesoamerican deity often represented as the god of wind, Ehecatl. He was recognized in Tenochtitlan but worshiped in Cholula. Quetzalcoatl and

around it were gold, silver, jewels, rich feathers, and very valuable clothing of different colors. It was represented as a man but had a bird's head with a red beak and above it a comb with wattles, and several rows of teeth, and the tongue hanging out. On its head was a painted paper miter, sharp pointed; there was a sickle in its hand, and many gold ornaments on its legs, and innumerable other ridiculous objects that were symbolic of all those things; and, indeed, they worshiped this god because he enriched those whom he loved, like the god Mammon or Pluto. And certainly the name given by the Cholulans to their god was appropriate, although they did not understand it. They called him Quetzalcoatl, which means "serpent of rich plumage," a description of the demon of greed.

These savages were not content to have gods but also had their goddesses, like those that the tales of poets introduced and the blind unbelief of Greeks and Romans venerated. The chief goddess that they worshiped was called Toci, which means "our grandmother," for according to the histories of the Mexicans she was the daughter of the king of Culhuacán, who was the first to be flayed by order of Huitzilopochtli, consecrating her in this way as his sister; and it was then that they began to flay men for the sacrifices and dress the living in the skins of those who had been sacrificed, for they believed that their god was pleased by it.[9] They also learned from their god to tear the hearts out of those whom they sacrificed, when he did this with those whom he punished in Tula, as will be described in its proper place. One of these goddesses whom they adored had a son who was a great hunter and was later adopted as a god by the faction opposed to the Mexicans, the Tlaxcallans, with whose help the Spaniards won Mexico.

The province of Tlaxcala is very suitable for hunting and the people are much given to it, and so they offered him great festivities. They represent the idol in a certain form, and I will not waste time in describing it; but the festivity that they offered to him is very colorful. And it was that at daybreak they blew upon a horn and everyone assembled with their bows and arrows, nets, and other hunting implements and went in procession with their idol, a large crowd following, to a high hill, on the top of which they had built a

---

Tezcatlipoca were represented as opposites in Aztec cosmology; the former provided order while the latter stirred up trouble.

9. The female deity Toci, or "our grandmother," was the earth mother goddess. Acosta explains her creation in book VII, chapter 6.

bower with a richly adorned altar in it, where they placed the idol. And marching along with a great noise of trumpets, conch shells, flutes, and drums they reached the place and surrounded the whole slope of the hill, and when they had set fire to it everywhere many and very diverse animals came out, such as deer, rabbits, hares, foxes, wolves, and so on, which ran toward the summit fleeing from the fire. Then the hunters went after them with much shouting and yelling, playing different instruments; they steered them to the summit before the idol, where the press of game was so great that some leaped, others rolled over and over, others jumped onto the people, and still others climbed on the altar, so that there was great rejoicing and merry-making. Then they took a great quantity of game and sacrificed the deer and large animals before the idol, tearing out their hearts with the same ceremony they used when sacrificing men. This done, they loaded the game onto their backs and returned with their idol in the same manner in which they had come and entered the city with all these things, rejoicing greatly and with much music of trumpets and kettledrums, until they reached the temple, where they replaced their idol with much reverence and solemnity. Then everyone went to cook the flesh from all that game and invited all the people to join them, and after the meal gave their usual performances and dances before the idol. They had many other gods and goddesses and a large number of idols, but the chief ones were in the Mexican nation and its neighbors and were those that we have described.

### CHAPTER 10 * OF A STRANGE KIND OF IDOLATRY THAT WAS PRACTICED BY THE MEXICANS

Just as (we said) the Inca kings of Peru substituted certain stone statues made in their likenesses, which they called their *guaioquies,* or brothers, and made their subjects offer them the same veneration as to themselves, the Mexicans did the same with their gods; but these went much further, for they made gods out of living men, and in the following manner: they would take a captive, the best one they could find, and before sacrificing him to their idols they gave him the name of the very idol to whom he was to be sacrificed; and they dressed and adorned him in the same fashion as their idol, and said that he represented the idol itself. And for the whole time that this representation lasted, which in some festivities was a year and in others six months, and in others less, they venerated and worshiped him like the idol itself, and he ate and drank and took his pleasure. And when he walked through the streets the people came out to worship him, and all of them offered him many alms, and they brought children and invalids to him to cure and bless them, and let him do everything he wanted, except that ten or twelve men always accompanied him everywhere he went to prevent him from escaping. And to cause folk to do him reverence wherever he passed, from time to time he played upon a little pipe, so that the people would come and worship him. When he was in prime condition and had grown quite fat, the festival arrived, and they opened him up and killed and ate him, making a solemn sacrifice of him. It is indeed painful to see how Satan holds these people in subjection, and is still master of many of them today, performing such mischievous and fraudulent tricks at the expense of the sad souls and miserable bodies that they offer him, while he laughs at the cruel pranks he plays on these unfortunates, whose sins justify Almighty God's leaving them in the power of the enemy whom they chose as god and protector. But, as I have said enough about the idolatry of the Indians, let us continue by describing the kind of religion, or rather superstition, that they employ in their rites, and their sacrifices, temples, and ceremonies and everything connected with these.

### CHAPTER 11 * HOW THE DEVIL HAS TRIED TO COPY GOD IN METHODS OF SACRIFICES AND OF RELIGION AND SACRAMENTS

But before we do this we must warn of something very worthy of consideration, and it is how the devil in his arrogance, and in competition with God, has taken over the things that God in his wisdom has ordained for his cult and honor, and for man's good and his salvation; these the devil strives to imitate and pervert so as to make himself honored and man more deeply damned. And so we see that, just as the Supreme God has sacrifices and priests, and sacraments, and religious persons, and prophets, and people dedicated to his divine cult and sacred ceremonies, so, too, does the devil have his sacrifices and priests, and his kind of sacraments, and people living in seclusion and feigned holiness, and a thousand kinds of false prophets. All of this, when described in detail, will give great pleasure and be of no little value in making us remember that the devil is the father of lies, as absolute truth tells us in the Gospel; and so he tries to usurp the glory of God for himself, and to counterfeit light with his darkness.[1] The enchanters of Egypt, taught by their master, Satan, tried to do other similar marvels in competition with Moses and Aaron.[2] And in the Book of Judges we read of that Michas who was the priest of a false idol, using the same implements that were used in the tabernacle of the true God, the ephod and teraphim and the rest.[3] No matter what the learned may say, there is scarcely anything instituted by Jesus Christ Our Lord in his Evangelical Law that the devil has not in some way falsified and transmitted to his heathen followers, as anyone may see who observes what we have learned from trustworthy accounts about the Indian rites and ceremonies with which we are dealing in this book.[4]

## CHAPTER 12 * OF THE TEMPLES THAT HAVE BEEN FOUND IN THE INDIES

Let us begin, therefore, with temples: just as the Supreme God decreed that a dwelling be dedicated to him, in which his holy name would be celebrated with special devotion, so the devil for his purposes persuaded the heathen to make him splendid temples and special places of worship and sanctuaries. In each province of Peru there was one chief *huaca,* or house of worship, and in addition to this there were several universal ones that served for all the realms of the Incas. Two were preeminent among them all. One was called Pacha-cama, which is four leagues from Lima, and even today the ruins of a very old and immense building can be seen, from which Francisco Pizarro and his men took that vast store of gold and silver vessels and pitchers that were

1. Saint John, 8, 44 (O'G).

2. Exodus, 7, 10 and 11 (O'G).

3. Judges, 18, 20 (O'G).

4. Whereas scholars today might see imagination and reason at work in the religious cultures of the Americas, Acosta saw the hand of the devil. The assertion that native religion was the devil's work was a widely held idea among Acosta's contemporaries. Acosta found no virtue in the form these practices took in the Indies, claiming in chapter 5 that worship in Peru was "exaggerated to the point of folly" and in chapter 8 that the funereal practices of the Mexicans were "full of absurdities." Nonetheless, the existence of temples, a priest-hood, monasteries, and rituals of penance (chapters 12–17), however demonic in nature, did suggest to Acosta that native peoples possessed a basis with which to reason. Such forms of organized religion influenced his classification of the Aztecs and Incas, and he labeled them superior to other groups of native peoples, like the Chichimeca and the Chiriguana, for whom he saw no evidence of organized religion.

brought them when they held the Inca Atahualpa prisoner.[1] There are reliable accounts that in this temple the devil spoke visibly and gave replies through his oracle and that sometimes a spotted snake was seen; and this speaking and responding by the devil in these false temples, and deceiving the wretched people, is a very common and proven thing in the Indies. However, in places where the Gospel has entered and raised the sign of the holy cross, the father of lies has fallen notably silent, as Plutarch wrote in his era, *Curcessaverit Pythias fundere oracula*.[2] And Saint Justin Martyr deals at length with the silence that Christ imposed on the devils who spoke through idols, as was prophesied much earlier in Holy Writ.[3] The method used by the heathen sorcerers and priests to consult the gods was in the manner that the devil had taught them: usually it was at night, and they entered turned away from the idol, walking backward. And, bending low and bowing their heads, they assumed an ugly posture and thus consulted with him. Usually the reply was a sort of horrible whistle, or a scream, which struck them with horror, and everything that they were told and commanded was intended for their deception and perdition. Thanks to God's mercy and the great power of Jesus Christ, little of this is found today. There was another even more important temple and place of worship in Peru, which was in the city of Cuzco, where the monastery of Santo Domingo is now, and from the building's blocks and stones that remain to this day it is easy to see that it was a very important place.[4] This temple was like the Roman Pantheon in that it was the house and

1. When the Spanish entered Peru in 1532, Atahualpa had recently ascended to the Inca throne by virtue of a military victory over his brother Huáscar. Taken prisoner by Francisco Pizarro and his Spanish forces in Cajamarca, he promised a sizable ransom of gold and silver in exchange for his freedom. During the period of collection for the ransom, the temple of Pachacamac was looted by Hernando Pizarro at his brother Francisco's behest. Atahualpa likely alerted the Spaniards to the pre-Inca temple of Pachacamac, located in a desert near the coast in the region of the Chimu. Despite Acosta's assertion that Pachacamac provided most of the ransom, Pizarro arrived only to find the treasure of Atahualpa's descriptions already hidden away by the priests of the temple. A firsthand account of the trip to Pachacamac is in Francisco de Jerez, *Conquista del Perú*, Biblioteca de Autores Espanoles, vol. 26 (Madrid: Imprenta de M. Riva de Neyra, 1853). John Hemming also describes the trek in his classic study of the Spanish conquest of Peru from a European perspective, *The Conquest of the Incas* (New York: Harcourt Brace Jovanovich, 1970), 55–63. The standard text on Cajamarca is James Lockhart, *The Men of Cajamarca* (Austin: University of Texas Press, 1972).
2. Plutarch, *Lib de Trac Re* (O'G).
3. Saint Justin Martyr, *Apologiae pro Christianis* (O'G).
4. Here Acosta refers to the temple of the sun, Coricancha, the central sacred edifice of the Inca Empire. Befitting the image of its deity, the sun god, shiny panels of gold covered the outer walls of the temple. In a common colonial practice, Spaniards forced Cuzco natives to destroy their revered temple and construct the Catholic monastery of Santo Domingo atop its solid foundation.

dwelling place of all the gods. For the Inca kings placed in it the gods of all the provinces and peoples that they conquered, and each idol was in its special place and the people of its province came to worship and venerate it, with enormous expenditure of things that they brought to minister to it; and thus the Incas believed that the conquered provinces were safe because their gods were being held hostage, as it were. The Punchao was there, which was an idol of the sun, made of very fine gold and with a great abundance of precious stones, set facing the east so cleverly that when the sun came up it struck the idol; and as it was very fine metal, it returned the sun's rays with such brilliance that it seemed another sun.[5] The Incas worshiped this idol as their god, and also as Pachayachachic, who is the maker of the heavens. They say that among the spoils of this rich temple a soldier received that beautiful gold plaque of the sun and that he gambled it away one night in the course of a protracted game; hence the origin of the proverb that circulates in Peru about great gamblers, saying, "he gambles away the sun before it rises."

CHAPTER 13 * OF THE SPLENDID TEMPLES
OF MEXICO

But the Mexicans' superstition was incomparably greater, in their ceremonies as well as the great size of their temples, which the Spaniards used to call *cu;* and this must have been a word taken from the islanders of Santo Domingo or Cuba, like many others in use that are not words from Spain or any other language employed in the Indies today, such as *maíz, chicha, vaquiano, chapetón,* and other similar words. There was, then, in Mexico the *cu,* the famous temple of Huitzilopochtli, whose very large enclosure formed a beautiful courtyard inside;[1] it was all built of great hewn stones carved to resemble

5. Arguably the single most central image of Inca state religion, the gold statue called the Punchao was housed in Coricancha, from whence it gave orders for the Inca Empire. The Spanish did not obtain the statue during their march into Cuzco because Manco Inca managed to usher it out of the city and carry it to Vilcabamba, where it continued to serve its political-religious role in the holdout Inca settlement. The Spanish seized the statue in 1571, when they captured the remaining Incas at Vilcabamba. The whereabouts of the Punchao after the capture are unclear.

1. Acosta describes the Templo Mayor, the central sacred site of Tenochtitlán dedicated to the deities Huitzilopochtli and Tlaloc. Construction of the temple was initiated under the rule of the first Moctezuma and enlarged under Tizoc. The first major archaeological excavation of the Templo Mayor, located in the very center of modern Mexico City, took place from 1978 to 1982. Studies on the historical function and signifi-

snakes, each joined to another, and that is why this enclosure had the name of *coatepantli,* which means "precinct of snakes." Above the chambers and chapels where the idols were there was a very handsome parapet made of small stones as black as jet, carefully and harmoniously arranged, and with the whole area plastered in red and white, which looked very fine from below. Above this parapet were handsome battlements made in spiral shape; the buttresses were finished off with two stone Indians in a sitting position, with candelabra in their hands, and from these emerged something like the hangings of a cross, with rich yellow and green feathers at their ends and long pennons of the same. Within the precinct of this courtyard were many apartments for religious, and others higher up for priests and *papas,* which was what they called the high priests who served the idol. This courtyard was so large and spacious that, although it seems incredible, eight or ten thousand men could assemble there to dance in a circle, as was the custom in that realm. It had four gates or entrances, east and west, north and south; each of these entrances marked the beginning of a very beautiful causeway two or three leagues long; and hence, in the middle of the lake, where the city of Mexico was founded, there were four very broad causeways in the form of a cross, which made the city very attractive. In these entrances were four gods or idols, each with its face turned toward one of the causeways. Opposite the door of this temple of Huitzilopochtli were thirty steps 180 feet long, divided by a street that ran between them and the courtyard wall. At the top of the steps was a broad walk 30 feet wide, all whitewashed; in the middle of this walk was a carefully constructed palisade made from tall trees placed in a row and 6 feet apart. These trunks were very thick and were all bored with small holes. From bottom to top, completely filling the palisade, were thin wands placed through the holes in the timbers, on which many human skulls were strung by the temples; each wand bore twenty heads.[2] These rows of skulls reached from the bottom to the top of the tree trunks and filled the palisade from end to end, and so many and so densely packed were the skulls that they caused amazement and horror. These were the skulls of the men they had sacrificed, for after they had killed and eaten them they would bring the skulls

---

cance of the temple include Elizabeth Boone, ed., *The Aztec Templo Mayor* (Washington, DC: Dumbarton Oaks, 1981); and Johanna Broda, David Carrasco, and Eduardo Matos Moctezuma, eds., *The Great Temple of Tenochtitlan: Center and Periphery in the Aztec World* (Berkeley: University of California Press, 1987).

2. The skull racks are known as *tzompantli* in Nahuatl.

and deliver them to the priests of the temple, and they would string them up there until they fell to pieces; and they took care to replace with others those that fell. At the summit of the temple were two chambers resembling chapels, and in them the two aforesaid idols, Huitzilopochtli and Tlaloc. These chapels were made with carved figures, and they were so lofty that a staircase of 120 stone steps led up to them. Before these apartments was a courtyard 40 feet square, in the middle of which was a green stone shaped like a sharp-pointed pyramid five handbreadths high, which was placed there for the human sacrifices that they performed; for when a man was thrown onto it face up his body was made to bend backward, and then they opened him and tore out his heart, as will be described later.

In the City of Mexico there were eight or nine other temples like this one I have described, adjoining each other within a large enclosure, with their own staircases and their courtyards with apartments and sleeping rooms. Some of them had their entrances on the west, others on the east, others on the south, others on the north, all very well built and possessing towers with different kinds of battlements and paintings and many stone figures and reinforced with large and broad buttresses. These were dedicated to different gods, but second to the temple of Huitzilopochtli was that of the idol Tezcatlipoca, who was the god of penitence and punishment, and it was very tall and beautifully built. There were 80 steps leading up to it, at the top of which was an open space 120 feet wide and next to it a room completely hung with curtains of different colors and workmanship; the door was low and broad and always covered with a veil, and only the priests could enter it. The whole temple was decorated very elaborately, with a number of effigies and carvings, for these two temples were like cathedral churches, and the rest in comparison to them were like parish churches and hermitages. And they were so spacious, and had so many chambers, that there were ministers in them, and colleges and schools and priests' houses, which will be described later. What I have said will suffice to make us understand the devil's arrogance, and the misfortune of the wretched folk who, at so much cost to their goods and labor and lives, served their own enemy, who wanted nothing more from them than to destroy their souls and consume their bodies; and yet they were happy, falsely believing that they had great and powerful gods to whom they did such service.

## CHAPTER 14 * OF THE PRIESTS AND THE
### OFFICES THEY PERFORMED

In every nation of the world men can be found who are specially dedicated to the cult of a god, either true or false, and these serve for the sacrifices and to declare to the people what their gods command. In Mexico there was very great emphasis upon this, and the devil, mimicking the usages of the Church of God, also established his order of lesser and greater and supreme priests and others resembling acolytes and others like the Levites of old. And the most astonishing thing for me is that apparently the devil tried to usurp the cult of Christ even in name, for the highest priests, and as it were the supreme pontiffs, were called *papas* by the Mexicans in their ancient tongue, as is proved today by their histories and accounts.[1] The priests of Huitzilopochtli succeeded by inheritance from certain districts assigned for this purpose. The priests of other idols succeeded by election or by being offered to the temple from childhood. The constant duty of the priests was to cense the idols, which they did four times on every ordinary day: the first time at dawn, the second at noon, the third at sunset, and the fourth at midnight. At this hour all the dignitaries of the temple arose, and instead of bells they blew on large trumpets and conch shells, and others played a mournful tune on little flutes for a long while. And after they had played the priest whose office it was came out dressed in a white garment like a dalmatic, with his censer in his hand full of coals, which he took from the brazier or stove that perpetually burned before the altar. In the other hand he had a bag full of incense, which he placed in the censer, and going in to the idol he censed it very reverently. Then he took a cloth and with it cleaned the altar and the curtains. This done, all went together to a room and there did a sort of very severe and cruel penance, cutting themselves and drawing blood in a way that will be described when dealing with the penance that the devil taught to his adherents. They never failed to perform these matins at midnight. No others could take part in the sacrifices, only the priests according to the rank and dignity of each. They also preached to the people during certain festivities, as we will

1. In Germán Vázquez Chamorro's edition of the "Tovar Manuscript," he suggests that while the general Nahua term for priest is *teopixqui* priests were called *papahua* in reference to their habit of wearing their hair in long locks. Acosta abridged *papahua* to *papa*, the Spanish word for pope. See Juan de Tovar, *Origen de los mexicanos,* edited by Germán Vázquez Chamorro (Madrid: Historia 16, 1987), 154, n. 178.

recount when we deal with these; they had their revenues and were also given ample offerings. The annointing with which they consecrated priests will also be described. In Peru they lived off the lands reserved for their gods, called *chácaras* there, which were numerous and very rich.[2]

## CHAPTER 15 * OF THE MONASTERIES OF VIRGINS THAT THE DEVIL INVENTED FOR HIS SERVICE

Because the religious life (which, in imitation of Jesus Christ and his holy apostles, so many servants of God, both male and female, have professed and still profess within the Holy Church) is so acceptable in the eyes of Divine Majesty, and so greatly honors his holy name and beautifies his church, the father of lies has not only tried to imitate that life but in a certain sense tries to compete with it and to make his ministers vie with it in austerity and observance. In Peru there were many monasteries of virgins, who could not be received if this was not their condition. There was at least one in every province, in which lived two kinds of women: old ones, whom they called *mamaconas,* to instruct the others, and young girls who stayed there for a certain time and were then taken for the gods or for the Inca. This house or monastery was called *acllaguaci,* which means "house of the chosen," and each monastery had its vicar or governor, called *appopanaca,* who had authority to choose all the girls he wished of whatever degree, of eight years of age or younger, if they seemed to him to be well grown and suitable.[1] Shut away in the monastery, these girls were instructed by the *mamaconas* in different things necessary for human life and in the rites and ceremonies of their gods; they were taken away from there at the age of fourteen or older and sent to the court under close guard. Some of them were appointed to serve in the temples and sanctuaries, where they preserved their virginity forever; some were used for the ordinary sacrifices that they made of virgins as well as other

2. The term *chácaras,* or *chacras,* designated a tilled plot of land, in this case the production of which was destined for the Inca leadership.

1. The *acclla* were indeed the chosen women of the Inca, who served as wives of the sun in the *accllaguaci* (also spelled *accllahuasi*), or house of the virgins, in Cuzco. The young *accllas* were collected under the supervision of the *apu-panaca* from areas dominated by the Inca. Irene Silverblatt's analysis of preconquest Inca life links the rise of the *acclla* tradition to the consolidation of the Inca state. See her *Moon, Sun, and Witches: Gender Ideologies and Class in Inca and Colonial Peru* (Princeton: Princeton University Press, 1987), esp. 81–108.

extraordinary sacrifices, such as those for the health, death, or wars of the Inca. Some also served as wives or concubines of the Inca and other kinsmen and captains of his, to whom he gave them, and this was held to be a great favor. This distribution was made every year. These monasteries, which contained a large number of virgins, possessed special revenues and lands from whose funds they were maintained. It was not lawful for any father to refuse his daughters when the *appopanaca* asked for them in order to shut them in those monasteries, and many even offered their daughters willingly, for they thought that they were earning great merit by having them sacrificed to the Inca. If it was found that one of these *mamaconas* or *acllas* had sinned against chastity, she was infallibly punished by being buried alive or suffering some other kind of cruel death.

In Mexico, the devil had his form of nuns as well, although their profession and holy state lasted no more than a year, and it was as follows: within that very large enclosure of the chief temple, as we described it above, were two houses of retreat, one opposite the other. One was for men and the other for women. The women's house contained only virgins of twelve or thirteen years of age, who were called "maidens of penitence"; there were as many of them as of the boys. They lived a chaste and cloistered life, as virgins appointed for the cult of the god. Their duty was to wash and sweep the temple and to feed the idol and its ministers every morning from the food collected as alms by the religious. The food that they gave the idol consisted of small loaves shaped like hands and feet and others that were twisted like our honey cakes. With this bread they made certain dishes and placed them before the idol daily, and its priests ate them, as did those of Bel, of which Daniel tells us.[2] These girls were shorn of their hair, and then they let it grow for a certain time. They arose at midnight for the matins of the idols that were invariably performed, carrying out the same duties as the other religious. They had their abbesses, who set them to making elaborately worked cloths to adorn the idols and temples. The dress that they always wore was pure white, with no embroidery or color whatsoever. They, too, did penance at midnight, making sacrifice by piercing the tops of their ears and smearing the blood that they drew on their cheeks, and in their house of retreat they had a pool where they washed off that blood. They lived chastely and discreetly, and if any was

2. Daniel, 14, 2 (O'G).

found to have committed an offense, even though the fault was very minor, she was quickly put to death without appeal, telling her that she had violated the house of their god. And they took it as an omen, and a sign that some bad thing of this kind had happened, if they saw a mouse or bat cross the chapel of their idol or that it had gnawed some veil. For they said that the mouse or bat would not have dared to commit such a discourtesy unless some crime had taken place. And so they would begin to investigate, and when they found the culprit, no matter of what rank, they sentenced her to death. Only maidens from one of six districts appointed for this purpose were admitted to this monastery, and their cloistered life lasted, as I have said, for the year during which they or their parents had vowed to serve the idol in that way, and they went from there to be married. There is some resemblance between these girls, and even more between those of Peru, and the vestal virgins of Rome of which historians tell us. This is an example of how the devil has been eager to be served by persons of chaste life, not because he likes chastity, for he is an unclean spirit by nature, but to deprive Almighty God in any way he can of the glory of being served with purity and chastity.

CHAPTER 16 * OF THE MONASTERIES OF
RELIGIOUS THAT THE DEVIL POSSESSES FOR
HIS SUPERSTITION

Well known from the letters of the fathers of our society, written from Japan, are the large number and great influence in that land of religious whom they call bonzes and their customs and superstitions and lies; and so nothing new need be said of them.[1] Fathers who have been in those countries tell of the Chinese bonzes or religious that there are of different styles or orders and that

1. Acosta is unique in his efforts to draw the peoples of the East Indies into a comparison and classification with the Inca and the Aztecs. His information on China and Japan likely came from his association, in Mexico and en route to Spain, with Fr. Alonso Sánchez, a fellow Jesuit, who was a missionary in the Philippines. At the time Acosta met him, Sánchez was traveling home to Spain to lobby for a military campaign against the Chinese, as his experience in the East Indies had convinced him that the evangelizing process would never progress without an accompanying military force.

Sánchez was one of many Jesuits active in both the New (Americas) and Old (China and Japan) Indies toward the end of the sixteenth century. Matthew Ricci is a better-known example. An abridged edition of his journal has been translated from the Latin and edited by L. J. Gallagher, in *China in the Sixteenth Century: The Journals of Matthew Ricci, 1563–1610* (New York: Random House, 1953). The classical study on the work of Ricci in China is Jonathan Spence, *The Memory Palace of Matteo Ricci* (New York: Viking Penguin, 1984).

they saw some in white habits with a sort of bonnet, and others in black habits without headgear or hair, and that ordinarily they are not held in much esteem, for the mandarins and ministers of justice whip them as they do the rest. These bonzes claim not to eat meat or fish or any living thing, only rice and greens; but secretly they eat everything and are worse than ordinary folk. They say that the religious at the court, which is in Peking, are highly regarded. Often the mandarins go to these houses or monasteries for recreation and almost always return drunk. Usually these monasteries are outside the cities; there are temples inside them, but there is not much zeal in China with regard to idols and temples because the mandarins pay little heed to idols and think them a subject for joking. Nor do they believe that there is another life or even any other paradise apart from being a mandarin, nor any other hell than the prisons that they have for offenders. They say that the common people must be entertained with idolatry, as the philosopher also says of his governors;[2] and even in Scripture this was a sort of excuse that Aaron gave for the golden calf that he made.[3] Nevertheless, the Chinese place on the stern of their ships, in a sort of chapel, a sculpture of a virgin seated in her chair, with two Chinese girls kneeling before her like angels and a flame burning night and day; and when they are about to embark they perform many sacrifices and ceremonies to her with a great noise of drums and bells, and throw burning papers off the stern.

To return to the religious orders, I do not know whether there was ever a house of retreat for men in Peru in addition to their priests and sorcerers, of whom there were vast numbers. But the place where the devil seems to have established such a house was in Mexico, for within the enclosure of the great temple were two monasteries, as referred to above: one of virgins, which I described, and the other for cloistered youths of eighteen to twenty years, whom they referred to as religious. They had tonsures on their heads like friars; their hair was scarcely longer, reaching halfway down their ears, except that at the back they let grow a lock of hair four fingers wide, which fell over their shoulders, and they tied and braided it like a tress. These youths who served in the temple of Huitzilopochtli lived in poverty, chastity, and obedience and did the office of Levites, supplying to the priests and temple

2. Aristotle, *Metaphysica,* book 12 (o'g).
3. Exodus, 32, 4 (o'g).

dignitaries the censer, the flame, and their vestments. They swept the sacred places and brought firewood to burn continually in the god's brazier, which was like a lamp and burned perpetually before the idol's altar. In addition to these youths there were other lads like acolytes, who carried out manual tasks such as embowering and arranging the temples with roses and reeds, giving water to the priests for their hands, supplying knives for sacrifice, and accompanying those who went begging alms to bring back the offerings. All these had governors who were in charge of them, and they lived so chastely that when they went out in public where women were present they walked with their heads down and their eyes on the ground, not daring to raise them to look at women. Their costume was a sort of sheet made of mesh. These cloistered youths were allowed to go into the city in groups of four or six, very humbly, to beg alms in its different districts; and when they were given none they had permission to go into the fields and pick the stalks of wheat or ears of maize that they needed, and the owner dared not speak to them or hinder their taking them. They had this permission because they lived in poverty and had no revenue other than alms. These youths could not number more than fifty; they practiced penance and rose at midnight to play conch shells and trumpets, with which they awakened the people. They watched over the idol in his chambers lest the flame before the altar go out; they supplied the censer with which the priests censed the idol at midnight, in the morning, at noon, and during prayers. These youths were very submissive and obedient to their elders and did not deviate a jot from what they were commanded to do. And after the priests had finished their censing at midnight these boys went to a special place and sacrificed, drawing blood from the fleshy parts of their limbs with hard, sharp knife points, and they daubed the blood that they drew in this way onto their foreheads and down past the ears; and when they had performed this sacrifice they went to bathe in a pool. These youths did not blacken their heads and bodies like the priests, and their dress was a kind of cloth that they make there, very rough and white in color. This training and harsh penance lasted for a whole year, during which they lived a life of seclusion and mortification. Truly it is a marvel that the false notion of religion could be so powerful in these youths and maidens of Mexico, causing them to do with such austerity in the service of Satan what many of us fail to do in the service of Almighty God. This is a severe reproach to those who, after doing a minor bit of penance, are very proud and satisfied.

However, because that discipline was not perpetual but lasted only a year, this made it more tolerable.

### CHAPTER 17 * OF THE PENANCES AND AUSTERITIES THAT THE INDIANS PRACTICED AT THE DEVIL'S BEHEST

Now that we have reached this point, it behooves us both to demonstrate Satan's accursed pride and shame and awaken the sense of our own lukewarm efforts in the service of Almighty God, to say something about the severe practices and strange penances that this wretched people made at the devil's behest, like the false prophets of Baal who wounded themselves and drew blood with knives,[1] and also like those who sacrificed their sons and daughters to the vile Beelphegor and passed them through the fire,[2] as Divine Scripture gives witness;[3] for Satan has always desired to be served by men, greatly to their cost. I have already said that the priests and religious of Mexico rose at midnight and that when the priests and dignitaries of the temple had censed the idol they went to a place where there was a large room with many seats. They sat down there, and each one took up a maguey thorn, which is like an awl or punch, or some other kinds of lancets or knives, and they pierced their calves with them near the bone, drawing a great deal of blood, with which they anointed their foreheads, bathing the lancets or points in the rest of the blood; and then they placed them on the battlements of the courtyard, stuck into globes or balls made of straw, so that all might see them and understand the penance that they had done for the people. They washed off this blood in a lake specially appointed for the purpose, called Ezapán, which means "blood water"; and there was a large quantity of these lancets or thorns in the temple, for none could be used a second time. In addition to this, these priests and religious underwent severe fasts, such as fasting for five and even ten days in succession before some of the important festivals, which were like our ember [fasting] weeks. They maintained continence so strictly that many of them, lest they succumb to any weakness, split their virile members up the middle and did any number of things to render

1. 3 Kings, 18, 28 (O'G).
2. Psalms, 105, 37 and 38; Numbers, 25, 3 (O'G).
3. 4 Kings, 21, 6 (O'G).

themselves impotent to avoid offending the gods. They did not drink wine and slept very little, for most of their disciplines were at night, and they did very cruel things to themselves, suffering for the devil, and all in exchange for being considered great fasters and very penitent. They were accustomed to discipline themselves with knotted ropes, and not only the priests but the people, too, used this discipline during the procession and feast that they made to the idol Tezcatlipoca, who, as we said above, was the god of penitence. For at that time all carried in their hands new ropes made of maguey fiber, six feet long with a knot on the end, and disciplined themselves with these, giving themselves great blows on their backs. For this same festivity the priests fasted for five consecutive days, eating but once a day and without contact with their wives; they did not leave the temple for those five days, striking themselves rigorously with the ropes I have described. Letters from the fathers of the Society of Jesus, written from India, describe at length the penances and harsh extremes used by the bonzes. But all this was sophistic, and done more for appearance than reality. In Peru, for the festivity of Itu, which was very great, everyone fasted for two days, during which time they had no congress with women nor ate anything with salt or chiles, nor drank *chicha,* and they were much given to this kind of fasting. For certain sins they did penance by lashing themselves with sharply stinging nettles; at other times they administered many blows on the back to one another, using a certain stone. In some places these misguided people, at the devil's behest, go into the wild mountains and lead a very rugged life there for a long time. At other times they sacrifice themselves by leaping from some high crag; and all of these are deceits of the being who loves nothing more than men's suffering and perdition.

### CHAPTER 18 * OF THE SACRIFICES THE INDIANS MADE TO THE DEVIL, AND OF WHAT THEY CONSISTED

The chief way in which the enemy of God and men has always demonstrated his cunning has been in the multitude and variety of offerings and sacrifices that he has taught the heathen for his worship. And, just as exhausting the creature's substance in the service and honor of the Creator is an admirable act and appropriate to religion, namely, by sacrifice, so the father of lies has

contrived to have God's creatures offered and sacrificed to him as their author and lord. The first kind of sacrifices made by men were very simple, with
Cain offering the fruits of the earth and Abel the firstlings of his flock; later,
Noah and Abraham and the other patriarchs also did this, until through
Moses God gave them that long ceremonial in Leviticus wherein so many
and different kinds of sacrifices are described, and for different aspects of
different things, and with different ceremonies.[1] So also Satan, in some nations, has been pleased to teach them to sacrifice their possessions to him,
no matter what they may be. In other nations he has progressed so much
in giving them rites and ceremonies of this kind, and so many observances,
that it is astonishing and clearly seeks to compete with the ancient law and
in many ways to usurp its very ceremonies. All the kinds of sacrifices used
by these heathen can be reduced to three: some are sacrifices of insentient
things, others are of animals, and others of men. In Peru they were accustomed to sacrifice coca, which is an herb that they value greatly, and maize,
which is their wheat, and colored feathers and beads, which they call *mollo*,
and seashells, and sometimes gold and silver, making little figures of animals
from it; also the fine cloth called *cumbi*, and fragrant carved wood, and very
often burned tallow.[2] These offerings or sacrifices were made to obtain good
growing seasons or health, or to deliver them from dangers and evils.

Their ordinary sacrifice of the second kind was of *cuies*, a type of little
animal resembling a rabbit that the Indians frequently eat.[3] And in matters of
importance, or in the case of wealthy persons, they offered the sheep of the
country, or alpacas (either smooth or fleecy), using great care and ceremony
as to their number and colors and times of sacrifice. The method used by the
Indians of killing any animal, large or small, according to their ancient ceremony, was the same as that of the Moors, who call it *alquible;* it consists of

1. Genesis, 4, 3 and 4; 8, 20; 15, 9 (O'G).

2. Acosta's reference to *mollo* as "colored feathers and beads" is an incorrect adaptation of Polo de Ondegardo's work. *Mollo* is in fact the term used to refer to *spondylu* shells used for offerings. They are found only
in warmer seas near present-day Ecuador, and their use in the central highlands signifies the variety of tribute
goods the Inca could demand from a range of ecological regions. For the reference in Polo, see the 1571 "Los
errores y supersticiones de los indios, sacadas del tratado y averiguación que hizo el Licenciado Polo," in
*Informaciones acerca de la Religión y Gobierno de los Incas,* edited by Horacio H. Urteaga and Carlos A. Romero,
Colección de Libros y Documentos Referentes a la Historia del Perú, vol. 3 (Lima: Imprenta Sanmarti,
1916), 39.

3. The *cuy,* plural *cuies,* is akin to a guinea pig and is still considered a delicacy in the Cuzco region.

seizing the animal by its right foreleg and turning its eyes to the sun, saying different words according to the quality of the animal being killed. For if it were mottled the words were spoken to the *chuquilla,* or thunder, so that rain would not fail; if it were smooth and white they offered it to the sun with certain words, and if it were fleecy with other words, and if it was a guanaco, which is a dark-colored animal, they addressed the sacrifice to Viracocha. And in Cuzco they killed a smooth-skinned animal with this ceremony every day and offered it to the sun and then burned it clad in a red garment, and while it was being burned they threw certain little baskets of coca on the fire (which they called *villcaronca*). There were people appointed to perform this sacrifice and flocks that served no other purpose. They also sacrificed birds, although this is not as frequent in Peru as in Mexico, where the sacrifice of quail was very common. In Peru they sacrificed birds from the *puna* (for that is what they call the desert there) when they were about to go to war in order to sap the strength of their enemies' *huacas.* This sacrifice was called *cuzco-vicza,* or *contevicza* or *huallavicza* or *sopavicza,* and was performed in the following manner: they captured very many kinds of desert birds and gathered a large quantity of thorny wood, called *yanlli,* and when it had been set alight they piled the birds together, and this pile they called *quizo,* and threw them on the fire, around which the officials of the sacrifice walked with certain stones both round and pointed, on which many snakes, lions, toads, and tigers were represented, saying *usachún,* which means "may our victory be successful," and other words with which they said, "may the strength of our enemies' *huacas* be lost"; and then they brought out some of their dark-colored sheep, which had been imprisoned without food for several days, which were called *urcu,* and when they killed them they said that just as the hearts of those animals were weakened so their enemies would weaken. And if they saw in these sheep that a certain piece of flesh that is behind the heart had not been consumed by the fast and imprisonment to which the animal had been subjected they thought it a bad omen. And they brought certain black dogs, called *apurucos,* and killed them and placed them on a plain and with certain ceremonies forced a certain kind of people to eat them. They also performed this sacrifice to prevent the Inca from being injured by poison, and for this ceremony they fasted from morning until the stars appeared and then stuffed themselves and feasted with music, as the Moors do. This sacrifice was the one most favored for use against their enemies' gods, and though nowadays almost all of this has ceased because wars have ceased, nevertheless fairly frequent traces of it have remained for private quarrels of Indians of the common sort, or of chiefs, or some towns with other towns.

They also sacrificed or offered sea shells, which they called *mollo,* and offered them to fountains and springs, saying that the shells were daughters of the sea, the mother of all waters. These have different names according to their color and so serve for different purposes. These shells are used in almost all kinds of sacrifices, and even today, out of superstition, some people put ground *mollo* into the native drink. Finally, if they thought it appropriate they offered sacrifices of everything that they sowed and cultivated. There were also Indians appointed to make sacrifices to the fountains, springs, or creeks that passed through their towns or farms or fields, and these were performed at the end of the sowing, so that they would not cease to run and would water their fields. The sorcerers chose these sacrifices according to the omens, and when they had finished they gathered up what was to be sacrificed out of the people's contribution and delivered it to those who were in charge of performing those sacrifices; and they performed them at the beginning of winter, which is the time when fountains and springs and rivers rise owing to the dampness of the season. And they attributed this to their sacrifices and did not sacrifice to the fountains and springs of uninhabited places. This veneration of fountains, springs, streams, creeks, or rivers that pass through a town or fields persists even today, and reverence is also felt for the fountains and rivers of unpopulated places. They pay particular reverence and veneration to the places where two rivers meet and wash there for healing, first rubbing on maize flour or other things and adding different ceremonies; and they do the same in their baths.

CHAPTER 19 * OF THE SACRIFICES OF MEN
THAT THEY MADE

But what is most painful about the unhappy lot of these wretched people is the vassalage that they paid to the devil, sacrificing men to him, who are made in the image of God and were created to enjoy God. As has been said above, in many nations they had the custom of killing, to accompany their dead, the persons who had been most pleasing to them and who they imagined could best serve them in the other life. Apart from this, in Peru they used to sacrifice children of from four to six years, up to the age of ten, and this was most frequently done in matters concerning the Inca, such as procuring health for him in his illnesses, and also when he went to war, to attain victory. And when the tassel was given to the new Inca, which was the insignia of the king just as the scepter or crown is here, they sacrificed as many as two hundred children from four to ten years of age, a ruthless and inhuman spectacle. The way they sacrificed them was to strangle them and bury them with certain grimaces and ceremonies; at other times they cut their throats and smeared themselves from ear to ear with their blood. They also sacrificed virgins from among those brought to the Inca from the monasteries, which we described above. A very great and widespread abuse of this kind existed, which was that when some Indian either important or ordinary was ill, and the soothsayer told him that he must surely die, they would sacrifice his son to the sun or to Viracocha, telling the god to be content with him and not to wish to take the father's life. Such cruelty resembled that which Scripture tells us was used by the king of Moab when he sacrificed his firstborn son upon the wall in sight of the Israelites, who thought this act so tragic that they refused to press him further and so returned to their homes.[1] Divine Scripture tells that this same kind of cruel sacrifice was used among those barbarous nations of Chanaanites and Jebusites and the others written about in the Book of Wisdom:[2] they call it peace to live in so many and so terrible evils, such as sacrificing their own children or making other hidden sacrifices, or staying awake all night doing mad things; and so they neither maintain cleanliness in their lives or in their marriages, but one man takes the life of another out of envy, another takes a man's wife and he has no objection, and everything is confused: blood, deaths, thefts, deceits, corruption, unfaithfulness, riots, wrongs, mutinies, forgetfulness of God, contamination of souls, changing sexes and birth, changing of marriage partners, and disorder of adulteries and filthiness, for idolatry is an abyss of all the evils. The sage says this of the people about whom David complained that the children of Israel were learning those customs, even sacrificing their sons and daughters to devils. God never wanted this, nor was it pleasing to him, for because he is the author of life and made all things for man he is not pleased when men take

---

1. 4 Kings, 3, 27 (O'G).
2. Book of Wisdom, 12, 5 and 6; 14, 23 (O'G).

the lives of other men; and, although the Lord tested and accepted the willingness of the faithful patriarch Abraham, he by no means consented to the killing of Abraham's son.[3] From this we can see the malice and tyranny of the devil, who in this has tried to surpass God, for he loves to be worshiped with the shedding of human blood and by this means attempts men's perdition in soul and body because of the ferocious hatred that he feels toward men as their cruel adversary.

### CHAPTER 20 * OF THE HORRIBLE SACRIFICES OF MEN THAT THE MEXICANS PERFORMED

Although the Peruvians surpassed the Mexicans in killing children and sacrificing their sons (for I have not read or learned that the Mexicans did this), yet in the number of men that they sacrificed and the horrible way in which they did it the Mexicans surpassed the Peruvians and even every other nation in the world. And so that we may see the great misery in which the devil so blindly held these people I will describe at length their inhuman custom in this regard. First, the men who were sacrificed had been taken in war, and they did not make these solemn sacrifices except with captives; in this, seemingly, they followed the style of the ancients, who according to what some authors say called the sacrifice *victima* because he had been vanquished, and they also called him *hostia, quasi ab hoste* because he was an offering made of their enemies, although usage gradually extended both words to any sort of sacrifice. Indeed, the Mexicans sacrificed only captives to their idols, and their usual wars were fought to provide captives for their sacrifices. And so they tried to take their enemies alive when they fought against each other and to capture but not kill them in order to rejoice in their sacrifice. This was the reason given by Moctezuma to the Marqués del Valle when he was asked why, when he was so powerful and had conquered so many kingdoms, he had not subdued the province of Tlaxcala, which was so near. Moctezuma replied to this that there were two reasons why they had not subdued that province, although it would have been easy to do so if they had wished. One was to have a place for the Mexican youth to exert themselves, lest they be reared in idleness and luxury; the other and principal reason was that he had

3. Psalms, 105, 37 (O'G).

reserved that province in order to have a place to obtain captives to sacrifice to his gods.[1]

The way in which they performed these sacrifices was that they gathered together those who were to be sacrificed at that palisade of skulls I described earlier and performed a ceremony with them at the foot of that palisade. They placed them all in a line at its foot, with many guards surrounding them. Then a priest came out dressed in a short alb with many fringes and descended from the summit of the temple with an idol made of a dough of amaranth and maize, kneaded with honey, whose eyes were green beads and whose teeth were grains of maize. He came with all possible haste down the temple steps and climbed upon a great stone that was set in a very lofty chapel in the middle of the courtyard. The stone was called *quauhxicalli,* which means "eagle stone." The priest climbed up a little stairway that was opposite the chapel and came down another that was on the other side; always clutching his idol, he went up to where those who were to be sacrificed were standing and walked from side to side, showing that idol to each man individually and saying, "this is your god." And when he had finished showing it to them he descended by the other side of the stairs, and all those who were going to die went in procession to the place where they were to be sacrificed, and there they found the ministers who were going to sacrifice them standing ready. The usual method of sacrifice was to open the chest of the man being sacrificed and, tearing out his heart still half alive, cast him aside to roll down the steps of the temple, which were bathed in blood.

To give a clearer understanding of this, be it known that six sacrificers appointed for this office came to the place of sacrifice: four to hold the feet and hands of the man who was to be sacrificed, another for his throat, and another to cut open the victim's chest and tear out his heart. They called these officials *chachalmua,* which in our language is the same as a minister of some sacred thing; this was a supreme office and held in great esteem among them and was inherited after the manner of an entailment. The minister who held

1. Moctezuma's supposed response to the Marqués del Valle, the postconquest title of Cortés, must be viewed within the context of the Mesoamerican practice of flower wars, the *xochiyaoyotl.* These wars, which lacked any element of a surprise attack, have been characterized as more ritual than battle. Ross Hassig suggests that these events, for which the date, location, and participants were announced in advance, were part of a long-term strategy to conquer formidable opponents by weakening and intimidating them over time. See his *War and Society in Ancient Mesoamerica* (Berkeley: University of California Press, 1992), 145–46.

the office of killing, the sixth of these men, was considered and revered as a supreme priest or pontiff and had a different name according to the difference in the times and solemnities when he sacrificed; also the clothing was different when they came out to exercise their office at different times. The name of their office was *papa* and *topilzin;* their apparel and clothing consisted of a red garment like a dalmatic with fringes on its edges, a crown of rich green and yellow feathers on their heads, in their ears something resembling gold earrings with green stones set into them, and under the lip, near the middle of the chin, a piece of jewelry like a little tube, made of blue stone. These six sacrificers had their faces and hands thickly daubed with black; five of them had their hair tightly curled and in disarray, with strips of leather fastened around their heads, and on their foreheads little rolls of paper painted in different colors. They were dressed in white dalmatics embroidered in black. In this garb they looked like figures of the devil himself, and seeing them come out with such a horrible appearance struck great fear into all the people. In his hand the supreme priest held a large flint knife, very sharp and broad; another priest had a wooden collar carved in the likeness of a serpent. When all six were in front of the idol they bowed low before it and ranged themselves in order next to the pyramidal stone that, as I mentioned above, was opposite the door of the idol's chamber. This stone was so sharp pointed that when the victim was thrown on his back on top of it, he was bent over in such a way that when the knife fell on his breast it was very easy to split a man down the middle with it.

After these sacrificers had ranged themselves in order, all those who had been taken in the wars and were to be sacrificed during this festival were brought out and, closely accompanied by guards, were led up those long staircases, all in rows and completely naked, to the place where the ministers were waiting. And as they arrived the six sacrificers took each of them in order, one seizing one foot and another the other, one holding one hand and another the other, and threw him backward over that sharp-pointed stone, where the fifth of these ministers placed the collar over his throat and the high priest used that knife to open his chest with extraordinary speed, tearing out the heart with his hands and holding it up still smoking to the sun, to whom he offered the heart's heat and steam. Then he turned to the idol and threw the heart in its face, and then they very easily sent the victim's corpse rolling down the temple steps, for the stone was placed so close to them that there was not two feet of space between the stone and the top step, and so with a kick they rolled the corpses down the stairs. And in this way they sacrificed all the victims one after another, and, when all were dead and the corpses had been rolled down the stairs, their owners — those by whose hands they had been made prisoner — picked them up and carried them off and distributed them among themselves and ate them, celebrating solemn rites with them. The smallest number of these victims was always above forty or fifty, for some men were very expert in taking captives. All the other nations round about did the same, imitating the Mexicans in their rites and ceremonies in the service of their gods.

### CHAPTER 21 * OF ANOTHER KIND OF HUMAN SACRIFICE THAT THE MEXICANS PERFORMED

In several festivals there was another kind of sacrifice that they called *racaxipe valiztli,* which means "flaying of persons."[1] It was so called because during certain festivals they took a slave or slaves, according to the number they desired, and after flaying off their skin dressed in it a person appointed for this purpose. This person went around to all the houses and markets of the cities, singing and dancing, and everyone had to offer him something; and if someone did not offer him anything he would strike him on the face with an edge of the skin, smearing him with the blood that was clotted on it. This performance lasted until the skin began to rot. During this time all those who went about in this way gathered a large quantity of alms, which were spent on things necessary for the cult of their gods. In many of these festivals a challenge was made between the sacrificer and the man to be sacrificed, as follows: they would tie a slave by one foot to a large stone wheel, and would give a sword and shield into his hands with which to defend himself, and then the one who was to do the sacrificing would come forth armed with another sword and shield. And if the prospective victim prevailed over the other he was freed from sacrifice and had the reputation of a famous captain and was treated like one ever afterward. But if he was vanquished they would sacrifice him on the very stone where he was tied. Another kind of sacrifice

1. Acosta is describing the festival of Tlacaxipeualiztli, the feast of the flaying of men, which was held to honor Xipe Totec, "Our Lord the Flayed One," a fertility and warrior deity. The festival included dances performed by men wearing the skins of flayed victims and actual sacrifices, both on the pyramids and at street level.

took place when they dedicated some captive to represent the idol, whose likeness they said he was. Every year they gave a slave to the priests so that the living likeness of the god would always be present; as soon as he entered into the office, after washing him very carefully, they dressed him in all the clothing and insignias of the idol and gave him the same name, and for a whole year he was as much honored and revered as the idol itself. He always had twelve men-at-arms with him to prevent him from escaping, and with this guard they allowed him to go freely wherever he wished; and if by chance he got away, the chief officer of the guard took his place to represent the idol and later to be sacrificed. This Indian had the most honored apartment in the temple, where he ate and drank, and where all the important men came to serve and revere him, bringing him food with all the pomp and order paid to the great lords. And when he went out into the city he was closely accompanied by lords and important persons and carried a little flute in his hand on which he played from time to time, giving the people to understand that he was passing by, and then the women would come out with their children in their arms and place them before him, greeting him as though he were a god; and so did all the rest of the people. At night they put him in a cage with very strong bars lest he escape, until, when the festival arrived, they sacrificed him in the way that has been described.

By these means and many others the devil kept those wretched creatures deceived and mocked, and so great was the multitude of those who were sacrificed with this infernal cruelty that it seems incredible; for they say that there were occasions when the number of victims was more than five thousand, and there was even a day when in different places more than twenty thousand men were sacrificed in this way.[2] For this horrible slaughter the devil used a ghastly stratagem through his ministers, and this was that whenever they felt like it the priests of Satan went to the kings and told them how the gods were dying of hunger and that they must be remembered. Then the kings took note of this and informed each other that the gods were asking for food and therefore they must call their people together for a

2. Four major festival dates in the Aztec calendar corresponded with massive sacrificial rituals. Although scholars have long debated how many people were put to death, no one suggests that these were other than mass killings of outsider victims captured through war or received as tribute payment. A study of the role of human sacrifice in the Mexica world that focuses on the significance, and not the quantity, of these ritual killings is Inga Clendinnen, *Aztecs* (New York: Cambridge University Press, 1991).

certain day, sending messengers to the enemy provinces to summon them to come to war. And when the people were congregated and their companies and squadrons were in order, they went out to the field where the armies were gathered; and the whole contest and battle was to take each other prisoner so as to sacrifice them, with each side trying to outdo the other in bringing more captives for sacrifice, so that in these battles they tried to capture rather than kill, for their whole aim was to bring live men to feed their idols. And this was the way in which they brought victims to their gods, and it must be noted that no king was crowned unless he first conquered some province, so that he could bring a large number of captives as sacrifices to their gods; and so an infinite amount of human blood was shed in every way in honor of Satan.

CHAPTER 22 * HOW THE INDIANS THEMSELVES
WERE EXHAUSTED AND COULD NOT ENDURE
THE CRUELTIES OF THEIR GODS

This excessive cruelty in shedding so much human blood, and the heavy tribute represented by constantly having to win captives to feed their gods, had exhausted many of those barbarians, seeming unbearable to them; and yet, because of the great fear aroused by the idol's ministers for their part, and the tricks with which they deceived the people, the Indians continued to carry out their harsh edicts; but inwardly they wished to be free of such a heavy charge. And it was the Lord's providence that the first men to bring the news of Christ's law found these people in this state of mind, for there is no doubt that it seemed a good law to them and a good God who wished to be served in that way. A worthy father in New Spain told me in this regard that when he went to that realm he had asked an old and important Indian why it was that the Indians received the law of Jesus Christ so quickly and why they had abandoned their religion without more proofs or verification or any dispute about the matter, for it seemed that they had changed without being moved by sufficient reason. The Indian replied, "Do not believe, Father, that we accept the Law of Christ as unthinkingly as you say, for I want you to know that we were so weary and unhappy with the things that the idols commanded us to do that we had tried to leave them and accept a different law. And, as it seemed that the one that you people preached to us had no cruelties and was much to our liking, and was so just and good, we realized that it was the true law, and so we received it very willingly." What this Indian said is fully confirmed by what we read in the first reports sent by Hernán Cortés to the emperor Charles V, where he relates that after he had conquered the City of Mexico and was in Coyoacán ambassadors came to him from the republic and province of Michoacán, asking him to send them his religion and someone to expound it, for they intended to leave theirs because they thought it wrong. Cortés did so, and today these are among the best Indians and best Christians in New Spain.[1] The Spaniards who witnessed those cruel human sacrifices were determined to do all in their power to destroy that accursed butchery of men; and they became all the more determined when one afternoon, before their very eyes, the Indians sacrificed sixty or seventy Spanish soldiers whom they had captured in a battle that occurred during the conquest of Mexico. And on another occasion they found in a room in Texcoco, written with charcoal: "Here was kept prisoner the unfortunate such-and-such a one and his companions, whom the Indians of Texcoco sacrificed." Another case occurred that was strange but true, for persons very worthy of belief attest to it; and this was that the Spaniards were watching one of those spectacles of sacrifice and they had split open and torn out the heart of a very handsome youth and cast him tumbling down the stairs as was their custom; and when he came to the bottom the youth said to the Spaniards in his own tongue, "My lords, they have killed me," which caused tremendous pity and horror in our people. And it is not incredible that he

1. For the English translation of the Cortés reports, see Hernán Cortés, *Letters from Mexico,* translated and edited by Anthony Pagden, introduction by J. H. Elliott (New Haven: Yale University Press, 1986). The anecdote from Cortés's letter glosses over the fact that the Tarascans, the people of Michoacán, had a long-standing enmity with the Mexica. Their entreaties to Cortés, which may have mentioned religious instruction, took place in the context of negotiations for a political alliance with the men who had defeated their former enemy, the Mexica. Despite Acosta's rosy representation of Spanish-Tarascan relations, the ruler of the Tarascans, Tangáxoan, was executed by the Spanish in 1530, a mere five years after his baptism. The Tarascans gained a reputation as model Christians through their participation in agricultural and artisanal communities established under the supervision of the bishop of Michoacán, Vasco de Quiroga. Quiroga drew on the ideas of Thomas More for his utopian settlements on the shores of Lake Patzcuaro. The classic sixteenth-century source for this is *The Chronicles of Michoacán,* translated and edited by Eugene R. Craine and Reginald C. Reindorp (Norman: University of Oklahoma Press, 1970). For a historical account of events in the region, see J. Benedict Warren, *The Conquest of Michoacán* (Norman: University of Oklahoma Press, 1985). For a textual analysis of the chronicles, see James Krippner-Martínez, *Rereading the Conquest: Power, Politics, and the History of Early Colonial Michoacán, Mexico, 1521–1565* (University Park: Pennsylvania State University Press, 2001).

could have spoken after his heart had been ripped out, for Galen reports that it happened sometimes during sacrifices of animals that they breathed after their hearts were removed and placed on the altar and even roared loudly and ran away for a short time.[2] Leaving aside for the moment the question of how this conforms with nature, my point is to show what intolerable servitude those savages suffered from the infernal murderer and what great mercy the Lord has done them by divulging to them his gentle, just, and wholly agreeable religion.

### CHAPTER 23 * HOW THE DEVIL HAS TRIED TO MIMIC THE SACRAMENTS OF HOLY CHURCH

What is most astonishing about Satan's envy and desire to compete with God is that not only in idolatries and sacrifices but also in certain kinds of ceremonies he has mimicked our sacraments, which our Lord instituted and his Holy Church employs, especially the sacrament of communion, the loftiest and most divine of them all. He tried in a certain sense to imitate it, to the great delusion of the heathen, and does so as follows: in the first month, which in Peru is called *raymi* and corresponds to our December, a very solemn festival was held called *capacraymi,* and during it great sacrifices and ceremonies were performed for many days, in which no *forastero,* or outsider, could remain at the court, which was in Cuzco. At the end of these days permission was granted for all outsiders to reenter the city, and they were made participants in the festival and sacrifices, being offered communion in the following form: the priestesses of the sun, who were like nuns of the sun, made small loaves of maize flour tinged and kneaded with the blood of white sheep that had been sacrificed that day. Then they ordered the strangers from every province to enter, and they lined up in order, and the priests, who were of a certain lineage and descendants of *lluquiyupangui,* gave each one a mouthful of these loaves, telling them that they were offered in order that they be confederated and united with the Inca, and they were warned not to speak or think ill of the Inca but always to have good intentions toward him, for that mouthful would be a witness of their intentions; and if they did not do as they should it would be discovered and would cause them to be attacked. These loaves were brought out on large gold and silver plates ap-

2. Galen, *On the Doctrines of Hippocrates and Plato,* book 2, chapter 4 (O'G).

pointed for this purpose, and all received and ate those mouthfuls, giving fervent thanks to the sun for this great boon, speaking words and making gestures of great contentment and devotion; and they protested that they would never do or think anything against the sun or the Inca for the rest of their lives and that they received the food of the sun on that condition, and that such food would remain in their bodies as witness of the faith they kept to the sun and to the Inca their king. This diabolical form of communion was also administered in the tenth month, called *coyaraymi,* which was September, in the solemn festival that they call *citua,* using the same ceremony; and in addition to taking communion (if this word can be used of such a diabolical thing) those loaves were also sent to all the *huacas,* or sanctuaries, or to other idols all over the realm, and people gathered from every place to receive them at the same time, and they were told that the sun had sent them that food as a sign that he wished all people to venerate and honor him; and some was also sent as a favor to the chiefs. Some may think that this is a tale or an invention; but indeed it is very certain that beginning with the Inca Yupanqui, the one who made the most laws concerning rites and ceremonies (as Numa did in Rome), this kind of communion lasted up to the time during which the Gospel of our Lord Jesus Christ did away with all these superstitions, offering the true bread of life that joins souls together and unites them with God. And if anyone wishes to satisfy himself more fully let him read the account that Licentiate Polo wrote to the Archbishop of Los Reyes, Don Jerónimo de Loaiza, and he will find this and many other things that Polo ascertained with great diligence and accuracy.

CHAPTER 24 * HOW THE DEVIL TRIED
IN MEXICO TO MIMIC THE FEAST OF CORPUS
CHRISTI AND THE COMMUNION USED
BY HOLY CHURCH

Even greater amazement will be caused by the feast and resemblance to communion that the devil himself, prince of the sons of pride, ordained in Mexico; this, although it is a trifle long, must be told, as it is described by persons worthy of credence. In the month of May the Mexicans held the chief festival of their god Huitzilopochtli, and two days before the feast those virgins who, as we said above, were secluded in the temple itself and resembled nuns ground a large quantity of amaranth seeds along with roasted maize. And after it was ground they kneaded it with honey, and with that dough made an idol of the same size as the wooden one, and gave it green or blue or white beads for eyes, and for teeth grains of corn, set forth with all the pomp we have described above. When it was finished all the nobles came and brought a rich and exquisite garment that resembled the idol's usual clothing, in which they dressed it; and after it was very well dressed and adorned they placed it upon a blue bench, on a litter, to be carried on men's shoulders. When the morning of the festival arrived, an hour before dawn all those maidens came out dressed in white, with new finery, and on that day they were called sisters of the god Huitzilopochtli. They came crowned with wreaths of toasted and popped corn, which resembles orange blossoms, and thick strings of the same around their necks, passing under their left arms. With rouge on their cheeks and bedecked with red parrot feathers on their arms from the elbows to the wrists, thus arrayed they took the litter on their shoulders and brought it into the courtyard, where all the youths were waiting, handsomely dressed in mesh garments and crowned in the same manner as the girls. When the maidens appeared with the idol the youths approached it very reverently and took the litter on their shoulders, carrying it to the foot of the temple steps, where all the people were kneeling, and taking some earth from the ground they put it on their heads, which was a frequent ceremony among them during the chief festivals of their gods. When this ceremony had been performed, all the people set off in procession as fast as they could and went to a hill about a league from Mexico called Chapultepec, and there they halted and made sacrifices. Then they went on with the same haste to a place nearby that is called Atlacuyauaya, where they made the second stop; and from there they went to another town a league farther on, called Coyoacán, from which they departed to return to the City of Mexico without a pause.

This journey of more than four leagues was made in three or four hours; they called this procession Ypayna Huitzilopochtli, which means "the swift and headlong way of Huitzilopochtli." When they had reached the foot of the temple steps they set down the litter and took heavy ropes and tied them to its carrying poles, and with great care and reverence, some pulling from above and others helping from below, they pulled the litter with the idol to the top of the temple with a great noise of flutes and blare of trumpets and conch shells and drums. They hauled it up in this fashion because the temple steps were very steep and narrow and the staircase very long, and so they could not climb with the litter on their shoulders. And as they were pulling up the idol all the people stood in the courtyard with great reverence and awe. When they had hauled it to the top and placed it in a bower of roses that had been prepared for it, the boys came and scattered many flowers of different colors, filling the temple with them both inside and out. This done, all the maidens came out, adorned as has been described, and took from their place of retreat pieces of dough made of toasted maize and amaranth, the same material of which the idol was made, kneaded into the shape of large bones. These they delivered to the youths, who in turn carried them up and laid them at the idol's feet all around that place, until there was no room for more. These pieces of dough were called the bones and flesh of Huitzilopochtli. After the bones were placed there all the ancients of the temple came out, priests and Levites and other ministers according to their degree of honor and length of service, for there was a strict hierarchy with regard to this, with their names and dignities. One rank after another came out with their mesh veils of different colors and workmanship, according to the dignity and office of each, with wreaths on their heads and garlands of flowers around their necks. After these came different images of the gods and goddesses that they worshiped, dressed in the same style. And ranging themselves in order around those pieces of dough they performed over them a certain ceremony of singing and dancing, as a result of which they were blessed and consecrated as that idol's very flesh and bones. When they had finished the blessing and rite of those pieces of dough representing the idol's bones and flesh, they worshiped them in the same manner as their god. Then the sacrificers came forth and performed the sacrifice of men in the way that has been described above, and these sacrifices were more numerous than on any other day because the festival was so important. When the sacrifices were finished all the youths and maidens came out of the temple, adorned as has been described. Ranked in order and in rows facing each other, they danced and sang to the sound of a drum that was played in praise of the festival and the idol they were celebrating; and all the nobles and elders and important people responded to this song by dancing around them in a ring, making a beautiful circle as they are accustomed to do, with the boys and girls always in the center, and the whole city came to see this spectacle.

On this day of the idol Huitzilopochtli, it was a carefully kept rule in all the land to eat no food save that dough mixed with honey, of which the idol was made; and this food had to be eaten at daybreak, and no water or anything else was to be drunk on top of it until midday, and if they did so it was considered a bad omen and a sacrilege. After the ceremonies were over they could eat other things. During this interval they hid water from the little children, and admonished all those who had the use of reason not to drink it, because the wrath of the god would come upon them and they would die; and they observed this precept with great care and strictness. When the ceremonies, dances, and sacrifices were finished they went to remove their costumes, and the priests and temple dignitaries took the idol made of dough and stripped it of its adornments and made many fragments out of the idol as well as out of the pieces that had been consecrated. Then, beginning with the eldest, they distributed them and gave them in a sort of communion to all the people, young and old, men and women. And they received it with so much reverence, awe, and tears that it was a remarkable thing to see, saying that they were eating God's flesh and bones and that they were unworthy to do so. Those who had invalids at home asked for fragments to be taken to them and carried the pieces away with much reverence and veneration. All who partook of the communion were obliged to give a tithe of the same seed of which the idol was made. When the solemn rite of communion was over an old man of great prestige climbed to the temple and in a loud voice preached their religion and ceremonies.

Who would not be astonished to see that the devil would take such care to have himself worshiped and received in the same way that Jesus Christ our Lord ordained and taught, and as Holy Church is used to doing? Truly, what was said at the beginning is perfectly clear, that Satan tries in every way he can to usurp and steal for himself the honor and worship that is due to God alone, although he always mixes his filthiness and cruelties into them, for he is a murderous and foul spirit and the father of lies.

## CHAPTER 25 * OF THE CONFESSION AND CONFESSORS USED BY THE INDIANS

That same father of lies also tried to mimic the sacrament of confession and to make himself honored by his worshipers in a ceremony very similar to the one used by the faithful. In Peru they believed that all adversities and illnesses came from sins they had committed and had recourse to sacrifices in order to atone for these; moreover, they also confessed orally in almost all the provinces, and they had both greater and lesser confessors appointed for this purpose and sins reserved for the greater confessor.[1] They received penances, sometimes harsh ones, especially if the person who committed the sin was a poor man and had nothing to give the confessor; and this office of confessor was also exercised by women. This use of confessors who are sorcerers (whom they call *ichuri* or *ichuiri*) was and is most universal in the provinces of Collasuyo.[2] They believe that it is a grave offense to hide some sin during confession, and the *ichuris*, or confessors, discover, either by casting lots or by examining the entrails of some animal, whether they are concealing some sin; and they punish this by striking the person's back many times with a stone until he confesses everything, and then they give him the penance and perform the sacrifice. They also use this confession when their children or husbands or wives are ill, or their chiefs, or when they are in great difficulties; and when the Inca was ill all the provinces confessed, especially the Collas. The confessors were bound to secrecy but with certain limitations. The sins that they chiefly confessed were, first of all, killing someone outside of war, also stealing, also taking someone else's wife, also administering herbs or spells to do evil. And carelessness in offering reverence to their *huacas,* violating festivals, speaking ill of the Inca, and not obeying him were considered very great sins.

They did not accuse themselves of secret sins and actions, but, according to what some of the priests have reported since the Christians came to the land, they do accuse themselves even of thoughts to their *ichuris* or confessors. The Inca confessed his sins to no man but only to the sun, so that the sun would tell them to Viracocha and pardon him. After the Inca had confessed he performed a ritual bath to cleanse himself wholly of his faults, and it took place as follows: entering a running stream, he spoke these words: "I have told my sins to the sun; thou, river, receive them and carry them to the sea,

1. It was of no small significance to many early missionaries that the native Andeans had a tradition of confession; some viewed this as evidence that they were primed to accept and practice Christianity. See Sabine MacCormack, "'The Heart Has Its Reasons': Predicaments of Missionary Christianity in Early Colonial Peru," *Hispanic American Historical Review* 65 (1985): 450.

2. Collasuyo, one of four quadrants of the Inca Empire, was located to the southeast of the capital city, Cuzco.

and may they never more appear." The others who confessed also used these ritual baths, in a ceremony very similar to the one the Moors use, which they call *guadoi* and the Indians call *opacuna*. And when it happened that a man's sons died he was held to be a great sinner and was told that it was because of his sins that the son died before the father. And such men, when they performed the ritual bath called *opacuna* (as has been said) following their confession, had to be beaten with certain nettles by some Indian who was a monstrosity: humpbacked, for example, or deformed from infancy. If the sorcerers or soothsayers established from the casting of lots or from omens that some sick person was going to die, they did not hesitate to kill his only son, even though he had no other; and they believed that he would regain his health by this, saying that he offered his son as a sacrifice in his place. And even since the Christians came into that land this form of cruelty has been found in some places. The persistence of this custom of confessing secret sins and doing such severe penances as fasting, giving away clothing, gold, and silver, going up into the mountains, or receiving heavy blows on the back, is certainly amazing; and the fathers of our society say that even today they stumble upon this plague of confessors, or *ichuris,* in the province of Chucuito and that many sick folk go to them.[3] But by the Lord's grace they are gradually seeing the light and now recognize the great benefit of our sacramental confession and come to it with great devotion and faith. And in part it has been the Lord's providence to permit that past usage, to the end that confession would not be difficult for them; and so the Lord is glorified in everything and that trickster the devil is tricked in his turn.

Because it is to the point here, I will speak of the remarkable use of confession that the devil brought to Japan, according to a letter received from there, which reads as follows: "In Osaka there are some very large cliffs, so tall that there are crags in them more than two hundred cubits high, and among those cliffs there is one with an overhanging promontory so awesome that as soon as the *xamabuxis* (which is what they call pilgrims) reach it their flesh

3. Chucuito was a province located on the shores of Lake Titicaca, inhabited mainly by the Lupaca people. It enjoyed special status as a royal province, which signified that no private *encomiendas* were granted within its boundaries. Priests, however, were welcome to enter. The Jesuits formed a mission in the province at Juli, which Acosta visited during his tenure in Peru. The history of Chucuito is documented in an extensive report drafted during a 1567 royal visit to the province. See *Visita hecha a la Provincia de Chucuito por Garci Diez de San Miguel en el año 1567* (Lima: Casa de la Cultura del Perú, 1964).

begins to tremble and their hair to stand on end, so terrible and frightening is the place. Here on this promontory is placed, with remarkable skill, a large iron beam three cubits or more in length, and on the tip of this beam is fastened a sort of balance whose pans are so large that a man can sit in one of them; and the *goquis* (who are demons in human shape) make these pilgrims enter one by one until none are left, and with a device moved by a wheel cause the beam to move outward, the balance going with it, so that at last both are hanging in the air with one of the *xamabuxis* sitting in it. And because the pan in which the man is sitting has no counterweight in the other it soon descends, and the other pan rises until it strikes the beam; then the *goquis* call out from the cliffs for the man to confess and speak all his sins, as many as he has committed and can remember, and in a voice loud enough for everyone to hear. And then he begins to confess, and some of the bystanders laugh at the sins they hear and others groan. And for each sin that they utter the other pan descends a little until finally, when all their sins are confessed, the empty pan is on the same level as the one in which the unhappy penitent is sitting. And when the pan is at last level with the other, the *goquis* make the wheel turn again and bring in the beam, and place another pilgrim on the scale until all have passed through. One of the Japanese recounted this after having become a Christian; he had made this pilgrimage seven times and sat in the scale an equal number, where he had confessed publicly. Moreover, he said that if by chance one of the pilgrims, when sitting in that place, did not confess his sins or concealed them, as sometimes happened, the empty pan did not descend. And if after having been urged to confess he persisted in his unwillingness to confess his sins, the *goquis* would let him fall from the pan, whereupon he was immediately dashed to pieces. But this Christian, whose name was Juan, told us that usually the fear and trembling of that place is so great for all who arrive there, and the danger that each one sees is so near at hand, of falling from that scale and being dashed on the rocks below, that very seldom is there anyone who does not confess all of his sins. Another name for that place is *sangenotocoro,* which means "place of confession." This account makes it very clear that the devil has tried to usurp divine worship for himself by turning the confession of sins that the Savior instituted to save men into a diabolical superstition intended for their greatest harm, no less among the heathens of Japan than in the provinces of Collao in Peru.

### CHAPTER 26 * OF THE ABOMINABLE UNCTION
### USED BY THE MEXICAN PRIESTS AND THOSE OF
### OTHER NATIONS AND OF THEIR SORCERERS

In the ancient law, God ordained the manner in which Aaron and the other priests were to be consecrated, and in the Gospel law we also have the holy chrism and unction that we use when priests of Christ are consecrated. There was also, in the ancient law, a kind of sweet-smelling substance that God commanded to be used only for divine worship. All this the devil has tried to mimic after his fashion but in the way that he is wont to work, inventing things so revolting and filthy that they themselves proclaim who their author is. In Mexico the priests of the idols anointed themselves in the following way: they smeared themselves from head to foot, and all their hair, and with this unction that they applied wet they made a kind of braid in their hair that looked like plaited horses' manes. In the course of time their hair grew so long that it reached well below their knees and weighed so much that it gave them a great deal of trouble, for they never cut or trimmed it until they died or until, when they were very old, they were retired and placed in affairs of governance or other horrible offices in the country. These priests had their hair plaited with strips of cotton six fingers wide. The soot with which they smeared themselves was usually of candlewood, for from very ancient times it had always been a special offering to the gods and for this reason it was greatly valued and revered. They were always smeared from head to foot with this color and looked like blacks; and this was their usual unction, except that when they were going to sacrifice and light incense in thickets and on mountaintops, and in the dark and fearful caves where they kept their idols, they used a different sort of unction, performing certain ceremonies to help them lose their fear and pluck up great courage. This unction was made from different poisonous creatures such as spiders, scorpions, centipedes, lizards, vipers, and so on, caught by the youths from the colleges; and they were so skillful at this that they always had a large supply of them for the occasions when the priests asked for them. Hunting those creatures was their special responsibility, and if they happened to see one in the course of another errand they set about hunting it down as if their lives depended on it. That is the reason why the Indians usually had no fear of these poisonous creatures, treating them as though they were not dangerous because they had been trained to perform this office. To make the salve from them, they took them all together and burned them in the temple brazier that stood before the altar until they were reduced to ashes; these they placed in mortars with a great deal of tobacco (which is an herb used by these people to numb the flesh and keep them from feeling pain). They mixed this with those ashes, which reduced their strength. Along with this herb and the ashes, they threw in live scorpions and spiders and centipedes and stirred everything together and kneaded it; and after all this they put in a ground seed that they call *ololuchqui,* which the Indians drink in order to see visions, whose effect is to deprive them of their senses.[1] They also ground together with these ashes some black, hairy worms, of which only the skin is poisonous. They kneaded all this together with soot and, putting it into little jars, placed it before their gods, saying that it was their food, and so they called it divine food.

By applying this ointment they became sorcerers and saw and spoke with the devil. Once the priests were smeared with it they lost all fear and acquired a spirit of cruelty, and so killed men very boldly in the sacrifices and went at night to the hills and to dark and fearful caves, scorning wild beasts and firmly believing that the lions, tigers, wolves, snakes, and other wild creatures who live in the hills would flee from them because of that divine salve; and even if they did not flee from it they would flee from seeing the picture of the devil into which the priests had transformed themselves. This ointment also served to cure the sick, and children, and so everyone called it divine medicine, and folk came from everywhere to the temple dignitaries and priests as to saviors, to have them apply it; and they anointed the ailing parts with it and said that it gave them great relief. And this must have been true, for tobacco and *ololuchqui* have great power to relieve pain, and if applied as a plaster would of themselves deaden the flesh, all the more so because so many different poisons were used. And since it relieved pain they thought it was the effect of a cure and of divine virtue. Thus they ran to those priests as to holy

1. Here Acosta is most likely referring to *oloiuhqui,* a flowering vine, the seeds of which were consumed by native peoples of Mexico for their hallucinogenic properties. Those who ate them experienced visions that served as signs through which priests could interpret the future. These and other native plants are described in Maximino Martínez, *Las plantas medicinales de México,* 4th ed. (Mexico City: Ediciones Botas, 1959). Mercedes de la Garza analyzes the uses of such plants in pre-Hispanic culture in *Sueño y alucinación en el mundo nahuatl y maya* (Mexico City: Instituto de Investigaciones Filológicas, Universidad Nacional Autónoma de México, 1990).

men, who kept the ignorant tricked and deceived, convincing them of whatever they liked and making them come to their medicines and diabolical ceremonies. Because they possessed so much authority, the priests had only to say anything whatsoever to the people to have it taken as an article of faith. And so they created innumerable superstitions in the common folk in the way of offering incense, in the way of cutting their hair, and in tying little sticks around their necks and strings of snakes' bones, telling them to bathe at such and such an hour, to stay up all night beside a hearth, and not to eat any other kind of food than that which had been offered to the gods; and then they made them come and witness their witchcraft, for they told fortunes with certain grains and made divinations by looking into pans and pools of water.

In Peru the sorcerers and ministers of the devil also used to anoint themselves freely, and there was an infinite number of seers, practitioners of witchcraft, sorcerers, soothsayers, and a thousand other kinds of false prophets; and even today a large part of this plague still persists, though in secret, for they dare not employ their devilish and sacrilegious ceremonies and superstitions openly. That is why their abuses and spells are described at more length in the confessional made by the prelates of Peru. Most particularly, there was a class of sorcerers among those Indians, permitted by the Inca kings, who are a sort of witch and take any form they choose and fly long distances through the air in a short time and see everything that happens and speak with the devil, who answers them in certain stones and in other things that they greatly venerate. These men serve as diviners and tell what is happening in very remote places before the news arrives or could possibly arrive, as happened even after the coming of the Spaniards; for even at a distance of two hundred or three hundred leagues news has been received of mutinies, battles, uprisings, and the death of tyrants as well as partisans of the king, and of private persons, on the same day and at the hour when those things happened, or the next day, something that in the natural order of things was impossible to learn so quickly. To perform this false divination they go into a house locked from the inside and drink until they lose their senses; after a day, they answer what they have been asked. Some aver and affirm that they use a certain kind of unction; the Indians say that usually it is the old women who ply this trade, old women from a province called Coaillo, and from another town called Manchay, and in the province of Guarochiri, and in other places that they do not specify.[2] These diviners also serve to tell where lost and stolen things can be found, and there are sorcerers of this kind everywhere, to whom the Anaconas and Chinas who serve the Spaniards go very regularly when they lose something belonging to their masters or wish to know some detail of things past or yet to come; for example, when the Spaniards go down to the cities on private or public business, they ask if their affairs will go well, or if they will fall ill or die, or if they will return safely, or if they will achieve what they are trying to do.[3] And the soothsayers answer yes or no after having talked with the devil in a dark place, so that they hear his voice but do not see whom they are talking to or what they are saying; and they perform any number of ceremonies and sacrifices for this purpose, using them to invoke the devil and getting outrageously drunk. For this particular purpose they use an herb called *villca,* pouring its juice onto their *chicha* or taking it in some other way.

It is clear from all this how great is the misfortune of those who have such ministers as teachers, whose whole purpose is to deceive. And it is a proven fact that there is no greater obstacle to receiving the truth of Holy Gospel, and to having the Indians persevere in it, than the communications of these soothsayers, who have been and still are innumerable, although by the grace of the Lord and the diligence of prelates and priests there are fewer of them now and they are less dangerous. Some of them have been converted and have preached publicly to the people, describing their errors and deceits and declaring their tricks and lies. Great good has come from this, as we also know, in letters from Japan, that the same has happened there, to the great glory of our God and Lord.

2. While women did play roles as confessors and diviners in Andean religion, Acosta's assertion that women *dominated* the trade in the province of Guarochiri is not borne out in colonial reports or historical monographs on the region. The Jesuit doctor Francisco de Ávila (1573–1647) compiled a comprehensive study of regional customs published as *The Huarochirí Manuscript: A Testament of Ancient and Colonial Andean Religion,* translated and edited by Frank Salomon and George L. Urioste (Austin: University of Texas Press, 1991). A masterful ethnohistory of the region is Karen Spalding, *Huarochirí: An Andean Society under Inca and Spanish Rule* (Stanford: Stanford University Press, 1984).

3. By Anaconas Acosta means *yanaconas,* the preconquest servants of the Inca leadership who often found postconquest placement in the service of Spaniards. In the colonial period, the word *china* referred to domestic servants.

CHAPTER 27 * OF OTHER CEREMONIES AND
RITES OF THE INDIANS THAT ARE
SIMILAR TO OURS

The Indians had innumerable other ceremonies and rites, and many of them
resemble those of the ancient law of Moses; there are others like those used
by the Moors, and others that somewhat resemble those of the Gospel law,
such as ritual bathing, or *opacuna*, as they call it, which was to bathe in water
in order to be cleansed of sins. The Mexicans also held their baptisms with
this ceremony, and it was that they cut the ears of newborn children, as well
as their virile member, which in some sense mimicked the Jews' circumci-
sion.[1] This ceremony was done chiefly with the sons of kings and lords. As
soon as they were born the priests washed them, and after they were washed
they placed a little sword in their right hand and in the left a little shield. The
insignias of their trades were placed on children of the common folk and on
baby girls' implements for spinning and weaving and needlework. This lasted
for four days, and all was performed before some idol. They had their own
method of solemnizing marriage ceremonies. Licentiate Polo wrote an entire
treatise about this, and I will say something about it later; and in other things
also, they carried out their ceremonies and rites with some show of reason.
The Mexicans were married by their priests in the following way: the bride
and groom stood before the priest, who took them by the hands and asked
them if they wanted to be married; and, when he knew the will of both, he
took an edge of the veil with which the bride's head was covered, and another
edge of the groom's clothing, and tied them together in a knot. Thus tied
together they were led to the bride's house, where there was a fire burning,
and they made her take seven turns around it, and the bride and groom sat
down together near it, and so the marriage ceremony was completed. The
Mexicans were extremely jealous of their wives' chastity, so much so that if
they found they were not virgins they announced the fact with insulting

1. Unlike the sole baptism ceremony in Christian tradition, several rituals followed birth in Aztec society. The
priests Acosta credits with washing the baby in the Nahua infant bathing rite were likely midwives, who are
reported to have bathed the newborn baby to remove pollution of conception and leave the child pure. See
Louise M. Burkhart, *The Slippery Earth: Nahua-Christian Moral Dialogue in Sixteenth-Century Mexico* (Tucson: University of Arizona Press, 1989), 113. Ear piercing took place during a separate ritual conducted by
local temple priests. In addition to rites practiced within hours or days of birth, Aztec children were introduced to society once every four years during the festival of Izcalli, the fire god. See Clendinnen, *Aztecs*, 190.

words and gestures, to the great confusion and shame of parents and relatives because they had not looked after her properly. And when they found that a bride had preserved her virginity they held a great feast, giving her and her parents many gifts, preparing large offerings to their gods and a great banquet, one in the bride's house and one in the groom's. And when they took them to their house they made a list of everything that he and she had brought in the way of houses, lands, jewels, and ornaments; and their parents kept this list so that if by any chance the marriage was nullified because they did not consort well together (which was the custom among them) they could divide the assets according to what each of them had brought, each partner having freedom to marry again whomever he or she pleased and giving the girls to her and the boys to him. They were strictly forbidden to join together again on pain of death, and this was observed very strictly.

And, although it seems that in many ceremonies those of the Indians concur with ours, the case is very different owing to the great admixture of abominations that always exists in them. The common and general feature of their ceremonies is to have one of three things, which are cruelty, or filth, or uselessness. For all of them were either cruel and harmful, such as killing men and shedding blood, or filthy and revolting, such as eating and drinking in the name of their idols, and urinating in the idol's name while carrying them, and smearing and daubing themselves so hideously, and an infinite number of other sorts of vileness; or at the very least they were vain and ridiculous and simply useless and more appropriate to the actions of children than those of men. The cause of this is the nature of the evil spirit himself, whose aim is to do evil, provoking men to murders or filth or at least to vanities and fruitless occupations. Anyone who looks with some attention at the devil's dealings with the men he deceives can see this, for all or part of what I have said can be found in all deluded men. The Indians themselves, after they have received the light of our faith, laugh and joke about the childish follies in which their false gods occupied them. They served them much more out of the fear they felt that the gods would treat them badly if they did not obey in everything than out of any love they bore them, although many of them also lived deceived with false hopes of temporal goods, for they could not imagine eternal good.

And it is worth noting that superstition increased wherever the temporal power was greatest, as can be seen in the realms of Mexico and Cuzco, where the number of temples that existed was incredible, for within the city of Cuzco itself there were more than three hundred.[2] Of the kings of Cuzco, it was Manco Inca Yupanqui who most increased the cult of their idols, inventing innumerable differences in sacrifices and festivals and ceremonies. And the same thing happened in Mexico with King Itzcoatl, who was the fourth of that realm. In other nations of Indians, such as those in Guatemala and the isles and the New Kingdom of Granada, and the provinces of Chile and others that resembled the free communities of Spain, although there was a great multitude of superstitions and sacrifices, they could not be compared with Cuzco or Mexico, where Satan was in his Rome or Jerusalem, as it were, until he was cast out, much against his will. And in his place the holy cross was planted, and the kingdom of Jesus Christ occupied everything that the tyrant had usurped.

### CHAPTER 28 * OF SOME FESTIVALS THAT THE INDIANS OF CUZCO HAD AND HOW THE DEVIL ALSO TRIED TO IMITATE THE MYSTERY OF THE HOLY TRINITY

To conclude this book, which contains matters pertaining to religion, we must say something of the festivals and solemn rites that the Indians celebrated, all of which cannot be described because they were many and varied. The Incas, lords of Peru, had two kinds of festivals: some were ordinary and occurred monthly at fixed times; and others were extraordinary, performed for important reasons, such as when a new king was crowned, and at the beginning of some important war, and when there was great need of rain. It must be understood that among the ordinary festivals there was a festival and sacrifice in each of the twelve months of the year; for, although in every month and its festival a hundred of their sheep were offered up, their colors or features had to be different. In the first of these, which is called *raymi* and falls in December, they had the leading and most important festival of all, and

2. Acosta classified the institutionalized practice of native worship (temples, priesthood, ritual calendar) as evidence of greater "superstition" in the more advanced Aztec and Inca societies. The abundance of these religious practices, which were intimately related to imperial governing structures, were at once abhorrent and notable to Acosta. He loathed the evidence of what he termed devil worship, yet he acknowledged that the level of sophistication indicated that the Aztec and Inca had progressed to a state more readily inclined toward Christianity.

for that reason they called it *capacraymi,* which means rich or chief feast. In this festival a large number of sheep and lambs were offered as a sacrifice, and burned with hewn and aromatic wood; and they brought sheep, gold, and silver and set up the three statues of the sun and the three of thunder — father, son, and brother — that they said the sun and thunder had. The Inca youths were dedicated during these festivities; they were dressed in breechclouts or loincloths and their ears were pierced, and the old men whipped them with ropes and smeared their faces with blood, all as a sign that they must be loyal knights of the Inca. No outsider could remain in Cuzco during this month and festival, and at the end of the festivities all outsiders entered the city and were given those maize loaves mixed with the blood of the sacrifice, which they ate as a sign of confederation with the Inca, as has been described above. And it is certainly worth noting that the devil, after his fashion, has also introduced a trinity into idolatry, for the three statues of the sun were called Apointi, Churiinti, and Intiquaoqui, which mean Father and Lord Sun, Son Sun, and Brother Sun; and they gave the same names to the three statues of Chuquiilla, the god who presides over the region of the air, where it thunders and rains and snows. I remember that when I was in Chuquisaca an honorable priest showed me a report, which I had in my possession for some considerable time, in which he had learned of a certain *huaca,* or temple, where the Indians professed to worship Tangatanga, who was an idol, about whom they said that he was three in one and one in three. And when the priest expressed astonishment at this I believe I told him that the devil stole everything he could from the truth for his lies and deceits and did so with that infernal and stubborn pride with which he always craves to be like God.[1]

To return to the festivals: in the second month, which is called *camay,* after the sacrifices were made they threw the ashes into a stream, following it with staffs in their hands for five leagues and begging the stream to carry the ashes

---

1. Acosta's perception of a holy trinity in the Andean religious tradition is the consummate example of the attempts within Spanish missionary imagination to identify imitations of Christian doctrine in native practices. While some Andean gods were represented or housed in groups of three, the example reveals more about Acosta's mind-set than indigenous beliefs. On this particular example, see MacCormack, *Religion in the Andes,* 269–71. Also in this passage the reference to Tangatanga, a regional deity in the province of Chuquisaca, recalls the distinction between state-level Inca religious cults and local religious practices. Although the Inca imposed worship of the sun deity on their subjects, people continued to revere local cults and *huacas.* Spanish missionaries often missed this distinction or tried to conflate the two traditions because they did not understand how both could be worshiped simultaneously.

to the sea, for Viracocha would receive that gift there. In the third, fourth, and fifth months a hundred black and mottled gray sheep were also offered in each festival, along with many other things that I do not describe lest I tire my readers. The sixth month was called *hatuncuzqui aymoray,* which corresponds to the month of May; a hundred more sheep of every color were also sacrificed. During this moon and month, which is when the maize is brought home from the threshing floors, a festivity took place that even today is much celebrated among the Indians, and they call it *aymoray.* This celebration is performed while coming from the farm or field to the house, reciting certain chants in which they pray that the maize (which they call *mamacora*) will last a long time. They take from their fields a certain part of the maize that has been most productive and place it in a little granary, which they call *pirua,* with certain ceremonies. They watch over it for three nights and place this maize in the richest garments they possess, and after it is covered and adorned they worship this *pirua* and hold it in great veneration; and they say that it is the mother of the maize on their farm and that by this rite the maize is given to them and preserved. And during this month they perform a special sacrifice, and the soothsayers ask the *pirua* if it has strength for the following year. If it answers no, they take it to the farm itself and burn it with as much solemnity as each man can muster, and then they make another *pirua* with the same ceremonies, saying that they are renewing it lest the seed corn be lost; and if it answers that it has the strength to continue they leave it for another year. This pagan nonsense persists to the present day, and it is a very common thing among the Indians to have these *piruas* and celebrate the festival of *aymoray.*

The seventh month, which corresponds to June, is called *aucaycuzqui intiraymi,* during which the festival called *intiraymi* takes place, when a hundred of the sheep known as guanacos are sacrificed; and they used to say that this was the feast of the sun. During this month they made a large number of statues carved of quinua wood, all dressed in rich clothing, and performed the dance that they called *cayo.* In this festival they used to spread many flowers on the road, and the Indians came with painted faces, and the nobles with little discs of gold on their chins, all singing. It should be noted that this festival comes at almost the same time when we Christians celebrate the solemn rites of Corpus Christi and that there is a certain resemblance in some aspects, such as the dances or representations or the chanting. And for this reason there has been, and still is, a great deal of superstitious belief among the Indians, who seem to be celebrating our solemn feast of Corpus Christi, that they are in fact celebrating their old festival of *intiraymi*. The eighth month is called *chahua huarqui,* during which a hundred more sheep were burned in the same way that I have described, all dark gray, the color of the Peruvian hare, and this month corresponds to our month of July. The ninth month was called *iapaquis,* during which another hundred brown sheep were burned, and a thousand *cuies* were likewise killed and burned to prevent ice and wind and water, and the sun, from damaging the crops. It seems that this month corresponds to August. The tenth month is called *coyaraymi,* in which another hundred white, fleecy sheep were killed. During this month, which corresponds to September, they held the festival called *citua* in the following manner: they all gathered together before the moon rose on the first day, and when they saw it they began to shout loudly with torches in their hands, say-ing, "Go elsewhere, evil," while striking each other with the torches. Those who did this were called *pancocos,* and after it was finished a general ceremony of bathing was performed in rivers and fountains, each person in his own irrigation canal or property, and they drank for four days in a row. During this month the *mamaconas* of the sun brought out a large quantity of loaves made with the blood of sacrifices, and a bite was given to each person from other parts of the country, and they were also sent to the temples of the entire country and to different *curacas* as a sign of confederation and loyalty to the sun and the Inca, as has been described.[2] These baths and drinking bouts, and some traces of this festival known as *citua,* still persist in some places but with somewhat different ceremonies and very secretly, although its chief and pub-lic manifestations have ceased.

The eleventh month was called *homaraymi punchaiquis,* during which an-other hundred sheep were sacrificed; and, if there was a drought, to bring on rain they tied a black sheep on a plain, spilling a great deal of *chicha* around it, and gave the animal nothing to eat until the rain came. This, too, is still done in many places nowadays at this same time of year, which is more or less in October. The last month is called *ayamara,* during which another hundred sheep were sacrificed and the festival called *raymicantará rayquis* took place.

2. The *curaca,* or *kuraka,* was an Andean ethnic lord, often called a *cacique* by Spaniards after the native Caribbean word for leader, which they took from the islands and applied to Mexico and Peru.

In this month, which corresponds to November, they prepared everything necessary for the youths whose ears were to be pierced the following month, and the youths and old men made a sort of muster, performing several maneuvers. This festival was called *ituraymi,* and is usually held when it rains either much or little or when there is a plague. Of the extraordinary festivals, although there were many, the most famous was the one called *ytu.* The festival of *ytu* had no special time, except that it was held on occasions of need. To perform it the people fasted for two days, during which time they had no congress with women nor ate anything with salt or peppers, nor drank *chicha,* and all gathered in a plaza where there were no strangers or animals; and for this festival they had certain mantles and garments and ornaments that were used only for this purpose. They walked very slowly in procession with their heads covered by their mantles, playing on their drums and not speaking to each other. This lasted for a day and a night, and on the following day they ate and drank and danced for two days and nights, saying that their prayer had been accepted. And, although nowadays this festival is not celebrated with all that ceremony, another, very similar festival that they call *ayma* is often held, with clothing that they save for the purpose; and, as I have said, this kind of procession with drums, and the preceding fast and subsequent drunkenness, is undertaken to meet urgent needs.

And, although they have abandoned the sacrifice of animals and other things, at least publicly, for they cannot hide it from the Spaniards, still they preserve many ceremonies originating from these festivals and ancient superstitions. Hence it is necessary to be aware of them, especially because the Indians perform the festival of *ytu* secretly during the dances of Corpus Christi, doing the dances called *llamallama* and *huacón,* and others according to their ancient ceremony; and this must be closely watched. In places where it has been necessary to warn of these abuses and superstitions that the Indians had in the time of their heathenness, lest they be permitted by the clergy, a longer account has been given regarding this matter; for the present it suffices to have touched upon the ways in which the devil occupied his devotees, so that despite him the difference that exists between light and darkness, and between Christian truth and pagan lies, may be made plain no matter what tricks have been used by the enemy of men and their God to imitate the things that are of God.

### CHAPTER 29 * OF THE FESTIVAL OF REJOICING
### CELEBRATED BY THE MEXICANS

The Mexicans were no less remarkable in their solemn rites and festivals, which were less costly in material things but incomparably more so in human blood. I have already described the chief feast of Huitzilopochtli. After it, the feast of the idol Tezcatlipoca was much solemnized. This festival came in May and in their calendar had the name of *toxcoatl,* but every four years it coincided with the festival of penance, during which plenary indulgences and remissions of sins were granted. On this day, which was the nineteenth of May, they sacrificed a captive who had the likeness of the idol Tezcatlipoca. On the eve of this festival the nobles came to the temple bringing a new garment identical to that of the idol; and the priests dressed the idol in it, taking off its other garments and storing them away with equal and even greater reverence than that which we use in handling holy vestments. In the idol's coffers were many ornaments and finery, jewels and other precious things and bracelets of rich feathers, which served no other purpose than to be there, and they worshiped all of this just as they did the idol itself. In addition to the garment with which they worshiped the idol that day, they invested it with special emblems such as feathers, bracelets, parasols, and other things. After it was thus arrayed they removed the curtain from the door so that it could be seen by everyone, and when the door was opened one of the temple dignitaries came out dressed in the same manner as the idol, carrying flowers in his hand and a little clay flute with a very shrill sound; turning to the east he played on it, and turning to the west and north and south he did the same. Then, having played to the four corners of the earth, indicating that all those both present and absent had heard him, he placed his finger on the ground and, picking up some earth with it, put it in his mouth and ate it as a sign of adoration. And all present did the same, flinging themselves to the ground weeping, invoking the darkness of the night and the wind, and begging the idols not to leave them comfortless or forget them or else to take away their lives and end the many travails that they suffered in them. While this little flute was being played, thieves and adulterers and murderers or any other sort of sinners felt great fear and sorrow, and some slashed themselves so cruelly that they could not hide the fact that they had sinned. And so all those Indians asked only one thing of their god, that their sins might not be made manifest, shedding many tears with great contrition and repentance and offering quantities of incense to placate their god. When they heard the flute all the brave and doughty men, and all the old soldiers who had served in the militia, along with other important persons, pleaded very vehemently and devotedly with the God of all creation and the lord through whom we live, and with the sun, to grant them victory over their enemies and strength to take many captives to honor their sacrifices. This ceremony was performed for ten days before the feast day, with the priest playing on the little flute, so that all could perform that act of worship of eating earth and asking the idols for anything they wanted, praying each day with their eyes lifted to Heaven and with sighs and groans, like people truly grieved by their faults and sins. However, their sorrow was only out of fear of the corporal punishment they received, and not of eternal punishment, for they insist that they did not know that there was such severe chastisement in the other life. And so they offered themselves up to death without much sorrow, believing that it gave all men rest.

When the day itself of this idol Tezcatlipoca's feast arrived, the whole city assembled in the temple courtyard to celebrate the calendar feast as well, which, as we have said, was called *toxcoatl,* meaning "dry thing." This entire festival is aimed at asking Heaven for rain, just as we perform rogations, and so they always had that feast in May, which is the time when there was most need of rain. The celebration began on the ninth of May and ended on the nineteenth. On the morning of the last day the idol's priests brought out a richly decorated litter, with curtains and trimmings of different kinds. This litter had as many handles as there were ministers to carry it, who came out all daubed in black, with white ribbons braided into their long locks and garments of the same colors as those of the idol. They placed on that litter the representation of the idol that had been chosen for that purpose, whom they called the likeness of the idol Tezcatlipoca; and, taking it on their shoulders, they brought it out to public view at the foot of the steps. Then the cloistered youths and temple maidens came out with a thick rope made of twisted strings of roasted maize, and after winding it all around the litter they placed a string of the same maize around the idol's neck and a wreath on its head. This rope was called *toxcatl,* denoting the dryness and barrenness of that season. The youths were swathed in net garments and wore wreaths and garlands of roasted maize; the maidens emerged wearing new clothes and ornaments, with strings of the same maize around their necks. On their heads they wore tiaras made of little rods all covered with that maize, and their feet and arms were decorated with feathers and their cheeks rouged. They also brought many strings of this roasted maize and put them on the nobles' heads and around their necks and placed flowers in their hands. After the idol had been set upon the litter the whole place was spread with a large quantity of maguey leaves, which are broad and spiny. When the litter had been set on the shoulders of those priests, they carried it in procession around the inner circuit of the courtyard, with two priests going before it carrying two braziers or censers. They censed the idol very frequently, and each time they threw on incense they would raise their arms as high as they could toward the idol and the sun, asking that their petitions might rise to heaven as that smoke rose on high. All the rest of the people who were in the courtyard, forming a circle around the idol, carried new ropes made of maguey fiber in their hands, a cubit long with a knot at the end, and they struck themselves with these, administering great blows on their shoulders, just as here in Spain people discipline themselves on Holy Thursday.[1]

The entire circuit of the courtyard, and the battlements, were full of green boughs and flowers, so well adorned and so fresh that they caused great delight. When this procession was over they returned the idol to its place, where they set it down; then a large number of people came out with flowers arranged in various ways and heaped the altar and the room and the whole courtyard with them, so that it seemed like the adornment of a monument. These roses were placed with the priests' own hands, the temple youths supplying them from outside, and on that day the room was open and the chamber left without its veil. This done, all came forward to offer cloth, draperies, jewels and precious stones, incense, resinous woods, ears of corn, and quail, and in a word everything that was customarily offered in such solemn rites. During the offering of the quail, which was that of the poor, they employed this ceremony: they gave them to the priest, and he took them and twisted off their heads and then threw them at the foot of the altar to bleed

---

1. Given the integral role of penitence in Christian doctrine, Spanish missionaries looked for examples of penitent practices among indigenous peoples, like this ritual flogging during the festival of Toxcatl. While the pre-Hispanic penance was considered misguided, missionaries believed that once the concept was identified in native thought it could be redirected. Louise M. Burkhart has evaluated notions of penance and other moral values in Nahua culture (*The Slippery Earth*).

there, and he did this with all the quail that were offered. Each person offered foodstuffs and fruits according to his means, which were the perquisites of the temple priests' altar, and so they were the ones who picked them up and carried them to their apartments in the temple. After this solemn offering had been made the people went off to their own villages and homes to eat, and the festival was suspended until they had finished eating. And at this time the temple youths and maidens, dressed in the way I have described, busied themselves with serving the idol everything that had been dedicated to it for its food; this was cooked by women who had made a vow to spend that day making the idol's meal, serving there for the whole day. Hence, all those women who had made a vow came at dawn and offered themselves to the temple priests to tell them what to do, and they did it with much diligence and care. Then they brought out such different and intricate dishes that it was a remarkable thing to see. After this meal had been prepared and the hour to eat it had arrived, all those maidens came out of the temple in procession, each with a little basket of bread in one hand and a small platter of food in the other; before them went an old man who served as chamberlain, in a very colorful costume. He was dressed in a white tunic that hung to his calves, under a sleeveless red leather doublet like a penitent's garment; instead of sleeves it had wings, and from them came broad ribbons from which was suspended, halfway down his back, a gourd of medium size. This gourd was full of flowers sticking out from little holes in it and inside were a number of superstitious talismans. This old man went before the whole procession dressed in this manner, very humble, sad, and hanging his head. When he reached the appointed place, which was at the foot of the steps, he made a deep bow. Then he stepped aside and the maidens came with the food and placed it in rows, coming forward one by one with great reverence. When they had set it down the old man again led them away and they returned to their place of seclusion.

After they had gone in, the youths and priests of that temple emerged and picked up that food and placed it in the apartments of the dignitaries and priests, who had been fasting for five consecutive days, eating only one meal a day and living apart from their wives; and during those five days they did not leave the temple, flogging themselves severely with ropes. They ate as much of that divine food (as they called it) as they could, and it was unlawful for anyone else to touch it. After all the people had eaten they again gathered in the courtyard to celebrate and witness the end of the festival, when a slave who had represented the god for a year was brought forth, dressed and adorned and revered like the idol itself; and, all bowing low, he was delivered to the sacrificers, who came out at the same time and seized him by feet and hands. The high priest cut open his breast and tore out his heart, holding it as high as he could and showing it to the sun and the idol, as we have already described. After the man who had represented the idol was dead, they went to a consecrated place set aside for the purpose, and the youths and maidens came forth adorned as has been described, where, with the temple dignitaries playing for them, they danced and sang in order around the drum; and all the lords, dressed in the same emblems that the youths wore, danced in a ring around them. As a rule but one victim died on this day, for only at intervals of four years were others killed with him, and the year in which these died was the year of jubilee and plenary indulgence. When they had had their fill of playing and eating and drinking, at sunset those maidens went back to their place of seclusion and took great earthenware platters full of bread kneaded with honey, covered with cloths embroidered with dead men's skulls and crossbones, and served it to the idol. Then they climbed to the courtyard in front of the oratory door, and, placing the meal there, with the chamberlain going before, they descended in the same order as they had come.

Then all the youths came out in order and with reeds in their hands raced up the temple steps, each trying to reach the platters of food more quickly than the others. And the temple dignitaries took care to observe the first, second, third, and fourth to arrive, paying no heed to the others, until all had snatched the food away and carried it off as if it were a relic of great value. This done, they took the first four to reach the food into the midst of the dignitaries and old men of the temple and brought them to the temple apartments with much honor, rewarding them and giving them very fine adornments, and from then on they were respected and honored as particularly distinguished men. When this snatching of food had been accomplished with much rejoicing and shouting, all those maidens and youths who had served the idol were given leave to go, and so they went off one after another. As the girls emerged the boys of the colleges and schools stood at the gate of the courtyard, all with balls made of reeds and grasses in their hands. They pelted the girls with these, jeering and making fun of them as folk who were leaving the idol's service. They were then free to do as they pleased, and this put an end to that solemnity.

## CHAPTER 30 * OF THE MERCHANTS' FESTIVAL
### PERFORMED BY THE CHOLULANS

Although a good deal has been said about the worship that the Mexicans offered to their idols, the one called Quetzalcoatl, who was the god of rich folk, received special veneration and solemn rites; therefore I will explain here what is told of his festival. The feast of this idol was solemnized in the following manner: forty days beforehand the merchants bought a slave who was well formed and without a blemish or mark of any kind, either of sickness or wounds or bruises; they dressed him in the habiliments of the idol itself so that he could impersonate it during those forty days.[1] And before dressing him they purified him, washing him twice in a lake that they called "lake of the gods," and after he was purified they dressed him in the same manner as the idol. During those forty days he was greatly revered because of what he represented; they put him in a cage at night (as has been said) to prevent him from escaping, and then in the morning they would take him out of the cage and put him in a place of honor and serve him there, giving him exquisite foods to eat. When he had eaten they hung strings of flowers around his neck and placed many nosegays in his hands; he had his own very respectful guard, along with many other people who accompanied him, and they went out into the city with him; he went through the whole city singing and dancing, so that he would be recognized as the likeness of their god. And when he began to sing women and children came out of their houses to greet him and make him offerings as to a god. Nine days before the festival two

1. The reference to slavery in Aztec society is a reminder that slavery did exist in the Americas before Spanish colonization, albeit in a radically different form than the image associated with colonial plantation slavery. Slaves in the Aztec world did not relinquish the right to personal freedom or property. Several paths to Aztec slavery existed. The majority of slaves were outsiders received as tribute or taken as captives in battle. However, slavery also was imposed within Tenochtitlán as punishment for misbehavior or crime, and impoverished individuals could contract to sell their own labor or the labor of a family member. Thus, sales took place at the slave market in Azcapotzalco, on the western shore of Lake Texcoco.

A word about the *pochteca,* the hereditary merchant class of the pre-Hispanic world, is in order here. The men of the *pochteca* engaged in long-distance trade from the region of modern New Mexico in the north to Guatemala in the south. In addition to their crucial role as suppliers of trade goods, like the prized *quetzal* feathers that came from the southeast, they also played military and cultural roles in the spread of the Aztec Empire. On the *pochteca* and pre- and postconquest trade more generally, see Ross Hassig, *Trade, Tribute, and Transportation: The Sixteenth-Century Political Economy of the Valley of Mexico* (Norman: University of Oklahoma Press, 1985).

very venerable old men among the temple dignitaries came to see him and prostrating themselves at his feet told him in a very low and humble voice, "Lord, you must know that nine days from now your labor of dancing and singing will come to an end, for then you must die," and he had to answer that he rejoiced in the thought. They called this ceremony Neyolo Maxitl Ileztli, which means "the summons," and after he had been summoned they took great care to notice whether he became sad or whether he danced as happily as before; and if he did not do so as cheerfully as they wished they enacted a loathsome superstition, and it was that they went and took the sacrificial knives and washed off them the human blood that clung to them from previous sacrifices, and with those washings made a draft mixed with another made of cocoa, and gave it to him to drink, because they said that it had such an effect on him that he would have no memory of what they had told him and would be almost insensible and would soon return to his usual singing; and they even say that by this means he joyfully offered to die, being bewitched by that draft. The reason that they tried to keep him from being downcast was that they considered it a very bad omen and the prediction of some great evil.

At midnight on the day of the feast, and after having paid him much honor with music and incense, the sacrificers laid hands on him and sacrificed him as I have described above, offering his heart to the moon and then throwing it at the idol and letting his body roll down the temple steps. Those who had offered him, the merchants whose feast this was, then took it up and, carrying it to the house of the chief among them, had it cooked in various ways to celebrate the banquet and meal of the festivity at break of day, first greeting the idol with a little dance that they performed as day was breaking and the victim was being cooked. Then all the merchants gathered together for this banquet, especially those whose business consisted of buying and selling slaves, whose responsibility it was to offer a slave each year to be the likeness of their god.

This idol was among the most important of that land, as we have said, and thus the temple in which it was placed was a very powerful one; there were sixty steps leading up to it and at the top of them a courtyard of moderate size, very scrupulously whitewashed. In the middle of it was a large, round room shaped like an oven, and the entrance was so narrow and low that it was necessary to stoop very low in order to enter. This temple had the same apartments as the others, where the priests and boys and girls and youths were cloistered, as has been said; they were cared for by a single priest who resided there permanently. He was something like the weekly official in a cathedral, for, since ordinarily there were three or four priests or dignitaries in the temples, each served for a week without leaving the place. The function of the weekly official of this temple, in addition to instructing the youth, was to beat on a big drum every day at sunset, making a signal with it, as we are accustomed to ring bells for prayers. This drum was so large that its harsh sound could be heard all over the city, and when the people heard it they fell so silent that it seemed not a soul was there; the markets emptied and the people went indoors, so that everything was left in great quiet and peace. It was played again at dawn, when the sun was starting to rise, and this gave the signal that day was breaking, and so on that signal travelers and persons from other cities hastened to begin their journeys, for until then they were forbidden to leave the city. This temple had a courtyard of middling size, where on the god's feast day great dances and celebrations were performed as well as very amusing theatrical performances. For this purpose there was a small theater about thirty feet square in the middle of the courtyard, thoroughly whitewashed, which they embowered and adorned for that day with all possible care, completely surrounding it with arches made of every kind of flowers and featherwork, and many birds and hares and other harmless creatures hanging between them at intervals, where the people gathered after having eaten. The actors came out and performed short comic pieces, pretending to be deaf, afflicted with colds, halt, blind, and missing an arm, all coming to the idol to ask for health. The deaf ones would give foolish answers and those with colds coughed. The halt, limping about described their miseries and complaints, and made the people laugh heartily. Others came out representing vermin, with some dressed as beetles, others as toads, others as lizards, and so on. When they had appeared they described their lives, and turning about they played little flutes, which pleased their listeners mightily, for they were very amusing. They also imitated butterflies and birds of many different colors, bringing out of the temple youths dressed in these costumes; they climbed into a grove of trees that had been planted there, and the temple priests shot at them with blowpipes, and there were comic verses in defense of some and against the others, with which they entertained the audience. After this was over they performed a *mitote,* or dance, with all these actors, and the festival ended; they usually did this at the most important festivals.

### CHAPTER 31 * THE BENEFIT THAT CAN BE DRAWN FROM AN ACCOUNT OF THE INDIANS' SUPERSTITIONS

I trust that what I have written will suffice to make my readers understand the pains that the Indians took to serve and honor their gods and the devil, which amounts to the same thing. For to tell in detail everything involved in this would take an infinite amount of time and serve for little, and some may even think that there is little or no benefit even in what I have told and that it is like wasting time by reading the nonsense that is invented in books of chivalry. But if they think carefully about it they will find it an entirely different matter and that it may be useful in many ways to know something about the rites and ceremonies practiced by the Indians. First, in the lands where they took place it is not only useful but absolutely necessary for Christians and teachers of the law of Christ to be familiar with the errors and superstitions of the ancients and to observe whether the Indians use them nowadays, either openly or secretly. And it is for this reason that grave and responsible men wrote long accounts of what they had learned, and the provincial councils have even commanded them to be written and printed, as was done in Lima, and in much greater detail than I have written here. Hence, in Indian lands, any information on this subject given to the Spaniards is important for the Indians' own good. For Spaniards themselves, both there and everywhere, this narration may cause them to feel gratitude toward God our Lord, offering infinite thanks to him for the great boon of giving us his Holy Law; for all of it is just, all pure, all beneficial, something that is easily understood when we compare it to the laws of Satan under which so many wretches have lived. It can also serve to make us recognize the devil's pride and envy and the deceits and tricks he has practiced on those whom he has enslaved; for on the one hand he wants to imitate God and compete with him and his Holy Law and on the other he mixes in an infinite number of vanities and filth, and even cruelties, since it is his role to wreak havoc on everything good and corrupt it. Finally, anyone who witnesses the blindness and darkness in which provinces and great kingdoms have lived for so many ages, and in which many people, and a large part of the world, still live in such deceits, cannot (if he has a Christian heart) fail to give thanks to Almighty God on behalf of those whom he has called out of darkness to the wonderful light of his Gospel, entreating the Creator's immense love to preserve and increase them in his knowledge and obedience and at the same time pitying those who still persist on the path of perdition, begging the Father of Mercy to reveal to them the treasures and riches of Jesus Christ, who with the Father and the Holy Spirit reigns forever and ever. Amen.

# BOOK VI

## CHAPTER I * HOW THE OPINION OF THOSE WHO BELIEVE THAT THE INDIANS LACK UNDERSTANDING IS FALSE

Having dealt with matters pertaining to the religion practiced by the Indians, in this book I intend to write of their customs and polity and government, with two aims in mind. One is to refute the false opinion that is commonly held about them, that they are brutes and bestial folk and lacking in understanding or with so little that it scarcely merits the name. Many and very notable abuses have been committed upon them as a consequence of this false belief, treating them as little better than animals and considering them unworthy of any sort of respect. Those who have lived among them with some degree of zeal and consideration, and have seen and known their secrets and their counsels, well know that it is a common and harmful delusion. In addition, little attention is paid to all Indians by those who think they know a great deal about them and who are usually the most ignorant and presumptuous of men. I see no better way of refuting this pernicious opinion than to describe their order and behavior when they lived under their own law. In it, although they had many barbaric traits and baseless beliefs, there were many others worthy of admiration; these clearly give us to understand that they have a natural capacity to receive good instruction and that they even surpass in large measure many of our own republics.[1] And it is no

---

1. Acosta rarely makes an explicit accusation about abuses, as he does in this chapter, where he critiques the Spanish treatment of native peoples, most likely at the hands of *encomenderos*. Moreover, he combines a critique of the Spanish with praise for the indigenous capacity for learning Christian practices. Acosta's assertion in chapter 1, which is echoed throughout book VI, shows that he finds value in some native abilities,

wonder that there were gross errors among them, for these are found even in the gravest legislators and philosophers, not excepting Lycurgus and Plato. In the wisest republics, such as those of the Romans and Athenians, we see signs of ignorance deserving of laughter; and, certainly, if the republics of the Mexicans and Incas had been described in the times of the Romans or Greeks, their laws and government would be respected. But if, knowing nothing of this, we enter by the sword and neither hear nor understand them, we do not believe that the Indians' affairs deserve repute but treat them like game hunted in the hills and brought to us for our service and whim.

The most diligent and learned men who have penetrated and attained their secrets, their ancient style, and their government judge them in a very different way, amazed that there could have been so much order and reason among them. One of these authors is Polo Ondegardo, whom I chiefly follow in things pertaining to Peru, and in matters of Mexico Juan de Tovar, a former prebendary of the Church in Mexico and now a religious in our Society of Jesus; on the orders of the viceroy Don Martín Enríquez, he made a diligent and lengthy study of that nation's old histories. And I do not mention other weighty authors who have informed me very fully, either in writing or orally, of everything I am going to recount.[2] The other aim that can be achieved with knowledge of the laws and customs and polity of the Indians is to help them and rule them by those very laws, for in whatever does not contradict the law of Christ and his Holy Church, they ought to be governed according to their statutes, which are as it were their municipal laws. Through ignorance of these, errors of no little importance have been committed, for those who judge and rule them have not known how to judge and rule their subjects. This, in addition to being an offense and an unreasonable

---

like the use of *quipus* for confession, and views such practices as evidence that the Indians "have a natural capacity to receive good instruction." This combination of critique and praise is unique for the late sixteenth century, an era that Sabine MacCormack has identified as a turning point for missionary activity in Peru, when conversion by persuasion "was supplanted by an ever-increasing insistence on the authority, not only of Christianity, but of European concepts of culture" ("The Heart Has Its Reasons," 446).

2. Here Acosta acknowledges Polo and Tovar as his primary sources on native peoples. The degree to which Acosta relied on Tovar was revealed with the 1856 discovery and subsequent analysis of the "Tovar Manuscript." While no one disputes that Acosta borrowed heavily from Tovar, scholars now agree that this practice was well within the boundaries of scholarly exchange in early modern Europe. In the prologue to the 1962 edition of Acosta's work, Edmundo O'Gorman studies and rejects a nineteenth-century accusation of plagiarism lodged against Acosta. See Acosta, *Historia natural y moral de las Indias* edited by Edmundo O'Gorman (Mexico City: Fondo de Cultura Económica, 1962), 12–23.

thing done to them, causes great harm, for it makes us Spaniards abhorred as men who are and always have been their enemies in both good and evil.

## CHAPTER 2 * OF THE METHOD OF CALCULATING TIME AND THE CALENDAR THAT THE MEXICANS USED

Beginning, therefore, with the divisions of time and the calculations that the Indians used, which is one of the most remarkable proofs of their cleverness and skill, I will first state how the Mexicans reckoned and distributed their year and will tell of their months and calendar and their reckoning of centuries or ages.[1] They divided the year into eighteen months and assigned twenty days to each month, making a total of three hundred and sixty days; the other five that remained to fill out the rest of the year were not assigned to any month but were counted separately, and these were called days of idleness, during which the people did nothing, nor did they go to the temple. They spent them only in visiting one another and wasting time, and the temple priests ceased to sacrifice. When those days were over they again began the calculation of their year, whose beginning and first month was March, when the leaves begin to turn green again, although they took three days from February, for the first day of their new year was the twenty-sixth of February, as is evident in their calendar. Our own calendar has been incorporated into it with remarkably accurate reckoning and skill, done by the early Indians first encountered by the Spaniards. I have seen this calendar and still have it in my possession, and it is worthy of study in order to understand the reasoning power and skill of these Mexican Indians.[2] Each of the eighteen months to which I referred has its special name and its own picture and sign, and this was commonly taken from the chief festival that took place in that

1. To clarify the account given by Acosta, the Aztec civilization used two calendars, one seasonal and one sacred, to calculate time on a fifty-two-year cycle. The seasonal, or *xiuitl*, had eighteen months of twenty days each plus a five-day period at the end. The sacred, or *tonalpoalli*, was made up of twenty signs matched with numbers from one to thirteen. Priests made calculations from the sacred calendar to determine a day sign, or *tonalli*, for each newborn baby.

2. Acosta had in his possession a reckoning of the Aztec day sign calendar sent to him by Tovar. The manuscript is located in the John Carter Brown Library, Brown University, and was published in George Kubler and Charles Gibson, *The Tovar Calendar: An Illustrated Mexican Manuscript ca. 1585* (New Haven: Memoirs of the Connecticut Academy of Arts and Sciences, 1951) 2:9–21. Tovar may well have discussed the calendar with Diego Durán, who wrote *The Book of Gods and the Ancient Calendar*, translated by Doris Heyden and Fernando Horcasitas (Norman: University of Oklahoma Press, 1971).

month or from the differences in appearance that the year causes. And they had certain days marked on their calendar for all their festivals. They counted weeks by thirteen days and marked each day with a zero or small round dot, multiplying the zeroes up to thirteen, and then began to count again: one, two, and so on. They also divided the years by using four signs, giving a sign to each year. These signs were four figures: one was a house, another a rabbit, the third a piece of cane, the fourth a flint; and they pictured them thus and used them to name the current year, saying, "In such and such houses or such and such flints of such and such a wheel, such a thing happened," for it must be understood that their wheel, which is like a century, contained four weeks of years, each week consisting of thirteen years, so that the sum of them all was fifty-two years. They painted a sun in the center, and then four arms or lines came out from it to the circumference of the wheel in the shape of a cross, thus dividing the circumference into four parts, each of them with its line of the same color, of which there were four different ones: green, blue, red, and yellow. And each of these had its thirteen compartments with its sign of house, rabbit, cane, or flint, each representing its year, and at one side they painted what had happened in that year. And so I saw in the calendar of which I have spoken an indication of the year when the Spaniards entered Mexico, with a picture of a man dressed in our style of clothing, painted in red, for that was the dress of the first Spaniard that Hernán Cortés sent.

At the end of the fifty-two years that closed the wheel they employed an amusing ceremony, and it was that on the last night they broke all the vessels they possessed and extinguished all the fires, saying that in one of the wheels the world was sure to come to an end and that perchance it was the one in which they were living, and that since the world was going to end there was no need to cook or eat, and for what did they need vessels or fire; and they would stay like this all night, saying that perhaps dawn would never come again, all of them watching very closely to see if the sun would rise. When they observed that dawn was coming they played on many drums and horns and flutes and other instruments of rejoicing and merriment, saying that God was granting them another century, which was fifty-two years, and then they began another wheel. On the day on which dawn ushered in another century they lit new fires and bought new dishes, pots, and everything necessary for cooking, and all went for new fire to the place where the high priest had lighted it, with a most solemn procession going before as a sign of thanksgiving because the dawn had come and granted them another century. This was their method of counting years and months and weeks and centuries.

### CHAPTER 3 * OF THE METHOD OF COUNTING YEARS AND MONTHS USED BY THE INCAS

In this calculation of the Mexicans, although for unlettered men it contains much reckoning and skill, yet I consider it a flaw not to count by moons or to distribute the months according to them. In this respect there is no doubt that the Peruvians surpassed them, for they reckoned their year correctly into a certain number of days, as we do, and divided it into twelve months or moons, using up the eleven lunar days that are left over, as Polo writes, by placing them within the months themselves. They used the following device to make the year's reckoning accurate and exact: in the hills around the city of Cuzco (which was the court of the Inca kings and also the greatest sanctuary of their realms, another Rome, as it were), they had twelve large pillars placed in order at such a distance and in such a position that each month one of the pillars indicated where the sun came up and where it set. They called these pillars *succanga,* and it was there that they announced festivals and the proper times for sowing and reaping and so on. They performed certain sacrifices to these pillars of the sun, according to their superstitions. Each month had its own distinct name and its special festivals. Formerly they began the year in January, as we do; but later an Inca king whom they called Pachacuti, which means "reformer of time," began the year in December, in consideration (as we may suppose) of the time when the sun begins to return from the farthest point of Capricorn, which is the tropic closest to them. It is not known whether either group had a correct reckoning of leap years, although some say that they did. The weeks reckoned by the Mexicans were not properly speaking weeks, for they were not of seven days, nor did the Incas make this division. And it is no wonder that they did not, for the reckoning of the week is not like that of the year, which is calculated by the course of the sun, nor like the month, which is calculated by that of the moon, except among the Hebrews, by the order of the creation of the world described by Moses,[1] and in the Greeks and Romans by the number of the seven planets, from whose names the days of the week take theirs. But for

1. Genesis, I (O'G).

men who lacked books and letters it is sufficient and more than sufficient that they had the year and the festivals and times calculated with such harmony and order as I have said.

## CHAPTER 4 * HOW NO NATION OF INDIANS HAS BEEN FOUND TO HAVE THE USE OF LETTERS

Letters were invented to refer to and immediately signify the words that we pronounce, just as words and terms themselves, according to the philosopher, are immediate signs of men's concepts and thoughts.[1] And one as well as the other (by this I mean both letters and words) were established to make us understand things: words for present things and letters for those that are absent or still to come. Signs that are not arranged in such a way as to signify words, but only things, are not called letters, nor are they truly letters even though they are written, just as a picture of the sun cannot be called writing, or letters representing the sun, but is simply a picture.[2] Nor can other signs that have no resemblance to the thing but serve only as reminders be described as writing, for the person who invented them did not do so to represent words but simply to denote that thing. Such signs are not called, nor are they properly speaking, letters or writing but ciphers or memory devices, like those used by spherists or astronomers to denote different signs or planets such as Mars, Venus, Jupiter, and so on. These are ciphers and not letters, for no matter by what name Mars is called, the Italian, the Frenchman, and the Spaniard denote it in the same way. Letters do not do this, for, although they denote things, they do so through words, and thus only those who know that language can understand them. For example: the word *sol* is written; neither Greek nor Hebrew knows what it means, for these languages do not know the Latin word itself. So that writing and letters are used only by those who signify words with them, and if they immediately signify the same things then they are not letters or writing but pictures and ciphers. From this

1. Aristotle (O'G).

2. Acosta's celebration of the letter responded to the widespread Renaissance belief that the alphabet was superior to other writing systems. This idea has been powerfully articulated by Elio Antonio de Nebrija in his *Gramática de la lengua castellana* (1492) and *Reglas de ortographia en la lengua castellana* (1517). In the twentieth century, the same ideology is still at work in the influential article by Jack Goody and Ian Watt, "The Consequences of Literacy," in *Literacy and Traditional Societies,* edited by Jack Goody (Cambridge: Cambridge University Press, 1968).

we may draw two important conclusions. One is that the remembrance of history, and of ancient times, can persist among men in one of three ways: either by letters and writing, as the Romans, Greeks, and Hebrews use, as well as many other nations; or by pictures, as have been used almost everywhere in the world (since, as was said in the second Nicene Council, pictures are a book for the illiterate); or by ciphers or characters, just as an arithmetical figure can stand for the numbers one hundred, one thousand, and so on, without necessarily meaning the word *hundred* or *thousand*. The other important conclusion to be drawn is the one stated in the title of this chapter, namely, that no nation of Indians discovered in our time uses letters or writing but employs the other two methods, which are images or figures. And by this I mean not only the Indians of Peru and New Spain but also in part the Japanese and Chinese, although what I have said may seem very wrong to some, since there have been so many accounts of the great libraries and places of study in China and Japan and of their printed blocks and writing supplies and letters. But it is the plain truth, as will be understood in the following chapter.

### CHAPTER 5 * OF THE KINDS OF LETTERS AND BOOKS THAT THE CHINESE USE

Many think (and indeed it is the common opinion) that the forms of writing employed by the Chinese are letters such as we use in Europe; I mean that words and terms can be expressed with them and that they differ from our letters and writing only in the fact that the characters are different, as Greek characters differ from Latin ones and from those of the Hebrews and Chaldeans. And for the most part this is not true; for they neither have an alphabet nor do they write any letters, nor does the distinction lie in the characters. Rather, their writing consists chiefly of making pictures or signs, and their letters do not signify parts of words like ours but are pictures of things such as sun, fire, man, sea, and so on. This is clearly proved by the fact that, although the languages spoken by the Chinese are innumerable and very different one from another, their writings and printed blocks are read and understood equally well in all languages, just as a single number is understood equally well in French and Spanish and Arabic. For this figure, 8, means eight everywhere, even though French expresses it with one word and Spanish with another.

From this it may be deduced that, since things themselves are innumerable, the letters or pictures used by the Chinese to denote them are almost infinite in number. For the person who needs to read and write in China, as the mandarins do, must know at least 85,000 pictures or letters, and those who must be perfect in that kind of reading have to know some 120,000. This is an astonishing thing and not to be credited were it not stated by persons as worthy of belief as the fathers of our society, who are even now in China learning their language and system of writing; and they have been studying this subject day and night for more than ten years with almost superhuman effort, for the love of Christ and the desire to save souls overcome all obstacles. This is the very reason why literate men are held in such esteem in China, because it is so difficult a thing, and only they hold positions as mandarins and governors and judges and captains. And hence parents take great care to have their children learn to read and write. There are many and excellent schools where children and youths learn this; and the master at school by day, and their parents at home by night, make them study so much that their eyes are constantly weary, and they are very often beaten with canes, though not such cruel ones as are used for malefactors. They call this the Mandarin language, and by the time a person has mastered it he has attained adult age; and it should be noted that, although the language spoken by the mandarins is a single language and different from the common ones, which are numerous, it is studied there like Greek and Latin among us, and only learned men (who are found everywhere in China) know it. But what is written in it is understood in every language, for, although the different provinces cannot understand one another by means of spoken words, they do understand the writing because the letters or pictures are the same for all and mean the same, even though they do not have the same name or pronunciation. For, as I have said, they serve to denote things and not words, as can easily be understood by the example I gave regarding numbers.[1] It also follows from this that even though

---

1. Contrary to Acosta's belief, today it is accepted that Chinese writing does not represent "things" but indicates things or ideas (ideograms) as they build on a conglomeration of words and meaning (logograms). Acosta's perspective on alphabetic writing and scientific knowledge was based on the written word, preventing him from understanding the complicity between painting, writing, and knowledge in Chinese culture. In an illuminating article D. N. Keightley observed: "A man absorbed with writing was absorbed not just with words but with symbols and, through the act of writing with the brush, with a form of painting and thus with the word itself. To the lover of high culture, the way in which something was written could be as important as

the Japanese and Chinese have such different nations and languages both can read and understand the language of the other; and were they to speak what they read and write they would not understand each other at all. These, then, are the letters and books used by the Chinese, which are so famous in the world, and they print by engraving a wooden block with the pictures they wish to print and then stamping as many pages as they wish, just as we print pictures by engraving copper or wood.

But any intelligent man will ask how they can express ideas by means of these pictures, for it is impossible to signify the different ideas that surround a picture, such as saying that the sun warms, or that he looked at the sun, or that the day is sunny; finally, how is it possible to denote in mere pictures the cases and conjugations and articles that many languages and systems of writing have? To this we reply that they indicate all this kind of meaning by different dots and flourishes and positions. It is more difficult to understand how they can write proper names, especially foreign ones, for these are things that they have never seen, nor could they have invented a picture for them. I tried to examine this when I was in Mexico with some Chinese, and I asked them to write this sentence, or something resembling it, in their language: "José de Acosta has come from Peru." The Chinese gentleman thought about it for a long time and at last wrote, and then the others read what was indeed the same sentence, although there was some variation in the proper name; for they use the device of taking the proper name and finding something in their language that resembles that thing, and then they write down the picture of it. And as it is difficult in so many names to find a resemblance between things and the way they sound in their own language it is very difficult for them to write such names. Father Alonso Sánchez told us that when he was in China and the mandarins took him from one tribunal to another they spent a long time writing his name on those blocks they use and at last would give him a name after their fashion in a ridiculous way that scarcely resembled it. This is the kind of letters and writing that the Chinese use. That of the Japanese is very similar to it, although Japanese who have been in Europe say that they can write anything in their own language, even European proper names, and showed me some writings of theirs that seem to

---

its content." See his "The Origins of Writing in China: Scripts and Cultural Contexts," in *The Origins of Writing,* edited by Wayne M. Senner (Lincoln: University of Nebraska Press, 1989).

indicate that they have some kind of letters, although most of their writing must be by characters and pictures, as has been said of the Chinese.

CHAPTER 6 * OF UNIVERSITIES AND
STUDIES IN CHINA

The fathers of our society who have been there say that they did not see colleges and universities that teach philosophy and other natural sciences, nor can they believe that there are any, and that their entire course of study is the Mandarin language, which is extremely difficult and very vast, as has been said. What they also study are things that are found in this language, such as histories, sects, civil laws, and moral precepts taught through proverbs, tales, and many other compositions; and the degrees that exist are in these studies of their language and laws. They have not a trace of divine sciences or theology, of the natural sciences hardly a trace, with little or no method or skill but only occasional propositions, according to the intellect and study of each in mathematics, knowledge of celestial movements and stars, and in medicine by acquaintance with herbs, which they use extensively, and many effect cures with them. They write with brushes; they have many manuscript and printed books, all of them badly put together.[1] They are fine actors and perform with a great show of scenery, costumes, bells, drums, and voices at intervals. The fathers tell of having seen plays that lasted for ten or twelve days and nights, with actors never absent from the stage and no lack of audience to watch; they present different characters and scenes one after another, and while some are performing others are sleeping or eating. Moral precepts and good examples are presented in these plays but mixed with other things that are clearly pagan. In short, this is what our members tell us of letters and the exercise of letters in China, which undeniably possess great cleverness and skill; but all of it is of very little substance, for the whole science of the Chinese amounts merely to knowing how to read and write.

1. In the realm of the materiality of sign carriers, Acosta had no less difficulty in understanding Chinese writing and the organization and transmission of knowledge (science). In the West by that time the material sign carrier had already been established in "book" form, after the medieval codex and its most recent printed version. In China, "rolls" were preferred. "Chinese books" is a misleading expression, as misleading as it would have been to talk about "Spanish rolls" from the point of view of the Chinese. On the Chinese and Japanese writing surfaces and sign carriers in the fifteenth and sixteenth centuries, see Sherman E. Lee, "Art in Japan, 1450–1550" and "Art in China, 1450–1550," in *Circa 1492: Art in the Age of Exploration* (Washington, DC: National Gallery, 1991), 315–27.

They do not grasp the higher sciences, and even their reading and writing is not genuine reading and writing, for their letters do not serve to make words but are little pictures of any number of things, which they learn by means of infinite labor and huge expenditures of time. And with all their knowledge an Indian of Peru or Mexico who has learned to read and write knows more than the wisest mandarin among them; for the Indian, with twenty-four letters that he knows how to write and join together, can write and read all the words in the world, and the mandarin with his hundred thousand letters will be hard put to it to write any proper name such as Martín or Alonso, and much less to write the names of things that he does not recognize. For, after all, the writing of China is merely a form of painting or making signs.

### CHAPTER 7 * OF THE KINDS OF LETTERS AND WRITING THAT THE MEXICANS USED

Among the nations of New Spain there is great knowledge and memory of their ancient customs. And when I desired to learn how the Indians could preserve their histories in so much detail I realized that, although they did not possess the care and refinement of the Chinese and Japanese, still they did not lack some kinds of letters and books, with which they preserved after their fashion the deeds of their ancestors. In the province of Yucatan, seat of the bishopric known as that of Honduras, there were some books with leaves in the Indian style, either bound or folded, in which the wisest Indians kept the distribution of time, and knowledge of plants and animals and other things pertaining to nature, as well as their ancient customs, and it was the result of great zeal and diligence. A missionary there thought that all of it must be witches' spells and magic art and insisted that they be burned, and indeed those books were burned, which was regretted afterward not only by the Indians but by curious Spaniards who desired to know the secrets of that land.[1] The same fate has befallen other things, which, because our people

---

1. The zealous Yucatan missionary who burned the sacred writings of the Maya was none other than the Franciscan Diego de Landa. Although Landa recognized the value of the sacred Maya books in his *Relación de las cosas de Yucatán* of 1566, he had them burned in 1562 along with other sacred objects during a brutal anti-idolatry campaign. Landa commented on the burning in one of the most famous passages on Spaniards' attitudes toward Mayan literacy: "These people also used certain characters or letters, with which they wrote in their books about the antiquities and their sciences; with these, and with figures, and certain signs in the figures, they understood their matters, made them known, and taught them. We found a great number of

thought that all of it was superstition, meant the loss of many memories of ancient and hidden things that might have been of no little use. This happens out of unhealthy zeal on the part of those who, without knowing or wanting to know anything about the Indians, indiscriminately dub everything witchcraft, and say that the Indians are all drunkards, and ask what they can know or understand.

Those who have tried to investigate these matters in the proper way have found many things worthy of consideration. One of the members of our Society of Jesus, a very sensible and clever man, brought together in the province of Mexico the old men of Texcoco and Tula and Mexico and conferred with them at length, and they showed him their collections of books and their histories and calendars, a sight very much worth seeing.[2] For they had their pictures and hieroglyphs with which they represented things in the following way: things that had shapes were painted in their own image, and for things that did not have actual shapes they had characters signifying this, and hence were able to express whatever they wanted. And for a reminder of the time when each thing happened they had those painted wheels, each containing a century, which as I said before was of fifty-two years; and they painted these things beside those wheels, corresponding to the year in which memorable events occurred, using the pictures and characters I have described. For instance, by placing a picture of a man with a red hat and jacket in the sign of the cane, which was the century at the time, they marked the year when the Spaniards came into their land; and they did the same with other events. But because their figures and characters were not as adequate as those of our writing and letters, this meant that they could not make the words conform exactly but could only express the essential part of ideas. But they also have the custom of repeating in chorus orations and speeches made by the ancient orators and rhetoricians, and many songs that their poets

---

books in these letters, and since they contained nothing but superstitions and falsehoods of the devil we burned them all, which they took most grievously, and which gave them great pain" (Diego de Landa, *Yucatan before and after the Conquest,* translated with notes by William Gates [New York: Dover, 1978], 82). Historian Inga Clendinnen explores the complex character of Landa in *Ambivalent Conquest: Maya and Spaniard in Yucatan, 1517–1570* (New York: Cambridge University Press, 1987), esp. 69–80.

2. The fellow Jesuit to whom Acosta refers is the aforementioned Juan de Tovar. The histories and calendars, again, are those that are found in the "Tovar Manuscript," also known as the *Codex Ramírez.* The critical point in Acosta's comment here is the assertion that Tovar's methodological approach, which privileges the native voice in the collection of historical sources, is valuable to the Spanish.

composed, which would have been impossible to learn through those hiero-
glyphics and characters. It is known that the Mexicans were very diligent in
making boys commit those speeches and compositions to memory, and for
this purpose they had schools, and as it were colleges or seminaries, where
the old men taught the youth these and many other things that are preserved
by tradition as fully as if they had been set down in writing.[3] In particular
they obliged the youths whom they had chosen to be rhetoricians and to
practice the office of orators to learn famous orations, and commit them to
memory word for word; and many of these, when the Spaniards came and
taught them to read and write our letters, were written down by the Indians
themselves, as responsible men who have read them can testify.

And I say this because some persons who read such long and elegant
speeches in Mexican history will easily believe that they were invented by the
Spaniards and not really composed by the Indians; but once they understand
the truth they will not fail to give proper credit to the Indians' histories. The
Indians also wrote down these same speeches after their own fashion, with
pictures and characters; and, to satisfy my mind about this, I have seen the
prayers of Our Father and Ave Maria, the Creed, and the general confession
written in the Indian way I have described; and surely everyone who sees it
will be astonished, because to signify the phrase "I, a sinner, do confess" they
paint an Indian kneeling at the feet of a religious, as if confessing; and then
for the expression "Omnipotent God" they paint three faces with crowns to
represent the Trinity; and for the glorious Virgin Mary they paint the face of
Our Lady and a bust of her with a child; and for Saint Peter and Saint Paul
two heads with crowns, and keys and a sword, and in this way the whole
confession is written in pictures. And where there are no pictures they put
characters, such as in "wherein I have sinned"; from this the keenness of the
Indians' minds can be inferred, for the Spaniards never taught them this way

3. The skill of oral communication was practiced as a high art form in Aztec society. Male children of the elite
attended the *calmecac*, where priests trained them in literary rules and memorization of songs, poems, and
histories. Young girls learned songs at the all-female schools called *cuicacalli*. Such forms of oral expression
were commonly practiced at public religious and political gatherings. In some instances, pictoral codices
served to jog the memories of the orators. In addition to songs and poetry, the speeches of the elders, called
*huehuetlatolli*, extolled the values of Aztec life at specific junctions like birth or death or the crowning of a new
ruler. Examples of these coronation speeches appear in the history of ancient Mexico in book VII of Acosta.
The basic colonial source for ancient Mexican oratory is book VI of Sahagún's *Florentine Codex*, "Rhetoric
and Moral Philosophy."

of writing our prayers and matters of faith, nor could they have thought of it had they not had a very clear idea of what they were being taught. I also saw written in Peru, in the same style of pictures and characters, the confession of all his sins that an Indian brought when he came to confession, painting each of the Ten Commandments in a particular way and then making certain signs like ciphers, which were the sins that he had committed against each commandment. I have no doubt that, if many of the most complacent Spaniards were given the task of memorizing such things by the use of pictures and signs, they would not succeed in committing them to memory in a whole year or perhaps even in ten.

CHAPTER 8 * OF THE MEMORY AIDS AND
RECKONINGS USED BY THE INDIANS OF PERU

Before the Spaniards came the Indians of Peru had no kind of writing at all, either by letters or characters or ciphers or pictures, like those of China or Mexico; but this did not prevent them from preserving the memory of ancient times, nor did they fail to keep a reckoning for all their affairs whether of peace, war, or government. For they were very diligent in passing tradition from one generation to another, and the young men received and preserved what their elders told them as a sacred trust and taught it to their successors with the same care. Apart from this task, they compensated in part for the lack of writing and letters with pictures like those of Mexico, (although those of Peru were very coarse and rough), and in part, indeed principally, with *quipus*.[1] *Quipus* are memory aids or registers made up of cords on which dif-

---

1. Acosta's praise of the *quipu* in this chapter is noteworthy given the fact that the *quipu*, originally deemed harmless by Spanish missionaries who only recognized religious histories in book form, became the subject of scrutiny after the Taki Onqoy rebellion of the 1560s. Indeed, the 1582 Third Council of Lima, in which Acosta played a major role, determined they were no longer to be used to decorate churches but should be destroyed. Examples of these complex memory devices still exist today.

The "coarse and rough" pictures Acosta mentioned were wooden boards painted with images that, when interpreted by a person familiar with them, revealed such information as Inca laws. Acosta's negative evaluation of the Andean images may suggest that the boards did not hold pictographic figures like those found in Mesoamerican codexes. "Figures" and "codexes" were more approximate to Acosta's notion of letters and books than these boards covered with *tocapu*, a geometric design structure that conveyed information. No examples of these wooden tablets are extant.

Acosta's comparison between Mexican and Andean forms of writing deserves further comment in light of recent scholarly comparisons. Tom Cummins observes that the adaptation of Mexican art forms for use in the

ferent knots and different colors signify different things. What they achieved in this way is incredible, for whatever books can tell of histories and laws and ceremonies and accounts of business all is supplied by the *quipus* so accurately that the result is astonishing. Appointed to possess these *quipus,* or memorials, were officials who today are called *quipucamayos,* and these men were obliged to render an account of each thing, like public notaries here in Spain, and hence they had to be believed absolutely. There were different *quipus,* or strands, for different subjects, such as war, government, taxes, ceremonies, and lands. And in each bunch of these were many knots and smaller knots and little strings tied to them, some red, others green, others blue, others white: in short, just as we extract an infinite number of differences out of twenty-four letters by arranging them in different ways and making innumerable words, they were able to elicit any number of meanings from their knots and colors.[2] This is true to the extent that nowadays in Peru every two or three years, when a Spanish governor is subjected to a trial of residency, the Indians come forward with their small proven reckonings, saying that in a certain town they gave him six eggs and he did not pay for them, and in such and such a house a hen, and in another place two bundles of hay for his horses, and that he paid only so and so many tomines and still owes so and so many; and all of this is accurately proved with a quantity of knots and bundles of strands, which they consider to be witnesses and authentic writing. I saw a bundle of these strings on which an Indian woman had brought a written general confession of her whole life and used it to confess just as I would have done with words written on paper; and I even asked about some little threads that looked different to me, and they were certain circumstances under which the sin required to be fully confessed.

Apart from these string *quipus* they have others composed of pebbles, from which they accurately learn the words that they want to commit to memory.

---

colonial period, specifically maps and genealogies, suggests compatibility with European forms. Andean art forms, on the other hand, like the *tocapu* designs in textiles or pottery, were so different that "there was an almost complete loss of Andean forms in official colonial culture." See his "Colonial Image of the Inca," in *Writing without Words: Alternative Literacies in Mesoamerica and the Andes,* edited by Elizabeth Hill Boone and Walter D. Mignolo (Durham: Duke University Press, 1994), 210.

2. Despite his general assertion as to the superiority of the written language, Acosta draws a parallel between the uses of the letters of the alphabet and the different knots and colors of the *quipu.* For further explication, see Walter D. Mignolo, "Signs and Their Transmission: The Question of the Book in the New World," in Boone and Mignolo, *Writing without Words,* esp. 234–37.

And it is something to see quite old men learning the Our Father with a circle made of pebbles, and with another circle the Ave Maria, and with another the Creed, and to know which stone represents "who was conceived by the Holy Ghost," and which "suffered under Pontius Pilate"; and you have only to see them correct themselves when they make an error, and the whole correction consists in looking at their pebbles. All I would need to forget everything I have learned by heart would be a circle of those pebbles. Not a few of these circles are found in the cemeteries of the churches for this purpose; and to see them use another type of *quipu* that employs grains of maize is a fascinating thing. For to make a very difficult calculation, to see how much each person must contribute, which an excellent accountant would have to do with pen and ink, these Indians, taking so many grains from that place and adding a certain number from this, and hesitating a hundred times, will take their grains and put one here, three there, and eight I don't know where; they will move one grain to another place, switch three from elsewhere, and their account comes out very accurately, without the slightest error; and they know much more clearly how to balance an account of what each one has to pay or give, than we could accomplish with pen and ink. If this is not intelligence, and these men are beasts, let anyone who likes judge of it; what I truly believe is that they surpass us considerably in the things to which they apply themselves.

### CHAPTER 9 * OF THE ORDER THE INDIANS MAINTAIN IN THEIR WRITINGS

It would be well to add to what we have stated about the Indians' writing, that their method was not to write one line after another but from top to bottom or in a circle. The Romans and Greeks wrote from left to right, which is the common and ordinary method that we use; the Hebrews do the opposite, for they start from right to left, and so their books have their beginning where ours end. The Chinese do not write like either the Greeks or the Hebrews, but from the top down, for since theirs are not letters but whole expressions in which each figure or character means one thing they have no need to connect some parts with others and hence can write from top to bottom. The Indians of Mexico, for the same reason, did not write in lines from one side to the other but the reverse of the Chinese, beginning at the bottom and going up; and they did this in the calculation of days and the other things that they wrote, although when they wrote in their wheels or signs they started in the middle, where the sun was represented, and continued to draw by years until they reached the edge of the wheel. Finally, all four of these differences are found in their writings: some write from right to left, others from left to right, others from top to bottom, and others from bottom to top. Such is the diversity of men's ingenuity.

### CHAPTER 10 * HOW THE INDIANS DISPATCHED THEIR MESSENGERS

To finish this subject of writing, some may rightly doubt how the kings of Mexico and Peru could receive news from all their realms, which were so great, or by what means they could send news of things that happened in their court, since they had no letters nor did they write dispatches. This doubt will be satisfied if we realize that, by word of mouth and pictures and memory devices, they were given information at very frequent intervals about everything that happened. For this purpose they had very swift runners, who served as couriers and went to and fro and were trained from boyhood in running; and they made sure that they were very well trained in breathing, so that they could run up a very steep hill without tiring. That is why they gave a prize in Mexico to the first three or four who could run up that long staircase of the temple, as has been described in the previous book. And in Cuzco the long-eared youths, in their solemn festival of Capacraymi, vied with each other in climbing the hill of Huanacauri; and in general it has always been, and still is, very common for the Indians to exercise by running. When it was a matter of importance, they carried a painting of the subject they wished to disclose to the lords of Mexico, as they did when the first Spanish ships appeared and at the time when they went to capture Toponchan. In Peru a strange importance was given to the mail, for the Inca established posts or mail stations all over his empire, which are called *chasquis* there, and of which I will speak in their proper place.

### CHAPTER 11 * OF THE GOVERNMENT AND MONARCHS THAT THEY HAD

It is a proven fact that barbarian peoples show their barbarity most clearly in their government and manner of ruling, for the more closely men approach to reason the more humane and less arrogant is their government, and those who are kings and nobles conform and accommodate themselves to their vassals, acknowledging that they are equal by nature and inferior only in the sense that they have less obligation to care for the public good. But among barbarians the case is the opposite, for their government is tyrannical and they treat their subjects like beasts while they themselves desire to be treated like gods. Therefore, many tribes and Indian peoples do not allow kings or absolute lords but live in free communities; and only for certain things, chiefly war, do they raise up captains and princes, who are obeyed while that occasion lasts and then return to their previous estate. This is the way most of this New World is governed, where there are no organized kingdoms nor established republics, nor hereditary and recognized princes or kings; however, there are some lords and principal men who are like knights, of higher status than the common herd. This is the case in almost the whole land of Chile, where the Araucanos, and those of Tucapel and others, have resisted the Spaniards for so many years. It was the situation in all the New Realm of Granada, and in Guatemala and the islands, and all of Florida and Brazil and Luzón, and other very extensive territories, except that in many of them their barbarity is even greater, for they scarcely recognize any head and all command and govern together. In those places everything is governed by whim and violence and unreason and disorder, and the most powerful man prevails and commands. In the East Indies there are extensive and well-organized kingdoms, like those of Siam and Bisnaga and others, which can put a hundred thousand and two hundred thousand men into the field whenever they wish; and superior to all the others is the greatness and power of the kingdom of China, whose monarchs have lasted for more than two thousand years according to them, thanks to their splendid form of government. In the West Indies only two established kingdoms or empires have been discovered, that of the Mexicans in New Spain and that of the Incas in Peru, and I could not easily say which of these has been a more powerful realm. For in buildings and the splendor of his court Moctezuma surpassed the rulers of Peru, but in treasures and wealth and extension of territory the Incas were greater than the Mexicans. In point of antiquity the realm of the Incas was older, though not by much, and I think they were equal in feats of arms and victories. One thing is certain, that these two realms greatly surpassed all the other Indian dominions that have been discovered in the New World as to good order and degree of civic organization as well as power and wealth, and exceeded them much more in superstition and the cult of their idols, for they were very similar in many ways.[1] In one thing they were very different, for among the Mexicans the succession of the kingdom was by election, as in the Roman Empire, and among those of Peru it was by inheritance and blood, as in the kingdoms of Spain and France. I shall deal with what seems most appropriate in these two types of government (for they are the chief and best known among the Indians), omitting many small matters and tedious details that are of no importance.

### CHAPTER 12 * OF THE GOVERNMENT OF THE INCA KINGS OF PERU

When the Inca who reigned in Peru died his legitimate son succeeded, and the legitimate son was deemed to be the one who had been born of the Inca's principal wife, whom they called Coya; and she, from the times of one who was called the Inca Yupanqui, was his sister, for the kings made a point of marrying their sisters, and though they had other wives or concubines, the succession of the kingdom resided in the son of the Coya. It is true that when the king had a legitimate brother he would succeed before the son, and after him his nephew and the son of the previous Inca; and the same order of succession was maintained by the *curacas* and lords in their estates and offices. Any number of ceremonies and exaggerated funeral honors were held, after their fashion, for the dead man. They had one very grandiose custom, and it was that no king who entered on his reign inherited any part of the table service and treasures and possessions of his predecessor but had to establish his household anew and gather silver and gold and everything else by himself, without touching anything belonging to the dead man. All of it was dedicated to his temple, or huaca, and for the maintenance and revenues of the family he left behind, who along with all their descendants were perpetually occupied in the sacrifices and ceremonies and cult of the dead king, for then they held him to be a god, and he had his sacrifices and his statues and all the rest. For this reason the treasure that existed in Peru was immense because

1. Since Acosta had no recourse to the extensive information available today on pre-Hispanic societies, he ignored cultures that exhibited a more organized governmental structure than a chiefdom at periods prior to Spanish conquest, such as the Maya.

each of the Incas tried to make his household and wealth greater than those of his ancestors.

The insignia with which they took possession of the kingdom was a red tassel of very fine wool, finer than silk, which hung in the middle of the forehead; and only the Inca could wear it because it was like a crown or royal diadem. Other lords could and did wear tassels, but on the side, hung near the ear; but the tassel in the middle of the forehead could be worn only by the Inca, as I have said. Very solemn festivals and a multitude of sacrifices took place at the time he assumed the tassel, with a large quantity of gold and silver vessels and many small figures of sheep made of the same metals, and great quantities of garments both large and small, of the fine cloth known as *cumbi* and very well made, and many sea shells of all kinds, and many rich feathers, and a thousand sheep, which had to be of different colors; and sacrifice was made of all this. And the high priest took a child of six or eight years in his hands and, addressing the statue of Viracocha, said in unison with the other ministers, "My lord, we offer you this child so that you will give us freedom from anxiety and help us in our wars, and keep our lord the Inca in his greatness and state, and may it always increase, and give him much wisdom to rule over us." Present at this ceremony or oath taking were people from the whole kingdom as representatives of all the *huacas* and sanctuaries that they had. And no doubt the reverence and adherence that these people had for their Incas was very great, for none of their people had ever been found to betray them, because in their government they ruled not only with great power but also with much rectitude and justice, allowing no one to be wronged. The Inca placed his governors in different provinces, and some of them were supreme and close to him in authority; others had less and still others much less, with such strange subordination, and to such a degree, that no man dared to get drunk or take so much as an ear of maize from his neighbor. These Incas held it axiomatic that it was good to have the Indians constantly occupied, and so we see today roads and highways and public works requiring immense labor that they say served to give the Indians exercise and keep them from being idle. When the Incas conquered a new province, it was their practice to immediately transfer most of the inhabitants to other provinces or to their court; these people are called *mitimaes* in Peru to this day. And in their place they settled folk of their nation of Cuzco, especially the Orejones or Long Ears, who were like knights of ancient lineage. Punishment for crimes was very severe. Those who know something of this subject agree that there could not have been a better government for the Indians, nor a fitter one.[1]

CHAPTER 13 * OF THE DISTRIBUTION THAT
THE INCAS MADE OF THEIR VASSALS

Adding more details to what has already been said, it must be understood that the distribution that the Incas made of their vassals was so exact that they could easily rule them all, even in a kingdom a thousand leagues long. For when they conquered a province they would quickly organize the Indians into towns and communities and count them by heads, and over each ten Indians they placed one who was responsible for them, and another for each hundred, and for a thousand another, and for each ten thousand another; and this man was called *huno*, which was an important office. And in each province a governor of the Inca lineage was set over all of these, whom all obeyed and to whom they made a detailed report annually about everything that had happened, namely, who had been born, who had died, the flocks, and the fields. These governors went out each year from Cuzco, which was the court, and returned for the great festival of *raymi* and at that time brought all the tribute of the kingdom to the court, which they could not enter unless they brought it. The whole kingdom was divided into four parts, which they called *tahuantinsuyo;* they were Chinchasuyo, Collasuyo, Andesuyo, and Condesuyo, according to the four roads that lead out of Cuzco, where the court was and where general assemblies were held. These roads and the provinces that belonged to them are at the four corners of the compass: Collasuyo to the south, Chinchasuyo to the north, Condesuyo to the west, and Andesuyo to the east. All their towns had two separate divisions, *Hanansaya* and *Urinsaya,* which is to say upper and lower. When orders were issued to do something, or to bring something to the Inca, there was an announce-

1. Postconquest sources often provided a unified image of the preconquest Inca rule. Acosta duplicates such a perspective when he exaggerates the seamlessness of the Inca Empire, particularly with regard to acquiescence to Inca rule. Active resistance on the part of tribes like the Araucanians continued throughout the history of the empire. Through an analysis of local pottery styles, Thomas C. Patterson explores how native groups incorporated into the Inca Empire carried out cultural resistance. See his "The Inca Empire and Its Subject Peoples," in *The Indian in Latin America,* edited by John Kicza (Wilmington, DE: Scholarly Resources, 1993).

ment of the part of it that was the responsibility of each province and town and municipal division; this was assessed not by equal parts but by quotas, according to the quality and possibilities of the land. So to deliver a hundred thousand bushels of maize, for example, they already knew that a certain province was responsible for a tenth part, and such and such another for a seventh, and such and such another for a fifth, and so on; and it was the same for the towns and municipal divisions and *ayllos,* or clans. And to make an accounting of it all there were the *quipucamayos,* the accounting officials, who with their strings and knots accurately reported what had been paid, even for a hen and a load of wood, and by means of their registers reckoned instantly what each of the Indians owed.

## CHAPTER 14 * OF THE BUILDINGS AND CONSTRUCTION METHODS OF THE INCAS

The buildings and constructions that the Incas made, in fortresses, temples, roads, country villas, and the like, were many and required enormous labor, as the ruins and fragments that remain today make plain. These can be seen in Cuzco and Tihuanaco and Tambo and other places, where there are stones so immense in size that we cannot imagine how they were cut and brought and placed where they are.[1] In order to construct the buildings and fortresses that the Inca ordered built in Cuzco and different parts of his kingdom, a large number of Indians came from every province, for the toil was enormous and is frightening to contemplate. They did not use mortar, nor did they have iron or steel to cut and carve the stones, nor machines or instruments to drag them, and yet with all this the stones are so cleanly put together that in many places you can scarcely see the joining of one to another; and many of these stones are so large, as I have said, that it would be called an impossible thing were it not actually witnessed. In Tihuanaco I measured one that was thirty-eight feet long and eighteen wide and about six feet thick, and in the wall of the fortress in Cuzco, which is of masonry, there are many much larger

1. *Tambo* refers to the Inca fortress called Ollantaytambo, which was located near Cuzco in the Sacred Valley. During the Inca uprising of 1536, led by Manco Inca, Hernando Pizarro's forces faced the seventeen imposing stone terraces at Ollantaytambo — each one filled with Inca soldiers and archers — and rode away in defeat. See Hemming, *The Conquest of the Incas* 213–16.

stones.[2] And what is most astonishing is the fact that, although the stones in the wall to which I refer are not cut uniformly but are very unequal among themselves in size and workmanship, they fit together with incredible smoothness and without the use of mortar. All of this was done by the work of many people and with terrible travail in the course of the work, for to fit one stone with another, the way they are adjusted, they had to test it many times because the other stones were not of the same size and thickness. Each year the Inca indicated the number of men who had to come and work on the stones and buildings; the Indians made the distribution among themselves, as in other things, without injustice being done to anyone. But, although these buildings were large, they were usually badly arranged and utilized and seemed no better than mosques or other barbarian buildings. They did not know how to build arches in their constructions, nor did they grasp the use of mortar to do so.[3] When they saw arches made over the River Jauja using trusses, they fled in fear as they watched the trusses being demolished after the bridge was finished, believing that the bridge (which is made of stone) would soon fall. And when they saw that it held fast and that the Spaniards walked on it, the chief said to his companions, "It is right to serve these people, for indeed they seem to be children of the sun." The bridges that they used were made of woven canes or reeds, with thick ropes fastened to the banks on either side, for they did not make bridges of stone or wood. The bridge that exists today at the outlet of the great lake of Chucuito, in Collao, is astonishing, for that stream is exceedingly deep and there is no possibility of placing any foundation in it; and it is so wide that no arch could span it, nor could there be more than one arch, and thus it was impossible to make a stone or wooden bridge. The ingenuity and craft of the Indians sufficed to make a very firm and safe bridge entirely of straw, which seems like a tall tale, but it is true. For, as was described in another book, they tied together

2. Acosta mistakenly identifies the ruins at Tiahuanaco as Incan. The buildings at Tiahuanaco were not constructed under Inca rule but as part of the earlier Tiahuanaco (Tiwanaku) civilization, which flourished in the Lake Titicaca region from 100 to 1200 A.D.

3. Although Acosta marvels at the Inca stonework he saw at Cuzco and Tiahuanaco, he notes that it is inferior to European monuments, "badly arranged," and "no better than mosques." Acosta's critiques of Inca construction reflect a European bias toward Old World architecture, the techniques of which were not always well suited to New World situations. In particular, Acosta's disdain for buildings without arches and mortar ignored the fact that Spanish constructions, like the Cathedral of Santo Domingo in Cuzco, crumbled with the tremors of Andean earthquakes while the Inca foundations and structures remained intact.

bundles of some reeds and canes that grow in the lake, which they call *totora,* and as it is a very light material the bundles do not sink. On top of these they place a large quantity of sedge and, with those bundles or rafts very firmly fastened on both sides of the river, men and beasts cross over at will. On several occasions when I crossed this bridge I was amazed by the Indians' skill, for with such simple materials they make a bridge that is better and safer than the pontoon bridge from Seville to Triana. I also measured the length of the bridge, and if I recall correctly it was more than three hundred feet. The depth of that outlet is said to be tremendous; seen from above, the water does not appear to be moving, but underneath the current is said to be very violent. Let this suffice about buildings.

CHAPTER 15 * OF THE INCA'S REVENUES AND
THE ORDER OF TRIBUTES HE IMPOSED
ON THE INDIANS

The Incas' wealth was incomparable, for, although no king inherited the property and treasure of his predecessors, the Inca had at his disposal all the wealth of his realms, which were very abundant in gold and silver as well as clothing and flocks; and the greatest asset of all was the innumerable multitude of his vassals, all occupied in and attentive to whatever pleased their king. They brought him everything he chose from each province: the Chichas contributed rich, sweet-smelling wood; the Lucanas, carriers to bear his litter; the Chumbibilcas, dancers; and the other provinces the best that each had to offer; and this was in addition to the general tribute that all had to pay. Indians designated for this service worked the gold and silver mines (of which there is a marvelous abundance in Peru), and the Inca gave them everything necessary for their expenditures, and everything that they mined was for the Inca. Because of this there was such treasure in that kingdom that in the opinion of many what came into the Spaniards' hands, although it was a vast amount, as we know, did not constitute a tenth part of what the Indians buried and hid, which the Spaniards have been unable to find despite the great efforts greed has spurred them to make to discover it. But the greatest wealth of those barbarian kings was that all their vassals were their slaves, from whose labor they profited as they pleased. And the remarkable thing is that they used them with such organization and good government that it did not seem to them like servitude but a very happy life.

To understand the order of tributes that the Indians paid to their lords, it must be understood that when the Inca settled the cities that he conquered he divided all their lands into three parts. The first part was for religion and rites, so that Pachayachachic, who is the creator and the sun, and Chuquiilla, who is thunder, and Pachamama and the dead, and other *huacas* and sanctuaries each had their own lands; the revenue from them was spent on sacrifices and maintaining the ministers and priests, for Indians were assignd to each *huaca* or temple. The greater part of this revenue was spent in Cuzco, where the universal sanctuary was located; another part was spent in the same city where it was collected, for in imitation of Cuzco every city had *huacas* and temples of the same kind and the same vocations, and thus they were served with the same rites and ceremonies as in Cuzco, which is surprising and very well attested to, for it was verified in more than a hundred towns, some of them almost two hundred leagues from Cuzco. Whatever was sown and harvested in those lands was placed in storehouses made expressly for the purpose, and this formed a large part of the tribute that the Indians paid. It is not known what proportion it was, for in some places it was more and in others less and in others almost everything; and this part was the one that benefited first.

The second part of the lands and fields was for the Inca; he maintained himself and his servants and family, and the nobles and garrisons and soldiers, from this part. And thus it formed the greater portion of his tributes, as the granaries or storehouses testify, for they are longer and broader than those of the *huacas*. This tribute was taken to Cuzco, or to places where it was needed for the garrisons, with remarkable speed and care, and when this was not necessary it was kept for as many as ten or twelve years against a time of need. These lands of the Inca were cultivated after those of the gods, and all the people without exception went to work in them, dressed in their best and singing songs in praise of the Inca and the *huacas;* and during the whole time they were cultivating or working they ate at the expense of the Inca, or the sun, or the *huacas* whose lands they were cultivating. But old folk and the ill, and widows, were excused from this work; and, although what was harvested belonged either to the Inca or the sun or the temples, the land belonged to the Indians or their ancestors.

The third part of the lands were given by the Inca to the community. It has not been ascertained just what proportion this was, if it was larger or smaller than the Inca's or the temples' portion, but it is certain that care was taken to make it sufficient to feed the people. No private person owned any of this part (nor did the Indians ever own anything privately unless by special favor of the Inca), and it could not be transferred or even divided among heirs. These communal lands were distributed annually, and each man was assigned the portion necessary to sustain his person and those of his wife and his children; and so in some years it was more and in others less, according to the state of his family, for which there were specific measures. Tribute was never exacted from the land that was distributed to each person, for all their tribute consisted of cultivating the lands of the Inca and the temples and placing their products in the storehouses. When the year turned out barren, food was given to the needy from these same storehouses, for there was always an abundance in reserve. The Inca made the same distribution of livestock as of the lands, which consisted of counting it and assigning pastures and boundaries for the temple flocks and the Inca's flocks, and for each town, and so from all the animals that were raised one part was for their religion, another for the kings, and a third for the Indians themselves. And the same order was followed even for hunters; it was unlawful to carry away or kill females. The Inca's flocks and those of the temples were many and large and were called *capaellamas*. Those of the councils or communities were few and poor, and so they were called *guacchallama*. The Inca took great care to preserve the flocks, for they were and are the whole wealth of that realm; as has been said, females were never sacrificed or killed for any reason, nor were they captured in the chase. If any animal suffered from mange or scab, which is called *carache* there, it had to be buried alive quickly so as not to infect others. The flocks were shorn at the proper season, and each man was given enough wool to spin and weave clothing for his children and his wife, and visits were made to see if they did the work, and the negligent were punished. Clothing for the Inca and his court was woven from his flocks; one kind, the same on both sides, was very fine and was called *cumbi;* the other was coarse and rough and was called *abasca*. There was no special number of these garments, only the numbers that each requested. The wool that remained was placed in their storage houses, and so when the Spaniards entered them they found them very full of this and all the other things necessary for human life. No sensible man could fail to be impressed with such a remarkable and provident form of government, for, although they were not religious or Christians, the Indians attained true perfection after their fashion by not having individual ownership, providing everyone with necessities, and supporting so amply all matters pertaining to religion and their lord and master.

## CHAPTER 16 ∗ OF THE TRADES THAT THE INDIANS LEARNED

There was another particularly admirable custom that the Indians of Peru had, and it was that from childhood all were taught every trade that a man needs for human life; for there were no special trades among them as among us, such as tailors and cobblers and weavers, but everyone learned everything needful for their persons and homes and provided for themselves. All of them knew how to weave and make their clothes; and thus when the Inca supplied them with wool he also gave them clothing. All knew how to till and cultivate the land without having to hire other workers. All built their own houses, and the women were the ones who knew most about everything and did not remain idle but worked with much care, serving their husbands.[1] Other trades that were not needed for the ordinary and everyday purposes of human life had their own craftsmen, such as silversmiths and painters and potters, and boatmen and reckoners and players of instruments; and in those same trades of weaving and farming, or building, there were master craftsmen for fine work whom the nobles used. But as for the common folk, as has been said, each took care of what was needed in his house, and one man did not pay another for this; and today it is the same, so that no man has need of another for the things of his house and his person, such as footwear and clothing and building a house, and sowing and reaping, and making the gear and tools necessary for the purpose. And in this the Indians almost copy the institutions of the monks of old of which the lives of the church fathers tell us. Truly, they are folk who are neither greedy nor spoiled, and so they are content with a modest living; and certainly, if their style of life were accepted

---

1. Acosta's observation that "women . . . did not remain idle" suggests an implicit contrast between women's roles in Peru and early modern Spain. This remark more accurately reflects Acosta's perception of his native society than it does the reality for women in Spain, the majority of whom toiled on a daily basis. On the struggles of women to procure labor and sustenance in sixteenth-century Seville, see Mary Elizabeth Perry, *Gender and Disorder in Early Modern Seville* (Princeton: Princeton University Press, 1990).

by choice and not by custom and nature, we would say that it was a life of great perfection and even contains sufficient preparation to receive the doctrine of the Holy Gospel, which is so inimical to pride and greed and idle pleasure. But the example that preachers offer does not always conform with the doctrine that they preach to the Indians. One thing is very noticeable, that, although the clothing and costume of the Indians is simple, still all the provinces are differentiated, especially by what they wear on their heads: for in some it is a woven braid wound around many times and in others it is broad and wound only once; in another there are little hats shaped like mortars, and in others a sort of tall round bonnet, and in others something like the hoops of sieves, and a thousand other differences.[2] And it was an inviolable law that no one might change the costume and habit of his province even though he moved to another, and the Inca considered this very important to good government. It is still true today, though not as much care is taken about it as formerly.

## CHAPTER 17 * OF THE POSTS AND *CHASQUIS* THAT THE INCA USED

Everywhere in his kingdom the Inca had a large service of posts and runners called *chasquis,* and they were the men who carried his orders to the governors and brought messages from them to the court. These *chasquis* were placed at every *topo,* which is a league and a half, in two huts where there were four Indians. These were supplied and changed every month by each district, and they carried the message they were given at top speed until they could give it to the next *chasqui,* and those designated to run were always on the alert and in readiness. They could run fifty leagues in a day and a night, even though most of the land was very rugged. They also served to bring things that the Inca wanted very swiftly, and so in Cuzco they had fresh fish from the sea (though the distance was a hundred leagues) within two days or a little more. After the Spaniards came these *chasquis* were used during troubled times and when there was much need of them. The viceroy Don Martín placed them as couriers at intervals of four leagues to bring and send dis-

2. A comprehensive reference guide to clothing in the colonial Andes, including descriptions of native dress, is Mary Money, *Los obrajes, el traje, y el comercio de ropa en la audiencia de Charcas* (La Paz: Taller Don Bosco, 1983).

patches, which is a very important thing in that realm, although they do not run as fast as those of former times, nor are there as many of them. They are well paid and serve as couriers do in Spain, handing over the papers that they carry every four or five leagues.

## CHAPTER 18 * OF THE LAWS AND JUSTICE AND PUNISHMENTS THAT THE INCAS IMPOSED AND OF THEIR MARRIAGES

Just as preeminence and advantages, such as lands of their own, insignias, and marriages with women related to the Inca, were given to those who served well in wars or other tasks, severe punishments were meted out to those who were disobedient or had committed some crime. Murder and robbery were punished by death and incest with either parents or children in the direct line was punished by the death of the culprit. But it must be noted that they did not consider it adultery to have many wives or concubines, nor did these women incur the death penalty if they were found with other men, except for the true wife with whom they contracted a genuine marriage, for there was only one of these and she was received with special solemnity and ceremony. This consisted of the husband's going to her house, or his taking her with him and placing an *ojota* on her foot. This is the name of the shoe that they use there, which is like a sandal or the open shoe of a Franciscan friar. If the bride was a virgin this sandal was of wool, but if she was not it was made of esparto grass. All the other wives served and recognized this one, and she wore black for a year for a dead husband and did not remarry for a year; usually she was younger than her husband. This wife was bestowed by the Inca, with his own hand, on his governors or captains, and the governors and chiefs in the towns gathered the boys and girls together in a public square and gave each man his wife; and they contracted matrimony with the ceremony I have described, of putting the sandal on her foot. If she was found with another man this wife was subject to the death penalty, and so was he; and even in cases in which the husband pardoned them he did not fail to punish them, though not with death. The same penalty applied to incest with a mother or grandmother or daughter or granddaughter; marriage or concubinage was not prohibited with other female relatives, only in the first degree of relationship. Nor was it permitted for brother and sister to have access to each other or to marry, on which point many in Peru are mistaken, believing that the Incas and nobles legitimately married their sisters, even if these were of the same father and mother; but the truth is that to marry within the first degree of relationship was always considered unlawful.

And this lasted until the times of Topa Inca Yupanqui, the father of Huayna Capac and grandfather of Atahualpa, during whose reign the Spaniards entered Peru. For the aforesaid Topa Inca Yupanqui was the first to break this custom and marry Mamaocllo, his sister on the father's side; and he commanded that only the Inca lords, and no others, could marry a sister on the father's side. That is what he did, and he had a son named Huayna Capac and a daughter named Coya Cussilimay; and when he died he commanded these children of his, who were full brother and sister, to marry, and that the other noble families could marry their sisters on the father's side. And because that marriage was illicit and contrary to natural law, God ordained that with the fruit that came of it, the Inca Huáscar and the Inca Atahualpa, the kingdom of the Incas would come to an end. If anyone wishes to understand more fully the matrimonial customs of the Indians of Peru, he should read the treatise written by Polo at the request of Don Jerónimo de Loayza, archbishop of Lima, for he made diligent inquiry about this as well as many other things concerning the Indians. And it is important to avoid the error made by many, who, not knowing which is the legitimate wife among the Indians and which the concubine, force a baptized Indian to marry his concubine, abandoning the legitimate wife. And we can also see how little justification there is for some who have tried to say that if husband and wife were baptized their marriage would be legal even though they are brother and sister. The Provincial Synod of Lima has determined, and correctly, that this is not true, for even among these same Indians that type of marriage is unlawful.[1]

## CHAPTER 19 * OF THE ORIGIN OF THE INCAS, LORDS OF PERU, AND THEIR CONQUESTS AND VICTORIES

By order of His Catholic Majesty the King, our lord Don Felipe, an investigation was made with all possible care into the origin and rites and statutes of

---

1. *Concilium provinciale Limense celebratum in civitate Regum. Anno MDLXXXIII* (O'G).

the Incas, although, because those Indians did not possess writing, it was impossible to verify the matter as thoroughly as might have been wished. But through their *quipus* and records, which as has been said serve them as books, what I shall recount here was ascertained.[1] First, in Peru in ancient times there was no kingdom or lord obeyed by everyone, but there were free inhabitants and communities, as today in the kingdom of Chile, and as has been the case in almost all the places conquered by the Spaniards in the West Indies except for the kingdom of Mexico. And so it must be pointed out that three kinds of government and styles of life have been found among the Indians. The first and chief kind, and the best, has been the realm or monarchy, as was that of the Incas and of Moctezuma, although these were in large part tyrannical. The second type is that of free associations or communities, where the people are governed by the advice of many, and are like councils. In time of war these elect a captain who is obeyed by a whole tribe or province. In time of peace each town or group of folk rules itself, and each has some prominent men whom the mass of the people respect; and at most some of these join together on matters that seem important to them to see what they ought to do. The third kind of government is absolutely barbarous, and these are Indians who have neither laws nor king nor fixed dwellings but go in herds like wild animals and savages.[2] As far as I have been able to understand it, the first dwellers in these Indies were of this kind, as are a large proportion of the Brazilians to this day, and the Chiriguanas and Chunchos, and Yscaycingas and Pilcozones, and most of the Florida Indians,

1. It is worth noting that efforts on the part of missionaries in Peru to teach reading and writing in Quechua by transcribing the native language with letters of the Latin alphabet never reached the degree witnessed in Mexico. Thus, written sources in Nahuatl far exceeded those found in Quechua, and this corpus of native-language documents influenced not only contemporary projects on colonial history but colonial investigations as well.

2. Forms of writing and government, both discussed in book VI, constitute the basis for Acosta's classification of native peoples on a scale according to their level of civilization. Acosta's scale of civilization has been singled out as one of the earliest attempts at comparative ethnology and heralded for its influence on the late-sixteenth-century intellectual world. According to Anthony Pagden, Acosta's "insistence that barbarism described not one but several different cultural types, [that] the peoples could be graded . . . had a direct influence on a number of writers." See chapter 7, "A Programme for Comparative Ethnology," in his *The Fall of Natural Man: The American Indian and the Origins of Comparative Ethnology* (New York: Cambridge University Press, 1982), 198. José Alcina Franch's introduction to the 1987 Spanish edition of Acosta provides an insightful discussion of Acosta's ethnology. See José de Acosta, *Historia natural y moral de las Indias* (Madrid: Historia 16, 1987), 26–30.

and in New Spain all the Chichimecas. From this kind of Indian, thanks to the ingenuity and wisdom of some of their principal men, was formed the other type of government, that of communities and free folk, where there is somewhat more order and permanence. Nowadays the Araucos and Tucapels in Chile are of this kind, as were the Moscas in the New Kingdom of Granada formerly and in New Spain some of the Otomíes; and in all these people there is less savagery and more reason. From this class of people, owing to the courage and wisdom of a few excellent men, arose the other sort of government, a more powerful and propitious one, that of kingdom and monarchy such as we find in Mexico and Peru. For the Incas conquered all that land and imposed their laws and rule.

According to their reckoning, the time that they have ruled is more than three hundred years and less than four hundred, although for a very long time their sovereignty did not extend for more than five or six leagues around Cuzco. Their beginnings and origin were in the Valley of Cuzco, and little by little they conquered the land that we call Peru, from beyond Quito as far as the Pasto River in the north and in the south as far as Chile, more than a thousand leagues in length. In breadth their kingdom reached to the west as far as the Southern Sea and as far as the great stretches of land on the other side of the Andes range, where today we can see Pucará del Inca, which was a fort that the Inca built for defense on the eastern side. The Incas went no farther than this owing to the very large expanse of water and swamps and lakes and the rivers that arise there. The breadth of their kingdom is less than a hundred leagues. These Incas were more advanced than any of the other nations of America in polity and government, and still more in arms and valor, although the Cañaris, who were their mortal enemies and favored the Spaniards, never wished to recognize this; and even today, if this subject arises, on the slightest provocation they will kill thousands over the question of who is the more valiant, as has happened in Cuzco. The justification by which they conquered and became lords of all that land was their claim that after the Universal Flood, of which all these Indians had knowledge, the world had been recovered by these Incas when seven of them emerged from the cave of Pacaritambo, and that in consequence all other men owed them tribute and vassalage as their progenitors.[3] In addition to this, they stated and

3. It is clear that Acosta's use of systematic reasoning was clouded by his desire to find evidence of Christianity in Andean myths of a flood. The cave Pacaritambo, or Pacariqtambo, cited by Acosta is the "inn of dawn" in

affirmed that only they possessed the true religion and knew how God ought to be served and honored, and that therefore they were obliged to teach all the others; hence they placed enormous emphasis on rites and ceremonies. There were more than four hundred temples in Cuzco, as their holy land, and all of these places were full of mysteries. And as they continued to conquer they gradually introduced their own gods and rites everywhere in that realm. The chief god whom they worshiped was Viracocha Pachayachachic, who is the creator of the world, and after him the sun. And so they said that the sun as well as all the other gods received virtue and existence from the Creator and that they were intercessors with him.

CHAPTER 20 * OF THE FIRST INCA AND
HIS SUCCESSORS

The first man named by the Indians as founder of the Incas was Manco Capac; and they imagine that after the flood he emerged from the cave or window of Tambo, which is five or six leagues from Cuzco.[1] They say that he founded two chief clans of Incas: one was called Hanancuzco and the other Urincuzco, and the lords who conquered and governed the land came from the former clan. The first of these lords to become head of a clan was named Inca Roca, and he founded a family, or *ayllo,* to which they give the name of Uizaquirao.[2] This man, although he was not a great lord, was served from gold and silver utensils, and he ordered that his whole treasure should be dedicated to the cult of his body and the support of his family. And hence his successor did the same; and it was a widespread custom, as has been said,

the Inca creation myth. See Gary Urton, *The History of a Myth: Pacariqtambo and the Origin of the Inkas* (Austin: University of Texas Press, 1990).

1. Colonial sources on the Inca dynasty include Juan de Betanzos, *Narrative of the Incas* (1551), Pedro Sarmiento de Gamboa, *Historia Indica* (1572), and the mestizo author El Inca Garcilaso de la Vega, *Royal Commentaries of the Inca* (1609). Garcilaso de la Vega, who composed his massive history of the Incas in Spain years after leaving his native Peru, had a personal as well as political interest in legitimating Inca history and culture. Both Betanzos and Sarmiento carried out their work in Peru at the behest of Spanish officials. Betanzos, widely regarded in Peru as a Quechua expert, collected oral testimonies for Viceroy Antonio de Mendoza (1551–52) and served as the translator for Viceroy Francisco de Toledo (1569–81) in his negotiations with the last Inca, Tupac Amaru. Sarmiento compiled his history for Toledo in the wake of the capture of Tupac Amaru at Vilcabamba; his account of the Inca lineage carried political ramifications for the survivors' socioeconomic status in the colonial world.

2. The *ayllo,* or *ayllu,* is the main organizational unit in Andean society. People belong to an *ayllu* based on kin and connections to land, which they hold in common.

that no Inca inherited his predecessor's possessions and house but instead founded a new house. At the time of this Inca Roca they used idols made of gold. After Inca Roca came Yahuar-huacac, who succeeded when he was already an old man. They say that he was given this name, which means "tears of blood," because on one occasion he was conquered and taken prisoner by his enemies and wept blood out of sheer sorrow. This Inca is buried in a town called Paulo, on the road to Omasuyo; he founded the family known as Ayllopanaca. He was succeeded by a son of his, Viracocha Inca; he was very rich and made large amounts of gold and silver plate and founded the clan or family of Coccopanaca. Gonzalo Pizarro sought the body of this Inca because of the rumor of great wealth buried with him, and after cruelly torturing many Indians he found it in Saqui Sahuana, where he was later defeated and taken prisoner and executed by President Gasca.[3] The aforesaid Gonzalo Pizarro ordered the body of this Viracocha Inca burned, and later the Indians took up his ashes and placed them in a jar, and preserved them and made great sacrifices to them, until Polo claimed them with the other bodies of the Incas. He found them carefully embalmed and whole, and with remarkable diligence and cunning took them out of the Indians' hands, and by this means ended the great number of idolatrous acts that were being performed for them. It was not considered proper that this Inca should be titled Viracocha, which was the name of God; and to excuse himself he said that Viracocha himself had appeared to him in a dream and told him to take his name. After this Inca came Pachacuti Inca Yupanqui, who was a very valiant conqueror and a great statesman and the inventor of most of the rites and superstitions of their idolatry, as I shall recount later.

3. The practice of raiding the sacred burial sites of the Inca became quite common as the conquistadors competed for loot. For an analysis of the cultural politics of a *huaca*-looting episode near Trujillo several decades after conquest, see chapter 4 of Susan Ramírez, *The World Upside Down: Cross-Cultural Contact and Conflict in Sixteenth-Century Peru* (Stanford: Stanford University Press, 1996).

The mention of President Gasca refers to his execution of Gonzalo Pizarro for instigating civil war among the Spanish in Peru. After his brother Francisco Pizarro's murder by Almagro supporters in 1541, Gonzalo Pizarro found himself in a weakened political position. He capitalized on the growing resentment of fellow *encomenderos* to Viceroy Blasco Núñez de Vela's intention to destroy the power of early conquistadors by enforcing the New Laws. A fierce civil struggle began between the viceroy and forces loyal to Gonzalo Pizarro. Into the midst of this crisis, the crown sent Pedro de la Gasca, the president of the *audiencia* of Lima, to end the war and revoke many of the New Laws that the colonists found objectionable, like the law that prohibited the inheritance of *encomiendas*. De la Gasca negotiated and fought his way to victory in the civil war for the royalist forces. Gonzalo Pizarro surrendered in 1548 only to face execution at the hands of de la Gasca.

CHAPTER 21 ∗ OF PACHACUTI INCA YUPANQUI
AND WHAT HAPPENED UP TO THE TIME
OF HUAYNA CAPAC

Pachacuti Inca Yupanqui reigned for sixty years and made many conquests. The first of his victories was that an elder brother of his, who had exercised overlordship during his father's lifetime and waged war with his permission, was defeated in a battle that he had with the Changas, the nation that possessed the valley of Andahuaylas, which is some thirty or forty leagues from Cuzco in the direction of Lima; thoroughly routed, he retired with a few followers. When the younger brother Inca Yupanqui saw this, he lied in order to gain power and said that Viracocha the Creator had spoken to him at a time when he was alone and very sad, and had complained that, although he was lord of the universe and creator of the world and had made the heavens and the sun and the whole universe and human beings, men did not obey him as they should even though everything was under his sway; rather, they equally revered the sun, and thunder, and the earth, and other things, although these had no virtue other than that which he gave them; and he told the Inca that in heaven where he lived he was called Viracocha Pachayachachic, which means "creator of the universe." And to make the Indians believe that this was true, even though he was alone, he must not hesitate to gather supporters under this name, for, although the Changas were numerous and had been victorious, the god would give him victory over them and make him a ruler, for he would send people to help him, even though they would be invisible. And so it happened that under this name he began to gather supporters and raised a very large number, and gained the victory and became ruler, and wrested power from his father and brother by defeating them in war; then he conquered the Changas and after that victory proclaimed that Viracocha must be held to be lord of the universe, and that reverence and respect must be paid to the statues of the sun and thunder; and from that time forward the statue of Viracocha was placed higher than those of the sun and thunder and the other gods. And, although this Inca Yupanqui set aside farms and lands and flocks to the sun and thunder and other gods, he set nothing aside for Viracocha, giving as a reason that he needed nothing because he was lord of the universe and the creator. When victory had been won over the Changas he told his soldiers that it was not they who had won the victory but certain bearded men whom Viracocha had sent, and that none but he could see them, and that these men had then turned into stones, and that they must be sought, and that he would recognize them. And so he brought together from the hills a large number of stones that he had chosen and made them into idols, and they worshiped them and made sacrifices to them. These were called Pururaucas and were carried into battle with great devotion in the belief that victory was certain with their aid. And this fantasy and fiction of the Inca was so powerful that he won notable victories with it. He founded the family called Inacapanaca and made a large gold statue that he named Indiillapa, and placed it on a litter made entirely of gold, of great value; much of this gold was taken to Cajamarca to free Atahualpa at the time when Marqués Francisco Pizarro was holding him prisoner.[1]

In Cuzco the Licentiate Polo found this Inca's house, and his servants and the priestesses who served his memory, and he discovered the body, which had been transferred from Patallacta to Totocache, where the parish of San Blas was founded. The body was so well preserved, and treated with a certain resin, that it seemed alive. The eyes were made of gold leaf so well placed that there was no need of the natural ones; and there was a bruise on his head that he had received from a stone in a certain battle. His hair was gray and none of it was missing, as if he had died that very day, although in fact his death had occurred more than sixty or eighty years before. This body, along with those of other Incas, was sent by Polo to the city of Lima under orders from the viceroy, the Marqués de Cañete, for it was necessary to root out the idolatry of Cuzco; and many Spaniards have seen this body, along with the others, in the hospital of San Andrés, founded by the aforesaid viceroy, although by now they are very much abused and in poor condition. Don Felipe Caritopa, who was the great-grandson or great-great-grandson of this Inca, has stated that the patrimony he left to his family was immense, and that it must be in

1. After Atahualpa's capture in 1532 at Cajamarca, the Inca ruler proposed a ransom of silver and gold that would fill the rooms where he was being kept. The Spanish readily accepted the offer, and over the next two months they watched as an estimated 13,000 pounds of gold and 26,000 pounds of silver arrived from various parts of the Inca Empire. Although he kept his end of the agreement, the Spanish accused Atahualpa of fomenting rebellion and executed him in July of 1533. Shortly thereafter, Manco Capac, yet another son of Huayna Capac, became the first puppet king crowned by the Spanish. He rebelled in 1536, however, and led the Inca retreat to Vilcabamba.

the hands of the *yanaconas* Amaro, Tito, and others. This Inca was succeeded by Topa Inca Yupanqui and he by another of his sons of the same name, who founded the family called Capac Ayllo.

That lord was succeeded by Huayna Capac, which means "rich or valiant youth," and he was both, more than any of his ancestors or descendants. He was very prudent and imposed great order everywhere in the land; he was determined and brave, and very fortunate in war, and achieved great victories. This Inca extended his kingdom much more than all his ancestors together. Death overcame him in the kingdom of Quito, which he had conquered, and which was four hundred leagues distant from his court. They opened him up and the intestines and heart remained in Quito because he had so commanded, and his body was brought to Cuzco and placed in the famous temple of the sun. Even today many buildings and roads and forts, and notable works of this king, are seen; he founded the family of Temebamba. This Huayna Capac was worshiped as a god by his people while he was alive, something that, according to the old men, was never done with any of his predecessors. When he died a thousand persons of his household were killed so that they could go and serve him in the other life, and they died very willingly in order to go and serve him, so willingly indeed that many, in addition to those chosen, offered themselves as victims for the same reason. The wealth and treasure of this Inca was something never seen before, and because the Spaniards came into Peru shortly after his death the Indians took great care to make it all disappear, although much of it was taken to Cajamarca to ransom his son Atahualpa. Men worthy of belief state that he had more than three hundred children and grandchildren in Cuzco. The mother of this Inca was greatly respected; her name was Mamaocllo. Polo sent her body and that of Huayna Capac, very well embalmed and preserved, to Lima, and thus eliminated a large number of idolatrous acts that were being performed with them.

Huayna Capac was succeeded in Cuzco by a son of his named Tito Cussi Hualpa, later called Huáscar Inca, and his body was burned by the captains of Atahualpa, who was also a son of Huayna Capac; he rose against his brother in Quito and opposed him with a powerful army.[1] What happened then was that two of Atahualpa's captains, Quizquiz and Chilicuchima, took Huáscar Inca prisoner in the city of Cuzco after he had been recognized as lord and king, for in fact he was the legitimate heir. In consequence the emotion caused everywhere in his realm was very great, especially in his court; and as always in case of need they had recourse to sacrifices, for they could not find men powerful enough to free their lord, both because the captains who had taken him prisoner were very strong and because of the numerous army with which Atahualpa was coming. They decided, and even say it was by Huáscar's orders, to make a great sacrifice to Viracocha Pachayachachic, creator of the universe, beseeching him, because they could not free their lord, to send people from heaven to get him out of prison. Having confidently performed this sacrifice, news came that certain people had come by sea, had disembarked, and had taken Atahualpa prisoner. And so, because the Spaniards who had taken Atahualpa in Cajamarca were so few, and also because this had happened immediately after the Indians had made the aforesaid sacrifice to Viracocha, they called them Viracochas, believing that they were people sent from God; and that is how this name, calling the Spaniards Viracochas, has endured to this day. And certainly if we Spaniards had given the example that we should have, those Indians would have been right in saying that we were people sent from God. The lofty aim of Divine Providence is greatly worthy of consideration, how it arranged for the entrance of our people into Peru, which would have been impossible had it not been for the division between the two brothers and their supporters and the great respect in which the Christians were held as folk who had come from Heaven; this certainly means that in winning the lands of the Indians their souls were all the more splendidly won for Heaven.

1. Shortly before the arrival of the Francisco Pizarro expedition to Túmbez in 1531, Huayna Capac died during a smallpox epidemic that swept the Andes in advance of the Spanish conquistadors. The Inca elite in Cuzco appointed his son Huáscar to take his place. His half-brother Atahualpa, however, commanded the Inca armies in Quito and decided to challenge Huáscar's rule. He neglected to travel to Cuzco for the coronation ceremonies, after which he sent his military forces south to take Cuzco. Huáscar was captured, though not executed, at this juncture. Atahualpa's clemency for his brother expired once the Spaniards imprisoned him and he conspired to preserve his reign.

## CHAPTER 23 ✳ OF THE LAST SUCCESSORS
## OF THE INCAS

The rest that follows what I have said has been dealt with at length in histo-ries of the Indies written by Spaniards, and because it is not to my present purpose I shall merely state the succession of the Incas that took place.[1] With Atahualpa dead in Cajamarca, and Huáscar in Cuzco, and Francisco Pizarro and his men having become masters of the realm, Manco Capac, the son of Huayna Capac, beseiged them in Cuzco and pressed them hard; and at last, wholly abandoning the land, he retired to Vilcabamba, far away in the moun-tains, and was able to maintain himself there thanks to their rugged nature.[2] The successor Incas stayed there up to Amaru, who was captured and put to death in the plaza in Cuzco, to the unbelievable grief of the Indians when they witnessed the man whom they considered their lord publicly killed. After this came the imprisonment of others from that lineage of the Incas. I met Don Carlos, grandson of Huayna Capac, son of Paulo, who was bap-tized and always favored the Spaniards' side against his brother Manco Ca-pac. During the viceroyalty of the Marqués de Cañete, Sayri Topa Inca left Vilcabamba and came to Ciudad de los Reyes in peace, and he was given the valley of Yucay, along with other properties, which a daughter of his inher-ited. This is the succession that is known today of that numerous and vastly rich family of the Incas, whose rule lasted for more than three hundred years, with eleven successors being counted in that realm up to the time when the line ceased altogether. In the other branch of the Urincuzco, which as stated above was also derived from the first Manco Capac, eight successors can be counted in the following order: Sinchi Roca was the successor to Manco

1. Colonial Spanish accounts of the conquest of Peru include Francisco Jerez, *Verdadera relación de la conquista del Perú y provincia del Cuzco llamada Nueva Castilla* (1534) and Pedro de Cieza de León, *Crónica del Perú* (1550). The work of Titu Cusi Yupanqui offers an indigenous Andean perspective on the same events. In 1570, Yupanqui, the penultimate Inca ruler at Vilcabamba, dictated his indigenous perspective of the history of the conquest, *Relación de la conquista del Perú*, to a priest shortly before dying.

2. Following Manco Capac's retreat to Vilcabamba, known thereafter as the "lost city of the Incas," the Inca maintained their rule despite persistent Spanish attempts to subjugate them. In 1571, under Viceroy Toledo's watch, the Inca stronghold at Vilcabamba finally was defeated. The Spanish brought the holdouts to Cuzco, where a public execution in 1572 of Tupac Amaru, the last Inca king, symbolized final defeat for the Inca Empire. The historical and cultural memory of Tupac Amaru has continued to serve as a powerful rallying point for Andean resistance to injustice.

Capac; successor to him was Capac Yupanqui; then came Luqui Yupanqui; then Mayta Capac, then Tarco Huaman; after him one of his sons, whom they do not name; and then Don Juan Tambo Maytapanaca. And let this suffice as to the origin and succession of the Incas who ruled the land of Peru, along with the rest of what has been said of their laws and government and the way in which they acted.

## CHAPTER 24 * OF THE KIND OF COMMONWEALTH THAT THE MEXICANS HAD

Although the kingdom, succession, and origin of the Mexicans, and the kind of commonwealth and government that they had, will become clear through the history that I intend to write, still I shall summarize here in a general way its most notable features, whose ampler declaration will be the history I will write later. The first way in which the government of the Mexicans seems to have shown civic organization was the method that they had, and always adhered to, of choosing a king. For from the first king that they had, named Acamapichtli, to the last, who was Moctezuma, the second of that name, none received the inheritance and succession of the realm except by legitimate nomination and election. This was at first the responsibility of the common people, although the nobles guided the affair. Later, at the time of Izcoatl the fourth king, through the counsel and orders of a wise and valiant man among them named Tlacaelel, four electors were appointed; and these, along with two lords or kings of peoples who were subject to the Mexican king, namely, the lord of Texcoco and the lord of Tacuba, were responsible for the election. As a rule they chose young men as kings, for their monarchs constantly went to war, and this function was almost exclusively what they wanted them for; and so they considered whether they were suitable for military action and took pleasure in it and valued it. After the election there were two kinds of festivities, one at the time the king took possession of his royal estate, when they went to the temple and performed great ceremonies and sacrifices over the brazier that they called divine, where fire always burned before the altar of their idol; and then there were many speeches and harangues by orators, for they were very diligent in this. The other and more solemn festivity was that of the coronation, for which the king first had to conquer in battle and bring a certain number of captives, who had to be sacrificed to their gods; and he entered in triumph with great pomp and was given a very solemn reception by the priests of the temple (who all went in procession playing different instruments and dispensing incense and singing) as well as laypeople and members of the court, who came out with sundry devices to receive the victorious king. The crown and royal insignia resembled a miter from the front and was lower behind, making it not entirely round because the front part was higher and came to a point at the top. It was the special privilege of the king of Texcoco to crown the king of Mexico with his own hands.

The Mexicans were very loyal and dutiful to their kings, and there is no evidence that they ever committed treason against them. Their histories tell that only their fifth king, named Tizoc, was killed with poison because he had been a coward and of little use. But there is no evidence that competition and ambition gave rise to dissension or factions among them, as often happens in communities. Rather, as will be seen in its proper place, there are accounts that the noblest of all the Mexicans refused the kingship because he believed that the commonwealth would be better served with another king. In the beginning, as the Mexicans were poor and lived in straitened circumstances, their kings were very moderate in their conduct and their court, but as they increased in power they increased in splendor and greatness until they reached the point of Moctezuma's opulence. Even if he had owned nothing more than his private zoo, it was a magnificent thing and its like has never been seen. For with all those fish and birds and reptiles and beasts there was something resembling a new Noah's Ark in his house; and for the ocean fish he had saltwater pools and for the river fish sweetwater pools, and food for the game birds and predatory birds, and for the wild beasts the same in great abundance, and a large number of Indians were occupied in maintaining and breeding these animals. When he saw that it was no longer possible to maintain some kind of fish or bird or wild animal, he had its likeness richly worked in precious stones or in gold or silver or sculpted in marble or stone. And for different kinds of living he had different houses and palaces: some were for pleasure, others for mourning and sorrow, and others for governing. And there were different rooms in his palace according to the rank of his lords, who served him with remarkable order and distinction.

### CHAPTER 25 * OF THE DIFFERENT RANKS AND ORDERS OF THE MEXICANS

They took great care to establish ranks for the lords and nobles, so that there would be recognition among them as to who was owed most honor. After the king, the highest rank was that of the four electors, who following the king's election were elected themselves, and were usually brothers or very close relatives of the king. These were called *tlacohecalcatl,* which means "princes of the throwing spears," a kind of weapon that they used a great deal. After these came the ones called *tlacatecatl,* which means "clipper or cutter of men." The third degree of dignity consisted of those called *ezuahuacatl,* which means "shedder of blood," but not by any means, only by scratching; all these titles were for warriors. There was another, fourth rank entitled *tlillancalqui,* which means "lord of the black house, or house of blackness" because of a certain soot with which the priests smeared themselves, which was used in their idolatries. These four ranks made up the supreme council, without whose opinion the king did not and could not do anything of importance; and when a king died, the man chosen as king had to come from one of these four ranks. There were other councils and courts in addition to those I have mentioned, and men who are experts on that land say that there were as many as in Spain, and different consistories with their judges and justices, and that there were other lower officials such as governors, councilors, lieutenants, constables of both higher and lower rank, and others of lesser degree, also under the command of these, in careful order; and all were subordinate to the four supreme princes who acted with the king, and only these four could issue a death sentence. The rest had to present a report to them about what they decreed and decided, and at certain times the king was informed of everything that was being done in his kingdom. There was also good administration and discipline in the system of taxation, for scattered all over the realm there were officials and accountants and treasurers who collected tribute and the royal revenues. Tribute was brought to the court at least once every month. The tribute consisted of everything that land and sea produced, clothing as well as food. In matters pertaining to their religion, or rather their superstition and idolatry, they used even greater care and precision, with a large number of ministers whose function was to teach the rites and ceremonies of their religion to the people. Hence an old Indian spoke well and wisely to a Christian priest who complained of the Indians, saying that they were not good Christians and did not understand God's law. "Have the fathers," he said, "make as much effort to turn the Indians into Christians as the ministers of our idols did in showing them their ceremonies, and with half of that effort we Indians will be very good Christians, for the law of Jesus Christ is much better, and the Indians do not accept it for lack of persons to teach them." Surely he spoke the truth, to our great humiliation and shame.

CHAPTER 26 * OF THE MEXICANS' WAY OF
FIGHTING AND THE MILITARY ORDERS
THAT THEY HAD

The Mexicans concentrated their chief point of honor on war, and so the nobles were the principal soldiers, and others who were not nobles rose to dignities and responsibilities through the glory of military exercise, and were counted among the nobles. They gave splendid prizes to those who had fought valiantly, and these enjoyed preeminence that no one else could possess. This made them fight fiercely. Their weapons were sharp knives made with flints set on both sides of a club, and this was so savage a weapon that it is said they could take off a horse's head with a downward stroke, cutting right through the neck. They used strong, heavy cudgels and also lances resembling pikes, and other spears for throwing, in which they were very skilled; they did a large part of their fighting with stones. For defense they used small bucklers and also shields, headpieces resembling helmets or morions, and a great deal of featherwork on their bucklers and helmets; and they dressed in the skins of tigers or lions or other savage beasts. They rapidly engaged the enemy hand to hand and were well trained in running and wrestling, for their principal way of winning was not so much to kill as to capture; and they made use of the captives, as I have said, in their sacrifices.[1] Moctezuma placed great emphasis on knighthood, instituting certain military orders and officers resembling the commanders of our military orders,

1. The main Aztec battle objective, namely, to capture and not to kill, appropriately distinguished by Acosta, has been identified by one scholar as a major reason for the defeat of the Mexica at the hands of the Spanish. See Inga Clendinnen, " 'Fierce and Unnatural Cruelty': Cortés and the Conquest of Mexico," *Representations* 33 (winter 1991): 65–100. Among the weapons described by Acosta, the "sharp knives" were made of obsidian. On Aztec methods of war and militarism, see Ross Hassig, *Aztec Warfare: Imperial Expansion and Political Control* (Norman: University of Oklahoma Press, 1988).

with different insignias. Among these the most preeminent were those who had the crown of their head tied with a red ribbon, and rich plumage from which strands hung to their shoulders, with red tassels of the same at the end; there were as many of these tassels as the feats of arms they had performed. The king also belonged to this order of knighthood, and so he is represented with this kind of plumage; and in Chapultepec, where Moctezuma and his son are carved on some rocks (a sight worth seeing), he is wearing the same costume made of a great deal of featherwork. There was another order that they called the Eagles, and others that were called Lions and Tigers. Usually these were the bravest warriors who distinguished themselves in war, and they always went to war wearing their insignias. There were others like Black Knights, who were not as important as the others; they had their hair cut above the ears all around. They went to war with their insignias like the other knights but armed only from the waist up; the more illustrious of them wore full body armor. All of these that I have mentioned could wear gold and silver and dress in fine cotton, and have gilded and painted vessels, and wear shoes. The common folk could use only earthenware vessels, nor could they use shoes or wear anything but *nequén,* which is a coarse sort of clothing. Each of the four orders had chambers of its own in the palace, with their titles: the first was called the chamber of the Princes; the second, of the Eagles; the third, of the Lions and Tigers; the fourth, of the Black Knights, and so on. The rest, the commoners, were below in more ordinary chambers, and if anyone lodged out of his proper place he incurred the death penalty.

### CHAPTER 27 * OF THE MEXICANS' GREAT CARE AND DILIGENCE IN BRINGING UP THEIR YOUTH

Nothing has amazed me more, or seemed more worthy of praise and remembrance, than the care and good order that the Mexicans had in bringing up their children. For, thoroughly understanding that all the good hopes of a commonwealth consist in the upbringing and instruction of the children and youth (with which Plato dealt at length in his books *De Legibus*), they took care to keep their children from idleness and license, which are the two plagues of that age, and to occupy them in useful and honorable pursuits. To this end there were in the temples places especially for children, like schools or boarding establishments, different from those of the temple boys and girls, which we discussed at length in their appointed place.[1] In these boarding establishments or schools there were a great many youths whom their parents had taken there voluntarily. They had tutors and teachers who taught and trained them in praiseworthy activities: to be polite, to respect their elders, to serve and to obey, giving them instruction about these matters; to make them agreeable to the great lords they were taught to sing and dance and were trained in the arts of war, such as shooting arrows and aiming at a target a dart or stick charred at one end, and handling a buckler skillfully, and wielding a sword. They were obliged to sleep badly and eat worse so as to accustom them from childhood to work and not be idle. Apart from the common number of these boys, there were others in these places who were the sons of lords and nobles, and they were given more special treatment. Their food was brought to them from home; they were entrusted to elders and ancients who looked after them and continually abjured them to be virtuous and live chastely, to be moderate in their diet, to fast, and to curb their gait and walk calmly and circumspectly. It was the custom to test them in difficult labors and exercises.

When they were grown, careful consideration was given to their inclinations: to the one whom they saw inclined toward war, occasion was given to prove it in battle; under the pretext of taking food and supplies to the troops, they sent them to war so that they could see what went on there and the travails that had to be undergone, to cause them to lose their fear by this means. Often they were loaded with very heavy burdens, so that if they showed good cheer in this they would more easily be admitted to the company of soldiers. And so it sometimes happened that a youth went into the field bearing burdens and returned a captain with signs of honor; others were so anxious to distinguish themselves that they were taken prisoner or killed, and they considered that the worst thing was to be taken prisoner, and so they outdid themselves not to become captives at the hands of their enemies. Hence those

1. Children aged twelve to fifteen, of both sexes, attended school at the temple in their *calpulli,* or district, where they received instruction in song and dance to prepare them to participate in public rituals. Each *calpulli* also had a *telpochcalli,* young men's house, where boys aged fifteen to twenty lived and worked. Sons of the nobility attended the *calmecac* during the same years. Military training and physical labor dominated the schedules of both commoners and nobles. The boys who trained in the *calmecac,* however, also learned the art of oration and might emerge with a special preparation for the priesthood.

who made efforts in this direction, who were usually the sons of noble and valiant folk, achieved their desires. Others who were inclined toward affairs of the temple and, to put it in our terms, wanted to be ecclesiastics, were taken out of the school when they reached a suitable age and placed in the temple apartments destined for the religious, also placing the insignias of priesthood upon them; and there they had their prelates and teachers who taught them everything concerning that ministry, and they had to remain in the ministry where they had dedicated themselves. The Mexicans used great order and method in bringing up their sons, and, if the same order existed nowadays in building houses and seminaries where these boys could be instructed, no doubt Christianity would flourish mightily among the Indians.[2] Some zealous persons have begun this, and the king and his council have showed that they favor it; but as it is not a profitable matter, it goes very slowly and is done without enthusiasm. May God lead us to feel shame, at least, for what the children of darkness did in their perdition, and not allow the children of light to lag so far behind in doing good.

### CHAPTER 28 * OF THE INDIANS' DANCES AND FESTIVITIES

Because it is an element of good government for a commonwealth to have its recreations and pastimes on appropriate occasions, it would be well to describe what the Indians — especially the Mexicans — were accustomed to do in this regard. No group of men living in common has been discovered that does not have some method of entertainment and recreation, with games or dances or pleasant exercises. In Peru I saw a sort of mock battle in which the competition between the two sides was so heated that the *puella* (for that was what they called it) became quite dangerous. I also saw any number of dances in which they imitated different occupations, such as those of shepherds, farmers, fishermen, and hunters; usually all these were danced with a very slow and deliberate sound, steps, and rhythm. There were others danced

2. In the aftermath of the Spanish conquest, formal education for the indigenous population was restricted to only a few male members of the elite, who attended schools run by missionaries, the most famous being Mexico's Colegio de Santa Cruz, run by Fray Bernardino de Sahagún in Tlatelolco. Native males received instruction in Latin and Nahuatl so they could learn Christian doctrine. Although Spanish priests expected them to become teachers of Christianity to their parents and their children, they banned the students from the priesthood based on their indigenous background.

by masked men, whom they call *huacones*, and both the masks and their movements were absolutely diabolical. Also, some men danced on the shoulders of other men, just as in Portugal they carry *pelas*, as they call them. The greater part of these dances were mere superstition and a kind of idolatry, for that was the way they worshiped their idols and gods. For this reason the priests have tried to avoid such dances as much as possible, although because a large part of them is pure recreation they still allow the Indians to sing and dance after their fashion. They play different instruments for these dances. Some are like flutes or pipes, others like drums, others like conch shells; the usual thing is for them to use their voices, all singing, with one or two reciting their poetry and the others coming in with the refrain. Some of these ballads of theirs were very ingenious and told a story; others were full of superstition, and still others were pure nonsense. The members of our society who work among them have tried to put things of our Holy Faith into their way of singing, and this has been found to be extremely useful, for they enjoy singing and chanting so much that they can spend whole days listening and repeating, never getting tired. They have also translated compositions and tunes of ours into their language, such as octaves and ballads and roundelays, and it is wonderful how well the Indians accept them and how much they enjoy them. Truly, this is a great way, and a very necessary one, to teach these people. In Peru these dances are generally called *taqui;* in other Indian provinces they are called *areitos;* in Mexico they are called *mitotes.*[1]

Nowhere was there such enthusiasm for games and dances as in New Spain, where even today one may see Indian acrobats dance admirably upon a tightrope and others standing on a tall, straight pole, where they dance and perform any number of variations. Others move and raise and twirl a very heavy piece of wood with the soles of their feet and their thighs, something that seems incredible unless it is seen. They do any number of other tricks of great skill, climbing, jumping, turning, carrying heavy weights, and accept-

1. The reference to dancing in Peru, the *taqui,* recalls the messianic movement of Taki Onqoy, literally "dancing sickness," that rippled through the Andean highlands in the early 1560s. Followers were thrown into frenzied movement as native deities took control of their bodies and danced to the theme of a nativist alliance that promised to rid the Andes of Spanish culture and control. For the reports by the main ecclesiastic sent to investigate Taki Onqoy, see Luis Millones, ed., *Las informaciones de Cristóbal de Albornoz,* in *El retorno de las huacas: Estudios y documentos sobre el Taki Onqoy Siglo XVI* (Lima: Instituto de Estudios Peruanos, Sociedad Peruana de Psicoanálisis, 1990).

ing blows heavy enough to break iron, and very remarkable examples of all of these can be seen. But the method of recreation most enjoyed by the Mexicans is the solemn *mitote,* which is a dance that had so much prestige among them that sometimes the kings danced it, and were not obliged to do so like the king Don Pedro of Aragon with the barber of Valencia. Usually this dance, or *mitote,* was performed in the courtyards of the temples and the royal palaces, which were the most spacious. In the center of the courtyard they placed two instruments: one was made like a drum and the other had the shape of a barrel, made all in one piece and hollow within, set upon a figure resembling a man or an animal, or on a pillar. Both were tuned in such a way as to be in good harmony with each other. With them they made different sounds, and the songs were many and various; all sang and danced to the beat, so uniformly that there was no difference between one and another, all moving in unison, in their voices as well as in the movements of their feet, which were so skillful that it was a wonderful thing to see. In these dances two circles of people were formed: in the center, where the instruments were, they placed the elders and the lords and most important people, and they danced and sang standing up, almost without moving. Around these, and at a good distance from them, the rest came out by twos, dancing in unison with more movement and making various changes in their steps and deliberate leaps, and among them made a very broad and spacious circle. In these dances they brought out the most precious costumes that they owned, and many jewels, according to the means of each. They took great care in performing them, and so these kinds of dances were taught them from childhood. Although many of them were performed in honor of the gods, they had not been instituted for that purpose; rather, as has been said, they were a form of recreation and rejoicing for the people. Hence it is not a good thing to deprive the Indians of them but rather to try to prevent any superstition from becoming mingled in them. In Tepotzotlán, which is a town seven leagues from Mexico, I saw the dance, or *mitote,* that I have described performed in the courtyard of the church, and it seemed to me a good thing to occupy and entertain the Indians on feast days; for they need some recreation, and recreation that is public and harms no one has fewer disadvantages than others that the Indians might perform by themselves should these dances be taken away from them. And generally speaking it is good to allow the Indians what we can of their customs and usages (if there is no admixture of their former errors), and this is in agreement with the advice of Pope Saint Gregory, to try to channel their festivals and rejoicings toward the honor of God and the saints whose feasts are being celebrated.[2] What I have said is probably sufficient, in general terms, concerning the usages and customs of the Mexicans, of their origin and development and empire, for it is a very long matter and to understand it fully would be most desirable; hence we will leave its full treatment for another book.

2. Acosta was surprisingly tolerant of these dancing rituals when he argued that "it is not a good thing to deprive the Indians" of this recreation. However, he also believed that the dances held the potential to promote idolatry and thus urged missionaries to "prevent any superstition" in the actions. Acosta's notion that Spanish missionaries could convince Andeans how to interpret the dances represented an attempt to divorce the practice of ritual dancing from native structures of meaning. Inga Clendinnen has explored the manner in which Mesoamerican structures of meaning continued to operate through religious practices of drinking and dancing. See her "Ways to the Sacred: Reconstructing 'Religion' in Sixteenth-Century Mexico," *History and Anthropology* 5 (1990): 105–41.

# BOOK VII

### CHAPTER I * WHY IT IS IMPORTANT TO KNOW OF THE INDIANS' DEEDS, ESPECIALLY THOSE OF THE MEXICANS

Any history, if it is a true one and well written, brings no little profit to the reader. For, as the sage says, "What is it that hath been? the same thing that shall be. What is it that hath been done? the same that shall be done."[1] Human affairs resemble each other greatly, and some peoples learn from what has befallen others. There are no peoples so barbaric that they do not have something worthy of praise, nor are there any people so civilized and humane that they stand in no need of correction. And so, even if the account or history of the Indians were to have no other result than that of being an ordinary history and account of events that indeed took place, it deserves to be received as a useful thing.[2] And an account of their doings must not be despised merely because they are Indians, for in the natural sciences we see that authors write not only about noble animals and famous plants and precious stones but also of the lower animals and common plants, and rocks

---

[1]. Ecclesiastes, 1, 9 (O'G).

[2]. In large part, the "account of the Indians" contained in book VII is a condensed version of the manuscript that Juan de Tovar passed to Acosta. Since Acosta had little influence in the production of the historical account of Mexican history, the way Acosta chooses to use and frame the information for his European audience is most revealing of his philosophical intent. His introductory chapter instructs the reader to approach the coming chapters with an open mind to the superb organization of the Aztec, and to a lesser extent the Inca, governments. To buttress the evidence of organized states, Acosta makes comparisons with imperial Rome. Given Rome's place at the Catholic center of the sixteenth-century world, these comparisons imply the potential for Mexico and Peru to evolve into centers of Christian knowledge and teaching. Like a priest delivering a sermon, Acosta highlights for his audience the lessons of this final book in his moral history: the European audience should respect the history of the Mexicans, as he refers to them, and use that history to learn how best to approach the evangelical project in the Indies.

and very ordinary things, for in them also there are properties worthy of
consideration. Thus, even if this account of mine were only history, as it is,
and not fable or fiction, it is a subject not unworthy of being written and
read. But there is another very particular reason, which is that because it deals
with peoples who are held in little esteem, we value what is worthy of memory in them for that very reason; and because those nations are in many ways
different from our Europe, our pleasure is all the greater in fully discovering
their origins, their ways of behaving, and the things that have happened to
them both for good and ill. And not only pleasure but also profit, particularly
for those who will be called upon to deal with them; for knowledge of their
affairs tends to make them trust ours and shows us to a considerable degree
how they should be treated. It even greatly diminishes the widespread and
foolish contempt in which they are held by Europeans, who deny that these
people can possess the qualities of reasonable and prudent men. To dissipate
this common opinion, nothing can serve better than a truthful narration of
these peoples' deeds. I shall therefore, with God's help, deal as briefly as I can
with the origin and successions and notable deeds of the Mexicans. And in
the last instance the reader will be able to understand the means chosen by
Most Holy God in sending to these nations the light of the gospels of his
only begotten son Jesus Christ Our Lord, whom I beseech to guide this little
work of mine and make it redound to the glory of his divine greatness, and be
of some use to these people, to whom he has communicated the law of his
Holy Gospel.

### CHAPTER 2 * OF THE ANCIENT DWELLERS IN NEW SPAIN AND HOW THE NAHUATLACAS CAME THERE

The first and ancient inhabitants of the provinces that we call New Spain
were very savage forest-dwelling men who lived solely from hunting, and for
this reason were called Chichimecas. They did not sow or cultivate the land,
nor did they live in groups, for their whole occupation and life was hunting,
and in this they were very expert. They dwelt among the crags and the
roughest places of the mountains, living like beasts without any form of
government, and totally naked. They hunted deer, hare, rabbits, weasels,
moles, mountain lions, birds, and even loathsome things like serpents, liz-

ards, mice, locusts, and worms, and nourished themselves with these things and with herbs and roots. They slept in the hills, in caves and thickets; the women went with their husbands on these hunting expeditions, leaving their little ones hanging from the branches of a tree, placed in a reed basket and sated with milk, until their return with the game. They had no chief, nor did they recognize one, nor did they worship any gods or have rites or any religion whatsoever.[1] Even today there are people of this sort in New Spain, who make a living with their bows and arrows, and they are very dangerous because they band together to do evil and launch attacks; and the Spaniards have been unable to reduce them to civilized behavior and obedience either by fair means or foul, by wiles or by force. For, because they have neither towns nor fixed abodes, fighting with them is exactly like hunting beasts, for they scatter and hide in the roughest and most thickly wooded parts of the mountains. This is the style of life in many provinces even today in different parts of the Indies. And it is this kind of wild Indians that the books *De procuranda Indorum salute* treat when they state that they must be compelled and tamed with reasonable force and that they must first be taught to be men and then to be Christians. It is said that the Indians called Otomíes in New Spain were of this sort, for they are commonly poor Indians and live in rough places; but they do live in towns and groups and have some sort of polity, even for matters connected with Christianity, and those who know them well find them no less apt and capable than Indians who are richer and held to be more civilized. To come to the point, these Chichimecas and Otomíes who were said to be the first dwellers in New Spain, because they did not reap or sow, left the best and most fertile part of it unpeopled; and that part was occupied by nations that came from elsewhere, and because they had some social organization they are called Nahuatlaca, which means "people who express themselves and speak clearly," unlike those others who were barbarous and did not possess the use of reason.

These second Nahuatlaca settlers came from a different and faraway land in the north, where a realm called New Mexico has recently been discovered.[2]

---

1. Acosta takes great pains to establish the unstructured society of the Chichimeca peoples, and his assertion that these people had no chief, gods, or religion is an exaggeration. His disdain for the Chichimeca stemmed in part from a fear acknowledged by contemporary Spaniards about the fierce nature of the seminomadic peoples who continued to challenge colonial insertions into northern New Spain.

2. Acosta's reference to New Mexico suggests that his portrayal of early Aztec history was colored by reports

In that land there are two provinces: one is called Aztlán, which means "place of herons," and the other is called Teuculhuacán, which means "land of those who have divine ancestors." In these provinces the Nahuatlacas have their houses and tilled fields and their gods and rites and ceremonies with good order and polity; they are divided into seven clans, or nations, and because in that land each clan has its recognized site and place the Nahuatlacas depict their origin and descendance as a cave and say that they came to settle the land of Mexico from seven caves; and they describe this in their books, depicting seven caves with their descendants. The time that has elapsed since the Nahuatlacas left their land, according to the computation in their books, is by now more than eight hundred years; by our reckoning it was the year of Our Lord eight hundred and twenty when they began to leave their land. It took them eighty full years to reach the land of Mexico where they now dwell. The cause of so long a journey was that their gods (who were undoubtedly demons that spoke visibly with them) had persuaded them to go seeking new lands with such and such characteristics; and so they moved along, exploring the land and looking for the signs that their idols had given them, and where they found good places they settled them one after another and sowed and reaped. And as they found better places they would abandon those already settled, but leaving some folk there still, mostly the old and sick and folk who were exhausted, and also leaving fine buildings, traces of which can be found today along the route that they took. In this slow march they spent eighty years on a journey that could be accomplished in a month, and thus entered the land of Mexico in the year nine hundred and two of our reckoning.

---

from the northern frontiers of the Viceroyalty of New Spain. Francisco Vásquez de Coronado led the first expeditions into New Mexico in 1540 looking for the mythic seven cities of Cibola. Although the expedition failed to find the fabled Cibola, they did meet up with Pueblo communities. Franciscan missionaries saw riches where the explorers did not because the native peoples were potential candidates for their evangelical projects. Hard pressed to find unbaptized communities in the Valley of Mexico, the Franciscans headed north to New Mexico in 1581 and 1582 to claim it as their new missionary territory. They made careful reports on the peoples, customs, and languages as they sized up their missionary task. Interested as he was in missionary methods and achievements, Acosta surely would have learned of these projects and reports during his stay in the City of Mexico. On exploration in this region, see David J. Weber, *The Spanish Frontier in North America* (New Haven: Yale University Press, 1992). On the establishment of the Franciscan presence, see Ramón Gutiérrez, *When Jesus Came, the Corn Mothers Went Away* (Stanford: Stanford University Press, 1991), esp. 38–94.

CHAPTER 3 * HOW THE SIX NAHUATLACA
CLANS SETTLED THE LAND OF MEXICO

These seven clans that I have mentioned did not all set out at the same time. The first were the Xochimilcas, which means "people of the fields of flowers." These settled the banks of the great lake of Mexico toward the south and founded a city of that name and many other places. Much later those of the second clan arrived, called Chalcas, which means "people of the mouths," and they also founded a city of that name, sharing boundaries with the Xochimilcas. The third to arrive were the Tepanecas, which means "people of the bridge," and they also settled on the western shore of the lake. These increased in numbers so much that they called the chief city of their province Azcapotzalco, which means "anthill," and for a long time they were very powerful. After these came the people who settled Texcoco, who are those of Culhua, which means "crooked people," for in their land there was a very crooked mountain. And thus the lake was surrounded by these four nations, for the last of them settled in the east and the Tepanecas in the north. These people of Texcoco were held to be very courtly and well spoken, and their language is very elegant.[1] Later came the Tlatluicas, which means "people of the mountains." These were the most uncivilized of all, and because they found all the level ground around the lake occupied as far as the mountains, they went over to the far side of them and discovered a very fertile and broad and warm land, where they established many large towns; and they called the chief town of their province Quauhnahuac, which means "place where the voice of the eagle sounds." Our common folk corrupt this name to Cuernavaca, and that province is the one known as the Marquesado today.[2] Those

1. The flattering description of the Texcocans, here and throughout book VII, must be read with the understanding that Diego Durán, a major source of information for Tovar, and hence for Acosta, lived most of his life in Texcoco and drew his material from native informants from the region.

2. Acosta's refers to the region of the Tlahuics as Quauhnahuac, "the place where the voice of the eagle sounds." Generally, Cuauhnahuac is the preconquest name attributed to the town and defined as "near the forest" or "place of the trees." Spaniards garbled the pronunciation of the word and sounded out Cuernavaca as the colonial and modern name of the town. Cuernavaca sat in the enormous province of the Marquesado del Valle de Oaxaca, Hernán Cortés's prize for his heroic efforts in the conquest of Mexico. Cortés resided in Cuernavaca and the town of Coyoacán but enjoyed tribute from the local native populations as well as civil jurisdiction in the Marquesado, an area including the modern states of Morelos, Oaxaca, Veracruz, and Mexico. The colonial history of region is explored by Robert Haskett in *Indigenous Rulers: An*

of the sixth generation, who are the Tlaxcaltecas, which means "bread people," went eastward over the mountains, crossing the Sierra Nevada, where the famous volcano is that lies between the City of Mexico and the City of Los Angeles.[3] They found very ample places; they spread out a great deal and built splendid buildings. They founded many towns and cities, and gave their own name to the chief city in their province, Tlaxcala. This is the nation that aided the Spaniards, and with their help the Spaniards won the land; and hence to this day they pay no tribute and enjoy a general exemption. At the time when all these tribes were settling the land, its ancient dwellers the Chichimecas showed no displeasure, nor did they make any resistance; they only departed and, seemingly astonished, concealed themselves in the most hidden part of the crags. But those who lived on the other side of the Sierra Nevada, where the Tlaxcallans settled, refused to allow what the other Chichimecas had countenanced; rather, they began to defend the land, and as they were giants, according to the Indians' histories, they tried to expel the intruders by force. But their great strength was overcome by the craft of the Tlaxcallans, who allayed their suspicions and, feigning peace with them, invited them to a great banquet; and they had folk lying in ambush, and when all of them lay in a drunken stupor the Tlaxcallans secretly stole their arms, which consisted of great clubs and wooden shields and swords and other kinds of weapons. Having done this, they suddenly fell upon them; and in trying to defend themselves and not finding their weapons the Chichimecas rushed to some nearby trees and, seizing the branches, stripped them off as if they had been so many leaves of lettuce. But at last, as the Tlaxcallans had come armed and in good order, they routed the giants and caused such ravages among them that not one was left alive. No one should be astonished or believe that the story of these giants is a fable, for even today bones of men of incredible size are still found. When I was in the City of Mexico in fifteen hundred and eighty-six, one of these giants was found buried on one of our properties, which we call Jesús del Monte; and they brought to show us a tooth, which, without exaggeration, was fully as large as a man's fist, and the

---

*Ethnohistory of Town Government in Colonial Cuernavaca* (Albuquerque: University of New Mexico Press, 1991).

3. The twin volcanoes, Popocatepetl and Iztaccihuatl, "smoking mountain" and "white woman," sit between the City of Mexico and the City of Los Angeles, or modern Puebla. Acosta probably referred to Popo, the higher of the two, although both would have been visible from Mexico City during the sixteenth century.

rest of the bones were in proportion.[4] I saw the tooth and was amazed by its extraordinary size.

After this victory the Tlaxcallans became peaceful and all the other clans were subdued, and the six foreign clans that I mentioned always maintained friendship among themselves, marrying their sons and daughters to each other and peacefully sharing boundaries, and each one with honest competition seeking to broaden and improve its polity, until they all attained great increase and power. The savage Chichimecas, seeing what was happening, began to acquire some civilized traits, and to cover their flesh and feel shame about things that had not caused them shame before, now that they had dealings with those other folk; and, with communication, they lost their fear and gradually learned from them. Now they made huts and rude dwellings to live in and had some social organization, choosing their chiefs and acknowledging their superiority. And so they emerged to a considerable degree from that bestial style of life they had had, but always in the hills and mountains and living separately from the others. I am convinced that most of the provinces and nations in the Indies have developed in this same way: the first of them were savages and, in order to maintain themselves by hunting, they little by little penetrated inhospitable lands and discovered a new world, living in it almost like beasts; they had no dwelling places nor roofs nor cultivated fields, nor livestock nor king, nor law nor God nor the use of reason. Later others, seeking new and better lands, settled the better parts and instituted order and polity and a sort of commonwealth, though still a very savage one. Later still, either from these or from other nations, men who possessed more energy and craft than the rest began to subdue and oppress the less powerful, until they formed great kingdoms and empires. Thus it was in Mexico, thus in Peru, and thus it undoubtedly is in all places where there are cities and commonwealths founded by these barbarians. Hence I have been confirmed in my belief, with which I dealt at length in my first book, that the first settlers of the West Indies came by land, and that in consequence all the territory of the Indies is contiguous with that of Asia, Europe, and Africa, and the New World with the Old World, although up to the present the

4. Acosta takes advantage of an eyewitness experience to embellish his information from the "Tovar Manuscript." The talk of giants, he informs the reader, is not as mythical as it might sound. He himself was privy to an excavation of giant bones at a Jesuit hacienda in Mexico. Unknown to Acosta, and others during this era, the bones were the remains of large prehistoric animals, probably mammoths, and not oversized humans.

land that joins these two worlds has not been discovered.[5] Or if a sea intervenes it is so narrow that animals and men can cross it by swimming, or in primitive boats. But, leaving aside these theories, let us return to our history.

### CHAPTER 4 * OF THE DEPARTURE OF THE MEXICANS AND THEIR ROUTE AND THE FOUNDING OF MICHOACÁN

Three hundred and two years having passed since the six clans I have described left their land and settled in that of New Spain, and when the land was well populated and reduced to order and polity, those of the seventh cave or family, which is the Mexican nation, arrived in it; like the others, it came from the provinces of Aztlán and Teuculhuacán. They were a well-organized and civil people and very warlike. These Indians worshiped the idol called Huitzilopochtli, which has been described at length above; and the devil, who resided in that idol, spoke to and easily influenced that nation. And so he ordered them to leave their land, promising to make them princes and lords of all the provinces that the other six nations had settled; that he would give them very extensive lands, much gold, silver, precious stones, feathers, and rich mantles. Accordingly they set forth with their idol placed in an ark made of reeds, carried by four chief priests with whom he communicated; and he revealed to them in secret the events of their journey, telling them what was going to happen, giving them laws and showing them rites and ceremonies and sacrifices. They took not a step without the consent and orders of this idol; he told them when to travel and when to stop and where, and they obeyed him unquestioningly. The first thing they did wherever they stopped was to build a house or tabernacle for their false god, and they always set it in the middle of the camp that they established, with the ark always placed on an altar such as the Christian church uses. Having done this, they would sow grain for bread and the other vegetables that they used; but they were so steadfast in obeying their god that if he thought it well to harvest the crop they would do so, and if not, when he ordered them to break camp, everything was left to feed the old and sick and exhausted folk, whom they

5. Again, Acosta moves beyond the Tovar text with a reiteration of his distinct theory, postulated in chapter 20 of book I, that "the first settlers of the western Indies came by land," an observation that serves to incorporate this book on early Mexican history into the structure of the entire work.

left behind everywhere they settled so that the whole land would be occupied by those of their nation.

Perhaps this departure and pilgrimage of the Mexicans may seem to resemble the exodus from Egypt and the journey made by the children of Israel; for the Mexicans, like the Israelites, were admonished to leave and seek the promised land, and both peoples carried their god with them as a guide, and consulted the ark and made tabernacles, and their god advised them and gave them laws and ceremonies, and one people as well as the other spent a large number of years in reaching the promised land. That there is a resemblance in all this, and in many other things as well, between what is told in the history of the Mexicans and that which Divine Scripture tells of the Israelites, is assuredly the case.[1] For the devil, prince of pride, tried when he dealt with these people and subjected them to his will to imitate what the most high and true God did with his people; because, as I have mentioned above, Satan has a strange compulsion to resemble God, whose familiarity and dealings with men this mortal enemy falsely attempted to usurp. A demon who conversed with men in this way, like this demon Huitzilopochtli, has never been seen before. And who he was is unmistakable, for rites more superstitious and sacrifices more cruel and inhuman than those he showed to his followers have never been witnessed or even heard of; in a word, they are dictates of the enemy of the human race himself.

The chief and captain whom these people followed was named Mexi, and from him was later derived the name of Mexico and the name of his nation the Mexicans. Traveling onward, therefore, as slowly as the other six nations had done, settling, sowing, and harvesting in different places (of which there are signs and ruins to this very day), and undergoing many trials and perils, after a long time they came to the province called Michoacán, which means "land of fish," for it has many large and beautiful lakes; and there, pleased with the location and coolness of the land, they determined to rest and remain. But on consulting their idol and learning that he was not content

---

1. Note that Acosta's description of the seventh clan, the Mexica, contains elements indicating the potential for civilization that other clans did not. They are "well-organized," "civil," and have laws, rites, and ceremonies, albeit ones urged upon them by a devilish deity. Moreover, he compares the journey of the Mexica to the journey of the Israelites. All of these attributes are clues to his European audience that the Mexica have traveled an evolutionary path to salvation through Christianity, the final destination for which will be cleared by the Spaniards among the ruins of Tenochtitlán.

with the place, they asked him at least to leave some of their people there to settle so good a land; and being satisfied with this, he taught them a trick in order to do it. And it was that, when the men as well as the women entered a beautiful lake called Pátzcuaro, they must steal the clothing of those who were to remain behind and then quietly break camp and go away, and this is what they did. When the others, who had not noticed the trick because of their pleasure in bathing, emerged and found themselves despoiled of their clothing, and thus deceived and left abandoned by their companions, they were very hurt and vexed; and in order to demonstrate the hatred they felt for them it is said that they changed their style of dress and even their language. At least it is certain that these folk of Michoacán were always enemies of the Mexicans and hence came to congratulate the Marqués del Valle for the victory he won when he conquered Mexico.[2]

### CHAPTER 5 * OF WHAT BEFELL THEM IN MALINALCO AND IN TULA AND CHAPULTEPEC

There is a distance of more than fifty leagues between Michoacán and Mexico. On the way lies Malinalco, where it happened that, when they complained to their idol about a woman in their company, a great sorceress whose name was Sister of their God (for with her evil arts she caused them much harm, trying in a certain way to make them adore her as a goddess), the idol spoke in a dream to one of those old men who carried the ark and commanded him to console the people in his name, again making them great promises; and he told them to leave that sister of his behind with all her family, for she was cruel and evil, breaking camp at night and in total silence, leaving not a trace of where they had gone. This they did, and the sorceress, finding herself tricked and left alone with her family, founded a town there

2. It is certain that the native peoples of Michoacán, the Tarascans, showed allegiance to the Spanish, and likely congratulated Cortés, the Marqués del Valle, for defeating them. The enmity between the Tarascans and the Mexica, however, likely grew out of fifteenth-century conflicts rather than the divisiveness by the lake of Paztcuaro described here. Doris Heyden, a scholar of preconquest Mexican history generally and the Durán manuscript specifically, asserts that "it is doubtful that the Aztecs passed by Patzcuaro on their migration" and suggests that their hatred for one another grew out of later battles where the Mexica tried unsuccessfully to conquer the Tarascans. See the introduction to Durán, *The History of the Indies of New Spain,* 23.

that is called Malinalco; and the natives of Malinalco are held to be great sorcerers, as children of such a mother.[1]

The Mexicans, because their numbers had greatly diminished through these divisions and through the numbers of sick and exhausted folk they had successively left behind, wanted to recuperate and stopped in a spot called Tula, which means "place of reeds." There the idol commanded them to dam a very large river and cause it to spread over a large plain, and by the arts that he taught them they surrounded with water a beautiful hill called Coatepec and made a large lake, around which they planted willows, poplars, junipers, and other trees. A large number of fish began to breed there, and many birds came, and a beautiful spot was created. As the place seemed good to them and they were tired of journeying, many wished to settle there and go no farther. The devil became terribly angry with this and, threatening his priests with death, ordered them to remove the dam from the river and let it return to its previous course; and he said that he would administer the punishment that they deserved to those who had disobeyed him. And because the devil's nature is to do evil, and because Divine Justice often permits those who take him as their god to be turned over to their executioner, it happened that at midnight a great noise was heard in a certain part of the camp; and in the morning, when they went there, they found lying dead all those who had wanted to stay there. And the manner in which they were killed was that their breasts were opened and their hearts torn out, for this was the way they were found; and thus their charming god showed those unhappy folk the kind of sacrifices that pleased him, which was to open men's breasts and tear out their hearts, as they did ever afterward in their horrible sacrifices.

After this punishment and after the land had dried up because the lake had lost its water, they consulted their god and by his will and command went forward little by little until they came to within a league of the City of Mexico, to Chapultepec, a place famous for its restorative qualities and coolness. They fortified themselves on this hill, fearing the nations that had already settled that land, for all were their enemies, chiefly because the Mexicans had been defamed by a certain Copil, son of that sorceress whom they had left behind in Malinalco; sent by his mother, after a long interval he had come in search of the Mexicans and tried to incite the Tepanecas and the

1. The woman Malinalxochitl or Wild Grass Flower, was the sister of the god Huitzilopochtli.

other neighboring nations, and even the Chalcas, against the Mexicans, so that they came in arms to destroy them. Copil went to a hill called Acapilco, which is in the midst of the lagoon, anticipating the destruction of his enemies; but warned by their idol they attacked him, and taking him unawares killed him and brought his heart to their god, who commanded them to throw it in the lake. And they fancy that from it grew a cactus, where the City of Mexico was founded. The Chalcas and other nations began to fight with the Mexicans, who had chosen as their captain a brave man named Huitzilihuitl, and in the course of the battle he was captured and killed by the other side; but the Mexicans did not lose heart on account of this, and, fighting valiantly despite their enemies, they hacked their way through their squadrons and, carrying their old folk and their women and children in their midst, reached Atlacuihuatan, a town of the Culhuas, whom they found celebrating a festival, and there they made themselves strong. Neither the Chalcas nor the others pursued them out of pure shame at seeing themselves defeated by so few when they were so many, and they retired to their towns.

## CHAPTER 6 * OF THE WAR THEY WAGED WITH THOSE OF CULHUACÁN

Following the idol's counsel, they sent their messengers to the lord of Culhuacán asking him for a place to dwell in; and after he had consulted with his people he assigned them to Tizaapán, which means "white waters," expecting that they would be lost and would perish; for there were a large number of vipers and serpents and other poisonous creatures in that place, which bred on a nearby hill.[1] But, persuaded and instructed by their devil, they willingly accepted what they were offered and by diabolical arts gathered up all those animals and even used them for sustenance, for they ate them willingly and without harm to themselves. When the lord of Culhuacán saw this, and observed that they had made fields and were tilling the land, he thought it

---

1. Culhuacán, believed to be one of the earliest settlements on Lake Texcoco, served as a refuge for the Toltecs in the wake of the destruction of their home of Tula, circa 1100 A.D. This Toltec legacy made the town distinct and even influential under the Aztec Empire, according to Nigel Davies, who has written extensively on the area, including *The Aztec Empire, The Toltec Resurgence* (Norman: University of Oklahoma Press, 1987). A richly detailed history of Culhuacán under Spanish rule, based largely on an analysis of indigenous wills, is S. Cline, *Colonial Culhuacán, 1580–1600: A Social History of an Aztec Town* (Albuquerque: University of New Mexico Press, 1986).

well to admit them to his city and deal with them on terms of friendship; but the god that the Mexicans worshiped (as is usual with the Evil One) never did anything good unless to do more evil. And so he said to his priests that it was not the place where he wanted them to stay, and that they would have to leave there by fomenting a war, and to do this they must seek out a woman who would be called the goddess of discord; and the scheme was to send and ask the king of Culhuacán for his daughter to be queen of the Mexicans and wife of their god. Their embassy pleased him, and he gave her to them with much finery and many attendants. On the very night that she arrived, by order of the murderer whom they worshiped, they cruelly killed the girl and, flaying her skin (which they do with great skill), dressed a boy in it and placed her clothing on it and set her beside the idol thus arrayed, dedicating her as a goddess and the wife of their god; and from that time onward they always worshiped her, later making an idol that they named Toci, which is to say "our grandmother."[2] Not content with this act of cruelty, they deceitfully invited the king of Culhuacán to come and worship his daughter, who was now consecrated as a goddess. And when he came with rich gifts and a great retinue they took him to the chapel where their idol was, which was very dark, so that he could offer sacrifice to his daughter, who was within. But it happened that the incense that they offered in a brazier, according to their custom, flamed up, and by the flame he recognized his daughter's skin. And when he realized the cruelty and deceit that had been practiced on him he came out, shouting loudly, and all his people attacked the Mexicans angrily and furiously until they forced them to retire to the lake, to the point that they nearly drowned in it. The Mexicans, while defending themselves and throwing certain spears that they used, with which they severely wounded their enemies, at last regained dry land; and, abandoning that place, they scattered around the lake, badly shattered and dripping wet, with the women and children weeping and howling against them and against the god who had placed them in such a plight. They had to cross a river in a place where

---

2. The actions of the Mexica toward the lord of Culhuacán, Achitometl, in this plot involving the marriage and sacrifice of the king's daughter symbolize, on the one hand, the desire of the Mexica to make political alliances with the more powerful Toltec-based town through the traditional practice of intermarriage. The tragic fate of the daughter illustrates the resentment the Mexica felt for having been sent by the king to dwell in the undesirable land at Tizaapán. Although the king's daughter died, she became a central part of Aztec history and religion as Toci, the powerful earth mother and goddess of fertility.

there was no ford, and devised rough rafts out of their shields and spears and reeds, and so crossed over. At last, circling around Culhuacán, they came to Iztapalapa and from there to Acatzintitlán, and then to Itzacalco, and finally, in a spot occupied today by the hermitage of San Antón, to the gates of Mexico and the district that today is called San Pablo; and their idol consoled them in their travails and encouraged them with promises of great things to come.

### CHAPTER 7 * OF THE FOUNDING OF MEXICO

Now the time had come for the father of lies to fulfill his promise to his people, who could no longer endure so many wanderings and travails and dangers.[1] It happened that some old men who were sorcerers or priests entered a dense thicket and came upon a spring of very clear, beautiful water that seemed to be made of silver; and as they looked around they observed that the trees were all white, and the ground white, and the fish white, and everything that they saw was white. Astonished by this, they recalled a prophecy made by their god, who had described this to them as a sign of the place where they were to rest and become lords over the other peoples; weeping for joy, they returned to the people with the good news. On the following night Huitzilopochtli appeared in a dream to an old priest and told him that they must search in that lake for a cactus growing out of a stone; according to what the god said, it was the place where, by his orders, they had thrown the heart of their enemy Copil, son of the sorceress. And on that cactus they would see a most beautiful eagle feeding on some very colorful birds, and when they saw this they would know that it was the place where their city was to be founded, a city that would prevail over all others and be famous in the world. In the morning the old man, gathering together all the people from the eldest to the youngest, made them a long speech about how much they owed their god and about the revelation he had had that night, though unworthy of receiving it; he concluded that all must go in search of that happy place that was promised to them, and this aroused so much devotion and joy in everyone that they undertook the task without delay. And, dividing into groups among all that expanse of reeds and canebrakes

1. Scholarly consensus cites the year 1325 A.D. as the approximate date of the founding of the Mexica capital Tenochtitlán.

and sedge in the lake, they began to search for signs of the revelation of this greatly desired place. That day they discovered the spring of the day before, but it was very different, for it did not run white but red as blood and divided into two streams, one of which was a very dark blue, something which astonished them and denoted a great mystery, as they believed.

At last, after much searching here and there, the cactus growing out of a rock appeared, and on it was a royal eagle with wings opened and spread wide, turned toward the sun and receiving its warmth; all around him was a great variety of rich bird feathers, white, red, yellow, blue, and green, of the fine quality they use to make pictures. The eagle had a very beautiful bird in its claws. As soon as they saw it and recognized the place of the oracle, all knelt and offered great veneration to the eagle, and it also bowed its head to them, looking all around. There were great cries and demonstrations of devotion and offerings of thanks to the creator and to their great god Huitzilo-pochtli, who was their father in everything and had always told them the truth. For this reason they gave the name of Tenochtitlán to the city that they founded there, which means "a cactus on a stone"; and to this very day on their arms and insignia there is an eagle on a cactus with a bird in one claw and the other on the cactus.

On the following day, by common accord, they built a hermitage next to the cactus where the eagle had been so that the ark of their god might rest there until they had the means of making him a splendid temple; and so they made it out of grass and mud and covered it with straw. Then, after some consultation, they decided to buy stones and wood and lime from their neighbors in exchange for fish and frogs and shrimp; and also ducks and widgeons and cormorants and other kinds of water birds, all of which they fished for and hunted with extraordinary diligence in that lake, which has an abundance of all these things. They went with them to the markets of the Tepaneca cities and towns and those of Texcoco, which were near each other, and by dint of much concealment and deception they gradually amassed what they needed to build their city; and, having made a better chapel for their idol out of stone and lime, they began to close off a large part of the lake with slabs of stone and masonry. After they had done this, one night the idol spoke to one of their priests as follows: "Tell all the Mexicans that the princi-pal lords must divide into four large districts, with their relatives and friends and dependents, taking as a central point the house you have made for my repose, and the members of each group shall build whatever they like in their district." This was put into practice, and these are the four principal districts of Mexico, which today are called San Juan, Santa María la Redonda, San Pablo, and San Sebastián. When the Mexicans had been distributed among these four districts, their god commanded them to divide among themselves the gods that he would indicate and that each of the four chief districts must name and designate other special areas where those gods would be worshiped; and thus many small districts were subordinated to each of these, according to the number of idols that their god ordered them to worship; and they called these *calpultetco,* which means "god of the districts." This is the way in which the city of Mexico, Tenochtitlán, was founded and how from small beginnings it grew to be very great.

### CHAPTER 8 * OF THE REBELLION OF TLATELOLCO AND THE FIRST KING CHOSEN BY THE MEXICANS

After the aforesaid division of districts and precincts was made, some of the elders and ancients, believing that they had not been given the advantage that they deserved, considered themselves ill treated, and they and their relatives and friends rebelled and went to seek a new dwelling place.[1] And as they traveled about the lake they found a small platform or terrace that the Indians call *tlatelolli,* which they settled and gave the name of Tlatelolco, meaning a sort of terrace. This was the third division of the Mexican people since they left their homeland, the first being that of Michoacán and the second that of Malinalco. Those who went to Tlatelolco were already restless and ill intentioned, and so they did their best to be bad neighbors to the Mexicans; they quarreled with them constantly and were a trouble to them, and their enmity and ancient rivalries persist to this day. The men of Tenochtitlan, therefore, seeing that the Tlatelolcans were their enemies and that their numbers were increasing, dreaded them and feared that in the course of time they might vanquish them. They consulted at length about the matter, and agreed that it

1. It should be noted here that the history of the Mexica dynasty, which Acosta portrays over the next twelve chapters, was a contested history, written and rewritten to serve current and future political purposes as well as the memory and honor of the past. One of the best scholarly studies of this dynasty is Susan D. Gillespie, *The Aztec Kings: The Construction of Rulership in Mexica History* (Tucson: University of Arizona Press, 1989).

would be well to choose a king whom they could obey and their enemies fear, for by this means they would be stronger and more united among themselves and their enemies would not dare to go against them. Having decided to choose a king, they agreed about something else that was very important and shrewd, which was not to choose him from among themselves, both to avoid dissension and to win over one of the neighboring nations, by whom they were surrounded and against whom they had no defense.

And when they had carefully considered, as much to placate the king of Culhuacán, whom they had gravely offended by killing and flaying his predecessor's daughter, as to have a king of their Mexican blood (for there were many such in Culhuacán), and because they had lived in peace with them for some time, they decided to choose as king a youth named Acamapichtli, son of a great Mexican prince and a lady who was the king of Culhuacán's daughter. They soon sent ambassadors to ask this of him, with a splendid gift, and explained their embassy thus: "Great lord, we your vassals and servants the Mexicans, placed and enclosed in the reeds and canebrakes of the lake, alone and abandoned by all the nations in the world, led only by our god to the place where we are now, which lies within the jurisdiction of your territory and that of Azcapotzalco and Texcoco, now that you have permitted us to stay in it, we do not wish, nor is it fitting, to be without a chief and lord to rule, correct, guide, and instruct us in our way of living and to defend and shelter us from our enemies. Therefore, we have recourse to you, knowing that in your house and at your court there are sons of our tribe who are connected with your own, having emerged from our entrails and yours, our blood and yours. Among these we have heard of one of your grandsons named Acamapichtli: we beseech you to give him to us as our lord, and we will honor him as he deserves, for he is descended both from Mexican nobles and the kings of Culhuacán." The king, realizing that it would not be a bad thing to ally himself with the Mexicans, who were valiant, told them to take his grandson and welcome him, although he added (referring to the wicked deed that has been described above) that had he been a woman he would not have given her.[2] And he ended his speech by saying, "Let my grandson go and serve your god and be his lieutenant and rule and govern all the children of

2. The wicked deed was the sacrificial flaying of the daughter of Achitometl, king of Culhuacán, described in chapter 6.

the god to whom we owe our life, lord of night and day and of the winds. Let him go and be lord of the water and the land that the Mexican nation possesses; take and welcome him, and be sure that you treat him like a son and grandson of mine." The Mexicans thanked him and also begged him to give the youth in marriage with his own hand, and so he gave him as wife a very noble lady from among them.

The new king and queen were brought with all possible honor, and they all received him, even the smallest among them coming forth to see their king; and then they took them to some palaces that at the time were very poor, and seating them on their thrones one of the old men and orators, who was much respected, rose and spoke as follows: "My son, our lord and king: you are very welcome to this poor house and city, among these canebrakes and reeds, where your poor parents, grandparents, and kinfolk suffer what only the Creator of all knows. Look, my lord, you have come to be the shelter, shade, and protection of this Mexican nation, for you are the semblance of our god Huitzilopochtli, for whose sake we give you command and jurisdiction. You know full well that we are not in our own land, for the land that we now possess is strange to us and we do not know what will become of us tomorrow or any other day. And so consider that you have not come here to rest or take your ease but to assume a new effort, with a burden so heavy that you will always have to work and be the slave of this whole multitude among whom your lot has fallen, and of all those other neighbors of ours whom you must try to keep happy and contented, for you know that we live on their lands and in their territory." And he ended his speech by repeating, "You and the queen our lady are very welcome to this your kingdom." This speech of the old man's, along with other speeches celebrated in the history of the Mexicans, was customarily recited in chorus by the young men. These speeches were preserved by tradition, and some of them merit being heard in their own words.[3] The king replied by giving thanks and offering all his diligence and care in defending them and helping them in every way he could. Upon this they swore allegiance to him after their custom and put

3. This speech is an example of the *huehuetlatolli*. Since these speeches are quoted at length in book VII, it is reasonable to believe that native history informants would have presented their version of ancient Mexica history to Tovar and Durán through such speeches. On the *huehuetlatolli*, see Miguel León-Portilla, *Literatures: Supplement to the Handbook of Middle American Indians*, edited by Munro S. Edmonson (Austin: University of Texas Press, 1985), 7–44.

upon his head the king's crown, which resembles that of the doge of Venice.[4] The name of this king, Acamapichtli the First, means "bundle of reeds." And thus his insignia is a hand holding many reed stalks.

## CHAPTER 9 * OF THE STRANGE TRIBUTE PAID BY THE MEXICANS TO THE AZCAPOTZALCANS

The choice of the new king was so successful that within a short time the Mexicans began to have a form of commonwealth, and to acquire a reputation and the respect of others; so their neighbors, moved by envy and fear, tried to subdue them, especially the Tepanecas, whose chief town was the city of Azcapotzalco and to whom they paid tribute as folk who had come from elsewhere and lived in their land. But the king of Azcapotzalco, fearing their increasing power, tried to oppress the Mexicans; having consulted with his people, he sent a message to King Acamapichtli that the tribute they were paying was very small and that in the future they would also have to bring him junipers and willows to build his city, and in addition to this they had to plant him a field in the water of various vegetables; and that when they had sprouted and been cultivated they would have to bring the field to him by water, every year without fail, and if not he would declare them his enemies and annihilate them. The Mexicans were devastated when they received this command, for they thought it an impossible thing to ask and that it was merely an excuse to destroy them. But their god, Huitzilopochtli, consoled them, appearing one night to an old man and commanding him to tell his son the king, in his name, that he should not hesitate to accept the tribute and that he would help him and all would be easy. Thus it was that when the time for tribute came the Mexicans brought the trees that had been demanded of them and also the field planted on the water and borne on the water, in which there was a great deal of maize (which is their wheat) already in ear; there were chiles, or *ají,* amaranth, tomatoes, beans, sage, squash, and many other things, all well grown and ready to harvest.

Those who have not seen the fields that they make in the lake of Mexico, in

---

4. Acosta employs a common early European reference to provoke the imagination of his audience as to the design of the crown of the Mexica king. The doge of Venice, or the duke of Venice, was the highest official of the republic of Venice. The duke wore a stiff, high crown, much like a bishop's headdress, bedecked with fine embroidery, jewels, and streamers in the back.

the midst of the water itself, will think that what I am describing here is an invention or at most will believe that it was a spell cast by the devil whom these people adored. But in truth it is a very practicable thing and has often been done to make a movable seedbed in the water; for they put earth atop the reeds and grasses in such a way that the water does not dissolve it, and they sow and cultivate there, and the crop grows and ripens and can be moved from one place to another.[1] But the fact that it was done so easily and on such a large scale, and was so ready to harvest, argues that Huitzilopochtli (who is also called Patillas), was involved in it, especially when such a thing had not been seen or done before.

And so the king of Azcapotzalco was very much astonished when he saw that they had accomplished what he had believed impossible and said to his people that those folk had a powerful god and that everything was easy for them. And he told the Mexicans that since their god gave them everything ready-made next year at tribute time he wanted them also to bring him in the vegetable bed a duck and a heron sitting on their eggs, and that it must be done in such a way that the chicks would hatch just as they arrived, and that it could not be otherwise on pain of incurring his enmity. The Mexicans continued to feel anguish because such an arrogant and difficult command was required of them. But their god consoled them by night (as he usually did) through one of his priests and said that he would take care of everything; they should not be sad, and they could be sure that the time would come when the people of Azcapotzalco would pay with their lives for those whimsical tributes, but at present they must maintain silence and obey. At tribute time, as the Mexicans were bringing everything from their field that had been asked of them, there appeared on the raft (they did not know how) a duck and a heron sitting on their eggs; and continuing on their way they came to Azcapotzalco, where the chicks hatched. And the king of Azcapotzalco was exceedingly astonished and told his people that these things were more than

---

1. The fields that Acosta describes are the *chinampas*. In truth the fields were not floating, but at times the gardens were moved, as explained by Acosta, from place to place. Of further interest here, Acosta inserts his authorial voice, rare in these chapters on ancient Mexican history, to call the system "practicable." Indeed, *chinampa* agriculture has been credited with providing the optimal agricultural production for the population in the Valley of Mexico. In spite of his praise for the system, Acosta accords the Mexica no particular credit, since *chinampa* technology was made known to man through the intervention of Huitzilopochtli during a night vision. Scientific experimentation or reason on the part of the Mexica themselves is denied by both the rendering of the Mexica historical myths and Acosta's observations.

human and that the Mexicans were in a fair way to become masters of everything. Yet the size of the tribute did not diminish one jot, and because the Mexicans were not powerful they suffered and remained in this subjection and servitude for fifty years. At this time King Acamapichtli died, after having enlarged the City of Mexico with many buildings, streets, and waterways, and great abundance of foodstuffs. He reigned in great peace and tranquility for forty years, always assiduous for the good and increase of his commonwealth. When he was on the point of death he did a memorable thing, which was that, although he had legitimate sons to whom he might have left the kingdom's succession, he did not do so and left his people free; for, as he had been freely chosen, they must choose whomever they thought best to govern them well, adjuring them to have a care for the good of the commonwealth. Displaying grief because he had been unable to free them from tribute and subjection, and entrusting his wife and children to them, he made his end, leaving all his people inconsolable over his death.

## CHAPTER 10 * OF THE SECOND KING AND WHAT BEFELL HIM DURING HIS REIGN

After the dead king's obsequies had been performed, the elders and important people, and some of the common folk, assembled to elect a king. The oldest man among them set forth their need and said that they should choose as head of their city a person who would have compassion on the old, and on widows and orphans, and would be the father of his people, for they were the feathers of his wings and the lashes of his eyes and the beard upon his countenance; and that he would have to be valiant, for they would soon need to rely on his strong arms, as their god had prophesied. They decided to choose as king a son of the previous monarch, reposing the same noble confidence in making his son his successor as he had done in confiding so fully in his people. This young man's name was Huitzilihuitl, which means "rich feather"; they placed the royal crown on his head and anointed him, as they had the custom of doing with all their kings, with an ointment that they called divine because it was the same with which they anointed their idol. Then an orator pronounced an eloquent discourse, exhorting him to be stout of heart in bringing them out of their troubles and the servitude and poverty in which they lived, oppressed by the men of Azcapotzalco; and when he had finished, all saluted the king and paid him homage. This king was unwed, and his council thought that it would be well to marry him to the king of Azcapotzalco's daughter in order to gain his friendship and by this means to temper the heavy weight of the tributes that they paid him, although they feared that he would not deign to give them his daughter because he considered them to be vassals. But, when they asked for her very humbly and with courteous words, the king of Azcapotzalco agreed and gave them one of his daughters, named Ayauhcihuatl, whom they carried off to Mexico with great festivity and rejoicing; and they performed the ceremony and rites of the marriage, which consisted of tying one corner of the man's mantle to one of the woman's as a sign of the marriage bond. A son was born to this queen, and they asked his grandfather, the king of Azcapotzalco, to name him. After taking the auguries, as was their custom (for they were extremely superstitious when it came to naming their children), he commanded that his grandson be named Chimalpopoca, which means "shield that smokes." The king of Azcapotzalco showed so much delight in his grandson that his daughter the queen took advantage of this to ask him, now that he had a Mexican grandson, to lift the heavy burden of tributes from the Mexicans; this the king did willingly, with the agreement of his counselors, substituting for the tribute that they paid the obligation of furnishing a pair of ducks every year, or a few fish, in recognition that they were his subjects and dwelled in his land. This relieved the Mexicans and made them very happy; but their happiness did not last long, for their protectress the queen died after a few years, and a year later Huitzilihuitl the king of the Mexicans died also, leaving his son Chimalpopoca a boy of ten years. He reigned for thirteen years and died at the age of little more than thirty. He was considered to be a good king, diligent in the cult of his gods, for the people believed that kings were made in their image, and that is why the kings were so zealous in the cult and veneration of their gods. He was also very wise in cultivating the friendship of their neighbors and in having many commercial relations with them; by this means he enlarged his city, exercising his people in warlike activities all around the lake and preparing them for the things that they were trying to accomplish, as will soon appear.

### CHAPTER 11 * OF THE THIRD KING,
### CHIMALPOPOCA, AND OF HIS CRUEL DEATH
### AND THE CAUSE OF THE WAR WAGED
### BY THE MEXICANS

By common consent the Mexicans chose as successor to the dead king his son Chimalpopoca, although he was a lad ten years of age, for they thought that it was still necessary to stay in the good graces of the king of Azcapotzalco by choosing his grandson as king; and so they placed him on his throne and gave him the insignia of war, with a bow and arrows in one hand and a knife-studded sword such as the Indians use in his right, meaning by this, as they explain, that they expected to free themselves by force of arms. The Mexicans were experiencing a serious shortage of water, for that of the lake was muddy and bad for drinking; and to remedy this they had the boy king send to his grandfather the king of Azcapotzalco to ask for water from the hill of Chapultepec, which is a league away from Mexico, as has been mentioned above. They achieved this easily and, by working diligently, made an aqueduct of turves and stakes and reeds along which the water reached their city; but because it was built upon the lake and the water conduit lay close to the surface, it crumbled and broke in many places, and they could not enjoy the water as they wished and needed to do. With this excuse, either because they purposely sought a pretext to break with the Tepanecas or because they acted rashly, what they did was to send a very uncompromising embassy to the king of Azcapotzalco, telling him that they could not make use of the water that he had granted them because the conduit had crumbled in many places; therefore, they asked him to provide them with wood and mortar and stones and to send his workmen to make a conduit of stone and mortar that would not break. The king was displeased with this demand, and his people liked it still less, for they thought it a very bold message and bad conduct for vassals to use such language with their lords. Therefore, the chiefs in the king's council were very angry, saying that this was a shameful thing, for, not content with letting them live on land that was not theirs and giving them water, the Mexicans now wanted them to go and serve them; what kind of behavior was that, and why were these people so proud, when they were fugitives and lived among canebrakes? They would have to teach them whether they were good enough to serve as workmen and would humble their pride by depriving them of their land and lives. Speaking thus angrily, they departed, leaving the presence of the king, of whom they were somewhat suspicious because of his grandson, and consulted again outside his presence. The result was that a public proclamation was issued forbidding any Tepaneca to trade with any Mexican, or to go to their city or admit them to theirs, on pain of death.

Thus we can see that the king did not have absolute command or authority over these councilors and that he governed more after the manner of a consul or *dux* than a king, although later on the kings' authority increased along with their power until it became irrefutable and tyrannical, as will be seen in the last of their monarchs. For it has always been the case with barbarians that the greater the power the greater the domination. And even in our histories of Spain we find in some of the ancient kings the kind of rule that these Tepanecas used, and even the early Roman kings were like this, except that Rome declined from kings to consuls and senate, until later it returned to having emperors; but barbarians, beginning with moderate kings, declined into tyrants, one sort of government and the other being the extremes and the best way being moderate rule.

But to return to our history: when the king of Azcapotzalco observed the intent of his people, which was to kill the Mexicans, he implored them first to steal his grandson the boy king away, and then they might do with the Mexicans whatever they wished. Almost all of them concurred in this in order to please the king and because they pitied the boy, but two of the great lords disagreed violently, saying that it was bad advice, for, although Chimalpopoca was of his blood he was so through the mother and his father's blood would influence him more. And with this they decided that the first one they had to kill would be Chimalpopoca, king of Mexico, and they vowed to do it. The king of Azcapotzalco felt so keenly their resistance and the decision to which they came that he soon fell ill of sorrow and frustration and quickly died; and upon his death the Tepanecas at last made up their minds and committed a great act of treason. One night, when the boy king of Mexico was sleeping untroubled and without a guard, the men of Azcapotzalco entered the palace and quickly killed Chimalpopoca, returning without being heard. The next morning when the Mexican nobles, according to their custom, went to greet their king and found him dead with grievous wounds, they raised such an outcry and weeping that all the city heard them; and all of them, blind with anger, armed themselves to avenge their king's death. As they set forth in a furious mob, one of their principal knights went out to meet them and tried to calm them and bring them to their senses with prudent arguments. "Where are you going, oh Mexicans?" he said to them. "Be calm, and quiet your hearts; remember that ill-considered actions are not well directed, nor do they lead to good results. Repress your grief, knowing as you do that, although your king is dead, the noble blood of the Mexicans did not end with him. We have sons of previous kings, with whose help you can better gain what you desire once the succession has been assured. What chief or leader do you have now to guide you in your aims? Do not go forward blindly; control your emotions. First choose a king to guide, strengthen, and inspire you against your enemies. Meanwhile, be wise and hide your feelings while you perform the obsequies of your dead king who lies here before you, and later a better time for vengeance will come." When they heard this they were brought to their senses, and to perform the funeral honors for their king they invited the lords of Texcoco and those of Culhuacán, to whom they reported the vile and cruel deed that the Tepanecas had committed, which moved them to pity for the Mexicans and inspired indignation against their enemies. The Mexicans added that their intent was either to die or avenge that great evil and asked them not to favor the unjust side of their enemies, for they did not want them to help the Azcapotzalcans by supplying them with arms and people. Rather they asked them to remain neutral to see what would happen; they only asked them, for their survival, not to cut off trade with them as the Tepanecas had done. When they heard these arguments the men of Texcoco and Culhuacán displayed great goodwill and satisfaction, offering their cities and all the association and trade they might desire, so that they could procure all the supplies they needed both by land and water. After this the Mexicans asked them to stay with them and attend the election of the king that they intended to hold, which the others also accepted in order to please them.

### CHAPTER 12 * OF IZCOATL, THE FOURTH KING, AND THE WAR AGAINST THE TEPANECAS

When all those who were to hold the election had assembled, an old man who was held to be a great orator rose to his feet, and according to what the histories tell he spoke as follows: "The light of your eyes is extinguished, oh Mexicans, but not the light of your heart; for, although you have lost the one who was your light and guide in this commonwealth of Mexico, the light of the heart remains to tell you that if one has been killed others remain who can make up for his lack exceedingly well. The nobility of Mexico did not die here, nor did the royal blood come to an end. Turn your eyes and look around you and you will see the nobility of Mexico drawn up in ranks, not one or two but many and very excellent princes, sons of the king Acama-pichtli, our true and legitimate lord. Here you may choose as you will, saying 'I want this one, and this other I do not want,' for, although you have lost a father, here you will find both father and mother. Recall, oh Mexicans, that the sun was eclipsed for a short time and the land was darkened and that the light soon returned to it. Although Mexico was darkened with the death of your king, let the sun come forth. Choose another king; take care where you turn your eyes and toward whom your hearts are inclined, for he will be the man that your god Huitzilopochtli chooses." And, continuing in this vein for a long time, the orator concluded much to the satisfaction of all. As a result of this council the choice fell on King Izcoatl, which means "serpent of knives," who was a son of the first king, Acamapichtli, begotten on a slave woman of his; and, although he was not legitimate, they chose him because he was the most gifted of them all in manners and valor and strength. All showed great pleasure, especially the men of Texcoco, for their king was married to a sister of Izcoatl's. After he was crowned and placed on his royal throne another orator came forward, who spoke at length of the king's obligations to his people and the zeal that he must put into his efforts, saying among other things the following: "Know that now we are all depending on you. Will you perchance let fall the load that is on your shoulders? Will you let the old man and the old woman and the orphan and the widow perish? Have pity on the babes that crawl across the floor, who will die if our enemies prevail against us. Oh my lord, begin to unfold and spread your mantle, to take upon your back your children, who are the poor and the common folk, who trust in the shadow of your mantle and the fresh breeze of your kindness." And there were many other words in the same vein, which (as I have said previously) the youths repeated in chorus as an exercise, and later they were taught as a lesson to those who were learning the skill of the orators for the first time.

Now at that time the Tepanecas were resolved to destroy the whole Mexican nation, and to carry out their purpose they made many preparations; and so the new king tried to foment war and do battle with those who had done them so much harm. But the common people, observing that their enemies excelled them greatly both in numbers and provision for war, went to the king filled with fear and begged him not to undertake so dangerous a war, saying that it would mean the destruction of their poor city and their people. When they were asked what means they wanted adopted, they replied that the new king of Azcapotzalco was merciful, and that they should ask him for peace and offer to serve him, and to take them out of those canebrakes and give them houses and land among his own people, and that all should be under the same lord, and that to accomplish this they should carry their god on his litter as an intercessor. This clamor from the people was so powerful, especially because some of the nobles approved of their opinions, that the king called on the priests and told them to prepare the litter with the god upon it in order to make the journey. When all this was done and everyone had agreed to make peace and submit to the Tepanecas, a handsome and spirited youth appeared among them and very boldly said to them, "What is this, oh Mexicans? Are you mad? How can there be such cowardice that we must submit thus to the men of Azcapotzalco?" And turning to the king he said, "My lord, how can you allow such a thing? Speak to these people and tell them to seek the means for our defense and honor and let us not place ourselves so basely and ignominiously in the hands of our enemies." This youth was named Tlacaelel, and he was a nephew of the king himself and the most valiant captain and the wisest counselor that ever the Mexicans had, as will be seen later. Izcoatl, heeding what his nephew had so wisely told him, stopped the people, telling them to let him first attempt a better and more honorable means. And then, turning to the nobles among his people, he said, "Here present are all of you who are my kindred and the flower of Mexico; the man who has the courage to take a message from me to the Tepanecas, let him stand up." They all stayed still, looking at one another, and there was not one who consented to expose himself to death. Then the youth Tlacaelel rose and offered to go, saying that since he had to die it mattered little whether it was today or tomorrow, and for what better occasion was he saving himself; that there he was, and the king must command him whatever he liked. And, although everyone thought that his deed was perilous, still the king decided to send him in order to discover the plans and intent of the king of Azcapotzalco and his people, believing that he would rather risk the life of his nephew than the honor of his commonwealth.

When Tlacaelel was prepared to leave he started off, and when he reached the guards, who had orders to kill any Mexican who might come by, he persuaded them by a ruse to let him in to see the king. The king was astonished to see him, and after hearing his embassy, which was to ask for peace by honorable means, answered that he would speak with his counselors, and told Tlacaelel to return next day for his answer. When Tlacaelel asked him for safe conduct, the king could only advise him to use his own good care. Upon this he returned to Mexico, giving his word to the guards that he would return. The king of Mexico, thanking him for his courage, again sent him for the reply. If it was a declaration of war, he commanded him to give the king of Azcapotzalco certain arms with which to defend himself and to anoint him and place feathers on his head, as was done to the dead, telling him that, since he did not wish peace, they would surely kill him and all his people. And, although the king of Azcapotzalco wanted peace, for he was of mild character, his people roused him to anger, so that the reply was that of open war. When the messenger heard this he did everything that his king had commanded, declaring by that ceremony of offering him arms and anointing the king with the unction of the dead that he challenged him in the name of his king. Because of all this the king of Azcapotzalco gladly allowed himself to be anointed and adorned with feathers and in exchange gave the messenger some very good weapons; and as he did this he warned him not to go out through the main gate of the palace, for many were waiting there to cut him to pieces, but to go out secretly through a postern that the king had opened in a courtyard of his palace. This the youth did, and going roundabout by secret paths he came to a safe place within sight of the guards, and from there he challenged them, saying, "Ho, Tepanecas! Ho, men of Azcapotzalco! How ill you do your office as guards! Know that you all must die, and that no Tepaneca will be left alive." At this the guards rushed upon him, and he defended himself so valiantly that he killed several of them, and seeing that reinforcements were arriving he returned boldly to his own city, where he informed the people that war had broken out and was now inevitable and that the Tepanecas and his king had challenged each other.

### CHAPTER 13 * OF THE BATTLE THE MEXICANS
### FOUGHT WITH THE TEPANECAS AND THE GREAT
### VICTORY THEY ACHIEVED

When the common people of Mexico learned of the challenge they went to the king with their usual cowardice, asking him to let them leave the city, for they felt that its loss was certain. The king consoled and encouraged them, promising that he would give them freedom after their enemies were defeated and that they must not doubt that they would be victorious. The people answered, "And if you are defeated, what shall we do?" "If we are defeated," he replied, "we must deliver ourselves into your hands, for you to kill us and eat our flesh in dirty pots and take vengeance on us." "That is what will happen," they said, "if you are not victorious; and if you do win, we promise to pay you tribute and build your houses, and prepare your fields and carry your weapons and your burdens whenever you go to war forever and ever, we and our descendants." After these agreements were made between the nobles and the common folk (who later did, either willingly or by force, all that they had promised), the king appointed Tlacaelel as his captain general; and when all his camp was drawn up in squadrons he gave authority as captains to his bravest relatives and friends. He delivered a very skillful and enthusiastic address to them, which increased the courage they already possessed (although it was no little), and commanded them all to follow the orders of the general he had appointed. He divided his people into two parts and ordered the bravest and most daring to make the first attack along with Tlacaelel and that all the rest should stay quietly with the king Izcoatl until they saw the first group break through their enemies. As they marched in their ranks the men of Azcapotzalco caught sight of them and charged furiously from their city, richly accoutered in gold and silver and splendid feathers and weapons of great value, as befitted those who held the power in all that land. Izcoatl gave a signal with a little drum that he carried on his back, and then, raising a great cry and calling, "Mexico, Mexico!" they closed with the Tepanecas; although their numbers were infinitely superior, the Mexicans broke through their ranks and forced them to retire to their city. Then those who had stayed behind advanced, shouting, "Tlacaelel, victory, victory!" and all rushed into the city together, where by the king's orders they spared neither men nor old folks nor women nor children, for they put all of them to death and looted and sacked the city, which was extremely rich. And, not content with this, they went after those who had fled and taken refuge in the wild sierras nearby, attacking them and doing cruel slaughter. From a hill where they had retreated the Tepanecas threw down their arms and begged for their lives, offering to serve the Mexicans and give them land and fields and stone and lime and wood and always to have them as their lords; and so Tlacaelel ordered his people to fall back and stop the battle, granting life to the others under the conditions they had offered and making them solemnly swear to uphold them.[1]

And so they returned victorious to Azcapotzalco and then to the City of Mexico with rich spoils. The next day the king called the nobles and common people together and, repeating to them the arrangement he had made with the latter, asked them if they were happy to keep it. They said that they had promised it and the nobles well deserved it, and so they were satisfied to serve them forever; and they took the oath, which has been kept inviolably ever since. This done, Izcoatl returned to Azcapotzalco and with the advice of his council distributed among the victors all the lands and property of those he had vanquished. The largest part went to the king, then to Tlacaelel, and then to the other nobles, as had been agreed upon during the war. And they gave some lands to a few of the common folk also because they had fought bravely; all others they spurned and drove out as cowardly folk. They also fixed common lands for the districts of the City of Mexico, some for each district, so that they could be used for religion and sacrifice to their gods. This was the order in which, ever afterward, they always distributed land and spoils from those whom they defeated and brought under subjection. The result was that the people of Azcapotzalco were left so poor that they had not even a field left for themselves, and the worst circumstance of all was that their king was taken from them as well as the prospect of having another, leaving them only the king of Mexico.

1. The Tepenacas' pledge to provide land, fields, stone, lime, and wood marked a turning point in Aztec history, for the Mexica had gained a position of preeminence that allowed them to demand tribute rather than pay it. The collection of tribute in Mesoamerica constituted one of the ways through which subjects paid homage to the Mexica ruler. In contrast to the labor tribute demanded under the Inca Empire, the Mexica collected most of their payment in kind. As an additional consequence of their victory over Azcapotzalco, Mexico-Tenochtitlán joined Texcoco and Tacuba, also called Tlacopan, to form the ruling group known as the Triple Alliance. The three powers jointly controlled the entire Aztec Empire until the late fifteenth century when the Mexica gained supremacy in this alliance.

## CHAPTER 14 ∗ OF THE WAR AND VICTORY OF
## THE MEXICANS OVER THE CITY OF COYOACÁN

Although the chief city of the Tepanecas was Azcapotzalco, there were other cities with lords of their own, such as Tacuba and Coyoacán. These, observing the havoc that had been wrought, tried to persuade the men of Azcapotzalco to renew the war against the Mexicans; and when they realized that they were unwilling, as a people entirely broken, the men of Coyoacán tried to make war on their own account.[1] To this end they stirred up the other neighboring nations, although these were unwilling to make a move or start a quarrel with the Mexicans. But, with their hatred and envy of the Mexicans' prosperity increasing, the people of Coyoacán began to mistreat and mock the Mexican women who went to their markets and did the same to the men whom they were able to ill treat; therefore, the king of Mexico forbade any of his subjects to go to Coyoacán, nor were any of its people admitted to Mexico. This caused the men of Coyoacán to decide to go to war with the Mexicans, and first they tried to provoke them with a humiliating insult. What they did was to invite them to a solemn feast of theirs, where, after giving them a good meal and entertaining them at a great dance such as the Indians have, as a final touch they sent them women's clothing and made them put it on and forced them to return to their city dressed in women's garments, telling them that they had not risen in arms after being provoked because the Mexicans were womanish and cowardly. It is said that the people of Mexico then took their revenge with another malicious trick, which was to build fires with poisonous smoke at the gates of the city of Coyoacán; this caused many women to miscarry and other folk to fall ill.[2] The result was that

1. Rebecca Horn provides a detailed analysis of Coyoacán life after their defeat by the Spanish in *Postconquest Coyoacan: Nahua-Spanish Relations in Central Mexico, 1519–1650* (Stanford: Stanford University Press, 1997).

2. Women figure prominently in the history of this struggle with Coyoacán. The men of Coyoacán taunted the Mexicans as cowards by forcing them to wear women's dress, an action described in other battles of central Mexico. Moreover, the principle acts of aggression were against women—ill treatment in the marketplace by those of Coyoacán and poisonous fires triggering miscarriage by those of Tenochtitlán. Childbirth and the local market were both areas of life dominated by women, yet, as focal points of reproduction and nourishment, acts against them represented threats to the whole of society. On the social status of Mexica women, see June Nash, "The Aztecs and the Ideology of Male Dominance," *Signs* 4, no. 2 (1978): 349–62; and Susan Kellogg, "The Woman's Room: Some Aspects of Gender Relations in Tenochtitlan in the Late Pre-Hispanic Period," *Ethnohistory* 42, no. 4 (fall 1995): 563–76.

open war broke out, and both sides gave battle with all their might. Victory was won by the strategy and efforts of Tlacaelel, for, leaving King Izcoatl fighting with the men of Coyoacán, he hit on the idea of lying in ambush with a few of his brave soldiers and took the rear of the men of Coyoacán by a flanking movement, and falling upon them forced them to retreat to their city. Observing that they intended to make a stand in the temple, which was very strong, he broke through their ranks with three very valiant soldiers and reached it before them; he captured the temple and burned it and forced them to flee through the fields, where, causing great havoc among the vanquished, he followed them inland for ten leagues until they surrendered to the Mexicans by casting down their weapons and crossing their hands. And they begged his pardon, with many tears, for their rashness in treating them as women and offered themselves as slaves, and in the end the Mexicans pardoned them. They returned from this victory with very rich spoils in clothing, weapons, gold, silver, jewels, gorgeous featherwork, and a large number of captives. Three lords of Culhuacán, who came to the aid of the Mexicans in order to win honor, were particularly prominent in this victory; and after they had been received by Tlacaelel and had proved faithful he gave them Mexican insignia and kept them always at his side, and they fought with great valor. It was quite clear that victory was wholly owed to these three, along with the general, for of all the captives that were taken two-thirds had been captured by these four. This was easily proved by the stratagem they used, which was that each time one of them took a captive he would cut off a bit of his hair and turn him over to the others, and they could see that those whose hair had been cut were much more numerous; this gave them great fame as valiant warriors, and as victors they were honored by receiving spoils and land in the very best places. The Mexicans always followed this practice, and it is the reason why their warriors were so eager to fight and gain fame by force of arms.

## CHAPTER 15 * OF THE WAR AND VICTORY THAT THE MEXICANS WON OVER THE XOCHIMILCANS

Now that the Tepaneca nation had surrendered, the Mexicans had the chance to do the same with the Xochimilcans, who, as has been said, were the first of those seven caves or clans to settle the land. The Mexicans did not seek this opportunity, although as victors they could have presumed to extend their sway; but the Xochimilcans worked to their own disadvantage, as happens sometimes to unwise and overzealous men who, to avoid the danger that they envision, end by incurring it. The men of Xochimilco believed that after the victories they had achieved the Mexicans would try to conquer them; and, as they spoke of this among themselves, although there were some who said that it would be well to recognize them as victors and ratify their good fortune, in the end the opposite opinion prevailed, namely, to forestall them and do battle with them. When Izcoatl the king of Mexico learned of this he sent his general, Tlacaelel, with his troops, and it chanced that the battle took place on the boundaries between the two nations. Although in number of soldiers and equipment the battle was not unequal, it was very much so in the order and discipline of the fighting, for the Xochimilcans attacked all together in a mob, without any sort of order. Tlacaelel had his men divided into squadrons and in excellent order, and so they quickly scattered their adversaries and made them retreat to their city, into which they soon entered, pursuing them until they were shut into their temple; and from there, by setting fire to it, they made them flee to the hills and at last to surrender with crossed hands. Tlacaelel, the captain, returned in great triumph, the priests coming out to receive him with the music of their flutes and scattering incense on him and the chief captains and performing other ceremonies and demonstrations of joy as they were wont to do. The king came with them, and all went to the temple to give thanks to their false god, for the devil was always very anxious to attribute honor to himself for things he had not done; for victory and power are given not by him but by the true God to those whom he wishes. The next day King Itzcoatl went to the city of Xochimilco and had himself sworn as king of the Xochimilcans, and to console them he promised to do them good. As a sign of this he commanded them to build a great causeway from Mexico to Xochimilco, a distance of four leagues, so that there would be more trade and intercourse between them. This the Xochimilcans did, and before long they thought so well of the Mexicans' government and good treatment that they felt very happy to have changed their king and their commonwealth.

Some neighbors of theirs, however, influenced by envy or fear of loss, did not learn from their example. Cuitlahuac was a city located on the lake, whose name and general location, though different, still exist today; these people were very skilled in plying the lake in boats, and they thought that they could do some damage to Mexico by water. When the king observed this, he commanded his army to go and fight with them. But Tlacaelel, believing that the war was unimportant and the cause too small for everyone to go against them, offered to defeat them only with boys, and that is what he did. He went to the temple and took from the youths secluded there those whom he judged worthy and from the boys that he found selected those between the ages of ten and eighteen who knew how to handle boats and canoes; and, giving them certain orders and instructions about the fight, he went with them to Cuitlahuac, where by his stratagems he pressed his enemies until they had to flee. And as he was pursuing them the lord of Cuitlahuac came out to meet him and surrendered himself, his city, and his people, and Tlacaelel ceased to attack them further. The boys returned with rich spoils and many captives for their sacrifices and were received very solemnly with a great procession and music and perfumes; and they went to worship their idol, taking earth and eating it, and with the priests lacerating their shins with lancets until the blood ran and other superstitions that they used in matters of such moment. The boys were greatly honored and encouraged, and the king kissed and embraced them and their parents and relatives accompanied them; and it was bruited throughout the land that Tlacaelel had conquered the city of Cuitlahuac with boys.

The news of this victory, and the thought of past victories, opened the eyes of those of Texcoco. They were a noble people and very intelligent for the level of culture that prevailed, and so the first person to think that they ought to surrender to the king of Mexico, and invite him to their city, was the king of Texcoco. With the approval of his council they sent ambassadors who were excellent orators, with lavish presents, to offer themselves as subjects and ask for his good peace and friendship. This was graciously accepted, although at the suggestion of Tlacaelel a ceremony was performed to seal the agreement. The men of Texcoco took the field with those of Mexico and fought and surrendered; this was a rite and ceremony of war in which no blood was shed and no wounds were suffered on either side. Thus the king of Mexico became supreme lord of Texcoco, not by depriving them of their king but by having him join the supreme council; and this arrangement continued until the time of Moctezuma II, during whose reign the Spaniards entered the country. Having subdued the city and territory of Texcoco, Mexico became mistress of that whole land and of the towns around the lake where it had been founded. Izcoatl, having enjoyed this prosperity and rule for twelve years, fell ill and died, leaving the kingdom that he had been given greatly increased because of his nephew Tlacaelel's valor and good counsel, as has been recounted. Tlacaelel thought it better to make kings than to be one himself, as will now be explained.

### CHAPTER 16 * OF MOCTEZUMA, FIFTH KING OF THE MEXICANS, FIRST OF THIS NAME

The election of the new king was the responsibility of the four chief electors (as has been said before) as well as the kings of Texcoco and Tacuba by special privilege. These six were joined by Tlacaelel as the one who had supreme authority, and when the matter was put to them the choice fell on Moctezuma, first of this name, who was a nephew of Tlacaelel himself. His election was very popular, and so very solemn festivities took place with more pomp than on previous occasions. As soon as he was elected they took him to the temple with a great retinue, and before the brazier that they called divine, where a flame always burned day and night, they set him on a throne and dressed him in royal accoutrements; and there, with tiger claws and sharp deer antlers that they kept for this purpose, the king sacrificed to their idol by drawing blood from his ears and the fleshy parts of his limbs and his shins, for that was how the demon liked to be honored. The priests pronounced their orations there, and so did the elders and captains, all of them congratulating him. At the time of these elections great banquets and dances were held and there was a great deal of illumination. And it was in the time of this king that the custom was begun, for the festival of his coronation, of having the king go to war in person in one place or another, from which he brought captives to make solemn sacrifices; and this became a law from that day forward. Hence Moctezuma went to the province of Chalco, which had declared itself an enemy, where he fought valiantly and took a large number of captives; with them he offered a notable sacrifice on the day of his coronation, though at that time he did not leave the province of Chalco, a place of very warlike people, completely defeated and laid waste. On the day of the coronation people came from many lands both far and near to see the festivities, and all were given lavish and splendid meals, and all, especially the poor, were dressed in new garments; hence on the same day the king's tributes were brought to the city with great order and pomp: clothing of all kinds, cocoa beans, gold, silver, rich featherwork, huge bundles of cotton, chiles, seeds, many vegetables, much fish roe from the sea and from rivers, and incalculable quantities of fruit and game, not counting the innumerable presents that other kings and lords sent to the new monarch. All the tribute was carried in squads according to the different provinces. The officers and tax gatherers marched in front with different insignias, all of this with so much order and in so civilized a fashion that the entrance of the tribute was as much worth seeing as the rest of the festivities. After the king was crowned he went off to conquer several provinces, and because he was both brave and virtuous he subdued the land from sea to sea, always relying on the counsel and astuteness of his general Tlacaelel, whom he justly loved and esteemed.

The war in which he engaged longest, and the one that gave him most trouble, was that of the province of Chalco, in which important things befell him. One very notable occurrence was that, having taken one of Moctezuma's own brothers prisoner, the Chalcans attempted to make him their king and to this end sent him very polite and compelling messages. Realizing what they wanted, he told them that if indeed they wished to make him their king they must raise a very tall pole in the main square, and on top of it make a platform to which he could climb. Believing that this was a ceremony designed to make him appear greater, they did so, and when all of his fellow prisoners, the Mexicans, had gathered around the pole he climbed to the top with a bunch of flowers in his hand and from that position spoke to them as follows: "Oh, valiant Mexicans! These others wish to raise me to be their king, but may the gods never permit me, for the sake of becoming a king, to act treasonably against my country. Instead, I want you to learn from me; die rather than go over to your enemies." So saying, he threw himself down and was dashed to pieces, and this spectacle aroused such horror and anger in the Chalcans that they immediately attacked the Mexicans and killed them with lances, dealing with them as savage and inflexible people and saying that they had the hearts of devils. On the following night two owls were heard exchanging mournful cries, and the people of Chalco took this as an omen that they would soon be destroyed. And so it was that King Moctezuma went against them in person with all his power and defeated them and laid waste their whole land, and crossing the Sierra Nevada he conquered as far as the

Northern Sea; and turning toward the Southern Sea he also won and subjected several provinces, so that he became a very powerful king, all this
with the aid and counsel of Tlacaelel, to whom is owed almost the entire
Mexican empire.

However, it seemed best to him (and he acted accordingly) not to conquer
the province of Tlaxcala, so that the Mexicans would have an enemy frontier
where the youth of Mexico could exercise their arms and also have a large
supply of captives with whom to make sacrifice to their idols. For, as we have
seen, they used a vast number of men in these sacrifices, and these had
necessarily to be taken in war. This King Moctezuma, or rather his general
Tlacaelel, is responsible for all the order and polity that Mexico has possessed
in councils and consistories, where there was great order and as large a
number of councils and judges as in any of the most flourishing states of
Europe. This same king established his royal household with great authority,
creating many and diverse officers, and was served with much ceremony and
pomp. He was no less notable in the cult of their idols, increasing the number
of priests, instituting new ceremonies, and holding strange observances in
their religion and vain superstition. He built that great temple to their god
Huitzilopochtli, of which I have made mention in another book. At the
dedication of the temple he offered innumerable sacrifices of men whom he
had taken captive in a number of victories. At last, enjoying great prosperity
in his empire, he fell ill and died, having reigned for twenty-eight years,
very unlike his successor, Tizoc, who resembled him in neither valor nor
good fortune.

CHAPTER 17 * HOW TLACAELEL REFUSED TO BE KING
AND THE ELECTION AND DEEDS OF TIZOC

The four electors met with the lords of Texcoco and Tacuba, and with Tlacaelel presiding they proceeded to elect a king. All the votes went to Tlacaelel
as the man who deserved the office more than any other, but he refused with
convincing reasons that induced them to elect another. For he said that it was
better for the state if another were king, and that he would be his executor
and associate as he had been up till then, and that they must not lay the
burden on him alone, for even though he was not the king he would work for
his commonwealth no less than as if he were. It is a very unusual thing to

reject supreme power and command and to wish to have the care and labor but not the honor and power; nor is it usual that the man who is capable of governing everything should wish another to have the chief power in exchange for the country's affairs being better. In this sense this barbarian outdid the wise Romans and Greeks; and if it is not so look at Alexander and Julius Caesar. To the former, ruling the world seemed a small thing, and he killed his best and most loyal men with cruel tortures because of flimsy suspicions that they wished to reign. And the other declared himself to be an enemy of his country, saying that if it had to be turned from the right way it would be turned, if only he might reign. Such is men's thirst for power, although Tlacaelel's deed could also have arisen from overweening confidence in himself, in the belief that he was a king without actually being one, for he almost commanded the king and they even let him wear a certain insignia resembling a crown, which belonged only to monarchs. But despite everything this deed of his merits praise and still more his belief that he could help his country more by being a subject than by being its supreme lord. For indeed this is true, just as in a play the actor deserves more glory who assumes and enacts the role of the most important person, although it be that of a shepherd or peasant, and leaves the role of captain or king to another who knows how to do it better. Just so, in sound philosophy, men ought to consider more the common good and exercise the office and state that they best understand. But this philosophy is beyond the scope of what we are presently discussing.

And so let us return to our tale and say that as a reward for his modesty, and because of the respect in which he was held by the Mexican electors, they asked Tlacaelel to say who he thought ought to reign, seeing that he did not wish to do so. He gave his vote to a son of the dead king named Tizoc, who was hardly more than a boy, and they told him that these were very slender shoulders to bear so much weight. He answered that his shoulders were there to help him bear the burden, as he had done with previous kings. This argument convinced them, and Tizoc was chosen. The accustomed ceremonies were performed with him; they pierced his nose and placed an emerald in it as an ornament, and that is the reason why this king is depicted in the books of the Mexicans by his pierced nose. This king turned out to be very different from his father and predecessor, for it was observed that he was not at all warlike and a coward; for his coronation he went to conquer a province that had risen in revolt and in the battle lost many more of his men than he captured from the enemy. However, he returned saying that he had brought the number of captives required for the sacrifices of his coronation, and so he was crowned with great solemnity. But the Mexicans, dissatisfied with having such an unwarlike king with so little spirit, determined to poison him, and so his reign lasted only four years. This clearly shows that sons do not always inherit the valor of their fathers and that the greater the glory of their predecessors the more abhorrent is the baseness and lack of courage of those who succeed them in command but not in merit. But another brother of the dead king, also a son of the great Moctezuma, successfully restored this loss; his name was Axacayatl, and he was elected at the suggestion of Tlacaelel, who chose better this time than on the previous occasion.

CHAPTER 18 * OF THE DEATH OF TLACAELEL
AND THE EXPLOITS OF AXACAYATL,
SEVENTH KING OF MEXICO

By this time Tlacaelel was very old, and because of it they brought him on their shoulders, in a chair, to be present at the consultations and business that presented themselves. At last he fell ill, and the new king, who had not yet been crowned, visited him and shed many tears because it seemed to him that he was losing a father and the father of his country. Tlacaelel earnestly commended his sons to him, especially the eldest, who had been valiant in the wars that he had waged. The king promised to look after him and to further console the old man invested him with the office and insignias of captain general before his father's eyes, bestowing on him all the privileges of his father; the old man was so happy with this that he soon ended his days. If these had not been the days when he passed to the other life they still could have been regarded as happy, for, starting from the poor and defeated city in which he was born, his efforts had established a great, rich, and powerful realm. As befitted the man who was almost the founder of their empire, the Mexicans performed his obsequies with more pomp and ceremony than they had done for any of their kings. To assuage the grief felt by the entire Mexican people on the death of this their captain, Axacayatl decided to organize an expedition, as was required for his coronation; and he very quickly led his host to the province of Tehuantepec, which is two hundred leagues from

Mexico, and there gave battle to a vast and powerful army, which had joined with neighboring provinces against Mexico. The first to stand before his army was the king himself, challenging his enemies; when they attacked he pretended to flee until he had drawn them into an ambuscade, where he had placed many soldiers covered with straw; these emerged unexpectedly and those who were fleeing turned around, so that they caught the men of Te- huantepec in the middle and attacked them and cruelly massacred them; then they went on to lay waste their city and temple and to chastise all the people severely. They continued without a pause to Huatulco, a port on the South- ern Sea that is very well known today. Axacayatl returned to Mexico from this campaign with large quantities of loot and riches, where he was very splen- didly crowned with great excess of sacrifices and tributes and all else, with everyone coming to see his coronation. The kings of Mexico received their crowns from the hands of the kings of Texcoco, which was their special privilege. He engaged in many other campaigns in which he won great victories, and was always first in leading his people and attacking his enemies, from which he earned the reputation of a very valiant captain.

And he was not content with defeating external enemies but quelled his own rebellious people, something that his ancestors had never been able to do or dared to attempt. We have already mentioned above how some restless and discontented people had left the Mexican commonwealth and founded another city near Mexico, which they named Tlatelolco, located where San- tiago is now.[1] These rebels formed a separate faction and multiplied rapidly and always refused to recognize the lords of Mexico or offer them allegiance. Therefore, King Axacayatl sent to tell them not to remain separate but rather, since they were of the same blood and the same people, to join together and recognize the king of Mexico. To this message the lord of Tlatelolco replied with great scorn and arrogance, challenging the king of Mexico to single combat; he then prepared his people, telling some of them to hide among the reeds of the lake. And to hide them better and mock the Mexicans, he com- manded them to disguise themselves as crows and ducks and birds and frogs

1. The Tlatelolcans, rebellious in Acosta's history, appear more favorably in the account of early Mexican history in the *Florentine Codex* amassed by the Franciscan Fray Bernardino de Sahagún. Most of Sahagún's native informants at the Colegio de Santa Cruz were native Tlatelolcans themselves. The tensions between the two peoples arose when the Mexica annexed Tlatelolco in 1473, abolishing its self-rule and making it subordi- nate to Tenochtitlán.

and other vermin that inhabit the lake, thinking to catch the Mexicans by a ruse when they passed through the paths and causeways of the lake.

Axacayatl, when he had heard the challenge and divined his enemy's stratagem, distributed his people and gave instructions to his general, Tlacaelel's son, to break up the ambush in the lake. Meanwhile he went to Tlatelolco by a little-used path and first of all called upon the man who had challenged him to keep his word. And when the two lords of Mexico and Tlatelolco went out to fight they told all their people not to move until they saw which of the two would be the winner. They obeyed, and the two attacked each other violently; they fought for a good while, and at last the lord of Tlatelolco had to turn his back, for the king of Mexico was attacking him more fiercely than he could withstand. When the men of Tlatelolco saw their captain fleeing they also lost heart and retreated, and the Mexicans followed them and attacked them furiously. The lord of Tlatelolco did not escape Axacayatl; he tried to make a stand at the top of his temple, but Axacayatl climbed after him and seized him violently and threw him down from the temple and then gave orders to set fire to both temple and city. While this was going on the Mexican general was angrily seeking vengeance on those who had tried to defeat them by a ruse, and after he had compelled them to surrender and beg for mercy the general said that he was not going to pardon them until they first behaved like the animals whose guise they had assumed. And so he forced them to croak like frogs and caw like crows, the creatures whose figures they had taken; and he told them that they would be pardoned by that means and no other. By this he meant to insult them and mock and deride their trick. Fear teaches very rapidly. In exchange for their lives they croaked and cawed in all the different voices they were commanded, although they were very resentful of the insulting joke that their enemies had enjoyed at their expense. They say that to this day the Mexicans make fun of the Tlatelolcans, and it is galling to them because they are greatly ashamed to be reminded of those pleasant caws and croaks. King Axacayatl also enjoyed the spectacle, and after it they returned to Mexico with great rejoicing. This king was held to be one of their best; he reigned for eleven years, and his successor was another king not inferior to him in exertions and virtues.

## CHAPTER 19 * OF THE EXPLOITS OF
### AHUITZOTL, EIGHTH KING OF MEXICO

Among the four electors of Mexico, who as I have explained gave the kingdom to whomever they pleased with their votes, there was a very gifted man named Ahuitzotl; the others gave him their votes, and his election was extremely popular with all the people, for in addition to being very brave all considered him to be affable and a friend of good words, a trait that, in those who rule, is the chief reason why they are loved and obeyed. For the celebration of his coronation, the campaign that he decided to undertake was to go and punish the rebellion of the people of Cuetlaxtlán, a very rich and prosperous province that today is one of the most important in New Spain.[1] These people had assaulted the overseers and stewards who were bringing tribute to Mexico and had risen against it; he had great difficulty in subduing them, for they had positioned themselves in a place where a large arm of the sea impeded the Mexicans' passage. To remedy this, with great labor and ingenuity Ahuitzotl had a sort of island made in the water, composed of faggots and earth and many other materials. By means of this construction he and his people could cross over to their enemies and give them battle, and he scattered and conquered and punished them with impunity and returned with great riches and triumph to Mexico to be crowned according to their custom. Ahuitzotl increased his kingdom by means of various conquests until he reached Guatemala, which lies three hundred leagues from Mexico. He was no less liberal than he was valiant: when his tributes arrived (which, as has been said, came with great pomp and abundance), he would emerge from his palace and, assembling all the people together where he wanted them, would order the tributes brought there; and on the spot he would distribute clothing and food and everything they needed, in great abundance, to all who were needy and poor. He distributed the things of value, such as gold, silver, jewels, featherwork, and precious gems, among his captains and soldiers and those who served him, according to the merits and deeds of each.

Ahuitzotl was also much concerned with the public welfare, pulling down buildings that were badly constructed and rebuilding many into sumptuous new ones. He thought that the City of Mexico had insufficient water and that

---

1. Cuetlaxtlán, a region whose name means "place with hides," was a Totonac lordship located on the coast of the Gulf of Mexico.

the lake was very muddy, and he decided to feed it with a very large spring of water that the people of Coyoacán used. To do this he sent for the most important person in that city, who was a famous sorcerer, and when he learned what the king proposed he told him to take care what he was doing, for that would be a very difficult matter and he must understand that if he took that water from its source and put it into Mexico the city would be inundated. The king believed that these were excuses not to do what he commanded, and he angrily expelled the sorcerer from his presence. On the following day he sent an officer of the court to Coyoacán to arrest the sorcerer; when he realized why those ministers of the court were coming he commanded them to enter and then assumed the form of a terrible eagle; frightened by the sight, they returned without arresting him. Now angry, Ahuitzotl sent others, to whom the sorcerer appeared in the guise of a ravening tiger, and they too dared not lay hands on him. A third group went and found him transformed into a horrible serpent, and they feared him still more. Considerably irritated by these tricks, the king sent warnings to Coyoacán that if they did not bring him that sorcerer in bonds he would promptly lay waste the city. In fear of this development the sorcerer at last went to Mexico, either of his own will or forced to it by his people, and when he arrived the king ordered him strangled. And, opening a conduit for the water to flow to Mexico, he at last achieved his end, allowing a large volume of water to flow into the lake. This they celebrated with great ceremonies and superstition, with some priests walking along and censing the banks, others sacrificing quail and sprinkling their blood on the edges of the conduit, and others blowing on conch shells and playing music to the water; the chief priest was attired in the dress of the goddess of water, and all of them were greeting the water and giving it welcome. To this day all of this is depicted in the *Annals of Mexico,* the book of which is in Rome; and it is located in the Holy Library or Vatican book repository, where a father of our society who had come from Mexico saw it and the other histories and explained them to His Holiness's librarian, who was extremely happy to understand that book, which he had never been able to comprehend before. Finally, the water reached Mexico, but its volume was so great that it nearly swamped the city, just as the other had foretold, and indeed ruined a large part of it. But Ahuitzotl's ingenuity repaired everything, for he had a drain made to save the city and he repaired all the parts that had fallen (which were poor dwellings) with strong and well-made work, and so he left his city surrounded with water like another Venice and very well built. The reign of this king endured for eleven years and was followed by that of the last and most powerful king of all the Mexicans.

## CHAPTER 20 * OF THE ELECTION OF THE GREAT MOCTEZUMA, LAST KING OF MEXICO

At the time when the Spaniards entered New Spain, which was the year of Our Lord fifteen hundred and eighteen, Moctezuma, the second of this name and last king of the Mexicans, was reigning. I say the last, although after he died the Mexicans elected another, and did so even during the life of Moctezuma himself, declaring him to be an enemy of the country, as will be seen later; but the one who succeeded him and the one who came into the hands of the Marqués del Valle as a captive had no more than the name and title of king, for almost all his realm had surrendered to the Spaniards.[1] Therefore, we correctly count Moctezuma to be the last, and as such he attained the summit of Mexico's power and greatness, which, although it occurred among barbarians, arouses great admiration in all. Therefore, and because this was the time when God willed that news of his Gospel and the kingdom of Jesus Christ should enter that land, I shall speak at a little more length about the affairs of this king. Moctezuma's character was very grave and deliberate; it was unusual to hear him speak at all, and when he spoke in the supreme council, of which he was a member, his prudence and good sense caused admiration; hence he was feared and respected even before becoming king. Ordinarily he lived apart, in a large room assigned to him in the great temple of Huitzilopochtli, where it was said that their idol communicated many things to him and spoke to him, and so he took pride in being very religious and devout. With these traits, and because he was very noble and courageous, his election was extremely easy and short, as a person on whom everyone's eyes were fixed for that office. Knowing that he was going to be elected, he went and hid in the temple, in that room to which he often withdrew. Whether he considered the office (that of ruling over so many people) very arduous, or whether (as I believe) it was out of hypocrisy and to show that he scorned power, he was at last found there and taken to his

1. The Mexican ruler Cuauhtemoc was elected in the wake of Moctezuma's capture by the Spanish.

consistory with all possible accompaniment and rejoicing. He came with such sobriety that everyone said that his name, Moctezuma, was fitting, for it means "fierce lord." The electors bowed low before him and gave him the news of his election; he went from there to the gods' brazier to burn incense and then to offer his sacrifices, drawing blood from his ears, the fleshy parts of the limbs, and the shins, as was the custom. They dressed him in his royal regalia and pierced his nose through its gristly parts, and hung from it a very rich emerald; these are barbarous and painful customs, yet the grandeur of reigning caused him not feel it. Then, seated on his throne, he heard the orations made to him, pronounced with elegance and skill as was their wont.

The king of Texcoco made the first oration, which, as it has been preserved fresh in men's memory and is worthy of being heard, I shall reproduce here. It runs as follows: "The great good fortune attained by this realm (oh most noble youth) in having deserved to have you at the head of it all, can easily be recognized by the ease and perfect agreement of your election and by the general rejoicing that everyone displays on account of it. They are surely right, for the Mexican empire is now so great and so extensive that to rule a world like this and carry such a heavy load requires no less strength and determination than that of your steadfast and fervent heart, nor less delibera-tion, knowledge, and prudence than yours. I clearly see that the omnipotent god loves this city, for he has given it light to choose what was best for it. For who can doubt that a prince who before reigning had studied the nine folds of the heavens will not now, obliged to it by the burden of his reign, achieve the things of earth with equal spirit, in order to assist his people? Who doubts that the great and valiant effort that you have always shown in impor-tant matters will not more than suffice now, when it is so necessary? Who could believe that, in a man of such valor, the orphan and the widow will lack recourse? Who is not convinced that the Mexican empire has reached the summit of its power, since the lord of all creation has taught you so much that whoever sees you receives that power? Rejoice, oh happy land, for the creator has given you a prince who will be a strong column upon which to lean; he will be father and refuge to whom you may go for help; he will be more than a brother in compassion and mercy toward his subjects. Surely you have a king who will not take advantage of his estate to pamper himself and lie abed, occupied in vices and mere pastimes; rather, in his deepest sleep his heart will be assailed and the care that he must take of you will leave him wakeful. He will not taste the most delicious mouthful of his food for thinking of your good. Tell me then, oh happy realm, if I am correct in bidding you to rejoice and be heartened in such a king. And you, most noble youth and our very powerful lord, be confident and of good cheer, for since the lord of all creation has given you this office he will also give you strength to hold it. And you may be sure that he who has always been so liberal with you in the past will not deny you his best gifts, for he has placed you in the highest estate; and may you enjoy it for many and prosperous years to come."

King Moctezuma listened very attentively to this speech, and when it was finished they say that he was so overcome with emotion that, although he tried to answer three times, he could not for his tears, those tears that are often shed from pure pleasure, combining the kind of devotion that arises from one's own contentment with a display of great humility. At last, over-coming his emotion, he spoke briefly as follows: "I would be blind indeed, good king of Texcoco, if I did not see and understand that the things you have told me have simply been a favor that you do me, for, although there are so many noble and great-hearted men in this realm, you chose the least deserving, who is myself. And certainly I feel that I have so little talent for such an arduous task that I do not know what to do except to appeal to the lord of all creation to favor me and to beseech you all to pray to him for me." When he had spoken these words he was again overcome and wept.

### CHAPTER 21 ∗ HOW MOCTEZUMA ORDERED THE SERVICE OF HIS HOUSEHOLD AND THE WAR HE WAGED FOR HIS CORONATION

This king, who had made such a show of humility and emotion upon his election, began to disclose his haughty intentions as soon as he became king.[1] First he commanded that no plebeian could serve in his house or hold royal office, as had been the custom of his ancestors up to that time, and he criticized them severely for having been served by persons of low estate; and he required all the lords and notable people to live in his palace and carry out

1. In comparison with his treatment of other leaders, Acosta presents a detailed description of Moctezuma. He reasons that this detail is necessary since Moctezuma governed when the Spaniards arrived. Sources, both native and Spanish, were more forthcoming about this leader in their midst. They also embellished the negative traits of their leader. "Haughty intentions" were less suited for a king memorialized through the lens of defeat.

the offices of his household and his court. In this he was opposed by an old man of great authority, a tutor of his who had reared him, telling him to take care because there were many dangers in such an action, for it would mean alienating and distancing himself from the common people and that they would not even dare to look him in the face when they saw themselves so spurned. He replied that that was what he wanted, and that he would not permit nobles and plebeians to be mingled as had been done until now, and that the service that such folk did represented what they were, so that the kings gained no repute from it. Finally, the question was settled by his calling his council and depriving lowborn persons of all the seats and offices that they had had in his household and court and giving them to nobles, and it was done. After this he set forth in person on the exploit necessary for his coronation. A very remote province in the direction of the Northern Sea had rebelled against the royal crown. He took with him to that province the flower of his people, all splendidly arrayed and well equipped.[2] He pursued the war with so much courage and skill that in a short time he had subjugated the whole province and severely punished those responsible and returned with a very large number of captives for the sacrifices and many other spoils. On his return all the cities received him with great solemnity, and the cities' lords served him water with their own hands, acting as his servants, something that they had not done with any of the previous kings; such was the fear and respect they had come to feel for him. In Mexico the festivities of his coronation were performed with such a display of dances, comedies, short theatrical pieces, illuminations, contrivances, games, and such a wealth of tribute brought from all parts of his realms that many strange people who had never been seen or heard of before came to Mexico, and even the Mexicans' enemies, such as those of Tlaxcala and Michoacán, came in very large numbers, in disguise, to see the celebrations. When Moctezuma learned of this he commanded that they be lodged and treated magnificently, like his own person, and stands as handsome as his own were built from which they could see the festivities, and at night both they and the king himself entered them and performed their games and masques. And because mention has been made of these provinces it is well to know that neither Michoacán,

2. The "flower of his people" is a reference to the most valiant warriors of Mexico-Tenochtitlán. Recall that the flower wars, *xochiyaoyotl*, were waged to demonstrate Mexica power and collect sacrificial victims.

Tlaxcala, nor Tepeaca ever consented to surrender to Mexico; rather, they fought valiantly against it, and sometimes the men of Michoacán defeated those of Mexico, and so did the men of Tepeaca.[3] It was there that Marqués Don Hernán Cortés, after he and the Spaniards were expelled from Mexico, decided to found the first Spanish city, which he called (if I remember correctly) Segura de la Frontera, although it never had many inhabitants, and with the later conquest of the City of Mexico all the Spaniards went to live there. Indeed, the men of Tepeaca and those of Tlaxcala and those of Michoacán always held out against the Mexicans, although Moctezuma told Cortés that he had deliberately foreborne to conquer them so as to have places to make war and take large numbers of captives.

### CHAPTER 22 * OF MOCTEZUMA'S HABITS AND GREAT STATE

This king insisted on being respected and even worshiped almost as a god. No plebeian could look him in the face, and if one did so he died for it; he never put foot to the ground but was always carried on the shoulders of his lords, and if he had to step down they placed a rich carpet on which he could tread. When he traveled he and the lords of his company went in a sort of park made for the purpose, and all the rest of the people were outside the enclosure, on either side of it. He never wore a garment twice or ate or drank from a vessel or plate more than once; everything had always to be new, and whatever he had used once he gave to his servants, who by this means became rich and sumptuously dressed. He was very insistent on keeping the laws; sometimes when he returned from a war he would pretend that he was going to some place of recreation and would disguise himself to see whether some part of the festivity or reception would be omitted because it was thought that he was not present; and if too much or too little was done he would invariably punish it. He also disguised himself many times to learn how his ministers performed their office and even sent people to offer bribes to his

3. The native enemies of the Mexica aided Cortés immeasurably in the conquest of Tenochtitlán. Evidence that preconquest identities and enmities lingered in the colonial period appears in texts authored by members of the mestizo elite, like the *Historia de Tlaxcala* by the Tlaxcala native Diego Muñoz Camargo, the *Crónica mexicáyotl* by Don Fernando Alvarado Tezozomoc of Tenochtitlán, and *Obras históricas* by Don Fernando de Alva Ixtlilxochitl of Texcoco, as well as works like the *Codex Chimalpahin,* penned by the nonelite Don Domingo de San Antón Muñón Chimalpahin Quauchtlehuacnitzin, a native of Amaquemecan Chalco.

judges or encourage them to do some bad thing, and if he learned about anything of the kind he would summarily sentence them to death. It made no difference to him if they were lords or even relatives, or even his brothers, for the offender invariably died. He had little contact with his people and rarely allowed himself to be seen; he secluded himself for long periods, pondering the government of his kingdom. In addition to being a harsh judge, and sober, he was very warlike and even daring, and so he achieved great victories and attained all that great state, which, because it is written of in histories of Spain, I do not think it necessary to describe further. And, as for what is said from this point onward, I will take care to write what the books and tales of the Indians write, of whom our Spanish authors make no mention because they have not fully understood the secrets of that land. And they are things very worthy of consideration, as will be seen.

### CHAPTER 23 * OF THE STRANGE OMENS AND PRODIGIES THAT APPEARED IN MEXICO BEFORE ITS EMPIRE PERISHED

Although Holy Scripture forbids us to credit omens and vain prognostications,[1] and Jeremiah warns us not to fear the signs of heaven as the heathens do,[2] that same Holy Scripture also shows us that in the course of some universal changes and chastisements that God wishes to perform the signs and monsters and prodigies that often precede them are not to be despised, as Eusebius of Caesarea tells us,[3] for the Lord of Heaven and Earth himself commands these strange new things in the heavens and the elements and in animals and others of his creatures, so that in part they may serve as a warning to men and in part be the beginning of chastisement, owing to the fear and terror they cause. In the second Book of the Machabees,[4] it is written that before that great change and upheaval of the people of Israel caused by the tyranny of Antiochus called Epiphanes, whom Holy Writ calls "a wicked root,"[5] it happened that for forty whole days great squads of horsemen were seen in the air, with gilded armor and lances and shields and ferocious horses,

1. Deuteronomy, 18, 10 and 11 (O'G).
2. Jeremiah, 10, 2 (O'G).
3. Eusebius of Caesarea, *De Demonstratione Evangelica*, book 9, 1st demonstration (O'G).
4. 2 Machabees, 5, 2 (O'G).
5. 1 Machabees, 1, 11 (O'G).

and with drawn swords, and they skirmished together, injuring and wounding one another; and they say that when the people of Jerusalem saw this they prayed to God to lift his wrath from them and turn those prodigies to good. In the Book of Wisdom also, when God wished to rescue his people out of Egypt and punish the Egyptians, we are told of visions and monstrous and terrifying things, such as sudden fires and horrible visions that appeared.[6] Josephus, in his book *De Bello Judaico,* tells of many and great prodigies that preceded the destruction of Jerusalem and the last captivity of the unhappy folk who so stubbornly held God to be their enemy. And Eusebius of Caesarea and others took this same account from Josephus, lending authority to those prophecies.[7] Historians are full of similar observations at the time of great changes in countries or commonwealths or religion. And Paulus Orosius recounts no few of them, and doubtless his observations are not erroneous, although to believe lightly in prophecies and signs is vanity and even superstition, prohibited by the law of our God. But in large matters and the changes of nations and kingdoms and very notable laws it is not erroneous but correct to believe that the wisdom of the Most High orders and permits things that give some indication of what is to be, so that it may serve, as I have said, to warn some and chastise others, and is a sign to all that the King of Heaven is concerned in the affairs of men. God has ordained the greatest and most terrible signs imaginable for the greatest change in the world, which will be the Day of Judgment; thus, to denote other lesser (but important) changes in different parts of the world, he does not fail to give some miraculous signs that he has at his disposal, according to the law of his eternal wisdom. It must also be understood that although the devil is the father of lies the King of Glory often forces him to tell the truth, and, out of pure fear and spite, he tells it quite frequently. Thus he cried out in the desert,[8] and through the mouths of those possessed with devils, that Jesus was the Savior who had come to destroy him; and through the girl possessed by the pythonical spirit he said that Paul was preaching the true God;[9] and by appearing to Pilate's wife and troubling her, he caused her to intervene for Jesus, that just man. Other histories in addition to sacred history tell of various testimonies by idols approving the Christian religion, of which Lactantius, Prosper, and others

6. Book of Wisdom, 17, 6 (O'G).

7. Eusebius of Caesarea, *Ecclesiastica Historia,* book 1 (O'G).

8. Saint Matthew, 1; Saint Luke, 4, 41 (O'G).

9. Acts, 16, 16 and 17 (O'G).

make mention. Eusebius may be read in the books of his *Evangelical Preparation,* and later in those of his *Demonstration,* which deals with this subject at length.

I have mentioned all this deliberately so that no one will scorn what is told in the histories and annals of the Indians about strange prodigies and the prophecies that they had concerning the end of their kingdom and the kingdom of the devil, whom they all worshiped.[10] As much because this happened in times very close to our own, whose memory is still green, as because it is very logical that the cunning devil should reject and lament so great a change, and that God at the same time should begin to punish those cruel and abominable idolaters, I say that these prodigies seem to be worthy of belief, and I consider them as such and so describe them here. What happened was that after Moctezuma had reigned in great prosperity for many years and become so proud that he was served and feared and even worshiped almost as a god, the Most High began to chastise him and in part to warn him, allowing those same demons whom he worshiped to give him lamentable warnings of the loss of his kingdom and to torment him with predictions never seen before, leaving him so melancholy and awestruck that he did not know what to do. The idol of the Cholulans, who is called Quetzalcoatl, announced that strange people were coming to possess those realms. The king of Texcoco, who was a great sorcerer and had made a pact with the devil, paid Moctezuma an unexpected visit and swore to him that his gods had told him that great losses and travails were being prepared for him and all his realm. Many sorcerers and wizards went to tell him the same, and among them was one in particular who foretold exactly what happened to him later, and while Moctezuma was speaking to him he observed that he had no thumbs on his hands or great toes on his feet. Angry about such news, he ordered all those sorcerers seized, but they soon disappeared from the prison. Moctezuma was so enraged by this that, unable to kill them, he had their wives and children put to death and their homes and property destroyed.

Harassed by these pronouncements, he tried to placate the wrath of his gods and for this purpose had a huge stone brought to make savage sacrifices

10. Although Acosta claims that the omens sighted by the Mexica people were signs supplied by God of a miraculous occurrence, it is highly plausible that the meaning of the omens was assigned in retrospect by native peoples looking for a rationale for the disastrous sequence of events that befell their homeland. For an account of these omens from the native perspective, see Miguel León-Portilla, ed., *The Broken Spears: The Aztec Account of the Conquest of Mexico* (Boston: Beacon, 1992).

upon it. When a large number of people went with their ropes and gear they could not move it, although they broke many very heavy ropes in the process; but as they continued to try they heard a voice near the stone telling them not to labor in vain, that they could not move it, for the lord of all creation did not want those things to be done anymore. When Moctezuma heard this he ordered the sacrifices to be made there. They say that another voice was heard: "Have I not told you that it is not the will of the lord of creation to do this? So that you may see that it is so, I will let myself be moved for a time, and then you will be unable to budge me." And the fact is that for a little while they moved it easily and then could not move it at all, until after many pleas the stone allowed itself to be dragged to the entrance of the City of Mexico, where it suddenly fell into a canal; and when they searched for it, it did not reappear, but they found it again in the very place from which they had brought it, which left them very bewildered and frightened.

At this same time a very large and shining flame of fire appeared in the sky, in the shape of a pyramid, which would begin to appear at midnight and rise little by little, and at dawn, when the sun came up, it would reach the zenith and disappear. It appeared in this way every night for a year, and every time it came out the people gave great cries, as was their custom, realizing that it was an omen of terrible evil. Also, once, when there was no fire either inside or outside the temple, everything caught fire, even though there had been no thunder or lightning, and when the guards began to cry out many people came with water, and nothing served to put it out until everything was consumed; they say that the fire seemed to be coming out of the beams themselves and that water made it burn even more fiercely. They also saw a comet appear in broad daylight, which moved from west to east scattering a large number of sparks; they say that its shape was like a very long tail, and at its front was something like three heads. With no wind or movement of the ground or any other reason, the large lake that lies between Mexico and Texcoco suddenly began to boil and rose bubbling so violently that all the buildings near it fell to the ground. At this time, they say, they heard many cries like that of a woman in anguish, which sometimes said, "Oh, my children, your destruction has come!" At other times it said, "Oh, my children! Whither shall I lead you so that you will not be wholly lost?"[11] Various two-

11. The weeping woman, known as La Llorona, has become incorporated into contemporary Mexican folklore.

headed monsters also appeared, which disappeared when they were brought before the king.

Among all these monsters two were the strangest. One was that the fishermen on the lake captured a bird the size and color of a crane but of a shape that was odd and outlandish. They took it to Moctezuma, who at that time was in some palaces known as places of weeping and mourning, all tinged with black, for, just as he had various palaces for recreation, he also had them for periods of sorrow; and his sorrow was very great because of the threats his gods were making through these dismal omens. The fishermen arrived at exactly noon and set that bird before him; on top of its head it had a shining and transparent thing like a mirror, in which Moctezuma saw that the heavens and the stars appeared. He was astonished by this, and turning his eyes to heaven and seeing no stars there he again looked into the mirror and saw that warriors were coming from the east, and that they were armed, fighting and killing. He sent for his soothsayers, for he had many, and when they had seen the same thing and did not know how to answer what was asked of them, the bird suddenly disappeared and was never seen again; and because of this Moctezuma was very sad and greatly perturbed.

The other thing that happened was that a farmer known to be a good and honest man came to talk to him. This man told him that he had been working in his field on the previous day when he saw a very large eagle flying toward him and that it seized him without hurting him and carried him to a certain cave, where it set him down, saying, "Mighty lord, I have brought the one you commanded me to bring." And the Indian farmer looked all around to see with whom it was speaking and saw no one, and then a voice said to him, "Do you know that man who is lying there on the ground?" And, looking at the ground, he saw a man in a deep sleep, with royal insignias and flowers in his hand, as well as a censer with incense burning in it, as the custom of that country was; and when the farmer recognized him he realized that he was the great king Moctezuma. After having gazed upon him the farmer answered, "Great lord, this appears to be our king Moctezuma." The voice spoke again, saying, "You speak truth; look upon him, how he is so deeply asleep and unaware of the great travails and evils that will surely come upon him; the time is at hand when he must pay for the many offenses he has committed against God and the tyrannies of his great pride, and he is so unaware of this, and so blind in his wretchedness, that he no longer feels. And in proof of this take this burning censer that he has in his hand and hold it to his thigh, and you will see that he feels nothing." The poor peasant dared not draw nearer or do what he was told because of the great fear that all the people had of the king, but the voice spoke again: "Do not fear, for I am incomparably greater than this king. I can destroy him and defend you; therefore, do as I command." With this the farmer, taking the censer from the king's hand, held it burning to the king's thigh, and he neither moved nor showed any awareness. When this was done the voice said to him that, since he saw the king so deeply asleep, he must go and awaken him and tell him everything that had happened; and then the eagle, by the same command, again carried him off and returned him to the same place from which he had been brought, and, carrying out what he had been told to do, he had come to warn the king. They say that Moctezuma then looked at his thigh and saw that it was burned, for until then he had not felt it, and he was extremely sad and troubled. It was possible that what the farmer had told him had happened in an imaginary vision.

It is not beyond belief that God devised by means of a good angel, or permitted by means of a bad one, to give that warning to the farmer (though a heathen) as a punishment for the king; for we read in Holy Scripture that heathens and sinners, like Nebuchadnezzar and Balaam and the pythoness of Saul, have had similar apparitions.[12] And even though some of these things may not have happened exactly as described it is certain that Moctezuma was very sad and greatly afflicted by many signs that his kingdom and authority were soon to come to an end.

## CHAPTER 24 * OF THE NEWS THAT MOCTEZUMA RECEIVED OF THE SPANIARDS WHO HAD REACHED HIS COUNTRY AND THE EMBASSY THAT HE SENT THEM

After Moctezuma had reigned for fourteen years, which was in the year of our Lord fifteen hundred and seventeen, some ships with people in them appeared in the Northern Sea, and the dwellers along the coast, who were vassals of Moctezuma, were greatly astonished by this; and wishing to satisfy themselves as to who they were the Indians went out in canoes to the ships,

12. Daniel, 2, 1; Numbers, 22, 31; 1 Kings, 28, 7–5 (O'G).

taking with them much food and rich clothing as if they wished to sell them.[1] The Spaniards welcomed them aboard their ships and in payment for the food and clothing that they were happy to receive gave them strings of red, blue, green, and yellow glass beads, which the Indians thought were precious stones. And after the Spaniards had found out who their king was, and how great was his power, they dismissed them, telling them to take those stones to their lord and say to him that for the present they were unable to go and see him but that they would soon return and visit him. With this message the coastal Indians went to Mexico, taking with them everything that they had seen painted on a cloth, the ships and the men and what they were like, together with the stones that they had been given. King Moctezuma was very thoughtful when he received this message and commanded them to say nothing to anyone. The next day he assembled his council and, showing them the cloth and strings of beads, consulted with them as to what he should do; and he decided to give orders to all the seacoasts to be watchful and inform him of anything that happened. The following year, which was early in the year fifteen hundred and eighteen, they saw coming over the sea the fleet in which the Marqués del Valle, Don Hernán Cortés, and his companions arrived. Moctezuma was greatly perturbed by this news, and when he consulted with his council they told him that undoubtedly their ancient and great lord Quetzalcoatl had come, for he had said that he would return and that he was coming from the direction of the east, whither he had departed. There was a belief among the Indians that in past times a great prince had left them and promised to return; I will discuss the foundation of this belief elsewhere. At last they sent five important ambassadors to welcome the Spaniards with rich gifts, telling them that they had known that their great lord Quetzalcoatl was coming there and that his servant Moctezuma had sent them to visit him, for he considered himself the god's servant. The Spaniards understood this message through Marina, an Indian woman they had brought with them who knew the Mexican language.[2]

1. Hernán Cortés did not reach Veracruz until April of 1519, but two previous Spanish expeditions had scouted the region. A 1517 junket explored the coast of the Yucatan, and a 1518 excursion went as far as the coast of Veracruz. This history likely refers to some sighting or contact with the 1518 group.

2. Marina was the Spanish name given at baptism to the native woman known as Malintzin or Malinche. Her role as interpreter for and companion to Cortés was noted by most Spanish chroniclers, yet her early life history remains unclear. Her language skills suggest she was born into a Nahuatl-speaking family and was sold

And, as it seemed to Hernán Cortés that this was a good opportunity for his entry into Mexico, he ordered his lodgings very well furnished and dressed himself with great pomp and adornment and had the ambassadors enter, and they all but worshiped him as a god. They presented their embassy, saying that his servant Moctezuma invited him to visit, and that as his lieutenant he held the whole land in his name, and that he, Moctezuma, knew that he was the Topilcin who had promised many years before to return to see them, and that they had brought him some of the vestments that he used to wear when he lived among them; and they begged him to accept them, offering him many and very fine presents. Cortés answered, accepting their offers and giving them to understand that he was the one they said he was, and they were very happy when they saw that he treated them with great love and benevolence (for in this, as in other things, this valiant captain was worthy of praise). And if his plan had been carried out, which was to win those people to him by good treatment, it seemed that the best imaginable occasion had been offered to bring that whole land to the Gospel in peace and love. But the sins of those cruel murderers and slaves of Satan cried out for punishment from Heaven, and the sins of many Spaniards were not small ones; and thus God's lofty plans decreed the salvation of peoples by first cutting off the damaged roots, and, as the Apostle says, the wickedness and blindness of one side meant the salvation of the other.[3] Indeed, on the day after the embassy that has been described, the captains and leaders of the fleet came to the flagship; understanding what was at stake, and the power and wealth of Moctezuma's kingdom, they thought it necessary to acquire the reputation among those people of being hardy and valiant men. Thus, although they were few, they would be feared and received in Mexico. For this purpose they fired all the guns in the ships, and as this was something the Indians had never seen before they were as terrorized as if the heavens had fallen on them. Later the soldiers had the idea of challenging them to fight, and when the Indians did not dare to do so they taunted and insulted them, showing them their swords, lances, javelins, halberds, and other weapons,

---

or traded into slavery in the Yucatan as a young girl. She spoke Nahuatl and Maya and translated between the Mexica leaders and Cortés with the assistance of Jerónimo de Aguilar, a Spaniard shipwrecked on the Yucatan Peninsula, who spoke Spanish and Maya. On her symbolic role in Mexican culture, see Sandra Messinger Cypess, *La Malinche in Mexican Literature from History to Myth* (Austin: University of Texas Press, 1991).
3. Saint Paul to the Romans, 11, 25 (O'G).

which frightened them very much. The poor Indians left the place so amazed and terrified that they changed their minds completely, saying that it was not their king and lord Topilcin who was coming but rather some enemy gods coming to destroy them.

When the ambassadors reached Mexico, Moctezuma was in his hall of audience, and before the embassy reported to him the unhappy king caused a number of men to be sacrificed in his presence, and he sprinkled the ambassadors with the blood of the sacrifices, believing that by this ceremony (which they used in especially solemn embassies) the news would be good. But when he had heard the whole story and received information about the manner of the ships and people and weapons he was confused and perplexed; and after holding his council he found no better plan than to try to delay the arrival of those strangers by magical arts and conjurations. The Indians often used these means, for they had great traffic with the devil, with whose help they often achieved strange effects. Therefore, the sorcerers, necromancers, and enchanters joined together and, persuaded by Moctezuma, undertook to make those people return to their own land; and for this purpose they went to certain places they deemed suitable to invoke demons and practice their art. It was a task worthy of consideration, and they did everything they could and knew. Seeing that nothing impeded the Christians, they returned to their king, saying that these were more than men, for none of their conjurations and enchantments did them any harm. So it seemed to Moctezuma that he should try another course, and pretending to be happy about the Spaniards' arrival he sent messages to his whole kingdom to tell his people to serve those celestial gods who had come to his land. All the people were in a state of great sadness and alarm. News arrived frequently that the Spaniards were asking many questions about the king and his ways of behaving and his household and possessions. He grieved excessively over this, and when his people and the sorcerers advised him to hide, and offered to place him where no living creature could find him, he thought it base to do so and decided to wait even though he died for it. And at last he left his royal houses for other dwellings that he had in order to leave his palace as a lodging for those gods, as the Indians called them.

CHAPTER 25 * OF THE SPANIARDS' ENTRY
INTO MEXICO

I do not intend to deal with the deeds of the Spaniards who won New Spain, nor the strange events that befell them, nor the invincible spirit and valor of their captain, Don Hernán Cortés, for there are many histories and reports about this, including those written by that same Hernán Cortés to the Emperor Charles V, which, though expressed in a plain style and in no way boastful, give sufficient information about what happened; and it was a great deal and very worthy of eternal memory. But to carry out my intent I must tell what the Indians recount of this matter, which has not been published in Spanish until now. When Moctezuma learned of the captain's victories and that he was coming to confront him, and that he had allied himself with the Tlaxcallans, Moctezuma's chief enemies, and had severely punished the men of Cholula, who were his friends, it occurred to him to deceive Cortés, or to test him, by sending a chief who would pretend to be Moctezuma, with his insignias and retinue; this fiction having been seen through by the *marqués* with the help of the Tlaxcallans who accompanied him, he sent him back with a gentle reproof for trying to deceive him. This left Moctezuma very perplexed, and in his fear, as he turned the situation over in his mind, he again tried to make the Christians turn back by using sorcerers and enchanters. For this purpose he assembled many more than he had done the first time, threatening to kill them if they returned without accomplishing what he had sent them to do. They promised to do it.

A very large group of these diabolical officers went to the Chalco road, which was the one on which the Spaniards were coming. As they mounted a hill, Tezcatlipoca, one of their chief gods, appeared to them; he was coming from the direction of the Spanish camp, dressed like a man of Chalco, and his breast was bound with eight turns of a hempen rope. He came like one beside himself and like a man drunk with passion and fury. When he reached the group of necromancers and sorcerers, he stopped and said to them very angrily, "Why do you come here? What is Moctezuma trying to do with your aid? Too late has he made his decision; it is ordained that his kingdom and his honor and everything he possesses will be taken from him because of the great acts of tyranny that he has committed against his vassals, for he has not reigned like a true lord but like a tyrant and a traitor." On hearing these words the sorcerers recognized him as their idol and prostrated themselves before him and made a stone altar there and covered it with flowers that were growing nearby. Paying no heed to this, he again railed at them, saying, "Why have you come here, traitors? Turn, turn and look at Mexico, so that you may know what is to become of her." It is said that they turned back to look at Mexico and that they saw the city burning and wholly consumed in living flames. Upon this the demon disappeared, and, not daring to take another step, they sent word to Moctezuma. For a time he was unable to speak, gazing thoughtfully at the ground, and after that time had passed he said, "What are we to do if the gods and our friends do not favor us but rather cause our enemies to prosper? Now I am determined, and let us all be determined, that whatever happens we will not flee, nor will we hide or display cowardice. I feel pity for the old and the children who have neither feet nor hands to defend themselves." And so saying he fell silent, for emotion had begun to overwhelm him.

At last, as the *marqués* was approaching Mexico, Moctezuma decided to make a virtue of necessity and went out to receive him some three-quarters of a league from the city, going with great pomp and carried on the shoulders of four lords, covered by a rich canopy of gold and featherwork. Moctezuma stepped down when they met, and they greeted one another very courteously; and Don Hernán Cortés told him not to be sorrowful, that he had not come to take his realm or diminish his authority. Moctezuma lodged Cortés and his companions in his chief palace, which was very great, and he went to other houses that he had. That night the soldiers fired off their artillery pieces in rejoicing and astonished the Indians no little, unused as they were to such music. On the following day Cortés assembled Moctezuma and the lords of his court in a large room. And when they were gathered together he told them, seated in a chair, that he was the servant of a great prince who had commanded him to go to those lands to do good and that in those lands he had found that the Tlaxcallans, who were his friends, complained bitterly about the affronts that the Mexicans constantly offered them. And he wished to know who was at fault and wanted to reconcile them so that from now on they would not do each other harm, and he and his brothers, who were the Spaniards, would stay there without doing them injury; rather, they would help them all they could. He made sure that everyone fully understood this speech, making use of his interpreters; when its purport was grasped by the king and the other Mexican lords their joy was great, and great also were the proofs of friendship that they gave to Cortés and the others.

Many believe that if matters had stayed as they were on that day the Spaniards could easily have done whatever they wished with both king and kingdom and could have given them Christ's law with great satisfaction and peace. But the judgments of God are sublime and the sins on both sides were many, and so the matter turned out very differently, although in the end God succeeded in his intent to do mercy to that nation with the light of his Gospel, first having judged and punished those who, in his divine view, deserved chastisement. Indeed, there were occasions when suspicions, complaints, and offenses arose on one side or the other; and Cortés, observing that the minds of the Indians had turned against him, seized King Moctezuma and arrested him and put him in irons, a deed that astonished the world, as did that other deed of his at the time when he burned the ships and was surrounded by his enemies, to conquer or die.[1] The worst thing of all was that because of Pánfilo de Narváez's unexpected arrival in Veracruz to take over the land, Cortés had to depart from the City of Mexico and leave poor Moctezuma in the power of his companions, who did not possess Cortés's discretion or moderation.[2] And so things came to a total break, with no possibility of peace.

### CHAPTER 26 * OF THE DEATH OF MOCTEZUMA AND THE SPANIARDS' DEPARTURE FROM THE CITY OF MEXICO

During Cortés's absence from Mexico, it occurred to the man he had left as his lieutenant to apply punishment to the Mexicans, and it was so excessive,

1. Despite Acosta's insistence that he will "tell what the Indians recount," his interpretation of this turn of events decidedly favors Cortés, whom he portrays as offering friendship and turning against Moctezuma only after being turned against himself. Diego Durán, for one, has a less Spanish-friendly interpretation of this. See his *The History of the Indies of New Spain,* 530–31.

2. The expedition of Pánfilo de Narváez arrived to the shores of Veracruz with orders to arrest Cortés. In 1519, Cortés was appointed by Governor Diego Velásquez to head the third expedition to the coast of Mexico. While Cortés prepared to set sail, gathering hundreds of men and sufficient supplies, Velásquez began to rethink his appointment of Cortés. When Cortés heard rumors to this effect, he rounded up his men and set sail as a rebel conquistador of sorts. Narváez arrived with the goal of halting the unauthorized Cortés expedition only to find that Cortés's might and successes had granted him authority anew in the eyes of the Crown.

and so many nobles died during a great *mitote,* or dance, which they held in
the palace, that all the people ran riot and with furious rage took up arms to
avenge themselves and kill the Spaniards; and so they surrounded the palace
and pressed them hard, nor did the harm done them by artillery and crossbows, which was great, cause them to desist.[1] They persisted in this for many
days, withholding food from the Spaniards and letting no one go in or out.
They fought with stones, throwing spears, their style of lances, and swords,
which are clubs with five or six sharp knives set into them, so sharp that the
histories tell that in one of those battles an Indian completely severed a
horse's head with one of these knives. As they were fighting one day with this
determination and fury, to quiet them the Spaniards made Moctezuma and
another lord climb to a rooftop, both of them sheltered by the shields of the
soldiers who accompanied them. When they saw their lord Moctezuma all of
them stopped fighting, and a great silence fell. Then Moctezuma called to
them, through that other lord, to desist and not to make war on the Spaniards, for because he was a prisoner, as they could see, it would do them no
good. On hearing this a noble youth named Cuauhtémoc, whom the Indians
were already trying to make their king, shouted to Moctezuma to retreat like
a knave, since he had been such a coward, and that they would no longer
obey him but would give him the punishment he deserved; and to insult him
still more, he called him a woman. Upon this, drawing his bow, Cuauhtémoc
began to shoot arrows at him, and the people again threw stones and continued their battle. Many say that it was then that Moctezuma was struck by a
stone, from which he died. The Indians of Mexico say that this was not the
case but that he later died as I will describe.

---

1. Unarmed soldiers danced in the Great Temple Square celebrating the feast of Toxcatl, held to worship the
gods Huitzilopochtli and Tezcatlipoca. Accounts differ on Cortés's whereabouts during this attack. The
*Florentine Codex* suggests Cortés was fending off the Narváez troops. Again, to compare Durán's account, he
places Cortés in the city at the time of the massacre. Further, he suggests that the story was fabricated to place
Cortés on the coast fighting Narváez for political expediency: "The killing in the temple courtyard was
attributed solely to Alvarado, and a certain conqueror told me that, while Cortés was in Veracruz fighting
with Narváez, in his absence Alvarado committed this atrocious massacre. However, I believe that this
account may have been invented so that such an appalling act would not be attributed to a person who
deserves to be praised and honored as one of the most valorous men. . . . What makes me think that in truth
Cortés was not absent from the city at this time is that immediately after the massacre the Indians rebelled
against the Spaniards and surrounded them, and not even a bird could have penetrated the city without
having been seen, much less Cortés with Narváez's men, who had increased his ranks." Durán also differs on
the account of Moctezuma's death, saying that the Mexica king was knifed by the Spanish. See Durán, *The
History of the Indies of New Spain,* 542, 545.

Alvarado and the other Spaniards, seeing themselves so hard pressed, sent to tell Captain Cortés of the great danger they were in. And he, who with wonderful skill and courage had taken Narváez into custody and brought most of Narváez's men over to his side, came by forced marches to help his people in Mexico; and, waiting for a time when the Indians were resting, for their custom was to rest one day after four days of fighting, he entered with skill and strength to bring them aid in the royal houses where the Spaniards had fortified themselves. They rejoiced greatly over this and fired off their cannon. But as the Mexicans' fury was increasing and there was no way to pacify them, and supplies of food were almost exhausted, Captain Cortés saw that there was no hope of defending themselves further and decided to depart by stealth one night; and, having made wooden bridges with which to cross two very large and dangerous canals, he set out at midnight in silence. And when most of his people had crossed the first canal an Indian woman heard them before they reached the second; she cried out that their enemies were leaving, and at her cries all the people rushed upon them with terrible fury, so that as the Spaniards crossed the second canal among those who were wounded and trampled more than three hundred died. On that spot today is a hermitage which is called, needlessly and wrongly, the hermitage of the martyrs. Many, because they tried to keep the gold and jewels that they carried, were unable to escape; others, because they stopped to collect their booty and bring it with them, were captured by the Mexicans and cruelly sacrificed before their idols.

The Mexicans found their king Moctezuma dead and, according to what they say, stabbed many times; and they believe that the Spaniards murdered him that night along with other lords. But in the account that he sent to the emperor the *marqués* says instead that the Mexicans killed one of Moctezuma's sons, whom he was taking with him, along with other nobles. And he says that all that wealth of gold and precious stones and silver that the Spaniards were carrying fell into the lake, where it never again appeared. However that may be, Moctezuma made a wretched end and paid what he owed for his arrogance and tyranny to the impartial judgment of God. For when his body came into the hands of the Indians they refused to do him funeral honors as a king or even as an ordinary man, casting the body away with great scorn and anger. One of his servants, grieving for the unhappy fate of a king who previously had been feared and worshiped like a god, made a bonfire on the spot and placed his ashes as best he could in a very humble place.

To return to the Spaniards who escaped, they endured great exhaustion and travail, for the Indians pursued them obstinately for two or three days and allowed them not a moment's rest; and they were so short of food that they shared a very few grains of maize to eat.[2] The accounts of both Spaniards and Indians agree that Our Lord saved them by a miracle and that Mary the Mother of Mercy and Queen of Heaven defended them miraculously on a little hill three leagues from the city of Mexico, where today a church has been established in memory of this, with the name of Our Lady of Succor. The Spaniards went to their friends in Tlaxcala, where they regrouped, and with their allies' help and the admirable valor and character of Hernán Cortés they again made war on Mexico on land and sea, with the stratagem of the brigantines that they launched on the lake; and after many battles and more than sixty very dangerous encounters they succeeded in taking the whole city on the day of St. Hippolytus, the thirteenth day of August in the year fifteen hundred and twenty-one. The last king of the Mexicans, who had stubbornly carried on the war, was at last captured in a large canoe in which he was fleeing and brought with other chiefs before Cortés. With extraordinary courage this young king took out a dagger, went up to Cortés, and said, "Until now I have done what I could in defense of my people; now I need only give you this, so that you may kill me with it on the spot." Cortés replied that he did not wish to kill him, nor had it been his intention to harm them but that their mad obstinacy was responsible for the great evil and destruction they had suffered and that they well knew how many times the Spaniards had offered them peace and friendship. With this he ordered a guard set on the king and ordered that he and all the others who had survived were to be well treated.[3] Many extraordinary things happened in this conquest of Mexico, and I do not believe that those who write about it are lying or exaggerating, for God favored the Spaniards' enterprise with many miracles, and without Heaven's favor it would have been impossible to overcome so many

---

2. At this point the Spaniards were losing the battle for Tenochtitlan. Following the assault at the festival of Toxcatl, the people of Tenochtitlán waged a battle that so beleaguered the Spaniards that they hatched an escape plan. Fierce fighting began on a causeway to the city after an indigenous woman took note of their nighttime flight and alerted Mexica soldiers. Loot shed by the escaping Spaniards and numerous casualties littered the canal at daybreak, earning the episode the title of "the night of sorrow." Cortés and his troops took refuge in a nearby town called Teocalhueyacan to regroup and plan a renewed attack along with their Tlaxcallan allies.

3. After blaming the destruction of Tenochtitlán on the Mexica, Cortés kept Cuauhtemoc for a few days and then gave orders that he be killed, a fact omitted by Acosta.

difficulties and conquer the whole land with so few men. For, although we may have been sinners and unworthy of such favor, the cause of God and the glory of our Faith, and the well-being of so many thousands of souls that the Lord had predestined from those nations, required that this change that we now see should take place by supernatural means, and means proper to him who calls the blind, and captives, to knowledge of him, and gives them light and liberty with his sacred Gospel. And so that this may be believed and comprehended more fully I shall recount some examples which I believe are germane to this history.

CHAPTER 27 * OF SOME MIRACLES THAT GOD
HAS PERFORMED IN THE INDIES IN FAVOR OF
THE FAITH, BEYOND THE MERITS OF THOSE
WHO BROUGHT THEM TO PASS

Santacruz de la Sierra is a very distant and large province in the realms of Peru, bordering on several nations of heathen who have not yet received the light of the Gospel, unless in the years since my departure the fathers of our society have gone there with that aim. But the province itself is Christian, and there are a large number of Spanish Indians in it who have been baptized. The way in which Christianity came there was as follows: a soldier who was leading a debauched and wicked life in the province of Los Charcas, fearing the law by which he was being pursued for his sins, traveled far inland and was received by the savages of that land. When the Spaniard saw that they were suffering greatly from lack of water, and that they were using many superstitions of the kind they practice to make it rain, he told them that it would soon rain if they would do as he said. They offered to do so willingly. Then the soldier made a large cross and raised it high and told them to worship there and ask for water, and they did so. Wonder of wonders, such copious rain soon fell that the Indians developed a great devotion to the Holy Cross, brought all their needs to it, and received everything for which they asked. They even cast down their idols and used the cross as their sign and asked for preachers to teach and baptize them, and for this reason the whole province is called Santacruz de la Sierra to this day. But to demonstrate by what means God worked these wonders it must be said that the soldier in question, several years after doing these apostolic miracles, had not improved his life; he went to the province of Los Charcas and, after behaving as he always had, was publicly hanged in Potosí. Polo, who must have known him well, writes of all this as a famous case that happened in his lifetime.

In the strange peregrination described by Cabeza de Vaca, later governor of Paraguay, which began in Florida with two or three companions who were the only survivors of a fleet, during which they spent ten years among the savages, journeying as far as the Southern Sea, he recounts (and he is a writer worthy of belief) that the savages compelled them to cure them of certain ill-nesses, and told them that if they did not do so they would be killed.[1] They knew nothing about medicine, nor did they have any instruments for it. But, driven to it by necessity, they became evangelical doctors and cured those sick men by saying the prayers of the Church and making the sign of the cross. With the fame they acquired for this they were obliged to carry on the same office for all the Indian peoples, who were innumerable; and our Lord as-sisted them miraculously, so that they were amazed by their own exploits, for they were perfectly ordinary men and one of them was a black man. There was a pikeman in Peru, a soldier about whom no merits are known except those of a soldier; he used to speak certain suitable words over wounds, making the sign of the cross, and they would be cured, from which the common saying, "the Pikeman's Psalm," came to be used. And when he was examined by those of authority in the Church his deeds and skill were approved.

In the city of Cuzco, when the Spaniards were surrounded and so hard pressed that it seemed impossible to escape without Heaven's aid, persons worthy of belief, from whom I heard it myself, tell that after the Indians had shot fire onto the roof of the place where the Spaniards dwelled (which was where the principal church is now), although the roof was made of a kind of straw called chicho there and the bundles of resinous wood they used were very large, the roof never caught fire nor was anything burned, for a lady who was on the upper floor quickly put out the fire; and this the Indians saw themselves, and told of it with great amazement.[2] Both from histories and from reports written by many persons we know for certain that in various battles the Spaniards fought, in New Spain as well as Peru, enemy Indians

1. The relation of his wanderings by Cabeza de Vaca is available in an English translation as *Castaways: The Narrative of Alvar Núñez Cabeza de Vaca*, edited by Enrique Pupo-Walker, translated by Frances M. López-Morillas (Berkeley: University of California Press, 1993).

2. *Chicho* is a reference to the coarse grass of the high Andes generally called *ichu*.

saw in the air a knight on a white horse with sword in hand, fighting for the Spaniards; this is the reason why the veneration in which the glorious apostle Santiago was held in the Indies has always been, and still is, so great.[3] At other times the image of Our Lady was seen in such battles, and the Christians in those parts have received incomparable benefits from her. And if these exploits of Heaven were to be told at length just as they occurred they would make a very long tale. It is sufficient to have mentioned this in connection with the favor the Queen of Glory extended to our people when they were so hard pressed and pursued by the Mexicans; all of the above has been written so that it may be understood that our Lord has taken care to favor the Faith and the Christian religion, defending those who professed it even though they may not have deserved such gifts and favors from Heaven through their own deeds. Along with this, it is desirable not to condemn so absolutely everything about the first conquerors of Mexico, as some scholars and religious have done, with no doubt admirable but excessive zeal. For, although most of them were rough and greedy men and very ignorant of how they ought to behave among heathen who had done nothing to offend the Christians, neither can it be denied that on the side of the heathen there were many sins against God and our people, which obliged them to use harshness and chastisement. And, what is more, the Lord of all wished to favor his cause and his side even though the faithful were sinners, to the benefit of those same heathen who would later be converted to his holy Gospel, for the ways of God are lofty and his purposes wonderful.

### CHAPTER 28, AND LAST * OF THE PLAN ORDAINED BY PROVIDENCE IN THE INDIES FOR THE ENTRY OF THE CHRISTIAN RELIGION THERE

I wish to end this history of the Indies by declaring the admirable purposes by which God planned and prepared the entrance of the Gospel into them, which is of great importance for praising and exalting the Creator's wisdom

3. Acosta accurately judged the popularity of Santiago but did not consider the new meanings attributed to the god in the Indies. In the colonial Andes, for instance, he was so popular that he became fused with the native god of thunder, Illapa, and according to Silverblatt was "drafted to serve in the defense of native religion." See Irene Silverblatt, "Political Memories and Colonizing Symbols: Santiago and the Mountain Gods in Colonial Peru," in *Rethinking History and Myth: Indigenous South American Perspectives on the Past,* edited by J. D. Hill (Urbana: University of Illinois Press, 1988), 186.

and benevolence. Through the account and discourse that I have written in these books, anyone may understand that, in Peru as well as in New Spain, those realms had reached their highest point and were at the peak of their power at the time the Spaniards arrived. For the Incas' possessions in Peru stretched from the realm of Chile to beyond Quito, a distance of a thousand leagues, and they were very well supplied and rich with gold and silver and all sorts of wealth. And in Mexico Moctezuma reigned from the Ocean Sea of the north to the Southern Sea and was feared and worshiped not as a man but as a god. It was then that the Almighty decreed that the stone mentioned in the Book of Daniel,[1] which broke the kingdoms and monarchies of the world, should also break those of this other New World; and just as the law of Christ came at a time when the monarchy of Rome had reached its height, thus it was also in the West Indies. And truly it was the most excellent providence of our Lord, for the fact that a head and temporal lord existed in the world at that time (as the holy doctors point out) made it possible for the Gospel to be communicated easily to many nations and peoples. And the same thing happened in the Indies, where the fact that the news of Christ reached the heads of so many realms and peoples made its transmission through all of them very easy. And there is still another detail to be noted: for the lords of Mexico and Cuzco, as they conquered territories, also introduced their language. Although there was and still is a great diversity of separate languages, the language of the court at Cuzco extended, and extends today, for more than a thousand leagues, and that of Mexico must extend for little less. This has not been unimportant, but indeed very important, to facilitate preaching at a time when preachers do not receive the gift of tongues as they did in old times.

How helpful the greatness of these two empires I have mentioned has been for preaching and the conversion of the people can be observed by anyone who cares to do so by the extreme difficulty that has been encountered in bringing to Christ the Indians who do not recognize an overlord. It can be seen in Florida and Brazil, and in the Andes and a hundred other places, where in fifty years less progress has been made than in five years in Peru and New Spain.[2] If I am told that the wealth of those lands was the cause I do not

---

1. Daniel, 2, 34 (O'G).

2. The reference to the Andes designates not Cuzco or the highland region but lowland territory inhabited by the Chiriguana and Guaraní peoples. The comparison between the pace of evangelization in areas where pre-Hispanic empires existed and those where chieftains ruled reinforces Acosta's scale of comparative ethnology.

deny it, but it would have been impossible to possess those riches, or preserve them, if there had not been a monarchy. And that is the very purpose of God at a time when we preachers of the Gospel are so cold and lacking in spirit that there are merchants and soldiers who, inspired by greed and power, seek and find new people to whom we may go with our spiritual wares. For, as Saint Augustine says, the prophecy of Isaiah was fulfilled when the Church of Christ spread not only to the right but to the left, which means, as he declares, that it increased by the human and earthly means of men who seek themselves rather than Jesus Christ.[3]

But it was also a special providence on the part of Our Lord that when the first Spaniards went there they found help among the Indians themselves because there were many factions and great divisions. In Peru it is obvious that the rift between the two brothers Atahualpa and Huáscar, the king Huayna Capac having recently died, provided an opportunity to Marqués Don Francisco Pizarro and to the Spaniards, for each of them wanted the Spaniards as friends and were occupied in making war on each other. In New Spain it is no less true that the help of the Indians in the province of Tlaxcala, owing to the permanent enmity they had toward the Mexicans, gave Marqués Don Hernán Cortés and his men the victory and sovereignty of Mexico; and without them it would have been impossible to win it or even to maintain themselves in the land. Those who have little esteem for the Indians, and believe that thanks to the Spaniards' advantage with their persons and their horses, and their offensive and defensive weapons, they can conquer any land or nation of Indians, are very much mistaken. Take the example of Chile, or rather Arauco and Tucapel, which are two valleys where for more than twenty-five years, even after fighting every year and doing everything they could, our Spaniards have scarcely been able to win a foot of land from them; for, once they have lost their fear of horses and harquebuses and have learned that the Spaniards can also be wounded by stones and arrows, the savages are very daring and stop at nothing and attack fiercely and do their deeds. For how many years have troops gone against the Chichimecas, who are a small group of naked Indians with bows and arrows, and to this day they have not been conquered; rather, are they not daily more daring and defiant? And did not the flower of Peru, with such quantities of arms and people as we wit-

---

3. Saint Augustine, *De Concordia Evangelistarum,* book 2, chapter 36 (O'G).

nessed, go against the Chuchos and Chiriguanas and Pilcozones? What happened? With what victory did they return? They returned happy to have escaped with their lives, almost all of them having lost their equipment and horses. Let no one believe that by saying Indians he means weak men; if he does, let him go and find out. Glory must be attributed to he who deserves it, chiefly to God and his admirable plan; for if Moctezuma in Mexico and the Inca in Peru had resisted the Spaniards' entry neither Cortés nor Pizarro, although they were excellent captains, would have gained a foothold in the land.

It was of no little help that the Indians received the Law of Christ so willingly, owing to the great subjection in which they were held by their kings and lords. And their very service and subjection to the devil and his tyrannies, and his heavy yoke, created an excellent opportunity for Divine Wisdom, which takes advantage of bad things to turn them into good, and makes its own good out of others' evil, with which it had nothing to do. It is apparent that none of the peoples of the West Indies have been more inclined to receive the Gospel than those who have been most subject to their lords and who have borne the heaviest weight of tributes and services as well as rites and death-dealing customs. All the territories possessed by the kings of Mexico and Peru are today the ones where Christianity is most cultivated and where there is less difficulty in both political and ecclesiastical government. We have already mentioned that the Indians were so weary of the heavy and intolerable yoke of Satan's laws, and his sacrifices and ceremonies, that they took counsel among themselves to seek a different law and different gods to serve. Hence Christ's law seemed to them, and still seems, just, easy, pure, good, equitable, and wholly full of good things. And what is difficult in our religion, that is, having to believe such lofty and sovereign mysteries, was made much easier among them because the devil had told them other things that were much more difficult; and the same things that he stole from our Gospel law, such as its style of Communion and Confession, worship of the three in one, and other such matters, helped the Indians against the enemy's will to receive in truth the things that they had received as lies. God is wise and marvelous in all his works and conquers the enemy with his own weapons and catches him with his own snare and kills him with his own sword.

Finally, our God (who had created these people and seemed to have forgotten them for so long when the happy hour arrived) wished to have those same demons, the enemies of men, give witness despite themselves of the coming of his true law, the power of Christ, and the triumph of his cross, which is amply proved by the many omens and prophecies and signs and prodigies mentioned above and by many others that took place in Peru and in other lands. And the ministers of Satan themselves, the Indian sorcerers and magicians, have confessed it and it cannot be denied; for it is evident and manifest to the whole world that, where the cross is planted and there are churches and the name of Christ is confessed, the devil dares not make a sound, and his speeches and oracles and replies and apparitions, which were so common everywhere in his heathen lands, have ceased. And if some accursed minister of his takes part in any of this today he does so in caves or on mountaintops or in very hidden places, entirely remote from the name and practice of Christians. May the Supreme Lord be blessed for his great mercies and for the glory of his holy name.

Surely, those who rule these people both temporally and spiritually ought to treat them as Christ imparted his law, with his easy yoke and light burden, and ought not to load them with more than they can carry, as ordered and disposed by the decrees of the good emperor of glorious memory. And if we made only half the effort to help them to their salvation as we expend on using their poor labors and exertions this would be the most peaceful and fortunate Christian realm in the world. Often our sins do not give us much room to improve. But in saying this I speak the truth, and it is a very certain truth for me: although the first entry of the Gospel in many places did not always occur with the sincerity and Christian means that it should have, God's mercy made good out of this evil and caused the subjection of the Indians to be their whole cure and salvation. If we look at everything that has been brought to Christianity in both East and West in our time, we will see how little sureness and firmness there has been in the Christian religion wherever the newly converted have had entire freedom to act according to their own wishes. Christianity is undoubtedly increasing and improving among the Indians who have been conquered and is giving more fruit every day, while in other places that have had different beginnings it is declining and threatening ruin.

And, although in the West Indies the beginnings were difficult indeed, Our Lord did not fail to send very good workers and faithful ministers of his, holy and apostolic men such as Fray Martín de Valencia of the Franciscans,

Fray Domingo de Betanzos of the Dominicans, and Fray Juan de Roa of the Augustinian order, along with other servants of the Lord who lived in a holy manner and performed superhuman deeds. There were also wise and holy prelates, and priests no less worthy of memory, of whom not only do we hear notable miracles and deeds worthy of the apostles but we know and associate with some men of this quality even in our time. But, because my intent has only been to deal with what concerns the history of the Indians themselves, up to the time when the father of Our Lord Jesus Christ deigned to communicate the light of his word to them, I shall go no further, leaving for another time or a keener intelligence the story of the Gospel in the West Indies, beseeching the Supreme Lord of all and entreating his servants to earnestly implore the Divine Majesty to deign to visit frequently and to increase by heavenly gifts the new Christendom that has been planted at the ends of the earth in recent centuries. Glory and honor and power be to the King of the Ages forever and ever, amen.

Everything that is written in these seven books of this *Natural and Moral History of the Indies* has been written subject to the judgment and correction of the Holy Catholic and Apostolic Church, in all and for all. In Madrid, February 21, 1589.

*José de Acosta's Historia natural y moral de las Indias:*
*Occidentalism, the Modern/Colonial World,*
*and the Colonial Difference*

## Introduction

José de Acosta has a distinctive place in sixteenth-century intellectual history, a century that produced a wealth of written works in Spain as well as in the Indias Occidentales, the name that was used by Acosta and his contemporaries. "Latin America" was not in sight in the early years of the emerging Atlantic commercial circuit and at the inception of the modern/colonial world system imaginary. In fact, Latin America could have only been conceived in the second phase of modernity, when the concept of "latinidad" became necessary to assert a southern, Catholic, and Latin identity in contradistinction to a northern, Protestant, and Anglo-Saxon one. This perspective was not available to Acosta, for whom the horizon of a triumphant Spanish Empire and the possibility of a global expansion of Christianity were at stake. He could have not anticipated that the idea of "natural and moral history" would undergo such a significant transformation between the first (dominance of the Spanish and Portuguese Empires) and second phase of modernity, which chiefly developed after the Industrial Revolution.

In this essay I would like to invite the reader (and I am particularly thinking of curious and inquisitive undergraduates) to think of Acosta's *Historia* beyond the canonical textual interpretation or the standard histories of sixteenth-century Spain and colonial Latin America. I am interested in understanding Acosta's contribution to the imaginary of the modern/colonial world as well as in understanding the turn of events when, ideologically, his reading of the "natural" and the "moral" began to be displaced by the philosophies emerging with new imperial powers (England, France, and Germany).

There are a few notions that I need to clear up before proceeding with my argument. The first is that of modernity/coloniality. The emergence of the Atlantic commercial circuit in the sixteenth century was a long process of historical events, the consolidation of capitalism and of planetary transformation. The terms *renaissance* and *early modern period* have been used to designate that moment; the first is common among humanists and the second among social scientists. I prefer to talk about the emergence of modernity/coloniality and describe it as the emergence of a world order under whose principles we are still living. *Christianity, capitalism, liberalism,* and *socialism* are some of the key words of the modern/colonial. The expression *modern/colonial* has the advantage over *early modern period* of introducing a spatial dimension that the latter lacks. *Early modern period* presupposes a linear narrative ascending from antiquity, to the middle age, the early modern, and the modern and contemporary. Spatially such a macronarrative is confined to the territory extending east and north of the Mediterranean to the North Atlantic and presupposes the Occident as an overall frame. *Modern/colonial world* instead brings the entire planet into the picture, as it contemplates, simultaneously, the emergence and expansion of the Atlantic commercial circuit, its transformation with the Industrial Revolution, and its expansion to the Americas, Asia, and Africa. Furthermore, *modern/colonial world* opens up the possibility of telling stories not only from the perspective of the "modern" and its outward expansion but from the perspective of the "colonial" and its constant subaltern position. Acosta's *Historia* was a signal contribution in building the imaginary of the modern/colonial world. It stands at the intersection of the "colonial difference" (e.g., the space in between Europe and its others) and the "imperial difference" (e.g., the north of Europe — Holland, England, France, and Germany — detaching themselves from the south since the seventeenth century) (Mignolo 2000).

José de Acosta's book, as we will see, had an enormous impact in building the imaginary of the modern/colonial world and in building the imaginary of the emerging Atlantic commercial circuit. Contemporaries of Acosta were Amerindian intellectuals like Guaman Poma de Ayala in the Viceroyalty of Peru, Fernando de Alva Ixtlilxochitl in Texcoco (New Spain), and Garcilaso de la Vega in Spain. From different perspectives and in different circumstances (although in the same period, the end of the sixteenth century and first quarter of the seventeenth), these intellectuals dealt with and from the colonial difference that Acosta's books contributed to making. What I will attempt to do is introduce you to Acosta's book from the intellectual perspectives opened up by Guaman Poma, Ixtlilxochitl, and Garcilaso de la Vega among others. Thinking from the colonial difference is, today in the Americas, an option similar to thinking from the Greek and Roman legacy in the intellectual history constructed in modern Europe. I do not believe that knowledge is "naturally" located in geographical spaces. I do believe in the fact that the coloniality of power and the making of the colonial difference "located" knowledge geohistorically. I do believe in the geopolitics of knowledge. As a matter of fact, the colonial difference in the domain of knowledge has been built, as we will see, as the epistemic colonial difference.

While in European history *Renaissance* and *early modern period* were two historiographic key words, *colonial period* was defined for Latin American history after independence in order to mark the "beginning" of nation-building processes. There was no colonial period, so to speak, but a set of Spanish viceroyalties in the Indias Occidentales and later in America. The nation-building process, in the first half of the nineteenth century, went together with the rearticulation of the colonial difference at the intersection of the demise of the Spanish Empire and the emergence of British Empire and French colonialism. It was from the perspective of new nation-states and the construction of national ideologies that the colonial period was conceived. Indeed, it was integrated into the rearticulation of the colonial difference, an important aspect that escaped or was not relevant to Benedict Anderson's emphasis on the original experience of nation building in the Americas ([1981] 1992). In the same way that, say, the European idea of renaissance and modernity needed "middle age" in order to build a macronarrative of distinction and difference, the very idea of Latin America also needed its difference from the colonial period as the ground for its distinction. The Spanish Indias Occidentales were erased after independence; Latin America took its place, and the frontier between the national and the colonial was constructed as the colonial period. One of the consequences can be seen today in how "Latin American studies" and "colonial Latin American studies" are understood and practiced. The former is conceived, in general, from Echeverria, Bello, and Sarmiento to Fidel Castro and Zapatismo. The second is conceived from "discovery" to "independence." Thus, the scenario has been set to have a third dimension farther removed in time, the precolonial period with an obscure beginning and a complex end: 1492 in the

Caribbean, 1520 in Mexico-Tenochtitlan, 1532 in the Maya area, and 1533 in the Andes.

I will look at Acosta in the geohistorical frame of the modern/colonial world (i.e., the emergence of the Atlantic commercial circuit) around 1500. The introduction of space here will allow me to escape from the modern/chronological construction of Latin America from the precolonial to the colonial to the national. By doing so I am honoring Acosta's own work, particularly in the first two chapters of the *Historia natural y moral de las Indias,* in which he has made a significant effort to locate, geographically and conceptually, the Indias Occidentales on a planetary scale. Certainly those were needs of the time, before the restrictions imposed by modern state building were at work. As a matter of fact, it was Acosta (and particularly his *Historia*) that largely contributed to building the imaginary of the Atlantic commercial circuit as planetary consciousness. The conception of the *oikoumene* in Ptolomy's representation of the known world contrasted and complemented the *mappae-mundi* common in Christian cosmology in the fifteenth century. The almost imperceptible combination of both, in the sixteenth century, became the interchangeable *Theatrum orbis terrarum* or *Orbis Universalis Christianus* (Ortelius 1574; O'Gorman 1958). And it was these changes in worldview to which the "discovery" of America greatly contributed and the first two chapters of Acosta's book are devoted.

### What We Know about Acosta's Historia

There have been two fundamental studies on José de Acosta to date: Edmundo O'Gorman's introduction to the 1940 edition of Acosta's book (Acosta [1940] 1962; O'Gorman 1972) and his addendum to the 1962 reprint (Acosta [1940] 1962), and Anthony Pagden's substantial chapter in *The Fall of Natural Man* (Pagden 1982). These studies lined up the two basic themes in Acosta's book: the emergence of the New World in the European consciousness in its "natural" (cosmological) and "moral" (ethnoracial) aspects. This was a foundational moment — indeed — of modernity/coloniality, a world in which we are still living. Thus, the natural and the moral worlds, the configuration of nature, and the nature of people required an unprecedented intellectual exercise to accommodate new realities into old patterns of thinking. There were of course deeds of Spanish soldiers and missionaries that deserved to be narrated, but that has been intentionally left out by Acosta. His mission was to contribute to the understanding of the place of the New World on the planet and the place of the Amerindians in the Christian order of things. The "natural" part of his history dealt with the transformation of *oikoumene* (or the inhabited world) into the concept of *orbis terrarum* (Acosta [1940] 1962; O'Gorman 1958). The "moral" part of Acosta's book should be read in relation to the debates of Valladolid (between Sepulveda and Las Casas) about whether war or conversion was the rule under which Amerindians should be integrated to Christianity. It should also be read in relation to the legal-theological investigations of the Salamanca school — which followed the debate of Valladolid — about the "rights of the people" (Vitoria), a forerunner of the "rights of man and of citizens" (Pagden 1982). The difference between them is that, while the first were stated in the domain of international relations and cross-religious understanding, the second were stated in the domain of the Europe of nations and national configuration. Returning to Acosta, the natural part of his *Historia* contributed to the place of the Indies in the *orbis terrarum;* the second contributed to understanding the place of the "(Amer)Indians" in the Christian chain of being and an emerging planetary consciousness that supplanted the *oikoumene*. These two moves have been easily related to modernity. They were simultaneously two moves related to coloniality.

O'Gorman's introductions ([1940] 1962), together with his groundbreaking book in between both, *La invención de América* (1958, 1961), reoriented the entire problematic. He rejected "discovery" as the Eurocentric version of events and replaced it with "invention." O'Gorman did not deny, of course, that a big lump was to be found there, between Europe and China, when navigating west, and that said lump was already inhabited. It was precisely because it was inhabited that the idea of discovery made sense from one side of the story only. By invention he meant that the Indias Occidentales and then America, and the division of the territories into viceroyalties, *audiencies,* and so on, was a decision and attribution to the Spaniards and the Portuguese, not of the original inhabitants. O'Gorman did not deny the ontological dimension of the lump and the people already inhabiting and naming it. He pointed out in a brilliant argument how the colonial difference (which is not his expression) was instituted by appropriating the lump through European names and at the same time denying naming power to the Amerindians and integrating the unknown into the known. The invention of

America is not an ontological problem but rather one of coloniality of power and the colonial difference in the foundation of an imaginary that I understand today as modernity/coloniality. More than thirty years after O'Gorman's publication of his seminal and groundbreaking book in the philosophy of history, two sociologists, one from Peru and the other from the United States, published a cornerstone article (Quijano and Wallerstein 1992). In an argument that is independent but at the same time complements O'Gorman's, Quijano and Wallerstein underlined the fact that the raising up of the Americas in the European consciousness was a fundamental moment for the constitution of the modern/colonial world, as we will see in the next section.

Finally, the third important contribution to understanding the relevance of Acosta's *Historia* is the chapter that José María López Piñero devoted to geography, cartography, and studies about the New World in his book on science and technology in Spain during the sixteenth and seventeenth centuries (López Piñero 1979, 212–39). Although there is no specific reference to Acosta's work in this book, it is important to keep in mind the official context in which the demarcation of Indias Occidentales occurred. Mapping territories and classifying nature were important aspects related to the business of states rather than to the business of missionaries and the Church.

### Indias Occidentales/America in the Imaginary of the Modern/Colonial World

The world *oikoumene* from 1250 up to 1500 was described by Abu-Lughod in her classic book *Before European Hegemony* (Abu-Lughod 1989). Two distinctive features of this world, or *oikoumene,* are of interest for my argument. One is that the center of attraction before 1500 was not Europe but China and India; people moved from west to east, and Portugal, during the fourteenth century, had gained control of the coast of Africa in its commerce with China (Dussel 1998). The mapping of the world and the rediscovery of Ptolemy during the fifteenth century was in part due to the heavy commercial traffic of the time (Brotton 1998, 17–45). The other feature is the fact that the Atlantic was not totally unknown but was not yet openly known and desired as a new space for commercial routing. The configuration of the Atlantic commercial circuit, which connected Spain to Anahuac and Tawantinsuyu and Portugal to a diversity of communities on the coasts of what is today Brazil, was not in place in the fourteenth century, "before European hegemony." The sixteenth century was indeed the century of heavy commercial traffic in the Atlantic. The Spaniards controlled the Caribbean, Anahuac, and Tawantinsuyu and transported gold, silver, and specie to Europe. The Portuguese began to explore the lands offered to them by the pope's partition and donation in the famous Inter Cetera's proclamation of May 4, 1508. Slavery became a historico-economic landmark in the Atlantic commercial circuit that fostered the imaginary of the emerging modern/colonial world.

There is an obvious connection among the pope's partition and donation, the Christian organization of the planet in three continents (Europe, Asia, and Africa), and the name Indias Occidentales, attributed to the newly "discovered" lands. The fact that Indias Occidentales became the fourth part of the world within the symbolic matrix of the medieval *mappae-mundi* (i.e., the T-in-O map) is not a simple coincidence.

Thus, if the pope's partition placed the Indias Occidentales, and later America, "within" the Christian cosmo-geography and domain, the donation made the (Amer)Indians (the people) automatically servants of God and vassals of the kings of Spain and Portugal. The consequences of this move for the "location" of Indias Occidentales/America in the imaginary of the modern/colonial world have indeed been enormous. A quotation from Anibal Quijano and Immanuel Wallerstein (1992) will complement what I said about O'Gorman in the previous section and will contribute to the point I am trying to make here. I am bringing together an existing symbolic Christian imaginary, the emergence of unknown lands and people on the European horizon, and the expansion of commercial capitalism.

> The modern-world system was born in the long sixteenth century. The Americas as a geosocial construct were born in the long sixteenth century. The creation of this geosocial entity, the Americas, was the constitutive act of the modern world-system. The Americas were not incorporated into an already existing capitalist world-economy. There could not have been a capitalist world-economy without the Americas. (549)

The quotation may give the impression of a certain exceptionalism, privilege, or glory in that it may echo similar statements claiming the ancestry of Greece, for example, in the foundation of Western civilization. My intention is not to celebrate the glory of an exceptional Americanism. It is my intention, instead, to give the event the historical relevance it has, not necessarily

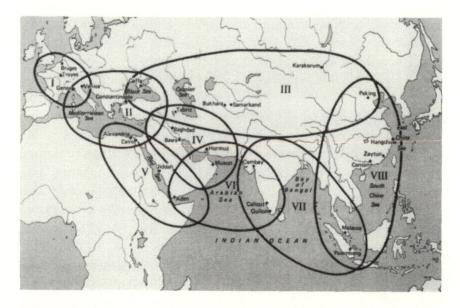

*Plate 1.* The eight dominant commercial circuits, with Peking as the attractive "center," between the thirteenth and fourteenth centuries or, as Abu-Lughod puts it, "before European hegemony." (From Janet Abu-Lughod, *Before European Hegemony: The World System,* A.D. 1250–1350. New York: Oxford University Press, 1989.)

for the glory of Spain or any kind of (Latin) American identity, but for the emergence of new commercial circuits and the imaginary of the modern/colonial world system. As Quijano and Wallerstein assert, the modern/colonial world system could not have developed without the transformation of Anahuac and Tawantinsuyu into Indias Occidentales/Americas. It is that transformation precisely which gave origin to a new imaginary and that, at the same time, suppressed the imaginary of the existing commercial circuits in today's America. "Modernity" has been construed and accepted, from left and right, as a description of the imaginary of the modern/colonial world, and "coloniality" was obscured as its incidental, not a constitutive, complement. One of the reasons for this turn of events in the imaginary is historical. Since the general idea of modernity has its foundation in the eighteenth century, by then the colonial side of modernity was already in place and to recognize coloniality would have implied recognizing Spain in the making of the Atlantic commercial circuit. However, imperial conflicts prevented that

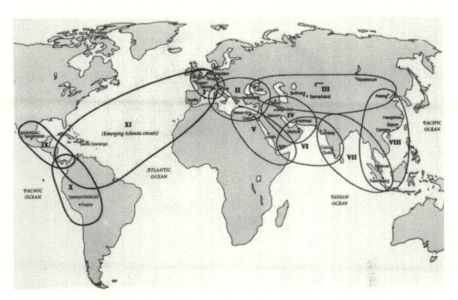

*Plate 2.* The emergence and consolidation of the Atlantic commercial circuit that connected the commercial circuits of Anahuac and Tawantinsuyu (the New World) to already existing circuits (the Old World), including an important circuit in northern Africa. The Atlantic commercial circuit created the conditions for fundamental changes in worldview, in the expansion of the economy, and in the foundation of the modern/colonial world and Christianity as its first global design.

recognition, and the "black legend" was invented precisely to rule Spain out of imperial contention. European imperial conflicts were not inconsequential. They became acute in 1898 in the U.S. intellectual justification of the war against Spain. Coloniality is what has made modernity possible at the same time that it was the discourse on and about modernity that maintained coloniality in the dark, as its incidental, though not its constitutive, side. The very conceptualization and debates on postmodernity reproduce today the same blindness, as if coloniality were the passive end of modernity in the making of history. Bringing coloniality to the foreground was the initial task of powerful postcolonial thinkers such as Aime Cessaire, Frantz Fanon, and Amilcar Cabral, who more often than not remain on the darker side of postmodernity. Thus, my conceptual genealogy goes back, on the one hand, to the late-sixteenth and early-seventeenth-century darker side of modernity, and it connects with Guaman Poma, Ixtlilxochitl, and Garcilaso de la Vega.

By 1590, when Acosta published his *Historia*, Copernicus had already

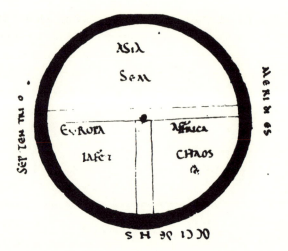

*Plate 3.* In the Middle Ages the T-in-O map linked the geographical distribution of the world with the three sons of Noah. It was a powerfully symbolic map. It was due to this map that we still conceive of the world as divided into four continents. (From Dennis Hay, *Europe.* England: Edinburg University Press, 1957.)

corrected the heliocentric conception of the universe. Once the fourth part of the world was incorporated into Christian cosmology, world maps after the sixteenth century showed the "visible" delineation of lands and waters, implying the "invisible" division in four continents upon which the symbolic T-in-O map was imposed. One of the main tasks, then, was to describe and explain the singularity and differences (mainly with Europe) of the fourth part of the world (the Indias Occidentales). This was one of the main contributions of José de Acosta's book. In the first two chapters Acosta undertook the task of finding the place of the new continent in the old order of things. The fourth continent was not enough, at the time, to change another tripartite Christian model: the division of the world was among the *mineralia, plantae,* and *animalia,* and Acosta organized the world accordingly. First, he took care of celestial matters and then of the tripartite division of beings on the planet. Certainly this tripartite division is insufficient by today's standards (Gould 1977, 115–18), but it was a distinction introduced by Aristotle and ratified in Christian cosmology (Crombie [1952] 1971, 1:80–180).

   This is basically what Acosta did and what he could do. He had at his disposal a closed and finite view of the world, not an infinite view of the universe. The revolution, in Koyré's term (1957, chap. 2), was parallel, I will argue, to a radical transformation that began to take place in the second half of the sixteenth century. Some of the main actors of this change were the Reformation; the displacement of capital and finance from Italy (Genoa and Venice) and Spain (Seville) to Holland (Amsterdam) and England (London) (Arrighi 1994); and the emergence of what, at the beginning of the twentieth century, Max Weber baptized as the "Protestant ethic" (1905). Briefly, a major internal frontier of the world system (that of imperial conflicts) began to be traced shortly after Acosta's book appeared. It was the beginning of a north-south distinction that became more visible and sharp after the nineteenth century. Acosta was at the end of a cycle and could hardly have anticipated that his "history" was being superseded by new developments in "northern" Europe. The geocentric imagery of the universe that Acosta embraced was reproduced from the end of the fifteenth century until far into the sixteenth.

The transition from the geo- to the heliocentric view of the universe took place in the seventeenth century, although it had its antecedents in the middle of the sixteenth, with the publication of Copernicus's *De revolutionibus orbium caelestium* (1543) and went on to Newton's *Philosophiae naturalis principia mathematica* (1726). Copernicus was apparently known in Spain by 1570. His work was mentioned as a suggested reading at the Academia de Matematicas around 1584 (López Piñero 1979, 187), although its influence was practically nonexistent. However, more important is the case of Diego de Zuniga, who, in his *In Iob commentaria* (1584), strongly supported Copernicus's theory, arguing that it does not contradict the Holy Book (López Piñero 1979, 187–88). There was more than one reason for Acosta not to seriously consider Copernicus in his cosmological discussions of the New World. In Peru, Acosta was able to confirm Aristotle's thesis that Heaven is round and moves around the entire planet earth, not just around certain of its parts, as previous authority had asserted. Acosta also stated that the planet earth was covered "above" by Heaven and "below" was surrounded by the abyss and a profound emptiness (book 1, chapters 1 and 2). He also complemented the knowledge available at his time by describing the southern sky, the stars that were observable from the south and not visible from Europe. The configuration of the sky made Amerigo Vespucci realize, at the beginning of the sixteenth century and on the coast of Brazil, that he was not in

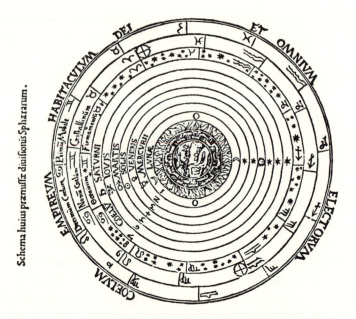

*Plate 4.* The pre-Copernican image of the universe had the earth in the center and the sun turning around it. Peter Apian's *Cosmographia,* of 1539, reminds us that this was a worldview held during the sixteenth century, in spite of Copernicus, and that this worldview was still held by José de Acosta. (From Alexander Koyré, *From the Closed World to the Infinite Universe.* Baltimore: Johns Hopkins University Press, 1957.)

India — as Columbus believed — but in a "Mondo Novo" (Vespucci 1504). Acosta's book is surrounded by two silent spaces in the domain of knowledge: one, underlined above, was developing in Europe; the other was developing in the Indias Occidentales, practically under the nose of Acosta but invisible to him.

Let us start with the first silent space, the one in Europe, as this is a scenario more familiar to most of Acosta's readers. The emergence of a "New World" in the European consciousness forced its intellectuals to reconsider their own conception of knowledge. They did this in two ways. One was clearly expressed and rationalized. The other was to extend a veil of silence in the construction of Western epistemic genealogy. What was clearly expressed and rationalized, and inspired pride even in sixteenth-century Spanish intellectuals, was a move from a concept of knowledge based on books to a concept of knowledge based on experience (Maravall 1963, 1966). The "discovery" of the New World contributed enormously to this change of conception. For example, in *Sumario de la natural Historia* (1526), followed by the more ambitious *Historia general y natural de las Indias* (1536–42), official chronicler Fernández de Oviedo distinguished himself from Pliny the Elder. Unlike Acosta, Oviedo did not have any philosophical or theoretical ambitions in his enterprise. Thus, he classified the history as general rather than moral. On the other hand, he made clear in his introduction that while Pliny the Elder (23–79 A.D.) wrote his *Naturalis Historia* on the basis of thousands of books consulted, Oviedo wrote his on the basis of thousands of lived experiences. This change in the conception of knowledge became prevalent, and *"philosophia natural"* was one of the dominant concerns, in connection with the New World, in sixteenth-century Spain (Ferreras-Savoye 1999). Acosta's book was by no means a unique case. On the contrary, it was preceded by a wealth of treatises, many of which were written in the field of pharmacology and medicine. One of the better-known examples was the result of a visit by Francisco Hernández, medical doctor at the court of Philip II, who spent several years in Mexico (between 1560 and 1580) collecting information on the flora and fauna of New Spain. He eventually wrote several detailed and descriptive volumes on the properties (some of them curative) of hundreds of plants (Somolinos d'Ardois 1960). The manuscript of his *Historia natural de Nueva España* was not published during his lifetime (he died in 1587). In book IV, chapter 29, Acosta referred to Francisco Hernández's contribution to the knowledge of the plants of New Spain, based on a summary of his manuscript that was published in 1589.

It is important to note, however, that José de Acosta and Francisco Hernández were not in the same ideological camp with regard to the intellectual history of the Spanish imperial domains. Francisco Hernández was a central figure in what Mexican historian Elias Trabulse (1988) identified as the first of three "heterodox" movements in New Spain. The first movement, from approximately 1550 to 1571, was in the domain of knowledge that endangered the dogma of the Holy Scriptures. Trabulse identified that first movement of dissent with the figures and influence of Erasmus of Rotterdam and Francisco Hernández, one of his followers. The second movement, around 1630, emerged with the arrival in Mexico of the new bent toward the "new sciences" (Bacon, Copernicus) and the radical critique of the canon of knowledge in the university (Aristotle, Ptolemy, and Galen). This second heterodox movement was also important because its main agents were no longer Spaniards in the New World (like Acosta or Hernández) but the emergent Creole intellectuals. Thus, the tension in the intellectual arena was intensified by the ideological conflict between "native" and "foreigner." The third movement of heterodoxy was located in the second half of the eighteenth century, with the impact of the Enlightenment in the New World. Of particular interest for my argument, as we will see, was Buffon's *Historie Naturelle*. In this scheme of things, Acosta's *Historia natural y moral de las Indias* can be read at the intersection of repressed ideas in the period of the Counter-Reformation and the intersection of Spanish, Amerindian, and Creole intellectuals in the New World.

Twenty years after Acosta's publication of *Historia natural y moral de las Indias,* Galileo Galilei published *Sidereus Nuncius* (*The Message of the Stars,* 1610). Thus, while Acosta was worried about whether the sky covered the New World and how different the southern sky was from the northern one, Galileo was reading the stars within a new conception of the universe and expanding beyond Copernicus. By doing so he was opening up the universe to its infinity and removing the sun from its very center (Koyré 1957, 88). Yet, in Spain and the New World *philosophia natural* and *philosophia moral* were two different paradigms. They were necessary to distinguish, on the one hand, Nature from Human Being (which will become Culture in the eighteenth century) and on the other to establish a connection between knowledge of the natural world as a step toward knowledge of God. When the humanistic paradigms of the Renaissance began to be replaced with the scientific paradigm that eventually generated the Enlightenment, God was displaced from the scene and Man was left alone in his confrontation with Nature. This paradigm that developed from Copernicus to Newton, and went on through Galileo, was enriched by the philosophical minds of Bacon and Descartes, who offered the rationale for the scientific knowledge of Nature through rigorous methodology and experimentation. Acosta's was perhaps the last glorious book within the humanist paradigms, and it was glorious three times over: first, because of his theoretical articulation of *philosophia natural y moral,* which he rendered as *historia;* second, because of his effort to modify the inherited paradigm from the Greco-Roman tradition; and, third, for his contribution to building the imaginary of the modern/colonial world system. At the edge of a paradigmatic epistemic change, Acosta was also contributing to the construction of the colonial difference, the most radical aspect of the imaginary of the modern/colonial world.

In this regard, concerning the construction of the colonial difference, we can introduce what Acosta left out of his book — reading, so to speak, the silences around it. The first silencing occurs when Acosta constructs a Greco-Roman intellectual genealogy to support his theoretical scheme (the number and disposition of the heavens, the four elements, the chain of being [mineral, plants, animals, humans]) and his empirical observations (the southern sky, the winds, water and land, plants and animals, culture, and Inca and Aztec societies). Acosta did not discuss Arabic contributions to the genealogy he was assuming. Such a debt was very well known, although the sixteenth century was oblivious, most likely intentionally, to that debt. Recognizing the Arabic contribution to the genealogy Acosta was building upon would have defeated the purpose of scholarship, with the making of the colonial difference as one unintended consequence. The geopolitical frontiers with the Moors had already been traced in 1492 with their final expulsion from the Iberian Peninsula. An intellectual contribution from those who had recently been expelled from the peninsula as religious enemies could not have been recognized. However, between the ninth and thirteenth centuries the traffic and epistemic interactions between Greek, Arabic, and Roman knowledge was impressive, according to the list of the translations from Greek to Arabic and from both to Latin, as provided by A. C. Crombie (1952, 1:55–63). Aristotle's *De animalibus (Historia animalium, Departibus animalium, De generatione animalium)*, for example, a classic work in the Western genealogy of natural history, was translated from Greek to Arabic by el-Batric in the ninth century and from Arabic to Latin by Michel Scot, in Spain, in the early thirteenth century, not to mention, of course, Avicenna's (980–1037) commentaries on Aristotle, which Kitab al-Shifa translated into Latin in Toledo in the twelfth and thirteenth centuries. In the early thirteenth century, Michel Scot also translated Averroes's commentaries on Aristotle into Latin. Crombie provides a narrative to help us better understand the impressive number of translations from Arabic to Latin.

> The Arabs themselves acquired their knowledge of Greek science from two sources. Most of it they eventually learned directly from the Greeks of the Byzantine Empire, but their knowledge of it came also at second

hand from the Syriac-speaking Nestorian Christians of Eastern Persia. . . . Gradually the learning which had been amassed by the Arabs began to penetrate into Western Christendom as trading relations slowly revived between Christendom and Islam. By the 9th century towns such as Venice, Naples, Bari and Amalfi, later joined by Pisa and Genoa, were carrying on trade with the Arabs of Sicily and the eastern Mediterranean. . . . The chief centers from which the knowledge of Arabic and ultimately of Greek science spread were Sicily and Spain. Toledo fell to Alfonso VI in 1085 and towards the middle of the 12th century became, under the patronage of its archbishop, the Spanish centre of translation from Arabic to Latin. ([1952] 1971, 1:51–52)

Up to the end of the sixteenth century, the Mediterranean was a center of trade and knowledge; consequently, Greek, Arabic, and Latin were three strong epistemic languages. Of course, there were other centers in China and India, as well as in Anahuac and Tawantinsuyu, but these were not connected to the epistemic genealogy Acosta was constructing. Crombie's narrative is also important for understanding the historical and epistemic break that took place when the Atlantic began to replace the Mediterranean not only as a major commercial center but as a center of knowledge. A new imaginary, that of the modern/colonial world, arose in the process of establishing the colonial differences on the southern frontier of the Mediterranean (with the Arabic world) and on the western frontier of the Atlantic (with the Amerindians). As I argue elsewhere, the formalization of the principle of *limpieza de sangre* (purity of blood) and the social control of the Spanish Inquisition took care of the first frontier. The discussions in the School of Salamanca about the rights of Amerindians, known today as the "right of the people," established the second frontier. It should also be remembered that *limpieza de sangre* played a crucial role in establishing the first internal frontiers; it contributed to the expulsion of the Jews from Spain and helped transform them into the "internal difference" (Mignolo 1999a). Acosta, of course, was not alien to this dispute. His *Historia moral* can be read as a continuation of the debate of Valladolid and the theological discussions in Salamanca (Pagden 1982).

Furthermore, Acosta's *Historia* was at the edge of a double epistemological break: on the one hand, the transition from the humanistic/Renaissance paradigm to the scientific/Enlightenment one. On the other hand, it contributed to establishing the epistemic frontier with Arabic as a language of knowledge, to the Islamic contribution to planetary civilization, and to erasing the knowledge of the Amerindians. *Historia natural y moral de las Indias* ignored Amerindian knowledge by converting the Amerindians into exotic objects of description: the people of Anahuac and Tawantinsuyu were certainly distinguished by their inclusion in the "moral" part of the history, but their own knowledge was not considered valuable or important. This silence in Acosta's work (as well as in all the texts written by Spaniards about the New World, including Bernardino de Sahagún's transcriptions and translations of reports provided by Amerindian intellectuals and informants), contributed to building an epistemic imaginary in which Amerindian knowledge did not count as sustainable. It was only considered an object of description and the work of the devil. Curiously enough, at the time Acosta was writing his history and — a few decades later — when Bacon and Galileo were providing the philosophy and method for the new sciences, Amerindian intellectuals were producing knowledge and suggesting — indirectly — the possibility of a new epistemology that could not have been recognized at the time. It is being recognized and used only today, as in this essay. Their work presupposed a border epistemology — that is, an awareness of Renaissance intellectual principles that they adapted to their own epistemic frame. One of the most notorious examples was the tension between the cyclical conception of time, which Amerindian intellectuals had to coordinate, and the Western linear one. This tension was more visible in chronicle and history writing. This was the most relevant discursive genre of the Renaissance and the colonization of the New World, as Florescano ([1992] 1994, 66–100) and Salomon (1982) demonstrated for Anahuac and Tawantinsuyu respectively. While Acosta's text was translated into various languages and distributed all over Europe, none of the texts written by Amerindian intellectuals in the New World (e.g., by Guaman Poma, Tezozomoc, Ixtlilxochitl, and Pachacuti Yamki) was printed until the late nineteenth and the twentieth centuries.

Let us explore this aspect, starting shortly after 1550, almost have a century before Acosta's book was published. The *Codice Badiano* (1552) is a case in point. This is a manuscript of healing instructions, written in Nahuatl by Martín de la Cruz and translated into Latin by Juan Badiano. Little or nothing is known about the authors. The manuscript, however, was sup-

*Plate 5.* Two indigenous intellectuals, Martín de la Cruz and Juan Badiano, composed, in colonial Mexico, a report that was at the same time a gift for Charles V, the emperor of Europe, and Charles I, the king of Spain. The *Codice Badiano,* composed around 1550, was written in part due to the educational activities of the Franciscan friars. The codicé, which also includes medicinal prescriptions, was written in Latin, and the drawing of the plants follows the visual imaginary of European Spaniards. (From *Libellus de medicinalibus Indorum herbis* [1552], written by Martín de la Cruz and translated into Latin by Juan Badiano. Facsimile edition. Mexico City: Instituto del Seguro Social, 1964.)

ported by the institutional prestige of the Colegio Santa Cruz de Tlatelolco, which had been founded in Mexico-Tenochtitlan in 1536 by the Franciscan order. The *colegio* was suspected of offering the "barbarians" access to knowledge. It began to decay during the reign of Phillip II and continued to do so until its closure in the second half of the sixteenth century. In a colonizing enterprise, the initial project of a learning institution, where Spanish, Latin, and Nahuatl were interacting languages and knowledges (analogous to Greek, Arabic, and Latin), was difficult to sustain. Angel Maria Garibay (1964) suggested also that the manuscript was a product of circumstances, destined to encourage Charles V to act in favor of the Amerindians, whose situation in Mexico and the *colegio* had become increasingly precarious. Garibay also noticed that no copy of the manuscript was ever found in Mexico, while the one known today traveled all over Europe. His third observation, which ties together the previous two, is that Bernardino de Sahagún, who was the mastermind and collector of all things Aztec, never mentioned the manuscript in his work. Garibay advanced a series of hypotheses to explain this fact. One is that Sahagún may not have been in Mexico-Tenochtitlan but traveling around New Spain when the manuscript was produced. The other is that, although Sahagún may have been familiar with the manuscript, it was a product whose meaning or relevance escaped him. It was, indeed, a manuscript produced and sent to the king by two Mexicans (Aztec and Nahuatl speakers) who also knew Latin and had mastered Western designs of flora. As can be seen in plate 5, there is no recognizable "Aztec" feature in this design.

The *Codice Badiano* (*Libellus de medicinalibus Indorum herbis,* Martín de la Cruz, 1552) can be looked at from two perspectives. One is the perspective of the Franciscan order (in this case) or the Jesuit order (in the case of Acosta), and the other is the perspective of the Amerindian intellectuals. Regarding the first perspective, the comparison between a text of the *Libellus* and the "translation" in Sahagún's *Florentine Codex,* provided by Vilchis, is revealing.

### *Libellus* (de la Cruz)

Cuando la irritación de los ojos es leve, se aplica hojas de *maizquitl* y de *xoxouhqui matlaxochitl,* bien molidas y en leche de mujer, o con rocio, o agua muy limpia. Esta mixtura se destila en los ojos. *Quien sufra de los ojos ha de abstenerse mucho del trato carnal, del ardor del sol y del humo y del viento. No debe tomar como condimento el chilmolli, ni ha de comer alimento caliente. Debe llevar junto al cuello un cristal rojo, no ha de ver cosas blancas, sino negras. Un ojo de zorra es maravillosamente provechoso para ojos danados, para eso se lo atara en la parte superior del brazo.* (Vilchis 1988, 38; my italics)

*Florentine Codex* (Sahagún)

Quando comienza el dolor de los ojos sera provechoso moler la yerba nombrada Iztecauhtic mixitl, y ponerla a la redonda dellos, o echar en los ojos ciertas gotas de pulque trasnochado, o serenado, o el zumo de las hojas del cerezo o la leche de la yerva o, cardo llamado en la lengua chicalotl, o el zumo de los grumos del arbol del *mizquite*. Y donde a pocos dias echar algunas gotas de la yerba llamada tonalchichicaquilitl, o la leche de la yerva nombrada *xoxouhca* patli, y mojarse con el la cabeza, y no sera malo sangrarse. (Vilchis 1988, 38)

The main difference between the two texts is the erasure of Amerindian prescriptions when they approach levels of knowledge and belief that conflict with those of Christians. Amerindian epistemology, contrary to Christian and secular ones, brings to the foreground the interactions and "common union" of the body and the cosmos (López Austin 1980) rather than the separation of the body and the spirit. Thus, from the perspective of Sahagún (and Acosta), a territorial epistemology justified erasure and suppression (e.g., "extirpation of idolatry"); yet, from the perspective of an Amerindian intellectual (in this case de la Cruz), there was, properly speaking, a border epistemology at work. That is, there is the possibility for Amerindians trained in Western knowledge to deal with both: manipulating Nahuatl and Latin, incorporating imported Spanish healing practices into local ones, and doing it on their own, without Spanish missionaries or men of letters acting as intermediaries. Such practices were out of the reach of Spanish missionaries. The Spanish had the Christian and Renaissance paradigms of knowledge under which to organize the known — for example, writing natural and moral histories. Amerindians, who had their own epistemic paradigm, found themselves in a subaltern epistemic position. Consequently, their paradigms had to interact with the Spanish ones, and the interesting result was not so much Amerindian organization of the known (which the Spaniards found significant) but the interference it produced in the ways of knowing. This "impurity," which established the foundation for border epistemology in the modern/colonial world system, gave an epistemological potential to the Amerindians that Spaniards could not reach and had to repress. However, by the end of the twentieth century border epistemologies that had been repressed for centuries began coming to the fore (Mignolo 1997, 2000a).

The same argument can be made taking Amerindian intellectuals at the end of the sixteenth and the beginning of the seventeenth century (approximately the time of Acosta's writing and the subsequent impact of his book) as a case in point. Let us remember the well-known example of Guaman Poma's "Mapamundi" and "Pontificial Mundo," wherein he drew, first, Tawantinsuyu on top of Spain; second, he drew the world organized in four spaces with one center; and, third, he made both Tawantinsuyu and Spain coexist. This "double consciousness" is not found in any Castilian chronicles of the time, Acosta's being one among many (Mignolo 1992, 27–48). Acosta can "see" Amerindian customs and society as something to be described, not as the products of human beings with their own knowledge. Acosta's perspective and consciousness is monotopic. He describes a "new" world and its people and offers a causal explanation of natural phenomena. Guaman Poma's perspective and consciousness is diatopic — that is, encompassing the perception of the world Amerindians lived in before the arrival of the Spaniards and the Spanish consciousness they were forced to incorporate. I am assuming, of course, that there *was* an Amerindian consciousness that did not match the Spanish one and from which Spanish patterns were interpreted and incorporated, although today it is difficult to grasp it in its purity, in the same way we believe and accept that we have access to ancient Greek cosmology and consciousness. Acosta, contrary to Guaman Poma, was not forced to incorporate the consciousness of the "other." Amerindian consciousness was, for Acosta, something to be described and suppressed (once again, the extirpation of idolatry). Amerindian double consciousness became an epistemic question under religious rhetoric. It also became an epistemological potential outside the reach of Spanish intellectuals; they were there to know and convert, not to learn and be transformed.

The Argentinean philosopher Rodolfo Kusch saw this problem clearly and articulated it around his notion of "the philosophical locus" (1971). Kusch realized that, while in Europe philosophy emerged and grew as a response to

*Plate 6.* Toward the end of the sixteenth century and the first two decades of the seventeenth, Waman Puma (Guaman Poma de Ayala) composed a report of around four hundred designs, each of them complemented with descriptive captions. While Acosta was living under the belief that the earth was the center of the universe, Guaman Poma had to deal with his "double consciousness," that is, to accommodate the coexistence of Inca-Aymara and Spanish and European cosmologies. First, he placed the east on top; second, he mapped the world according to the four *suyus* with Cuzco in the center; third, he mapped Spain in the same way that he mapped Tawantinsuyu (the Spaniards, remember, did the same; they mapped Tawantinsuyu according to their cartographic conceptions); and, fourth, he conceived Spain (Castille) and Tawantinsuyu (Cuzco) as coexistent. None of the Spaniards thought about the coexistence of both worlds. Spaniards, as conquerors, remained in their single consciousness. Guaman Poma, as the conquered, was forced into a double consciousness. (From Guaman Poma, *Nueva corónica y buen govierno,* completed circa 1610. Facsimile edition by John Murra and Rolena Adorno. Mexico City: Siglo Ventiuno, 1982.)

vital daily problems, in South America, as it was colonized by the Spanish (and, I will add, the Portuguese), philosophy was an imported academic exercise. Kusch stated that he came upon this problem when he saw Guaman Poma's "Mapamundi," a map that is not "scientifically accurate" but articulates a powerful "lived experience," a subjectivity. Kusch underlined other aspects of the map — not what I am describing here as Guaman Poma's double consciousness, borrowing obviously from Du Bois's expression ([1905] 1990). Double consciousness (as in the *Libellus* manuscript) became the philosophical place first of the Amerindians and later of Creoles (white and black). That is, double consciousness was and is the philosophical locus of those who live and think from the colonial experience. What about those who do not, I am frequently asked. Those who do not, simply do not. This answer will also apply to the nonprivileged positions of Guaman Poma and Du Bois, whose double consciousness was the necessary outcome of being, and consequently feeling, marginalized from hegemonic ways of being and thinking. The problem is not so much who is "in" or "out" but the sheer fact that the conditions for being in or out are the very foundations of the colonial difference. This, of course, was difficult to articulate in the sixteenth century, although examples abound.

The repression of the Amerindian intellectual elite in the remainder of the colonial period, and later on, the project of national homogeneity enacted by Creole nation builders after independence, made Amerindians' double consciousness (and that of people of African descent) invisible. The Creole intelligentsia managed to take the place of the former colonizer and repress their own double consciousness (which became a cause of complaint for not being at the same civilizing stage that Europe was) and play the game of the monotopic and homogeneous consciousness of the nation. What I am saying here is that double consciousness is the most visible outcome of the colonial difference and that it is not particular to one or another ethnic group. We owe the term to W. E. B. Du Bois, although the term is apt to describe the situation of Amerindians and white or "mestizo" Creoles in Latin America. Among Latin American Creoles, double consciousness manifested itself as a desire to be what the European civilizing model offered and the awareness that, in (Latin) America, the force of barbarism was the reality. This double consciousness was manifested as being neither Amerindian nor European but wanting to be European on the margins. Mestizo Creole double consciousness has a tragic sense that sharply contrasts with the subversive and rebellious black double consciousness articulated by Du Bois or with the black Creole version offered by Caribbean writers and thinkers (Glissant, Confiant, Bernabé, Chamoiseau).

### The Rift in Western Epistemology: The Colonial Difference
### Revisited and the Imperial Difference Invented

The reader may feel that I went off track at the end of the previous section. Indeed, I was preparing the ground to introduce the subsequent discussion on "natural" and "moral" history and the transformation of the imaginary of the modern/colonial world system in the eighteenth century. Acosta had a bag full of tricks with which to write the moral and natural history of the Indias Occidentales. Yet his tricks were becoming outdated by the time he implemented them. The rift that was taking place at the end of the sixteenth century was pushing him closer to the *"antiguos,"* although he himself insisted in his text in distinguishing between the *antiguos* and the *"modernos"* and aligning himself with the *modernos'* history (Western history). Acosta criticized the *antiguos* (from Aristotle to biblical authorities) for several reasons. He criticized them for ignoring the fact that "this New World was inhabited"; some of the *antiguos* did not even believe that there was land in that part of the planet. It should be noted that Acosta's first two "books" were written in the New World; books 4 through 7 were written in Spain. Acosta used deictics accordingly: *this* and *here* in the first part of the book and *that* and *there* in the second in reference to the New World. Thus, while criticizing the *antiguos* for ignoring all the marvels of the New World, he retained the overall theoretical model that Copernicus was debunking in the sixteenth century (Ferris 1988, 61–83). At the time Columbus landed in the Indies (one century before Acosta's book was written), Copernicus was a student at the University of Kraców. Although Copernicus did not release his revolutionary book on astronomy (*De revolutionibus*) until the end of his life, it was not because of personal doubts about his theory but because of social and justified fears generated by the beliefs supported by state institutions. It was not easy, halfway through the sixteenth century, to state that the sun was fixed and the planet turned around it or to convince people that this statement was not heresy but was simply based on observation. There were good reasons for Acosta not to know of this, and to know even less of the investigation carried on, after Copernicus, by Tycho Brahe and Johannes Kepler. Some of the path-breaking findings came at the end of the sixteenth century.

My point is not to criticize Acosta for adhering to an old conception of the universe, one in which the sun turns around the earth and not vice versa, but to underline the emergence of what I have termed elsewhere the "internal borders" of the modern world system (Mignolo 2000a, 2000b). In this case, the dividing lines within Christianity, as traced by the Reformation, manifested themselves in other domains. While Acosta was proclaiming that knowing the natural world was a way of knowing and admiring its creator, a few decades later Francis Bacon was advocating a method that would replace the search for causes with the search for laws. Knowledge of nature would no longer be justified as a means of knowing its creator; instead, knowledge of nature would lead to knowledge of the laws governing it (Merchant 1980). The very concept of reason was being displaced. From Bacon's time on, reason, knowledge, and law placed the human being in front of nature in a confrontational manner, like that between the knowing subject and the known object. The common union between knowledge of nature and of its creator, which maintained a certain link between the knowing subject and the known object, began to be replaced with a more rigorous experimental method whose final destination was knowing the laws of nature rather than using nature to know its creator. From Bacon to Newton there is a logical trajectory and a break with the Christian/Renaissance paradigm. This trajectory implanted new ways of reasoning and a linear model of history. All other possible models of the universe and relationships between human beings and nature were denied. Knowledge became "naturalized" as Western knowledge, from Aristotle and Ptolemy to Copernicus and Newton to Bacon, Descartes, and Kant. Renaissance models began to fade away, becoming invisible on the other side of the internal (European) borders. The "south" of Europe was constructed in the late eighteenth century at the same time as the "Orient."

It is not surprising that early missionaries dealing with nature and cosmology, and with the New World and cartography, paid little attention to what Amerindians had to say on each of these topics or even whether the issues they were concerned with made sense from the perspective of Amerindian cosmology. It was, and continues to be, as if "nature" that does not have its own discourse (as human beings do) has no discourse at all beyond the tradition extending from Aristotle to Acosta, which is another way of saying that Amerindians were considered part of nature. This assumption was due, in my understanding, to the fact that European missionaries and men of letters describing New World nature took it for granted that people were indeed part of nature itself. Acosta was aware, as he stated and argued in book 7, that Amerindians were far from deprived of intelligence, and he described particular instances in which this intelligence was manifested. He recognized their intelligence — though not their knowledge, their conceptualization of themselves, and their relation to the cosmos, a relation that we now know did not distinguish between moral and natural or propose to "know" nature or "admire" God. Amerindian epistemology was embodied, so to speak, in the sense that it presupposed an interaction among living organisms rather than a separation between human beings and nature that human beings could know, exploit, and use. The success of this move during the colonial period was such that the Creole intelligentsia never questioned it after independence. The Amerindian intelligentsia was silenced from colonial times until today, when a wild and all-absorbing capitalism proposes to appropriate all natural resources to produce artificial objects. Today Amerindian intellectuals build on an epistemic memory that was cut off and fragmented in the sixteenth century but has all the elements needed to argue against and build on projects alternative to capitalism. Furthermore, the picture gets more complicated since governments and the current nation-states in "emerging economies" are hesitant in their positions and consequently are not contributing to the restitution of subaltern knowledges and discourses about nature. The state can "recognize" subaltern knowledges, but it cannot create the conditions for their enactment. Indeed, the state faces a constant dilemma. One is to support the claims of economic/capitalist projects; the other is to support the opposite claims made by social movements, particularly indigenous social movements where an alternative to Western epistemology is at stake. Finally, there are the claims of social movements interested in maintaining the biodiversity of the planet (Global Biodiversity Strategy 1992; Escobar 1998). Arguing for decolonization of knowledge in this domain is not a return to the 1970s but a move toward a future in which the natural silence of nature has to face an increasingly powerful technological discourse on biodiversity. I shall offer a couple of examples, remembering that the imaginary of the modern/colonial world system was put in place by the subalternization of knowledges from the sixteenth to the twentieth centuries.

Taking just one example from the Andes, where Acosta has his experience and the information for his "natural" and "moral" histories, nature as such did not have a name or place in Aymara cosmology. This was, so to speak, another lack of the Amerindians: they had neither writing, history, nor natural philosophy. They had, however, the technology to produce food and a sophisticated cosmology that complemented their technological knowledge. Nature, in other words, was not something there, in front of human beings, but was (and still is today, in the epistemology of Amerindian communities, even if they have interacted with the modern world) part of the living universe. As is well known, "Mother Earth" is considered both life and the source of life in Amerindian cosmology, as Carlos Lenkersdorf (1996) has documented among the Tojolabales of southern Mexico in connection with the statements and claims of the Zapatistas' uprising. This conceptualization is not easy to reconcile with either the discourse of capitalist expansion and exploitation or the discourse of the state on "natural resources" and on the exhibition of nature in museums and natural gardens. National parks projects, which had their inception in the proliferation of botanical gardens in the eighteenth century and developed throughout the nineteenth (Navarro 1801), were a natural consequence of this latter case. With respect to the "exploitation" of nature, Acosta was already articulating a discourse on nature as external to the moral. Furthermore, with the Industrial Revolution and Kant's concept of "physical geography" (*Anthropology From a Pragmatic Point of View,* [1797] 1996) it became natural to assume that nature is dead and at the same time is raw material for the production of artificial objects or for the commodification of "natural" products. With the Industrial Revolution, the colonial difference acquired a new face. As Coronil (1997) has demonstrated, the planetary distribution of nature paralleled the planetary distribution of labor. Nature was identified more and more with three continents (the Americas, Asia, and Africa) where "natural disasters" seemed to happen more frequently and spectacularly. Nature conceived as dead but enjoyable became an object to enjoy and observe, linked to the tourist industry.

Now let me pause here and say that my effort to understand the Amerindian conceptualization of nature is not oriented toward a "restitution" of Amerindian knowledge, restitution that may end up placing that knowledge in a museum or valuing it as an object of study. My point is quite different. What I am arguing is that the subalternization of knowledge in the modern/ colonial world system produced the impression that what was subalternized was already "behind" a triumphal march of the Christian ethos, Renaissance scholarship, and Enlightenment scientific progress. What I am arguing is that the subalternization of non-Western knowledge did not leave it behind but aside: on the margins, in the colonial difference. It also resulted in the impoverishment of human intelligence and creativity in the name of a superior way of knowing. What I mean, then, by restitution is not recuperation but reinscription. This argument is necessary because of the colonial difference in the making of the modern/colonial world system. Furthermore, the argument shall be made from the subaltern perspective of the colonial difference and not from the perspective of the subalternization of knowledge that, today, "recognizes" and laments that things have been as they were.

The Amerindian cosmology is closer, indeed, to contemporary views of the universe modeled on the Greek concept of Gaia (Lovelock 1987). The proponents of Gaia have, of course, a more sophisticated discourse than that of Amerindians in the Andes or southern Mexico, but the general destination of their thought is quite similar. Amerindian discourse was articulated "before" the hegemony of Western epistemology, but it is still constantly rearticulated in the "present," particularly when transnational corporations intend to appropriate Amerindian lands for the implementation of capitalist economic designs. Neither Amerindian languages nor their knowledge were allowed to compete or even remain parallel to the languages and knowledges of modernity. Gaia comes "after" as a critique of modern science and its complicity with capitalism. But both Amerindian discourse and Gaia science are "contemporary" discourses today that can join forces in searching for new ways of thinking beyond the human/nature dichotic paradigm. Amerindian discourse had to yield and be condemned to the "traditional" in front of a victorious modernity that had stripped itself of any kind of tradition. Modernity, indeed, and the imaginary of the modern/colonial world system, was defined precisely as that which does not have tradition, even if the foundational discourse of modernity has its foundation in ancient Greece! The discourse of Gaia is more sophisticated in a sense because it builds on the vocabulary and grammar of three hundred years of scientific discourse, whereas Amerindian discourse was castrated with the castration of Amerindian languages (Guzman de Rojas 1995). Yet the general orientation of Amerindian cosmology is very compatible with the Amerindian conception of and attitude toward Mother Earth. Certainly Amerindians did not reach the point of making predictions about the future of the universe, as did those scientists who studied Gaia (Lovelock 1987, 96–97; 1990). But they coincide in this: there is no earth on the one hand and life on earth on the other. Earth is part of life in the universe and, as such, is life itself generating reproduction over death and being maintained in the process of reproduction. Lovelock says it in a different way.

> I see through Gaia a very different reflection. We are bound to be eaten, for it is Gaia's custom to eat her children. Decay and death are certain, but they seem a small price to pay for life and for the possession of identity as an individual. It is all too easily forgotten that the price of identity is mortality. The family lives longer than one of us, the tribe longer than the family, the species longer than the tribe; and life itself can live as long as it can keep this planet fit for it. (96)

The imagination of nature in the formation and transformation of the modern/colonial world system has gone a long way. Now that we have a general picture, or, even better, a general drawing, let us return to Acosta at the end of the sixteenth century.

### De Caelo and Utchatha: The Subalternization of Knowledges in the Making of the Colonial Difference

By all modern (and I mean since the Renaissance) accounts, the history of science was conceived as an ascending line from some invented origin to a teleological destination guided by a metaphysical principle, namely, progress. In retrospect, and following this model, Acosta was utterly wrong in maintaining a geocentric conception of the universe when Copernicus had already determined that the sun was the center. Acosta was as wrong as his contemporary, Guaman Poma, who was drawing a "Pontificial Mundo" on the basis of a fourth division of space that did not correspond to the four continents in Christian, and later scientific, cosmologies. Acosta was as wrong as Copernicus, who placed the sun at the center of the universe when we know today that it is not. On the other hand, however, Acosta was as right as Guaman Poma and Copernicus. Right and wrong in my previous sentences only make sense from a denotative epistemology and a progressive conception of knowledge fabricated by the modern/colonial imaginary. The first characterizes Western modern epistemology claiming its foundations in the Platonic, denotative philosophy of language. The second is a succession of steps leaving behind what has been changed, as if knowledge operates under the same logic as car models. Right and wrong make no sense from the perspective of an enactive philosophy of language (Maturana 1991; Varela, Thompson, and Rosch 1991, 133–84). Acosta's description of the Indias Occidentales and its people was enacted from his own "philosophical place" — not the correspondence between his discourse and the "reality" of the world but the correspondence between his discourse and the reality of the cosmology to which he was attached. Yet, if the same could be said about Copernicus, what makes us believe that Copernicus was right and Acosta wrong? What makes us believe that Amerindian cosmology does not count next to Acosta's and Copernicus's? The question here is not the correspondence of a given cosmology to reality but of the coloniality of power and knowledge. The above three examples are a blueprint of the making of the internal (imperial) and external (colonial) borders of the modern/colonial world system. The rift between Acosta and Copernicus marks the internal (imperial) epistemic frontier and the moment in which the south falls behind the scientific and philosophical production of the north — or, as López Piñero (1979, 371–403) states, the "absence of Spain from the scientific revolution of the seventeenth century." The break between Acosta's and Amerindian cosmologies signals the making of the external (colonial) difference, which, of course, was more brutal than the first, internal one.

Nicolaus Copernicus and Acosta, in the first and second halves of the same century, respectively, were in opposite positions vis-à-vis knowledge. Copernicus drew all his knowledge from books since he was among the first generation to enjoy the impressive changes in scholarship enacted with the invention of the printing press. At the beginning of the sixteenth century approximately nine million books reproducing about thirty thousand titles circulated in Europe. In 1526, Fernández de Oviedo (in the Caribbean), a man of letters in the Indias Occidentales and a forerunner of Francisco Hernández and Acosta in writing natural history, announced with pride that his knowledge of nature came from thousands of direct experiences rather than thousands of books (Mignolo 1982). This connection between knowledge and experience constituted the splendors and miseries of Spanish men of letters vis-à-vis the scientific revolution that was taking place in the north, away from the colonial experience. It was a great challenge to traditional ways of knowing, but it lost out to the transformation of knowledge generated by the consequences of the printing press. Direct experience, however, allowed Acosta to make several corrections to inherited wisdom about the earth and also contribute to building the imaginary of the modern/colonial world system in two directions: enlarging existing wisdom and suppressing Amerindian knowledge about the cosmos, both natural and moral. The distinction between nature and humanity was already in place in Acosta and was reinforced, in the eighteenth century, with Kant's ([1797] 1996) distinction between anthropology (Acosta's moral history) and physical geography (Acosta's natural history). Then again, the crack between Acosta and Kant is not just a temporal distance but the imperial epistemic difference distinguishing the north from the south that will be articulated clearly by Hegel in the last part of his introduction to *The Philosophy of History* ([1822] 1991, 79–102).

By the time of Acosta's writing, there was a significant amount of information available, more in Mexico (Gruzinski 1988; Florescano [1992] 1994) than in Peru, (MacCormack 1991, 139–205), about Amerindian societies, histories, and cultures. Acosta did not say much about the Mayan people (Farriss 1984; Clendinnen 1987). However, all the information available (Cieza de León, Betanzos) provided a flat description of Amerindians and did not engage in substantial conversations with Andean intellectuals. Yet there were intellectuals in both the Andes and Mesoamerica. In Mexico, *Colloquio and Doctrina Christiana,* a dialogue between Spanish missionaries and Mexican *tlamatini* (both intellectuals in their own right) that took place toward the end of the 1520s and was edited by Sahagún around 1565, is perhaps the early manifestation of an attempt to achieve a dialogue that soon became "ethnographic description" (Leon-Portilla in Sahagún [1565] 1981). These intellectuals, in the Andes and Mesoamerica, had their own cosmology (as Acosta and Copernicus did), but it was not recognized by Spanish missionaries and men of letters as being at the same level. Amerindians did not have a voice in the Spanish discussions, and we do not have much documentation concerning the way they reacted to these discussions. This lack of recognition was indeed the fundamental step in establishing the colonial difference that made a distinction between "sustainable" and "dispensable" knowledge. Among the former, one can mention Acosta's genealogy from Greek and Latin thinkers to his own time and place. Among the latter, one can think of the new genealogy that was establishing the internal borders of the modern world, from Copernicus to Newton, bypassing Spanish contributions to Western knowledge. Indirectly, knowledge from the Arabic world and Chinese knowledge, as rendered by the Jesuits toward the end of the sixteenth century were also considered dispensable rather than sustainable, adding other dimensions to the colonial difference.

When we look at Guaman Poma's diagram of the "Pontifical Mundo" and see four divisions and a center, we do not necessarily understand that such a spatial arrangement cannot be detached from time. The drawing itself was not something that was already in the Andean cultural practice; it is entirely an adaptation of European drawing, adapted in the same way that the Amerindians adapted the Latin alphabet. However, very much like the Latino/Latina literature currently being written in English, there is the adaptation of a medium that renders and constructs memories that were not attached to the invention and use of such memory. In fact, the division of space in four parts and the center render simultaneously the spatial and temporal organization of the cosmic and social. Cuzco is at the center of space and present time. That basic matrix is further complicated, in the Andes, by a complex *ceque* system that R. Tom Zuidema has described in wondrous detail (1964, 1986, 1995), and is impossible to reproduce here. The *ceque* system is basically a matrix of 328 sacred places that includes human-made artifacts in human-identified places (e.g., a rock, a river, or a mountain). It is included and organized on the basis of the four *suyus* (Zuidema [1964] 1995, 68–77). *Ceque* were imaginary lines linking each place with Cuzco, the center of Tawantinsuyu, including stones, rivers, or houses that were and had been relevant to the Inca memory and social organization. Each *ceque* crossed a stone, a river, or a house, and that reference point was called *guaca,* as Acosta mentioned. The *ceque* system was organized within each *suyu*. When towns and communities were incorporated into the Inca's administration, the town system of *ceque* was redrawn to make it fit with the central system, with Cuzco as its point of origin and destination. This was indeed a spatial conceptualization but an organization of the "state" space that did not have frontiers in the same sense that the Spanish imposed frontiers in the New World and nation-state builders redrew them. Mapmaking of the modern state underlined the frontiers as markers of an enclosed territory. The Incas' "map" was different: they marked an open and extended territory linked to the "state" by means of the *ceques,* which were signposts of governmental organization. Today, Mexico or the United States, for instance, would have been conceivably integrated into the *chinchaysuyu.* Perhaps this is still difficult to understand for the reader of the twenty-first century. It was not easier for Acosta at the end of the sixteenth.

For the point I am making here, suffice it to say that beyond the general conceptualization of the space-time relation that I have sketched spatial organization divided Cuzco and the Inca sociopolitical organization into four parts called *suyu,* and each *suyu* was described with regard to its social and spatial properties. Family relations and social hierarchies were organized around the four *suyus.* Spatially, the four *suyus* had approximately the following distribution, arranged according to the four cardinal points familiar to the Western reader: *chinchaysuyu* (northwest), *antisuyu* (northeast), *cuntisuyu* (southwest), and *collasuyu* (southeast).

This was happening at the time when Acosta was conducting research and writing his book. The detailed description of the *ceque* system, which was not available to Acosta, was described in detail by Bernabé Cobo in his *Historia del Nuevo Mundo,* which was published in 1653. When you combine the four *suyus* with the *ceque* system, you end up with something like the diagram reproduced in plate 9, in which you should imagine Cuzco at the center. As is well known, one possible meaning of *Cuzco* is "navel of the world."

What I just presented is much less than an introduction to the complexity and sophisticated rationality of Inca sociocosmological and historical organization. Before moving to the next level, the vocabulary of philosophical-cosmological conceptualization that complements the sociocosmological diagrams, I would like to offer a cautionary note. When Zuidema wrote his classic book on the topic, he was aware of the contributions as well as the limitations of Granet's work (1934) on ancient China and Held's work (1935) on ancient India. Their limitations, according to Zuidema, were that they designed their schemes beforehand and then described and explained Chinese and Indian civilizations in terms of them. As a result, Granet and Held en-

*Plate 7.* The well-known *Mapamundi del Reino de las Indias* by Guaman Poma. The east is on top, and it follows the division of the four *suyus.* (From Guaman Pomo, *Nueva corónica y buen govierno,* completed circa 1610. Facsimile edition by John Murra and Rolena Adorno. Mexico City: Siglo Ventiuno, 1982.)

countered a difficult barrier: cultural incommensurability, for which Granet in particular has been criticized by a young generation of Chinese scholars working on translation and cross-cultural understanding (Liu 1999). Zuidema's project had a different orientation. He considered his work a "translation" of the complex conceptual Andean cosmology into the language of modern anthropology. Zuidema's work has made an enormous contribution to understanding Bernabé Cobo's *Historia del Nuevo Mundo.* In his effort to translate Andean cosmology into "Western cosmology," for which disciplines such as anthropology have been created to deal with the colonial difference, Zuidema has contributed to the idea that it was possible for Amerindian intellectuals to "think," and think well, without going back to Aristotle.

However, the lack of documentation and coherent narratives makes it difficult, if not impossible, to come up with accounts of Amerindian history of thought. A macronarrative framed in sentences such as "from the closed world to the infinite universe" or "from Saint Augustine to Galileo" is unthinkable in the Amerindian legacies. The unthinkable here is a consequence of the colonial difference that not only contributed to suppressing the possibility of epistemic expansion and continuity but fragmented what before the conquest, and from the perspective of the Andean intellectuals, was coherent and continuous. With this caution in mind, I would like to move now to the legacies of the Aymara, a civilization that preceded the Incas, and make some observations on its cosmological "philosophical" vocabulary. These observations will complement what I said about the Quechua imaginary in Guaman Poma. Furthermore, I will be moving from a supposed Andean cosmology "before" the conquest (similar to our imagining of Greek cosmology before the European Renaissance) to a double consciousness

*Plate 8.* A reconstruction of Guaman Poma's *Mapamundi del Reino de las Indias,* reconstructed in order to show the four *suyus* by Bolivian art historian Teresa Gisbert de Mesa in her "Reply to Walter Mignolo's 'Misunderstanding and Colonization.'" (From Serge Gruzinski and Nathan Wachtel, *Le Nouveu Monde, Mondes Nouveaux: L'Experience Americaine.* Paris: Editions de l'Ecole des Hautes Etudes en Sciences Sociales, 1996.)

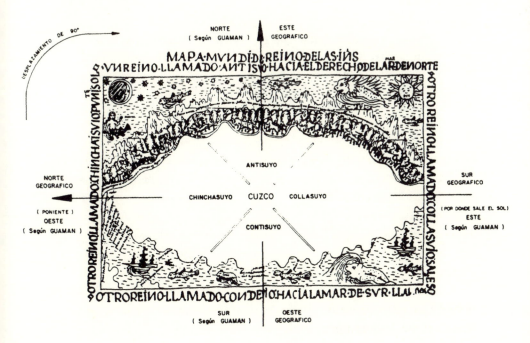

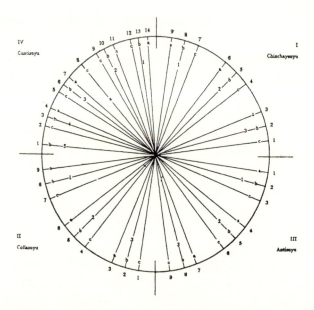

*Plate 9.* Tawantinsuyu (the four corners of the world, very similar to the Christian three continents in the T-in-O map), was organized by means of a system of *ceques,* a series of radial lines emanating from Cuzco, the center of Tawantinsuyu, outward. The *ceque* system not only organized space but also time and social relations. When the Incas subjugated a town or community, they asked the inhabitants to realign their *ceque* system to make it coincide with the *ceque* system emanating from Cuzco. Territoriality and frontiers had a different logic in the Inca Empire in comparison with the West and both the Roman and Spanish empires. (From R. Tom Zuidema, *The Ceque System of Cuzco: The Social Organization of the Capital of the Inca.* Leidin: Brill, 1964.)

and border epistemology that emerged after the conquest, which was going on during Acosta's time in Peru and was reframed by the golden age of Amerindian intellectuals between 1570 and 1670 in both the Andes and Mesoamerica.

Let us begin with four drawings from Guaman Poma de Ayala.

### A Philosopher or "Astrólogo"

The story that goes from plates 10 to 13, and is a significant silence in Acosta's book VII, is more or less the following. Guaman Poma describes the person in plate 10 as either philosopher or astrologer (i.e., a sage).

*Indios* philosophers or astrologers knew "the hours and Sundays and days and months, years, to seed and to harvest the food of each year." The "broken" Spanish and the apparent ambiguity in this vocabulary should not surprise us. It is part of the border epistemology emerging from the colonial difference. It is also a sign of indifference and indifferentiation between "philosopher" and "astrologer" (those who read the sky and the world instead of reading the books and the words, as is stated in the *Colloquios* and *Doctrina Christiana*). What we have here is a merging of Andean and Western categories in conflictive dialogue with the hegemonic colonial discourse Guaman Poma had in front of him and which he was addressing. Thus, it is not (once again) a question of hybridity but of the *subaltern reason* in conflictive dialogue with hegemony, of which Acosta's book could be an example. "That is fine, but do it my way" seems to be the underlying statement of inclusive and benevolent authoritarianism. Furthermore, we can see that the philosopher or astrologer carries a quipu in his hand, a sort of "text" in Andean culture (or literally a text if we go back to the root of the word and link *text* and *textile* [Ascher and Ascher 1981]). Guaman Poma refers to it as a "book of Khipu." This drawing is located in the section in which Guaman Poma describes idolatry (folio 883). The section in which he describes the *quipucamayocs* is the section devoted to the administration of the Inca Empire (plate 11, folio 335). Guaman Poma introduces two social roles not known before the conquest: the author and the *quilcaycamayoc*. The *quilcaycamayoc* is a new social role that embodies border epistemology in its very name since it was a name created to describe the function of the Spanish notary in terms of the vocabulary the Inca had in Quechua. Finally, Guaman Poma's conceptualization of himself as an author while writing and drawing his *Nueva corónica y buen gobierno* introduces a social role unknown among Amerindians.

Let us move to the Aymara language, which provides us with a rich vocabulary connected to the words *philosopher* and *astrologer.* I will not elaborate here on why there is no such family of words in Quechua. Ludovico Bertonio was a Jesuit, like Acosta, who arrived in Lima around 1581 and published a dictionary of the Aymara language in 1612. Due to his presence in Lima at that time, he witnessed the increasing importance of the Jesuit order in the Andes at the end of the sixteenth and the beginning of the seventeenth centuries. Some statistics show that, while around 1576 there were approximately 75 missionaries of the Jesuit order, around 1600 the number had

*Plate 10*. Guaman Poma's description of the *astrólogo* (*amauta* or philosopher) in an Inca cosmological setting, with the sun and the moon, the masculine and feminine, as complementary opposites. He also carries a string of quipus, implement of the Inca writing system, within the same logic of the *ceque* system (Guaman Poma, *Nueva corónica y buen govierno*). The drawing reveals the coexistence, as in "El Pontificial Mundo," of Spanish and Inca concepts of representation. This is a good example of what Serge Gruzinski analyzes as "*metiss* thinking" (la pensée metisse). (From Serge Gruzinski, *La pensée metisse*. Paris: Fayard, 1999.)

*Plate 11.* The *quipu,* like any other writing system, was a good tool in the hands of the philosophers as well as the accountants for keeping track of goods in the stores of the Inca, the head of Tawantinsuyu. *Kipucamayoc* (or *quipucamayoc*) was the name given to accountants, those who were skillful in the use of the quipu. (From Guaman Poma, *Nueva corónica y buen govierno,* completed circa 1610. Facsimile edition by John Murra and Rolena Adorno. Mexico City: Siglo Ventiuno, 1982.)

*Plate 12.* The *astrólogo* (*amauta* or philosopher) has been converted, by colonization, into an author. This plate is captioned "Camina el autor" (the author is walking). While the *amauta* carried quipus in his hands, the author carries a rosary. Furthermore, the author is being followed by a horse, a companion that was unavailable to the *amauta.* (From Guaman Poma, *Nueva corónica y buen govierno,* completed circa 1610. Facsimile edition by John Murra and Rolena Adorno. Mexico City: Siglo Ventiuno, 1982.)

*Plate 13.* The *quipucamayoc* became the *quilcaycamayoc,* since *quilcay* was the name invented in the Quechua language to name the Spanish writing system. In this plate we see the transformation of the *quipucamayoc* into the *quilcaycamayoc,* a good portrait of what could have been the kind of double consciousness experimented with (in different ways and to different degrees) by the people of the Inca Empire. (From Guaman Poma, *Nueva corónica y buen govierno,* completed circa 1610. Facsimile edition by John Murra and Rolena Adorno. Mexico City: Siglo Ventiuno, 1982.)

increased to 282. Acosta, once again, was in the middle of that effervescence. Bertonio is important here because he will help us make sense of the transformation from the *quipucamayoc* to the *quilcaycamayoc* (and from the *amauta* to the author) and help us to understand what remained obscure and hidden to Acosta and many of the Spanish missionaries. First, let me introduce a word of caution. I am not saying that "we" (scholars) are the great bearers of a truth that the missionaries were unable to grasp. I am just saying that the missionaries were blind to the colonial difference they were establishing (perhaps they were blind because of that) and that we now are no better than the missionaries. We have a different project — to undo the colonial difference not only in the Americas at the inception of the modern/colonial world but also later in Asia and Africa, when new and renewed global designs emerged from the European Enlightenment rather than from the European Renaissance.

Be that as it may, Bertonio ([1612] 1984) collected the words *amaotta* and *chuymakhtara* and translated them as "Very sage and prudent man." There are other words, such as *amaotana,* which Bertonio translated as "wisdom"; *amahuatha,* which he rendered as "to love"; and *querer* (to want), which in Spanish is equivalent to "to love" when employed in indirect form (te quiero, I love you). However, a direct construction such as "quiero un pedazo de pan" is better rendered into English as "I want (a piece of bread)." A related word, *amahuasitha,* is translated by Bertonio as "to love each other" and also as "to desire something." Now, *chuymakhtara,* which is equivalent to *amaotta* according to Bertonio, is related to other words such as *chuyma* and *chuymana. Chuyma* seems to have a certain distinction in Aymara, as it is the root of a whole array of words. Bertonio translated it generously: "the entrails properly, although it applies more specifically to the heart, to the stomach, and to the insides of the body." However, Bertonio observed that *chuyma* also meant "everything belonging to the mood and the frame of mind of the state of a person (estado interior del animo), bad or good, vice or virtue." To make this idea clear, Bertonio felt the need to add a series of related words.

*Chuymarochatha:* to entrust or confide something to memory (history?!)
*Chuymachasita:* to beg understanding of something by means of difference or definition (philosophy?!)
*Chuymanisa:* stupid person, someone without judgment

*Chuymakhtara:* sage, learned

*Chuymakapa:* the chest or the part of the body aligned with the heart (i.e., thinking in Amerindian cosmology was not located in the brain but in the heart, where feeling was also located; see López Austin for this point based on Méxican cosmology)

I will stop here, but we could go on for a while, running our fingers through Bertonio's dictionary in search of families of words relating the body to understanding. I would emphasize that *understanding* is a better word than *knowledge* for what is going on here. This is one of the ways of "understanding" why among Amerindian people Nature was not distinguished from Human Being and was far from being something to be "known." Thus, one can make sense of the fact that *chuyma* is also the "heart of plants, trees and other things." Bertonio further elaborates by saying that it is "like the peach's heart and other fruits that have it." An obvious conclusion is that understanding in Aymara is attached to the body and metaphorically located in the heart. In this configuration, it is also understandable that *philosopher* and *astrologer* will be translated into Aymara as *amauta* and *chuyman,* as in *tocapu amaotta* and *tocapu chuymani,* which Bertonio renders as "man of great understanding (*entendimiento*)." Thus, while Acosta's sense of rationality found its grounding in Aristotle's logic, Renaissance humanistic learning, and the New World experience, *chuyma* and *ammaota* in the Aymara world deployed a rational calculus in which Nature was not understood as something outside of or different from Human Beings. It was a totality called *pacha.* What in Western Christianity (and in Acosta) was a three-pronged differentiated order of things (God, Nature, and Man), and the knowledge *of* nature was at the same time an understanding *of* its creator, this in Aymara was a unified totality rather than a differentiated trilogy. Rengifo Vásquez explained that the concept of *runa* includes the notion of "man," as in Western cosmology, but also incorporates within it the notions of *sallqa* (nature) and *huacas* (deities). You can say that these are incommensurable cosmologies. I prefer to think that we have here cosmologies structured by the colonial difference, as we cannot understand one without the other. The colonial difference is structured on a power relation, although one is in a subaltern relationship with the other (Rengifo Vásquez 1998, 90). *Pacha* is not a god in Andean cosmology but an *order* of things. Rengifo Vásquez specifies that

"Form of life" is used in this text to mean not the exterior aspect or customs of a person or a collectivity, but rather the distinctive singularity with which each one of the living beings that inhabit the Andean *Pacha* present themselves in any particular circumstances. Similarly, each form of life, be it a llama, the chulpi corn or don Juan Quispe, has its cycle of life, its manners of being, its attributes which differentiate it from other runas, potatoes or corn. (90)

This epistemological structure or force remained hidden to Acosta. Or perhaps it was too strange for him. But it was also even stranger to the epistemological rift that transformed humanistic learning into experimental and scientific thoughts. The humanistic concept of *saber* (wisdom) was closer to Andean epistemology than the scientific rationality that has dominated Western epistemology since the seventeenth century. Curiously enough, contemporary critics of modern epistemology, from the perspective of ecology, bring back what was suppressed in the early sixteenth century by means of the colonial difference. I mentioned Lovelock and his concept of Gaia. Let me add a couple of references from an ecofeminist critique that encompass both gender and ethnicity in the making of the colonial difference and in the subalternization of non-Western forms of knowledge. Maria Mies employs a forceful metaphor that captures one of the points I am trying to make here when she writes: "Women, nature, and foreign peoples and countries are the colonies of White Man. Without their colonization, that is, subordination for the purpose of predatory appropriation (exploitation) the famous Western civilization would not exist, nor its paradigm of progress and, above all, natural sciences and technology either" (Mies and Shiva 1993, 43).

Mies's coauthor, Vandana Shiva, also helps in complementing Mies' point, which is what I was trying to say about Acosta ignoring or dismissing Amerindian knowledge. If today modern science — as Shiva says — is projected as "a universal, value free system of knowledge, which by the logic of its method claims to arrive at objective conclusions about life, the universe and almost every thing" (Shiva 1993, 23), such logic was being put in place with the double articulation of the colonial epistemic difference (Acosta vis-à-vis Amerindian epistemology) and the imperial epistemic difference (Bacon and Copernicus vis-à-vis Renaissance humanistic epistemology). The correspondence between contemporary critics of modern epistemology and Amerindian epistemology takes place at the level of "experience," a concept criticized by postmodern feminist thinkers (Donna Haraway) and countercriticized by postcolonial and "third world" feminist thinkers (Alcoff, Moya, and Mohanty). Shiva's argument is that central to such domination is an arbitrary barrier (I would say both the colonial and the imperial difference) between "knowledge" (the expert) and "ignorance" (the nonspecialist, like Amerindians in relation to knowledge according to Renaissance humanistic standards) (Fernández 1983). "This barrier," adds Shiva, "operates effectively to exclude from the scientific domain the consideration of certain vital questions relating to the subject matter of science, or certain forms of non-specialist knowledge" (1993, 22). Shiva's observation could be transferred to what Amerindian intellectuals such as Guaman Poma, Garcilaso de la Vega, Muñoz Camargo, and Muñóz Chimalpahin were doing, although not so clearly articulated. It was the beginning of the colonial epistemic difference and not easy to figure out. The denial of knowledge beyond epistemic hegemony joins the past experience of the Amerindians with contemporary experiences among third world ecofeminists. Shiva offers us this story to think about.

> when I was pregnant and already in labour, I again encountered this (expert and non-expert forms of knowledge) arbitrary boundary between expertise and ignorance. The doctor insisted that I needed to be delivered by Caesarean section because, she said, it would be a difficult birth. I had experienced no problems, had prepared myself for a natural childbirth and informed myself about the potential problems, including medical mal practices. As a mother, however, I was denied the status of "expert" in child bearing; that status was restricted to the doctor. (23)

It would be wrong to say that "experts" in medical knowledge are useless in giving birth or in making decisions about Andean life. This is as wrong, indeed, as the ignorance and dismissal of the expert on "nonexpert knowledge." The solution is not, of course, a synthesis. In a synthesis, or a celebration of hybridity, there will be a terrain in which the hegemony of expert knowledge will always be ahead. The solution should be looked at in terms of border epistemologies from subaltern perspectives, as Mies and Shiva are doing now and as Guaman Poma, Muñoz Chimalpahin, and Sor Juana did in the sixteenth and seventeenth centuries.

The grammatical and lexicographic work of Spaniards, including Bertonio, contributed to the development and enrichment of Amerindian languages such as Aymara and Quechua even though Spanish ended up overpowering them. Thus, their epistemological potential was cut off and absorbed into the language of the colonizing empire. When Spanish was increasingly superseded by the epistemic potential of English, German, and French (which began to happen a few years after Acosta's book appeared), Aymara and Quechua were twice suppressed: through both the colonial and the imperial difference. I am aware that it is not easy today to understand Andean cosmology as a result of the pollution introduced by early missionaries, soldiers, and men of letters. The problem is similar to the difficulties in understanding ancient Greek cosmology. However, we have the illusion that this is easier because the West has made Greece its cosmological ancestor and transformed the difference into the continuity of sameness. A careful comparison among Greek, Andean, and Mesoamerican cosmologies will show that they have much more in common with each other than Greek has with modern Western cosmology. Irene Silverblatt (1995) has shown that in the late sixteenth and seventeenth centuries the making of the colonial difference and the imposition of Spanish hegemony transformed the complexity of Andean society under Inca rule before 1532. Incas, as well as other Amerindian non-Inca communities, became "Indians." As a consequence, an ideal Inca society began to emerge in the imaginary of "Indians" and Spaniards and persists today, revamped by a twentieth-century form of "*indigenista*" and "*indianista*" literary and political projects. Our vocabulary and cosmology today, in the West, is entrenched in the Greek, while on the other side of the colonial difference it is related to ancient Andean cosmology. In the transformation, and at the same time in the construction of the imperial epistemic difference (e.g., the epistemic difference from Copernicus to Newton locating knowledge production in the north of Europe, concomitant with new emerging empires and colonial powers), Acosta is a pivotal case. On the one hand, he contributed to the making of the colonial difference and asserting Spanish hegemony. On the other, his own position was becoming subalternized by the epistemic imperial difference that was in the making under his nose, so to speak.

Let us now pause and undo this knot. Acosta was, as I said, at the edge of Renaissance intellectual life, moving from an idea of knowledge (*saber*) based on books to an idea of knowledge (*conocer*) linked to direct experience. The New World gave an edge to those who were able to capitalize on direct experience and distinguish themselves from other Spaniards who were writing about the New World from Europe, without direct experience (Mignolo 1982). At the same time, Acosta was blind to Amerindian epistemology and contributed to repressing the Arabic contribution to Christian and Western scholarship. That is, he was contributing to a double articulation of the epistemic colonial difference: across the Mediterranean and across the Atlantic. The imaginary of the "modern" world was being shaped in the exercise of the coloniality of power and the establishment of the colonial difference. Furthermore, Acosta was becoming the "victim" of the imperial difference that in Europe began to distinguish between north and south. The trajectory that goes from Bacon and Copernicus to Kant and Newton, through Galileo, is the trajectory linked to the movement of the history of capitalism as told by Arrighi (1994): from Genoa to Amsterdam and London. Spain and the Latin countries, enacting and supporting the Counter-Reformation, began to slip out of the march of progress, the rearticulation of the modern world, and the remaking of the colonial difference.

### After Acosta: Buffon, the Colonial Difference, and Spanish Creoles' Double Consciousness

I call "imperial" the difference established within the modern/colonial world system, the internal as opposed to the external "colonial" difference. Since the eighteenth century, European intellectuals have begun to locate the core of Europe in the countries that were becoming the new imperial powers. By the same token, and since to do so they needed to establish the geopolitical difference, the south began to shape up. The "south of Europe" was a place close to Africa and the Orient, and it coincided with the previous imperial powers (Spain and Portugal) as well as with the sources of Europe's own intellectual history (Greece and Italy). Buffon was a pivotal figure in redrawing the external colonial difference as well as a contributor to drawing the internal one.

In the middle of the eighteenth century a new reading of America's nature emerged. The first interesting aspect of this reading was the fracture it established from the previous histories, descriptions, and narratives. From Fernández González de Oviedo (1526, 1536–42) to Francisco Hernández (around 1580) to José de Acosta (1590) and Bernabé Cobo (1653), the question of the "nature of the New World" was in the hands, the pen, and the language of imperial Spain. From Buffon to Hegel, proceeding through De Pauw and Abbée Raynal, the question was in the hands, the pen, and the language of northern European (French and German) intellectuals whose countries did not have the same investment (political, religious, or economic) in the New World that Spain had had for three centuries. What was at stake? Why were Buffon, De Pauw, and Hegel interested in the Americas and in literally taking the expression "New World" to the point of linking nature and people with youth and primitiveness and consequently placing the Americas in the future of universal history, since its present was in Europe and not in America? Not only the conceptualization of nature has changed, but the conceptualization of history has as well. In both cases, the external colonial difference was rearticulated, since the Americas were not only related to Spanish imperial power but also to the raising of new ones. Furthermore, the displacement and transformation of capitalism paralleled the transformation in the conceptualization of knowledge and science. Rhetoric was the master matrix during the Renaissance. Philosophy became the new one during the Enlightenment. The transformation moved from discourse (which was the classificatory pleasure of Renaissance rhetoricians) to system (which was the toy of Enlightenment philosophers), even though in Buffon there is still a remnant of Renaissance legacies in the compilation of all kinds of information related to a given item (Flourens [1850] 1971). His interest in systems went with the territory, just as in the second half of the nineteenth century the idea of the law of nature replaced the presence of God as the "nature maker" and "man" was directly confronted with nature. It was no longer necessary to have knowledge of God as a final destination and nature as a mediator toward that final end.

Paul Henri Thiery, Baron d' Hollbach wrote an illuminating paragraph about this transition.

> Let man cease, then, to search out of the world he inhabits for beings who can procure him a happiness that nature denies him; let him study this nature, let him learn her laws, let him contemplate her energies and the immutable rules by which she acts; let him apply these discoveries to his own felicity, and let him submit in silence to her laws, which nothing can alter; let him consent to be ignorant of causes hid from him under the most impenetrable veil; let him submit without murmuring to the decrees of a universal necessity which can never be brought within his

comprehension nor even emancipate him from those rules his essence has imposed upon him. (Hollbach [1797] 1834, vol. I, 17)

Two hundred years after Acosta, God was erased as a transcendent signified of which nature was its signifier. Nature became viewed as a sign whose signified was immanent to it: the "law" of nature. A need to know was posited at the same time that man's dependence on nature was recognized. This was the first step. The second step was to replace the religious ethic with a secular one based on the ties between man and nature: "The morality of nature is the only religion that the interpreter of nature offers to his fellow citizens, to nations, to the human species, to future races weaned from those prejudices which have so frequently disturbed the felicity of their ancestors. . . . The friends of mankind cannot be friends of the gods . . . , the adorer of truth will not compromise with falsehood" (Hollbach [1797] 1834). We are far from Acosta's language. The articulation of nature with society and the need to "discover" nature, to know its law, has moved nature closer to the human being, at the same time depriving it of its "life." The distinction between natural and moral in Acosta's history became sharper. It was, in the happy expression of Carolyn Merchant (1980), "the death of nature."

This death of nature was obvious at the end of the eighteenth century, but the idea emerged a few decades after the publication of Acosta's history. Francis Bacon's concern with the reorganization of knowledge led to a radical transformation of the ways of conceiving the relationships between the human being and nature. Merchant summarizes it in a convincing manner: "Bacon's *New Atlantis* postulated a program of scientific study that would be a foundation for the progress and advancement of the 'whole of mankind.' But whereas Andrea and Campanella had in mind the improvement of the lot of the peasantry, beggars, cottagers, and artisans, Bacon can be identified with the interests of the clothier capitalists, merchants, mine owners, and the state" (1980, 177). This observation was rooted in the history of England during the second half of the sixteenth century, when it was not yet involved in colonial expansion and consequently in the production of the external colonial difference. England was occupied instead with state building. The thirty years that mediate between Acosta's book and Bacon's *New Atlantis* are the years in which the internal imperial colonial difference began to emerge, though not programmed as such by Bacon, as far as his interest in the reorganization of knowledge was concerned. There is a significant difference, to start with, between Acosta's Counter-Reformation Catholicism and the education of Bacon, whose "mother [was] a Calvinist whose Protestant values permeated his early home life" (167).

If Bacon established the reference point for a new discourse about the knowledge of nature, he also created the conditions for the links between knowledge and the "exploitation" of nature. This change in thinking coincided with the displacement of capital power from south to north, from Seville to Amsterdam — creating the short hegemony of Dutch imperialism that would soon be displaced to London in the emerging British Empire (Arrighi 1994). This transformation is expressed in the following text by Carolyn Merchant who observes that the "development of science as a methodology for manipulating nature, and the interest of scientists in the mechanical arts, became a significant program during the latter half of the seventeenth century. Bacon's followers realized even more clearly than Bacon himself the connections between mechanics, the trades, middle-class commercial interests, and the domination of nature" (Merchant 1980, 186). When writing his *Treasure of Traffike,* or a *Discourse of Foreign Trade,* published 1641, Lewes Roberts noted:

> The earth, though notwithstanding it yieldeth thus naturally the richest and most precious commodities of all others, and is properly the fountain and mother of all the riches and abundance of the world, partly . . . bred within its bowels, and partly nourished upon the surface thereof, yet is it observable, and found true by daily experience in many countries that the true search and inquisition thereof, in these our days, is by many too much neglected and omitted. (Webster 1975, 356, quoted in Merchant 1980, 187)

It so happened that Bacon himself made a few references to America in his *New Atlantis,* and he also equated America with New Atlantis. The "dispute over the New World" (Gerbi [1955] 1982) was in the making, and with it the internal/imperial borders were drawn.

The main lines in which this dispute took place during the eighteenth century, mainly following Buffon's publication of *Histoire Naturelle* and extending to Hegel's *Lessons in the Philosophy of History,* as studied by Gerbi ([1955] 1982), are the following.

First, Buffon set the stage for the transformation of a metaphor into its literal meaning. The New World, in the eighteenth century, became "young" in relation to the Old World, and so was its nature. The explanation given by Buffon started from a description offered by Fernández de Oviedo and José de Acosta concerning the humidity, great rivers, and abundant rain that characterized the New World. Buffon used the descriptions of the Spanish authors to create an explanation for the lack of development and immaturity of New World nature. According to Buffon, the climate of the New World was not conducive to the proper growth of plants and animals. This, in turn, impinged on the characteristics of the people inhabiting it. Humidity was the cause of the abundance of insects and reptiles that summarized the basic state of putrefaction and the degraded state of nature. The ultimate cause of humidity, abundant rain, and large rivers was explained by the fact of the "newness" of the New World, which had supposedly remained underwater for much longer than the other three continents. As such, *America,* which was used as a term equivalent to *New World,* was a continent that had not yet been inhabited by man.

A new dimension of the colonial difference entered the imaginary of the modern/colonial world system, in French, under the name of science. France's imperial drive was significantly different before and after the reign of Napoleon. French possessions in Canada and the Antilles did not have the force of the Spanish Empire, which extended from modern Argentina to Colorado in the United States and westward to California. However, the "debate on the New World" contributed to reinforcing the imperial differences (e.g., France in relation to Spain) and redrawing the colonial difference (e.g., French intellectual writing on the New World, instead of the Indias Occidentales, which diminished the contribution of Spain and Portugal to what they were doing). Acosta told the "natural" and "moral" history at the intersection of a geocentric conception of the universe, a chain of being model of the order of Creation and the experience in the New World. From Buffon on, the heliocentric view was accepted, the organic conception of the universe organized, and the chain of being replaced with a mechanistic and systematic one. Yet the idea of progress was also being articulated in the history of nature. The "youth" of the New World had become the blueprint of an evolutionary model that was not yet apparent in Acosta but became more prevalent in the eighteenth century and culminated in the well-known place that Hegel attributed to America in the concert of world history. Although Hegel's text is relatively well known, it would be worthwhile to quote it again here.

> The World is divided into Old and New; the name of New having originated in the fact that America and Australia have only lately become known to us. But these parts of the world are not only relatively new, but intrinsically so in respect of their entire physical and psychical constitution. Their geological antiquity we have nothing to do with. I will not deny the New World the honor of having emerged from the sea at the world's formation contemporaneously with the old: yet the Archipelago between South America and Asia shows a physical immaturity. The greater part of the islands are so constituted, that they are, as it were, only a superficial deposit of earth over rocks, which shoot up from the fathomless deep, and bear the character of novel origination. . . . Of America and its grade of civilization, especially in Mexico and Peru, we have information, but it imports to nothing more than that this culture was an entirely national one, which must expire as soon as Spirit approached it. America has always shown itself physically and psychically powerless, and still shows itself so. . . . In comparing South America (reckoning Mexico as part of it) with North America, we observe an astonishing contrast. In North America we witness a prosperous state of things; an increase of industry and population, civil order and firm freedom; the whole federation constitutes but a single state and has its political centers. In South America, on the contrary, the republics depend on military force. . . . From the Protestant religion sprang the principle of the mutual confidence of individuals. . . . Among Catholics, on the contrary, the basis of such a confidence cannot exist; for in secular matters only force and voluntary subservience are the principles of action. ([1822] 1991, 80–81)

Hegel apparently did not have much knowledge of the geology or history of the Americas, but his summary captured the internal (imperial) difference (the south and north of Europe, Counter-Reformation and Reformation, Spain and Portugal as colonial powers replaced with Holland and England, etc.) quite well. This internal (imperial) difference, already apparent in Buffon's *Histoire Naturelle,* was reinforced and expanded by Voltaire, Marmontel, Raynal, and De Pauw (Gerbi [1955] 1982, 8–70).

Instead, for Spaniards and Jesuits like Acosta, the question was the difference (but not the hierarchy) of nature and the place of the Amerindians in the order of humanity. In the line of reflections that extends from Buffon to Hegel, the question was the hierarchy of America's nature and the quality of its inhabitants, Amerindian as well as Creole. Here things get very complicated because the emergence of the internal imperial difference (on the one hand) went together with the rearticulation of the external colonial difference after the independence of the Americas from Spain and England. The distinction between north and south in the Americas mirrored the same distinction in Europe. Thus, one aspect of the rearticulation of the external colonial difference was its becoming a reflection of the internal one. In the "south" however, things became unclear for different reasons and in different directions. The starting point was the power of northern discourse in transforming the imaginary of the modern/colonial world system. That is, the south began to respond to the north (from Spain and the Americas), which was not at all the situation when Acosta published his *Historia natural y moral*. The leading counterdiscourse was in the hands of the Jesuits, exiled from South America, who learned about the debate on the New World when they arrived in Europe. An outstanding reference is the work of Fr. Francisco Clavijero, who, following his exile from Mexico, published in Italy in 1780–81 his *Historia antigua de México*. This work was quickly reprinted and translated into several languages. The Jesuits were the avant-garde of white and mestizo Creole intellectuals in South America. At that time, black Creole intellectuals in the Caribbean were not yet leaving their mark.

The Jesuit order, which was important in the Spanish colonization of the New World, should not be quickly identified with Spanish colonialism. Jesuits in China and in the New World had a similar religious mission that was tangentially related to the interest of the Crown. Matthew Ricci, who worked in China toward the end of the sixteenth century, is one example among many of the fact that the Jesuit order transcended the confines of a language and the cultures built around that language. Clavijero was in a still different situation, not because he was in Mexico but because he identified himself as a Jesuit and Creole, different from Acosta, who was a Castilian Jesuit. Clavijero took great pride in reestablishing the achievements of Aztec civilization and defending the image of a Creole sense of "Americaness." Clavijero tangentially contributed to building the imaginary space of the

Creoles, white and mestizo, in confrontation with Europeans (Spanish as well as northern European) in the "debate on the New World." The space of knowledge, before the Creole imaginary, was mainly covered by Spanish missionaries (Sahagún), men of letters (Las Casas, Acosta), and soldiers (Cortés, Cieza de León). Mestizo and indigenous writers such as Guaman Poma, Pachacuti Yamki in the Andes, and Tezozomoc, Ixtlilxochitl, and Muñoz Camargo in Mesoamerica, were not published until the sixteenth century or later (Florescano 1994). Garcilaso de la Vega was the exception and as such offered a distorted image of Amerindian intellectuals. There was no opportunity for a debate on the New World until the eighteenth century, when a strong Creole community appeared on the intellectual scene. However, it is important to remember Gerbi's statement that from the very beginning of the Spanish administration in the Americas a rift was created between peninsular Spanish and Spanish born in the Americas (Creoles). This rift grew throughout the colonial period with the increasing number of Creoles and the continuous number of peninsular Spanish going to the Americas (Gerbi [1955] 1982, 226–40). Gerbi suggests that this conflict, interestingly enough, was not ethnic at the beginning, since both groups were white and Christian Spanish; nor was it necessarily economic or social, since the groups in conflict more often than not belonged to the same economic strata and social milieu. The conflict, therefore, was geographic. Those who were born in the Americas considered themselves to be opposed by and subordinated to the Spanish peninsular population.

If the Spanish presence in the Americas was a result of conquest and the British presence one century later (1601) was due to colonization — as Hegel reminded us — then there was no rift among English colonizers equivalent to that between Creoles and peninsular Spanish. Perhaps this is also one of the reasons why the term *Creole* does not apply to those born in the British colonies in the Americas, as it applies to the Spanish-descendant population in the Caribbean, where the rift and the conflict were indeed both ethnic and economic. Creoles in Spanish America developed a sense of location as their grounding for political determination. Jesuits like Clavijero (in exile) and intellectuals like Eguiara y Eguren in Mexico (Mignolo 1995, 163–69) struggled to establish the values of "things" American at the end of the eighteenth century. Culture rather than Nature was their concern in setting up and implementing Creole intellectual values in a transatlantic ideological struggle. But Nature was reasserted in a different way when Creole intellectuals of the colonial period were replaced with a new category, the nation-building intellectuals. They were indeed Creole, in the etymological sense of the word, and from that time on Latin American intellectuals can be designated as Creole, except that Creole was a category basically of the colonial period defined in relation to Spanish peninsulars. As a consequence, the difference between "white" Spaniards born in America and "white" Spaniards born in Spain became complicated as a restriction to the categorization of Creole in Spanish America. *Mestizaje* as a historical necessity ended up with the Spanish purity of blood "here" and "there" that characterized the sixteenth century. In Mexico for instance, the image of the Creole became, during independence, the image of the national intellectual. However, later, toward the end of the nineteenth century, early "Creole patriotism" after independence was converted into a "mestizo nationalism" during the Mexican Revolution of 1910. I am using *mestizaje* here in a general sense to refer to the mixing of the Spanish and Amerindian populations as well as the mixing of the Spanish with people of African descent and even European immigrants of the late nineteenth century, particularly in the Southern Cone. The national intellectuals of the nineteenth century, for example, Creoles like Clavijero and Egiara y Eguren, had a different project. National intellectuals assumed the responsibility of building the nation and the national imaginary, while "Creole intellectuals" under colonial rule were striving for autonomy. In that process, Nature was reconceptualized no longer in the sense of "newness," as in Acosta, but in the nature-culture opposition. Domingo Faustino Sarmiento expressed it in the rhetorical figure of "civilization-barbarism." Sarmiento, who articulated a powerful model of internal colonialism for Latin America, considered Nature, concomitantly with the French philosophers of the eighteenth century, as an enemy of civilization. A significant inversion took place in the nineteenth century, and in the national imaginary, in relation to Acosta's concept of Nature as the expression of God. The inversion was not, of course, insignificant. This powerful model engendered the classic Latin American novels of the twentieth century (Ricardo Guiraldes, *Don Segundo Sombra*, 1926; Eustaquio Rivera, *La Vorágine*, 1926; Romulo Gallegos, *Doña Bárbara*, 1928; Alejo Carpentier, *Los pasos perdidos*, 1948) in which Nature was the locus of both miseries and splendors. But, above all, it became a feature of a Latin American profile that became internationally known through "magical or marvelous realism." The break between Acosta and Sarmiento in Latin American history goes through the imperial difference and the complicity of the Latin American nationalists' program in it. To read Acosta now implies awareness of that historical break and the relentless presence of the coloniality of power.

We seem to have left Acosta far behind. Indeed, all of what I have been saying was prompted and invited by my recent rereading of his *Historia natural y moral de las Indias*. I would not have engaged myself in these meditations in the late 1980s or early 1990s, when colonial studies in and about what is modern Latin America (which was unthinkable at the time of Acosta) were limited to the chronology of the "colonial period." Today I am looking at coloniality at large, and at the coloniality of power and the colonial difference in a modern/colonial world in which we are still living and struggling. Globalization and neoliberalism are new names, new forms of rearticulating the colonial difference. The colonial period may have ended, but the coloniality of power continues to order planetary relations and the colonial difference continues to be a place of control and subalternization and at the same time a site of struggle and imagination of new possible futures. While internal colonialism characterized the national period, the future demands new approaches to the question of nature — not only in the terms I suggested, both as subaltern forms of knowledge and an approach to nature in the broken genealogies of Amerindian and Native American thoughts and in the new perspectives emerging from ecofeminism, but also in what Fernando Coronil (1997) described as the "global distribution of nature" parallel to the "global distribution of labor." The paradigmatic texts (*Don Segundo Sombra, La Vorágine,* etc.) of Latin American narrative and essays mentioned above were all written before the cold war. During the cold war nature was resemanticized and linked to the underdeveloped third world as a source of natural goods to be transformed and commodified in the developed, industrial, and civilized first world. If the above is a description that replaced, at the end of the twentieth century, the discourse of Enlightenment philosophy with regard to the New World, and was extended to the planet in general, then the emerging social movements linking ethnology to ethnicity are perhaps the equivalent of Creole intellectuals reacting to the misreading of French philosophers (Escobar 1998). Of course, this is a different story in the remaking of the colonial difference and the reproduction of the modern/colonial world order.

## Moral History, Epistemic Purgation, and
## "Rights of the People"

Let us go back to the sixteenth century, to history and the order of knowledge. I shall be brief in this last section since I have written extensively about this topic in several publications (Mignolo 1981; 1994; 2000c). The only point I would like to reinforce here is one that is only indirectly articulated in my previous publications: history and the making of the colonial difference.

The most striking move among missionaries and men of letters in the sixteenth century was to assume that because Amerindians did not have letters (Acosta, book VI) they did not have history. Accordingly, Spaniards appointed themselves to write this "missing" history. The colonial difference appears in all its sharpness when we look at the question of how Amerindians and Spaniards kept records of past events and organized their memories. Spaniards assumed that their own way of dealing with the past, which they called "history," was a universal feature of human communities and that those who did not have the same conception of recording the past did not have history. In a way this was right: Amerindians did not have history in the sense that the Spaniards understood it. On the other hand, this was not important, although the Spaniards could not accept or see this. In fact, they were blind to the colonial difference, and that blindness is still being reproduced today in different forms. Certainly, Acosta was not directly guilty of it. He did not have access to the narratives written by the distinguished Amerindian intellectuals mentioned above. Guaman Poma, Tezozomoc, Ixtlilxochitl, and others were struggling to articulate a cyclical concept of time reconciled with a linear one. This leads to the second assumption in the sixteenth-century concept of history: alphabetic narrative of a linear sequence of events. Mexican scholar Enrique Florescano ([1992] 1994, 1–183) wrote extensively about the group of Mexican intellectuals (self-identified as Amerindian) and touched also upon Andean ones (like Guaman Poma and Pachacuti Yamki), who had to deal with the colonial difference itself. Amerindian intellectuals were not in a position to exploit the academic potential of their double consciousness. The alphabet and the printing press were not in their hands, and their own concept of space / time / nature was not accepted as a valid and sustainable one by missionaries and men of letters. They became informants whose texts were not published during their lifetimes and eventually only circulated among Spanish intellectuals and church and state officers. Florescano (1994) analyzes, for example, how in the case of Texcocan historian Alva Ixtlilxochitl two concepts of time intervene in his one narrative. One is the cyclical and renewed concept of time among the Mexicans. The other is the linear and terminal Christian time, from Jesus to the Final Judgment. When the Spaniards wrote about "the origins of the Amerindians according to their own histories," they of course could not write at the intersection of two concepts of time and space (Guaman Poma) as Amerindians did. They could only describe, and reduce to an object of description, what for Amerindians was inscribed in their bodies (and of course in their minds, which are part of the body).

Before Acosta's book (1590), which was mainly written in the Andes and partly in Spain — based on Andean experiences — but included substantial information about Mexico provided by his fellow Jesuit, Francisco de Tovar (circa 1580; Ramirez 1987), two substantial sequences of events occurred. One was the debate of Valladolid, between Sepúlveda and Las Casas, about the Spanish right to conduct conquest and war, which prompted the investigation of the School of Salamanca about the "Rights of the People," in this case the Amerindians, to their own land and government. The other was the enormous work written by the Franciscan Bernardino de Sahagún, in Mexico, between 1528 and 1578. This was an impressive work of ethnography in which Latin, Spanish, and Nahuatl were interactive languages. While Amerindians learned Spanish, Spaniards learned Nahuatl. The foundation of the School of Tlatelolco, which made all of this work possible and also created the conditions for the strong group of Amerindian intellectuals, flourished between approximately 1580 and 1620 (Florescano [1992] 1994). Members from indigenous groups had access to Christian education, while receiving, at home, the "lore" of their Mexican ancestors. Muñóz Chimalpahin and Alvarado Tezozomoc were from noble Mexican families. Juan Bautista Pomar, Alva Ixtlilxochitl, and Muñoz Camargo were from Mexican mothers of noble families and Spanish fathers. Contrary to the rest of the group, Muñoz Camargo opted for translating and reducing indigenous memories to Spanish narrative codes. The rest struggled at the intersection, conceding to alphabetical writing but not entirely to Spanish narratives. What distinguished Muñoz Camargo from the rest is that he opted for straightforward assimilation while the others preferred to stand for a "critical assimilation" — that is, maintaining their right to be different and assuming their human equality with the Spaniards (120–31).

Although most of these processes were going on during Acosta's time in the Andes and Mexico, none of it is found in his narrative. When he moved from "natural" to "moral" history, he devoted an entire book (book V) to idolatry and its extirpation. Acosta, as was common among the religious orders, attributes to the devil all the wrongdoing of the Amerindians. The extirpation of idolatry was seen from a historical perspective as a brutal institution of the colonial difference and a justification for an epistemic lobotomy. Compare, for instance, what Acosta has to say about idolatry (in book V) with Florescano's reconstruction of the epistemic violence consecrated by the conquest and you will soon realize that it is not merely a theological question. It is basically an epistemic one, since reason — and consequently epistemology — was linked to the Christian cosmology in a pre-secular West. Here is Florescano's description.

For the indigenous mentality, the destruction of their gods was a catastrophe of cosmic proportions. The conquest and destruction of Tenochtitlan represented not only the loss of the Mexica capital, it was the demolishing of the center of the cosmos, a disruption of the sacred order that, beginning in Tenochtitlan, the navel of the world, united the celestial powers with those of the underworld and established the relationship with the four directions of the universe. The demolishing of Tenochtitlan appears, then, as a dislocation of the forces that endowed the cosmos with energy and organized territorial space, as a general destruction of the cosmic balance. The indigenous witnesses who give accounts of the effect produced by the Conquest express this sensation of cosmic disasters with great drama:

> Castrate the sun, that is what the foreigners have come to do.
> The tearful lament is extended, the tears drop
> there in Tlatelolco. . . .
> Where are we going? Oh friends?
> Later was it true? They are already abandoning México City:
> the smoke is lifting; the fog
> Is spreading . . .
> Weep my friends,
> Understand that with these events
> we have lost the Méxican nation.
> (Florescano [1992] 1994, 100–101)

Florescano's description, followed by quotations from Amerindian documents, was not known during the sixteenth century, partly because of Amerindians' own practice of not disclosing their sayings and feelings but organizing themselves to survive, revolt, or adapt. However, it is essential today to reread texts like Acosta's, or those of the entire debate of Valladolid and the subsequent discussions in the School of Salamanca, in light of documentation available to us today (see also Gruzinski 1988, Lockhart 1991, and MacCormack 1991 for more detail about Amerindian activities "beyond" the Spanish reports). If these texts continue to be read as texts, starting from what they are saying and ignoring their silencing (intentional or not), the colonial difference will continue to be reproduced. Amerindian agency will continue to be ignored, as texts such as Las Casas's or Acosta's will "fill" that space with their care and description "about" the Amerindians, since Amerindians had no say in Spanish discussions about what to do with them. In this context, the epistemic lobotomy with which Acosta opens his "moral" history is a telling case of producing the epistemic difference by disavowing Amerindian epistemology.

There is a logical connection, in Acosta, between letters (i.e., alphabetic writing), *sciencia* (knowledge and civility), and reason. Idolatry, which was imputed to the devil, was related to the lack of all of this. Acosta, like Las Casas, distinguished between three types of barbarians, judged of course from the perspective of those who have letters, *sciencia*, reason, and the right God. The first type of barbarian, that is, those closer to "us," was the Chinese, since they have all the things Europeans have (like writing, for example), although they are in "imperfect" form. The Mexicans and the Incas constituted for Acosta the second type of barbarian. Although they had a certain way of writing, it was less "precise" than Chinese writing. They also had social practices that were not condoned by sixteenth-century standards of civilization, as Norbert Elias described them in the twentieth century. The third type of barbarian was the savages, who were closer to beasts and consequently to nature. Acosta observed that the Incas and the Mexicans were, so to speak, "sophisticated" barbarians and as such distanced themselves from nature (or the third type of barbarian). Consequently, they were on the right track and ready for conversion. They had the "mental structure" but were wrongheaded regarding "content." They were idolaters.

Acosta defined *idolatry* as the "cause of all evil." He defined two types (or, as he says, lineages) of idolatry. One is close to "natural things," the other close to "imagined things." Now the first type (and Acosta here is following the rhetorical logic of definition by classification) shall be subdivided in two: one occurs when worship is offered to "general" things like the sun, the moon (and it is not easy to understand why Acosta understands the sun and the moon as being "general"), air, fire, and so on, or of particular things like a river, tree, or forest. He adds that this lineage of idolatry was practiced in excess in Peru and that they call it *huaca* (book V, chapter 2). Now in this simple logico-rhetorical classification of Andean idolatry Acosta missed the entire epistemic universe and established, for posterity, the colonial epistemic difference. Today both native and foreign anthropologists, are trying to reconstruct Andean systems of thought, many times using information available in the missionaries' reports. This anthropological work is very helpful in reconstructing what was misunderstood by missionaries. But in these works the colonial difference as a system of epistemic values remains intact. That is, the reconstruction of the system of knowledge that has been misunderstood does not question the very foundation of the anthropologist's or historian's understanding. It is, mutatis mutandis, still in the same logic, though with different content than the missionaries' reports. Revealing what Acosta missed should contribute to redressing the imbalance of the coloniality of power, maintaining still the values of modern epistemology and disavowing as such, although recognizing as "object," epistemologies with different lineages — that is, the epistemologies that belong to the "three kinds of barbarian" in Acosta's classification. This can be termed "barbarian epistemologies," like the contribution at least of China, on the one hand, and of Aztecs and Incas on the other. However, the reader may have noticed that in Acosta a planetary classification of people and places, the Arabic-Islamic world (the Moors), and the Jews are not mentioned. One supposes that they are not mentioned because in Acosta's view these people are not barbarians but belong to the "civilized" world of reference. This could be due to the fact that Acosta's classification is based on the possession of alphabetic writing. Certainly, Arabic and Hebrew are alphabetic writing systems, and these people are not exactly idolaters. The difference, then, we can suppose because Acosta does not mention it, is in the realm of religion among people considered to be at the same level. If this is so, then at this point the Arabic-Islamic world is part of the internal colonial difference. It will be translated and rearticulated as external colonial difference at the beginning of the nineteenth century when France colonized North Africa.

Now that we have an idea of how people of the world have been classified by their degree of barbarism and idolatry, let us explore further the first type of idolatry to better understand Acosta's (as well as other missionaries') making of the colonial difference. Hopefully, we can suggest some ways of undoing it. What Acosta saw as "worshiping nature" was a mixture of theoretical and practical knowledge engrained in social practices from the perspective of Andean people. I am referring mainly to Aymara- and Quechua-speaking people, who in Acosta's time were more tightly bonded than the current national divide between Bolivia, Peru, Chile, and Ecuador leads us to believe. That is, there is a nation beyond the modern nation-state, and both are separated by the colonial difference redefined by the nation-state. I am aware of entering here into a terrain of suspicion, particularly among leftist intellectuals, who will see arguments of this kind as nativist, romantic, New Age, and so on — pretty much like the postmodern feminist denial of "experience," a category that women of color and third world women revindicate in their "barbarian theorizing." The difference here is that I have not myself been raised and educated within Amerindian communities and my approach to their form of knowledge is as foreign as a postmodern white feminist vis-à-vis women of color and third world feminists' experience. The colonial difference is at work in precisely what I said but mainly in the situations I described. To undo the colonial difference it is necessary, first, to avoid the pure reinscription of the white epistemology that maintained its purity precisely by making and reproducing the colonial difference. White epistemology cannot be avoided; it is hegemonic. But it can be diversified by the consideration of the epistemic domains created by the colonial difference. That is to say, the task is not to reconstruct a pure system of thought outside Western epistemology but to remove the wall by means of which other systems of thought were labeled "idolatry" and placed "outside" in the very act of establishing the epistemic colonial difference.

The first lineage of idolatry, as Acosta defined it, was indeed a cosmo-logic different from his, which he could not understand. He could not understand it because, for Acosta, Nature was something to be known, while in the Andes nature was a cosmo-community and part of a cosmo-logic. Indeed, Andean people were not properly "worshiping nature," as Acosta "saw" it, but engaged in dialogic relations in a space of reciprocity: if Nature provides food and sustains life, it is "natural" in a social system of reciprocity to give to Nature (as a living organism) something in return. Now you can see how the pollution emerges in the very act of describing something, for example, a system of knowledge, that is encroaching on your own description and not pushed back and silenced by the colonial difference, as in the missionaries' description of idolatry. You can understand, also, that it was a better project for missionaries to "extirpate idolatry" by performing an epistemic lobotomy rather than worrying about how the logic they were confronting could encroach on their own. Yet by so doing Acosta, after describing Nature, pushed aside the Amerindians' own relationship and conceptualization of it. Juan van Kessel, an anthropologist studying the links between the current Aymara population and the colonial extirpation of idolatry, provides a helpful description of the epistemic and technological devastation that was hidden beyond the missionaries' conceptualization of idolatric behavior among Amerindians.

Los erradicadores de idolatrías, a su vez, atentaron contra la tecnología andina, por cuanto pretendieron eliminar la religión andina, con su mitología y cosmovisión, que es, precisamente, la matriz gestadora del sistema tecnológico andino. El ritual que acompaña la medicina andina, y en general todos los rituales religiosos de producción, eran los que más molestaban a los españoles. Ellos consideraban estos rituales como brujería, como idolatría y como un culto al diablo. De este modo grandes sectores de la tecnología andina tuvieron que replegarse en la clandestinidad, mientras que los demás tuvieron que camuflar sus rituales de producción con nombres y envolturas cristianas. Estos últimos representan mucho más que un adorno o un agregado folklórico . . . *el ritual productivo constituye la dimensión simbólica y el marco conceptual de la tecnología andina.* (1992, 190–191; my italics)

The sentence in italics is a concise description of what Acosta "saw" and described as the first lineage of idolatry. However, Acosta's description, purged of its Christian dogmatic undertones, could easily be recast in terms of modernity and development in Latin America after World War II (Escobar 1995). The productive rituals, engrained in the yearly cycle of the rotation of the earth around the sun, and the conceptual frame of Andean technology would please any executive officer of a transnational corporation attempting to sell modern technology in view of the progress and well-being of indigenous communities. Van Kessel may be right. The problem is that he, like Acosta, continues to dismiss the knowledge that *he does not have, and that he is not willing to let in, in its own right.*

That is, technology does not necessarily overrule indigenous knowledge. It only requires that the indigenous knowledge be conversant with new technologies. The question is not a matter of "either/or" but of "critical assimilation" from the perspective of the subaltern: how to "use" Western technology and absorb it into the indigenous way of doing things. Acosta, as well as our imagined executive officer, would have difficulty sharing his knowledge and recognizing that his knowledge is not the totality. Recognition is not a problem as long as the belief in the totality of one's own epistemic paradigm remains intact. The problem is not to recognize the "other's paradigm" but to recognize that I do not have an epistemic monopoly and that to let the other's knowledge in means at the same time to lose one's epistemic power. This kind of epistemic power is what Quijano calls the "coloniality of power." It is precisely in the exercise and agency of the coloniality of power that the colonial difference can be maintained and reproduced.

When I refer to Andean epistemology or technology, I am not implying a spiritual or metaphysical force furnishing a transcendental identity of "Andean." I am instead talking about local histories in which technology is produced because of local necessity, geographical as well as geopolitical conditions. If we can talk, for example, about Chinese, European, or Andean technology, it is a post facto description of a practice that was demanded by local necessities. As far as it cannot be claimed that an Andean or European epistemology or technology is more than a post facto description of a local practice, it cannot be maintained either that a universal epistemology and technology exist. What exist are power relations. In the making and reproduction of the modern/colonial world what exists is the coloniality of power. From this statement two conclusions can be derived. One is that in confronting and comparing European and Andean epistemologies and technologies, it is important not to fall into binary conceptualizations since the European and the Andean are not the totality. Beyond and next to them is a diversity of local epistemologies and technologies that Europeans encroached upon in the past five hundred years in the process of making the modern/colonial world. The second conclusion is that the main problem is not the coexistence of diverse epistemologies and technologies but the coloniality of power through which they are organized and related. Thus, Andean technology is inscribed in a paradigm oriented toward bio-logical production. Again, the term *bio* should not be read within a Western "vitalism" supporting authoritarian regimes and racial cleansing. Remember, *bio* here is in a different paradigm, although we have to use the same words. The Zapatistas, for instance, have to use the word *democracy* and at the same time give it a meaning that is not oversteeped in the (neo)liberal paradigm. A technology that is oriented toward reproduction of the life cycle and parallels nature (the earth) as a living system was, and still is, difficult for a hegemonic technology oriented toward the mechanical reproduction of objects to accept. Acosta was looking all over for causes. He was confronted with a paradigm in which causes have no function. R. Kusch labeled this paradigm "seminal thinking" and distinguished it from "causal thinking." Remember that this is not a binary operation since it does not imply totality. It is the circumstantial comparison of two among many. Now let us look a little closer at this idea of seminal thinking.

Acosta noted in passing (book V, chapter 4) that "They also worshiped the earth, which they called Pachamama, like the ancients celebrated the goddess Tellus." What the Andeans did with Pachamama was not exactly worshiping, nor was it exactly like the celebration of Tellus. Above all, it was not an additional activity ("They also . . . "). Pachamama was and is a central concept in Andean cosmology or, if you prefer, the epistemic and technological paradigm embedded in cosmology (or religion, as it is more common to say). To explain the meaning of pacha is not a simple operation, and I have no other choice here than to be schematic. *Pacha* has been rendered as "time" by Bouysse-Cassagne and Harris (1992, 18). Kusch understood it to mean "habitat," that is, space but more than that — space as environment (1970, 98). Kusch objected to general translations of *pacha* as "time" or "ground" (as it is reproduced in Bouysse-Cassagne and Harris) and suspected that there is in the concept "something much more engaged with the very life" of Andean people. Kusch goes through a laborious reading and meditation on the Aymaran concept of the aforementioned *ceque* system that Tom Zuidema reconstructed in painstaking scholarly work (1964). The first detailed description of the *ceque* system, it should be remembered, was not available to

Acosta since it was only provided later by Bernabé Cobo in his *Historia del Nuevo Mundo,* published in 1653.

But where is *pacha* in the *ceque* system? Kusch, interpreting Cobo's narrative, surmises that each *guaca* was like a "deployment" of the Pacha Master. What is that? Kusch looks into several compound words having *pacha* as a prefix, for example *Pacha-Kuti* and *Pacha-yachachic. Kuti,* it is well known, means "abrupt turn of events," "revolution," and "judgment," as the Aymara integrated the Christian notion of Final Judgment into their cosmology. Understandably, a cyclical concept of time/space like the Andean one has no final destination, just the end of a cycle and the beginning of the next one. *Pacha-kuti* was used precisely to refer to abrupt and drastic changes of events such as the transition from one "time/sun age or cycle" to the next one. Cuzco, then, was not only the center of space but also the present of the current "time/sun age or cycle." Consequently, *Pacha-Kuti* could be rendered as a drastic change of space/time, a revolution in Marxist terms. There should be no surprise, then, that *Pacha-Kuti* was the term used to describe, from the Andean perspective, the arrival and establishment of Spanish men, law, and religion.

Apparently *pacha* is not something that can be changed, but it is something that can be taught. *Pacha-yachachic,* as "Master of Pacha," is an unnamed force whose "deployments" are the *guacas.* I cannot go into more interesting details here, since I have introduced these terms to make *Pachamama* better understood. If an equivalent with ancient Greece is necessary to understand its meaning, then I would say that it is more like *Gaia* than *Tellus.* Let me remind you of Lovelock's introduction of the term *Gaia* in relation to what he was observing and trying to identify.

> How is it that the Earth keeps so constant an atmospheric composition when it is made up of highly reactive gases? Still more puzzling was the question of how such an unstable atmosphere could be perfectly suited in composition for life. It was then that *I began to wonder if it could be that the air is not just an environment for life but is also a part of life itself.* To put it another way, it seemed that the interaction between life and the environment, of which the air is a part, is so intense that the air could be thought of as being like the fur of a cat or the paper of a hornet's nest: not living, but made by living things to sustain a chosen environment. (1987, 87–88)

What is the point here? That "Gaia as a way of knowing," as it is conceived today (Thompson 1987), could be imagined as a logical outcome of Andean cosmology if it had been given the chance to expand and evolve. As Lovelock conceived, it is instead the result of the limits he encountered in the logic that was rearticulated by and since Copernicus but already had its foundation in Ptolemy. Be this as it may, the Andean conception of Pachamama was far removed. In fact, it was so far removed from Acosta's logic that Acosta and other missionaries found a shortcut — idolatry, or worshiping natural "things," bypassing the fact that it was not a question of "things" but of living organisms in an encompassing living universe. This is, on the other hand, the description of *Pachamama* offered by van Kessel: "La *Pachamama* . . . no *confecciona* flora, fauna y humanos: todos éstos 'nacen' de ella. La divinidad es inmanente en el mundo, está dentro del mundo y se identifica plenamente con la tierra. La relación entre *Pachamama* y sus criaturas es la de una madre a sus hijos y de estos hacia ella: cargada de afecto" (1992, 194–95). This is very close to Gaia being conceived as a living organism, a biosphere without a transcendent entity and without a center. In this conception, living entities are circumstantial and momentary (they are born and they die); life is what is maintained. Gaia is more than the planet earth; it is "an entity comprising a whole planet and having the powerful capacity to regulate its climate and chemical composition" (Lovelock 1990, 88). We have here the vocabulary of sciences instead of the vocabulary of philosophy and religion (Acosta) or the vocabulary of two languages (Aymara and Quechua) that the colonial difference did not allow to expand.

What is the point here? The point is that "expurgation of idolatry" is a double epistemic lobotomy. It demonizes at the same time as it ignores the complex frame of knowledge and the fact that the distinction between "moral" and "natural" history did not make sense to Amerindians. Yet Amerindians did not have the opportunity, for complex reasons, to make this point and this argument. This argument can be made today by practicing a sort of border epistemology from a subaltern perspective (which in this case was materialized in the Amerindian epistemology). Second, and later in the colonial world, idolatry was recognized as some kind of knowledge (generally associated with the devil) but was not described as sustainable knowledge. Occidentalism was born with the construction of "the Indias" (Occidentales) and the first semantization of the colonial difference. The third moment is the one I intended to contribute to in this commentary: the emergence of a border epistemology that will imagine the colonial difference from the colonial difference — that is to say, from a subaltern perspective, which in this case is from the perspective of current Amerindian legacies, in the Andes as well as in Mexico, as the Zapatistas' discourse made clear to the world. Finally, thinking about the coloniality of power and from the colonial difference allowed me to identify the imperial difference that emerged shortly after Acosta's book. The imperial difference contributed to the making of the north/south distinction at the time when, as Said (1978) showed, European scholarly and intellectual discourse was producing orientalism. Orientalism was a resemantization of the colonial difference that obviously presupposed the existence of a discursive formation, which put occidentalism in place in the first articulation of the colonial difference and the creation of the Atlantic commercial circuit. Acosta, finally and pedagogically, is at the edge of the first phase of the modern/colonial world. A decade after the publication of his book, the works of Copernicus and Bacon were already announcing the second phase of the modern/colonial world, which concluded with the Enlightenment, the Industrial Revolution, and the fabrication of orientalism and southern Europe.

# BIBLIOGRAPHY

Abu-Lughod, Janet L. 1989. *Before European Hegemony: The World System, A.D. 1250–1350*. New York: Oxford University Press.

Acosta, José de. [1940] 1962. *Historia natural y moral de las Indias, en que se tratan de las cosas notables del cielo, y elementos, metales, plantas, y animales dellas: Y los ritos, y ceremonias, leyes, y gobierno de los Indios, compuesto por el padre Joseph de Acosta*. Edited by Edmundo O'Gorman. Mexico City: Fondo de Cultura Económica.

Adorno, Rolena. 2000. *Guaman Poma: Writing and Resistance in Colonia Peru*. 2d ed. Austin: University of Texas Press, 2000.

Anderson, Benedict. [1983] 1992. *Imagined Communities*. Rev. ed. London: Verso.

Arrighi, Giovanni. 1994. *The Long Twentieth Century*. London: Verso.

Ascher, Marcia, and Robert Ascher. 1981. *Code of the Quipu: A Study in Media, Mathematics, and Culture*. Ann Arbor: University of Michigan Press.

Bertonio, Ludovico. [1612] 1984. *Vocabulario de la lengua Aymara*. Cochabamba: Centro de Estudios de la Realidad Económica y Social.

Bouysse-Cassagne, T., and O. Harris. 1992. "Pacha: En torno al pensamiento aymara." In *Tres reflexiones sobre el pensamiento andino*, edited by T. Bouysse-Cassage, O. Harris, T. Platt and V. Cereceda, 11–60. La Paz: Hisbol.

Brotton, Jerry. 1998. *Trading Territories: Mapping the Early Modern World*. Ithaca, NY: Cornell University Press.

Clendinnen, Inga. 1987. *Ambivalent Conquests: Maya and Spaniard in Yucatan, 1517–1570*. Cambridge Latin American Studies, vol. 61. Cambridge: Cambridge University Press.

Cobo, Bernabé. [1653] 1943. *Historia del Nuevo Mundo*. Madrid: Ediciones Atlas.

Coronil, Fernando. 1997. *The Magical State: Nature, Money, and Modernity in Venezuela*. Chicago: University of Chicago Press.

Crombie, A. C. [1952] 1971. *Augustine to Galileo*. Vol. I: *Science in the Middle Ages (5th to 13th Centuries)*. Vol. 2: *Science in the Later Middle Ages and Early Modern Times (13th to 17th Centuries)*. Cambridge: Harvard University Press.

Cruz, Martín de la. [1552] 1964. *Libellus de medicinalibus Indorum herbis*. Translated from Nahuatl to Latin by Juan Badiano. Mexico: Instituto Mexicano del Seguro Social.

Debus, Allen G. 1978. *Man and Nature in the Renaissance*. Cambridge: Cambridge University Press.

Du Bois, W. E. B. [1905] 1990. *The Souls of Black Folk*. New York: Vintage.

Dussel, Enrique. 1998. "Beyond Eurocentrism." In *The Cultures of Globalization*, edited by F. Jameson and M. Miyoshi, 10–35. Durham: Duke University Press.

Escobar, Arturo. 1995. *Encountering Development: The Making and Unmaking of the Third World*. Princeton: Princeton University Press.

——. 1997. "Cultural Politics and Biological Diversity: State, Capital, and Social Movements in the Pacific Coast of Colombia." In *The Politics of Culture in the Shadow of Capital*, edited by L. Lowe and D. Lloyd, 201–26. Durham: Duke University Press.

——. 1998. "After Nature: Steps to an Anti-essentialist Political Ecology." *Current Anthropology* 40:1–30.

Farriss, Nancy. 1984. *Maya Society under Colonial Rule: The Collective Enterprise of Survival*. Princeton: Princeton University Press.

Fernández, Luis Gil. 1983. *Panorama social del humanismo español (1500–1800)*. Madrid: Editorial Alhambra.

Ferreras-Savoye, Jacqueline. 1999. "El paradigma de la Naturaleza en el siglo xvi Castellano." *Cuadernos Americanos* 73:78–89.

Ferris, Timothy. 1988. *Coming of Age in the Milky Way*. New York: Morrow.

Florescano, Enrique [1992] 1994. *Memory, Myth, and Time in Mexico: From the Aztecs to Independence*. Translations from Latin America series. Austin: University of Texas Press.

Flourens, Pierre. [1850] 1971. *Histoire des travaux et des idées de Buffon*. Geneva: Slatkine Reprints.

Garibay, Angel Maria. 1964. Introduction to Martín de la Cruz, *Libellus de medicinalibus Indorum herbis*, 1–8. Mexico City: Instituto Mexicano del Seguro Social.

Gerbi, Antonello. [1955] 1982. *La disputa del Nuevo Mundo*. Translated from the Italian to Spanish by Antonio Alatorre. Mexico City: Fondo de Cultura Económica.

Gisbert, Teresa. 1996. "Commentaires." In S. Gruzinski and N. Wachtel, eds. *Les Nouveau Monde, Mondes Nouveaux: L'expérience Américaine*, 332–34. Paris: Éditions de l' École des Hautes Études en Sciences Sociales.

Gould, Stephen Jay. 1977. *Ever since Darwin: Reflections in Natural History*. New York: Norton.

——. 1987. *Time's Arrow, Time's Cycle: Myth and Metaphor in the Discovery of Geological Time*. Cambridge: Harvard University Press.

Granet, Marcel. 1934. *La pensée chinoise*. Paris: La Renaissance du livre.

Gruzinski, Serge. 1988. *La colonisation de l'imaginaire: Société indigénes et occidentalisation dans le Mexique espagnol, xvi–xvii siècles*. Paris: Gallimard.

——. 1999. *La pensée métise*. Paris: Fayard.

Guzmán de Rojas, Iván. 1995. "Técnicas lexicográficas para relacionar el aymara con los idiomas latinos." In *Lenguas y culturas latinas*, compiled by Norma Campos Vera, 77–98. La Paz: Union Latina de Bolivia.

Hay, Dennis. 1957. *Europe*. Edinburgh: Edinburgh University Press.

Hegel, G. W. F. [1822] 1991. *The Philosophy of History*. Translated by J. Sibree. New York: Prometheus.

Hernández, Ramon, comp. 1984. *Derechos humanos en Francisco de Vitoria: Antología*. Salamanca: Editorial San Esteban.

Hollbach, Paul Henri Thiery, Baron d'. [1797] 1834. *Système de la Nature*. London: J. Watson.

Kant, Immanuel. [1797] 1996. *Anthropology from a Pragmatic Point of View*. Translated by Victor Lyle Dowdell, with an introduction by F. P. Van de Pitte. Carbondale: Southern Illinois University Press.

Karrow, Robert W. 1993. *Mapmakers of the Sixteenth Century and Their Maps: Bio-bibliographies of the Cartographers of Abraham Ortelius, 1570*. Chicago: Speculum Orbis. Based on Leo Bagrow's A. Ortelii Catalogus Cartographorum.

Kessel, Juan van. 1992. "Tecnología aymara: Un enfoque cultural," In *La cosmovisión Aymara*, compiled by H. van den Berg and Norbert Schiffers, 187–220.

Koyré, Alexandre. 1957. *From the Closed World to the Infinite Universe.* Baltimore: Johns Hopkins University Press.

Kusch, Rodolfo. 1971. *Pensamiento Indígena y Pensamiento Popular en America.* Buenos Aires: Hachette.

Lenkersdorf, Carlos. 1996. *Los hombres verdaderos: Voces y testimonios de los tojolabales.* Mexico: Siglo XXI.

Liu, Lydia, ed. 1999. *Tokens of Exchange: The Problem of Translation in Global Circulations.* Durham: Duke University Press.

Lockhart, James. 1991. *Nahuas and Spaniards: Postconquest Central Mexican History and Philology.* UCLA Latin American Studies Series, vol. 76. Stanford: Stanford University Press.

López Austin, Alfredo. 1980. *Cuerpo humano e ideologia: Las concepciones de los antiguos náhuas.* Mexico City: Universidad Nacional Autónoma de México.

López Piñero, Jose María. 1979. *Ciencia y técnica en la Sociedad española de los siglos XVI y XVII.* Barcelona: Labor Universitaria.

Lovelock, James. 1987. "Gaia: A Model for Planetary and Cellular Dynamics." In *Gaia, a Way of Knowing: Political Implications of the New Biology,* edited by W. I. Thompson, 83–97. Great Barrington, MA: Lindisfarne.

———. 1990. *The Ages of Gaia: A Biography of Our Living Earth.* New York: Bantam.

MacCormack, Sabine. 1991. *Religion in the Andes: Vision and Imagination in Early Colonial Peru.* Princeton: Princeton University Press.

Maravall, José Antonio. 1963. *Los factores de la idea del progreso en el Renacimiento español.* Madrid: Real Academia de la Historia.

———. [1966] 1967. "La concepción del saber en una sociedad tradicional." In *Estudios de historia del Pensamiento Español,* 201–60. Madrid: Ediciones de Cultura Hispanica.

Maturana, Humberto. 1991. "Reality: The Search for Objectivity or the Quest for a Compelling Argument." In *Die Gedankenwelt Sir Karl Poppers: Kritischer Rationalismus im Dialog,* edited by N. Leser, J. Seifert, and K. Plitzner, 283–357. Heidelberg: Carl Winter Universitätsverlag.

Merchant, Carolyn. 1980. *The Death of Nature: Women, Ecology, and the Scientific Revolution.* New York: Harper and Row.

Mies, Maria, and Vandana Shiva. 1993. *Ecofeminism.* Halifax: Fernwood.

Mignolo, Walter D. 1981. "El metatexto historiográfico y la historiografía indiana." *Modern Languages Notes* 96:358–402.

———. 1982. "Cartas, crónicas, y relaciones del descubrimiento y de la conquista." In *Historia de la Literatura Hispanoamericana: Epoca Colonial,* edited by I. Madrigal, 65–126. Madrid: Catedra.

———. 1992. "On the Colonization of Languages and Memories: Renaissance Theories of Writing and the Discontinuity of the Classical Tradition." *Comparative Studies in Society and History* 34:301–335.

———. 1994. "Literacy and the Colonization of Memory: Writing Histories of People without History." In *Literacy: Interdisciplinary Conversations,* edited by Deborah Keller-Cohen, 91–114. Norwood, NJ: Ablex.

———. 1995. "Decires fuera de lugar: La cuestión del sujeto en las crónicas indianas." In *Revista Latinoamericana de Critica Literaria* 41:9–32.

———. 1996. "Misunderstanding and Colonization: The Reconfiguration of Memory and Space." In *Le Nouveau Monde, Mondes Nouveaux: L'expériénce Américaine,* edited by S. Gruzinski and N. Wachtel, 271–350. Paris: Éditions de l'Ecole des Hautes Études en Sciences Sociales.

———. 1997. "Espacios geográficos y localizaciones epistemológicas o la ratio entre la localización geográfica y la producción de conocimientos." In *Canones and Contextos,* 91–106. Fifth Congresso Abralic-Anais, vol. 1. Rio de Janeiro: Facultade de Letras, Universidade Federal de Rio de Janeiro.

——. 1998. "Diferencia colonial y razon postoccidental." In *Anuario Mariateguiano*. Vol. X, no. 10: 171–188. Lima: Centro de Ciencias Sociales.

——. 2000a. *Local Histories/Global Designs: Coloniality, Border Thinking, and Subaltern Knowledges*. Princeton: Princeton University Press.

——. 2000b. "The Many Faces of Cosmo-Polis: Border Thinking and Critical Cosmopolitanism." *Public Culture* 12:721–748.

——. 2000c. "Coloniality at Large: Time and the Colonial Difference." In *Time in the Making and Possible Futures*, edited by Candido Mendes and Enrique Rodriguez Larreta, 237–272. Rio de Janeiro: UNESCO, International Social Science Council and Universidad Candido Mendes.

Mires, Fernando. 1990. *El discurso de la naturaleza: Ecología y política en América Latina*. San José, Costa Rica: DEI.

Navarro, Juan. [1801] 1992. *Historia natural o jardin Americano*. Mexico City: Universidad Nacional Autónoma de México.

O'Gorman, Edmundo. 1958. *La invención de America: El universalismo de la cultura de occidente*. Mexico City: Fondo de Cultura Económica.

——. 1961. *The Invention of America: An Inquiry into the Historical Nature of the New World and the Meaning of Its History*. Bloomington: Indiana University Press.

——. 1972. *Cuatro historiadores de Indias, siglo XVI: Pedro Mártir de Anglería, Gonzalo Fernández de Oviedo y Valdés, Bartolomé de Las Casas, Joseph de Acosta*. Mexico City: Secretaría de Educación Pública.

Ortelius, Abraham. 1574. *Theatrvm orbis terrarvm; opus nunc denuo ab ipso auctore recognitum, multisque locis castigatum, & quamplurimis nouis tabulis atque commentarijs auctum*. Antwerp: apud Ant. Coppenium Diesth.

Pagden, Anthony. 1982. *The Fall of Natural Man: The American Indian and the Origins of Comparative Ethnology*. Cambridge: Cambridge University Press.

Pagden, A., and N. Canny, eds. 1987. *Colonial Identity in the Atlantic World, 1500–1800*. Princeton: Princeton University Press.

Pozo, Candido. 1959. *La teoría del progreso dogmatico en los teólogos de la escuela de Salamanca, 1526–1644*. Madrid: Instituto "Francisco Suarez."

——, comp. 1962. *Fuentes para la historia del metodo teológico en la Escuela de Salamanca*. Biblioteca teológica granadina, vol. 6. Granada: Facultad de Teología.

Quijano, Anibal, and Immanuel Wallerstein. 1992. "Americanity as a Concept, or the Americas in the Modern World System." *International Journal of Social Science* 134:549–54.

Ramirez, José Fernando. 1987. *Relación del origen de los indios que habitan esta Nueva España, según sus historias. Origen de los mexicanos*, edited by Germán Vázquez. Madrid: Historia 16.

Rengifo Vásquez, Grimaldo. 1998. "'The Ayllu.'" In *The Spirit of Regeneration: Andean Culture Confronting Western Notions of Development*, edited by Frederique Apffel-Marglin with PRATEC, 89–123. London: Zed Books.

Rostworowski, Maria. 1998. "Pachacamac and El Señor de los Milagros." In *Native Traditions in the Postconquest World*, edited by E. Hill Boone and T. Cummins, 345–60. Washington, DC: Dumbarton Oaks.

Sahagún, Bernardino de. [1565] 1981. *Coloquios y doctrina Christiana*. Translated and with an introduction by Miguel-León Portilla. Mexico City: Universidad Nacional Autónoma de Mexico.

Said, Edward. 1978. *Orientalism*. New York: Vintage Books.

Salomon, Frank. 1982. "Chronicles of the Impossible: Notes on Three Peruvian Indigenous Historians." In *From Oral to Written Expression: Native Andean Chronicles of the Early Colonial Period*, edited by R. Adorno, 9–40. Latin American Series, vol. 4. Syracuse: Foreign and Comparative Studies, Syracuse University.

Shiva, Vandana and Vanaja Ramprasad. 1993. *Cultivating Diversity: Biodiversity Conservation and the Politics of the Seed.* Dehra Dun: Research Foundation for Science, Technology and Natural Resource Policy, distributed by Nataraj Publishers.

Silverblatt, Irene. 1995. "Becoming Indian in the Central Andes of Seventeenth-Century Peru." In *After Colonialism: Imperial Histories and Postcolonial Displacements,* edited by G. Prakash, 279–98. Princeton: Princeton University Press.

Somolinos D'Ardois, German. 1960. *Vida y obra de Francisco Hernández: Obras completas de Francisco Hernández.* Vol. 1. Mexico City: Universidad Nacional Autónoma de México.

———. 1964. "Estudio histórico." In *Libellus de medicinalibus Indorum herbis,* 301–28. Mexico City: Instituto Mexicano del Seguro Social.

Spence, Jonathan D. 1998. *The Chan's Great Continent: China in Western Minds.* New York: Norton.

Thompson, W. I., ed. 1987. *Gaia, a Way of Knowing: Political Implications of the New Biology.* Great Barrington, MA: Lindisfarne.

Trabulse, Elias. 1988. "Tres momentos de la heterodoxia científica en el México colonial." *Quipu: Revista Latinoamericana de Historia de las Ciencias y la Tecnología* 5, no. 1:7–18.

Varela, F., E. Thompson, and Eleanor Rosch. 1991. *The Embodied Mind: Cognitive Science and Human Experience.* Cambridge: MIT Press.

Vespucci, Amerigo [1604] 1951. *El Mundo Nuevo: Cartas relativas a sus viajes y descrubrimiento.* Edited by Roberto Levillier. Buenos Aires: Editorial Emecè. Text in Italian, Spanish, and English.

Vilchis, Jaime B. 1988. "Medicina novohispana del siglo XVI y la materia médica indígena: Hacia una caracterización de su ideología." *Quipu: Revista Latinoamericana de Historia de las Ciencias y la Tecnología* 5, no. 1: 19–48.

Wallerstein, Immanuel. 1974. *The Modern World-System.* Vol. 1: *Capitalist Agriculture and the Origins of the European World-Economy in the Sixteenth Century.* New York: Academic Press.

Wallerstein, Immanuel, et al. 1996. *Open the Social Sciences: Report of the Gulbenkian Commission on the Restructuring of the Social Sciences.* Stanford: Stanford University Press.

Weber, Max. [1905] 1992. *The Protestant Ethic and the Spirit of Capitalism.* London and New York: Routledge.

Wolf, Eric R. 1982. *Europe and the People without History.* Berkeley: University of California Press.

World Resources Institute. 1992. *Global Biodiversity Strategy: Guidelines for Action to Save, Study, and Use Earth's Biotic Wealth Sustainably and Equitably.* Washington, DC: World Resources Institute.

Zuidema, R. Tom. 1964. *The Ceque System of Cuzco: The Social Organization of the Capital of the Incas.* Translated by Eva M. Hooykaas. Leiden: Brill.

———. 1986. *Reyes y guerreros: ensayos de cultura andina.* Lima: FOMCIENCIAS.

———. 1990. *Inca Civilization in Cuzco.* Translated by Jean-Jacques Decoster, with a foreword by Francoise Heiritier-Auge. Austin: University of Texas Press.

———. 1995. *El sistema de ceques del Cuzo: la organización de la capital de los Incas, con un ensayo preliminar.* 1. ed. Lima: Fondo Editorial de la Pontificia Universidad Católica del Perú.

# INDEX

Crombie, A. C., 465–66

Cuauhtémoc, 422n, 439, 441n

Cuba, 28, 78, 107–8, 144, 168, 201

Cuernavaca, 383n

Cuetlaxtlán, 420

Cuitlahuac, Mexica war with, 411–12

Culhua (clan), 383, 390

Culhuacán, 273, 390–92, 395–97

Cummins, Tom, 342n

Cuzco: ceremonies and rites in, 265, 282, 290, 300, 315; Chumbibilca tribe, 173; on Guaman Poma's map, 482; Inca court at, 314, 349; stone construction in, 350–51n

Dancing: festival to Tezcatlipoca, 323; *mitote,* 326–27, 375, 376; *puella* (mock battle), 374; ritual dances, 296n, 303, 316, 318

Davies, Nigel, 390n

de la Cruz, Martín, 11n, 467–70, 468 (plate 5)

Demographics: climate and habitation, 34–39, 75–77, 144, 145; Creoles and, 504–5; migration and, 51–53, 143, 386–88, 390–94; population transfer, 143–44, 255n, 348–49; of Windward Islands, 150, 168

*De procuranda Indorum salute* (Acosta), xxi, xxiii–xxvi, 6

Diseases: altitude sickness *(soroche),* 98n, 118n, 119–21, 145n; bezoars, medicinal properties of, 66, 243, 246–48; *carache* (llama's disease), 246; *chicha* as medicine, 199; *cocoliste* (fever), 144; and depopulation of coastal regions, 143–44; hypothermia, 121–22; medicinal plants, 140, 210–11, 220–21, 222, 223, 309; mercury poisoning, 184; mine accidents, 144; seasickness, 118–19; vicuña meat, medicinal properties of, 243

Dominica Islands, 27, 107

Drake, Francis, 125–26, 127, 128

Dreams and omens, 72n, 277, 306, 427–31

DuBois, W. E. B., 473–74

Durán, Diego, 4n, 10n, 11n, 69–70, 250n, 383n

Dyes, 213, 223, 245

Earth: antipodes, 26, 29–32, 51; cosmology of, 15–26, 112; Earth (Pachamama) as deity, 258, 515–17; habitation of, 32–33, 34–39; ocean navigation and, 27–29

Earthquake, 155–59

Education, 341n, 372–73n, 375, 469, 508

El Dorado, 82–83, 141, 152

Elias, Norbert, 510

Elites: coca as food of, 211; and literacy, 336; marriage in Incan kingdom, 358; men of wisdom *(amautas, tlamatinimes),* 23 n.1, 481, 488 (plate 10), in Mexico, 370, 373n; Quetzalcoatl as god of, 324; tributes to, 218, 268–69. *See also* Priests

Enlightenment, New World, 464, 466–67

Enríquez, Martín, 127, 330

Ercilla, Alonso de *(Araucana),* 124, 209

Ethiopia, 35, 41, 79, 95

Europe: astronomy, 19, 24–26; capitalism, 457, 476, 498, 499, 500; climate in, 79, 96–97, 120–21, 151; eurocentrism, 29 n.6, 30 n.3; Indias Occidentales explained to, 460; invention of Amerindians, 455–56; New World and reconsideration of knowledge, 89n, 462–64; New World diet compared to, 197n, 198n, 200n; and northern European conception of New World, 498

Fanon, Frantz, 459

Fire, 100, 112–13, 211

Fishing, 132–39, 143

Flaying rite *(racaxipe valiztli),* 273, 296–98

Flogging, 287, 306, 315, 321, 322

Floods, 72–73, 79–80, 82, 170, 360

*The Florentine Codex,* 8n, 100n, 470

Florescano, Enrique, 8n, 507, 508, 509–10

Florida, 28, 63, 74, 128–29, 160

Flowers, 218–19, 303, 321

France, 49–50, 501

Gaia, 478–79, 494, 516–18

Galilei, Galileo, 464

Gama, Vasco da, 56n

Games, 323, 374–76

Garcés, Enrique, 187

Garibay, Angel María, 469

Gasca, Pedro de la, 10n, 362n

José de Acosta (1539–1600) was a Spanish Jesuit historian.

Jane E. Mangan is Assistant Professor in the Department of History at Harvard University.

Walter Mignolo is William Hanes Wannamaker Professor of Romance Studies, Professor of Literature and Cultural Anthropology, and Director, Institute for Global Studies in Humanities, John Hope Franklin Center, Duke University. His publications include *The Darker Side of the Renaissance: Literacy, Territoriality, and Colonization* (1995) and *Local Histories/Global Designs: Coloniality, Subaltern Knowledges, and Border Thinking* (2000). He is coeditor along with Elizabeth Hill Boone of *Writing without Words: Alternative Literacies in Mesoamerica and the Andes* (1994). He is editor of the journal *Nepantla: Views from South,* published by Duke University Press.

Frances M. López-Morillas has translated numerous Spanish-language works into English, including Alvar Nuñez Cabeza de Vaca's *Naufragios.*

Library of Congress Cataloging-in-Publication Data
Acosta, José de, 1539–1600.
[Historia natural y moral de las Indias. English]
Natural and moral history of the Indies / José de Acosta ; edited by Jane E. Mangan ;
with an introduction and commentary by Walter Mignolo ; translated by Frances López-Morillas.
p. cm. — (Chronicles of the New World encounter) (Latin America in translation/en traducción/em tradução)
Includes bibliographical references and index.
ISBN 0-8223-2832-1 (cloth : alk. paper) — ISBN 0-8223-2845-3 (pbk. : alk. paper)
1. America — Early accounts to 1600. 2. America — Description and travel. 3. Indians of Mexico — Early works to 1800. 4. Indians of South America — Early works to 1800. 5. Natural history — America. 6. Acosta, José de, 1540–1600 — Journeys — America. I. Mangan, Jane E.–    II. Mignolo, Walter. III. Lopez-Morillas, Frances. IV. Title. V. Series. VI. Series: Latin America in translation/en traducción/em tradução
E141 .A28313 2002    980′.013 — dc21    2001059859